KI

KITCHENS

VOLUME I

For Cookbooks Call
Vaughn 334-872-0868
Small 334-227-4475
Selma
Tucker 334-624-3822
Greensboro

Telephone Pioneers of America
Kentucky Chapter No. 32

This cookbook is a collection of our favorite recipes which are not necessarily original recipes.

Manufactured by
Favorite Recipes® Press
an imprint of

P. O. Box 305142
Nashville, Tennessee 37230

ISBN: 0-9662212-0-6

Manufactured in the United States of America

Expression
of
Appreciation

On the following pages is a collection of mouth-watering recipes contributed by Life, Regular, Future Pioneers, Pioneer Partners and Friends.

These recipes are not necessarily originals but are favorites of the contributors and represent a warm cross-section of kitchens throughout the southeastern United States.

We wish to thank and gratefully acknowledge all our friends who contributed in so many ways to make this cookbook a reality.

Cookbook Committee

Chairpersons

Gwen Mills   Mary T. Thompson

Members

Oleta Bryan	Rose Pero
Martha Denning	Rowena Pipes
Lil Green	Kathy Ryan
Thelma Hardin	Barbara Sumner
Ruthie Marty	Carol Wilson
Bernie Mills	Dot Young
Aggie Noonan	George Young

Telephone Pioneers of America

Kentucky Chapter No. 32

Councils

A.T.&T.	Louisville Central-West
Big Sandy	Louisville South-East
Blue Grass	Pennyrile
Capital	Purchase

Life Member Clubs

Big Sandy	Lexington
Bowling Green	Louisville
Capital	Madisonville
Daniel Boone	Owensboro
Hopkinsville	Paducah

Winchester

TERMS USED IN COOKING

APPETIZER — A small serving of food served before or as the first course of a meal.

ASPIC — A transparent jelly, usually meat, which has been boiled down to become firm when cold.

BATTER — A mixture of flour or liquid that can be beaten or stirred.

BISQUE — A rich thick cream soup made from fish.

BLANCH — To place fruits or nuts in boiling water to remove skins, also to dip vegetables in boiling water in preparation for freezing, canning or drying.

BOUILLABAISE — A chowder made from several varieties of fish and wine.

BOUILLON — Clear soup made from lean beef.

BRAISE — To brown meat or vegetables in hot fat, then to cook slowly in small amount of liquid.

CARAMEL — Burnt sugar syrup used for coloring and flavoring. Also a chewy candy.

CHICORY — A plant root that is cut into slices, dried and roasted into coffee. The plant leaves are used for salad and sometimes called curly endive.

CIDER — The juice from pressed apples used as a beverage or to make vinegar.

CLARIFY — To make a liquid clear by adding beaten egg white and egg shells. The egg coagulates in hot liquid and cloudiness adheres to it. The liquid is then strained.

COBBLER — A fruit pie with a rich biscuit dough made in a deep-dish.

COCKTAIL — An appetizer served before or as the first course of a meal. An alcoholic beverage served before the dinner or cut shellfish with tart sauce served at the start of a meal.

CRACKLINGS — Crisp particles left after fat has been fried out.

CROQUETTES — Chopped meat held together by eggs, shaped and dipped into crumbs then fried.

DOUGH — A mixture of flour, liquid that is stiff enough to be kneaded.

DRIPPINGS — Liquids resulting from meat being cooked.

ENTREE — A dish served between the chief courses, before the roast.

FONDUE — A dish made of cheese, eggs, etc.

FRITTERS — Vegetables or fish covered with batter then fried in deep fat.

FROSTING — A sugar that has been cooked and used to cover cakes, and other foods.

GIBLETS — The liver, gizzard or heart of poultry.

HORS d'OEUVRES — Tart, salty or crisp foods served as appetizers.

INFUSION — Liquid taken from tea, herbs or coffee.

JULIENNE — Food cut into very thin strips.

MACEDOINE — A mixture of fruits or vegetables.

MARINATE — To let foods stand in an acid mixture of oil and vinegar, then flavored with spices and herbs.

MINCE — To cut foods in very fine pieces.

FOOD PROCESSES

BAKE — To cook by dry heat, usually in an oven.

BARBECUE — To roast or broil whole, as a hog, fowl, etc. Usually done on a revolving frame over coals or upright in front of coals. To cook thin slices of meat in a highly seasoned vinegar sauce.

BOIL — To cook in liquid, usually water, in which large bubbles rise rapidly and continually so that all the liquid is agitated.

BOILING POINT — The temperature reached when a mixture maintains a full bubbling motion on its surface.

BREW — To cook in hot liquid until flavor is extracted.

BROIL — To cook by exposing the food directly to the heat.

BRAISE — To cook meat by searing in fat, then simmering in a covered dish in small amount of moisture.

CANDY — To conserve or preserve by boiling with sugar. To incrust or coat with sugar.

COAT SPOON — When a mixture forms a thin even film on the spoon.

CODDLE — To cook slowly and gently in a liquid just below the boiling point.

CREAM — To work foods until soft and fluffy. Usually applied to shortening and sugar.

CUBE — To cut in even sliced pieces.

CUT — To divide foods with a knife or scissors.

DICE — To cut into small cubes.

DISSOLVE — To pass into solution.

FOLD — To combine, using a motion beginning vertically down through the mixture, continuing across the bottom of the bowl and ending with an upward and over motion.

TABLE OF CONTENTS

1546-85

FAVORITE RECIPES
FROM MY COOKBOOK

Recipe Name	Page Number

Appetizers,
Pickles,
Relishes

HERB CHART

Use fresh whole herbs when possible. When fresh herbs are not available, use whole dried herbs that can be crushed just while adding. Store herbs in airtight containers away from the heat of the stove. Fresh herbs may be layered between paper towels and dried in the microwave on High for 2 minutes or until dry.

Basil	Can be chopped and added to cold poultry salads. If the recipe calls for tomatoes or tomato sauce, add a touch of basil to bring out a rich flavor.
Bay leaf	The basis of many French seasonings. It is added to soups, stews, marinades and stuffings.
Bouquet garni	A bundle of parsley, thyme and bay leaves tied together and added to stews, soups or sauces. Other herbs and spices may be added to the basic herbs.
Chervil	One of the traditional *fines herbes* used in French cooking. (The others are tarragon, parsley and chives.) It is good in omelets and soups.
Chives	Available fresh, dried or frozen, it can be substituted for raw onion or shallot in nearly any recipe.
Garlic	One of the oldest herbs in the world, it must be carefully handled. For best results, press or crush the garlic clove.
Marjoram	An aromatic herb of the mint family, it is good in soups, sauces, stuffings and stews.
Mint	Use fresh, dried or ground with vegetables, desserts, fruits, jelly, lamb or tea. Fresh sprigs of mint make attractive aromatic garnishes.
Oregano	A staple, savory herb in Italian, Spanish, Greek and Mexican cuisines. It is very good in dishes with a tomato foundation, especially in combination with basil.
Parsley	Use this mild herb as fresh sprigs or dried flakes to flavor or garnish almost any dish.
Rosemary	This pungent herb is especially good in poultry and fish dishes and in such accompaniments as stuffings.
Saffron	Use this deep orange herb, made from the dried stamens of a crocus, sparingly in poultry, seafood and rice dishes.
Sage	This herb is a perennial favorite with all kinds of poultry and stuffings.
Tarragon	One of the *fines herbes*. Goes well with all poultry dishes whether hot or cold.
Thyme	Usually used in combination with bay leaf in soups, stews and sauces.

APPETIZERS, PICKLES, RELISHES

APPETIZERS

ASPARAGUS ROLLS

20 slices sandwich bread
1 c. asparagus spears
1 (8 oz.) pkg. cream cheese
3 oz. Blue cheese

4 dashes of Worcestershire
   sauce
¾ c. melted butter

Remove crusts from bread. Roll bread out flat with rolling pin. Mix cheeses and sauce together. Spread on bread. Drain asparagus on paper towels. Roll up 1 spear for each slice of bread. (Seam side down.) Brush with melted butter. Freeze, cut, thaw and bake until brown.

Alice Ritchey

NO LOS BALONEY

Slice baloney to desired thickness. In skillet, saute onions in bacon grease. Throw in baloney. When baloney is half done, cover with slice of American cheese. Cook until cheese melts. Scoop works on toasted bun; add lettuce and tomato; salt and pepper to taste. It's great!

Chef Keno

BATTER FRIED BANANA PEPPERS

Banana peppers
1 egg, beaten
1 tsp. salt
1½ tsp. baking powder
⅔ c. water

1 c. flour
1 Tbsp. salad oil
1 Tbsp. lemon juice
½ tsp. red pepper
Cooking oil for frying

Mix together baking powder, salt, flour and red pepper. Add beaten egg, water, salad oil and lemon juice. Dip peppers in batter and fry in hot cooking oil.

Note: If using hot banana peppers, omit ½ teaspoon red pepper.

Mary Baxter

BENEDICTINE

1 (8 oz.) pkg. Philadelphia
   cream cheese
1 (5 inch) piece peeled
   cucumber

¼ onion (size of an egg)
1 tsp. sugar
1 Tbsp. salad dressing
1 drop of green food coloring

Cut cucumber in small pieces. Put in blender. Add chopped onion. Blend until pulp. Add sugar. Add mixture to cream cheese. Add salad dressing. Stir until it will spread on crackers or bread. Add more pulp if a dip is desired. Add food coloring. Add pulp to cheese a little at a time until you reach the thickness desired.

Alleen S. Gray

CHICKEN LOG

2 (8 oz.) pkg. cream cheese,
   softened
1 Tbsp. bottled steak sauce
½ tsp. curry powder
1½ c. minced cooked
   chicken

⅓ c. minced celery
¼ c. chopped parsley
¼ c. chopped toasted
   almonds

Beat together first 3 ingredients. Blend in next 2 ingredients and 2 tablespoons of parsley. Refrigerate remaining parsley. Shape mixture into a 9 inch log. Wrap in plastic wrap and chill 4 hours or overnight. Toss together remaining parsley and almonds; use to coat log. Makes 3 cups of spread.

Brenda Bishop

CHICKEN NUGGETS

½ c. flour
1 tsp. salt
¼ tsp. pepper
3 tsp. sesame seeds
1 egg, slightly beaten

¼ c. water
1 lb. chicken breasts, cut into
   bite-size pieces
Cooking oil

Combine first 6 ingredients. Roll chicken in batter. Fry in hot cooking oil until golden brown. Drain.

Pam Thompson

CHILI CHEESE MOLD

1 env. unflavored gelatin
1 c. chili sauce
1 c. cottage cheese
½ c. whipping cream,
    whipped

½ tsp. salt
½ c. mayonnaise

Soften gelatin in ¾ cup cold water; dissolve over low heat. Combine chili sauce, cottage cheese, mayonnaise and salt. Add gelatin. Fold in whipped cream. Turn into 1 quart mold. Chill until firm. Unmold on plate. Arrange with an assortment of crackers around it.

Peggy Kessinger

COCKTAIL MEAT BALLS

2 lb. ground round
1 c. corn flake crumbs
⅓ c. dried parsley flakes
2 eggs
2 Tbsp. soy sauce
1 tsp. pepper
1 tsp. garlic powder

⅓ c. catsup
2 Tbsp. minced onions
1 (1 lb.) can jellied cranberry
    sauce
1 (12 oz.) bottle chilli sauce
2 Tbsp. dark brown sugar
1 Tbsp. lemon juice

Heat oven to 350°. Combine the first 9 ingredients. Form into walnut size meat balls. Arrange in baking dish. Cook cranberry sauce, chilli sauce, sugar and lemon juice in saucepan until cranberry sauce is melted. Pour over meat balls and bake 30 minutes.

I like to cook meat balls in the oven about 20 minutes; drain and then add the sauce and cook at least 20 minutes more.

Nadiene Ward

CRABMEAT NIPPIES

1 (6 oz.) can crabmeat
2 tsp. mayonnaise

1 tsp. grated onion
½ c. grated Cheddar cheese

Flake crabmeat and toss with mayonnaise and onion. Spoon onto Melba toast. Sprinkle generously with cheese. Broil 3 inches from heat 1 to 2 minutes until cheese is melted and slightly browned. Serve hot. Makes 20 to 24 canapes.

CREOLE SPREAD

1 (8 oz.) pkg. cream cheese
½ c. dried beef
1 Tbsp. mayonnaise

1 tsp. horseradish
1 tsp. chili sauce
½ tsp. Salad Herbs

Soften cream cheese at room temperature. Beat until smooth. Shred dried beef fine and mix with cream cheese. Add mayonnaise, horseradish, chili sauce and Salad Herbs; mix thoroughly. Store in refrigerator. Makes 1½ cups.

Cristy Lewis

SALAD HERBS

¼ c. parsley
¼ c. dried tarragon leaves
1 Tbsp. dried oregano leaves

1 Tbsp. dried dill weed
1 Tbsp. celery flakes

With blender set on lowest speed, sprinkle parsley, tarragon, oregano, dill and celery flakes into blender a little at a time and blend a few seconds after each addition. Use ½ teaspoon for 4 servings. Store in airtight container. Makes ½ cup.

Cristy Lewis

CURRY LOAF

1 (2¼ oz.) can Underwood
  deviled ham
1 (5 oz.) can Swansons boned
  chicken with broth
1 (8 oz.) pkg. cream cheese
  (room temperature)

A little grated or chopped
  green onion, chopped
  fine
Curry powder
Crisp crackers

Mix together all but curry powder and crackers. Shape into a loaf and cover entire surface with sprinkling of curry powder. Chill. Serve with crisp crackers.

Brownie - Lois Bruner

DELICES DE GRUYERE

3 Tbsp. butter
4 Tbsp. flour
1½ c. milk
1 tsp. salt
Dash of white pepper and
    nutmeg

4 egg yolks
½ lb. (2½ c.) grated Swiss
    cheese
2 Tbsp. flour
1 egg, well beaten
1 c. fine dry bread crumbs

Melt butter in saucepan and stir in flour until smooth; cook 1 to 2 minutes. Stir in milk and cook; stir constantly until thick and smooth. Continue cooking over low heat for 5 minutes. Stir in salt, pepper, nutmeg, egg yolks and grated cheese. Heat thoroughly and remove from heat. Pour into a flat platter and refrigerate 2 to 3 hours. After cheese mixture has been refrigerated, mold into balls the size of large walnuts. Coat with flour; dip in beaten egg; roll in crumbs. Fry in deep fat at 375° for 3 to 4 minutes or until golden brown. Drain on paper toweling. Serve with or without hot tomato sauce as hors d'oeuvres. Serves 4.

Cristy Lewis

EGG AND BACON PIE

1 recipe Basic Pastry plus ½
    c. grated cheese
2 Tbsp. butter
2 - 3 onions, chopped
6 slices bacon, chopped
3 eggs

2 c. milk
½ tsp. dry mustard
2 tsp. chopped parsley
Salt
Pepper

Preheat oven to 375°. Line a deep (8 inch) pie plate with pastry. Heat butter; add onion and bacon; fry for 3 to 4 minutes. Beat eggs; add warm milk; drain onion and bacon. Add salt, pepper, mustard and parsley. Pour into pastry shell; cook 35 to 40 minutes. Extra slices of rolled bacon can be broiled and used as a garnish.

Cristy Lewis

EGG AND MUSHROOM CASSEROLE

½ lb. mushrooms, sliced thin
4 hard-boiled eggs, sliced
3 Tbsp. butter
2 Tbsp. flour
1½ c. milk

Pinch of nutmeg
2 tomatoes, peeled and sliced
Cracker crumbs
Chopped parsley

Preheat oven to 400°. Make a sauce with 2 tablespoons butter, flour and milk. Add salt, pepper and a good pinch of nutmeg. Add mushrooms and simmer for 10 minutes. Arrange slices of egg and tomato in a casserole; pour over the sauce and sprinkle with cracker crumbs. Dot with the remaining 1 tablespoon butter and cook for 20 to 25 minutes, until the top is crisp and brown. Sprinkle with parsley.

Denise Figg

DEVILED EGGS

8 eggs, hard-boiled, sliced
   lengthwise (remove
   yolks)
2 Tbsp. butter

½ tsp. dry mustard
¼ tsp. salt (more if desired)
3 Tbsp. vinegar

Mix and beat butter, mustard, salt and vinegar together. Add mashed yolks and mix well. If mixture is dry, add enough mayonnaise to make creamy mixture. Fill egg halves; sprinkle with paprika.

DEVILED EGGS

12 hard cooked eggs
½ c. salad dressing
¼ c. chopped red or green
   pepper

½ c. chopped celery
¼ c. pickle relish
Salt
Pepper

Cut eggs in half lengthwise. Remove yolks; mash. Blend in salad dressing, celery, red pepper and relish; season to taste. Refill egg whites. Serves 12.

Mary V. Stanley

COUNTRY HAM BALLS

2 lb. country ham, ground
1 lb. pork sausage
2 c. bread crumbs

2 c. milk
2 eggs

   Sauce:

2 c. brown sugar
2 c. cider vinegar

1 c. water
2 Tbsp. mustard

Mix first 5 ingredients together and chill. Roll into small balls and put in a baking dish. Mix the sauce ingredients together and pour half of the sauce over the ham balls and bake at 350° for about 45 minutes. Heat remaining sauce and pour over baked ham balls and serve hot. Yield: About 2 dozen.

Gwen Mills

DEVILED COUNTRY HAM APPETIZER

2 jars Smithfield deviled ham
(from gourmet shop)
1 Tbsp. orange French
dressing (more or less)

2 pkg. cocktail size beaten
biscuits

Mix ham and French dressing and mound onto serving dish. Surround with beaten biscuits and serve as an appetizer or party fare.

LEEKS ON TOAST

2 bunches (approx. 12) leeks
4 slices buttered toast
Melted butter
4 Tbsp. grated Cheddar
cheese

½ tsp. salt
¼ tsp. paprika

Trim leeks; slit through core and wash carefully to remove all sand. Simmer in salted water, to cover, until tender, 20 to 25 minutes. Drain. Place on toast; brush with melted butter and sprinkle with grated cheese, salt and paprika. Place under broiler until cheese is bubbly and just barely browned. Serves 4.

Zella Mae Cox

BAKED MUSHROOMS
(Hors d'oeuvres, side dish or cookout)

1 lb. fresh mushrooms
Butter or margarine
Salt

2 bay leaves
Dry red dinner wine
Fresh ground black pepper

Wipe mushrooms with damp cloth. Place in glass baking dish and add bay leaves, salt and pepper. Dot with butter and sprinkle wine over all. Cover and bake at 450° for about 20 minutes. Arrange on platter garnished with parsley sprigs and cherry tomatoes as hors d'oeuvres. Serve hot as a vegetable, or prepare in foil and cook on back of grill for a great steak accompaniment.

MUSHROOM HOR D'OEUVRES

1 (8 oz.) pkg. cream cheese
8 oz. diced mushrooms
2⅛ oz. minced onions
½ stick butter
12 pieces diet thin white
  bread

Soften cheese. Wash and drain mushrooms. Saute butter, onions and mushrooms for 10 minutes. Cool. Mix everything together and salt to taste. Toast bread on one side; cut off crust. Spread on untoasted side thickly. Place on cookie sheet. Broil 5 minutes or until bubbly. Makes 8. (Freezes well.)

Peggy Graviss

MUSHROOM MOUTHFULS

8 oz. pkg. cream cheese,
  softened
1 stick margarine
1 c. flour
¼ stick margarine
½ lb. (about 2 doz. small)
  mushrooms, chopped
Salt and pepper to taste
1 medium onion, chopped

Blend cream cheese and 1 stick oleo; work in flour and chill. Saute mushrooms and onion in 2 tablespoons margarine until it appears transparent and very slightly browned. Add salt and pepper to taste and cool. Roll out dough on floured board and cut in 3 inch circles. Place a teaspoon of filling in each of the circles and pinch into triangles. Bake on a lightly greased cookie sheet for 10 to 12 minutes at 450°. Serve warm. Makes 2 to 3 dozen.

Barbara C. Hendrick

MUSHROOM AND ONION QUICHE

Pate Brisee pastry
3 Tbsp. butter
2 onions, chopped
1 can (about 1 c.) button
  mushrooms
2 eggs
½ can (about 1 c.) evaporated
  milk
½ c. grated cheese
Pinch of dry mustard

Preheat oven to 400°. Line a deep (8 inch) pie plate with the Pate Brisee. Heat 2 tablespoons of butter in a pan and cook onion until transparent. Drain; put in pastry shell with most of the mushrooms, cut in halves. Leave a few uncooked for decoration. Beat eggs; stir in milk, grated cheese and seasoning. Pour over mushrooms. Bake about 35 minutes. Saute the remaining mushrooms in remaining butter. Drain and cut into thin slices. When pie is done, decorate with sliced mushrooms. Serves 4 or 5.

Bill Farris

STUFFED MUSHROOMS

1 lb. medium to large
   mushrooms
1 stick butter
¼ c. onion, chopped fine
¼ c. celery, chopped fine

1 tsp. Worcestershire sauce
½ tsp. salt (if desired)
Pinch of pepper
Pinch of monosodium
   glutamate

Wash mushrooms; drain; remove stems and chop fine. In large skillet, heat ½ stick of butter. Add onion, celery and mushroom stems. Simmer until celery is tender. Stir in Worcestershire sauce, salt and pepper. Add a pinch of monosodium glutamate. Brush mushroom caps with butter, then fill with onion and celery mixture. Arrange mushroom caps with stuffed sides up in skillet. Simmer 5 minutes or until slightly browned (cover first 2 or 3 minutes). Serve with steak, roast pork, chops or chicken. Also may be used as hors d'oeuvres.

Pam Thompson

STUFFED MUSHROOMS

Season to taste a cake of cream cheese with:

Tabasco
A.1. Sauce
Salt

Mayonnaise
Worcestershire sauce

Remove stems from fresh mushrooms, using those about the size of a quarter to a half dollar. Wash and allow to dry. Stuff the raw caps with the preceding mixture; sprinkle with paprika and serve.

COOKED OLIVES

1 lb. green olives, pitted	Parsley, chopped
6 cloves garlic	Salt
Red pepper	1 c. water
3 Tbsp. oil for frying	1 lemon slice
Juice of ½ lemon	

Saute garlic in oil until golden. Add red pepper, water, parsley and olives; cook over very low heat for 30 minutes until most of the liquid evaporates. Add lemon juice shortly before dish is ready. Decorate with a lemon slice and serve as appetizer or with grilled or stuffed chicken. Preparing time: 10 to 15 minutes. Cooking time: 30 minutes. Serves 5.

Traditional for Oriental Jews.

Paula White

ONIONS VIENNESE

Cut 2½ pounds of onions into quarters. Cover with water and allow to reach good boil. Drain.

Add to them:

2 Tbsp. sherry wine	½ tsp. marjoram
½ c. chopped celery	Pinch of thyme
¼ c. pimentos	1 Tbsp. monosodium
1 c. mushrooms	glutamate

Melt ½ stick butter and slowly blend in 2 tablespoons flour and 1½ cups milk. Cook until mixture thickens, then combine with onions. Place layers of onion mixture, cracker crumbs and cheese (½ pound at least) in casserole. Top with paprika. Bake at 325° for 1 hour.

Mrs. Ken Ford

PIGS IN BLANKETS

6 frankfurters	Flaky pastry
Prepared mustard	Egg or milk to glaze
6 thin fingers of cheese	

Preheat oven to 450°. Split the frankfurters; spread lightly with mustard and insert a finger of cheese in each. Roll the pastry thin and cut into 6 inch squares. Place 1 frankfurter diagonally on each square and bring together the other 2 diagonal corners of the pastry, so that the ends of the frankfurters are exposed. Put on a baking sheet; glaze with egg or milk and bake 20 minutes.

Melanie Davis

DEEP DISH PIZZA

1 lb. ground beef	1 pkg. cheese pizza mix
¼ c. chopped onion	2 (6 oz.) pkg. Mozzarella
¼ c. chopped green pepper	cheese
1 (16 oz.) can tomatoes	

Brown meat; drain. Add onion and green pepper. Cook until tender. Stir in tomatoes and pizza sauce from mix; simmer 15 minutes. Heat oven to 425°. Prepare pizza dough as directed. Press into bottom and halfway up sides of greased 13x9 inch pan. Cover with half of Mozzarella and meat sauce; repeat with remaining cheese and meat sauce. Sprinkle with grated Parmesan cheese from pizza mix. Bake at 425° for 20 to 25 minutes. Let stand for 10 minutes before serving.

Betty Jo Yeary

LITTLE PIZZAS

Split English muffins and toast. Spread with tomato paste. Top with thin slice of cheese or grated cheese. Sprinkle with a pinch of oregano. Broil until cheese is bubbly.

Mary Beeler

SAUSAGE PIZZA

1 pizza crust mix with sauce	½ medium green pepper
½ lb. hot Webbers sausage	1 c. Mozzarella cheese
½ medium onion, chopped	

Fix pizza crust mix according to directions. Let stand. Cook the sausage over medium heat, breaking up sausage; drain. Spray pizza pan with Pam. Butter hands well; knead dough for 5 minutes; spread over pan. Cover with sauce; sprinkle sausage, onion and green pepper; cover with shredded cheese. Bake at 425° for 20 minutes or until crust is brown.

Renee Rapier

SALMON PARTY BALL

1 (1 lb.) can (2 c.) salmon
1 (8 oz.) pkg. cream cheese,
   softened
1 Tbsp. lemon juice
2 tsp. grated onion

1 tsp. prepared horseradish
¼ tsp. salt
¼ tsp. liquid smoke
½ c. chopped pecans
3 Tbsp. snipped parsley

Drain and flake salmon, removing skin and bones. Combine salmon, cream cheese, lemon juice, onion, horseradish, salt and liquid smoke; mix. Chill several hours. Combine pecans and parsley. Shape salmon mixture into ball; roll in nut mixture. Chill.

Linda Y. Borden

SALMON SPREAD

1 (15½ oz.) can salmon,
   drained
1 (8 oz.) pkg. cream cheese,
   softened
1 Tbsp. lemon juice

1 tsp. grated onion
1 tsp. prepared horseradish
½ c. chopped pecans
2 Tbsp. parsley

Flake salmon; discard skin and bones. In a mixing bowl, stir together cream cheese, lemon juice, grated onion and horseradish. Add salmon. Mix well. Chill thoroughly. Form into an 8 inch long log. Combine pecans and parsley; roll log in nut mixture. Chill. Serve with assorted crackers.

Sharon Duke

SAUERKRAUT BALLS

8 slices bacon
½ c. onion, finely chopped
½ c. mashed potatoes
1 Tbsp. parsley flakes
2 tsp. caraway seeds
2 eggs, beaten

1 clove garlic, finely chopped
1 (16 oz.) can sauerkraut,
   drained
1½ c. Special K cereal,
   crushed
Oil

Fry bacon in large skillet until crisp; drain and crumble. Pour off all but 2 tablespoons fat. Saute onion and garlic until tender. Stir in bacon, sauerkraut, potatoes (can use instant) and parsley. Drop by rounded teaspoonfuls onto waxed paper lined baking sheet and form into balls. Cover with wax paper and refrigerate until firm. Mix cereal and caraway seeds. Dip sauerkraut balls in eggs and roll in cereal mixture. Fry balls until brown in oil heated to 375°. Drain on paper towel.

Beverley Piatkowski

SAUSAGE BALLS

1 lb. Webbers (mild) sausage   1½ c. Bisquick
1 (8 oz.) jar Cheez Whiz

Mix with hands. Roll into small balls. Freeze. Then bake at 400° for 20 minutes.

Flora Montgomery

SAUSAGE BALLS

1¼ lb. pork sausage   6 c. Bisquick
10 oz. grated sharp cheese
    (such as Cracker Barrel
    Cheddar)

Mix all ingredients and blend thoroughly with your hands. Roll into balls the size of small marbles. Bake in 350° to 400° oven until brown.

Note: These freeze well and can be baked at the last minute.

Ruth Ackerman

SAUSAGE BALLS

1 lb. hot sausage   1 lb. Cheddar cheese, grated
3 c. Bisquick   1 Tbsp. onion, minced
1 tsp. hot sauce

Crumble sausage and mix with cheese. Add Bisquick 1 cup at a time. Add minced onion and hot sauce. Mix well. Form into 1 inch balls and place on ungreased cookie sheets. (At this point, you can freeze them for later use.) Bake in preheated 350° oven for about 15 minutes or until light brown. If frozen, may take a few extra minutes. Serve warm.

Denise Figg

SAUSAGE PINEAPPLE TIDBITS

1 lb. smoked sausage   ½ c. currant jelly
½ c. chili sauce   1½ tsp. prepared mustard
1½ tsp. lemon juice   1 large can pineapple chunks

Slice sausage into bite-size chunks. Drain pineapple chunks. Mix all ingredients in a saucepan and simmer for 15 minutes. Serve in a chafing dish.

Sharon Duke

SCANDINAVIAN GINGER SAUSAGES

2 egg yolks
1 lb. pork sausage
½ c. chopped dill pickle

1 tsp. ginger
2 Tbsp. all-purpose flour

Beat egg yolks; mix with sausage, pickles and ginger; blend well. Chill for 2 to 3 hours. Shape into very small sausages and roll in flour. Fry in deep fryer at 375°. Serve warm. Yield: 4 to 5 dozen.

Paula White

SWEET AND SOUR SAUSAGE

1½ lb. smoked sausage
1 large can pineapple chunks
½ c. soy sauce
4 Tbsp. cornstarch

1 c. pineapple
1 c. vinegar
1½ c. sugar
1 c. water

Mix liquid and cornstarch in saucepan. Cook 10 minutes over low heat until thick. Add pineapple chunks and sausage which has been cut into bite-size chunks. Simmer 15 minutes. Serve hot.

Sharon Duke

SHRIMP MOUSSE

1 can condensed tomato
  soup
9 oz. pkg. cream cheese
2 Tbsp. gelatin
4 tuna sized cans shrimp,
  drained and mashed
½ c. green pepper, minced

½ c. celery, minced
1 small onion, minced
Garlic salt
Juice of 1 lemon
1 c. mayonnaise
Crackers

Over low temperature, heat together the tomato soup and cream cheese until melted and blended. Meanwhile, dissolve the gelatin in ⅓ cup cold water. When mixed thoroughly, add to the warm soup and cheese mixture. Cool the mixture in the refrigerator while completing the next part of the recipe. Combine the remaining ingredients, stirring until completely mixed. Combine with the refrigerated mixture and put in

5 to 6 cup mold. Refrigerate for several hours and serve with crackers. (The mousse keeps well for several days in refrigerator.)

Note: I use 3 cans of shrimp and it is just as delicious.

Wilma Crowdus

SNACK

½ c. oil, heated
1 pkg. Kroger oyster crackers
1 pkg. Hidden Valley original
    dressing

1 tsp. dill
½ tsp. lemon pepper

Pour hot oil over crackers and mix well. Sprinkle Hidden Valley dressing, dill and lemon pepper and mix.

Chris Stagner

TURTLES HORS D'OEUVRES

1 lb. ground chuck
1 lb. hot Italian sausage

Brown together. Add 1 pound Velveeta cheese, chopped. Stir until melted. Spread on small rye party rounds. Place on cookie sheet and freeze. Then bag. Makes 5 dozen.

You are always ready for guests. No need to thaw. Bake at 375° until brown and bubbly.

Doris Beeler

APPETIZER CHEESECAKE

2 c. sour cream
½ c. finely chopped green
    pepper
½ c. finely chopped celery
¼ c. finely chopped pimento
    stuffed olives
¼ c. finely chopped onion

2 tsp. lemon juice
1 tsp. Worcestershire sauce
5 drops of bottled hot pepper
    sauce
1⅓ c. rich round cracker
    crumbs
Dash of paprika

Combine all ingredients, except crumbs. Line 4 cup bowl with clear plastic wrap. Spread ½ cup of sour cream mixture in bottom of bowl. Layer with ½ cup of the crumbs, then 1 cup sour cream mixture, ½ cup crumbs and the remaining sour cream mixture. Cover; chill for 24 hours. Store remaining cracker crumbs. *Before serving,* unmold on serving plate; remove wrap. Top with remaining crumbs. Serve with assorted crackers.

Barbara C. Hendrick

AUNT IRENE'S CHEESE ROLL

2 (8 oz.) pkg. cream cheese
2 pkg. smoked ham, chipped
Green onions
¼ tsp. salt
1 tsp. Worcestershire sauce

Let cream cheese soften at room temperature. Finely chop green onions. Mix with cheese along with 1 package of ham, salt and sauce. Shape into ball and refrigerate. When cool, roll in other package of ham. Makes 2 cheese rolls.

Sharon Sherman

BACON AND CHEESE PUFF PIE

Fry 10 slices of bacon; drain. Place 1 can of crescent roll dough in 9 inch ungreased pie pan to form crust. Sprinkle bacon over crust. Top with tomato slices (2 medium tomatoes); season with salt and pepper. Place 4 thin slices of Kraft American cheese over top. Beat 3 egg whites until stiff. Set aside. In large mixing bowl, combine 3 egg yolks, ¾ cup sour cream, ½ cup all-purpose flour, ½ teaspoon salt and a dash of pepper. Blend well. Gently fold beaten egg whites into mixture until a few lumps of egg white remain. Do not overblend. Pour mixture over cheese layer. Sprinkle with paprika. Bake at 350° for 35 to 40 minutes or until knife comes out clean.

Edna Flanders

BACON-CHEDDAR CHEESE SPREAD

2 c. shredded Cheddar
  cheese
⅓ c. sour cream
2 Tbsp. green onion,
  chopped fine
3 slices cooked bacon,
  crumbled

Beat together cheese, sour cream, onion and bacon.

Melanie Davis

BEER CHEESE

2 lb. Kraft American cheese,
   grated
7 oz. ketchup
1/5 bottle Louisiana hot sauce

3/8 oz. garlic powder
1 (12 oz.) can beer (opened
   for 2 days)

Grate cheese. Add remaining ingredients. Blend in blender or food processor.

Pablo Briseno

BEER CHEESE

1 lb. sharp Cheddar cheese
1/2 tsp. cayenne
1/4 c. beer (or a little less; just
   enough to moisten)*

8 oz. pkg. Philadelphia cream
   cheese
1/2 tsp. garlic juice

Have cheeses at room temperature. Grate Cheddar cheese, then add cream cheese and other ingredients; mix thoroughly. Shape into log and roll in a mixture of 1 tablespoon chili powder, 1 teaspoon cayenne and approximately 1/2 cup paprika. Wrap in wax paper and store in refrigerator. Will keep a week or longer.

* Olive juice can be substituted for beer if preferred.

BEER CHEESE BITES

2 c. Bisquick
2/3 c. Cheddar cheese,
   shredded

1/2 c. beer
2 Tbsp. margarine, melted
Sesame seed or poppy seed

Heat oven to 450°. Mix Bisquick, cheese and beer; make a soft dough. Beat vigorously about a minute. Form dough into a ball on a floured board. Knead 5 times. Roll into rectangle about 10x16 inches. Cut into 2 inch squares, then cut squares diagonally into halves (triangles). Spread with melted margarine, then sprinkle with sesame or poppy seeds. Place on ungreased baking sheet and bake about 8 minutes or until brown. Yield: 80 appetizers.

Peggy Kessinger

CASHEW CURRY SPREAD

½ c. cream cheese
½ c. cottage cheese

1 tsp. curry powder
½ c. cashews, chopped fine

Mash cheeses together. Add curry powder and nuts; mix together. Chill in refrigerator.

CHEESE BALL

2 (8 oz.) pkg. cream cheese
1 (8½ oz.) can crushed
   pineapple, drained
¼ c. green pepper, minced

2 Tbsp. onions, chopped
1 tsp. seasoned salt
1 c. chopped nuts
Nuts to roll ball in

Mix cheese and pineapple. Add other ingredients. Chill until firm enough to roll in nuts.

Patricia Embry

CHEESE BALL

6 slices crisply cooked
   bacon, crumbled
3 Tbsp. Kraft cold pack Blue
   cheese
½ c. chopped pecans
¼ c. milk
1 (8 oz.) pkg. Philadelphia
   Brand cream cheese
2 c. (8 oz.) shredded Cracker
   Barrel brand sharp
   natural Cheddar cheese

1 tsp. Tabasco sauce
1 (8 oz.) can crushed
   pineapple, drained
1 tsp. chopped candied
   ginger
1 (3 oz.) pkg. Philadelphia
   Brand cream cheese

Combine softened cream cheese, Blue cheese, pineapple, nuts and ginger until well blended. Spoon into 1 quart mold. Chill. Combine softened cream cheese with milk until well blended. Stir in shredded cheese; add bacon, onion and Tabasco sauce. Spread over first layer. Refrigerate overnight; unmold. Garnish top layer with coconut and pecan halves if desired.

CHEESE BALL

1 lb. Colby or Cheddar
    cheese
1 small pkg. cream cheese
    (room temperature)
1 Tbsp. chopped green
    peppers

1 Tbsp. chopped onion
1½ Tbsp. chopped pimento
2 dashes of Worcestershire
    sauce
1 tsp. lemon juice
Crushed nuts (optional)

Mix together. Roll in crushed nuts if desired.

Allouise Davidson

CHIP BEEF CHEESE BALL

2 (8 oz.) pkg. cream cheese
1 (3 oz.) pkg. smoked beef,
    cut fine
¼ c. pecans
1 Tbsp. Worcestershire sauce

1 Tbsp. diced onion
Few dashes of Tabasco
Pecan chips
Parsley flakes

Mix all but pecan chips and parsley flakes with an electric mixer. Place and shape into a ball. Cover with pecan chips and parsley flakes.

Donna Barrett

CHRISTMAS-RED CHEESE BALL

½ lb. natural Cheddar
    cheese, finely grated
¼ c. coarsely chopped pitted
    ripe olives
Dash each of onion, garlic
    and celery salts

1 (3 oz.) pkg. soft cream
    cheese
3 Tbsp. sherry
½ tsp. Worcestershire
½ c. coarsely snipped dried
    beef (optional)

Several days ahead or day before: In large bowl, with mixer at medium speed, thoroughly combine cheeses, sherry, ripe olives, Worcestershire and salts. Shape mixture into a ball; wrap in foil and refrigerate until needed. About 30 minutes before serving, remove foil, reshape if necessary, and roll in dried beef. Makes about a 3 inch ball.

COLORADO CHEESE BALL

1 (3 oz.) pkg. cream cheese
(room temperature)
1 Tbsp. Worcestershire sauce
¼ tsp. salt
6 drops of Tabasco sauce

¼ lb. Blue cheese, grated
½ lb. sharp Cheddar cheese,
grated
½ tsp. Accent
1 tsp. lemon juice

Blend together. Form 2 balls; roll in 1 cup chopped pecans and parsley flakes. Refrigerate. Serve with your favorite saltines.

CREAM CHEESE CARROT BALLS

8 oz. pkg. cream cheese
½ c. raisins

1 c. carrots, grated
½ c. pecans

Blend a small amount of milk into the cream cheese. Add raisins and pecans; mix well. Form into balls. Roll in grated carrots. Serve on lettuce leaves with mayonnaise or your favorite salad dressing.

Cristy Lewis

CHEESE BALL

2 (8 oz.) pkg. Philadelphia
cream cheese
1 pkg. Cracker Barrel
Cheddar cheese spread
(bell shaped container)
1 Tbsp. green pepper

1 Tbsp. onion
1 Tbsp. pimento
1 Tbsp. bacon bits
2 Tbsp. Worcestershire sauce
1 Tbsp. lemon juice
¼ tsp. garlic

Mix together; form ball or mound. Cover with nuts.

Ouida Brown

CREAM CHEESE BRAIDS

1 c. sour cream
½ c. butter
2 pkg. yeast
½ c. sugar

1 tsp. salt
½ c. warm water (105°)
2 eggs, beaten
4 c. plain flour

Heat sour cream over low heat; stir in sugar, salt and butter. Cool to lukewarm. Sprinkle yeast over water in a large mixing bowl, stirring until yeast dissolves. Add sour cream mixture, eggs and flour. Mix well; cover tightly and refrigerate overnight or for several hours (until good and cool).

To make braids: Divide dough into 4 equal parts. Roll out each part on a well floured board into a 12x8 inch rectangle (or close to it). Spread ¼ of Cream Cheese Filling on each rectangle. Roll up jelly roll fashion, beginning on the long side. Pinch ends together and fold under. Place the rolls, seam down, on greased baking sheet. Slit each roll to resemble a braid (I just make XXX on top). Cover and let rise until doubled, about an hour. Bake at 375° for 12 to 15 minutes. Spread with glaze while warm.

Cream Cheese Filling:

2 (8 oz.) pkg. cream cheese, softened	1 egg, beaten
¾ c. sugar	⅛ tsp. salt
	2 tsp. vanilla

Combine cream cheese and sugar. Add other ingredients. Mix well.

Glaze:

2 c. powdered sugar	2 tsp. vanilla
4 Tbsp. milk	

Mix well and spread over bread while warm. Add extra milk or water if too thick.

Patsy S. Brown

CHEESE ROLL

1 lb. sharp cheese, grind	½ c. mayonnaise
¼ c. tomato catsup	1 Tbsp. mustard
1 small can pimentos	Dash of Worcestershire sauce
Dash of Tabasco sauce	

Mix until smooth. Let stand in refrigerator until cold, then roll in ground peanuts or pecans.

For a change, instead of pimentos, substitute crisp bacon crumbs, garlic, onion, olives and green pepper.

CHEESE SPREAD

¾ c. beer
10 oz. Blue cheese, crumbled
10 oz. Cheddar cheese,
    grated
1 Tbsp. butter, softened

1 Tbsp. onion, minced
1 tsp. Worcestershire sauce
Dash of Tabasco sauce
½ tsp. dry mustard

Blend beer and cheese in blender. Add remaining ingredients and blend until smooth. Chill.

Paula White

DEVILED HAM BALLS

3 (2¼ oz.) cans deviled ham
¼ c. pretzels, coarsely
    crushed
½ tsp. Worcestershire sauce

Dash of pepper
3 (3 oz.) pkg. cream cheese,
    softened
Chives

Form into 25 small balls and freeze 30 minutes. Roll each ball in 1 tablespoon of softened cream cheese to cover it completely. Roll in chives. Refrigerate until served.

Freddie Clinton

DEVILED HAM BALL

2 large jars deviled ham
1 (8 oz.) pkg. cream cheese
    (room temperature)
Garlic powder

Dried minced onion (about 2
    tsp.)
A little milk

Mix deviled ham with minced onion to taste. Form in mound and place in center of plate. Beat cream cheese, at room temperature, with enough milk to make it spread easy. Season with garlic powder. Frost deviled ham ball with cream cheese mixture and garnish with parsley. Serve with assorted crackers.

Melanie Davis

HAM BALLS

1½ lb. ham, ground
1½ lb. pork, ground
2 eggs, beaten
1 can tomato rice soup
1 c. corn flake crumbs

1 c. crushed pineapple
¼ c. vinegar
½ c. brown sugar
Small jar maraschino
    cherries, quartered

Mix ham and pork together; add 2 eggs, tomato rice soup and corn flakes. Mix well and form into small balls. Mix crushed pineapple, vinegar, brown sugar and maraschino cherries; spread over ham balls. Bake at 350° for 1 to 1½ hours.

Pam Thompson

HAM AND EGG BALLS

3 boiled eggs
¼ lb. cooked ham
1 tsp. chives
Salt to taste

½ tsp. paprika
Mayonnaise
Crushed corn flakes

Mash egg yolks, chives and mayonnaise to make a smooth paste. Add paprika; salt to taste. Grind egg whites; add ham and combine mixtures. Add more mayonnaise if needed. Form into balls and roll in crushed corn flakes. Serve on toothpicks.

Peggy Kessinger

HERBED CHEESE SPREAD

1 (8 oz.) pkg. cream cheese
½ c. crumbled Blue cheese

3 tsp. Salad Herbs (see index)

Let cream cheese and Blue cheese soften to room temperature, then blend together in blender until smooth. Add Salad Herbs and mix well. Chill. Yield: 1 ¼ cups.

Cristy Lewis

HOLIDAY CHEESE BALL

1 (8 oz.) pkg. cream cheese,
   softened
1 (8½ oz.) can crushed
   pineapple, drained
2 c. chopped pecans
¼ c. chopped green pepper

3 Tbsp. chopped onion
1 tsp. seasoned salt
2 Tbsp. chopped chutney
Maraschino cherries
Parsley

Beat cream cheese slightly; gradually stir in pineapple, 1 cup pecans, green pepper, onion, seasoned salt and chutney. Chill well. Shape into a ball and roll in remaining pecans. Chill until serving time. Garnish with maraschino cherries and parsley. Serve with assorted crackers. Yield: 4½ cups.

Paula White

HUNGARIAN CHEESE SPREAD

8 oz. pkg. cream cheese
2 Tbsp. whipped butter
2 Tbsp. green pepper,
   chopped fine
2 Tbsp. chives, chopped

2 tsp. capers, chopped
¼ tsp. dry mustard
1 tsp. Hungarian paprika
¼ tsp. salt
¼ tsp. pepper

Mix cream cheese with whipped butter. Blend in all the other ingredients. Shape into a ball and chill.

Denise Figg

LEEK BALLS - PRASAH

2 large leeks
5 oz. lean beef
2 eggs
½ slice white bread, soaked
   in water and drained

1 egg (hard-boiled)
Oil for frying
Bread crumbs
Salt
Pepper

Cook leeks in water for 15 minutes; drain and cool. In a bowl, mince together meat, cooked leeks, hard-boiled egg and bread. Mix well and add 2 beaten eggs, seasoning and bread crumbs. Form into balls and fry in oil. Serve as first course or a side dish to the main course. Preparing time: 30 minutes. Cooking time: 30 minutes. Serves 6.

Traditional for Bulgarian Jews.

Paula White

FRIED CHEESE MELTAWAYS

1 c. Bisquick
½ c. milk
1 egg
1 lb. Cheddar, Swiss,
   Monterey Jack, Colby or

Mozzarella cheese, cut
into ¾ inch cubes
Cooking oil

Heat cooking oil (2 inches) in deep fryer to 375°. Mix 1 cup baking mix, milk and egg until smooth (use hand beater). Coat cheese cubes lightly with baking mix. Insert a wooden pick in each cheese cube; dip in batter and fry several cubes at a time; turn until golden brown, about 1 or 2 minutes. Drain on paper towels. Yield: About 45 appetizers.

Peggy Kessinger

NOODLES CHEDDAR

1 c. cottage cheese
1½ c. sour cream
1 crushed clove of garlic
1 tsp. Worcestershire sauce
2 Tbsp. grated onion

½ tsp. salt
8 oz. hot cooked, drained egg
   noodles
1 c. shredded Cheddar
   cheese

Mix all ingredients, except ¼ cup shredded cheese. Place in 2 quart casserole; sprinkle remaining cheese on top. Bake in 400° oven 25 to 30 minutes.

Denise Figg

OLIVE CHEESE BALLS

2 c. shredded sharp natural
   Cheddar cheese
1¼ c. all-purpose flour

½ c. margarine
36 small pimento stuffed
   olives, drained

Mix cheese and flour mix in margarine (work dough with hands if it seems dry). Mold 1 teaspoon dough around each olive. Shape into a ball. Place 2 inches apart on ungreased cookie sheet. Cover and refrigerate at least 1 hour. Heat oven to 400°. Bake 15 to 20 minutes.

Pat Vinscom

CHEESE WAFERS

1 lb. sharp Cheddar cheese
1 lb. butter
¼ tsp. salt

4 c. flour
¼ tsp. cayenne

Grate cheese and mix with butter at room temperature. Add flour, salt and cayenne. Mix well, using hands. Make small balls, rolling in palms of hands. Place on ungreased baking sheet. Press half a pecan in center of each ball, mashing in well. Bake at 425° for 20 to 25 minutes.

These do not get brown. These freeze really well.

Barbara C. Hendrick

PIMENTO, CREAM CHEESE, PECAN SPREAD

1 lb. cream cheese
1 (4 oz.) jar pimentos plus
   juice

Dash of pepper

Put in large bowl and mix with electric mixer until well blended.

1 Tbsp. sugar
½ Tbsp. salt
1½ Tbsp. flour

1 well beaten egg
¼ c. vinegar
4 Tbsp. melted butter

Mix sugar, salt, flour, egg and vinegar in a small saucepan. Add melted butter and cook over medium heat until thick. Pour into cream cheese mixture and beat until well mixed. Add 1 cup chopped pecans; mix well and chill. Serve on a variety of crackers or use as dip.

Mrs. Clarence Ebelhar

PIMENTO CHEESE SPREAD

1 c. milk
1 large can or jar pimentos
1 lb. American cheese
5 Tbsp. flour
1 egg

2 Tbsp. sugar
5 Tbsp. vinegar or pickle
    juice
¼ tsp. salt

Place milk into double boiler; cut cheese in small chunks into milk. Cook until cheese is melted. Remove from heat and cool. Chop pimentos. Add egg and pimentos to cheese mixture. Mix flour, sugar, salt and vinegar; add to cheese mixture. Place back on heat; cook until moderately thick. Remove from heat and beat slightly before pouring into container. Cool. Keep in refrigerator. Good for lunches.

Fay Smith

PIMIENTO CHEESE SPREAD

¾ lb. mild cheese
1 large can pimientos
6 hard-boiled eggs

4 medium pickles
Salad dressing

Grind cheese, pimientos, eggs and pickles in food chopper. Mix with juice from can of pimientos and enough salad dressing to give mixture a good spreading consistency.

Lila Stovall

PINEAPPLE CHEESE BALL

2 (8 oz.) pkg. cream cheese,
  softened
1 small can crushed
  pineapple, drained
2 c. chopped pecans

¼ c. finely chopped green
  pepper
2 Tbsp. finely chopped onion
1 Tbsp. seasoned salt

In a medium bowl, with fork, beat cream cheese until smooth. Gradually stir in pineapple, 1 cup pecans, green pepper, onion and salt. Shape into ball. Chill until firm enough to roll into ball and roll in remaining nuts. Wrap in foil. Refrigerate until well chilled, preferably overnight. Any leftover cheese mixture can be reshaped and refrigerated for use another day. Serves 40.

Patricia Jewell

PINEAPPLE CHEESE BALL

2 (8 oz.) pkg. cream cheese
2 c. chopped pecans
1 Tbsp. grated onion, drained

1 small can crushed
  pineapple
¼ c. grated green pepper

Soften cream cheese and mix pineapple, pepper and onion. Add 1 cup of pecans. Refrigerate until chilled. Work into a ball and roll in rest of nuts.

Donna Barrett

POLISH CHEESE SPREAD

½ lb. cottage cheese
½ lb. chopped chives or
  green onions
8 small radishes, chopped

2 pickled gherkins, chopped
2 Tbsp. sour cream
Salt and pepper to taste

Mix ingredients together well. Serve on dark rye or pumpernickel.

Kim Clinton

SAGE CHEESE

1 (3 oz.) pkg. cream cheese
1 c. cottage cheese
2 Tbsp. Roquefort cheese,
  crumbled
2½ tsp. ground sage

½ tsp. salt
⅛ tsp. pepper
¼ tsp. garlic powder
½ tsp. lemon juice
Paprika or parsley flakes

Soften cream cheese to room temperature; combine with cottage and Roquefort cheeses; mix well. Add sage, salt, pepper, garlic powder and lemon juice; mix well. Chill 2 or 3 hours. Garnish with parsley or paprika. Yield: 1½ cups.

Cristy Lewis

HOT SWISS CANAPES

3 egg whites
3 slices uncooked bacon, chopped
1½ c. shredded Swiss cheese
¾ c. green pepper, chopped fine
¼ c. green onions, chopped fine
½ tsp. salt
⅛ tsp. pepper
24 slices party rye bread

Have egg whites at room temperature. Beat until stiff (peaks form). Have the next 6 ingredients ready; fold into egg whites. Spread about 1 tablespoon mixture on each bread slice. Place on cookie sheet and broil 5 inches from heat 5 to 7 minutes, until bacon cooks. Serve immediately.

Brownie - Lois Bruner

TEATIME TASSIES

11 oz. (1 (8 oz.) pkg. and 1 (3 oz.) pkg.) cream cheese
½ c. butter
2 eggs
2 Tbsp. soft butter
Dash of salt
1 c. sifted flour
1½ c. brown sugar, packed
2 tsp. vanilla
2 c. chopped pecans

Cheese Pastry: Let the cream cheese and the ½ cup of butter soften at room temperature. Blend and stir in flour. Chill, about 1 hour. Shape into 2 dozen (1 inch) balls and place into miniature muffin tins (ungreased). Press dough on bottom and up sides to form cups.

Pecan Filling: Beat together eggs, sugar, 2 tablespoons butter, vanilla and salt until smooth. Divide ½ of the pecans among pastry lined cups. Add egg mixture equally among cups and top with remaining pecans. Bake in a slow oven, 350°, for 25 minutes and cool before serving.

Ruth Ackerman

28

DIPS

APRICOT FRUIT DIP

8 oz. cream cheese
9 oz. Cool Whip
4 Tbsp. mayonnaise

2 Tbsp. lemon juice
12 oz. jar apricot jelly
Dash of curry powder

Mix all ingredients, except Cool Whip. Blend well.

Note: Pears, apples, pineapple and bananas are especially good to dip.

Sarah A. Drewes

HOT BEAN DIP

½ c. Cheddar cheese, grated
1 (No. 2) can pork and beans
1 or 2 tsp. chili powder
2 Tbsp. vinegar

2 Tbsp. tomato juice
2 tsp. Worcestershire sauce
1 tsp. garlic salt
Dash of cayenne pepper

Blend all ingredients together in blender until smooth. Serve with potato chips or crackers.

Melissa Jackson

BEAU MONDE DIP

4 oz. sour cream
¾ c. Hellmann's mayonnaise
1 tsp. Beau Monde seasoning

1 tsp. dill weed (not seed)
½ tsp. garlic powder
1 tsp. parsley flakes

Mix together; serve with vegetables.

J. W. Borden, Jr.

CHEESE DIP/SPREAD

1 (5 oz.) jar Old English
　cheese

1 (8 oz.) pkg. cream cheese
1 green onion, chopped

Let cheese reach room temperature. With mixer, blend until smooth. Stir in green onion. Put mixture in a container with lid that can be placed in freezer. Leave in freezer overnight. Let thaw at room temperature, about 2 hours. Serve with crackers or veggies.

Rose Briseno

CREAMY BEEF CHEESE DIP

1 (8 oz.) pkg. cream cheese
1 pkg. chipped beef, chopped
   fine
½ c. walnuts, chopped
   coarse
½ c. sour cream or cottage
   cheese

2 Tbsp. onion, chopped fine
2 Tbsp. green pepper,
   chopped
3 Tbsp. milk
¾ tsp. pepper

Place block of cream cheese in a 1 quart glass bowl. Mix until soft. Add remaining ingredients and stir well. Serve with crackers or vegetables.

Opal Willis

DRIED BEEF DIP

2 c. sour cream
2 (8 oz.) pkg. cream cheese
1 small onion, diced

1 green pepper, diced
1 or 2 (4 oz.) jars dried beef

Heat sour cream; add onion and green pepper. Add 1 package cream cheese. Pull dried beef into shreds and blend in until cheese is soft. Add other package of cream cheese and heat until evenly blended.

Beth Howard

HOT BEEF DIP

1 c. (2½ oz. jar) dried beef
¼ c. chopped onion
1 Tbsp. margarine
1 c. milk
1 (8 oz.) pkg. cream cheese,
   cubed

½ c. sliced mushrooms,
   drained
¼ c. grated Parmesan cheese
2 Tbsp. chopped parsley

Rinse dried beef in hot water; drain and chop. Cook onion in margarine until tender. Stir in milk and cream cheese; mix well until blended. Add dried beef and remaining ingredients. Mix well. Serve hot. Makes 2 cups.

Melanie Davis

BENEDICTINE DIP

1 (8 oz.) pkg. Philadelphia
    cream cheese
1 Tbsp. cucumber, grated

¼ tsp. onion, grated
1 drop of green food coloring

Moisten cheese with cream to make a paste; add other ingredients and mix well.

Paula White

BLEU CHEESE DIP

8 oz. cream cheese
¾ c. Bleu cheese
¼ tsp. garlic salt

3 Tbsp. milk
1 Tbsp. mayonnaise
1½ tsp. lemon juice

Soften cream cheese. Grate Bleu cheese into cream cheese. Add remaining ingredients; blend thoroughly after each addition.

Pam Thompson

COTTAGE CHEESE DIP

1 c. small curd cottage
    cheese
¼ c. creamy cucumber
    dressing
2 Tbsp. green onion,
    chopped fine

3 slices bacon, cooked crisp
    and crumbled
1 Tbsp. pimento, minced

Combine all ingredients; mix well and chill.

Melissa Jackson

EASY CHEESE DIP

1 jar Kraft's Cheez Whiz
Kraft mayonnaise (enough to
    "dip" consistency)

1 Tbsp. Worcestershire sauce

Blend all ingredients well. Serve with raw vegetables.

Ruth Ackerman

HOT CRAB DIP

1 (8 oz.) pkg. cream cheese
1 can Campbell's cream of
   shrimp soup
1 Tbsp. chopped chives

1 (6 oz.) can crabmeat
1 (6 oz.) shrimp (more crab
   and shrimp may be
   added if desired)

Cook until heated through in top of double boiler. Serve while hot in a fondue pot. Serve with Triscuits or other crackers.

Thin with milk or cream and serve over rice for dinner.

Barbara C. Hendrick

CURRY DIP

1 c. mayonnaise
1 tsp. curry powder
1 tsp. onion, minced

1 Tbsp. catsup
1 Tbsp. Worcestershire sauce
1 garlic clove, crushed

Mix ingredients together. When ready to serve, take out garlic clove. Make day before you want to use it. Serve with raw vegetables.

Mildred Zack

CURRY DIP

1 c. mayonnaise
1 tsp. curry powder
2 tsp. minced onion

1 tsp. horseradish
1 tsp. prepared mustard
1 tsp. cider vinegar

Combine all ingredients and mix well. Serve with raw vegetables.

Trudy Frazier

CURRY DIP

1 c. mayonnaise
1 tsp. curry powder
1 tsp. grated onion

1 tsp. cider vinegar
1 tsp. horseradish

Mix all ingredients thoroughly. Chill until ready to serve. Serve in center of platter with raw vegetables of carrots and celery sticks, broccoli and cauliflower.

Sharon Duke

DILL DIP

⅔ c. mayonnaise
⅔ c. sour cream
1 Tbsp. chopped parsley

1 Tbsp. chopped green onion
1 tsp. Beau Monde
1 tsp. dill weed

Mix all together and refrigerate overnight. Makes 2 cups.

Dorothy O'Neal

HOT SEAFOOD DIP

½ c. chili sauce
1 Tbsp. grated onion
1 Tbsp. horseradish
1 Tbsp. mayonnaise
1 tsp. Worcestershire

3 Tbsp. lemon juice
¼ tsp. salt
3 to 6 drops of liquid hot
    pepper sauce
Dash of pepper

Mix all ingredients together. This is good on any seafood plate.

Lynnette Bonn

SHRIMP DIP

1 (6½ oz.) can shrimp,
    drained and cut up
    (reserve a little of shrimp
    juice)
1 (8 oz.) pkg. cream cheese,
    softened

1 tsp. Worcestershire sauce
1 Tbsp. lemon juice
1 Tbsp. horseradish
1 Tbsp. minced onion

Add enough shrimp juice to cheese for right consistency for dipping, then add rest of ingredients.

SOUR CREAM DIP

1 c. sour cream
½ c. mayonnaise
½ tsp. garlic powder
¼ tsp. onion salt

½ tsp. dried basil
½ tsp. paprika
1 Tbsp. dried parsley
Dash of red pepper

Combine all ingredients and mix well. Chill. Yield: 1½ cups.

Cristy Lewis

SPINACH DIP

1 c. (8 oz.) sour cream
1 pkg. *Knorr* vegetable soup
   mix
1 (10 oz.) pkg. frozen
   chopped spinach,
   thawed, drained and

extra moisture pressed
out between paper
towels (use raw, do not
cook)
1 c. *Kraft* mayonnaise
1 round loaf onion-rye bread

Blend all ingredients in a blender. Store in refrigerator overnight. Scoop out center of a round loaf of onion-rye bread and fill cavity with the dip. Use the center of the bread you removed, torn into bite-size pieces, and all types of raw vegetables and potato chips as dippers.

Ruth Ackerman

SPINACH DIP

1 c. Hellmann's mayonnaise
1 c. sour cream
1 pkg. Knorr vegetable soup
   mix
1 c. chopped water chestnuts

1 pkg. frozen spinach
   (uncooked), drained and
   squeezed
French or Vienna bread

Mix all, but bread, well. Serve on bread.

Shirley Harrison

SPINACH DIP

6 oz. Hellmann's mayonnaise
1 pt. sour cream
1 pkg. Knorr vegetable soup
   mix
¼ c. chopped water
   chestnuts

2 (10 oz.) pkg. chopped
   spinach, thawed
¼ c. chopped onion

Mix the preceding ingredients together and refrigerate overnight. Hollow out the center of a large loaf of bread (rye, wheat, etc., round loaf) and spoon the dip into it.

Mary Quandt

SUMMER COTTAGE DIP

1 c. creamed cottage cheese
1 small avocado, diced
1 tsp. minced onion
2 hard cooked eggs, finely
   chopped

½ c. dairy sour cream
Salt to taste
Dash of pepper sauce
1 tsp. fresh lemon juice

Drain cheese, if too moist, and beat with avocado until smooth and creamy. Add onion and eggs; blend. Fold in sour cream and seasonings; chill. Serve with crisp vegetables, relishes or small, crisp crackers. Yield: 2½ cups.

Lou Perry

TACO DIP

1 (8 oz.) pkg. cream cheese,
   softened
1 (8 oz.) pkg. sour cream
1 pkg. taco seasoning

1 - 1½ c. chopped lettuce
1 medium size tomato, diced
¾ c. grated Cheddar cheese

Mix cream cheese and sour cream until smooth. Stir in taco seasoning until well mixed. In glass pie plate or other shallow serving dish, spread lettuce on bottom, then sour cream mixture. Sprinkle cheese and tomato on top. Serve with Tostitos or your favorite corn chips.

Galena Gronefeld

TEMPURA

3 eggs
1⅔ c. flour
1 tsp. salt

2½ tsp. soy sauce
2 Tbsp. sugar
1¼ c. water

Make batter just before using. Beat eggs with mixer; add soy sauce and water. Gradually add flour, sugar and salt, beating until smooth. Dip meat or vegetables into batter to coat lightly. Deep-fry a few pieces at a time.

Ruth Ackerman

VEGETABLE DIP

1 c. mayonnaise
1 c. sour cream
3 Tbsp. parsley flakes

3 Tbsp. fresh minced onion
3 tsp. dill weed
3 tsp. Beau Monde seasoning

Mix all together and chill.

Debbie Rigdon

DIP FOR VEGETABLES OR CHIPS

4 tsp. beef stock (liquid
    bouillon)
1 medium onion, grated or
    cut fine

Dash of Worcestershire sauce

Mix with 8 ounces of cream cheese. Fold in a pint of mayonnaise (use less if you like). Add chives to taste.

Flora Montgomery

VEGETABLE DIP

Small jar dried beef
Can deviled ham
2 (8 oz.) pkg. cream cheese
½ to 1 c. Hellmann's
    mayonnaise

Large onion
Garlic powder

With food processor or mixer, chop beef and onion; add ham, cheese, mayonnaise and garlic powder to taste. Beat until smooth; add more mayonnaise if needed to make good dip consistency. Serve with fresh vegetables: Green onions, peppers, carrots, celery, radishes, cucumbers, etc.

Phyllis Muncy

VEGETABLE GARDEN DIP

1 c. sour cream
½ c. mayonnaise
¼ c. radishes, chopped
¼ c. green pepper, chopped
½ c. green onions, chopped
¼ c. unpeeled cucumber,
　　chopped

1 Tbsp. sugar
1 tsp. salt
Dash of pepper
Dash of garlic salt

Combine all ingredients in a bowl; refrigerate. Serve with raw vegetables. Yield: 2 cups.

Beverly Craft

GREEK VEGETABLE DIP

1 c. cottage cheese
½ tsp. oregano
¼ tsp. garlic powder
1 (8 oz.) pkg. Feta cheese

½ c. cucumber, chopped
½ c. ripe olives, chopped
½ c. green pepper, chopped
1 small jar pimientos, diced

Combine cottage cheese, oregano and garlic powder; blend in blender until smooth. Add Feta cheese; blend until smooth. Stir in cucumber, olives, green pepper and pimientos. Chill 2 hours. Serve with assorted crackers.

Gwen Mills

RAW VEGETABLE DIP

⅔ c. mayonnaise
⅔ c. sour cream
1 tsp. dill weed

1 tsp. seasoned salt (Lawry's)
1 Tbsp. grated onion
1 Tbsp. parsley

Mix all together and chill before serving.

Brownie - Lois Bruner

YOGURT VEGETABLE DIP

1 c. shredded cucumber
½ c. green onion, minced
¼ c. pimento pepper, minced
1½ c. plain yogurt

½ tsp. salt
⅛ tsp. pepper
1 or 2 garlic cloves, minced
1 Tbsp. lemon juice

Shred cucumber and press out as much moisture as possible. Combine cucumber, onion and pimento. Combine remaining ingredients and mix with vegetables thoroughly. Chill.

Peggy Kessinger

QUICK VEGETABLE DIP

1 (8 oz.) pkg. sour cream   1 tsp. dill weed
1 tsp. seasoned salt

Mix together and refrigerate.

Peggy Graviss

PICKLES AND RELISHES

FREEZER PICKLES

2 qt. sliced, peeled   2 Tbsp. salt
  cucumbers   1½ c. sugar
1 medium onion, sliced thin   ½ c. vinegar

Mix cucumbers, onion and salt. Let set 2 hours in refrigerator. Drain off liquid. Add sugar and vinegar. Mix thoroughly with pickles and onions. Put in containers and freeze. When thawed, pickles are crisp.

Phyllis L. Davis

MRS. HESTER'S CRISP OLD FASHIONED PICKLE SLICES

4 qt. unpeeled cucumbers,   5 c. sugar
  sliced thin   3 c. white vinegar
6 medium white onions,   2 Tbsp. mustard seed
  sliced thin   1½ tsp. celery seed
1 green pepper, cut in strips 1½ tsp. turmeric
⅓ c. canning salt   Ice cubes
¼ tsp. garlic powder

Combine all vegetables and salt; cover with ice cubes and mix thoroughly. Let stand 3 hours. Drain well. Combine other ingredients in a kettle, dissolving sugar, then pour over vegetables. Bring to just boiling. Put in clean, hot jars and seal. Chill before serving.

Using same recipe, deleting onions and green pepper is just as good. I make both ways each summer.

Brownie - Lois Bruner

REFRIGERATOR PICKLES

6 c. thinly sliced cucumbers   1 c. thinly sliced green
  (unpeeled)   peppers
1 c. thinly sliced onion

Mix:

1 Tbsp. salt   1 c. vinegar
1 tsp. celery seed   1 c. sugar

Pour this mixture over sliced vegetables and place in covered dish in refrigerator until ready to serve. Best if made day before or at least several hours.

Mrs. Richard (Joyce) Edwards

SOUR PICKLES

1 c. salt	1 gal. water
1 c. vinegar	Small cucumbers

Mix together and heat to boiling. Pour over pickles and seal in hot sterilized jars.

Lillie Emerson

BANQUET SWEET PICKLES

7 lb. cucumbers	2 qt. vinegar
1 tsp. cloves	5 lb. white sugar
1 tsp. pickling spices	1 tsp. celery seed
2 c. lime (buy slaked lime from druggist; follow label directions)	1 Tbsp. plain salt (not iodized)

Wash and slice 7 pounds of cucumbers; let stand 24 hours in cold water and 2 cups lime. Drain; wash well 3 or more times to remove all lime. Cover with cold water and let stand 3 hours. Drain; mix 5 pounds white sugar, cloves, celery seed, pickling spices, plain salt and vinegar. Mix all this together cold and pour over cucumbers and let stand overnight. Boil 35 minutes; can while hot.

Few Tips: I stir the cucumbers several times while in lime water. Lime and water are hard to mix. Sugar will dissolve in cold vinegar; stir well and add spices and salt. Be sure to use crock or stone jar for cucumbers to stand overnight.

VIRGINIA CHUNK SWEET PICKLES

Use 75 cucumbers 4 or 5 inches long or 2 gallons of small ones. Or use what you have; most any nice solid cucumber makes a nice pickle.

Make brine of a proportion of 2 cups salt to 1 gallon water; boil and pour over cucumbers, boiling hot. Weight down to keep under brine. Let stand 1 week. In hot weather, skim daily. Drain and cut in chunks. For the next 3 mornings, make a boiling hot solution of 1 gallon water and 1 tablespoon powdered alum and pour over the pickles. Make this fresh hot bath for 3 mornings. On the fourth morning, drain and discard alum water. Heat 6 cups vinegar, 5 cups sugar, ⅓ cup pickling spice and 1 tablespoon celery seed to boiling point and pour over the pickles. On the fifth morning, drain this liquid off and add to it 2 cups more sugar; heat again to boiling point and pour over the pickles. On the sixth morning, drain liquid; add 1 cup sugar; heat and pack the pickles into sterilized *Kerr* jars and fill to within ½ inch of top of jar with the boiling liquid. Seal at once.

Ouida Brown

BEET RELISH

6 c. cooked beets, chopped
  (about 3 lb.)
6 c. cabbage, shredded
  (about 1½ lb.)
¾ c. fresh grated horseradish
3 tsp. coarse salt
½ tsp. ground pepper
3 c. cider vinegar
1½ c. sugar

Combine beets, cabbage, horseradish, salt and pepper; mix well. Combine vinegar and sugar in large kettle and heat until sugar is dissolved. Bring mixture to a boil. Add vegetable mixture; return to boil and simmer, uncovered, for 5 minutes.

Gwen Mills

CRANBERRY RELISH

1 lb. fresh cranberries
1 medium orange
1 c. raisins
1 onion, chopped
½ c. green pepper, chopped
1 garlic clove, minced
2 Tbsp. fresh ginger, minced
1 c. cider vinegar
1 (6 oz.) can frozen cranberry
  juice concentrate
2 c. sugar
½ tsp. coarse salt
¼ tsp. cayenne pepper
¼ tsp. ground cloves
1 tsp. mustard seed

Wash cranberries; put them through a food chopper using the coarse blade. Put in a large kettle. Remove orange peel from the orange, be careful not to include any of the white membrane. Cut peel in slivers and add to cranberries. Remove all white membrane from orange, section the orange and add to cranberries. Add raisins, onion, green pepper, garlic, ginger, vinegar and cranberry juice. Bring to a boil; stir occasionally. Boil, uncovered, for 10 minutes. Add remaining ingredients. Bring to a boil and simmer, uncovered, about 20 minutes or until mixture becomes thick; stir often. Pour into hot, sterilized jars, leaving ⅛ inch head space. Seal immediately. Process 10 minutes in boiling water bath.

Gwen Mills

EIGHT PINTS CUCUMBER RELISH

12 large cucumbers　　　　**3 sweet red peppers**
6 large onions

Peel cucumbers and onions. Put through small food chopper. Add 1 cup salt. Let stand overnight and drain in morning.

1 qt. vinegar　　　　　　　**3 c. white sugar**
4 Tbsp. dry mustard　　　　**3 tsp. celery seed**
4 Tbsp. flour　　　　　　　**2 Tbsp. turmeric**

Mix dry ingredients with a cup of cold water. Add to boiling vinegar and, when all is boiling, add chopped vegetables. Boil 10 minutes and put in sterile jars.

Helen Russman

HOT DOG RELISH

18 large green tomatoes　　**1 Tbsp. salt**
9 sweet green peppers　　　**1 Tbsp. celery salt**
9 sweet red peppers　　　　**1 qt. salad dressing**
4 large onions　　　　　　　**1 qt. prepared mustard**
3 c. sugar

Grind through food chopper and let set in colander for 1 hour. Add 3 cups sugar, 1 tablespoon salt and 1 tablespoon celery salt. Bring to a boil and let boil for ½ hour. Add salad dressing and mustard. Let all this come to a boil; be careful to not let it stick. Seal in jars.

Ladonna Darnell

INDIAN RELISH

Put through food chopper or chop until very fine:

12 green tomatoes　　　　　**3 peeled onions**
12 tart peeled and cored
　　apples

Boil:

5 c. vinegar	**3 tsp. ginger**
5 c. sugar	**1 tsp. turmeric**
1 tsp. red pepper	**1 tsp. salt**

Add the chopped ingredients. Cook them for ½ hour. Pack the relish in jars and seal. Yield: 4 quarts.

J. W. Borden, Jr.

PEPPER RELISH

12 green peppers (sweet)	**1 pt. vinegar**
12 yellow onions	**2 c. sugar**
12 red peppers (sweet)	**2 Tbsp. salt**
4 - 6 mild hot peppers (yellowish green)	

Grind all. Cook (at a boil) 15 minutes. Put in sterilized jars. Very good with roast.

Mary Beeler

HOT PEPPER RELISH

14 red peppers (no seeds)	**6 c. cider vinegar**
14 green peppers (no seeds)	**¼ c. salt**
16 hot peppers (use seeds)	**1 tsp. cinnamon**
12 onions	**3 Tbsp. allspice**
1¼ c. dark brown sugar	

Coarsely grind peppers and onions; combine with remaining ingredients. Bring to a full boil, then remove from heat. Do not overcook. Put into hot jars and seal. Makes about 12 pints.

Wear rubber gloves to cut hot peppers.

Gwen Mills

MOMIE MATT'S PEPPER RELISH

12 large red sweet peppers	**1½ c. sugar**
6 large, sour, hard apples	**1 c. brown sugar**
1 hot pepper	**1 qt. 5% vinegar (white)**
1 Tbsp. salt	**½ pt. water**

Put peppers, onions and apples through food chopper and pour enough boiling water over this to cover. Let stand ½ hour. Drain thoroughly. Add sugars, salt and vinegar; boil 30 minutes. Pack in sterilized jars and seal while hot.

Mrs. Ken Ford

RAISIN RELISH

4½ lb. apples
2 lb. seedless raisins
1 large onion, chopped
4 c. brown sugar
6 c. cider vinegar

½ c. salt
1 oz. ginger, ground
1 oz. white mustard seed
1 oz. celery seed
¼ oz. red pepper

Peel and chop cooking type apples. Combine with other ingredients in a heavy kettle. Boil 30 minutes. Seal in hot, sterile jars. Makes 4 pints. Serve with baked ham or pork.

Gwen Mills

SWEET RELISH

4 c. shredded cabbage,
 packed well
2 c. sweetened cooked
 applesauce
½ c. onions, cut fine
1 c. carrots, shredded fine
3 Tbsp. salt
⅛ tsp. black pepper

1 c. water
3½ c. sugar
½ tsp. cinnamon
½ tsp. cloves
½ tsp. allspice
8 c. ground green tomatoes
3 c. vinegar

Mix all ingredients in large 10 quart kettle or dishpan. Mix well for several minutes. Cook over high heat, stirring at all times for about 25 to 30 minutes or until all vegetables are tender. Place quickly in clean, hot pint jars while boiling hot. Makes 9 to 10 pints.

Bev Sowders

SQUASH RELISH

8 c. chopped yellow squash
2 c. chopped sweet onions
1 c. chopped sweet peppers
 (half red and half green)
1 Tbsp. uniodized salt
3½ c. granulated sugar

2 c. vinegar
1 tsp. celery seed
1 tsp. mustard seed
¼ tsp. mace
¼ tsp. turmeric

44

Combine chopped vegetables with salt. Let stand for 2 hours. Drain well. Combine sugar and remaining ingredients; heat to boiling. Add drained vegetables and bring back to boiling point. Pack in hot, sterilized jars and seal.

Rosaleen Robertson

GREEN TOMATO AND CABBAGE RELISH

1 doz. medium size onions, chopped
6 green peppers, chopped
6 red sweet peppers, chopped
1 gal. cabbage, chopped
½ gal. green tomatoes, chopped
⅔ c. canning salt
6 c. sugar

10 c. apple cider vinegar
1 Tbsp. whole cloves (cloves tied in bag using cheesecloth)
½ c. ground mustard
3 Tbsp. celery seed
6 Tbsp. mustard seed
Chopped red pepper to taste (I use 2 Tbsp.)

Cover onions, green peppers, red sweet peppers, cabbage and green tomatoes with ⅔ cup canning salt and mix well. Let mixture stand overnight (at least 12 hours). Drain well. In an enamel kettle, bring to a boil the following ingredients: 6 cups sugar, 10 cups apple cider vinegar, 1 tablespoon whole cloves (cloves tied in a bag using cheesecloth), ½ cup ground mustard, 3 tablespoons celery seed, 6 tablespoons mustard seed and chopped red pepper to taste (I use 2 tablespoons). Pour over vegetable mixture; after is brought to a boil, cook about ½ hour. Put in clean hot jars and seal. Makes approximately 15 pints.

Brownie - Lois Bruner

TOMATO AND APPLE RELISH

2 qt. ripe tomatoes, peeled and chopped
1 c. onions, chopped
1 c. celery, chopped
2 green and 2 red peppers, chopped
2 c. tart apples, peeled and chopped

2¾ c. sugar
1½ c. vinegar
1 Tbsp. salt
2 Tbsp. mustard seed
½ Tbsp. whole cloves
1 stick cinnamon

Tie last 3 ingredients in a thin cloth. Cook all ingredients until thick and clear, about 45 minutes.

Pat Whisman

ZUCCHINI RELISH

10 c. zucchini, peeled and ground up
4 c. onions, ground
5 Tbsp. salt
2¼ c. cider vinegar
6 c. sugar
1 Tbsp. nutmeg
1 Tbsp. turmeric
2 Tbsp. cornstarch
2 Tbsp. celery seed
½ tsp. pepper

Grind zucchini and onions; add salt and let stand overnight. Drain and rinse in cold water; drain again. Be sure all water is drained off or relish will be thin. Add remaining ingredients and cook 30 minutes; stir often while cooking. Seal.

Red and green peppers may be added for color.

Gwen Mills

ZUCCHINI RELISH

6 c. ground zucchini
4 c. ground onions
1 sweet red pepper, ground
1 sweet green pepper, ground
5 Tbsp. pickling salt

Let mixture stand overnight in water. Water should cover mixture. Next morning, drain and rinse.

3 c. vinegar
6 c. sugar
1 Tbsp. nutmeg
1 Tbsp. turmeric
1 Tbsp. dry mustard
1 Tbsp. cornstarch
1 Tbsp. celery seed
1 Tbsp. black pepper

Combine dry ingredients and mix well; add vinegar. Stir in drained vegetable mixture. Cook, stirring often, 30 minutes or until thickened. Put in sterile jar and seal, according to directions on jar box. Serve with hot dogs, hamburgers, etc.

Ruthie Marty

ZUCCHINI RELISH

10 c. ground zucchini squash
4 c. ground onions
5 Tbsp. salt
2¼ c. vinegar
1 Tbsp. dry mustard
¼ tsp. black pepper
1 Tbsp. cornstarch
6 c. sugar
2 tsp. celery seed
1 Tbsp. turmeric
1 Tbsp. nutmeg
2 or 3 red peppers for coloring

Mix zucchini, onions and salt. Let stand overnight. Drain and rinse twice. Add vinegar, dry mustard, black pepper, cornstarch, sugar, celery seed, turmeric, nutmeg and red peppers. Cook slowly until clear (about 30 minutes). Seal hot. Makes 6 pints.

Phyllis L. Davis

Notes

Soups,
Salads,
Vegetables

SPICE CHART

Spices should be stored in airtight containers away from the heat of the stove or in the refrigerator. Add ground spices toward the end of the cooking time to retain maximum flavor. Whole spices may be added at the beginning but should have a small amount of additional spices added near the end of cooking time also.

Allspice	Pungent aromatic spice, whole or in powdered form. It is excellent in marinades, particularly in game marinade, or in curries.
Caraway seed	Use the whole seeds in breads, especially rye, and with cheese, sauerkraut and cabbage dishes.
Celery seed	Use whole or ground in salad dressings, sauces, pickles or meat, cheese, egg and fish dishes.
Chili powder	Made from dried red chili peppers, this spice ranges from mild to fiery depending on the type of chili pepper used. Used especially in Mexican cooking, it is a delicious addition to eggs, dips and sauces.
Cinnamon	Ground from the bark of the cinnamon tree, it is delicious in desserts as well as savory dishes.
Coriander	Seed used whole or ground, this slightly lemony spice adds an unusual flavor to soups, stews, chili dishes, curries and desserts.
Curry powder	A blend of several spices, this gives Indian cooking its characteristic flavor.
Cumin	A staple spice in Mexican cooking. Use it in meat, rice, cheese, egg and fish dishes.
Ginger	The whole root used fresh, dried or ground is a sweet, pungent addition to desserts or oriental-style dishes.
Mustard (dry)	Ground mustard seed brings a sharp bite to sauces or may be sprinkled sparingly over poultry or other foods.
Nutmeg	Use the whole spice or a bit of freshly ground for flavor in beverages, breads and desserts. A sprinkle on top is both a flavor enhancer and an attractive garnish.
Pepper	Black and white pepper from the pepperberry or pepper-corn, whether whole, ground or cracked, is the most commonly used spice in or on any food.
Poppy seed	Use these tiny, nutty-flavored seeds in salad dressings, breads, cakes or as a flavorful garnish for cheese, rolls or noodle dishes.
Turmeric	Ground from a root related to ginger, this is an essential in curry powder. Also used in pickles, relishes, cheese and egg dishes.

SOUPS, SALADS, VEGETABLES
SOUPS

BACON AND POTATO SOUP

8 slices bacon, fried crisp
1 c. onions, chopped
2 c. cubed potatoes
1 c. water
1 can cream of chicken soup
1¾ c. milk

1 (4 oz.) ctn. sour cream
½ tsp. salt
Pepper to taste
2 Tbsp. fresh parsley,
    chopped
Bacon fat

In bacon fat, saute onions 2 to 3 minutes. Drain. In a pot with sauteed onions, add potatoes and water; bring to a boil. Cover and simmer for about 15 minutes, or until potatoes are tender. Stir in soup, sour cream and crumbled bacon. Add milk, salt, pepper and parsley. Heat to serving temperature. *Do not boil.*

Mildred Mattingly (submitted by Brownie - Lois Bruner)

BEAN SOUP

1 qt. water
1 lb. Northern beans
1 ham hock
2 ribs celery, diced
¼ lb. bacon

1 small onion, chopped
1 c. diced potatoes
1 c. water
Salt and pepper to taste

Put 1 quart water, beans, ham hock and celery in large kettle. Brown bacon with onion and add to beans. Simmer about 3 hours. Add 1 cup diced potatoes and simmer 1 hour longer with 1 cup water. Add salt and pepper to taste.

Mary Lauder

BEAN SPROUT SOUP

1 c. skim milk
2 Tbsp. soy sauce
½ tsp. salt
¼ tsp. pepper

1 tsp. prepared mustard
4 oz. cooked chicken, cut in
    chunks
½ c. bean sprouts

In saucepan, combine milk, soy sauce, salt, pepper and mustard. Cook over low heat 10 minutes or until heated through. Add chicken and bean sprouts to milk mixture and reheat. Serve immediately. Serves one.

Judy Smith

BEER CHEDDAR SOUP

1 qt. beer
2 Tbsp. butter
2 Tbsp. flour
½ tsp. salt
¼ tsp. coarsely ground
   pepper

1 garlic clove
2 egg yolks
3 Tbsp. sour cream
1¼ c. grated Cheddar cheese
Toast

Bring beer to a boil. Cream butter, flour, salt, pepper and garlic; gradually stir into beer. Beat egg yolks lightly with sour cream and add to soup. Add 1 cup cheese and simmer until cheese is melted. Pour over toast in soup bowls and sprinkle with remaining Cheddar. If a thinner soup is desired, stir in a little more beer just before serving and correct seasoning to taste. Serves 6.

Paula White

BEER CHEESE SOUP

1½ qt. milk
2½ lb. American cheese,
   diced fine

2 (12 oz.) cans beer

In a heavy saucepan, heat milk. Add cheese and cook; stir constantly until cheese is melted. Add beer. Cook, stirring until heated and thickened.

Sharon Duke

HOT BORSCHT

3 c. water
1 c. tomato pulp or puree
1 onion, diced
1 c. carrot, shredded
1 c. beets, shredded

1 c. potatoes, shredded
2 c. cabbage, shredded
2 tsp. salt
1 Tbsp. lemon juice
Sour cream

Combine water and tomato and bring to a boil. Add vegetables; season with salt; cover and simmer about 30 minutes or until vegetables are tender. When done, add lemon juice. Add a spoon of sour cream to each bowl.

BOUERNSUPPE - PEASANT SOUP

1 lb. stewing beef, cut into ½
    inch pieces
1 large onion, sliced
2 Tbsp. butter or drippings
1 tsp. salt
1 bay leaf
1 clove garlic, crushed
Dash of paprika
2 Tbsp. vinegar

2 qt. hot beef broth or 1 qt.
    beef broth and 1 qt. hot
    water
3 medium potatoes, peeled,
    diced
1 Tbsp. minced dill
2 Tbsp. grated Parmesan
    (optional)
3 Tbsp. flour

Saute beef and onion in butter or drippings until well browned. Add salt, bay leaf, garlic and paprika. Sprinkle with flour. Stir and cook over low heat until flour is absorbed and browned. Sprinkle with vinegar and stir thoroughly over low heat. Add hot broth and simmer 45 minutes. Add potatoes; cook slowly another hour. Sprinkle with dill and cheese. Makes 6 to 8 servings.

Lila White

BROCCOLI SOUP

2 Tbsp. butter
¼ c. chopped onion
2 c. chicken broth
½ tsp. salt

1 c. milk
¼ tsp. pepper
1 bunch broccoli, chopped

Saute onion in butter until tender. Add broth, broccoli, salt and pepper. Cook until tender, covered. Puree in blender. Add milk and re-heat. Serve hot.

Sue Tipton

BROCCOLI SOUP

1 box frozen chopped
    broccoli
2 c. water

1 medium onion, minced
1 stalk celery (if you have it)

Simmer 15 minutes.

Add:

1 c. cream of chicken soup　　**½ stick butter**
1½ c. milk

Simmer another 15 minutes.

Flo Gish

BROTSUPPE - BREAD SOUP, FRANCONIAN STYLE

6 slices slightly stale　　　　**1 medium onion, chopped**
**　pumpernickel or dark rye**　**1 or 2 Tbsp. meat drippings**
**　bread**　　　　　　　　　　**2 or 3 Tbsp. leftover gravy**
8 c. beef broth or water,　　　**　(preferably pork gravy)**
**　heated to boiling**

Break bread into cubes; cover with boiling hot broth or water. Let stand until soft. Separately saute onion in meat drippings until soft and yellow. Add bread and broth; simmer ½ hour. (If water is used, add salt to taste.) Stir in gravy. Makes 6 to 8 servings.

Mit Rahm (with cream): Instead of leftover gravy, add 2 table-spoons heavy cream.

Lila White

CREAM OF CARROT SOUP

6 medium carrots, peeled and　**3 c. chicken stock or broth**
**　coarsely chopped**　　　　　**¾ c. light cream**
3 medium spring onions (tops　**Salt and freshly ground white**
**　and roots removed),**　　　　**　pepper to taste**
**　coarsely chopped**
3 Tbsp. butter or margarine
1 medium potato, peeled and
**　coarsely diced (this is for**
**　thickness)**

In large saucepan or pot, place carrots, onions and butter. Cook over medium heat, stirring occasionally, for 3 to 4 minutes or until onions are limp. Add potato and chicken stock to the pot. Cover; reduce heat to low and simmer 20 to 25 minutes or until carrots are just tender. Place mixture in a blender; cap and blend on high speed for 30 seconds or until pureed. Add cream to the puree, stirring well. Add salt and white pepper to taste. Soup can be returned to the stove and reheated until hot, but not boiling, or thoroughly chilled before serving. If served cold, correct seasoning and stir well before placing in bowls. Chilled soup may be garnished with fresh or dried chives.

I usually double this, due to the fact it's such a small amount.

Wilma Crowdus

GOLDEN CREAM SOUP

3 c. chopped potatoes
1 c. water
½ c. celery slices
½ c. carrot slices
¼ c. chopped onion
1 tsp. parsley flakes

½ tsp. salt
Dash of pepper
1 chicken bouillon cube
1½ c. milk
2 Tbsp. flour
½ lb. Velveeta cheese, cubed

Combine potatoes, water, celery, carrots, onion, parsley flakes, seasonings and bouillon cube. Cover; simmer 15 to 20 minutes or until vegetables are tender. Gradually add milk to flour; stir until well blended. Add milk mixture to vegetables; cook until thickened. Add cheese cubes; stir until melted.

Terri Ramage

CANADIAN GREEN TOMATO SOUP

3 c. green tomatoes
   (unpeeled), chopped
1 onion, chopped
¼ tsp. cinnamon
⅛ tsp. ground cloves
1 tsp. sugar

¼ tsp. pepper
4 c. water
¼ tsp. soda
3 Tbsp. butter
3 Tbsp. all-purpose flour
4 c. milk

Put the tomatoes, onion, cinnamon, ground cloves, sugar, pepper and water in a kettle. Bring to a boil and boil for 20 minutes. Add the soda. Melt butter; add flour; mix well and add milk. Cook until creamy, stirring constantly. Add the green tomatoes to the mixture. Mix well. Salt to taste. Serves 6.

Gwen Bond

HOPPIN-JOHN SOUP

2 lb. sausage
6 cans black-eyed peas
2 medium onions, chopped

2 c. cooked Minute rice*
1 c. water
Salt and pepper (to taste)

Fry sausage and drain off the grease. Drain 3 cans of the black-eyed peas; add juice and all on the other 3 cans. In a Dutch oven size pot, stir in the black-eyed peas, chopped onions, salt, pepper, water and sausage. Bring to a boil and cook on medium for 45 minutes. Then add your cooked rice and let simmer for about 20 minutes. The soup will be thick so you'll have to stir frequently so it won't stick to the bottom of the pot.

* You can add more or less rice, depending on how thick or thin you prefer your soup.

Cindy Stewart

OYSTER AND SPINACH SOUP

½ c. onion, finely chopped
1 clove garlic, minced
½ c. butter or margarine
2 (12 oz.) cans fresh oysters, drained and chopped
½ c. all-purpose flour
1½ qt. milk
2 c. chicken broth
1 (10 oz.) pkg. frozen thawed and pureed spinach (I cook 2 or 3 minutes before pureed)
1 Tbsp. salt
Pepper to taste

Saute onions and garlic in butter until tender. Add oysters and cook until edges begin to curl. Blend in flour and cook until bubbly. Gradually add milk, cook, stirring constantly, until thickened. Stir in broth and spinach. Bring to a boil. Remove from heat; add salt and pepper. Serves 8.

Brownie - Lois Bruner

PEANUT BUTTER SOUP

1 qt. chicken stock
3 oz. onion, minced
3 oz. celery, minced
8 oz. peanut butter
3 oz. butter
1 Tbsp. flour
1 c. half & half
1 tsp. salt
¼ tsp. pepper
Bacon crumbs or minced country ham

Mix together chicken stock, onion and celery; simmer for about 1 hour. Strain out onion and celery; discard. Stir in peanut butter and dissolve. Mix flour with remaining ingredients and simmer together 15 minutes. If too thick, thin with milk. Garnish with bacon crumbs or minced country ham. Serves 6.

Cristy Lewis

POTATO SOUP

Cook together:

6 potatoes, diced	**2 tsp. salt**
½ c. onion, chopped	**1 tsp. celery salt**
2 stalks celery, chopped	**⅔ tsp. pepper**

Cover all with water and cook until tender. Fry 8 slices bacon; save 6 tablespoons drippings. Make white sauce of 6 tablespoons drippings, 2 tablespoons flour and 2 cups milk. Add white sauce to soup; crumble bacon and add. Heat thoroughly.

Donna Browning

SABRA SOUP - MORAK CHEMDAT HAORETZ

Fresh vegetables in season (about 12 oz.)	**Margarine**
	1 Tbsp. parsley, chopped
1 chicken bouillon cube	**Salt**
6 c. water	**Pepper**

Peel vegetables and cube. Stir them in a little margarine; add water and simmer over medium heat for 45 minutes. During cooking, add seasoning and bouillon cube. Serve hot; garnish with chopped parsley or dill. Preparing time: 15 minutes. Cooking time: 45 minutes. Serves 6.

Paula White

EUROPEAN SPLIT PEA AND SAUSAGE SOUP

1 c. dried split peas	**3 ribs celery, diced**
4 c. boiling water	**½ c. evaporated milk**
1 tsp. salt	
3 cooked sausages, sliced thin	

Cook peas in boiling water for 1 hour. Add salt, sausages and celery. Simmer for another hour; add boiling water if necessary. Just before serving, add milk and enough boiling water to make 6 cups of soup. Serves 6.

D. L. Bond

TURKEY NOODLE SOUP

Meaty turkey frame
3 qt. water
4 c. turkey broth
1 onion, finely chopped
1 c. mushrooms

Pinch of poultry seasoning
3 oz. uncooked noodles
2 c. diced cooked turkey meat
1 - 2 Tbsp. salt

Put a meaty turkey frame into a large pot. Add 3 quarts of water and 1 to 2 tablespoons salt. Heat to boiling; skim foam. Cover and simmer 2 hours or longer. Strain broth and refrigerate. Remove fat from surface. When turkey frame is cool, pick off meat. Combine broth with vegetables and seasonings. Heat to boiling. Simmer 10 minutes. Stir in noodles. Simmer until noodles are tender, about 5 to 10 minutes. Stir in turkey and heat through.

Peggy Hunter

SALADS

AMBROSIA

1 can fruit cocktail, drained
1 can mandarin oranges,
   drained
2 bananas, sliced

1 can pineapple chunks,
   drained
½ c. coconut
½ c. powdered sugar

Mix all ingredients together and chill.

Peggy Kessinger

AMBROSIA SALAD

2 oranges, peeled and sliced
   ¼ inch thick
1 grapefruit, peeled and
   sectioned

1 c. seedless grapes
1 banana, sliced ½ inch thick
¼ c. coconut
2 tsp. sugar

Combine all ingredients; toss lightly. Refrigerate. Serves 8.

Rosalie Smith

TROPICAL APPLE SALAD

1 c. red apple, diced
   (unpared)
1 c. yellow apple, diced
   (unpared)
1 large banana, sliced
1 c. celery, diced
½ c. walnuts, broken
½ c. coconut flakes

¼ c. mayonnaise
1 Tbsp. sugar
½ tsp. lemon juice
Dash of salt
½ c. whipping cream,
   whipped
Romaine lettuce leaves

Combine apples, banana, celery, walnuts and coconut. In a separate bowl, blend together the mayonnaise, sugar, lemon juice and salt. Fold whipped cream into mayonnaise mixture, then gently fold into apple mixture. Chill. Arrange lettuce leaves in bowls. Spoon in salad. Sprinkle with additional coconut.

Phyllis L. Davis

WALDORF OR APPLE SALAD DRESSING

Juice of 1 lemon
Juice of 1 orange
½ c. sugar

1 Tbsp. flour (heaping)
1 egg

Mix together and cook in double boiler until thick.

Thelma Barnett

APPLESAUCE CHRISTMAS SALAD

¼ c. cinnamon candies
1 c. water
1 (3 oz. size) pkg. strawberry
Jello

2 c. applesauce

Heat water to boiling. Add ¼ cup cinnamon; melt until dissolved. Add Jello. Stir until dissolved. Add 2 cups applesauce. Chill.

Flo Gish

BANANA SALAD

8 or 9 bananas, sliced
crosswise
1 c. sugar
1 egg

¼ tsp. salt
¼ c. white vinegar
1 c. pecans

Beat egg and sugar together. Add vinegar and salt. Heat slowly until thickened. Pour over bananas and chill for a few hours or overnight.

Maxine Welch

DRESSED BANANAS

4 or 5 nice sized bananas
Creamy peanut butter

Pecans

Cut the bananas in halves, then split lengthwise. Spread peanut butter on one half and stick it back together with other half. Do each banana this way and then place in serving dish (or on lettuce on individual salad plates). Prepare dressing (recipe follows) and pour over banana halves. Sprinkle with finely chopped or ground pecans.

58

Dressing:

¼ c. vinegar
¼ c. water

½ c. sugar
1 well beaten egg

Cook until thick and pour over banana halves.

Ruth Ackerman

FROZEN BANANA SALAD

4 bananas, mashed
1 (8½ oz.) can crushed
    pineapple (undrained)
1 Tbsp. lemon juice
1 (6 oz.) jar maraschino
    cherries, drained and
    quartered

½ c. chopped pecans
1 tsp. salt
¾ c. sugar
2 (8 oz.) ctn. sour cream
Lettuce

Combine all ingredients, except lettuce; stir well. Pour into a 9 inch square pan. Freeze until firm; cut into squares; serve on lettuce.

Kim Clinton

BETTY'S SALAD

1 (3 oz.) pkg. raspberry Jello
¾ c. sugar
1 small can crushed
    pineapple

1 (8 oz.) pkg. Philadelphia
    cream cheese
2½ pt. whipped cream

Mix sugar, pineapple and juice with Jello in small pan and bring to a boil. Pour in an 8 or 9 inch bowl and put in refrigerator until it sets. Soften cream cheese and mix with whipped cream on low speed in the blender until it thickens. Fold in at low speed the Jello mixture. Put in refrigerator until mixture is set.

Betty Coogle

BLUEBERRY SALAD

2 pkg. grape Jello
2 c. boiling water
1 can pineapple, drained
1 can blueberry pie filling
Pecans, chopped

1 (8 oz.) pkg. cream cheese
1 small ctn. sour cream
½ c. sugar
½ tsp. vanilla

Mix Jello and boiling water, then add pineapple and blueberry pie filling to mixture. Add chopped pecans and let jell. For topping, beat cream cheese and sour cream well. Then add sugar and vanilla; mix well and place on top of Jello mixture. Garnish with pecans if you like.

Maxine Welch

ROQUEFORT OR BLEU CHEESE MOUSSE

6 egg yolks
6 Tbsp. cream
1½ Tbsp. gelatin
4 Tbsp. cold water

¾ lb. Roquefort or Bleu
   cheese
1½ c. heavy cream, whipped
3 egg whites, stiffly beaten

Beat egg yolks with cream in saucepan over low heat until mixture is creamy. Soften gelatin in cold water. Dissolve gelatin over hot water and add to eggs. Chop cheese fine and add to gelatin mixture. Cool. Fold in whipped cream and egg whites. Pour mousse into an oiled mold and chill several hours. Unmold on serving dish and garnish with parsley, mint or watercress. Serves 8.

Paula White

BROCCOLI AND CAULIFLOWER SALAD

1 lb. fresh cauliflower,
   chopped
1 lb. fresh broccoli, chopped
1 small onion, chopped
⅓ c. vinegar

⅓ c. sugar
⅔ c. mayonnaise
1 tsp. salt
Chopped radishes (optional)

Combine cauliflower, broccoli and onion; toss well. Combine remaining ingredients; pour over vegetables. Let stand in refrigerator overnight. Makes 6 to 8 servings.

Barbara C. Hendrick

BROCCOLI SALAD

1 large head broccoli,
   chopped
½ c. sunflower seeds
½ c. raisins

½ lb. bacon, fried and
   crumbled
½ large red onion, sliced thin
1 c. mushrooms, sliced

Combine 1 cup mayonnaise, ¼ cup sugar, 2 tablespoons vinegar and a dash of salt. Pour over salad. Toss lightly. Serves 6 to 8.

Melanie Davis

MARINATED BROCCOLI SALAD

1 large bunch broccoli
  flowerets
2 chopped green onions
1 can red kidney beans,
  washed and drained

1 (8 oz.) pkg. gourmet
  shredded Swiss cheese

Marinate overnight in bottled Zesty Italian dressing or use Good Seasons Zesty Italian dressing.

Mrs. Ron Martin

BUTTER BEAN SALAD

1 c. cooked butter beans
⅓ c. chopped celery
3 green onions, chopped
2 hard cooked sliced eggs

4 tsp. chopped pimiento
4 tsp. chopped parsley
4 tsp. green pepper, chopped
French dressing

Drain beans. Chill all ingredients and combine. Toss with generous amount of French dressing. Serve on crisp lettuce leaves.

BETTY'S CABBAGE SALAD

Keep this delicious cabbage salad covered and refrigerated and it will keep indefinitely. Makes a great accent for summer meals.

In a large container, arrange the following ingredients in layers:

1 large head cabbage,
  shredded
1 green pepper, sliced paper
  thin
2 medium onions, thin sliced,
  separated into onion
  rings

1 medium can or jar pimento,
  drained

Do not stir.

For the dressing, mix together the following ingredients and boil for 2 minutes:

1 c. salad oil
1 c. sugar
¾ c. white vinegar

1½ tsp. salt
1 tsp. celery seed

Pour the hot dressing over the vegetables. Cover tightly and refrigerate at least 4 hours before serving. Makes about 15 servings.

Betty T. King

CARDINAL SALAD

2 (3 oz.) pkg. lemon Jello
2 c. warm water
¾ c. beet juice
¼ c. vinegar
½ tsp. salt
1 tsp. grated onion

1 c. diced celery
1 (1 lb.) can whole beets,
   shredded coarsely
1 (8 oz.) can crushed
   pineapple (juice
   included)

Dissolve Jello in warm water. Add beet juice, salt, vinegar and onion. Chill. When slightly thick, fold in celery, beets and pineapple. Pour in a 7 or 8 cup mold. Chill until firm.

Maxine Welch

CARROT RAISIN SALAD

3 c. grated carrots
1 c. raisins
1 Tbsp. honey
¼ c. milk

1 Tbsp. lemon juice
¼ tsp. salt
¼ tsp. nutmeg

Mix carrots and raisins together. Blend remaining ingredients together. Stir into carrot mixture. Chill for 1 hour before serving. Yield: 6 servings.

Gwen Mills

CAULIFLOWER BROCCOLI SALAD

1 head cauliflower
1 bunch broccoli
1 red onion

1 green pepper
Small jar of pimentos
Salt to taste

Dressing:

½ c. sugar
½ c. vinegar
½ c. oil

1 c. mayonnaise
1 tsp. dry mustard

Mix dressing well and pour over cut up vegetables. Let stand several hours or overnight.

Tourist Commission

CAULIFLOWER SALAD

1 large cauliflower, cut
   bite-size
½ lb. bacon, cooked and
   crumbled
2 large tomatoes, chopped

1 bunch green onions,
   chopped bite-size
1 c. Cheddar cheese, diced
½ c. mayonnaise

Mix all together; serve and be ready for everyone asking "What is this? It's good!"

Perry

CAULIFLOWER SALAD

1 head cauliflower, broken
   into tiny pieces
1 (8 oz.) pkg. cream cheese,
   softened

2 or 3 carrots, finely grated
1 small green onion, sliced
   fine (use tops also)
½ c. mayonnaise

Mix all ingredients well and chill thoroughly.

Ruth Ackerman

CHEESE PARTY MOLD

1 (3 oz.) pkg. lemon gelatin
2 c. boiling water
½ c. heavy cream, whipped
1 c. canned crushed
   pineapple

1 c. chopped walnuts
¼ c. stuffed green olives,
   sliced
1 c. American cheese, grated

Dissolve gelatin in boiling water. Chill until mixture begins to thicken. Whip gelatin and fold in whipped cream, pineapple, walnuts, stuffed green olives and American cheese. Pour into mold; chill until firm. Serve with creamy salad dressing. Serves 6 to 8.

Terry White

MOLDED CHEESE SALAD

2 small pkg. lemon gelatin
3 c. boiling water
3 c. cottage cheese
1 c. grated Cheddar cheese
½ c. green onions, chopped

3 Tbsp. green pepper, chopped
3 Tbsp. cucumber, chopped
½ c. lemon juice
1 c. mayonnaise

Dissolve gelatin in boiling water and cool. Stir in remaining ingredients. Pour into mold and chill until firm. Serves 8.

Denise Figg

BING CHERRY SALAD

1 (No. 2) can pitted Bing cherries

1 c. sherry wine
1 pkg. black cherry gelatin

Drain cherries thoroughly. Add water to cherry juice, if necessary, to make 1 cup of liquid. Heat juice. Dissolve gelatin in hot liquid. Let cool and add sherry wine. Divide cherries equally into 4 or 5 individual molds. Pour gelatin into molds and chill until set. Makes 4 or 5 servings. Serve on crisp lettuce with mayonnaise or sour cream.

BLACK CHERRY JELLO SALAD

1 large pkg. black cherry Jello
1 carrot, shredded

1 rib celery, diced fine
1 c. pecans, chopped

Make Jello according to package directions and chill until partially set. Stir in carrot, celery and pecans. Pour into mold and chill until set.

Peggy Kessinger

CHERRY COKE JELLO SALAD

1 large pkg. cherry Jello
1 can red cherries
   (unsweetened)
1 (No. 2) can crushed
   pineapple

¾ c. sugar
1 c. Coke or Pepsi

Heat cherries until almost boiling. Add the sugar and stir until dissolved. Pour over Jello and stir until dissolved. Add the can of pineapple, juice and all. Then add cup of Coke. Refrigerate for several hours before serving.

Donna Browning

DOUBLE DECK CHERRY SALAD

1 (No. 2) can sliced pineapple
1 pkg. cherry Jello
1 (3 oz.) pkg. cream cheese
3 Tbsp. canned milk (cream)

1 (No. 2) can Bing cherries
⅓ c. lemon juice
1 pkg. orange Jello
½ c. sliced stuffed olives

Drain pineapple; add water to pineapple syrup to make 1¾ cups. Heat to boiling; dissolve cherry Jello in hot liquid. Chill until partially set. Add pineapple slices, cut thin. Pour into oiled 8 inch square pan; chill until firm. Soften cheese with cream and spread over Jello. Chill until firm. Drain cherries. Add water and lemon juice to cherry syrup to make 1¾ cups liquid. Heat to boiling and dissolve orange Jello in this. Chill until partially set. Add cherries and olives. Spread over cheese and chill until firm. Cut in squares to serve 8 or 9.

Mark A. Cowan

CHERRY SALAD

2 small pkg. cherry Jello
1 can red cherries
   (unsweetened)
1 (No. 2) can crushed
   pineapple

¾ c. sugar (scant)
1 small (8 oz.) bottle Coke

Heat cherries until almost boiling. Add ¾ cup sugar and stir until dissolved. Pour over Jello and stir until dissolved. Add can of pineapple (juice and all). Add Coke last. Refrigerate until completely set.

Jewell Hundley

CHERRY SALAD

1 can cherry pie filling
1 pkg. chopped pecans
1 can crushed pineapple,
    drained

1 can Eagle Brand milk
1 bowl Cool Whip

Fold all ingredients together and chill until set (approximately 2 hours).

Linda Y. Borden

CHERRY MOLDED SALAD

2 small pkg. cherry gelatin
1½ c. hot water
1½ c. Coca-Cola or other cola
    drink

3½ c. black pitted cherries
    and juice
3½ c. crushed pineapple,
    drained

Dissolve gelatin in hot water; add Coca-Cola, black cherries and juice. Add pineapple. Refrigerate until firm. Serves 6.

Paula White

CHERRY SALAD

1 can pie cherries
1 c. sugar
1 c. boiling water
2 pkg. cherry gelatin

1 (No. 2) can pineapple
1 c. nuts
Juice of 1 lemon

Cook cherries and sugar 5 minutes. Dissolve gelatin in boiling water. Cool. When cool, add pineapple, nuts and lemon juice. Refrigerate until solid. Serves 6.

Bina Cloyd

FESTIVE CHERRY SALAD

1 (3 oz.) pkg. lemon Jello
1 (3 oz.) pkg. apricot Jello
1½ c. boiling water
1½ c. orange juice
1 (16 oz.) can dark pitted
    cherries, drained and
    chopped

1 (15 oz.) can crushed
    pineapple, drained
1 c. finely chopped celery
¾ c. chopped pecans

Dissolve gelatin in boiling water. Stir in orange juice. Chill until thickened; fold in remaining ingredients. Spoon into 5 cup mold. Chill until set. Yield: 8 to 10 servings.

Dot Berry

HOT CHICKEN SALAD

3 c. cooked chicken, cubed
1½ c. celery, chopped
¾ c. slivered almonds
1 (6 oz.) can sliced water
    chestnuts
½ tsp. salt
2 tsp. grated onion
3 Tbsp. lemon juice

1½ c. mayonnaise
1 (11 oz.) can condensed
    cream of chicken soup
¾ c. grated sharp Cheddar
    cheese
1½ c. crushed potato chips
    (about 4 oz.)

Combine everything, but the cheese and potato chips, in a greased 9x13 inch casserole dish. Combine cheese and crushed potato chips; sprinkle on top. Bake in a preheated 325° oven for 45 minutes or until lightly browned. Serves 8.

Clarine Ballard

CHICKEN SALAD

½ c. chopped onions
½ c. chopped celery
½ c. sweet pickles
1 baked chicken

½ lb. grapes
¾ c. mayonnaise
¼ c. pimentos

Remove the chicken from the bone and chop into small pieces. Mix remaining ingredients with chicken and chill.

Sue Sympson

CHICKEN SALAD

2½ - 3 lb. (approx. 12)
    chicken breasts
20 oz. water chestnuts, sliced
2 lb. seedless white grapes
2 c. diced celery
2 - 3 c. slivered almonds
    (optional)

3 c. mayonnaise
2 tsp. curry powder
2 Tbsp. soy sauce
2 Tbsp. lemon juice

Stew chicken breasts; remove bone and chop. Toss ingredients together and serve on pineapple slices and lettuce leaves. Makes 2 quarts of salad.

Barbara C. Hendrick

BAKED CHICKEN SALAD

3 c. cubed cooked chicken
1½ c. celery
¾ c. almonds
¾ tsp. salt
3 Tbsp. lemon juice

1½ c. mayonnaise
1 small can mushrooms
1½ c. potato chips
1½ c. grated cheese

Mix together first 7 ingredients. Sprinkle top with cheese and crumbled potato chips. Bake 10 to 12 minutes at 450°. Serves 6 to 8.

Dorothy O'Neal

CANADIAN CHICKEN SALAD

1 Tbsp. unflavored gelatin
¼ c. cold water
¾ c. mayonnaise
1 c. cooked chicken, chopped
½ c. celery, chopped

¼ c. olives, chopped
2 Tbsp. pimientos, chopped
Dash of salt
Dash of paprika

Dissolve gelatin according to package directions. Add to mayonnaise and mix well. Let cool. Fold in chicken, celery, olives and pimientos. Season to taste with salt and paprika. Chill in refrigerator.

Mary Lauder

CHOICE CHICKEN SALAD

6 eggs
½ c. chopped pickles
Nuts (if desired)

1 (5 or 6 lb.) chicken, cooked
 and chopped

Mix preceding together well. Add special dressing which follows.

68

Special Dressing for Chicken Salad:

1½ c. sugar
½ tsp. mustard
½ tsp. salt
1 Tbsp. flour

2 beaten eggs
1 c. sweet milk
1 c. vinegar
Dash of red pepper

Mix dry ingredients and add beaten eggs, milk and vinegar. Cook until thick or the desired consistency is reached.

CHILI SALAD

1 medium head lettuce, cut in chunks
3 c. corn chips
1 large tomato, chopped

1 c. shredded Cheddar
4 oz. pepperoni, sliced thin
¼ c. ripe olives, sliced
15 oz. can chili beans

Combine lettuce, corn chips, tomato, cheese, pepperoni and olives. Heat chili until bubbly, immediately pour over top of salad; toss lightly to coat. Serves 6.

Helen Sykes

CABBAGE SLAW

1 head cabbage, sliced
2 green peppers, sliced
1 large onion, sliced
1 c. sugar plus 2 tsp.
1 c. vinegar

¾ c. oil
1 Tbsp. salt
1 tsp. ground mustard
1 tsp. celery seed

Slice cabbage in thin shreds. Make alternate layers of cabbage, green peppers and onion. Pour 1 cup sugar on top. Mix 1 cup vinegar, ¾ cup oil, 1 tablespoon salt, 1 teaspoon ground mustard, 1 teaspoon celery seed and 2 teaspoons sugar; let it reach a boil. Pour boiling mixture over slaw. Refrigerate 4 hours or longer.

Debbie Rigdon

COLE SLAW

1 pt. white vinegar
2½ c. white sugar
1 tsp. celery seed

½ tsp. mustard seed
¼ tsp. thyme

Mix all together and boil 2 minutes and cool.

Chop and mix together:

1 pepper
1 large onion

1 large head cabbage

Pour vinegar mixture over cabbage mixture and store in refrigerator. Will keep for several weeks.

D. White

COLE SLAW
(With vinegar dressing)

3 lb. cabbage
2 green peppers

1 red pepper
1 onion

Shred the preceding all together. Sprinkle 2 cups of white sugar on the preceding. Chill for 2 hours.

Boil together:

¾ c. vinegar
¾ c. vegetable oil

1 Tbsp. salt
2 tsp. celery seed

Pour this hot syrup over cabbage mixture. Chill 2 hours before serving.

Phyllis L. Davis

COTTAGE COLE SLAW

½ c. cottage cheese
½ c. mayonnaise
3 Tbsp. vinegar
1½ tsp. onion juice
6 c. fine shredded cabbage
¾ tsp. salt

½ tsp. pepper
1 tsp. caraway seeds
(optional)
½ medium green pepper,
chopped
2 c. diced apples

Combine cottage cheese and mayonnaise. Add vinegar, onion juice, seasonings and caraway seeds. Combine dressing with cabbage, apples and green pepper. Place in large bowl lined with cabbage leaves. Garnish with cottage cheese and green pepper. You may decorate to suit occasion. Chill. Makes 8 to 10 servings.

CRUNCHY COLESLAW

1½ qt. shredded cabbage
1 c. chopped red and green
   pepper
1 c. celery slices

½ c. Italian dressing
1 Tbsp. brown sugar
1 Tbsp. celery seed

Combine cabbage, pepper and celery. Add combined dressing, sugar and celery seed; mix lightly. Chill. Toss again just before serving. Garnish with pepper rings if desired. Serves 6 to 8.

Mary V. Stanley

HOT SLAW

1 (4 oz.) can hot green chili
   peppers, drained, seeded
   and chopped

1 (1 lb.) can tomatoes
1 tsp. salt
1 small onion, quartered

Place all ingredients in electric blender until smooth. Refrigerate until serving time.

Judy Smith

SLAW

1 large head cabbage, grated

1 medium onion, diced

Mix:

½ c. vinegar
1 tsp. celery seed
1½ tsp. salt

1 c. Wesson oil
¾ c. sugar
1 Tbsp. prepared mustard

Bring to rolling boil; pour over cabbage and onion. Refrigerate 8 hours before serving.

Mrs. Delbert (Gloria) Murphy

RAINBOW COLE SLAW

2 c. green cabbage, shredded
1 c. red cabbage, shredded
1 carrot, grated
⅓ c. onion, chopped fine
⅓ c. green pepper, chopped
    fine
¼ c. sweet red pepper,
    chopped fine
1 Tbsp. fresh parsley,
    chopped

1 c. red apple, diced
    (unpeeled)
½ c. sour cream
½ c. mayonnaise
2 tsp. sugar
1 tsp. cider vinegar
Salt and pepper to taste

Combine all vegetables, parsley and apples. In a separate bowl, whip together the remaining ingredients. Pour this over vegetables and mix gently. Cover and refrigerate until chilled. Mix gently before serving.

Lila White

FREEZER SLAW

1 medium cabbage, shredded
1 carrot, shredded

1 green pepper, shredded

Sprinkle 1 tablespoon salt over and let stand 1 hour. Then squeeze excess liquid out by hand.

Combine in pan:

2 c. sugar
1 c. vinegar
½ c. water

1 Tbsp. mustard seed
1 tsp. celery seed

Bring to a boil for 1 minute. Pour over cabbage mix. Cool and freeze. Serve slightly thawed.

Peggy Graviss

SLAW TO FREEZE

1 c. vinegar
2 c. sugar
2 tsp. salt
½ c. water
1 tsp. celery seed

1 tsp. mustard seed
1 large head cabbage
2 sweet peppers
1 carrot
1 onion (very small)

Boil the vinegar, sugar, salt, water, celery seed and mustard seed together for 3 minutes. Then pour mixture over last 4 ingredients. Place in freezer boxes and freeze.

Erdean Lee

LONG KEEPING SLAW

Shred 1 head cabbage and slice 1 large onion, separating into thin rings. Sprinkle with 2 tablespoons sugar, then set aside.

Mix:

1 c. vinegar	**1 tsp. celery seed**
1 Tbsp. mustard	**½ c. oil**
1 Tbsp. salt	**1 c. sugar (approx.)**

Pour mixture over cabbage and onion. Store in refrigerator. Will keep for 1 to 2 weeks.

Mrs. T. C. (Marge) Terry

SWEET-SOUR SLAW

Shred 1 medium head of cabbage and chop small green pepper into it. Pour dressing over cabbage and pepper.

1½ c. sugar	**¼ c. onion, grated**
1 c. vinegar	**½ tsp. dry mustard**
1 tsp. salt	**1 tsp. celery seed**
½ c. salad oil	**1 tsp. paprika**

Mix sugar, vinegar and salt; bring to a boil. Cool. Add remaining ingredients, mixing well. Store in refrigerator. Will keep for an indefinite period of time.

Mrs. Richard (Joyce) Edwards

CORN SALAD

2 (12 oz.) cans corn	**2 Tbsp. mayonnaise**
¾ c. cucumbers, diced	**1 Tbsp. vinegar**
¼ c. onion	**½ tsp. salt**
2 small tomatoes	**¼ tsp. dry mustard**
¼ c. sour cream	**¼ tsp. celery seed**

Mix and chill.

Jean Lyle

CONGEALED SALAD

1 small can crushed
   pineapple (not drained)
¼ c. sugar
1 pkg. lemon Jello

½ c. cold water
1 c. grated cheese
1 pkg. nuts
1 pt. whipping cream

Mix pineapple and sugar; bring to boil. Mix lemon Jello with water. Add to pineapple mixture and refrigerate to thicken. After thickened, whip cream and add cheese and nuts to the cream. Fold this into Jello mixture and *wow!*

Norma Combs

CONGEALED SALAD

1 pkg. orange Jello
1 c. boiling water

1 pkg. mixed fruit Jello

Dissolve Jello with water. Then take juices from 1 can mandarin oranges and 1 can peaches. Heat and into this dissolve 1 envelope Knox gelatine. Then mix that with Jello and let almost congeal in refrigerator. While it is congealing, cut up oranges and peaches in small pieces. (You may also use other fruit, I cut up a few dark cherries.) When Jello mixture is almost congealed, fold into fruit and whipped cream until well mixed, then put in mold.

FROSTED CONGEALED SALAD

2 pkg. lemon Jello
2 c. 7-Up or Upper 10
2 or 4 bananas, sliced
½ c. small marshmallows

2 c. boiling water
1 (No. 2) can crushed or
   chunk pineapple, drained

Dissolve Jello in boiling water; dilute with 7-Up; chill. Combine bananas, pineapple and marshmallows. Stir mixture into gelatin. Chill until firm.

Topping:

½ c. sugar
1 or 2 Tbsp. butter
¼ c. American cheese,
   shredded
1 egg, slightly beaten

2 Tbsp. flour
1 c. whipped cream (I use
   Dream Whip)
1 c. pineapple juice

Cook pineapple juice, egg, flour, butter and sugar until sauce is thick. Cool. Fold cooked sauce into whipped cream. Frost salad. Sprinkle with shredded cheese.

CREAM CHEESE SALAD

1 large can crushed
   pineapple
2 pkg. unflavored gelatin
½ c. sugar

1 c. water
1 (8 oz.) pkg. cream cheese
½ pt. whipping cream
½ c. pecans

Dissolve gelatin in water and cook the pineapple and sugar until dissolved. Add cream cheese, whipping cream and pecans. Chill until set.

Elaine Cady

CRANBERRY SALAD

1 lb. cranberries
1 large orange (unpeeled)
1 large apple (unpeeled, use
   red apple)
1 (No. 1) flat can crushed
   pineapple

2 c. sugar
1 pkg. lime gelatin
1 pkg. orange gelatin

Remove seeds from orange and core apple. Put through food chopper together with raw cranberries. Add pineapple and sugar; let stand 2 hours. Dissolve both packages of gelatin together in 3 cups hot water and add fruit.

Erdean Lee

CRANBERRY SALAD

2 c. raw cranberries
½ c. celery
1 c. orange (peel and all)

1 c. sugar
½ c. nuts (pecans)

Grind all and add to 1 package lemon Jello dissolved in 1 cup hot water and 1 cup cold water. Mold as desired.

CRANBERRY SALAD

2 c. cranberries
1 orange
1½ c. sugar

½ c. chopped nuts
½ c. chopped celery
1 pkg. strawberry Jello

Dissolve Jello in ¼ cup hot water. Grind cranberries, orange, nuts and celery in meat grinder. Add sugar; stir; let set at least 1 hour. Add cooled Jello and serve when set. Whipped cream is a nice topping.

CRANBERRY SALAD

1 (13½ oz.) can crushed
   pineapple
2 (3 oz.) pkg. lemon flavored
   gelatin
1 (1 lb.) can whole cranberry
   sauce

7 oz. ginger ale or 7-Up
1 (2 oz.) pkg. whipped
   topping mix
1 (8 oz.) pkg. cream cheese
½ c. pecans
1 Tbsp. butter or margarine

Drain pineapple, reserving syrup. Add water to make 1 cup liquid. Heat pineapple liquid to boiling point; add lemon gelatin and stir until dissolved. Cool; gently stir in ginger ale and refrigerate mixture until partially set. Mix drained pineapple with whole cranberry sauce and fold into gelatin. Pour into square pan and chill firm. Whip topping mix according to package directions and fold in softened cream cheese. Spread over cranberry gelatin. Toast pecans in butter for 10 minutes in a 350° oven. Sprinkle over salad. Serves 8 to 10. Keeps well in refrigerator.

Mary T. Thompson

CRANBERRY SALAD

1 c. ground cranberries
   (fresh)
2 large apples, cored (but not
   peeled)
1 c. crushed pineapple

1 c. sugar
1 pkg. lemon Jello
4 drops of red food color
½ c. pecans

Mix food color to 1 cup hot water and Jello; let partially jell and then add remaining ingredients.

Patsy Akers

CHRISTMAS CRANBERRY SALAD

1 qt. cranberries
2 c. sugar
½ to 1 c. pecans

2 pkg. lemon Jello
2 oranges

Put cranberries and oranges through food grinder. Dissolve Jello and, when cool, add preceding ingredients. Mold as desired.

CRANBERRY RING SALAD

4 c. fresh cranberries
1½ c. sugar
1 c. water
1½ Tbsp. unflavored gelatin
¼ c. water (cold)

2 Tbsp. lime or lemon juice
⅔ c. walnuts, coarsely
   chopped
1 c. celery, diced

Pick over and wash cranberries. Boil sugar and water for 5 minutes; add berries. Cook slowly, without stirring, until berries break open, about 5 minutes. Soften gelatin in cold water and dissolve in hot cranberry juice. Add lime or lemon juice. Cook until mixture begins to thicken; add walnuts and celery. Pour into ring mold and chill until firm. Unmold on watercress or lettuce and serve with a creamy salad dressing. Center may be filled with cottage cheese whipped with a little sour cream. Serves 6 to 8.

Trudy Frazier

CREAMY CRANBERRY SALAD

1 (3 oz.) pkg. cream cheese,
   softened
2 c. frozen whipped dessert
   topping, thawed
1 (11 oz.) can mandarin
   orange sections, drained

1 (11 oz.) jar
   cranberry-orange relish
1½ c. tiny marshmallows
1 (8¾ oz.) can crushed
   pineapple, drained
⅓ c. chopped nuts

Combine; chill several hours. Serve on lettuce.

Jo Ann Thompson

FROZEN CRANBERRY SALAD

2 (3 oz.) pkg. cream cheese,
   softened and whipped
2 Tbsp. salad dressing
2 Tbsp. sugar
1 (8¼ oz.) can crushed
   pineapple (do not drain)

1 (16 oz.) can whole
   cranberries
½ c. chopped nuts
½ pt. whipping cream,
   whipped

Combine cream cheese, salad dressing, sugar and pineapple. Mix in cranberries and nuts. Fold in whipped cream. Put into individual molds or 2 inch deep pan. Freeze until ready to eat. Yield: 8 to 10 servings.

Madeline Ogden

FROZEN CRANBERRY SALAD
(For dessert)

1½ pkg. (12 oz.) cream
   cheese
3 Tbsp. sugar
2 cans whole cranberry sauce
1 large can crushed
   pineapple

½ to 1 c. chopped walnuts
⅓ pkg. small marshmallows
1 c. whipping cream

Cream cream cheese with sugar; add cranberries, pineapple and walnuts. Mix together thoroughly. Fold in whipped cream and marshmallows. Pour into a large Pyrex dish (9x13 inches) or salad mold. Freeze about 8 hours. Let set at room temperature a few minutes before serving.

Phyllis L. Davis

TANGY CRANBERRY MOLD

½ c. water, boiled
2 c. V-8
1 small orange, peeled, cut in
   ½ inch pieces
1 c. chopped walnuts

1 (6 oz.) orange Jello
1 (16 oz.) can whole
   cranberry sauce
Leaf lettuce
Sour cream

Stir Jello into boiling water in bowl; stir until dissolved. Stir in V-8 and cranberry sauce. Refrigerate until mixture mounds slightly when dropped from a spoon. Fold in orange and nuts. Pour into a 6 cup mold. Cover and refrigerate about 4 hours or until firm. Unmold on lettuce lined plate; garnish with sour cream.

Ruthie Marty

CUCUMBER-LIME SALAD

1 (3 oz.) pkg. lime gelatin
¾ c. boiling water
¾ c. cucumber, grated
1 Tbsp. onion, grated

1 c. cottage cheese
1 c. mayonnaise
⅓ c. pecans, chopped

Dissolve gelatin in boiling water. Cool until partially set. Fold in remaining ingredients. Chill until firm. Serves 6 to 8.

Paula White

CUCUMBER SALAD

2 cucumbers, sliced thin
½ onion, sliced thin
1 tsp. tarragon vinegar
2 Tbsp. sour cream

Salt and pepper to taste
½ tsp. paprika
Black olives

Combine cucumbers, onion, vinegar, sour cream, salt and pepper; mix well and chill. Sprinkle with paprika just before serving and garnish with black olives.

Mary Lauder

CUCUMBER SALAD

1 pkg. lime Jello
1 c. hot water
1 cucumber, grated
1 small onion, grated

1 c. cottage cheese
1 c. mayonnaise
½ c. nuts

Make Jello according to directions. When partially jelled, add other ingredients. Mix well and refrigerate.

Gwen Bond

CUCUMBER SOUR CREAM SALAD

1 Tbsp. sugar
1½ tsp. salt
1 c. sour cream
3 Tbsp. grated onion

2 Tbsp. white vinegar or
  lemon juice
4½ c. thin sliced peeled
  cucumbers

Blend sugar, salt, sour cream, onion and lemon juice. Stir in cucumbers. Chill 2 hours. Serve on lettuce.

Patti Roby

EASY SALAD

1 (8 oz.) pkg. Philadelphia
  cream cheese
1¼ c. sugar
1 large or 2 small cans fruit
  cocktail

1 small can crushed
  pineapple, well drained
1 small can apricots, drained
  and chopped
1 (6 oz.) container Cool Whip

Mix cream cheese and sugar; beat well. Add fruit cocktail, pineapple and apricots. Stir in Cool Whip. Freeze in large aluminum pan. When frozen, can be cut into pieces and refrozen.

Izetta Stephens

STUFFED EGGPLANT SALAD

2 large eggplants
4 medium tomatoes, peeled
  and diced
⅓ c. thinly sliced scallions
2½ tsp. salt
¼ tsp. pepper

1 Tbsp. sugar
⅓ c. oil
½ c. lemon juice
¼ c. chopped parsley
2 tsp. oregano

Place eggplants on baking sheet. Bake in 375° oven 35 to 45 minutes or until tender when pierced with fork. Allow to cool. Cut a lengthwise slice from the side of each eggplant and carefully remove inside pulp. Dice pulp and mix with tomatoes and remaining ingredients. Chill eggplant mixture and eggplant shells. Pour off excess liquid from mixture and spoon into eggplant shells to serve. Serves 6.

Mary Baxter

FIVE-CUP SALAD

1 c. pineapple chunks,
    drained
1 c. mandarin oranges,
    drained

1 c. coconut
1 c. miniature marshmallows
1 c. sour cream

Combine all ingredients and chill.

Mary Lee Chaney

FIVE CUP SALAD

1 c. miniature marshmallows
1 c. pineapple tidbits
1 c. sour cream

1 c. shredded coconut
1 c. mandarin oranges

Combine all ingredients. Let stand at least a few hours, preferably overnight, in refrigerator.

FRUIT SALAD

2 c. pineapple juice
1 large can pineapple chunks
2 cans mandarin orange
    slices
1 small bottle maraschino
    cherries

2 boxes *instant* vanilla
    pudding mix
2 or 3 large, sliced bananas

Drain all canned fruits (juice can be added to pineapple juice to make 2 cups). Beat juice and pudding mix until thick; fold in fruit and chill.

Ruth Ackerman

FROSTED FRUIT SALAD

1 (6 oz.) pkg. lemon or lime
    Jello
1 c. boiling water
2½ c. 7-Up or 1 (16 oz.) bottle
1 large can crushed
    pineapple, drained (save
    juice)
4 bananas, sliced
2 c. miniature marshmallows

1½ c. shredded Cheddar
    cheese
1 c. sugar
2 Tbsp. cornstarch
1 c. pineapple juice
1 egg, slightly beaten
1 c. whipped cream or Dream
    Whip

First Layer: Mix Jello, boiling water, 7-Up, crushed pineapple and bananas together and pour into 9x13 inch dish.

Second Layer: Add miniature marshmallows.

Third Layer: Add shredded Cheddar cheese.

Fourth Layer (Topping): Mix sugar, cornstarch, pineapple juice and egg in pan. Stir and cook until thickened. *Completely cool.* Add whipped cream or Dream Whip. Pour on top of Jello mixture and refrigerate.

Donna Browning

FROSTED FRUIT SALAD

2 (3 oz.) or 1 (6 oz.) pkg.
    lemon or lime Jello
1 c. boiling water
2½ c. 7-Up or 1 (16 oz.) 7-Up

1 large can pineapple,
    drained (save juice)
4 bananas

Pour all this into 9x13 inch dish.

Second Layer: 2 cups miniature marshmallows.

Third Layer: Sprinkle 1 cup shredded Cheddar cheese over marshmallows.

Topping:

1 c. sugar
2 Tbsp. cornstarch

1 c. pineapple juice
1 egg, slightly beaten

Stir and cook until thickens. *Completely cool.* Add 1 cup Dream Whip or whipped cream. Pour on top of congealed mixture and refrigerate until set.

Jewell Hundley

FROZEN FRUIT SALAD

1 (3 oz.) pkg. cream cheese
1 Tbsp. mayonnaise
2 c. Cool Whip
1 (13 oz.) can crushed
    pineapple, drained
1 (17 oz.) can fruit cocktail,
    drained

1 small can mandarin
    oranges, drained
1 c. miniature marshmallows
2 or 3 bananas, sliced

Mix cream cheese and mayonnaise. Add drained fruit, sliced bananas and marshmallows. (Bananas will not darken.) Fold in Cool Whip. Place in an 8x8x2 inch pan and freeze.

Judy Puckett

HOT FRUIT SALAD

1 can fruit cocktail, drained
1 can peaches, drained
1 can white Queen Ann cherries, drained and pitted
½ c. white raisins
2 or 3 oranges, sliced with peel on, then sliced in halves
¾ c. sugar

3 Tbsp. real butter
1 can pears, drained
1 can pineapple chunks, drained
½ c. sherry
3 Tbsp. flour
¼ tsp. salt
¾ c. mixed fruit juices (including juice of 1 lemon)

Pour hot water over raisins to plump. Cut fruit in hunks. Cook oranges until tender, with extra fruit juice and salt. Drain and add to mixed fruit. Add sugar. Combine butter, flour and fruit juice; cook until very thick. Add sherry. Fold into fruit. Refrigerate overnight or freeze until needed. Heat in 350° oven until mixture bubbles. This goes real well with baked ham.

GARDEN VEGETABLE SALAD

1 (No. 2½) can green beans
1 large sweet onion
4 stalks celery
1 large green pepper

1 (No. 300) can green peas (small)
1 large cucumber
1 large can pimentos

Drain vegetables and combine with sliced onion. Chop celery, pimento and pepper. Mix all ingredients in 4 quart bowl (except cucumber; add just before serving).

Dressing:

1 tsp. salt
¼ c. tarragon or wine vinegar
¾ c. sugar (more if desired)

½ c. white vinegar
⅜ c. salad oil
1½ tsp. cold water

Shake or stir until sugar is dissolved. Pour over vegetables and refrigerate 24 hours. Toss 3 or 4 times during the 24 hours so dressing can marinate all vegetables. Serves 12 to 14.

GORDON SALAD

Green onions or scallions,
    sliced
Black olives
Lettuce
Garlic salt
Ground red pepper

Fresh mushrooms, sliced
Cucumbers, sliced
Salt
Celery salt
Freshly ground black pepper

Combine preceding ingredients and toss first with olive oil and then with juice of 1 lemon.

Salad Tips: Wipe mushrooms with damp cloth; do not soak or peel. Wash and dry lettuce leaves; wrap in terry cloth towel and place in refrigerator until the last minute. Break leaves; never cut. Always toss with oil before adding lemon juice or vinegar as the oil keeps the leaves from being burned or wilted by the liquid. Freshly ground black pepper is a must.

GREEK COUNTRY SALAD

1 lb. fresh spinach, washed
    and chilled
2 tomatoes
1 small onion

½ cucumber
1 c. crumbled Feta cheese
½ c. black olives

Salad Dressing:

½ c. oil
½ c. vinegar
2 Tbsp. water

½ tsp. oregano or dill
½ tsp. sugar

Break spinach into bite-size pieces into a salad bowl. Add tomato wedges, thinly sliced cucumbers, cheese and olives. Mix together the dressing ingredients and shake well. Pour the dressing over the salad and toss just before serving. Makes 6 medium servings.

Mary Goff

GREEN BEAN SALAD

1 can wax beans   1 can French green beans
1 can kidney beans

Drain; mix and add 1 green pepper (sliced) and 1 onion (sliced).

Heat and add to the preceding mixture:

½ c. vinegar   ¼ tsp. pepper
¾ c. sugar   1 tsp. salt
¾ c. oil

Mix well; allow to cool and refrigerate.

GUACAMOLE SALAD

2 ripe avocados, pitted and   2 Tbsp. onion, grated
    peeled   1 garlic clove, minced
4 jalapeno chili peppers,   ½ tsp. ground coriander
    seeded, minced   ½ tsp. salt
1 tomato, peeled, chopped   ¼ tsp. pepper
    fine   Shredded lettuce
3 Tbsp. fresh lime juice   Tortillas

Mash avocados into a coarse puree. Stir in remaining ingredients, except lettuce and tortillas. Spoon over lettuce on salad plate. Serve with tortillas.

Beverly Craft

HEAVENLY HASH SALAD

1 pkg. Philadelphia cream   1 pkg. lime Jello
    cheese   Pecans (if desired)
1 c. milk
1 large can crushed
    pineapple

Mix cream cheese and milk until smooth. Drain pineapple juice (1 cup) and bring to a boil; remove from stove. Add Jello. Add this to cream cheese and milk mixture. Add pineapple and nuts. Refrigerate.

Mary Baxter

HOMINY SALAD

1 can hominy, drained
½ c. celery, chopped fine
½ c. green onions, chopped
    fine
½ c. olive oil
1 clove garlic, chopped fine

1 Tbsp. lemon juice
1 Tbsp. red wine vinegar
½ tsp. basil, crumbled
½ tsp. dry mustard
½ tsp. salt
¼ tsp. pepper

Combine hominy, celery and green onions; mix. Combine oil, garlic, lemon juice, vinegar, basil, dry mustard, salt and pepper. Mix well. Pour over hominy and mix. Chill.

Gwen Mills

HONEYMOON SALAD

1 (8 oz.) bar cream cheese
¼ c. salad dressing
1½ c. small marshmallows

1 can crushed pineapple
1 small pkg. cocoanut
1 (8 oz.) container Cool Whip

Let cream cheese set at room temperature until soft, then fold in remaining ingredients. Chill until firm.

Mary T. Thompson

JELLO SALAD

1 pkg. Jello (cherry or
    strawberry)
1 c. cold water

1 c. hot water
⅓ c. sugar

Mix Jello. Stand until set, then add 2 bananas (cut up), 4 slices pineapple (cut up), 1 cup cottage cheese (small curd), and nuts. Let set a little more, then fold in ½ pint whipped cream.

I used Dream Whip. I used an 8x12 inch glass dish and cut and served in squares on lettuce.

KIDNEY BEAN SALAD

1 (No. 2) can kidney beans,
   drained
½ c. chopped dill pickles
2 Tbsp. chopped green
   pepper (optional)
Dash of pepper
Bibb lettuce (optional)

1 c. thinly sliced celery
2 Tbsp. chopped pimento
   (optional)
1 Tbsp. minced onion
1 tsp. salt
⅓ c. mayonnaise (scant)

Combine beans, celery, pickles, pimento and green pepper, onion, salt and pepper. Toss lightly with mayonnaise.

LETTUCE AND ONION SALAD

Dressing:

2 Tbsp. melted bacon grease
2 Tbsp. vinegar

1 Tbsp. sugar

Heat to boiling point and pour over 1½ quarts shredded lettuce and 3 green onions, chopped. Add salt and pepper to taste. Toss to mix. Serve at once.

LIME JELLO SALAD

1 c. milk
1 c. miniature marshmallows
1 (3 oz.) pkg. lime Jello
1 (No. 2) can crushed
   pineapple

Small pkg. chopped pecans
1 (8 oz.) pkg. softened cream
   cheese
1 pkg. Cool Whip or Dream
   Whip

Melt marshmallows in milk over low heat and add dry Jello. Beat until Jello is mixed and dissolved; add softened cream cheese and pineapple (and juice). Let congeal a little, then fold in Cool Whip. Let congeal and cut into squares.

Peggy Graviss

LIME COTTAGE CHEESE SALAD

1 pkg. lime Jello
1½ c. hot water
½ c. pineapple juice
1 c. cottage cheese
¼ tsp. salt
½ c. mayonnaise

1 Tbsp. vinegar
1 c. crushed pineapple
1½ c. diced celery
¼ c. pimiento
¼ c. chopped nuts

Dissolve Jello in water; add pineapple juice. When slightly thickened, whip. Add remaining ingredients and chill.

Note: May be prepared the day before using.

LIME MOLD

2 pkg. lime Jello
1 (8 oz.) pkg. cream cheese
Maraschino cherries and
    pecans

1 large can crushed
    pineapple
3 c. water

Dissolve Jello in 3 cups hot water; allow to congeal. Allow cheese to remain at room temperature until soft. Add cheese and pineapple to Jello and whip; add small bottle cherries and about ½ cup broken pecans. Pour in mold and refrigerate.

This is a nice salad for Christmas.

LINGUINE SALAD

Cook 1 (16 ounce) package linguine as package directs, but cook 10 minutes. Rinse and drain well. Cool. Mix together 1 (16 ounce) bottle Italian dressing and 1 bottle McCormick's Salad Supreme. Chunk up tomatoes, cucumbers and onions (optional). Add to the linguine along with your dressing. Mix well and refrigerate overnight.

I put in a Tupperware bowl, then you can turn easily to mix.

Nadiene Ward

MACARONI SALAD

16 oz. cooked and cooled
    macaroni
1 bell pepper, chopped
1 onion, chopped
4 carrots, grated

2 c. mayonnaise
1 can condensed milk
½ c. white vinegar
Sugar (to your taste)

Blend all in large bowl. Store in refrigerator.

Fay Smith

MACARONI SALAD

3 Tbsp. mustard (prepared)
1½ c. sugar
½ pt. Miracle Whip
⅓ c. vinegar
1 large can evaporated milk
¼ tsp. salt

1 lb. macaroni
4 hard-boiled eggs
1 large green pepper
Celery
Onion

Mash egg yolks with mustard. Add milk, sugar, Miracle Whip, vinegar and salt. Add chopped egg whites, celery, green peppers and onion. Add cooked and drained macaroni.

Nancy A. Thiry

MACARONI-TUNA SALAD

7 oz. pkg. macaroni, cooked
½ c. mayonnaise
½ c. sour cream
½ tsp. celery seed
½ tsp. onion salt
1 (7 oz.) can tuna, drained
1 can green peas (very small
    peas)

¾ c. diced mild Cheddar
    cheese
2 Tbsp. green pepper
1 Tbsp. pimento
1 Tbsp. diced onion
Salt and pepper to taste

Mix all ingredients; refrigerate. Best if mixed ahead to allow flavor to set.

Shirley Cates

MARINATED VEGETABLES

1 can peas
1 can green beans (French
   style or regular)
1 c. chopped celery

1 bell pepper, chopped
1 bunch green onions,
   chopped
1 can water chestnuts, sliced

Dressing to be poured over vegetables:

1½ c. water
1 c. vinegar

1 c. sugar
½ c. oil

Marinate overnight. Drain before serving.

MEXICAN SALAD

1 large head lettuce,
   shredded into bite-size
   pieces
1 large onion, chopped
1 large tomato, chopped into
   bite-size pieces

1 can kidney beans, drained
Salt and pepper to taste
Green olives, sliced
Grated cheese
Crushed corn chips
Catalina dressing

Mix the preceding ingredients, excluding the corn chips. Let each individual add the corn chips and Catalina dressing as they wish.

Linda Y. Borden

MILLIONAIRE SALAD

2 c. cooked rice
2 Tbsp. sugar
1 (8 oz.) pkg. cream cheese
1 medium can crushed
   pineapple

1 Tbsp. salad dressing
1 c. whipping cream
1 c. pecans
1 pkg. miniature
   marshmallows

Combine cream cheese and sugar. Mix everything else, except whipping cream. Add it last.

Virginia Stith

MOUNTAINEER SALAD

Small head cabbage   1 c. crushed pineapple
½ c. cooked peanuts   2 c. small marshmallows

  Combine ingredients and add mayonnaise as desired just before serving. (Grate cabbage or slice as you prefer.)

OLIVE WREATH SALAD

1 (No. 2) can (2½ c.) crushed Juice of 4 lemons
 pineapple   ¼ tsp. salt
1 (3 oz.) pkg. lime Jello   1 c. chopped nuts
½ c. grated American cheese 1 c. cream, whipped
½ c. chopped pimientos
½ c. small stuffed olives,
 sliced

  Drain pineapple. Heat pineapple syrup to a boil. Add to lime Jello. Stir until Jello dissolves. Cool. When gelatin begins to thicken, add pineapple, cheese, pimientos, celery, nuts and salt. Fold in whipped cream. Place roll of sliced olives to bottom of 9 inch ring mold. Pour small amount of gelatin mixture into mold. Chill until firm. Then pour in other mixture and let chill until firm. Serves 8 to 10.

ORANGE-MANDARIN SALAD

1 large orange Jello   1 large ctn. Cool Whip
1 pt. orange sherbet
1 can mandarin oranges,
 drained (save juice)

  Dissolve Jello in 1 cup boiling water. Add juice from drained oranges, then sherbet and Cool Whip. Mix well, then add orange sections and put into large mold which has been rinsed in cool water. Refrigerate until set. Unmold and serve.

Mrs. James Tucker

MANDARIN ORANGE SALAD

1 (3 oz.) pkg. orange Jello
1 c. boiling water
1 pt. orange sherbet
1 (11 oz.) can mandarin
    orange segments,
    drained

2 c. miniature marshmallows
    or 1 c. Cool Whip

Dissolve Jello in boiling water. Add sherbet and stir until dissolved. Chill until almost set. Fold in marshmallows or Cool Whip. Chill until firm.

Newland Stanfill

MANDARIN ORANGE SALAD

1 small pkg. orange Jello
1 c. hot water
1 small can crushed
    pineapple (do not drain)

⅓ c. sugar

Mix; let cool slightly.

Then add:

1 c. chopped nuts
1 c. (small can) mandarin
    oranges, drained

1 c. coconut
1 c. sour cream

Pour into rectangle cake pan and allow to set. Cut into squares and serve.

Phyllis L. Davis

ORANGE SHERBET SALAD

2 small pkg. orange Jello
2 c. hot water
1 pt. orange sherbet
1 can pineapple tidbits,
    drained

1 can mandarin oranges,
    drained

Dissolve Jello in hot water; add sherbet. Stir until melted. Add drained fruit; chill until firm. Cover with topping.

Topping - Cook in double boiler:

1 c. pineapple juice
2 Tbsp. flour
2 Tbsp. butter

½ c. sugar
1 egg, beaten

Cook and let cool. Then add 1 cup Cool Whip 1 hour before serving.

Sharon Sherman

ORANGE SALAD

1 small box orange Jello
1 small box curd cottage
cheese
1 small bowl Cool Whip
1 small can crushed
pineapple, drained

1 small can mandarin
oranges, drained
½ c. English walnuts
(optional)

Mix together and let set.

Virginia Moran

ORANGE SHERBET MOLD

1 (3 oz.) pkg. orange gelatin
1 c. boiling water
1 pt. orange sherbet
1 (11 oz.) can mandarin
oranges, drained
1 c. miniature marshmallows

1 (8½ oz.) can crushed
pineapple, drained
⅔ c. pecans, chopped
Small jar maraschino
cherries, cut up

Dissolve gelatin in boiling water. While hot, stir in orange sherbet. Chill until thick and syrupy. Fold in mandarin oranges, marshmallows, pineapple, pecans and maraschino cherries. Pour into lightly oiled mold. Chill until firm. Serves 4 to 6.

Lora Martin

ORANGE SHERBET SALAD

2 (3 oz.) boxes orange Jello
1 pt. orange sherbet
1 c. miniature marshmallows
1 (8½ oz.) can crushed
pineapple

1 (1⅓ oz.) can mandarin
oranges
1 c. whipping cream
1 c. boiling water

Dissolve Jello in water. Let it begin to set, then add orange sherbet and other ingredients. Fold in cup of whipped cream. Chill for several hours.

Allouise Davidson

ORZA SALAD

4 oz. uncooked orza
2 medium tomatoes, coarsely
   chopped
4 oz. Feta cheese, crumbled
½ c. minced fresh parsley

½ c. minced fresh basil
   leaves or dill
¼ c. fresh lemon juice
1 Tbsp. plus 1 tsp. olive oil
Salt and pepper to taste

Cook orza according to package directions. Drain with cold water. Add tomato, Feta cheese, parsley, basil or dill. Combine remaining ingredients and pour over salad and toss. Salad is better if rice is put in the refrigerator and let set for several hours before you make salad.

Note: Orza is a type of rice that can be found in health food stores.

Terry White

PEA SALAD

1 head lettuce
1 pkg. frozen peas
1 c. celery, diced
1 small onion, diced
½ lb. bacon

2 c. mayonnaise
Dash of sugar
3 boiled eggs, sliced
Cheddar cheese

Place pieces of lettuce in bottom of flat baking dish. Sprinkle peas over lettuce. Sprinkle celery and onion over mixture. Crumble crisp cooked bacon over mixture. Add slices of boiled eggs. Mix 2 cups of mayonnaise with a little sugar and spread over mixture. Grate Cheddar cheese over top. Refrigerate and serve.

Elizabeth Hensley

PEAR-CRANBERRY SALAD

1 (6 oz.) pkg. raspberry
   gelatin
1 c. boiling water
2 c. cold water
½ tsp. lemon juice

1 (16 oz.) can whole
   cranberry sauce
1 (29 oz.) can pear halves,
   drained and chopped
½ c. chopped pecans

Dissolve gelatin in boiling water; stir in cold water, lemon juice and cranberry sauce. Chill until consistency of unbeaten egg whites. Fold in pears and pecans. Spoon in 7 cup mold. Chill until firm. Yield: 10 servings.

Dot Berry

PEPSI JELLO

1 small pkg. lemon Jello
1 (12 oz.) cold Pepsi Cola
1 small can crushed
    pineapple, drained

½ c. finely chopped pecans

Empty Jello in bowl. Bring to boil half of the Pepsi. Pour over Jello, then add the rest of the cold Pepsi. Then add nuts and drained pineapple. Store in refrigerator until set.

Ruth Ackerman

PINEAPPLE-COTTAGE CHEESE SALAD

1 (No. 2) can crushed
    pineapple
2 env. unflavored gelatin
1 lb. (2 c.) cottage cheese
¼ c. mayonnaise or cooked
    salad dressing
1 Tbsp. sugar
1 c. coarsely chopped
    walnuts

1 medium green pepper,
    chopped (cut and reserve
    1 ring for garnish)
1 drained (4 oz.) can
    pimentos, chopped
1 c. heavy cream, whipped

Set aside 2 tablespoons pineapple. From rest of pineapple, drain syrup into glass measuring cup; soften gelatin in this syrup. Set measuring cup in pan of boiling water, stirring occasionally, until gelatin dissolves. Now, stir gelatin into pineapple and cottage cheese combined with rest of ingredients. Pour into mold. Refrigerate until firm; unmold; garnish top with reserved pepper ring filled with the reserved pineapple. Makes 12 servings.

Jimmie Dillman

PINEAPPLE CREAM CHEESE SALAD

2 pkg. plain Knox gelatine
⅔ c. sugar
1 small ctn. whipping cream
1 c. water

1 (No. 2) can crushed
  pineapple
½ c. pecans

Dissolve gelatine in water; add sugar and pineapple, including juice. Bring to a boil for 5 minutes. Set aside. Add cream cheese; stir until smooth. Let cool. Add whipping cream and nuts. Pour into mold and chill overnight in refrigerator.

Lynnette Bonn

PINEAPPLE SALAD SUPREME

2 eggs
1 c. sugar
1 c. milk

1 Tbsp. flour
2 Tbsp. butter

Mix preceding and cook until thick. Cool; add ½ cup apple cider vinegar; stir.

Pour over:

1 lb. grated mild Cheddar
  cheese
1 c. chopped pecans

1 large can drained pineapple
  chunks

Chill overnight.

Mrs. Jene (Mary Dixion) Baker

PISTACHIO SALAD

1 box instant pistachio
  pudding
1 (No. 2) can crushed
  pineapple, drained
  (reserve juice)

½ c. chopped nuts
1 c. miniature marshmallows
  (mixed colors)
1 (9 oz.) ctn. Cool Whip

Drain pineapple; mix pudding with pineapple juice. Add Cool Whip; mix well. Fold in marshmallows, pineapple and nuts. Chill until firm.

Sharon Shepherd

96

POTATO SALAD

8 - 10 potatoes
1 good size cucumber
About 9 or 10 red radishes
6 Tbsp. salad dressing

1 tsp. yellow mustard
3½ Tbsp. sugar
Salt and pepper to taste

Cut up potatoes; peel cucumber and slice. Do not peel radishes; slice thin. Mix salad dressing, yellow mustard, sugar, salt and pepper. Pour on top of vegetables. Let set a while. Then blend all in bowl. Cover and put in refrigerator. Goes well with baked beans and beer bread.

Mary Beeler

CANADIAN POTATO SALAD

6 nice size red potatoes,
    scrubbed
1 c. mayonnaise

1 Tbsp. celery seed
1 c. chopped purple onion
Salt and pepper

Boil potatoes in jackets just until tender. While potatoes are still warm, chop with jackets into bowl. Add remaining ingredients. Serve warm.

All ingredients can be altered to taste.

Rose Briseno

MRS. CHANDLER'S POTATO SALAD
(Must be prepared the day before)

8 boiled medium potatoes (in
    jackets)
1½ c. mayonnaise
1 c. commercial sour cream
1½ tsp. horseradish
1 tsp. celery seed

½ tsp. salt
1 c. fresh chopped parsley
    (do not omit or decrease)
2 medium onions, finely
    minced

Peel potatoes; cut in ⅛ inch slices. Combine mayonnaise, sour cream, horseradish, celery seed and salt; set aside. In another bowl, mix parsley and onion. In large serving bowl, arrange layer of potatoes, salt lightly; cover with layer of mayonnaise-sour cream mixture. Continue layering, ending with parsley and onion. *Do not stir!* Cover and refrigerate at least 8 hours before serving. Salad is better if made the day before. Yield: 8 to 10 servings.

Double the recipe for a cocktail supper for about 20.

Wilma Crowdus

DEVILED HOT POTATO SALAD

4 c. hot, cooked, cubed
   potatoes
¼ c. chopped green onions
   (with tops)

1 c. sour cream
2 Tbsp. prepared mustard
1 tsp. salt
1 tsp. sugar

Mix potatoes and onions. Heat sour cream. Don't boil. Blend in seasonings. Pour over potatoes and onions; toss. (Top with smoked sausage, hot dogs or ham slices.)

Patti Roby

GERMAN POTATO SALAD

10 lb. potatoes
1 lb. bacon
2 medium onions, chopped
5 stalks celery, chopped
¼ c. flour
Salt to taste (about 2 Tbsp.)

¼ tsp. pepper
2 c. sugar
2 c. vinegar
2 c. water
1 large green pepper,
   chopped

Boil potatoes, peel and slice. Add onions, celery, green pepper, salt and pepper; mix. Cut bacon in small pieces and fry. Remove bacon from fat and set aside. Add flour to fat; stir until smooth. Add sugar, vinegar and water to fat; bring to boil. Pour over potato mixture. Add bacon and mix well. Serve warm.

Dorothy Young

GERMAN POTATO SALAD

8 slices bacon
3 Tbsp. flour
4 tsp. chopped onion
⅔ c. vinegar
⅔ c. water

½ c. sugar
4 tsp. salt
½ tsp. black pepper
2 qt. cooked, diced potatoes
½ c. chopped fresh parsley

Fry bacon crisp. Remove from pan and drain (reserve ¼ cup of fat) and crumble. To ¼ cup of bacon fat left in pan, add flour and onions. Stir in vinegar, water and sugar. Add salt and pepper. Cook only until medium thickness. Add to potatoes. Add parsley and crumbled bacon. Mix carefully with 2 forks to prevent mashing the potatoes.

Erdean Lee

ITALIAN STYLE POTATO SALAD

¼ c. low calorie Italian salad
   dressing
1 tsp. Worcestershire sauce
1 tsp. prepared mustard
1 tsp. salt

1 egg
4 potatoes (1½ lb.), pared
   and boiled
4 pitted ripe olives, sliced
1 Tbsp. chopped parsley

Combine Italian dressing, Worcestershire sauce, mustard, salt and egg in a bowl; beat until well blended. Dice potatoes into a bowl; add sliced olives. Pour dressing over potatoes; toss to coat evenly. Refrigerate until ready to serve. Sprinkle with parsley. Serves 8, 58 calories each.

Melanie Davis

MOM'S OLD FASHIONED POTATO SALAD

Peel, dice and cook potatoes in salted water. Rinse with cold water when potatoes are done.

Chop and add:

4 boiled eggs
3 or 4 Tbsp. pickles

1 medium onion

Dressing:

½ c. vinegar
½ c. water
½ c. sugar
2 Tbsp. flour or cornstarch
1 egg

Dash or 2 of prepared
   mustard
Butter the size of a walnut
Dash of salt

Cook until thick. Cool and pour over potato mixture and stir. Refrigerate.

D. White

PATIO POTATO SALAD
(An ideal outdoor barbecue dish)

⅓ c. sugar
1 Tbsp. cornstarch
½ c. milk
¼ c. vinegar
1 egg
4 Tbsp. butter
¾ tsp. celery seed

¼ tsp. dry mustard
¼ c. chopped onion
¼ c. mayonnaise
7 medium potatoes, cooked,
   peeled and diced
3 hard cooked eggs, chopped
Paprika

In saucepan, combine sugar and cornstarch. Add next 6 ingredients and ¾ teaspoon salt. Cook and stir over low heat until bubbly. Remove from heat; add onion and mayonnaise. Cool. Combine potatoes and hard cooked eggs; gently fold in dressing. Chill. Just before serving, sprinkle with paprika. Serves 6.

Mrs. Bill (Sharon) Kurtz

PATIO POTATO SALAD

4 c. (6 medium) sliced,
   cooked potatoes
½ stick butter
½ c. chopped onion
½ c. chopped green pepper
1 Tbsp. flour

2 Tbsp. sugar
1½ tsp. salt
Tall can Pet milk
⅓ c. cider vinegar
4 tsp. prepared mustard
Bacon curls

Melt butter; add onions and peppers. Cook until tender. Blend in combined sugar, flour and salt. Gradually add milk, stirring constantly. Cook until thick. Add vinegar and mustard. Place potatoes in a 1½ quart casserole. Pour over sauce. Toss lightly. Top with bacon curls. Serves 6.

Dorothy O'Neal

PRETZEL SALAD

2 (3 oz.) boxes strawberry
   Jello
1 large ctn. Cool Whip
2 (10 oz.) pkg. frozen
   strawberries
1 (8 oz.) pkg. cream cheese

1 c. sugar
2½ c. crushed pretzels
⅓ c. margarine
3 Tbsp. sugar
2 c. boiling water

Mix well crushed pretzels, margarine and 3 tablespoons sugar. Bake at 350° for 10 minutes in 9x13 inch pan. Cool completely! Mix cream cheese and 1 cup sugar; add Cool Whip and *mix well!* Spread over cooled pretzels. Dissolve Jello in boiling water; add frozen strawberries. Break up with fork while stirring. Chill until slightly thickened. Pour over Cool Whip layer. Chill until set.

Patricia Jewell

RIBBON SALAD

1. Dissolve large package lime Jello by directions - ½ cup of water; let congeal in large pan such as bread pan or large casserole dish.
2. Dissolve lemon Jello in cup of hot water in top of double boiler

and add ½ cup marshmallows and juice from Number 2 can of crushed pineapple. Let marshmallows dissolve and remove from fire. Add 8 ounce package of Philadelphia cream cheese. Beat with rotary beater until dissolved. Then add crushed pineapple, 1 cup Miracle Whip and 1 cup cream (whipped); mix well. Pour over green Jello; let congeal.

3. Mix large package cherry Jello as directed - ½ cup water. Cool and pour over lemon Jello mixture. Makes very large amount.

Very good for Christmas salad. Cut in half for small group. Use orange and green for Easter.

Izetta Stephens

RICE SALAD

1 large pkg. marshmallows
1 large can crushed
   pineapple
2 c. cooked rice
8 oz. pkg. cream cheese
2 Tbsp. mayonnaise

2 Tbsp. sugar
1 c. Cool Whip
12 or more maraschino
   cherries, well drained
1 c. nuts (optional)

Combine the cheese, sugar and mayonnaise together until smooth. Add cooked rice, well drained pineapple, cherries, marshmallows and Cool Whip. Mix well. One cup of nuts may be added. Chill in refrigerator.

Kim Clinton

NEW ZEALAND RICE SALAD

1 c. rice, cooked in 2½ c.
   chicken stock
2 Tbsp. vinegar
2 tsp. prepared mustard
1½ tsp. salt
Pinch of pepper
¼ c. salad oil

1 c. olives, cut in pieces
2 hard-boiled eggs, diced
1 c. celery, sliced
¼ c. dill pickles
¼ c. red pepper, chopped
1 small onion, minced
¼ c. mayonnaise

Blend together salad oil, vinegar, mustard, salt and pepper. Pour over hot rice; toss and set aside to cool. Add remaining ingredients; toss gently and chill. Serves 8.

Gwen Mills

SANGRITA SALAD

1⅓ c. orange juice
¼ c. lime juice
3 Tbsp. dry red wine
3 Tbsp. grenadine syrup
3 Tbsp. minced onion

1 tsp. salt
1 tsp. Tabasco sauce
1 Tbsp. plain gelatin
1 medium avocado, cubed

Combine all ingredients, except gelatin and avocado. Put ½ cup of mixture in saucepan and stir in gelatin. Stir over low heat until gelatin dissolves, then return to original mixture. Add avocado and pour into oiled mold. Chill until firm. May be served with mayonnaise. Serves 6.

Judy Smith

SAUERKRAUT SALAD

1 large can sauerkraut
1 tsp. salt
1 medium size green pepper
2 c. onions
2 c. sugar

2 cans bean sprouts
½ tsp. pepper
2 c. celery
1 c. vinegar (white)

Dissolve sugar, vinegar and salt; add pepper. Chop celery, onions and green pepper; add to vinegar and sugar mixture. Mix well with drained sauerkraut and bean sprouts. Let marinate several hours before serving. This will keep several days in a sealed Tupperware bowl.

KRAUT SALAD

1 c. drained sauerkraut
1 c. diced celery
½ c. diced peppers
½ c. chopped onions

1¼ c. sugar
¼ c. cooking oil
¼ c. vinegar
¼ tsp. salt

Mix ingredients for dressing. Chill. Mix with salad ingredients. Chill and serve.

SAWDUST SALAD

1 small pkg. lemon Jello
1 small pkg. orange Jello
1 (No. 2) can crushed
   pineapple, drained

2 - 3 sliced bananas

Combine 2 packages Jello with 2 cups boiling water and 1½ cups cold water. Add bananas and pineapple (nuts if desired). Let mixture set until firm.

Boil until thick the following:

2 eggs
1 c. pineapple juice

¾ c. sugar
2 Tbsp. flour

Cool this thickened mixture and spread over set gelatin.

Top with layer of Cool Whip *or* beat together the following:

½ pt. whipping cream
1 (3 oz.) pkg. Philadelphia
  cream cheese

2 Tbsp. sugar

Spread on top.

Myrna Blackman

SEVEN LAYER SALAD

1 medium head lettuce
  (bottom layer)
½ c. chopped green pepper
  (second layer)
½ c. chopped onion (purple,
  third layer)
½ c. chopped celery (fourth
  layer)

1 pkg. small frozen peas
  (Birds Eye), cooked,
  cooled (fifth layer)
1 pkg. shredded Cheddar
  cheese (sixth layer)

Mix together:

1 c. sour cream
½ c. salad dressing

2 Tbsp. sugar

Pour over all (seventh layer). Crumble 9 slices crisp bacon on top.
Anna Smyth

SEVEN-UP SALAD

2 pkg. lemon Jello
2 c. hot water
1 7-Up
1 (20 oz.) can crushed
  pineapple

3 bananas, sliced
1 c. miniature marshmallows

Let jell partly, then add pineapple, banana and marshmallows. Save pineapple juice for topping.

Topping:

1 c. pineapple juice
2 tsp. flour or cornstarch

1 beaten egg
2 tsp. butter

Cook juice, cornstarch and egg until thick; add butter and cool. Fold in ½ pint whipping cream. Sprinkle ½ cup grated cheese over top.

Anna Smyth

SEVEN-UP SALAD

1 large box lemon or lime
   Jello
2 c. 7-Up
1 (No. 2) can crushed
   pineapple

2 c. hot water
1 c. miniature marshmallows

Dissolve Jello in hot water. Add 7-Up. Add pineapple (which has been drained, save liquid). Pour mixture into baking dish. Spread marshmallows on top and let chill until set.

Topping: Beat 1 egg. Add ⅓ cup sugar and 1 tablespoon flour. Add juice saved from pineapple. Cook over low heat until thickened. Cool completely; fold in 1 package Dream Whip (beaten according to package directions). Spread mixture on top of Jello. Garnish with nuts and cherries.

SPAGHETTI SALAD

1 cucumber, sliced
2 tomatoes, chopped
½ green pepper, chopped
1 small can mushrooms
1 (8 oz.) bottle Italian
   dressing

1 bottle McCormick's salad
   dressing
1 lb. spaghetti

Cook spaghetti and wash well in cold water. Mix in all ingredients and place in refrigerator for 4 hours; stir occasionally.

Anna Keene

GERMAN SPINACH SALAD

1 lb. fresh spinach
½ c. mayonnaise
½ c. sour cream
2 Tbsp. green onions,
    chopped
2 Tbsp. parsley, minced

1½ Tbsp. vinegar
1½ Tbsp. fresh lemon juice
1 garlic clove, minced
Cheddar cheese cubes or
    garlic croutons

Wash and dry spinach. Mix next 7 ingredients and add to spinach. Garnish with cheese or garlic croutons. Serves 4.

R. A. Bratcher

FRESH SPINACH SALAD

1 lb. fresh spinach
½ lb. fresh mushrooms
6 - 8 green onions, chopped
8 slices bacon, cooked and
    crumbled
1 boiled egg, sliced
Salt and pepper to taste

1 c. salad oil
½ c. sugar
½ tsp. dry mustard
½ tsp. onion juice
½ tsp. salt
⅓ c. cider vinegar

1. Combine spinach, mushrooms, onions, egg and bacon in a large bowl; set aside.
2. Combine salad oil, sugar, mustard, onion juice and salt in container of electric blender; blend well. Remove lid of container; slowly add vinegar while blender is running.
3. Toss spinach mixture with dressing. Season with salt and pepper. Yield: About 8 servings.

Marsha Golden

WILTED SPINACH SALAD WITH BACON DRESSING

1½ lb. fresh spinach, washed
    well
3 or 4 strips bacon
1 clove fresh garlic, chopped
1½ tsp. dry mustard

1½ tsp. sugar
¼ c. red wine vinegar
Freshly ground coarse black
    pepper to taste

After washing spinach, pat or spin in a salad spinner until dry. Remove stems; rip leaves and place in salad bowl. Fry bacon until crisp; drain and set aside. Add garlic, mustard, sugar and vinegar to bacon grease in pan; bring to a boil and simmer 30 seconds. Pour over spinach. Crumble crisp bacon on top. Add pepper. Serves 4 to 6.

Variation: Add ¼ cup brandy to the wine vinegar. This can be flamed in the pan, or not.

Jean Lyle

SPINACH SALAD

½ lb. bacon
8 c. torn spinach
2 hard-boiled eggs, sliced
¼ c. celery, sliced
3 Tbsp. green onions, sliced
½ tsp. coarse ground pepper

¼ tsp. salt
2 Tbsp. brown sugar
½ c. red wine vinegar
2 Tbsp. lemon juice
1 Tbsp. Worcestershire sauce

Fry bacon until crisp; drain; reserve ½ cup drippings. Crumble bacon and set aside. In a large salad bowl, place spinach, eggs, celery, green onions, pepper and salt. In a saucepan, combine brown sugar, ½ cup reserved bacon drippings, vinegar, lemon juice and Worcestershire sauce. Heat just to boiling; stir in bacon. Pour over spinach; toss gently. Serves 6.

Lynnette Bonn

SPINACH RICE SALAD

1 c. cooked rice
½ c. bottled Italian salad
   dressing
1 Tbsp. soy sauce
½ tsp. sugar
2 c. fresh spinach, cut into
   thin strips

½ c. sliced celery
½ c. sliced green onions
   (including tops)
⅓ c. crumbled crisp bacon

Combine dressing, soy sauce and sugar. Stir into warm rice. Cover and chill. Fold in remaining ingredients before serving. Makes 6 to 8 servings.

Betty T. King

STRAWBERRY SALAD

Strawberry Sauce:

1 large pkg. strawberry Jello
3 large bananas, diced
1 pt. strawberries (with juice)
1 c. hot water

1 c. cold water
1 small can crushed
   pineapple

Mix all ingredients together and jell.

Topping: Beat together Cool Whip, ½ cup powdered sugar and small package cream cheese. Spread over Jello mixture.

Paula White

STRAWBERRY SALAD

1 small pkg. strawberry
   gelatin
½ c. boiling water
1 (10 oz.) pkg. frozen
   strawberries, thawed

½ c. chopped nuts
1 (8 oz.) can crushed
   pineapple
1 banana, mashed
½ pt. sour cream

Dissolve gelatin in boiling water. Combine fruits and nuts; add to gelatin. Put half of mixture into a 6x10 inch dish and refrigerate until firm. Spread sour cream over this layer and pour remaining gelatin over sour cream. Refrigerate until firm. Serves 6.

Paula White

STRAWBERRY SALAD

1 box strawberry Jello,
   dissolved in 1 c. hot
   water
10 oz. pkg. frozen
   strawberries, thawed

1 small can crushed
   pineapple

Mold. Dissolve 1 box lemon Jello in 1 cup hot water. Let cool. Fold in ½ pint whipped cream, 1 small package Philadelphia cream cheese and ½ cup chopped pecans. Pour over the top of salad already molded and mold.

HAWAIIAN STRAWBERRY SALAD

1 (6 oz.) pkg. strawberry Jello
1 c. boiling water
2 (10 oz.) pkg. thawed frozen
   strawberries
1 large can crushed
   pineapple

3 mashed bananas
1 c. chopped pecans
1 (8 oz.) pkg. cream cheese
1 c. sour cream

Dissolve Jello in boiling water. Add strawberries, pineapple, bananas and pecans. Pour half of the mixture into rectangular bowl. Place in refrigerator to set. Combine cream cheese and sour cream until well blended. Pour on top of chilled mixture. Top with remaining fruit mixture. Chill until firm. Yield: 15 servings.

Betty T. King

STRAWBERRY HOLIDAY MOLD

1 (3 oz.) pkg. strawberry Jello
1 c. boiling water
¼ c. cold water
1 (8 oz.) can crushed
   pineapple with juice

1 (21 oz.) can cherry pie filling
½ tsp. ground cinnamon

Dissolve Jello in boiling water; stir in cold water. Combine with pineapple, pie filling and cinnamon. Chill until slightly thickened; stir well. Spoon into 5 cup mold. Chill until firm. Unmold and serve with sauce.

Sauce:

½ c. heavy cream, whipped   ½ c. sour cream

Fold whipped cream into sour cream; spoon into serving dish and pass with mold.

Ruthie Marty

STRAWBERRY SALAD

1 can strawberry pie filling
1 can Eagle Brand milk
1 large ctn. Cool Whip

2 small cans crushed
   pineapple
¼ c. lemon juice

Mix together and chill. Good with cherry also.

Betty King

TEA SHOP SALAD

1 can pineapple tidbits
1 can Queen Anne cherries,
  pitted
½ lb. marshmallows
½ c. chopped pecans

1 c. sugar
1 pt. Cool Whip
3 eggs
1 Tbsp. Knox gelatine
Liquid from pineapple tidbits

Dissolve gelatine in 4 tablespoons of cold water. Mix eggs and sugar; add pineapple juice. Cook in double boiler over medium heat. Stir constantly until thick. Remove from heat and add gelatine. Let cool. Pour over fruit and pecans. Add Cool Whip. Mix well. Refrigerate overnight.

M. Gorey

TACO SALAD

1 ripe avocado, peeled
1 (8 oz.) pkg. cream cheese,
  softened
½ c. sour cream

2 Tbsp. milk
1 tsp. lemon juice
½ tsp. chili powder
Dash of salt

Mix in blender. Spread evenly in bottom of pan with sides. On top of this, add 1½ cups of lettuce (shredded). Next, put 2 small tomatoes (chopped finely) on top, then add onion or green onions. Finally, spread 1 cup shredded Cheddar cheese on top. Chill 5 to 7 hours.

Wilma Crowdus

TOMATO ASPIC

2 c. V-8 juice
1 small box lemon Jello

Few dashes of pepper sauce

Heat 1 cup of V-8 juice until boiling. Pour over Jello. Stir until dissolved. Add second cup V-8 juice and pepper sauce. Stir together. Pour into individual molds or square pan. Serves 4 to 6.

Dorothy O'Neal

TOMATO SOUP SALAD

1 can tomato soup
1 env. gelatin (plain)
1 c. cold water
3 oz. pkg. cream cheese
1 c. chopped nuts

1 c. chopped celery
1 green pepper, chopped
1 onion, chopped
1 c. mayonnaise

Let soup come to a boil and add gelatin which has been dissolved in cold water. Add next 5 ingredients. When cold, add mayonnaise. Chill overnight. Serves 10 to 12.

Paula White

TUNA MOLD OR SALAD

1½ c. tomato juice
3 oz. pkg. lemon Jello
3 oz. cream cheese, softened
½ c. mayonnaise

½ c. chopped celery
½ c. chopped green pepper
2 tsp. grated onion
6½ oz. can tuna, drained well

Bring tomato juice to boil. Add lemon Jello. Stir until dissolved. Add cheese and mayonnaise; stir until mixture is smooth. Add celery, green pepper, onion and tuna to cooled Jello (not necessary to let Jello set up). Pour into mold or a flat dish.

Madrid Shaw

TUNA FISH OR CHICKEN SALAD

Warm a can of chicken with rice soup to dissolve 1 small package lemon Jello. Cool. Drain and flake 1 can tuna (solid, packed in water). Add to preceding before *set.* Add 1 small can crushed pineapple, drained, ½ cup nuts (pecans or walnuts) and 1 cup chopped celery. Mix together and add ½ cup mayonnaise. Fold in ½ pint whipping cream, whipped. Pour in oblong dish and let set in refrigerator. Serve with sliced tomatoes and ripe olives on plate and pass crescent rolls.

Clara Nance

CURRIED TUNA SALAD

1 (6½ oz.) can tuna
1 onion, chopped fine
¼ c. pickle relish
¼ c. mayonnaise
1 can black olives, pitted and
    sliced

1 tsp. curry powder
Dash of salt
2 hard-boiled eggs, diced

Mix all ingredients together and chill.

Gwen Mills

TWENTY-FOUR HOUR SALAD

Lettuce
Green onions
Cucumbers

Radishes
Small can peas

Seal over top of salad with:

2 Tbsp. sugar

2 c. mayonnaise

Sprinkle on top of the preceding 5 ounces Parmesan cheese. Top with bacon bits. Chill and serve.

Phyllis L. Davis

VEGETABLE SALAD

1 (8 oz.) pkg. frozen peas
1 small head cauliflower
1 bunch broccoli
1 bunch (6) green onions
    (only white part)

4 stalks celery
1 jar pimentos

Cut all into small bite-size pieces.

Add the following dressing:

1 (8 oz.) ctn. sour cream
1 (8 oz.) jar mayonnaise

1 pkg. Hidden Valley original
    (buttermilk)

Mix all together and let set 5 to 7 hours. We have tried this recipe and it is delicious!

Phyllis L. Davis

GREEN VEGETABLE SALAD

2 medium cans French style
    green beans
1 medium can peas
1 can pimentos

1 c. grated carrots
½ c. cut celery
½ c. green mango
¼ c. chopped onion

Drain first 3 ingredients well and chop pimentos; mix well.

Add:

½ c. vinegar
¾ c. sugar

1 tsp. salt

Mix well and pour over salad.

Tourist Commission

JELLIED WALDORF SALAD

1 (3 oz.) pkg. Jell-O orange
    gelatin
Dash of salt
1 c. boiling water
¾ c. cold water

1 Tbsp. lemon juice
¾ c. diced unpeeled apple
¼ c. chopped celery
¼ c. chopped nuts (pecans)

Dissolve gelatin and salt in boiling water. Add cold water and lemon juice. Chill until thickened; stir in remaining ingredients. Pour into a 4 cup mold. Chill until firm, about 4 hours.

Mary T. Thompson

MARSHMALLOW WALDORF SALAD

3 c. diced apples (unpeeled if
    you like)
1 Tbsp. lemon juice
1 c. miniature marshmallows
1 c. chopped celery

¼ c. chopped pecans or
    walnuts
Kraft mayonnaise
Lettuce
Thin, unpeeled apple wedges

Sprinkle apples with lemon juice. Add marshmallows, celery and nuts. Add enough mayonnaise to moisten. Toss lightly. For each serving, place a mound of salad on a lettuce covered plate. Arrange apple wedges on salad, petal fashion.

Bessie Litchford

WATERGATE SALAD

1 (No. 2) can crushed
    pineapple (juice and all)
1 (3 oz.) box Jell-O pistachio
    pudding
1 c. small marshmallows
1 c. finely chopped nuts (I
    prefer pecans)

1 large (9 oz.) container Cool
    Whip
Green food coloring
    (optional)

Mix all together and chill in square dish, 2 or 3 inches deep.

Mary T. Thompson

WATERGATE SALAD

9 oz. Cool Whip
½ c. chopped pecans
½ c. small marshmallows

1 can crushed pineapple
1 box pistachio pudding

Mix preceding ingredients together; refrigerate. Can be served immediately.

Vinetta Wills

WATERMELON BOAT

Watermelon
Cantaloupe balls
Honeydew melon balls

Strawberries
Miniature marshmallows

Cut off top third of watermelon. Cut zig-zag pattern 1 inch deep around top of watermelon. Scoop out melon balls, leaving shell intact. Combine melon balls, strawberries and marshmallows; mix lightly. Spoon fruit mixture into shell.

Mary V. Stanley

SALAD DRESSINGS

ASPIC DRESSING

1 (3 oz.) pkg. cream cheese | 1 tsp. honey
1 Tbsp. lemon juice | 1 tsp. Salad Herbs (see Index)
3 Tbsp. cream

Let cream cheese soften to room temperature, then combine with other ingredients. Blend until smooth. Yield: ⅔ cup.

Cristy Lewis

WALDORF OR APPLE SALAD DRESSING

1 lemon and 1 orange (juice) | 1 Tbsp. flour
½ c. sugar | 1 egg

Cook in double boiler until thick.

Thelma Barnett

HOT BACON DRESSING

6 slices bacon | ½ tsp. salt
2 Tbsp. bacon fat | 1 c. milk
¼ c. sugar | 1 egg, beaten
1½ Tbsp. flour | ¼ c. vinegar

Fry bacon; drain and crumble. Reserve 2 tablespoons bacon fat and place in skillet. Stir in sugar, flour and salt. Remove from heat. Gradually stir in milk. Cook over medium heat; stir constantly, until thickened. Blend small amount of hot mixture into egg; return to pan. Cook additional minute. Stir in vinegar and bacon. Good on Bibb lettuce.

Melissa Jackson

BLEU CHEESE SALAD DRESSING

Combine:

¾ c. sour cream | ½ tsp. salt
½ tsp. dry mustard | ⅓ tsp. garlic powder
½ tsp. black pepper | 1 tsp. Worcestershire

Blend 2 minutes on low speed. Add 1⅓ cups mayonnaise. Blend on low 30 seconds, then 2 minutes on medium speed. Crumble 4 ounces Bleu cheese into very small pieces. Blend at low speed, no longer than 4 minutes. This must set for 24 hours.

Note: This takes a little time, but the taste surpasses the bottled dressing and is well worth the effort.

Anita Picklesimer

BOILED SALAD DRESSING

2 Tbsp. all-purpose flour
2 Tbsp. sugar
1½ tsp. dry mustard
1 tsp. salt
2 egg yolks

½ c. evaporated milk
¼ c. milk
⅓ c. vinegar
2 Tbsp. butter

Mix flour, sugar, mustard, salt and egg yolks together in top of double boiler. Add evaporated milk and mix well. Cook over boiling water; stir constantly, until mixture is heated. Add milk and vinegar alternating a few drops at a time. Beat mixture until thick and smooth. Remove from heat and stir in butter. When butter is melted, strain dressing and store in scalded glass jars. Dilute with more cream.

Paula White

BOILED SALAD DRESSING

1½ tsp. salt
1 tsp. dry mustard
1 Tbsp. sugar
4 egg yolks

1½ c. milk
½ c. vinegar
4 Tbsp. (½ stick) margarine

Mix dry ingredients. Beat egg yolks well; stir in dry ingredients, next the milk, then slowly add vinegar. Place in top of double boiler with the butter and cook over simmering water; stir constantly, until sauce thickens. Cool.

Sharon Duke

BLUE CHEESE DRESSING

1 c. buttermilk
1 c. mayonnaise
2 garlic cloves, crushed

½ lb. Blue cheese
Salt to taste

1546-85

115

Blend buttermilk and mayonnaise. Add crushed garlic and crumble cheese into mixture. Pour into a jar and store 1 day before using. When ready to serve, spoon onto salad instead of shaking the dressing onto the salad.

Renee Wallace

BLUE CHEESE DRESSING

Mix:

1 c. crumbled Blue cheese	2 Tbsp. sugar
1 c. mayonnaise	½ c. dairy sour cream
¼ c. vinegar	Clove garlic, minced

Beat until fluffy. Chill.

Wilma Crowdus

BUTTERMILK DRESSING

1½ c. cottage cheese	¼ c. soy sauce
¼ c. mayonnaise	¾ tsp. oregano
¼ c. buttermilk	¾ tsp. thyme
1½ c. tomato puree	½ tsp. garlic
¼ c. tomato juice	

Mix in blender until smooth.

Mary Lauder

CELERY SEED DRESSING

¼ c. vinegar	¼ tsp. sugar
3 Tbsp. salad oil	¼ tsp. celery seed
¼ tsp. salt	⅛ tsp. pepper

Combine all ingredients in a jar; cover and shake well.

Beverly Craft

CENTURY DRESSING

1 large onion, grated	2 tsp. celery salt
1 c. water	½ c. sugar
½ c. lemon juice	⅓ c. vinegar
1 c. catsup	2 c. oil (less if desired)
½ tsp. white pepper	½ tsp. salt

Boil sugar and water 10 minutes; add lemon juice and grated onion; boil 5 minutes more. Add seasoning and stir well. Pour in quart bottle and add vinegar, catsup and oil.

CHIMNEY CORNER DRESSING

1½ c. salad oil
2 c. catsup
1½ c. sugar

2 tsp. onion powder
1 tsp. salt
3 Tbsp. vinegar

Mix all of the preceding ingredients and serve over tossed salads.

Norma T. Hibbs

FRENCH SALAD DRESSING

1 large sweet onion, cut in
   quarters
2 c. sugar
1 c. catsup (Heinz)
¾ c. vinegar
⅛ tsp. garlic salt or 1 toe
   fresh garlic, minced

1 tsp. mustard
1 tsp. paprika
3 tsp. salt
1 Tbsp. Worcestershire sauce
1 c. Wesson oil

Put all ingredients in blender and puree. Make at least 24 hours in advance. Keep in refrigerator.

Joyce Eaton

FRENCH DRESSING

½ tsp. salt
¼ tsp. pepper
2 Tbsp. lemon juice

4 Tbsp. olive oil
3 Tbsp. sweet cream

Combine all ingredients in the order given and mix well.

Lynnette Bonn

FRENCH DRESSING

¼ tsp. pepper
½ tsp. salt
⅛ tsp. paprika
⅛ tsp. dry mustard

1 tsp. sugar
3 Tbsp. lemon juice
6 Tbsp. white vinegar
1 c. salad oil

Put all ingredients in a glass jar; cover and shake thoroughly. Store in refrigerator; shake well before using. Yield: 1½ cups.

Zora Lawson

DELICIOUS FRENCH DRESSING

Part No. 1:

1½ c. sugar   1 c. tarragon vinegar

Cook until sugar is dissolved and cool.

Part No. 2:

4 tsp. tarragon vinegar
2 tsp. salt
2 small onions, grated
4 tsp. Worcestershire sauce

2 tsp. paprika
1½ c. Wesson oil (or any
    good salad oil)

Combine Part Number 2 after beating well and add to cooled Part Number 1 and beat well again. Add 1 or 2 whole cloves of garlic and store in covered jar in refrigerator.

This recipe came from a very fine restaurant in Meridian, Mississippi, which was established in 1870. They were paid $25.00 for the recipe.

GREEK SALAD DRESSING

2 Tbsp. salad oil
2 Tbsp. olive oil
2 Tbsp. cider vinegar
2 tsp. paprika

1 tsp. sugar
1 tsp. dry mustard
Salt to taste

Combine all ingredients in a jar and shake well to mix. Chill well before using. Shake well before using. Yield: ½ cup.

Cristy Lewis

GREEN GODDESS DRESSING

1 c. mayonnaise
1½ c. sour cream
¼ c. vinegar
1 small can anchovies

½ c. fresh parsley, chopped
½ c. onion, chopped
½ tsp. salt

Thoroughly blend all ingredients. Let stand overnight before using. Keeps for a long time in refrigerator.

Mildred Zack

SPECIAL ITALIAN DRESSING

1⅓ c. vegetable oil
½ c. tarragon vinegar
2 Tbsp. minced garlic
1 tsp. salt
2 tsp. freshly ground pepper
3 Tbsp. chopped fresh
    parsley
1 tsp. whole basil leaves
1 tsp. whole oregano
1 Tbsp. plus 1 tsp. anchovy
    paste

⅓ c. pimiento stuffed olives
1 Tbsp. capers
¼ c. grated Parmesan cheese
1 Tbsp. plus 1 tsp. lemon
    juice
2 tsp. sugar
4 green onions with tops,
    coarsely chopped

Combine all ingredients in container of electric blender; blend well. Refrigerate at least 1 hour before serving. Yield: About 2 cups.

Clarine Ballard

ITALIAN SALAD DRESSING

1½ c. salad oil
12 Tbsp. wine vinegar
1 tsp. garlic powder
½ tsp. dried oregano

1 tsp. dried basil
½ tsp. sugar
Salt and pepper to taste

Combine all ingredients and beat with a rotary beater. Chill and beat again when ready to use. Yield: 2 cups.

Cristy Lewis

GRANDMA'S DELICIOUS MAYONNAISE

Beat 3 eggs well. Add ½ cup sugar with ½ teaspoon mustard, 1 cup cream and ½ cup vinegar (add vinegar very slowly). Cook in double boiler until thick. *Do not boil.* Add ½ teaspoon salt when mixture is cool. Makes 1 pint of dressing.

MOM'S MAYONNAISE

2 eggs
½ c. sugar
1 large Tbsp. flour

½ tsp. salt
½ tsp. dry mustard

Mix together.
Then add:

⅓ c. vinegar

⅔ c. milk

Cook until thick. Add large teaspoon butter and cool.

Nadiene Ward

POPPY SEED FRUIT SALAD DRESSING

¾ c. sugar
1½ tsp. onion salt
1 tsp. dry mustard

⅓ c. vinegar
1 c. Crisco oil
1 Tbsp. poppy seed

In small bowl, combine sugar, salt and dry mustard. Stir in vinegar. Beat at medium speed while gradually adding oil. Beat 5 to 10 minutes longer, until thickened. Add poppy seed and refrigerate. Serve on fresh fruit salads.

Ruth Ackerman

JIM PORTER'S TAVERN DRESSING

¼ c. sugar
1 tsp. dry mustard
2 tsp. salt
1 c. cider vinegar
½ c. water

1 c. olive oil
1 garlic clove
1 Tbsp. poppy seed
1 Tbsp. celery seed

120

Dissolve salt, sugar and mustard in vinegar. Stir in water. Gradually beat in oil until well blended. Add rest of ingredients. Pour into bottle. Shake well before serving.

Note: Especially good over Bibb lettuce.

Bill Farris

SUBTLE RANCH DRESSING

2 c. buttermilk
1 c. sour cream
1 c. Hellmann's mayonnaise
1 tsp. white pepper

2 oz. dill leaf
1 tsp. garlic, grated
1 tsp. onion powder

Mix all ingredients. It is better to let the dressing set overnight to marry the flavors.

Doris Beeler

ROQUEFORT DRESSING

1 pkg. Roquefort cheese
½ c. mayonnaise
1 c. sour cream

3 cloves garlic
1 Tbsp. minced onion
Salt and pepper to taste

Crumble Roquefort cheese; add mayonnaise and blend well. Add sour cream, minced garlic, minced onion, and salt and pepper to taste. Let set at least a couple hours before serving.

Melissa Jackson

ROQUEFORT DRESSING

1 large (8 oz.) pkg. cream
    cheese
½ pt. sour cream
2 Tbsp. mayonnaise (milk to
    thin)
Garlic powder

Salt
Pepper
Parsley flakes
Chopped onion tops
    (optional)

Crumble Roquefort, as much as desired. Chill. Delicious as dressing or dip.

Nadiene Ward

ROQUEFORT DRESSING

1 clove garlic, crushed
6 oz. Roquefort cheese
1 c. oil

¼ c. lemon juice
Grated lemon rind
1 pt. sour cream

Mix well and serve on salad.

Helen Russman

ROQUEFORT CHEESE DRESSING

1 c. French dressing
1 c. Wesson oil
1 Tbsp. dry mustard
1 Tbsp. garlic salt
¼ lb. Roquefort cheese (Blue
   cheese can be
   substituted)

Red pepper to taste
1 c. mayonnaise
1 Tbsp. Worcestershire sauce
2 Tbsp. sugar
4 Tbsp. vinegar (wine
   vinegar)

Mix well all ingredients. Pour cheese in last after it has been broken up in chunks with fork.

ROQUEFORT OR BLUE CHEESE DRESSING

⅓ c. evaporated milk
4 oz. cream cheese
1 c. mayonnaise
4 oz. Roquefort or Blue
   cheese

Dash of white pepper
½ tsp. Beau Monde
   seasoning

Put ⅓ cup evaporated milk into a 2 cup measuring cup and chill in the refrigerator. Soften 4 ounces of cream cheese in a bowl. When soft enough, cream it. Blend in 1 cup mayonnaise and 4 ounces of a crumbled wedge of Roquefort or Blue cheese. Whip the milk still in the measuring cup with your electric mixer, until fluffy and doubled in quantity. Add this to other ingredients. Blend together. Add a dash of white pepper and Beau Monde seasoning; mix again.

Lena March

ROQUEFORT SALAD DRESSING

1 c. sour cream
1 Tbsp. mayonnaise
¼ tsp. garlic salt
¼ tsp. pepper
3 oz. Roquefort cheese,
    crumbled

1 Tbsp. wine vinegar
½ tsp. salt
¼ tsp. celery salt
¼ tsp. paprika

Combine ingredients and chill to blend flavors. Makes 1½ cups.

Lynnette Bonn

SESAME DRESSING

2 Tbsp. lemon juice
1 Tbsp. sesame oil

1 Tbsp. honey
⅛ tsp. ground ginger

Combine all ingredients in a bottle; shake well before using.

Annette Anderson

SPINACH SALAD DRESSING

1 c. oil
¾ c. sugar
⅓ c. catsup
¼ c. vinegar

1 tsp. Worcestershire sauce
1 medium onion, diced
1 clove garlic, crushed

Mix until sugar is well blended. Let stand in refrigerator overnight before using.

J. W. Borden, Jr.

SOUR CREAM DRESSING

½ c. sour cream
2 Tbsp. vinegar
½ tsp. paprika

½ tsp. salt
1 tsp. onion juice

Combine all ingredients and beat until thick and smooth.

Note: Good with potato, cucumber, cabbage or lettuce salad. Yield: ½ cup.

Melissa Jackson

SWEET AND SOUR SALAD DRESSING

¾ c. water
¼ c. vinegar
½ c. sugar, divided
½ tsp. salt

1 Tbsp. cold water
2 tsp. flour
1 egg

Heat to boiling ¾ cup water, ¼ cup vinegar and ¼ cup sugar. Meanwhile, mix ¼ cup sugar, ½ teaspoon salt, 1 tablespoon cold water, 2 teaspoons flour and 1 egg. When this is mixed to a smooth paste, stir the paste slowly into the boiling liquid and cook slowly until thickened. Remove from heat and beat with a rotary beater to make smooth.

Excellent on Waldorf Salad.

Ruth Ackerman

SWEET AND SOUR SALAD DRESSING

5 slices bacon
½ tsp. paprika
¼ tsp. dry mustard
⅓ c. water

⅓ tsp. salt
¼ tsp. pepper
3 Tbsp. cider vinegar
1 tsp. sugar

Chop finely 5 slices of bacon and cook the pieces in a skillet over low heat until they brown. Stir in salt, paprika, pepper and dry mustard. Add cider vinegar mixed with water and sugar; cook over low heat. Cool the dressing before tossing it with salad greens.

THOUSAND ISLAND DRESSING

1 c. mayonnaise
¼ c. chili sauce
2 hard cooked eggs, chopped
2 Tbsp. green peppers,
    chopped

2 Tbsp. celery, chopped
1½ Tbsp. finely chopped
    onions
1 tsp. paprika
½ tsp. salt

Mix all of the preceding well. Chill. Makes 2 cups.

Wilma Crowdus

VEGETABLES

APPLE YAMBAKE

2 apples, sliced
⅓ c. chopped pecans
½ c. brown sugar, packed
½ tsp. cinnamon

2 (17 oz.) cans yams, drained
¼ c. margarine
2 c. miniature marshmallows

Toss apples and nuts with combined brown sugar and cinnamon. Alternate layers of apples and yams in 1½ quart casserole. Dot with margarine. Cover. Bake at 350° for 35 to 40 minutes. Sprinkle marshmallows over yams and apples. Broil until lightly browned. Makes 6 to 8 servings.

Marsha Golden

ASPARAGUS AU GRATIN

1½ c. cracker crumbs
2 c. cooked asparagus, diced
2 c. milk
2 Tbsp. margarine

2 Tbsp. flour
1 tsp. salt
1 c. cheese, grated

Place a layer of asparagus in a buttered 2 quart baking dish. Sprinkle with cracker crumbs. Blend butter, flour and salt in a double boiler. Add milk and stir until thick. Remove from heat and add cheese. Pour part of this sauce over the layers of asparagus and cracker crumbs. Repeat to use remaining ingredients. Bake at 350° until top is brown.

Brenda Chitty

ASPARAGUS AU GRATIN
(Cabbage Patch Circle Bazaar Luncheon Dish)

No. 2½ can asparagus tips
 (or pieces, for economy)
Small can mushrooms (or
 pieces, for economy)
4 eggs (hard-boiled), sliced

Cheese Sauce (made by
 adding 1 cup grated
 Cheddar cheese to 1½ c.
 white sauce)
Bread crumbs (about 1 c.)

Place asparagus, mushrooms and egg slices in layers in a buttered casserole; pour Cheese Sauce over all; put buttered bread crumbs on top. Add salt, pepper and paprika. Bake at 350° until brown on top and bubbly, about 20 to 30 minutes. Serves 6.

The Cabbage Patch Circle

CREAMED ASPARAGUS WITH ALMONDS

2 Tbsp. butter
2 Tbsp. flour
½ tsp. salt
1 c. milk

1 c. slivered almonds
1 (13 oz.) can asparagus
Cracker crumbs

Melt butter, but do not brown. Add flour and salt; stir until smooth. Add milk slowly and cook over medium heat until smooth and just the right thickness for sauce. Drain asparagus and put in 1½ quart casserole. Mix almonds with sauce and pour over asparagus. Crumble cracker crumbs on top and place in oven (350° or 375°) about 20 minutes or until hot.

Wanda Harris

ASPARAGUS PARMIGIANA

1½ lb. fresh asparagus, cooked
1 onion, chopped
1 garlic clove, chopped
3 Tbsp. oil
½ tsp. salt

¼ tsp. Tabasco
1 (1 lb.) can tomatoes
¼ tsp. thyme
1 (8 oz.) can tomato sauce
8 oz. Mozzarella, sliced
2 Tbsp. Parmesan cheese

Drain asparagus. Arrange in shallow baking dish. Saute onion and garlic in oil until golden brown. Add salt, Tabasco sauce and tomatoes. Simmer, uncovered, for 10 minutes. Add thyme and tomato sauce. Simmer 20 minutes. Pour sauce over asparagus; place Mozzarella cheese over top. Sprinkle with Parmesan cheese. Bake at 350° for 30 minutes.

J. W. Borden, Jr.

ASPARAGUS CASSEROLE

Melt 1 stick butter and add 1½ cups crushed cracker crumbs. Line bottom of casserole with 1 cup of crumbs. Drain 1 (Number 2) can of asparagus and place on crumbs.

Make Cheese Sauce from following:

4 Tbsp. butter, melted
3 Tbsp. flour
1½ c. milk

1 glass Old English cheese
1 tsp. salt

Cook until thickens. Pour over asparagus. Top with remaining crumbs. Bake for 12 minutes at 425°.

ASPARAGUS CASSEROLE

2 cans asparagus
1 can mushroom soup

1 c. grated cheese
2 hard-boiled eggs

Mix soup with little juice from asparagus. In a casserole dish, place a layer of asparagus-soup mixture, sliced eggs and cheese. Repeat until casserole is filled. Top with crushed cracker crumbs and heat in moderate oven at 300° to 350° until hot.

Martha Harper

ASPARAGUS CASSEROLE

2 medium cans asparagus
2 c. grated American cheese
2 c. cracker crumbs (I use
    Ritz)

Slivered almonds
1 stick butter, divided
½ c. milk
2 Tbsp. cornstarch

Drain liquid from asparagus into saucepan; add ½ stick butter and heat. Make a paste of the ½ cup milk and cornstarch; add to the hot liquid. Stir until it thickens. Spread ½ of the asparagus into a casserole dish, then add ⅓ of the cheese and ⅓ of the crumbs and ½ of the sauce; add the rest of the asparagus and ⅓ cheese and ⅓ crumbs and the rest of the sauce. Sprinkle remaining ⅓ cheese and ⅓ crumbs over the top of the sauce. Sprinkle almonds over the top of the cheese and crumbs and, lastly, pour the rest of the butter (melted) over the almonds. Bake at 375° for 30 minutes or until brown.

Ruth Ackerman

AUNTIE'S BOSTON BAKED BEANS

1½ lb. Great Northern beans
½ lb. salt pork, scored
1½ c. molasses

1½ c. tomato puree
1 Tbsp. salt

Wash beans and soak overnight. Cook in same water as beans were soaked in. Cook until tender, then drain. Reserve 1½ quarts of the water. Mix all together, except salt pork. Put in bean pot and cover with reserved water, then push the salt pork down into center of pot. Bake 6 hours adding reserved water if necessary. Bake in oven at 350°. Cover first 5 hours, then uncover last hour.

Alleen S. Gray

BAKED BEANS

1 large can pork and beans
3 Tbsp. bacon drippings
Salt to taste
Pepper to taste
1 bottle chili sauce

1 Tbsp. vinegar
3 Tbsp. brown sugar
1 tsp. paprika
1 small onion

Stir all together and pour into covered baking dish and bake ½ hour in 350° oven. Put strips of bacon on top and bake ½ hour longer.

Peggy Kessinger

BAKED BEANS

3 (1 lb. 12 oz.) cans pork and
   beans
1 medium onion, chopped
1 tsp. prepared mustard

¾ c. plus 1 Tbsp. ketchup
1½ c. firmly packed brown
   sugar
5 slices bacon, diced

Mix all together. Put in 3 quart baking dish. Cover. Bake at 300° for 3½ to 4 hours. Remove the cover and bake 30 minutes longer. Stir 2 or 3 times during baking.

Patti Roby

BAKED BEANS

2 cans pork and beans
½ c. brown sugar
½ c. chopped onion
½ to 1 c. catsup

1 tsp. chili powder
½ lb. cooked hamburger
2 cooked sausage patties

Drain hamburger and sausage. Mix all together and simmer in crock pot or a pan on top of stove. If using large cans of beans, increase all other ingredients to your taste.

Patsy S. Brown

128

BARBECUED BEANS

2 cans pork and beans
1 c. brown sugar
1 c. catsup

1 small onion, diced
2 tsp. prepared mustard
3 slices bacon, cut in pieces

Mix all ingredients, except bacon. Put into baking dish and top with bacon. Bake at 250° for 1½ to 2 hours. Serves 10.

Mrs. Bernard (Bobbie) Sublett

BAKED BEAN MEDLEY

1½ lb. ground beef
1 small onion, chopped
1 tsp. salt
1 (15½ oz.) can kidney beans
1 (16 oz.) can lima beans

1 (16 oz.) can pork and beans
½ c. catsup
¼ c. brown sugar
2 Tbsp. vinegar

Combine ground beef, onion and salt in a skillet. Brown and drain. Combine beef mixture with remaining ingredients and stir well. Place in lightly greased casserole dish. Bake at 350° for 30 to 35 minutes.

Mrs. William (Eloise) Froehlich

DURGIN-PARK BAKED BEANS

1 lb. navy or pea beans
½ tsp. baking soda
⅓ c. molasses
1 tsp. dry mustard
½ lb. salt pork, cut into ½
    inch pieces

6 c. water
1 small onion
¼ c. sugar
¼ tsp. pepper

Soak beans overnight in 6 cups of water. In the morning, add baking soda; bring to a boil. Lower heat and continue to boil for 10 minutes. Drain, reserving liquid. Place salt pork, onion and beans in a two quart casserole or bean pot. Combine molasses, sugar, dry mustard, pepper and 1 cup reserved liquid. Pour over beans and stir. Add just enough reserved liquid to cover beans (about 1 cup). Cover casserole or bean pot and bake at 300° for 2 hours. Add remaining liquid and stir. Bake an additional 1½ to 2 hours (or until beans are tender and liquid is absorbed). Serves 8.

HONEYED BEANS WITH BACON

2½ c. lima or navy beans,
   soaked overnight
6 slices bacon
1 onion, peeled and chopped
1 tsp. dry mustard

1 Tbsp. chopped candied
   ginger
2 Tbsp. chopped chutney
¾ c. honey

Preheat oven to 325°. Drain beans from water in which they were soaked and simmer in boiling salt water until tender. Dice bacon; put in a saute pan with the onion; stir until fat begins to melt and saute until onion is transparent. When beans are done, drain and put into a deep casserole. Add bacon and onion, seasoning, mustard, ginger and chutney; mix well. Stir in the honey. Cover and cook for about 1 hour. Then uncover and cook for another ½ hour. Serves 4 to 5.

Dee Dee Millen

GREEN BEANS WITH GARLIC DRESSING

4 c. green beans
1 tsp. salt
2 slices bacon

½ c. garlic French dressing
2 Tbsp. green onion, minced
¼ tsp. oregano leaves

Cook beans in boiling water until tender crisp. Cook bacon until crisp; drain on paper toweling, then crumble. Add bacon to beans. Mix French dressing, onion and oregano; pour over the beans. Heat.

Patti Roby

DILLED GREEN BEANS

2 lb. green beans
1 c. vinegar
2 Tbsp. pickling salt

2 tsp. dill weed
¼ tsp. cayenne
2 cloves garlic, crushed

Wash beans; drain and cut in 2 inch lengths. Cover beans with boiling water; cook 3 minutes. Drain. Pack in hot sterilized jars; leave ½ inch head space. In a large kettle, combine vinegar, 3 cups water, pickling salt, dill weed, cayenne and garlic; bring to a boil. Cover beans with pickling liquid, leaving ½ inch head space. Seal. Process in boiling water bath 10 minutes. Makes 4 pints.

Gwen Mills

GREEK GREEN BEANS

1 lb. green beans
1 onion, chopped fine
¼ c. butter
1 garlic clove, minced
1 tsp. fresh mint leaves,
    minced or ½ tsp. dried
    mint

1 Tbsp. parsley, minced
1 tsp. fennel seeds
½ c. tomato sauce
¼ c. water
Salt and pepper to taste

Saute onion in butter until golden brown. Wash and trim beans. Cut beans into 2 inch lengths. Add to onion and saute, stir constantly, until beans have turned a bright green. Add remaining ingredients and simmer 30 minutes or until tender. Makes 4 to 6 servings.

Trudy Frazier

GREEN BEAN CASSEROLE

1 (16 oz.) can French style
    green beans, drained
1 (10¾ oz.) can cream of
    celery soup

1 (2.8 oz.) can French fried
    onions
¾ c. milk

Combine beans, soup, milk and ½ can of French fried onions; pour into casserole. Bake, uncovered, at 350° for 20 minutes. Top with remaining onions and bake 5 minutes longer.

Annette Crossfield

PENNSYLVANIA DUTCH GREEN BEANS

3 strips bacon
1 small onion, sliced
2 tsp. cornstarch
¼ tsp. dry mustard
¼ tsp. salt

1 (No. 303) can Del Monte
    brand cut green beans
1 Tbsp. brown sugar
2 tsp. vinegar
1 hard cooked egg, sliced

Fry bacon in skillet until crisp. Remove bacon and crumble. Drain off all but 1 tablespoon drippings. Add onion and brown lightly. Stir in cornstarch, salt and dry mustard. Drain beans, reserving ½ cup liquid. Stir reserved liquid into skillet. Cook, stirring until mixture boils. Blend in brown sugar and vinegar. Add green beans and heat thoroughly. Turn into serving dish and garnish with egg and crumbled bacon.

Barbara Montgomery

STRING BEAN CASSEROLE

1 or 2 cans string beans
1 can mushroom soup
½ can milk

½ can dried onions (French
    fried in can)

Mix together in casserole. Then sprinkle the rest of dried onions on top. Bake at 350° for 45 minutes with lid on. Take lid off and brown 15 minutes.

Kitty Wright

MIXED BEAN BAKE

1 (20 oz.) can pork and beans
1 (16 oz.) can kidney beans,
    drained
1 (16 oz.) can baby lima
    beans, drained
½ c. chopped green pepper

1½ c. chopped celery
1½ c. chopped onion
1½ c. brown sugar
1 c. catsup
Salt and pepper to taste
Garlic salt (optional)

Mix together and put in 3 quart Pyrex. Place bacon strips across dish or mix in bacon drippings. Bake 45 minutes at 350°. Best baked beans ever! Serves 12.

Debbie Owens

BORSCHT

1 small cabbage, quartered
    (about 2 lb.)
¼ lb. fresh beets
½ lb. ground beef
1 onion, chopped
6 c. beef bouillon
1 bouquet garni (1 sprig
    thyme, 4 peppercorns
    and 1 bay leaf tied in
    cheesecloth)
1 c. canned white kidney
    beans, drained and
    rinsed

¼ c. grated fennel bulb
1 (16 oz.) can tomatoes,
    drained, sieved
2 Tbsp. red wine vinegar
Salt
Black pepper
Sour cream
1 Tbsp. vinegar

Cook cabbage and beets separately in boiling salted water until tender, about 10 minutes for cabbage and 20 minutes for beets. Drain and rinse with cold running water. Shred cabbage and skin; grate beets. Saute beef and onion; add 1 tablespoon vinegar; stir occasionally until meat is light brown. Add bouillon and bouquet garni. Simmer about 20 minutes; stir occasionally; remove bouquet garni. At serving time, stir in cabbage, beets, beans, fennel, tomatoes and 2 tablespoons red wine vinegar. Heat to boiling. Season to taste with salt and pepper. Serve with a dollop of sour cream.

Annette Anderson

HARVARD BEETS

1 (1 lb.) can beets, sliced	¾ tsp. salt
3 Tbsp. flour	Dash of pepper
½ c. sugar	¼ c. vinegar

In small saucepan, stir together flour, sugar, salt and pepper. Reserve beet liquid to measure ⅔ cup. If needed, add water to beet liquid to measure to ⅔ cup. Gradually stir in beet liquid and vinegar to flour mixture. Cook, stirring constantly, until mixture thickens and boils. Boil and stir 1 minute. Stir in sliced beets and heat through. Yields 4 servings.

Variation: Don't use pepper; add little butter.

Sue Parker

PICKLED BEETS

2 (16 oz.) cans sliced beets	⅔ c. vinegar
1 c. onions, sliced	1 cinnamon stick
⅔ c. brown sugar	5 whole cloves

Drain beets, reserving ⅔ cup liquid. If necessary, add water to liquid to make ⅔ cup. In large saucepan, combine all ingredients. Bring to a boil. Simmer 10 minutes; stir occasionally. Refrigerate. Before serving, drain; remove cinnamon stick and cloves. Serves 8.

Beverly Craft

BROCCOLI CASSEROLE

3 pkg. frozen broccoli	4 oz. jar mushrooms
8 oz. sour cream	8 oz. Cheddar cheese
Small jar pimentos	½ tsp. salt
1 can mushroom soup	¼ tsp. pepper

Cook broccoli; drain well and place in bottom of greased casserole. Mix together all other ingredients and pour over broccoli. Bake 30 minutes at 350°.

Dot Berry

BROCCOLI CASSEROLE

Cook 2 (10 ounce) packages frozen cut broccoli following package directions; drain. Cook 3 medium onions (quartered) in boiling, salted water until tender. Drain.

In saucepan, melt:

2 Tbsp. all-purpose flour   **Dash of pepper**
¼ tsp. salt

Add 1 cup milk; cook and stir until bubbly. Reduce heat; blend in 1 (3 ounce) package cream cheese until smooth. Place vegetables in 1½ quart casserole. Pour sauce over; mix lightly. Top with ¾ cup shredded sharp Cheddar cheese. Crush a small box of Tidbit cheese crackers and sprinkle evenly over top. Bake at 350° for 40 to 45 minutes. Serves 6.

Patricia Jewell

BROCCOLI CASSEROLE

2 pkg. frozen broccoli,   **½ stick butter or margarine**
  chopped (I like Winn   **½ lb. Velveeta cheese**
  Dixie's Astor brand)

Cook broccoli about 5 minutes. Drain well. Put butter and cheese into broccoli while hot and let melt. Pour into greased casserole dish. Crush 1 stack of Ritz crackers from 12 ounce box. Mix with 1 stick of melted butter and spread over top of casserole. Bake 20 to 30 minutes at 350°. Serves 8.

This may be made a day ahead of time, but is best to fix crust on day of baking.

Mary T. Thompson

BROCCOLI CASSEROLE

4 c. cooked broccoli (1 inch pieces)
1 (10 oz.) can cream of mushroom soup
1 (2 oz.) jar pimentos, drained
¾ c. sour cream

1 c. diced celery
1 tsp. salt
½ tsp. pepper
½ c. grated cheese
¼ c. slivered almonds

In large bowl, combine all ingredients, except cheese and almonds. Place in greased casserole. Top with cheese and nuts. Bake at 350° for 25 to 30 minutes. Can be prepared day before and kept in refrigerator.

Newland Stanfill

BROCCOLI-RICE CASSEROLE

½ c. chopped onion

½ c. chopped celery

Saute in 1 stick margarine.

2 c. raw rice, cooked
2 pkg. chopped broccoli, thawed

1 can condensed cream of chicken soup
1 (8 oz.) jar Cheez Whiz

Combine all ingredients in 9x13 inch casserole. Cook at 350° for 30 minutes.

Clara Nance

CALLYE'S BROCCOLI CASSEROLE

2 (10 oz.) pkg. frozen broccoli, chopped
½ c. mayonnaise
½ c. sharp cheese, grated
1 c. cheese crackers, crushed
½ c. almonds or pecan meats, slivered, broken

1 can cream of mushroom soup
1 Tbsp. lemon juice
1 (2 oz.) jar pimientos, chopped

Cook broccoli in salted water and drain. Arrange broccoli in a buttered 1½ quart casserole. Mix soup, mayonnaise, lemon juice and cheese. Spoon over broccoli. Top with pimientos, crackers and nuts. Bake at 350° for 20 minutes until bubbly hot. Serves 8.

Oleta Bryan

BROCCOLI CASSEROLE

Cream together:

1 can cream of mushroom soup or golden mushroom	**½ c. butter** **1 small jar Cheez Whiz**

Mix cheese mixture with:

10 oz. pkg. frozen broccoli **½ c. onion**	**1¼ c. raw Minute rice**

Bake at 325° for ½ hour uncovered. Use 1¾ quart dish.

Peggy Graviss

BROCCOLI CASSEROLE

Broccoli **1 ctn. sour cream** **1 can cream of mushroom soup**	**Parmesan cheese**

Cook broccoli until almost done. Drain. Put in casserole dish. Mix sour cream and soup together. Pour this mixture over broccoli. Sprinkle with Parmesan cheese. Bake in 350° oven until it bubbles (about 20 minutes).

Georgetta Montgomery

BROCCOLI-RICE CASSEROLE

½ c. finely chopped celery	**1 pkg. chopped broccoli,**
½ c. chopped onion	**cooked and drained**
4 Tbsp. bacon drippings	**2 c. cooked rice**
1 can cream of chicken soup	**Salt and pepper to taste**
1 soup can milk	**1 (8 oz.) jar Cheez Whiz**

Saute celery and onion in bacon drippings. Add soup and milk. Mix with broccoli, rice, salt and pepper in buttered 9x13 inch pan. Cover with Cheez Whiz. Bake at 300° for 1 hour. Serves 6.

Maxine Welch

BROCCOLI CASSEROLE

2 pkg. chopped broccoli,
  cooked according to pkg.
  directions, then drained
2 c. Minute rice
1 small jar pimentos
1 can water chestnuts, sliced
1 jar medium mushrooms,
  sliced
1 (medium size) jar Cheez
  Whiz
1 can cream of celery soup
  (undiluted)
1 can cream of mushroom
  soup *(undiluted)*
1 c. shredded Cheddar
  cheese (for top)
Salt and pepper to taste

Mix all of the preceding, except Cheddar cheese. Pour into a greased 9x12 inch dish. Cover with Cheddar cheese. Cook at 325° about 30 to 35 minutes.

Wilma Crowdus

BROCCOLI AND CHEESE CASSEROLE

2 pkg. frozen chopped
  broccoli, thawed
1 c. Minute rice
1 can cream of chicken or
  celery soup
1 small jar Cheez Whiz
¼ c. chopped onion
¼ c. margarine

Stir onion in margarine until tender. Turn heat off and add Cheez Whiz, melt; add chicken or celery soup, rice and broccoli. Mix and bake in 370° oven until hot and bubbly, about 20 to 30 minutes.

Thelma Barnett

BROCCOLI CASSEROLE

2 boxes chopped broccoli
1½ c. cooked rice (no Minute
  rice)
1 can cream of mushroom
  soup
1 (medium size) jar Cheez
  Whiz
Ritz crackers or saltines
  (stack)
1 stick melted butter

Cook broccoli as directed and drain. Add the rice, cream of mushroom soup and Cheez Whiz. Mix well and place in a baking dish. For topping, crumble Ritz crackers or saltines. Mix with 1 stick melted butter. Spread on top of casserole. Bake in 350° preheated oven for about 30 minutes or until it bubbles.

Clara Burd

BROCCOLI CASSEROLE

1 pkg. frozen chopped
  broccoli
½ can cream of mushroom
  soup
½ c. grated sharp cheese

1 egg, well beaten
½ c. mayonnaise
1 Tbsp. grated onion
½ c. Ritz cracker crumbs

Cook broccoli and drain. Combine all ingredients, except cracker crumbs, into greased casserole dish. Place cracker crumbs on top and bake at 400° for 20 minutes.

Lil Pasinski

BROCCOLI CASSEROLE

2 small pkg. broccoli (frozen)
1 c. cooked rice
1 can cream of mushroom
  soup
1 can cream of chicken soup

8 oz. Velveeta cheese *or* 8 oz.
  jar Cheez Whiz
1 c. celery, chopped
½ tsp. thyme
1 clove garlic

Boil broccoli until tender. Drain; let cool. Melt soups and cheese together. Saute onions and garlic until clear. Mix all together and pour into buttered casserole dish. Sprinkle with cracker crumbs (Ritz) and oleo. Bake at 300° for 1 hour.

J. W. Borden, Jr.

BROCCOLI CASSEROLE

1 pkg. frozen broccoli,
  chopped
1 can cream of chicken soup
1 Tbsp. butter

3 slices cheese
1 tsp. salt
12 to 15 Ritz crackers

Cook broccoli according to directions on package. Drain and stir in chicken soup, butter and salt. Break up cheese and add to mixture. Crumble Ritz crackers and add. Pour into baking dish and crumble some Ritz crackers over top. Sprinkle with paprika. Bake in 350° oven for 35 to 40 minutes.

Bonnie J. Riggs

BROCCOLI CASSEROLE

Cook 2 packages broccoli spears, drain *well.* Boil 3 eggs (hard). When cool, chop. Boil 3 or 4 chicken breasts (cool). When cool, remove from bone and cut into chunks.

Cheese Sauce:

1 stick margarine   **3 c. milk**
¾ c. flour

Melt margarine. Add flour; stir until blended. Add 3 cups milk; cook and stir until thick. Add ½ cup grated Cheddar cheese powder or American cheese. When blended, add 4 slices American cheese and stir until blended. Put about 1 cup Cheese Sauce in bottom of casserole, then broccoli, chicken and egg. Pour rest of Cheese Sauce over top. Melt 1 stick margarine; add 2 stacks Ritz crackers (crumbled) and stir until coated. Pour over top of casserole. Bake in 350° oven about 20 minutes.

Myrna Blackman

CHOPPED BROCCOLI CASSEROLE

1 pkg. chopped broccoli   **1 egg, beaten**
½ c. mayonnaise   **2 Tbsp. grated onion, cooked**
½ c. mushroom soup   **in a little butter**
Salt (to taste)   **½ c. Cheddar cheese**

Cook broccoli 5 minutes. Mix all the other ingredients. Pour into a casserole dish; top with buttered bread crumbs or cracker crumbs. Bake at 350° for 30 or 35 minutes.

Willie Summers

BROCCOLI DISH

1 pkg. chopped broccoli,   **1 small onion, chopped fine**
cooked and drained   **½ c. mayonnaise**
1 can mushroom soup   **1 egg**
½ c. Cheddar cheese, grated

Mix; top with more cheese. Cook 40 minutes at 350°.

Kathy Ryan

GOURMET BROCCOLI

3 lb. or 3 (10 oz.) pkg.
   broccoli
¼ c. butter
¼ c. flour
1½ Tbsp. chicken seasoned
   stock base
½ tsp. salt

2 c. milk
6 Tbsp. butter
⅔ c. hot water
⅔ (8 oz.) pkg. herb seasoned
   stuffing mix
1 Tbsp. salt

Cook broccoli in boiling water in which 1 tablespoon salt has been added; drain and chop. To make white sauce, melt ¼ cup butter; add flour, chicken base, salt and milk; cook until thickens to right consistency. Melt 6 tablespoons butter in hot water; pour over stuffing mix and toss. Put broccoli in 2 quart dish. Pour on white sauce and top with dressing. Press down and bake in 400° oven for 20 or 25 minutes.

Patti Roby

BRUSSELS SPROUTS

2 qt. Brussels sprouts
2 Tbsp. butter
¼ c. lemon juice
1 c. dairy sour cream

¼ c. minced parsley
½ tsp. salt
⅛ tsp. pepper
Sliced olives (optional)

Cut stem ends off the sprouts and make an X cut in the top for faster cooking. Let stand a few minutes in cool salted water. Heat butter in skillet over medium heat. Drain sprouts; add to hot butter. Cover and steam 10 minutes. Check with fork to see if tender crisp. Add lemon juice and steam 2 minutes. Add sour cream, parsley, salt and pepper. Heat, but don't boil. Top with olives.

Patti Roby

CABBAGE FOR A KING

1 large head cabbage,
   shredded
1 large onion, chopped
3 Tbsp. butter
3 Tbsp. flour
1 can tomatoes

1 Tbsp. Worcestershire sauce
¾ tsp. salt
¼ tsp. pepper
3 slices buttered bread,
   cubed and toasted
½ lb. Cheddar cheese, grated

Cook cabbage in boiling salted water for 15 minutes. Saute onion in butter until tender. Stir in flour; add tomatoes, Worcestershire sauce, salt and pepper. Toast in oven the buttered bread, cubed; drain cabbage. Grease 2 casseroles. Put in layer of cabbage, layer of sauce, then bread cubes and cheese; layer cabbage again, sauce, bread cubes and cheese (make 2 or 3 layers). Bake at 375° for 30 minutes (15 minutes covered and 15 minutes uncovered). Freezes well.

CABBAGE CASSEROLE

1 medium size cabbage
1 can cream of celery soup
1 c. mayonnaise
1 c. shredded Cheddar
   cheese

2 eggs, beaten
Sugar (optional)
Ritz crackers

Cut up cabbage and parboil in salt water. Add a little sugar if desired. Drain. Mix well mayonnaise, soup, cheese and eggs. Put cabbage in casserole dish and stir mixture through it. Cover with crumbled Ritz crackers. Bake 30 minutes at 350°.

Georgetta Montgomery

CABBAGE CASSEROLE

Medium size head cabbage,
   cut up
1 can cream of celery soup
2 eggs, well beaten
1 c. shredded Cheddar
   cheese

1 c. mayonnaise or salad
   dressing (I prefer
   mayonnaise)
Ritz cracker crumbs

Cook cabbage 10 to 15 minutes and drain. Add soup, eggs, shredded Cheddar cheese and mayonnaise. Mix and put into a 2 to 2½ quart casserole. Sprinkle Ritz cracker crumbs over the top. Bake at 350° for 30 minutes.

Mae Bagby (submitted by Brownie - Lois Bruner)

CABBAGE AND CELERY CASSEROLE

4 Tbsp. butter
1 onion, sliced
1 small stalk celery, sliced
½ small head cabbage,
   shredded
2 Tbsp. butter
3 Tbsp. flour

1¼ c. milk
Salt
Pepper
½ c. fresh white bread
   crumbs
2 Tbsp. butter

Melt butter; add onion and celery; cook gently for 5 minutes; stir occasionally. Add cabbage and allow to simmer on gentle heat for another 5 minutes. Melt the butter in a saucepan and add the flour to make a roux. Add milk gradually; stir until a smooth sauce is formed. Season well. Put the vegetables into a casserole and season. Pour sauce over vegetables and sprinkle with bread crumbs dotted with butter. Cook in 350° oven for 20 minutes until the crumb topping is golden brown.

Brenda Chitty

FIVE MINUTE CABBAGE

1¼ c. milk
8 c. shredded cabbage
2 Tbsp. flour
¼ c. milk

2 Tbsp. butter
1 tsp. salt
⅛ tsp. pepper

Heat 1¼ cups milk in skillet over medium heat; add cabbage; simmer 2 minutes. Blend flour with ¼ cup milk; add to cabbage. Add butter, salt and pepper. Stir until it comes to a boil and thickens. Cover and cook over low heat 2 minutes, then stir.

Patti Roby

FRESH BUTTERED CABBAGE

1 large head cabbage
1 stick margarine

Salt and pepper to taste

In large cooking pot, place cut and chopped up cabbage in boiling water. Add salt and pepper to taste. Add 1 stick of margarine and cook until done, leaves will be tender and be slightly limp looking.

Norma T. Hibbs

FROZEN CABBAGE

Wash cabbage; remove outer leaves; quarter heads; remove core. Put in wire basket, then lower in boiling water. Let come to a boil; boil 3 minutes. Remove from boiling water. Cool in ice cold water; let drain in colander. Put in freezer bags and freeze immediately. When ready to use, put ½ cup water and ½ teaspoon salt in pan; bring to boil. Add frozen cabbage; let boil for 15 minutes; drain. Add bacon grease or butter. Serve hot.

Phyllis L. Davis

HUNGARIAN CABBAGE ROLLS

1 can sauerkraut
1 large cabbage (a large leaf cabbage is best)
¼ c. uncooked rice (Minute rice)
¼ c. chopped onion
1 egg, slightly beaten

2 Tbsp. ketchup
1 tsp. salt
¼ tsp. pepper
1 can of tomato soup
1 can tomatoes
2 Tbsp. lemon juice
2 Tbsp. brown sugar

Take the center (stalk) out of cabbage head; place cabbage head in boiling water to wilt leaves, 1 to 2 minutes. Take cabbage head out of water. Mix ground beef, rice, onion, egg, salt, pepper and ketchup. Roll some meat mixture in a cabbage leaf and roll up. Place in large pot which has been covered with sauerkraut. Mix together last ingredients and pour over rolls. Cook, covered, 2 hours (approximately) on simmer. Add a little water if needed.

Use same recipe for stuffed peppers!

Frances Crum

SCALLOPED CABBAGE

6 c. cabbage, shredded
½ c. boiling water
3 eggs, slightly beaten
1 tsp. salt

6 Tbsp. vinegar
¾ c. mayonnaise
1½ c. crushed potato chips

Parboil cabbage about 3 minutes in just a little boiling water in which about ½ teaspoon salt has been added. Do not drain. Combine eggs, ½ teaspoon salt, vinegar and mayonnaise. Add cabbage and any liquid that clings to it. Pour into greased 1½ quart casserole. Sprinkle potato chips on top. Bake at 350° for 25 minutes.

Patti Roby

CANDIED CARROTS

2 c. carrots, cooked
¼ c. butter or margarine
¼ c. brown sugar

Salt to taste
Pepper to taste

Combine all ingredients and bake at 350° for 30 minutes.

Allouise Davidson

CANDIED CARROTS

8 medium carrots
1 tsp. salt

6 Tbsp. brown sugar
2 Tbsp. margarine

Pare and scrape carrots and cut in quarters, then lengthwise. Cook until tender. Melt margarine and brown sugar in heavy skillet. Add the drained carrots and simmer over low heat. Turn over occasionally until the carrots are coated with margarine and sugar. Remove from heat and serve.

Stella Moore

CARROTS AU GRATIN

3 c. carrots, diced
6 soda crackers, crushed (¼
   c.)
1 tsp. onion salt

¼ c. chopped green pepper
Dash of pepper
2 Tbsp. melted butter
½ c. grated sharp cheese

Cook carrots in ½ inch boiling salted water 10 minutes or until tender. Heat oven to 425° (hot). Combine cracker crumbs, onion salt, green pepper and pepper. Alternate layers of carrots and crumb mixture in greased 1 quart baking dish. Spoon any remaining carrot liquid on. Pour on butter and sprinkle with cheese. Bake 15 to 20 minutes or until cheese melts. Serves 6.

Paula Brauner

HONEY GLAZED CARROTS
(Microwave)

4 medium carrots, sliced
2 Tbsp. butter
2 Tbsp. honey

2 Tbsp. water
¼ tsp. salt

Combine carrots, butter, honey and water in a 1 quart casserole dish. Cover and cook 7 to 8 minutes on HIGH or until carrots are just about tender. Be sure to stir occasionally. Stir in salt at the end.

Sharon Sherman

144

MARINATED CARROTS

5 c. carrots (I use the frozen)
1 medium size onion, sliced
    thin
1 green pepper, sliced thin
1 can Campbell's tomato
    soup
¼ c. salad oil

1 c. sugar
¾ c. white vinegar
1 tsp. prepared mustard
1 tsp. salt
1 tsp. pepper
1 tsp. Worcestershire sauce

Cook carrots until tender. Drain. Combine all ingredients, except carrots, mixing well. Add carrots; mix well. Marinate 12 hours before serving. Keeps well in Tupperware for several days.

Brownie - Lois Bruner

MARINATED CARROTS

2 bunches carrots
1 bell pepper, chopped
1 onion, chopped
1 can bisque of tomato soup
½ c. vinegar
½ c. oil

1 c. sugar
1 tsp. salt
1 tsp. pepper
1 tsp. mustard
1 tsp. Worcestershire sauce

Peel and slice thin 2 bunches of carrots. Cook and drain. Add 1 bell pepper (chopped) and 1 onion (chopped). Set aside. Mix together and bring to a boil 1 can bisque of tomato soup, ½ cup vinegar, ½ cup oil, 1 cup sugar, salt, pepper, mustard and Worcestershire sauce. Pour over carrots and let stand overnight. Heat to serve.

This is wonderful for a big dinner or a crowd.

Mary Harrod

CAULIFLOWER CASSEROLE

1 cauliflower
1 stick margarine
3 Tbsp. flour
2 c. milk

2 c. diced Velveeta cheese
Paprika
Boiling salted water

Cook cauliflower in boiling salted water until tender, about 10 minutes. Drain. Place in large baking dish. For your cheese sauce, melt 1 stick margarine in saucepan. Add 3 tablespoons flour; mix until smooth. Add 2 cups milk. Cook until slightly thickened. Add 2 cups diced Velveeta cheese; cook until melted. Pour over cauliflower. Sprinkle paprika over top. Bake in hot oven until slightly browned.

Bessie Litchford

CAULIFLOWER WITH SHRIMP SAUCE

1 head cauliflower
1 can frozen condensed
   cream of shrimp sauce,
   thawed

½ c. sour cream
1½ tsp. salt
⅛ tsp. pepper

Separate into flowerets and cook in boiling salted water in which 1 teaspoon salt was added. When tender, drain. Blend soup, sour cream, ½ teaspoon salt and pepper. Heat until boiling point, but don't boil. Pour over cauliflower.

Patti Roby

CELERY CASSEROLE

2 c. celery, sliced
1 (8 oz.) can water chestnuts
1 can cream of chicken soup

1 stick melted butter
1 tube Ritz crackers

Cook celery 7 minutes and drain. Mix with water chestnuts, soup and half of melted butter. Crush crackers and toss with remainder of the butter. Put on top of the casserole. Bake at 350° for 30 minutes.

Mary Baxter

CHILI RELLENO CASSEROLE

1 layer green chilies, seeded
1 layer grated Cheddar
   cheese
1 layer green chilies, seeded

1 layer grated Monterey Jack
   cheese
1 layer crumbled Ritz
   crackers

Beat together 2 eggs with 2 cups milk and pour over casserole. Bake at 350° about 30 minutes until top is light brown.

Betty Jo Yeary

146

BAKED CORN

3 eggs, separated
½ c. evaporated milk
1 tsp. salt
3 Tbsp. sugar

1½ Tbsp. flour
2 c. canned or cooked corn
2 Tbsp. butter, melted

Beat egg yolks. Add rest of ingredients. Fold in stiffly beaten egg whites. Pour into a greased casserole. Bake 40 to 45 minutes at 300°. Serves 6.

Dorothy O'Neal

CORN OYSTERS

6 ears corn
3 egg yolks, well beaten
¼ c. flour
½ tsp. baking powder

¾ tsp. salt
¼ tsp. pepper
3 egg whites, stiffly beaten

Cut corn off cob, ⅔ the depth of kernel. Scrape cob. Add yolks; blend together. Sift flour, baking powder, salt and pepper. Stir into corn and egg mixture; blend well. Gently fold in egg whites. Drop by spoonful on hot greased griddle. Fry until brown; turn and brown other side.

Patti Roby

CORN PUDDING

1 can yellow cream style corn
2 eggs, beaten
¼ c. milk

1 tsp. flour
2 tsp. sugar
1 tsp. salt

Mix all ingredients. Pour into Pyrex casserole. Bake at 300° for 45 minutes. Serves 6.

Lil Pasinski

CORN PUDDING

1 (16 oz.) can corn (no juice)
3 eggs, slightly beaten
1 tsp. salt
½ tsp. pepper

3 Tbsp. melted margarine
3 Tbsp. sugar
1⅛ c. scalded milk, cooked
    until almost boiling

Mix all the preceding. Bake in preheated oven at 325° for 30 to 40 minutes.

Bernadette Mills

CORN PUDDING

1 egg, beaten
¼ c. sugar
½ c. milk
1½ Tbsp. flour

1 can whole corn
1 small can cream corn
Chunk of butter

Mix all of the preceding and bake 30 to 40 minutes at 375° or until seems like custard.

Virginia Moran

CORN PUDDING

1 can cream style corn
1 small can whole kernel corn
4 eggs, well beaten

4 Tbsp. sugar
3 Tbsp. flour
1 ctn. half & half

Mix all ingredients together. Bake at 350° about 1 hour or until knife comes clean when testing from center.

Barbara Haddix

CORN PUDDING

2 c. whole kernel corn
4 eggs
8 level Tbsp. flour
2 pt. milk

4 rounded tsp. sugar
4 Tbsp. butter, melted
1 tsp. salt

Stir into the corn the flour, salt, sugar and butter. Beat the eggs well; put in the milk. Then stir into the corn and put into pan or Pyrex. Bake inside of oven slowly about 40 to 45 minutes. Stir from bottom 3 times while baking.

Beaumont Inn

CORN PUDDING

2 c. fresh corn
6 eggs
8 Tbsp. flour
4 c. milk

3 tsp. sugar
2 Tbsp. butter
1 tsp. salt

Stir into the cut off corn the flour, salt, sugar and butter. Beat the eggs well and pour into the milk, then put in the corn mixture and bake in a glass dish or greased pan in a 350° to 400° oven for 30 to 35 minutes, stirring from the bottom about 3 times.

Mrs. Coy E. (Trilby) Ball

148

CORN PUDDING

2 c. corn
½ c. bread cubes
2 tsp. minced onion
¾ c. shredded cheese

½ tsp. salt
2 eggs
½ c. hot milk

Mix and pour into baking dish. Bake in 350° oven until brown and set. Can add green pepper.

Madrid Shaw

SOUTHERN CORN PUDDING

2 c. corn
4 Tbsp. flour
1 Tbsp. butter
2 level tsp. sugar

1 level tsp. salt
2 well beaten eggs
2 c. milk

Mix corn, flour, sugar and salt together. Combine well beaten eggs, melted butter and milk. Mix with corn mixture. Pour into a greased baking dish. Bake at 350° for 1 hour. Stir from bottom 2 or 3 times during first 30 minutes of baking. Serves 4 to 5 people.

Bonnie J. Riggs

OVEN ROASTED CORN

Corn (fresh)
¾ c. butter
2½ tsp. salt

1½ tsp. oregano
2 tsp. dried chopped chives

Alternate:

2 tsp. minced green onion

1½ tsp. barbecue spice

Pull back husks and remove silks. Mix together butter, salt, oregano and chives (or the alternate of minced green onion or barbecue spice). Spread this savory butter on the corn and pull husks back around the corn and tie with string. Put in roasting pan and bake at 350° for 40 minutes.

Patti Roby

CHINESE STYLE PICKLED CUCUMBERS

2 medium cucumbers	2 tsp. fresh ginger root,
2 tsp. salt	minced
½ c. vinegar	2 tsp. sesame seed
⅓ c. sugar	

Wash cucumbers and peel lengthwise in ¼ inch strips, leaving every other strip of green skin on. Cut in halves lengthwise; remove seeds and slice thin. Put in bowl and add salt. Mix well and let stand 1 hour. Pour off water and pat dry with paper toweling. Mix remaining ingredients and bring to a boil. Pour over cucumbers and chill. Makes 4 servings.

R. A. Bratcher

CUCUMBERS WITH MUSTARD DRESSING

3 large cucumbers, peeled	1 Tbsp. prepared mustard
and sliced thin	1 tsp. salt
2 Tbsp. salad oil	Pepper to taste
4 Tbsp. vinegar	

Place sliced cucumbers in a bowl and cover with ice. When ready to serve, drain and mix well with the other ingredients which have been mixed well.

Rosalie Smith

SOUR CREAM CUCUMBERS

2 - 4 cucumbers	½ tsp. salt
1 c. sour cream	2 Tbsp. chopped chives
2 Tbsp. vinegar	1 tsp. celery seed
1 Tbsp. sugar	2 Tbsp. dill, chopped

Slice cucumbers very thin. Mix all other ingredients together and pour over cucumbers and marinate overnight.

Peggy Kessinger

DANDELION GREENS, ITALIAN STYLE

1 lb. dandelion greens	¼ c. cooking oil
1 onion, diced	Salt and pepper to taste
1 garlic clove, minced	Parmesan cheese
½ small dried red pepper,	
crushed	

Wash greens thoroughly in salted water; cut leaves in 2 inch pieces. Cook in about an inch of boiling salted water until tender, about 10 minutes. Saute onion, garlic and red pepper in oil. Drain greens; add to onion mixture and season to taste. Heat slowly. Serve with grated cheese. Makes 4 servings.

R. A. Bratcher

BAKED EGGPLANT

1 large eggplant
1 tsp. salt
1 egg
1 small, chopped onion or
   onion flakes

1 c. soft bread crumbs
¼ c. pecans
Butter

Pare eggplant and cut in slices. Cook in boiling salted water until tender. Drain well and mash with a lump of butter. Add onion, crumbs, egg (well beaten), and pecans. Put in greased casserole; top with buttered crumbs and bake in moderate oven 20 to 30 minutes.

Kim Clinton

CREOLE EGGPLANT

2 small eggplants
4 slices bacon
¼ c. chopped onion
¼ c. chopped green pepper
½ c. fresh sliced mushrooms

2 c. chopped peeled
   tomatoes
1 c. Mozzarella cheese
¼ tsp. pepper

Wash eggplants; cut in halves lengthwise. Remove pulp, leaving ¼ inch shell. Chop pulp. Combine bacon, onion, green pepper and mushrooms in large skillet. Saute until bacon is crisp. Add eggplant pulp, tomato, salt and pepper. Bring to a boil, then simmer 10 minutes. Place eggplant shells in 10x6x2 inch pan. Place hot mixture into shells. Add ½ inch water. Sprinkle cheese on top and bake at 350° for 30 minutes.

Helen Russman

EGGPLANT CASSEROLE

1 eggplant
Buttered crackers, crumbled
1/3 c. finely chopped green
 pepper
1/3 c. finely chopped celery
Poultry seasoning
Salt and pepper to taste

Few pats of butter
2/3 c. shredded Cheddar
 cheese
1 can cream of mushroom
 soup
Parmesan cheese
Milk

Peel and cube eggplant. Boil until tender. In casserole, crumble a layer of crackers. Put in layer of eggplant. Sprinkle a layer of peppers and celery over this. (These can be used raw or sauteed in butter.) Sprinkle a small amount of poultry seasoning over this, then a little salt, butter and pepper. Top with a layer of Cheddar cheese, then a layer of soup. Repeat layers, ending with soup. Crumble crackers on top and sprinkle on Parmesan cheese and some butter. Pour some milk over top and bake at 350° until bubbly, about 30 to 35 minutes.

Ora Johnson

CHEESY EGGPLANT PIE

9 inch unbaked pastry shell
1/4 c. chopped green pepper
1/4 c. chopped onion
1/4 c. butter
8 oz. tomato sauce

1/2 tsp. salt
3 c. sliced, diced eggplant
2 c. shredded Cheddar or
 Mozzarella cheese

Saute onion and green pepper in butter. Stir in tomato sauce. Boil. Add eggplant. Cook 10 minutes. Put half in pie crust, half cheese on top, other half eggplant and rest of cheese. Bake 35 minutes at 400°. Let stand 10 minutes or more before serving.

Mrs. Patsy Meredith

MOUSSAKA

1 large or 3 medium
 eggplants
Salt
Oil
1 onion, chopped
1 1/2 lb. ground chuck
Pepper
1/4 tsp. cinnamon

1 (8 oz.) can tomato sauce
3 Tbsp. tomato paste
3 Tbsp. fresh parsley
8 oz. Feta cheese
2 1/2 Tbsp. oleo or butter
2 1/2 Tbsp. flour
1 1/4 c. hot milk
1 egg yolk

Peel and thinly slice the eggplant. Brush with oil and place on cookie sheet. Broil 8 minutes on 1 side and 7 minutes on the other. While eggplant is cooking, brown onion and ground beef in a skillet until browned. Add salt, pepper and cinnamon. Add tomato sauce, tomato paste and parsley. Stir well. Moisten with a few tablespoons of water and simmer about 10 minutes. Heat milk in a small pan. Melt oleo in a sauce-pan; add flour and stir until very smooth. Add hot milk gradually, stirring constantly, and cook until it boils. Add salt and pepper to taste. Simmer until the sauce thickens. Beat the egg yolk. Stir in a little of the sauce and beat well. Add back to the sauce, stirring constantly. Remove from heat. Spray 8x11 inch casserole with Pam. Put a layer of eggplant, then a layer of tomato and beef mixture, then a layer of crumbled Feta cheese. Repeat until you have used all ingredients. Pour milk sauce over the top and bake in 350° oven for 1 hour. Serve immediately. Serves 6.

Mary Goff

STUFFED EGGPLANT-OLD STONE INN

1 large eggplant
½ c. water
½ tsp. salt
1 (10½ oz.) can condensed
    cream of mushroom soup
1 tsp. Worcestershire sauce
1 c. Ritz cracker crumbs,
    rolled fine (about 24
    crackers)

1 c. chopped onion
1 Tbsp. butter
1 Tbsp. chopped parsley
1 Tbsp. butter, melted
1½ c. cold water

Slice off one side of eggplant. Remove pulp to ½ inch of skin. Heat water and salt until boiling. Cook eggplant in water until tender, about 10 minutes. Drain thoroughly. Cook onion in butter until tender. Add eggplant, parsley, soup, sauce and all but 2 tablespoons of crack-ers. Fill eggplant shell with mixture. Place in a 10 x 6 x 1½ inch baking dish. Pour melted butter over eggplant and sprinkle with reserved crumbs. Carefully pour 1½ cups of water in bottom of dish. Bake at 375° for 1 hour or heated through. Serves 4 to 6.

Dorothy O'Neal

MIXED GREENS

¾ lb. salt pork, rinsed
6 c. water
¼ tsp. crushed red pepper
2 lb. mustard greens

2 lb. turnip greens
Onions and tomatoes
   (optional)

In large pot, combine meat and water. Cover; bring to boil. Reduce heat; simmer 60 minutes. Skim off any fat. Add seasonings and greens; cook 45 to 60 minutes or until tender. Serve with onions and tomatoes if desired. Serves 8 to 10.

Mary V. Stanley

GRITS CASSEROLE

4 c. water
1 tsp. salt
1 c. instant grits
1 stick butter or margarine
1 roll garlic cheese

2 eggs
Milk
Bacon crumbs or corn flakes
   (optional)
French fried onions (optional)

Add salt to water and bring to a boil. Slowly stir in grits. Cook 3 minutes, stirring constantly. Remove from heat and stir in butter and garlic cheese. Put eggs in a cup and add enough milk to make a cup. Beat eggs and milk mixture well and add to grits. Bake in greased 2 quart casserole at 300° for an hour. Makes 6 servings.

Note: You can sprinkle French fried onions or crisp bacon crumbs or corn flakes on top if you like.

Bessie Litchford

FRIED GRITS

1⅓ c. water
1 tsp. salt
⅔ c. grits
3 Tbsp. butter

2 eggs, beaten with 2 Tbsp.
   water
Flour
3 Tbsp. butter

Bring water to a boil. Add salt. Slowly stir in grits. Add 3 tablespoons butter. Cover pot; cook over low heat for 20 minutes; stir occasionally. Pour grits into a greased 2 quart ovenproof casserole. Refrigerate for 2 hours or overnight. Cut chilled grits into slices about ½ inch thick. Dip slices in eggs, then in flour. Saute in butter until golden brown. Serves 4 to 6.

Brenda Chitty

154

GRITS CASSEROLE

4½ c. boiling water
1 tsp. salt
1 c. grits
⅔ c. milk

2 eggs
1 stick margarine
1 - 1½ rolls garlic cheese
2 c. crushed corn flakes

Cook grits in boiling salt water; add margarine and cheese (cut up fine), then add beaten eggs and milk, a little at a time. Put in well greased baking dish. Spread with crushed corn flakes and dot with butter. Bake 1 hour at 350°. Serves 10 to 12.

Flo Gish

GRITS CASSEROLE

4 c. water
1 tsp. salt
1 c. hominy grits
1 stick butter
1 c. milk
4 eggs, slightly beaten

12 oz. grated Cheddar cheese
Ritz or cheese crackers
Worcestershire sauce (to
   taste)
Garlic (to taste)

Add salt to water; bring to boil. Add grits slowly, keeping water at a brisk boil. Cover and cook slowly for about 1 hour or until grits are soft, stirring occasionally. Remove from heat. Stir in butter and milk, then cheese and garlic and Worcestershire sauce. Cool to lukewarm. Beat in eggs and pour into greased 2 quart casserole. Bake at 350° for 1 hour.

Debbie Owens

HOMINY A LA OLD HOUSE

2 c. cooked hominy
1 c. grated Swiss cheese
3 eggs, slightly beaten
1 tsp. salt
1 tsp. Worcestershire sauce

1 Tbsp. chopped chives
1 Tbsp. chopped parsley
1 Tbsp. chopped pimiento
1¼ c. light cream, scalded

Heat oven to 350°. Combine all ingredients and pour into a well buttered casserole. Bake, uncovered, at 350° in a pan of hot water for 30 minutes or until set. Serves 6.

Paula White

HOMEMADE HOMINY

1 qt. shelled corn (Hickory
    Cane)
2 Tbsp. lye

1 gal. boiling water
1 tsp. salt

For each quart of shelled corn, add 2 tablespoons lye and 1 gallon boiling water. Boil about 30 minutes or until hull loosens. Rinse corn several times, then cover with cold water. Rub to remove hulls and black tips. Let stand in fresh water 2 to 3 hours. Change water and cover with boiling salted water, 1 teaspoon salt to each quart of water. Boil until tender; drain. Season to taste with bacon drippings, and pepper and salt, if needed.

Josie Bratcher

HOMINY GRITS

1 c. hominy grits
1 tsp. salt

5 c. boiling water

Cook slowly 25 to 30 minutes, stirring frequently. Serve with gravy or with butter or with cream and sugar. Chill the leftovers; slice and fry in butter until golden brown.

HOMINY PUDDING

1½ c. cooked hominy
2 eggs, beaten
1 c. milk
1 Tbsp. sugar
¼ tsp. salt

1 c. sliced peaches or apples,
    sweetened
Nutmeg
Cinnamon

Mix hominy with eggs, milk, sugar, salt and sliced fruit. Place in buttered deep baking dish and sprinkle with nutmeg and cinnamon. Set dish in a pan with ½ cup water; water should come halfway up sides of dish. Bake in a preheated 400° oven for about 45 minutes. Test after 45 minutes by inserting tip of knife into pudding 1 inch from edge of dish. If knife comes out clean, pudding is done. (Center will set as pudding cools.) Serves 4 to 6.

Heidi Thompson

HOMINY WITH CHEESE SAUCE AND CHIVES

2 c. cooked hominy	¾ c. grated sharp cheese
2 Tbsp. butter	1 tsp. salt
2 Tbsp. flour	¼ tsp. pepper
1½ c. milk	2 Tbsp. chives

Reheat hominy in top of double boiler. In a saucepan, melt butter; blend in flour; add milk; stir until sauce boils. Add cheese, salt and pepper; stir until cheese is melted. Pour cheese sauce over hot hominy and sprinkle with chives. Serves 4.

Denise Figg

HOMINY CROQUETTES WITH PECANS

1 c. cooked hominy	1 egg
1 Tbsp. soft butter	½ c. dry bread crumbs
⅓ c. chopped pecans	White Sauce (optional)
¼ tsp. onion salt or onion	
powder	

Mix hominy with butter, pecans and onion salt or powder. Shape into 8 croquettes. Beat egg slightly with about 1 tablespoon cold water. Dip each croquette into crumbs, then in egg, then into crumbs again and fry 1 minute in hot fat. Drain and serve plain or with White Sauce. Serves 4.

Denise Figg

HOMINY GRITS SOUFFLE

4 oz. uncooked hominy grits	4 oz. grated sharp Cheddar
3 c. boiling water	cheese
1 tsp. salt	4 eggs, separated
1 Tbsp. plus 1 tsp. margarine	1 tsp. Worcestershire sauce
½ c. chopped onion	Dash of hot sauce
1 garlic clove, minced	
⅓ c. seeded and diced	
canned jalapeno peppers	

Preheat oven to 350°. Stir grits into boiling salted water; cook, stirring until soft. Melt margarine in small skillet; add onion and garlic; saute until soft. In a bowl, combine cooked grits, onion mixture and peppers; add cheese, egg yolks, Worcestershire and hot sauce. In separate bowl, beat egg whites until stiff; gradually fold into grit mixture. Transfer to 2 quart casserole and bake 30 to 35 minutes or until a thin knife when inserted in center comes out clean. Serves 4. Per serving: 345 calories.

Jeffrey Cox

TWENTIETH CENTURY HOMINY

1 qt. shelled corn (Hickory Cane)

2 Tbsp. baking soda
1 tsp. salt

Wash corn; add 2 quarts cold water and soda. Cook in enamel kettle for 3 hours or until hulls loosen. Add more water if necessary. Drain off water when tender. Wash corn in cold water, rubbing until all hulls are removed. Then bring corn to boil in more water. Cook until tender; drain and add salt. Fry in bacon drippings.

Louisa Rosser

HOMINY GRITS SOUFFLE

¾ c. grits
1 c. boiling water
2 c. milk

¼ c. melted butter
4 egg yolks, well beaten
6 egg whites, stiffly beaten

Pour ¾ cup grits into 1 cup boiling water and cook 5 minutes; stir constantly. Stir in 1 cup milk and cook 30 minutes slowly. Remove from heat and stir in another cup milk and ¼ cup melted butter. Place again over low heat and stir until mixture is smooth and heated through. Remove from heat and stir in well beaten egg yolks. Cool to lukewarm and fold in stiffly beaten egg whites. Bake in a buttered baking dish for 45 minutes in 350° oven. Makes 6 servings.

Denise Figg

BAKED HOMINY AND CHEESE

2 c. canned tomatoes
3 Tbsp. onion, chopped
2 cloves
½ tsp. salt
1 Tbsp. sugar
⅛ tsp. cayenne

3 Tbsp. margarine
2 Tbsp. flour
2½ c. cooked hominy
½ c. grated Cheddar cheese
½ c. bread crumbs

Mash up tomatoes and simmer with the onion, cloves, salt, sugar and cayenne for 20 minutes. Strain. Melt 2 tablespoons of margarine and blend with flour. Add strained tomato juice and bring slowly to a boil; stir constantly. Put a layer of hominy in a greased baking dish. Add layer of cheese, then a layer of tomato sauce. Repeat layers. Spread top with crumbs. Dot with remaining margarine. Bake in hot oven at 425° for 20 minutes or until crumbs are brown. Serves 6.

Lora Martin

KOHLRABI IN CREAM SAUCE

1 qt. kohlrabi bulbs, peeled
    and cubed
Kohlrabi leaves
2 Tbsp. butter

3 Tbsp. flour
½ c. milk
Salt and pepper to taste
2 Tbsp. salt

Cook cubes in salted water; add about 1 tablespoon salt; cook about 15 or 20 minutes or until tender. Cook leaves in salted water; add about 1 tablespoon salt; cook about 20 minutes. Drain cubes; save ½ cup liquid. Drain leaves and chop coarsely. Melt butter; add flour and cook; stir in reserved liquid and milk gradually. When thickened to desired consistency, add cubes and greens. Add salt and pepper to taste.

Patti Roby

LEEKS AU GRATIN

8 - 12 leeks (according to
    size)
3 Tbsp. butter
2 Tbsp. flour
1 c. milk

1 c. grated Cheddar cheese
½ tsp. prepared mustard
Lemon juice
4 Tbsp. bread crumbs

Preheat oven to 375°. Wash leeks thoroughly and trim off coarse green tops. Cook only until just tender in boiling salted water; drain and put in a buttered baking dish. Make a sauce with 2 tablespoons butter, flour and milk. Add cheese; stir until it melts; add salt, pepper, mustard and a squeeze of lemon juice. Pour sauce over leeks; sprinkle with bread crumbs and dot with remaining 1 tablespoon of butter. Cook about 25 minutes until top is crisp and brown.

Denise Figg

FESTIVE LIMAS

2 Tbsp. butter
1 chicken bouillon cube
1 tsp. instant minced onion
1 pkg. frozen Fordhook limas

2 Tbsp. chopped chives
2 c. pea pods (Chinese)
2 Tbsp. chopped pimento
2 tsp. parsley flakes

Melt butter in a pan. Add chicken cube and minced onion. Cook, stirring constantly, until cube is dissolved. Add limas and pea pods (sliced); then add pimento, chives and parsley flakes. Add your salt and pepper. Cover and cook over medium heat until limas and pea pods are tender. Cook 12 minutes.

Optional: Add garlic powder and a little sage.

Barbara C. Hendrick

LIMA BEAN CASSEROLE

2 pkg. frozen lima beans
1 small onion, cut fine
½ green pepper
1 stick butter

1 can celery soup
8 oz. Cheddar cheese,
   shredded
Ritz crackers

Cook limas until barely tender. Brown onion and pepper in butter. Mix with limas, which have been drained. Mix in celery soup. Place in a greased casserole. Cover with cheese and crumbled crackers. Bake at 350° for 40 minutes.

Mary Baxter

MACARONI AND CHEESE

½ lb. macaroni
2 c. milk
1 tsp. salt
¼ c. margarine

¼ c. flour
1 (8 oz.) pkg. Cracker Barrel
   cheese (mild), shredded

Cook macaroni in boiling, salted water, according to package directions. Rinse in *hot* water and drain well. Make a white sauce with the margarine, flour, milk and salt. Place half of the macaroni in a greased 1½ quart casserole. Cover with half the white sauce. Sprinkle with half of the shredded cheese. Repeat with remaining macaroni, white sauce and cheese. Bake in a moderate oven (350°) for 20 minutes.

Ruth Ackerman

MACARONI AND CHEESE CASSEROLE

2 c. Ready Cut Red Cross
   macaroni
3 qt. boiling water
1 Tbsp. salt
1 stick margarine

3 Tbsp. flour
2 c. milk
2 c. diced Velveeta cheese
Bread crumbs or paprika

Bring 3 quarts water to a brisk boil; add 1 tablespoon salt. Slowly add 2 cups Ready Cut Red Cross macaroni. Cook vigorously for 10 minutes. Drain. Put in large casserole.

For your cheese sauce, melt 1 stick margarine in saucepan. Add 3 tablespoons flour. Mix well. Add 2 cups milk. Cook until slightly thickened. Add 2 cups diced Velveeta cheese. Stir constantly until melted. Pour over macaroni. Sprinkle bread crumbs or paprika over top. Bake until slightly browned.

Bessie Litchford

MACARONI CASSEROLE

3 Tbsp. butter
1 can mushrooms and juice
½ lb. grated mild Cheddar
   cheese
1 c. mayonnaise
1 can mushroom soup
⅓ c. chopped onion
⅓ c. pimentos
⅓ c. chopped green onions
1 box macaroni
1 box Blue cheese crackers,
   crumbled

Cook 1 box macaroni and drain off some water, but not all. Mix the following with the macaroni in a large casserole dish. Top all this with 1 box Blue cheese crackers, crumbled and mixed with 3 tablespoons butter. Bake 20 minutes at 350°. Serves 12.

Lil Pasinski

MUSHROOMS A LA GRECQUE

½ lb. mushrooms, washed
   and sliced
1 onion, sliced
2 Tbsp. olive oil
1 Tbsp. tomato paste
2 bay leaves
6 peppercorns
⅔ c. chicken stock
2 Tbsp. dry white wine
Salt
Pepper

Slice mushrooms through the stems and blanch for 2 minutes. Saute the onion in oil. Arrange mushrooms in a casserole and add the remaining ingredients. Cover and cook in the oven for 30 to 40 minutes at 325°. Remove bay leaves and peppercorns. Serve sprinkled with paprika and chopped parsley.

Dee Dee Millen

MUSHROOMS AU GRATIN

2 lb. mushrooms, sliced
¼ lb. butter
1 c. sour cream

¼ c. minced fresh parsley
1½ - 2 c. Cheddar or Swiss
   cheese, grated

Saute mushrooms in butter. Cool. Preheat oven to 350°. Blend sour cream and parsley into mushrooms. Transfer to a baking dish and sprinkle cheese over it. Bake 15 minutes or until bubbly.

Heidi Thompson, Melanie Davis

MUSHROOMS AND ONIONS IN WINE SAUCE

1 lb. mushrooms
½ c. butter, melted
16 tiny white onions
2 Tbsp. flour
4 Tbsp. parsley, chopped
½ bay leaf

¼ tsp. fresh grated nutmeg
6 Tbsp. bouillon
¼ c. sherry or Madeira
Croutons
Parsley sprigs

Melt butter; add tiny onions and saute for 5 minutes. Add mushrooms and when they are coated with butter, add 2 tablespoons flour, parsley, ½ bay leaf, nutmeg and bouillon. Cook and stir until onions are tender. Add sherry or Madeira. Stir and cook until hot. Garnish with croutons and sprigs of parsley.

Peggy Kessinger

SCALLOPED MUSHROOM CASSEROLE

1 lb. fresh mushrooms
¼ lb. soda crackers
1¼ c. milk

1 tsp. salt and pepper (or to
   taste)
¼ stick butter

Wash and dry mushrooms. Cut into pieces. Mix with crushed crackers, milk, salt and pepper. Place in casserole. Dot with butter. Bake 45 minutes at 350°. Serves 6.

Dorothy O'Neal

STUFFED MUSHROOMS

Sherry
1 lb. medium size mushrooms
Butter or margarine
Grated American cheese
Grated fresh onions and
parsley

Grated hard-boiled egg
Bread crumbs or Ritz cracker
crumbs
Salt and pepper to taste

Remove stems from mushrooms. Put stems through meat grinder. Melt butter in skillet and saute onions. Add all ingredients and mix well. Add salt and pepper to taste. Stuff mushroom heads with this mixture. Place in buttered casserole, stuffed side up. Pour some sherry directly onto mushrooms and into casserole. Bake at 325° about 45 minutes.

Ruth Ackerman

NOODLE CASSEROLE

1 Tbsp. salt
3 qt. boiling water
8 oz. medium egg noodles
2 Tbsp. butter
2 Tbsp. flour
2 c. milk
½ lb. Cheddar cheese,
shredded

Salt and pepper to taste
1½ c. cooked or canned
tomatoes, chopped and
drained
6 Tbsp. buttered crumbs

Add salt to boiling water; gradually add noodles and cook, uncovered, stirring occasionally, until tender, then drain and rinse in cold water. Melt butter over low heat. Add flour and blend. Add milk and cook until smooth and thickened. Add all, but ½ cup of the cheese, and stir until melted. Add salt and pepper to taste. Combine with noodles and tomatoes; transfer to a buttered 1½ quart casserole. Sprinkle with the remaining cheese and crumbs. Bake in a 350° oven 25 to 30 minutes or until bubbly and lightly browned. Good served with oven fried chicken or meat loaf.

Ruthie Marty

ONION PIE

1 recipe Basic Pastry
3 Tbsp. butter
2½ lb. Bermuda onions, sliced
3 eggs

1 c. sour cream
¼ c. dry sherry
1 tsp. celery salt
1 egg white
4 slices bacon

Preheat oven to 450°. Line a 9 inch pie plate with pastry; prick bottom and let chill while preparing the filling. Heat butter and saute onion until transparent. Remove from heat. Beat eggs; add sour cream, sherry, celery salt and seasoning; heat just long enough to blend ingredients together. Stir into onions. Brush bottom of pie shell with lightly beaten egg white and pour in the filling. Arrange strips of bacon on top. Bake 10 minutes, then reduce heat to 300° and bake for ½ hour or until pastry is cooked.

Paula White

COCKNEY PIE

1 onion, sliced
½ lb. mushrooms, sliced
2 oz. butter
1 oz. flour
½ pt. beef stock

2 tsp. wine vinegar
Black pepper
1 lb. sliced boiled beef
¾ lb. cooked carrots, sliced
1 Tbsp. Demerara sugar

Slice onion and mushrooms. Heat butter and cook onion and mushrooms until tender. Stir in flour, then add stock and wine vinegar. Season with salt and pepper. Bring to a boil and simmer 2 minutes. Put sliced meat into an ovenproof dish and pour over the sauce. Cover the dish with sliced carrots. Sprinkle brown sugar over the carrots. Bake at 350° for about 30 minutes.

Eldred Sykes

PEAS WITH ONION AND MUSHROOMS

1 (10 oz.) pkg. frozen peas
1 (4 oz.) can mushrooms (stems and pieces), drained

1 small onion, chopped
3 Tbsp. butter
¼ tsp. salt
Dash of pepper

Cook peas as directed on package; drain well. Saute mushrooms and onion in butter. Add remaining ingredients. Cook another couple of minutes and then serve. Serves 4.

Lynnette Bonn

164

BLACK-EYED PEAS

2 c. dried black-eyed peas
2 smoked ham hocks
2 qt. water
2 c. thinly sliced onion

1 c. chopped celery
2 cloves garlic, minced
½ tsp. crushed red pepper
½ tsp. salt

Soak peas overnight in enough water to cover; drain. In large pot, combine hocks, water, onion, celery and seasonings. Cover; bring to boil. Reduce heat; simmer 30 minutes. Add peas; cover. Cook, stirring occasionally, over low heat 1½ hours or until peas are tender. Garnish with green onion slices if desired. Serves 8.

Mary V. Stanley

SPICY BLACK-EYED PEAS

2 c. dried black-eyed peas
2 qt. water
1 tsp. salt

1 lb. hot pork sausage with sage flavoring, cut in 4 pieces

Wash peas. Discard any bad ones. Place peas in a pot; add water and salt. Bring to a boil. Lower heat; cover pot. Brown sausage. Add meat and its fat to the peas. Cover; continue cooking over low heat for 1 to 1½ hours or until peas are cooked. Serves 4.

Zella M. Cox

HOPPIN' JOHN

1 lb. black-eyed peas
½ lb. smoked ham, cut up
1 onion, diced
¼ tsp. cayenne pepper

¾ c. uncooked rice
Salt to taste
Pepper to taste

Put peas and ham cut in pieces in kettle and cover with water; bring to a boil and then turn down to simmer. If necessary, add boiling water as needed. Cook until tender. Add all other ingredients and simmer until rice is tender, about 20 or 25 minutes. If necessary, add more boiling water to cook rice.

Sharon Duke

FRIED BANANA PEPPERS

1 jar hot banana peppers
1½ c. milk
1½ c. flour
½ c. cracker meal

1 egg
½ or 1 can beer
3 bowls

Split peppers and seed. Bowl Number 1 - Milk, egg and beer. Bowl Number 2 - One cup flour. Bowl Number 3 - ½ cup cracker meal and ½ cup flour. Dip peppers into milk and bread with flour; set aside 10 minutes. Re-dip peppers into milk and bread with flour and cracker meal mixture. Set aside 10 minutes; drop in deep fat (360° to 365°). Cook until golden brown.

Mary Raney

STUFFED PEPPERS

8 peppers
1 lb. ground beef
1 onion, chopped
1 rib celery

1 c. Minute rice
1 small can (1 c.) tomatoes
1 small can tomato sauce
4 Tbsp. butter

Cut peppers in halves and remove seeds. Parboil for 5 minutes. Put butter in skillet and add chopped onion and celery. Let cook 4 or 5 minutes, then add meat and cook until meat changes color. Then add cooked rice, tomatoes and tomato sauce. Cook until thick or suitable to put in peppers. Add the liquid from meat for the sauce on top.

Note: These may be frozen when stuffed and baked later.

Rosaleen Robertson

STUFFED GREEN PEPPERS

6 green peppers
1 lb. ground beef
2 c. dry bread crumbs
2 Tbsp. onion, chopped

2 tsp. salt
¼ tsp. pepper
1 (16 oz.) can tomato sauce

Cut thin slice from stem end of peppers and remove seeds and membranes; wash peppers. Mix remaining ingredients. Stuff mixture into peppers. Place in baking dish; cover and bake 45 minutes. Uncover and bake 15 minutes longer. Serves 6.

Rosetta Humphries

AU GRATIN O'BRIEN POTATOES

2 c. thin sliced raw potatoes
1 qt. boiling water
1 c. chopped green pepper
⅓ c. pimiento, chopped
3 Tbsp. margarine, melted

⅓ c. flour
2 c. warm milk
1 c. Cheddar cheese, grated
1 tsp. salt
½ tsp. pepper

Drop potato slices into 1 quart boiling water; allow water to return to boiling. Add onion and green pepper; let water return to boiling point again. Remove from heat and drain. Add pimiento and mix. In top of double boiler, blend melted margarine and flour. Add warm milk; cook and stir until smooth. Add grated cheese; stir until a smooth thick sauce. Season with salt and pepper. Pour into potato mixture. Pour into a greased baking dish; bake at 350° for 1½ hours or until potatoes are done. Serves 6 to 8.

Lynnette Bonn

BAKED BARBEQUE POTATOES

1 Tbsp. flour
1½ tsp. salt
¼ tsp. pepper
5 c. thin sliced raw potatoes
½ c. chopped onion
2 Tbsp. butter
1 c. shredded process
    American cheese

⅓ c. ketchup
1 tsp. Worcestershire sauce
3 drops of Tabasco sauce
1½ c. scalded milk
4 slices bacon, fried crisp,
    drained, crumbled

Mix flour, salt and pepper. Arrange potatoes, flour mixture and half the cheese in layers in 2 quart casserole. Mix catsup, Worcestershire sauce, Tabasco sauce and milk. Pour over potatoes; dot with butter. Cover and bake at 375° for 50 minutes. Uncover and stir. Continue baking until potatoes are tender, about 20 minutes. Sprinkle with rest of cheese and bacon.

Patti Roby

BOY SCOUT POTATOES
(Individual servings)

Heavy foil

1 sliced potato (medium)

1546-85

167

Sprinkle with onion, Cheddar cheese, salt, pepper and parsley flakes. Wrap in heavy foil and place on charcoal grill for 30 minutes and serve.

Beverly (Goldilocks) Wilhite

COMPANY POTATOES

2 lb. bag frozen hash browns
  (Southern style)
1 lb. shredded Cheddar
  cheese
2 (10½ oz.) cans cream of
  celery soup

1 (16 oz.) ctn. sour cream
1 stick margarine
1 c. chopped celery
1 large onion, chopped

Saute celery and onion in margarine until onions are clear (do not brown). Combine all ingredients and mix well. Put in a buttered or Pam sprayed 9x13 inch casserole dish. Bake for 1 hour at 350°. Casserole is done when potatoes are tender.

Recipe can be halved.

Donna Browning

COMPANY CREAMED POTATOES

1 qt. cubed, boiled potatoes
¼ tsp. pepper
2 Tbsp. butter

1 pt. half & half
1 tsp. salt
½ c. Ritz cracker crumbs

Prepare the day before. Boil potatoes in their skins until tender, but not mushy. Skin and cut into small cubes. Put in a heavy saucepan and pour half & half and seasoning over the potatoes. Cook over low heat until the boiling point is reached. Remove from heat immediately. Cool and refrigerate, covered, overnight. Put potatoes in a 2 quart casserole and heat, covered, in a preheated 325° oven 1 hour. Remove cover the last 15 minutes. In the meantime, brown cracker crumbs in butter. When ready to serve, sprinkle browned cracker crumbs on top.

Ruth Ackerman

HASH BROWN POTATO CASSEROLE

2 lb. bag hash brown
  potatoes
1 stick melted butter
1 can cream of chicken soup

1 (8 oz.) ctn. sour cream
1 c. grated Cheddar cheese
¼ c. chopped onion
Salt and pepper

168

Mix all ingredients together and pour into greased casserole. Top with paprika and more grated cheese if desired. Bake at 350° for approximately 45 minutes. Makes 1 large or 2 small casseroles.

Jane Brashear

HOT JACKET POTATOES

4 large potatoes
1 large or 2 medium onions,
   sliced
2 firm tomatoes, chopped
1 c. grated mild Cheddar
   cheese

Salt to taste
Pepper to taste
4 Tbsp. butter

Clean potatoes; wrap in foil. Place on baking sheet. Bake in preheated 450° oven for 1 hour. Cook onion slices in small amount of water until just tender. Drain and cool. Toss tomatoes, cheese and onion together. Make an "X" cutting on top of potatoes; press sides to open. Do not cut all the way through the potatoes. Add salt, pepper and 1 tablespoon butter to each potato. Place ¼ of the tomato mixture in each potato. Potatoes should be hot enough to melt the cheese. May be broiled until heated if potatoes have cooled.

Heidi Thompson

IRISH POTATO CASSEROLE

8 - 10 medium potatoes,
   peeled
1 (8 oz.) pkg. cream cheese,
   softened
1 (8 oz.) ctn. commercial sour
   cream

½ c. butter or margarine,
   melted
¼ c. chopped chives
1 clove garlic, minced
2 tsp. salt
Paprika

Cook potatoes in boiling water about 30 minutes or until tender. Drain potatoes and mash. Beat cream cheese with an electric mixer until smooth. Add potatoes and remaining ingredients, except paprika; beat just until combined. Spoon mixture into a lightly buttered 2 quart casserole; sprinkle with paprika. Cover and refrigerate overnight. Remove from refrigerator 15 minutes before baking. Uncover and bake at 350° for 30 minutes or until thoroughly heated. Yield: 8 to 10 servings.

Jo Ann Thompson

OVEN BAKED POTATOES

8 large unpeeled baking
potatoes, cut in 8
lengthwise strips
½ c. salad oil
2 Tbsp. Parmesan cheese
½ tsp. garlic powder
½ tsp. salt
½ tsp. paprika
¼ tsp. pepper

Cut potatoes into strips and lay skin side down in shallow baking dish. Mix all ingredients and baste. Put in 350° oven for approximately 45 minutes or until done, basting frequently.

Betty Carrier

POTATOES

1 pt. sour cream
10 oz. Cheddar cheese
Grated small onion
3 Tbsp. milk
2 Tbsp. melted margarine
⅓ c. bread crumbs
1 tsp. salt
⅛ tsp. pepper
6 medium potatoes

Boil potatoes in skins; let cool, peel and grate. Mix sour cream, Cheddar cheese, onion, milk, pepper and salt. Spread buttered crumbs on top. Bake at 300° for 50 minutes.

Can be fixed ahead of time and baked when needed. Also good reheated.

Mrs. Doris R. Buckner

POTATO PUFFS

2 c. mashed potatoes
1 c. flour
2 eggs
1½ tsp. baking powder
Salt to taste
Onion (optional)
Parsley flakes

Mix well; shape into puffs and deep-fry, maybe 10 minutes or so.

Jean Lyle

REFRIGERATOR MASHED POTATOES

9 large potatoes, peeled
2 (3 oz.) pkg. cream cheese
2 tsp. onion salt
½ tsp. salt
¼ tsp. pepper
2 Tbsp. butter
1 Tbsp. salt

Cook peeled potatoes until tender in boiling water in which 1 tablespoon salt has been added. Drain. Mash until smooth. Add remaining ingredients and beat until light and fluffy. Cool. Cover and put in refrigerator. May be used any time within 2 weeks.

To use, place desired amount in greased casserole; dot with butter and bake at 350° about 30 minutes.

Patti Roby

SCALLOPED POTATOES

8 small potatoes, thinly sliced
1 large onion, thinly sliced
2 Tbsp. pimentos, finely cut
1 c. grated American cheese

Salt and pepper
1 can cream of celery soup
¼ c. milk

Layer potatoes, onion, pimentos and cheese in a greased baking dish. Season each layer with salt and pepper. Blend soup and milk. Pour over potatoes. Bake at 300° for 2 hours. Serves 4.

Mary Harrod

SOUR CREAM FRIED POTATOES

4 - 6 medium potatoes,
   washed
1 pkg. sour cream

1 - 1½ sticks butter
   (margarine)
Salt and pepper to taste

Slice potatoes ½ inch thick with the peelings on; fry in butter at medium to low heat, adding ½ cup of water to help steam them done. Take them up on a serving plate; spread with sour cream, and serve while hot.

Wynola Sharon Davis

SWISS POTATOES

5 boiled potatoes, cubed
2 Tbsp. chopped green onion
   (with tops)
2 Tbsp. salad oil

2 Tbsp. butter
2 Tbsp. grated Swiss cheese
1 tsp. salt
¼ tsp. pepper

Cook potatoes and onions in oil and butter in a skillet until potatoes are lightly browned. Add cheese, salt and pepper; toss.

Patti Roby

SWEET POTATOES

1 large can sweet potatoes
½ c. seedless raisins
¼ c. light cream or milk
4 Tbsp. butter
⅔ c. sugar
Pinch of salt
2 Tbsp. bourbon
Marshmallows

Place potatoes in saucepan with raisins; add 1 cup water and simmer 20 minutes. Drain and mash thoroughly. Add sugar, salt, butter and bourbon. Beat well and add cream. Top with marshmallows and brown in oven.

Shirley Cates

CANDIED YAMS

2 large yams or sweet
   potatoes
½ tsp. nutmeg
1 tsp. cinnamon
½ c. white sugar
2 Tbsp. margarine
⅔ c. evaporated milk
⅓ c. water

Heat oven to 350°. Peel and slice raw potatoes. Place a layer in a greased ovenproof casserole. Mix nutmeg, cinnamon and sugar. Sprinkle half the mixture over the potatoes. Dot potatoes with half of the butter. Add another layer of potatoes. Sprinkle with remaining sugar mixture and butter. Mix the milk with water. Pour over potatoes. Cover casserole and bake 45 minutes. Remove cover and turn oven up to 400°. Bake 10 to 15 minutes more or until potatoes are done and the top is light brown. Serves 4.

Melissa Jackson

STUFFED BAKED SWEET POTATOES

6 medium sweet potatoes
3 Tbsp. butter
½ c. orange juice
1 tsp. salt
1 (8 oz.) can crushed
   pineapple
½ c. chopped pecans

Scrub and bake sweet potatoes at 375° for 45 minutes to 1 hour. Cut thin slice off top of potatoes. Scoop potato out of shell; combine with butter, orange juice and salt; whip. Stir in pineapple. Spoon back into shells. Sprinkle with nuts. Bake at 375° for about 12 minutes or until real hot.

Patti Roby

172

SWEET POTATO CASHEW BAKE

½ c. packed brown sugar
⅓ c. broken cashews
½ tsp. salt
¼ tsp. ground ginger
2 lb. sweet potatoes (5 or 6 medium), cooked, peeled

and cut crosswise into thick slices
1 (8 oz.) can peach slices, well drained
3 Tbsp. butter or margarine

Combine brown sugar, cashews, salt and ginger. In a 10x6x2 inch baking dish, layer half the sweet potatoes, half the peach slices and half of the brown sugar mixture. Repeat layers. Dot with butter or margarine. Bake, covered, at 350° for 30 minutes. Uncover and bake mixture about 10 minutes longer. Spoon brown sugar syrup over before serving.

This recipe can be made in triplicate for group.

Barbara C. Hendrick

SWEET POTATO CASSEROLE

3 c. mashed sweet potatoes
1 c. granulated sugar
1 stick margarine, melted
1 tsp. vanilla
2 eggs, well beaten

1 c. brown sugar (light)
⅓ c. melted margarine
½ c. all-purpose flour
1 c. chopped pecans

Mix sweet potatoes, granulated sugar, 1 stick margarine, 1 teaspoon vanilla and eggs well. Put into buttered casserole dish. Next, mix 1 cup brown sugar, ⅓ cup melted margarine, ½ cup all-purpose flour and 1 cup chopped pecans until crumbly. Cover the sweet potato mixture with this. Bake, uncovered, at 350° for 30 minutes. Cut into 1½ inch squares. Serve warm.

Note: One teaspoon dehydrated parsley flakes is equivalent to two sprigs of fresh parsley.

Brownie - Lois Bruner

SWEET POTATO CASSEROLE

2 c. mashed sweet potatoes
¾ stick (6 Tbsp.) butter
1¼ c. sugar
2 eggs

¼ tsp. cinnamon
¼ tsp. nutmeg
1 c. milk

Bake at 400° for 20 minutes.

Add Topping:

¾ stick butter, melted | ½ c. brown sugar
¾ c. crushed corn flakes | ½ c. pecans

Bake for 10 minutes at 400°.

Phyllis L. Davis

SWEET POTATO CASSEROLE

3 c. drained sweet potatoes | ½ c. melted butter
1 c. sugar | ½ c. milk
2 eggs, beaten | 1 tsp. vanilla

Combine all ingredients in 2 quart baking dish.

Topping:

1 c. brown sugar | ½ c. flour
1 c. pecans | ½ c. melted butter

Crumble mixture over potatoes. Bake at 350° for 30 minutes.

Doris McCord

SWEET POTATO CASSEROLE

3 c. sweet potatoes, mashed | ½ c. milk
1 c. white sugar | ½ tsp. vanilla
½ tsp. salt | 1 c. brown sugar
2 eggs, beaten | ⅓ c. flour
½ stick margarine, melted | ⅓ c. melted margarine

Preheat oven to 350°. Combine first 7 ingredients as listed and beat well. Put in baking dish. Mix by hand brown sugar, flour and ⅓ cup melted margarine. Crumble over top. Bake about 40 minutes or until set.

Clara Burd

SWEET POTATOES WITH CRUNCHY TOPPING

3 c. mashed sweet potatoes | 1 c. sugar
½ tsp. salt | 2 eggs
⅓ stick margarine or butter | ½ c. milk
1 tsp. vanilla

Mix all ingredients and then turn into greased baking dish. Cover with topping.

Topping:

1 c. brown sugar
⅓ stick melted margarine

1 c. chopped nuts
⅓ c. flour

Mix together to form lumps and then sprinkle over potatoes. Bake 35 minutes at 350°.

Note: This amount of topping can be used for a doubled amount of potatoes.

Grace Murphy

CRUNCHY-TOP SWEET POTATO SOUFFLE

3 c. mashed sweet potatoes
½ c. milk
1 c. sugar
⅓ stick margarine, melted
1 c. chopped pecans

2 eggs, lightly beaten
1 tsp. vanilla
½ tsp. salt
1 small can crushed
     pineapple, drained

Mix together all ingredients and beat until fluffy. Pour into a greased baking dish.

Topping:

⅓ c. margarine
⅓ c. flour

1 c. brown sugar
1 c. chopped pecans

Sprinkle topping mixture over sweet potato mixture and bake at 350° for 35 minutes. (Longer if deep dish is used.)

Ruth Ackerman

QUICK 'N EASY QUICHE

1 green pepper, chopped
1 bunch green onions,
    chopped
3 eggs
1½ c. Swiss cheese

3 - 4 scoops cottage cheese
Dash of cayenne
Dash of basil
1 small jar sliced mushrooms
½ pkg. Ritz crackers

Grease quiche pan. Make crust out of mushrooms and crackers; line quiche pan. Sprinkle with cayenne and basil. Lay green pepper and onion on. Mix cheeses and eggs in blender or with mixer until smooth and pour over vegetables. Bake in 350° oven for 30 minutes. Serve with fruit salad.

Lou Ann Crouch

CREAMED RADISHES

4 pkg. fresh radishes
2 Tbsp. flour
1 c. milk

⅛ tsp. curry powder
2 Tbsp. margarine
Salt to taste

Pare and cut off ends of radishes; cover radishes halfway with cold water in saucepan. Cover; cook for 10 minutes. Remove from heat. Add flour and milk; stir well. Add curry powder, blending well. Cook until sauce is smooth. Add margarine; salt to taste. Yield: 4 servings.

Lynnette Bonn

BEEFY RICE

1 c. regular long grain
  uncooked rice
1 stick butter or margarine
1 small can (or 2 if you like
  more) mushrooms

2 cans beef consomme soup
Chopped onions to taste
Salt and pepper

Put all of this in an uncovered casserole dish and bake at 350° for approximately 1 hour. It will look really soupy, but by the end of the hour it will have absorbed the juice.

This is delicious as a side dish for beef, chicken or Oriental dishes. *Do not* use Minute rice as it is already cooked rice.

Sherry Jones

CAJUN RICE

1 c. uncooked regular rice
1 tsp. salt
½ tsp. Tabasco sauce
10 oz. water
1 can drained crabmeat or
  shrimp

1 can mushroom soup
1 small onion, chopped
¼ c. celery, chopped
¼ c. bell pepper, chopped

Mix all ingredients and bake, covered, at 350° for approximately 1 hour or until done. Stir once.

John H. Drewes

CHEESE PILAF

2 Tbsp. butter
1 Tbsp. cooking oil
2 cloves garlic

1 c. uncooked rice
2 c. chicken bouillon
¼ c. grated Parmesan cheese

Preheat oven to 350°. Heat butter and oil; add garlic, crushed fine with a little salt, and the rice. Saute until rice begins to color. Pour into a baking dish; add bouillon; cover and cook for 25 to 30 minutes or until liquid is absorbed. Remove from the oven; add cheese; stir until cheese has melted and is mixed well with the rice. Serves 4. (This is good with chicken.)

For variety, stir in raisins, red or green pepper strips, seeded black or white grapes or nuts.

Heidi Thompson

CURRIED RICE

½ c. rice
2 c. hot water
½ c. canned tomatoes
½ c. finely sliced onion

½ c. thin sliced red or green pepper
2 Tbsp. melted butter
¾ tsp. curry powder

Preheat oven to 350°. Put rice in a casserole; add water and allow to stand about ¾ hour. Add all other ingredients and mix well. Cover and cook for 1 ½ hours; stir occasionally. Most of the liquid should now be absorbed, but serve the rice while it is still moist. Serves 4.

Eldred Sykes

FRIED RICE

1 oz. cooking oil
2 c. cooked rice
¼ c. chopped fresh shrimp or canned shrimp
¼ c. chopped ham
¼ c. chopped barbecued pork
¼ c. chopped green onions

¼ c. chopped, well done, fried eggs
2 oz. bean sprouts
⅔ tsp. salt
¼ tsp. Accent
1 oz. Chinese soy sauce
Few drops of sesame oil

Prepare medium hot pan with 1 ounce cooking oil. Saute shrimp, pork and ham about 1 minute. Put rice in to cook about 2 minutes. Add salt, Accent, and Chinese soy sauce with a few drops of sesame oil mixed into it. Serves 2.

Pam Thompson

FRIED RICE

5 c. cooked rice
2 eggs
1 c. chopped onion

2 c. chopped ham
Soy sauce

Get skillet hot and put about 1 tablespoon of grease; add cooked rice and cook about 1 minute. Add eggs (scrambled), green onions and chopped ham; cook about ½ minute, then add soy sauce as desired. Cook about 2 or 3 minutes.

Marie Nguyen

HAM FRIED RICE

1⅓ c. long grain rice, soaked
    in cold water for 30
    minutes and drained
2 c. water
1 tsp. salt
1 Tbsp. butter
2 eggs, lightly beaten

¼ c. vegetable oil
4 oz. green beans, cut into 1
    inch lengths
10 oz. cooked ham, diced
½ tsp. black pepper
4 scallions
6 average mushrooms

Put the rice into a saucepan; pour over the water and 1 teaspoon of salt. Bring to boil; reduce the heat to low and cover the pan. Simmer for 15 to 20 minutes or until the water has been absorbed and the rice is cooked and tender. Remove from heat. Melt butter in a large frying pan. Add the eggs and cook for 2 to 3 minutes or until they are set on the underside. Stir eggs and cook 2 to 3 minutes more or until they are just set. Remove from heat and transfer eggs to a bowl, breaking them up with a fork. Set aside. Add oil to the frying pan and heat over moderately high heat. Add the cooked rice, beans, ham and pepper. Cook for 2 minutes, stirring constantly. Reduce heat to moderately low and add the scallions, eggs and mushrooms. Cook for 2 minutes, stirring constantly, or until mixture is very hot. Transfer the mixture to a warmed serving dish and serve at once.

J. W. Borden, Jr.

INDIAN FRIED RICE

2 lb. rice
4 medium onions
½ tsp. powdered cloves
½ tsp. shelled cardamon
    seeds

¾ tsp. ground cinnamon
4 oz. butter or margarine
Salt to taste
3 pt. water

178

Slice onions and fry in hot butter until a golden brown and re-move. Fry spices in same butter until they crackle. Add rice and fry a few minutes. Add salt and water. Cover and cook until all the water has been absorbed. Serve hot. Garnish with sliced fried onions. Serves 8.

Peggy Larrison

JAPANESE FRIED RICE

1. First of all dice ½ large bell pepper and 1 medium onion. Also, 2 large carrots. (Celery is optional.) Set aside.

2. Beat 2 eggs and fry hard; taking them out of skillet, slice in thin strips. Set aside.

3. Tear up or cut in relatively small pieces ½ pound of sausage and fry on medium heat (not too fast).

4. While sausage is frying, put diced vegetables in another skillet with enough margarine to fry. Fry these slowly. When sufficiently done, remove from heat.

5. I generally use 2 cups of Minute rice for 1 family.

6. Combine vegetables, sausage and rice; mix well. Add soy sauce to your liking.

Clarine Ballard

RAVISHING RICE

1 lb. hot sausage	4½ c. boiling water
1 medium onion, chopped	2 env. chicken soup mix
1 medium green pepper	½ c. raw rice
1 c. celery, chopped	Slivered almonds

Brown sausage; drain. Add onion, pepper and celery. Bring water to boil; add soup mix and rice; boil 7 minutes. Mix together; pour into casserole dish. Top with almonds.

Loretta Picklesimer

RICE CAKES

1 c. rice	2 c. milk
1 c. boiling water	1½ tsp. salt

Put 1 cup rice and 1 cup boiling water in top of double boiler; cover with lid and cook until rice absorbs all water. Then add 2 cups milk and 1½ teaspoons salt. Heat to boiling point, but don't let it boil. Cook until milk is absorbed. Chill. Make into rice cakes or rice balls and fry.

This was Helen's mother's recipe. These cakes are real crisp when fried and you don't use any butter on them; use regular cooking rice, *don't* use Minute rice.

Helen Russman

RICE CASSEROLE

1 stick margarine	2 cans beef consomme
1 onion, chopped fine	Mushrooms (optional)
1 c. rice (regular)	

Brown rice and onion in melted margarine. Add consomme. Bake in casserole in 350° oven about 45 minutes or until consomme is absorbed.

Good with small can of mushrooms.

Georgetta Montgomery

SESAME-RICE FRITTERS

¼ c. sesame seed	⅛ tsp. pepper
2 Tbsp. skim milk powder	Dash of salt
¼ c. water	⅔ c. brown rice, cooked
2 egg yolks	2 egg whites
2 Tbsp. whole wheat flour	Oil for frying

Toast sesame seed until golden, about 20 minutes, in a 200° oven. Mix skim milk powder and water. Add egg yolks, flour, pepper and salt. Combine milk mixture, sesame seed and rice; mix well. Fold in stiffly beaten egg whites. Drop by tablespoon onto hot, oiled griddle and fry until brown. Drain on paper towel. Yield: 16 fritters.

Sharon Duke

SPANISH RICE

4 slices bacon	½ c. rice
1 c. chopped onions	½ c. water
¼ c. chopped green pepper	4 whole cloves
2 (10 or 11 oz.) cans tomato	1 bay leaf
soup	½ tsp. salt

Cut bacon in small pieces. Fry until crisp. Remove bacon. Cook onions and pepper in bacon fat until golden. Add remaining ingredients. Cover tightly and cook slowly 50 minutes. Stir occasionally. Remove cloves and bay leaf. Sprinkle crisp bacon over top.

Linda Y. Borden

SPANISH RICE

½ c. raw rice
4 Tbsp. margarine
3 Tbsp. onion, chopped
3 Tbsp. green pepper,
   chopped

¼ tsp. salt
⅛ tsp. sage
2 Tbsp. flour
2 c. tomato pulp
1½ c. hot water

Saute rice in 1½ tablespoons of margarine until light brown. Add 1½ cups hot water. Boil until dry. Cover and steam slowly 10 minutes. Put remaining margarine, onion, pepper, sage and salt in another pan and brown lightly. Add flour and ½ cup tomato pulp. Blend well. Add remaining pulp and boil 5 minutes. Pour over rice. Let steam until sauce has desired consistency. Serves 6.

Lora Martin

TURKISH PILAF

2 c. instant rice (uncooked)
¼ c. butter or margarine
1 (16 oz.) can tomatoes, cut
   up
2 beef bouillon cubes
¼ tsp. pepper

1 bay leaf
1 c. boiling water
1 onion, diced
1 clove garlic, minced
1 tsp. salt
1 tsp. sugar

Brown rice in butter in a medium saucepan; stir in remaining ingredients. Bring to boil, then reduce heat. Cover and simmer 15 to 17 minutes, stirring occasionally. Remove bay leaf before serving. *Delicious!*

Linda Y. Borden

WILD RICE CASSEROLE

½ pkg. sliced bacon, diced in
   small pieces
1 c. onion, diced
1 c. celery, diced

1 small can mushrooms,
   diced
1 can mushroom soup
½ c. uncooked wild rice

Rinse wild rice and boil until done (triples in size). Drain in colander, but do not rinse cooked rice. Brown bacon until crisp in frying pan. Remove and drain. Saute celery and onion in bacon grease until tender. Mix all ingredients and place in covered casserole. Bake at 350° for 30 minutes.

J. W. Borden, Jr.

SAUERKRAUT BALLS

½ c. onion, chopped fine
1 small garlic clove, minced
   or ⅛ tsp. garlic powder
1 Tbsp. butter
1 (16 oz.) can sauerkraut,
   squeezed dry
½ c. crisp bacon bits or 6 - 8
   slices or 1 c. fine
   chopped ham

1 Tbsp. chopped parsley
½ c. cold mashed potatoes
½ - ⅔ c. evaporated milk
   (undiluted)
½ c. fine dry bread crumbs

Cook garlic and onion in butter over medium heat until soft. Chop sauerkraut very fine. Add cooked onion and garlic, bacon bits or ham, parsley and potatoes; mix thoroughly. Shape into 30 (1 inch) balls. Dip balls in milk, then coat with bread crumbs. Use at once or chill until needed. Fry in deep fat at 375° about 2 minutes. Balls can be frozen before or after frying.

Daisy Mace

SPINACH CASSEROLE

4 (10 oz.) pkg. frozen
   chopped spinach
1 pkg. cream cheese
Salad dressing mix

1½ c. sour cream
½ (4 oz.) can mushroom juice
   (save drained
   mushrooms for topping)

Cook spinach and drain well; add rest of ingredients and put in casserole. Top with whole mushrooms. Bake for 15 to 20 minutes, uncovered, at 350°.

Helen Russman

EXOTIC SPINACH CASSEROLE

2 (10 oz.) pkg. chopped
   spinach
1½ pt. sour cream

1 pkg. onion soup mix
2 Tbsp. sherry wine

Cook spinach; drain thoroughly. Add sour cream, onion soup and wine. Place in a 1½ quart casserole. Bake 15 to 20 minutes at 325°. Serves 8 to 10.

Dorothy O'Neal

SQUASH AU GRATIN

3 medium yellow squash	¼ tsp. pepper
½ c. onion, chopped	3 Tbsp. butter
¼ c. water	1 c. herb seasoned croutons
1 tsp. salt	½ c. grated Cheddar cheese

Wash and trim squash; slice ¼ inch thick. Put in skillet with onion, water, salt and pepper. Cook until tender, 10 or 12 minutes. Drain. Put in 1 tablespoon butter; stir. Melt 2 tablespoons butter in skillet. Stir in croutons. Heat over very low heat. Put squash in bowl. Top with croutons and cheese.

Patti Roby

SQUASH CASSEROLE
(Yellow summer squash)

2 c. cooked squash, drained	1 tsp. salt
1 stick butter	Dash of pepper
½ c. milk	1½ c. cheese, diced
1 small or medium onion,	1 - 1½ c. cracker crumbs
diced	(save part for topping)
2 eggs	

Combine all ingredients and pour into a buttered casserole dish. Top with reserved crumbs and bake 30 to 40 minutes at 325°.

Betty Jo Yeary

SQUASH CASSEROLE
(Tastes like dressing - only better)

1 qt. squash	1 stick butter
1 large onion	Corn bread crumbs (1 - 2 c.
1 egg	approx. or until liquids
Dash of sugar	are absorbed)
Salt and pepper to taste	Sage to taste

1546-85

Cook squash and onion together until tender and drain off water. Add egg, sugar, salt, pepper, butter, corn bread crumbs and sage. Place in a baking dish and bake at 450° until brown.

Shirley Cates

SQUASH CASSEROLE

2 lb. yellow summer squash
1 medium onion
½ tsp. salt
1 stick butter, melted
1 can cream of chicken soup

1 (8 oz.) ctn. sour cream
1 can water chestnuts
1 (8 oz.) pkg. Pepperidge
    Farm herb seasoned
    stuffing

Cut up squash; dice onion and cook until tender. Drain. Dice water chestnuts and add all remaining ingredients to squash and mix well. Place in large casserole and bake 30 minutes at 350°. Serves 16.

A small amount of stuffing can be spread over top, if you like.

Jimmie Dillman

YELLOW SQUASH CASSEROLE

1½ - 2 c. cooked squash
1 medium size onion
1 (4 oz.) pkg. grated cheese
1 c. (about 2 slices) cubed
    bread

1 egg
1 c. milk

Cook, drain and mash squash. Stir in chopped onion. Season with salt and pepper. Arrange squash, cheese and bread in alternate layers in buttered baking dish. Beat egg and milk together. Pour over layers in casserole. Bake in 375° oven 30 to 40 minutes.

Betty T. King

SQUASH ON GRILL

¼ c. vegetable oil
3 Tbsp. lemon juice
½ tsp. salt
¼ tsp. pepper
1 clove garlic, crushed

¼ tsp. crushed rosemary
½ tsp. Worcestershire sauce
2 zucchini
2 yellow squash

Combine lemon juice, salt, pepper, garlic, rosemary, and Worcestershire sauce. Stir well. Cut squash in two lengthwise. Score cut sides with ½ inch deep diagonal cuts and put in baking dish, cut side down.

Pour oil mixture over and let stand several hours. Drain squash and put on grill 4 inches above heat. Cook 15 minutes or until tender when pierced with a fork.

Patti Roby

SUMMER SQUASH ITALIANE
(Microwave)

3 Tbsp. butter
1 onion, minced
1 garlic clove, minced
1 small green pepper
4 medium tomatoes, peeled
    and sliced

Oregano to taste
½ tsp. salt
1 - 1½ lb. squash, sliced
1 c. Parmesan cheese

Cook butter on HIGH with first 4 ingredients for 4 minutes. Stir in squash, tomatoes, and salt. Cover and cook on HIGH for 8 minutes. Stir. If necessary, cook 2 minutes more. Top with Parmesan cheese and brown cheese 4 to 5 minutes.

Sharon Sherman

SAUTEED CHAYOTE SQUASH WITH TOMATOES

2 chayote squash
2 Tbsp. unsalted butter
1 medium onion, minced
1 (16 oz.) can tomatoes,
    drained and chopped
1 Tbsp. fresh parsley,
    chopped
Pinch of sugar

Pinch of thyme
1 Tbsp. fresh parsley,
    chopped
1½ tsp. salt (or to taste)
¼ tsp. pepper (or to taste)
Fresh parsley, chopped (for
    garnish)

Cut chayotes into 1 inch cubes; discard center seed. Saute onion in melted butter over medium low heat until soft, but not brown, 5 to 7 minutes. Add chayotes; stir to coat with onion; add tomatoes, parsley, sugar, thyme, and salt and pepper to taste. Bring to a boil; cover; reduce heat and slowly simmer for 20 minutes or until tender. Adjust seasonings to taste and serve garnished with fresh parsley.

Dee Dee Millen

BROILED TOMATOES WITH SOUR CREAM

4 tomatoes
Salt and pepper to taste
⅓ c. sour cream

⅓ c. mayonnaise
⅛ tsp. curry powder

Wash and core tomatoes. Do not peel. Cut in half, crosswise. Sprinkle with salt and pepper. Blend remaining ingredients. Spread on cut sides of tomatoes. Broil until mixture is bubbly, 5 to 10 minutes.

Patti Roby

CHEESE STUFFED TOMATOES ON GRILL

3 large tomatoes, cut in
   halves
¼ c. soft Italian bread crumbs
2 Tbsp. butter, melted

Dash of salt and pepper
2 oz. Monterey Jack or
   Mozzarella cheese
Chopped parsley

Scoop out center of each tomato and chop into pulp; set aside. Combine crumbs, butter, salt and pepper. Stir in cheese and tomato pulp; fill tomato shells with crumb mixture. Wrap each stuffed half in foil. Place on grill and cook 10 to 15 minutes until cheese is melted. Remove foil; sprinkle with parsley.

Patti Robey

ESCALLOPED TOMATOES

1 can tomatoes
1 onion, chopped
2 or 3 slices toasted bread
½ c. brown sugar

2 Tbsp. butter
Dash of salt
¼ c. dried parsley

Mash up tomatoes. Saute onion in butter. Add to tomatoes. Add brown sugar, dash of salt and broken up toasted bread. Mix well and cook for a few minutes over low heat. If it gets too dry, add a tablespoon of water. Add parsley and mix well.

Zella Mae Cox

GREEN TOMATO PIE

Slice small green tomatoes thin. Fill unbaked pie crust with tomatoes, 2 tablespoons flour, ¾ cup sugar, 3 tablespoons butter, ¼ teaspoon nutmeg and 2 tablespoons vinegar. Cover with crust and bake at

450° until crust begins to brown. Then set at 350° and bake until tomatoes are tender.

You can slice the tomatoes thin in the fall and freeze for winter pies. Delicious with roast.

Helen Russman

MARINATED TOMATOES

5 large, ripe tomatoes
¼ c. salad oil
1½ Tbsp. lemon juice
½ garlic clove, minced

½ tsp. salt
½ tsp. oregano leaves
⅛ tsp. pepper

Peel tomatoes and cut in thick slices. Combine ingredients; pour over tomatoes. Chill. Stir once or twice.

Patti Roby

SCALLOPED TOMATOES

2 Tbsp. butter or margarine, divided
3 slices bread, toasted
1 (14½ oz.) can tomatoes, drained (liquid reserved)
¼ c. onion, chopped

1 tsp. minced parsley
½ tsp. basil
¼ tsp. salt
¼ tsp. sugar
⅛ tsp. pepper

Spread 1 teaspoon butter on each slice of toast; cut in quarters. Place 6 pieces buttered side down in shallow 1 quart baking dish. Cut tomatoes in halves; place cut side up over bread; set aside. In small saucepan, saute onion in remaining 1 tablespoon butter until tender. Stir in remaining ingredients and the tomato liquid; heat through. Pour over tomatoes. Arrange remaining toast around sides of baking dish. Bake in preheated 350° oven 10 minutes or until heated. Serves 4.

Paula Brauner

VEGETABLE CASSEROLE

3 cans mixed vegetables
1 can sliced water chestnuts
1½ sticks butter

1 (16 oz.) jar Cheez Whiz
1 pkg. Ritz crackers

Butter 2½ quart dish; melt ½ stick butter; pour over drained vegetables. Place on drained water chestnuts; melt Cheez Whiz and pour over other ingredients; cover with crushed Ritz crackers; dot with 1 stick of butter. Bake at 350° for 30 minutes.

Patsy Ford

VEGETABLE CASSEROLE

1 pkg. frozen French green
    beans
1 pkg. frozen green peas

1 pkg. frozen small green
    limas

Cook separately and drain.

1 can water chestnuts (not
    chopped fine)
1 medium onion
1¼ c. mayonnaise
1 tsp. mustard (prepared)

1 tsp. Worcestershire sauce
¼ tsp. Tabasco
Juice of lemon
Garlic salt to taste
Salt to taste

Mix and bake 30 minutes at 350°. Chop 3 hard-boiled eggs and place on top (after cooking). Serves 8 or 9.

Clara Nance

VEGETABLE NECKLACE

1 pkg. frozen Brussels
    sprouts
1 head cauliflower
2 Tbsp. chopped onion
2 Tbsp. chopped green
    pepper

2 Tbsp. pimento
1 can Cheddar cheese soup
2 Tbsp. margarine

Cook Brussels sprouts; steam head of cauliflower. While cooking, saute green pepper and onion. Remove from heat; add pimento. Drain Brussels sprouts and cauliflower. Place cauliflower on plate and place sprouts around head. Add cheese to sauteed mix and pour over vegetables.

Lil Pasinski

TANGY WINTER VEGETABLES

½ c. salad oil
1 (16 oz.) bag carrots, cut into
   ½ inch thick slices
2 medium onions, each cut
   into quarters
Salt
Pepper

4 (10 oz.) containers Brussels
   sprouts, each cut in half
½ c. water
2 Tbsp. white wine vinegar
¾ tsp. sugar
½ tsp. basil

About 3 hours before serving or day ahead: In 8 quart Dutch oven, over medium high heat, in hot salad oil, cook carrots, onions, ¾ teaspoon salt and ⅛ teaspoon pepper until vegetables are tender, about 10 minutes, stirring frequently. With slotted spoon, remove carrot mixture to large bowl. To oil remaining in Dutch oven, over high heat, add Brussels sprouts, 2 teaspoons salt and ⅛ teaspoon pepper. Stir until Brussels sprouts are coated with oil. Add water; heat to boiling. Reduce heat to medium; cover Dutch oven and cook Brussels sprouts about 10 minutes or until tender crisp, stirring occasionally. Remove Brussels sprouts and liquid to bowl with carrot mixture. Add vinegar, sugar and basil to vegetables in bowl; with rubber spatula, toss gently to mix well. Cover and refrigerate vegetable mixture at least 2 hours to blend flavors, tossing occasionally. Makes 12 accompaniment servings.

Mary V. Stanley

BAKED ZUCCHINI

1½ c. cracker crumbs
¼ c. butter or margarine
1 lb. unpared zucchini,
   shredded
1½ tsp. onion

1 egg, beaten
1½ tsp. salt
¼ tsp. pepper
½ c. Cheddar cheese,
   shredded

Mix together cracker crumbs and butter; set aside ½ cup for topping. Mix shredded zucchini, onion, egg, salt, pepper, shredded cheese and cracker crumbs. Place in 1½ quart greased casserole. Top with cracker crumbs. Bake at 325° for 1 hour.

CREOLE ZUCCHINI

2 lb. sliced zucchini
1 c. onion, chopped
1 garlic clove, minced
¾ c. green pepper, chopped
¼ c. salad oil or butter
4 tomatoes, peeled and
　　chopped

1½ tsp. salt
¼ tsp. pepper
¼ c. chopped parsley
¼ c. Parmesan cheese

In a skillet, saute onion, garlic and green pepper in oil until soft. Add zucchini, tomatoes, salt and pepper. Cover and cook over medium heat until tender, about 20 minutes. Serve topped with parsley and cheese.

Patti Roby

ZUCCHINI CHEESE PUDDING

4 small zucchini, sliced thin
1 Tbsp. fresh thyme, minced
2 Tbsp. butter
4 eggs
1 c. milk

½ c. heavy cream
¾ c. grated Parmesan cheese
1 c. grated Swiss cheese
Tabasco sauce to taste
Soda crackers

Preheat oven to 350°. Saute the zucchini and thyme in butter until squash is tender. Beat the eggs, milk, heavy cream, Parmesan and Tabasco until thoroughly mixed. Arrange a layer of crackers in a well buttered ovenproof dish. Top with half each of egg mixture, squash, and Swiss cheese. Repeat layers. Let stand 20 minutes, then bake about 35 to 40 minutes or until puffy and browned. Serve hot. Serves 4 to 6.

Paula Childress

GARDEN ZUCCHINI

2 or 3 sliced zucchini
　　(depending on size)
2 or 3 sliced tomatoes
2 thinly sliced dry onions or 4
　　or 5 chopped green
　　onions

1 Tbsp. Mrs. Dash seasoning
　　(optional, but good)
Butter or margarine
Parmesan cheese, grated
Salt and pepper to taste

Preheat oven to 350°. Layer half of zucchini, tomatoes and onions in buttered baking dish. Sprinkle with half of Mrs. Dash seasoning, Parmesan cheese, salt and pepper. Dot liberally with butter or margarine. Layer remaining ingredients in the same manner. Cover with foil and bake 30 minutes or until onion is tender.

Joyce Dean

RATATOUILLE

Olive oil
2 onions, chopped fine
2 peppers, chopped
3 - 4 zucchini, sliced thin
1 small eggplant

4 tomatoes, peeled, seeded, chopped
½ c. parsley, chopped
1 clove garlic, crushed
Grated Parmesan cheese

Preheat oven to 250°. Heat some oil in a skillet; saute onions until they begin to color. Add peppers; saute a few more minutes. Add zucchini and eggplant; add a little more oil if necessary. Cook about 5 minutes, then put all vegetables in a baking dish and add tomatoes. Cover and cook in the oven for 1¼ hours. Add parsley, garlic and seasoning; cook 20 more minutes. Sprinkle generously with cheese before serving.

Zella M. Cox

ZUCCHINI CASSEROLE

3 c. diced zucchini
2 c. shredded carrots
1 grated onion (can be left out)

1 can cream of chicken soup
½ c. sour cream

Pour into 2 quart dish.

Topping:

½ pkg. Pepperidge Farm stuffing

½ c. melted butter

Bake 25 to 35 minutes at 350°.

Mary Leslie Bogar

ZUCCHINI PIE

3 medium zucchini
3 Tbsp. butter
½ clove garlic
¼ tsp. salt
⅛ tsp. dill weed

⅛ tsp. pepper
2 eggs, beaten
1 c. Monterey Jack cheese,
 cubed

Slice zucchini into ¼ inch pieces. Saute in butter until crispy tender, about 5 minutes. Pour into a buttered 9 inch pie pan. Pour eggs over zucchini and top with cheese. Bake at 325° for 45 minutes.

Mary Leslie Bogar

ZUCCHINI PIE

3 medium zucchini
3 Tbsp. butter
½ clove garlic
¼ tsp. salt
⅛ tsp. dill weed

⅛ tsp. pepper
2 eggs, beaten
1 c. Monterey Jack cheese,
 cubed

Slice zucchini into ¼ inch pieces. Saute in butter until crispy tender, about 5 minutes. Pour into a buttered 9 inch pie pan. Pour eggs over zucchini and top with cheese. Bake at 325° for 45 minutes.

Mary Leslie Bogar

Main Dishes

COOKING MEAT AND POULTRY

ROASTING
- Use tender cuts of beef, veal, pork or lamb and young birds.
- Place meat fat side up, or poultry breast side up, on rack in foil-lined shallow roasting pan. Do not add water; do not cover.
- Insert meat thermometer in center of thickest part of meat, being careful that end does not touch bone, fat or gristle.
- Roast at 300 to 350 degrees to desired degree of doneness.

BROILING
- Use tender beef steaks, lamb chops, sliced ham, ground meats and poultry quarters or halves. Fresh pork should be broiled slowly to insure complete cooking in center. Steaks and chops should be at least 1/2 inch thick.
- Preheat oven to "broil". Place meat on rack in foil-lined broiler pan.
- Place meat on oven rack 2 to 5 inches from the heat source, with thicker meat placed the greater distance. Brush poultry with butter.
- Broil until top side is browned; season with salt and pepper.
- Turn; brown second side. Season and serve at once.

PANBROILING
- Use the same cuts suitable for broiling.
- Place skillet or griddle over medium-high heat. Preheat until a drop of water dances on the surface.
- Place meat in skillet; reduce heat to medium. Do not add water or cover. The cold meat will stick at first, but as it browns it will loosen. If juices start to cook out of the meat, increase heat slightly.
- When meat is brown on one side, turn and brown second side.

PANFRYING
- Use comparatively thin pieces of meat, meat that has been tenderized by pounding or scoring, meat that is breaded and chicken parts.
- Place skillet over medium-high heat. Add a small amount of shortening—2 tablespoons will usually be sufficient.
- When shortening is hot, add meat or poultry. Cook as in panbroiling.

BRAISING
- Use for less tender cuts of meat or older birds. You can also braise pork chops, steaks and cutlets; veal chops, steaks and cutlets; and chicken legs and thighs.
- Brown meat on all sides as in panfrying. Season with salt and pepper.
- Add a small amount of water—or none if sufficient juices have already cooked out of the meat. Cover tightly.
- Reduce heat to low. Cook until tender, turning occasionally. Meats will cook in their own juices.

COOKING IN LIQUID
- Use less tender cuts of meat and stewing chickens. Browning of large cuts or whole birds is optional, but it does develop flavor and improve the color.
- Brown meat on all sides in hot shortening in saucepan.
- Add water or stock to cover meat. Simmer, covered, until tender.
- Add vegetables to allow time to cook without becoming mushy.

MAIN DISHES

PORK

AUSTRIAN HAM AND NOODLE DISH

½ lb. wide noodles, broken
1 lb. cooked ham, diced
1 c. light cream
2 eggs, beaten
2 Tbsp. melted butter

¾ tsp. salt
½ tsp. pepper
½ c. grated Parmesan or
   Swiss cheese

Cook and drain noodles. Combine with ham. Place in buttered baking dish. Beat cream and eggs together. Add salt and pepper to taste. Pour over ham and noodles. Sprinkle with cheese and butter. Bake in preheated oven (350°) for 45 minutes. Makes 4 to 6 servings.

R. A. Bratcher

BAKED PICNIC HAM

1 (4½ lb.) picnic ham
1 c. brown sugar
1 c. water

½ c. vinegar
1 small Coke

Wash ham; place in roaster, skin side down. Pour remaining ingredients over ham. Cover and bake at 400° for 2 hours and 30 minutes or until tender. Remove skin and top fat from ham. Sprinkle with additional brown sugar; brown top slightly. Cool; slice. Yield: 8 servings.

Phyllis L. Davis

BROCCOLI AND HAM CASSEROLE

10 oz. fresh or frozen broccoli
1 c. cooked chopped ham
2 Tbsp. green peppers,
   chopped
2 hard-boiled eggs, chopped
¼ c. American cheese,
   grated

1 Tbsp. chopped parsley
1 Tbsp. chopped onion
4 Tbsp. lemon juice
1½ c. light cream sauce
1 c. buttered bread crumbs

Cook broccoli; cut into 1 inch pieces and place in buttered casserole. Combine ham with parsley, green peppers, eggs, cheese, onion, and lemon juice; cover broccoli with ham mixture. Top with cream sauce. Sprinkle buttered crumbs on top. Bake at 350° for 20 minutes.

Helen Russman

CANNED HAM

Scrape gelatin off Armours canned ham. Put ham in pan. Coat ham with honey or syrup. Pat brown sugar on it and sprinkle powdered cloves all over. Cover with 2 layers of aluminum foil. Bake in 325° oven for 2 hours.

Raisin Sauce: Use as many raisins as you want (½ cup). Cover well with water and boil until tender, but don't let them get mushy. Pour in the juice that cooked out of the ham; pour in some orange juice (to cut down on sweetness), taste, may need more cloves. Thicken with cornstarch, thinned with cold water. You may pour Raisin Sauce over ham. Keeps it from drying out.

Clara Nance

CREAMED HAM AND CHICKEN

1 c. fresh mushrooms, chopped
2 green peppers, cut in 1 inch pieces, blanched
1 Tbsp. melted butter
1 boiled chicken, diced
4 c. cooked ham, diced
2 c. medium thick cream sauce
½ c. sweet cream
2 egg yolks, beaten
1 can pimientos, drained, cut in 1 inch pieces

Saute mushrooms and green peppers in the butter. Add chicken and ham, then cream sauce and simmer until well heated. Season with salt. Combine cream with beaten eggs and add to chicken mixture. Add pimientos last. Stir well, bring to boiling point only; sauce will curdle if allowed to boil. Serve on toast. Serves 6.

Eldred Sykes

HAM AND APRICOT PIE

1 slice (about 1½ lb.) ham (1 inch thick)
Prepared mustard
1 c. dried apricots, soaked overnight
3 Tbsp. seedless raisins
3 - 4 Tbsp. gravy or water
6 medium potatoes, peeled and sliced
1 Tbsp. butter or margarine

Preheat oven to 375°. Brown ham lightly on both sides. Put it into a deep baking dish; spread lightly with mustard and sprinkle with pepper. Arrange apricots and raisins on top. Add gravy or water and cover with slices of potato. Sprinkle very lightly with salt and dot with butter. Cover with waxed paper and bake for ¾ hour. Remove the paper and bake for 15 to 20 minutes more.

Paula Childress

HAM AND EGG PATTIES

Filling:

1½ c. ground cooked ham	2 - 3 Tbsp. medium cream
2 boiled eggs, chopped	sauce
⅛ tsp. prepared mustard	Egg or milk to glaze

Preheat oven to 425°. Roll out pastry (for a 9 inch (2 crusted) pie) to ⅛ to ¼ inch thick and cut into rounds about 4½ to 5 inches across. Mix ham and eggs; add salt, pepper, mustard and enough sauce to bind. Divide mixture between the pastry rounds; moisten edges and fold over. Crimp edges together; glaze with egg or milk and bake about 25 minutes.

Teresa Stroup

OLD KENTUCKY HAM

12 - 15 lb. country ham	Pineapple slices
2 c. brown sugar	Apricot halves
½ c. mixed pickling spices	Cherries
Cloves	

Let ham stand in cold water to cover overnight. Next morning, drain; cover again with cold water. Add 2 cups brown sugar and ½ cup mixed pickling spices. Bring to a boil and simmer for 4 or 5 hours. Take off stove and let cool in own liquor, usually overnight. Remove from liquor; cut off skin and trim off excess fat. The ham may be decorated with pineapple slices, apricot halves, cherries, cloves and brown sugar. Put under broiler long enough to glaze and brown. When ham is cold, cut in paper thin slices and serve with beaten biscuits.

Paula White

OLD KENTUCKY HAM CROQUETTES

1 c. ground ham	½ tsp. dry mustard
1 c. thick white sauce	1 egg, beaten
1 Tbsp. Worcestershire sauce	Toasted bread crumbs

Grind ham; mix all ingredients, except bread crumbs. Shape into croquettes and roll in bread crumbs. These can be prepared ahead and frozen, then baked for 30 minutes in 350° oven when needed.

Dee Dee Millen

HAM LOAF

1½ lb. cooked lean pork,
  ground
1½ lb. cooked ham, ground
1 (10½ oz.) can tomato soup
1½ c. milk
2 eggs
1 c. cracker crumbs

½ c. onion, chopped
½ c. green pepper, chopped
1½ tsp. monosodium
  glutamate
½ tsp. salt
¼ tsp. pepper

Grind pork and ham together. Mix all ingredients together. Pack mixture into a greased loaf pan. Bake in 350° oven for 1½ hours. Pour off juices before unmolding.

Rosemary Ramirez

HAM AND POTATO BAKE

1 can cream of mushroom
  soup
½ - ¾ c. milk
Dash of pepper
4 c. sliced potatoes

1 c. diced cooked ham
1 small onion
1 Tbsp. butter
Dash of paprika

Combine soup, milk and pepper. In buttered 2 quart casserole, arrange layers of potatoes, ham, onion and soup. Be sure ham is covered to prevent drying. Dot top with butter. Sprinkle with paprika. Cover; bake in 375° oven for 1 hour. Uncover and bake 15 more minutes or until potatoes are done. May substitute 1 cup diced cooked chicken for ham. Yield: 6 servings.

Lil Pasinski

HAM AND POTATO

1 can cream of celery soup
½ c. milk
1 tsp. salt
½ tsp. pepper
1 c. diced ham (cooked)

3 c. thinly sliced potatoes
1 onion, sliced thin or
  chopped
3 Tbsp. margarine
Paprika

196

Combine first 4 ingredients. Place ham, potatoes and onions in layers in 2 quart casserole. Pour first 4 ingredients over preceding; sprinkle with paprika and dot with margarine. Bake, covered, for 45 minutes at 375°. Uncover and bake 15 minutes.

Velma Pace

HAM AND POTATO CROQUETTES

3 potatoes
½ c. minced leftover ham
1 egg
Salt to taste

Pepper to taste
Nutmeg
3 Tbsp. cooking oil
3 Tbsp. margarine

Peel potatoes; grate and rinse. Mix with ham and egg; season with salt, pepper and nutmeg. Mix well. Shape into small croquettes. Heat oil and butter in a skillet; saute the croquettes until golden on both sides. Place on a hot serving dish and keep warm. Makes 12 to 15 croquettes.

Note: You can roll the croquettes in flour.

Heidi Thompson

HAM AND RICE CASSEROLE

¼ c. margarine
½ c. onion, chopped
2 c. cooked ham, chopped
1 c. cooked rice
3 c. chicken broth
1 can tomatoes, mashed

2 Tbsp. parsley flakes
½ tsp. dried thyme
Salt to taste
Pepper to taste
1½ c. Cheddar cheese,
  grated

Saute onion in margarine; add ham and cook about 10 minutes. Add other ingredients and simmer until rice has absorbed most of the liquid, about 25 minutes. Pour into a well greased baking dish. Sprinkle grated Cheddar cheese on top and bake in 350° oven about 30 minutes or until cheese melts and is nicely browned.

Melanie Davis

HAM STEW

3 c. water
3 cans mixed vegetables
1 onion, chopped
Salt to taste

1 (6 oz.) can tomato sauce
½ can (6½ oz.) ham, chopped
2 Tbsp. cornstarch
½ c. water

Mix together first 6 ingredients and cook for 30 minutes. Mix 2 tablespoons cornstarch in ½ cup cold water. Gradually pour into soup and stir constantly. Let it come to a boil again, then serve.

Ann Brawand

HAM STUFFED POTATOES

6 potatoes
¾ c. diced ham
¼ c. chopped green pepper
2 Tbsp. onion, chopped fine

½ tsp. salt
¼ tsp. black pepper
1¼ c. sour cream
½ c. Swiss cheese, shredded

Bake potatoes at 400° for 1 hour until done. Cut thin slice off top of potatoes. Scoop out potato. Break up potato with a fork, but don't mash. Combine potato, ham, green pepper, onion, salt and pepper. Add enough sour cream to moisten. Put back into shells. Top with cheese. Bake at 400° for 15 or 20 minutes or until golden.

Patti Roby

SWEET AND SOUR HAM LOAF

1 lb. ground cooked ham
½ lb. ground fresh pork
½ c. soft bread crumbs
½ c. water
1 egg
¼ c. celery, minced

1 Tbsp. instant minced onion
¼ tsp. pepper
⅓ c. brown sugar
1 Tbsp. prepared mustard
1 Tbsp. vinegar

Mix together ham, pork, crumbs, water, egg, celery, onion and pepper. Pack firm into a baking dish. Mix sugar, mustard and vinegar; pour over top. Bake at 350° for 50 minutes.

Bill Tomes

HAM TETRAZZINI

2 c. diced cooked ham
6 Tbsp. butter or margarine
6 Tbsp. flour
2 c. milk
⅛ tsp. marjoram
½ c. grated sharp Cheddar
    cheese

½ lb. fresh mushrooms,
    sliced
2 Tbsp. chopped pimento
1 (8 oz.) pkg. spaghetti
1 c. buttered bread crumbs
Dash of black pepper (if
    desired)

Melt butter and blend in flour. Gradually add milk, pepper and marjoram; cook, stirring constantly, until thickened. Add cheese and stir until blended. Add mushrooms, pimento and ham. Cook spaghetti in boiling salted water. Drain. Arrange spaghetti in a greased 2 quart casserole. Pour ham mixture over spaghetti and sprinkle with buttered bread crumbs. Bake in moderate oven (350°) for 20 to 30 minutes. Serves 6 to 8 people.

Emylie E. DeLong

BACON AND APPLE PIE

½ lb. bacon slices, cut in
    strips
1 large onion, chopped
1 lb. cooking apples, peeled
    and sliced thin
2 tsp. dried sage

3 tsp. sugar
Pie crust for an 8 inch pie
Milk
Salt
Pepper

Line an 8 inch pie pan with the strips of bacon. Arrange layers of onion and apples on top; sprinkle each layer with sage, salt, pepper and sugar. Cover with pastry; brush with a little milk to glaze and bake for 25 minutes. Reduce heat to 350°. Cover with foil if browning too quickly and cook 10 to 15 minutes longer. Serves 4 or 5.

Dee Dee Bond

BACON CRUST PIE

Bacon Crust:

2 c. ground lean bacon
1 small can tomato puree
½ c. bread crumbs

1 small onion, chopped fine
¼ c. green pepper, chopped

Mix all ingredients for the crust together; knead well and press into the bottom of an 8 to 9 inch pie plate. Flute around the edge.

Filling:

1 c. cooked rice
1 small can tomato puree

⅛ tsp. oregano
1¼ c. grated Gruyere cheese

Preheat oven to 375°. Mix rice, tomato puree, oregano, salt, pepper and 1 cup of cheese and spoon into the pie shell. Cover with wax paper and bake for 15 to 20 minutes. Remove paper; sprinkle with remaining cheese and brown lightly under a hot broiler. Serves 4 to 5.

Melissa Jackson

CHEESE, BACON AND TOMATO PIE

Pastry for an 8 - 9 inch (2
   crust) pie
6 oz. bacon slices
2 - 3 tomatoes, peeled and
   sliced

½ lb. Cheddar cheese, cut in
   thin slices or slices of
   process cheese
Cayenne pepper
1 egg or milk to glaze

Preheat oven to 450°. Line an 8 to 9 inch pie plate with half the pastry and prick the bottom. Cut bacon slices in 2 or 3 pieces and put half in the bottom of the pie shell. Cover with half the tomatoes; sprinkle sparingly with salt and generously with cayenne pepper. Cover with half the cheese slices and repeat layers. Dampen edge of pastry and cover with remaining pastry. Press edges together. Make a hole in center and decorate pie with pastry leaves made from trimmings. Glaze with beaten egg or milk; bake 30 to 40 minutes. Serve hot with tomato sauce or cold with salad. Serves 4 or 5.

Denise Figg

EGG AND BACON PIE

1 recipe Basic Pastry plus ½
   c. grated cheese
2 Tbsp. butter
2 or 3 onions, chopped
6 slices bacon, chopped
3 eggs

2 c. milk
½ tsp. dry mustard
2 tsp. chopped parsley
Salt
Pepper

Preheat oven to 375°. Line a deep 8 inch pie plate with pastry. Heat butter; add onion and bacon; fry for 3 or 4 minutes. Beat eggs in a bowl; add warmed milk; drain onion and bacon. Add salt, pepper, mustard and parsley. Pour into pie shell and cook for 35 to 40 minutes. If desired, garnish with extra pieces of bacon. Serves 6.

Note: Basic Pastry is used for this pie, but the flavor is improved with a little cheese. It can be added to the flour before cutting in the shortening.

Denise Figg

CHEESE CORN MEAL MUSH WITH BACON

1 tsp. salt
½ c. corn meal
1 c. grated Parmesan cheese

¼ tsp. paprika
8 strips bacon

200

Add salt to 1 cup water in top of double boiler and bring to a boil. Mix corn meal with 1 cup cold water and stir into boiling water. Boil; stir constantly until corn meal thickens. Then place over simmering water in the bottom part of double boiler; cover and simmer 30 minutes. Stir in ¾ cup cheese and paprika. (Recipe may be made ahead to this point and kept in refrigerator.) Fry bacon until crisp; drain on paper towel. Keep warm and pour off most of fat from pan. Spread mush in same pan and fry until brown on bottom. Turn mush to brown other side and sprinkle with remaining grated cheese. Serve with bacon. Serves 4.

Denise Figg

BACON CROQUETTES

10 oz. cooked bacon, minced
4 oz. mushrooms, minced
1 oz. green pepper, minced
1 oz. onion, minced
2 oz. cheese, grated

3 Tbsp. fresh bread crumbs
¼ tsp. thyme
2 eggs
Bread crumbs
Fat for frying

Mix all minced ingredients together with the cheese. Stir in the fresh bread crumbs and season with salt, pepper and thyme. Bind with beaten egg to a firm paste. Shape into croquettes on a floured board; chill in the refrigerator. Coat croquettes in egg and bread crumbs and fry in hot fat until golden brown. Drain on paper towel. Serve with chutney. Serves 4 to 6.

Denise Figg

BAKED PORK CHOPS WITH DRESSING

6 pork chops
¼ tsp. salt
⅛ tsp. pepper
1 Tbsp. cooking oil
½ c. onion, chopped
½ c. margarine
4½ c. bread cubes
½ c. water
½ tsp. poultry seasoning

¼ tsp. celery salt
¼ c. water
½ c. celery, chopped
3 medium potatoes, peeled
    and quartered
Cooking oil
1 (10½ oz.) can cream of
    mushroom soup

Season pork chops with salt and pepper. Brown in 1 tablespoon hot oil in a skillet. Remove from skillet and place in baking dish. Saute onion and celery in margarine in a small skillet. Combine with bread cubes, poultry seasoning, celery salt and ¼ cup water. Mix lightly. Shape dressing into mounds on top of chops. Coat potatoes with oil and place around chops. Combine soup and ½ cup water; pour over chops and potatoes. Bake in 350° oven for 1 hour or until meat is tender. Serves 6.

Paula White

CROCKPOT ISLANDER PORK

1 (3 lb.) pork roast	2 Tbsp. orange juice
5 or 6 whole cloves	2 Tbsp. honey
½ tsp. nutmeg	2 Tbsp. soy sauce
¼ tsp. paprika	2 tsp. lemon juice
¼ c. catsup	½ tsp. Kitchen Bouquet

Place roast on rack and broil 15 to 30 minutes or until brown. Stick the cloves in the meat. Place roast in crock pot. Sprinkle with nutmeg and paprika. Stir together catsup, orange juice, honey, soy sauce, lemon juice and Kitchen Bouquet. Pour over roast. Cover and cook on LOW 10 to 12 hours. (HIGH 4 to 6 hours.) Remove meat from crock pot. Juices may be thickened with 1½ tablespoons cornstarch and 2 tablespoons water. Cook on HIGH until thickened.

Ellen Jones

PORK PIE

1 medium size head cauliflower	Pinch of thyme
1 Tbsp. cooking oil	¼ tsp. paprika
2 small onions, chopped fine	3 Tbsp. flour
1 garlic clove, crushed	3 c. diced cooked pork
3½ c. canned tomatoes	Pastry for a 9 inch (1 crust) pie

Preheat oven to 450°. Cook cauliflower until just tender in boiling salt water. Drain and divide into small flowerets. Heat oil in a saute pan; add onion and garlic; saute for a few minutes. Add tomatoes, thyme, salt, pepper and paprika. Simmer 10 minutes, then press through a sieve. Blend the flour with a little cold water; add to the sauce and stir until boiling. Put the pork and cauliflower into a deep dish (about 2 quarts) and pour the sauce over. Cover with pastry and bake about 25 minutes or until crust is well browned.

Heidi Thompson

BAR-B-QUE PORK CHOPS "POR DOC"

6 - 8 extra thick loin pork
   chops (1½ inches thick)
Bacon drippings
⅓ lb. butter or margarine
1 c. very finely chopped
   onion
1 can frozen lemon juice

6 Tbsp. red wine vinegar
4 Tbsp. sugar
3 Tbsp. Worcestershire sauce
2 tsp. dry mustard
2 tsp. paprika
½ tsp. garlic powder
Few dashes of Tabasco sauce

Salt and pepper chops. Dust with flour and brown in bacon drippings. Place in baking dish in single layer. Melt butter. Add all other ingredients. Simmer for 5 minutes. Pour over chops. Cover baking pan and bake in 350° oven for 1½ hours or until fork tender. Baste from time to time with sauce.

Mrs. Jim (Ann Murphy) Kincheloe

PORK CHOPS AND RICE

4 pork chops
1 can beef broth (or bouillon
   cubes)
1 can pineapple tidbits

¼ c. chopped green peppers
¼ c. catsup
1 Tbsp. vinegar
1 Tbsp. brown sugar

Brown chops; pour off fat. Add remaining ingredients; cover and simmer 45 minutes. Stir occasionally. Mix 2 tablespoons water and 1 tablespoon of cornstarch. Stir into sauce. Cook until thickened. Serve with rice.

Flora Montgomery

PORK CHOP-POTATO CASSEROLE

6 potatoes, peeled and sliced
3 medium onions, sliced
½ lb. (2 c.) shredded Cheddar
   cheese
All-purpose flour

Salt
Pepper
Milk
6 large pork chops

Grease a large casserole. Place potato slices, onion slices and cheese in layers on bottom of casserole. Sprinkle each layer lightly with flour, salt and pepper. Pour enough milk over layers to fill pan 1 inch deep. Top with pork chops. Bake at 300° for 45 minutes or until pork chops are browned. Yield: 4 to 6 servings.

Phyllis L. Davis

1546-85

PORK CHOPS AND WILD RICE

4 loin pork chops, cut ¾ inch
 thick
½ c. chopped onion
1 c. uncooked rice, washed

1 (10½ oz.) can condensed
 beef broth
1⅓ c. water
1 medium tomato, sliced

Trim fat from chops and cook trimmings in skillet until 2 table-spoons of drippings have accumulated; remove trimmings. If you have an electric skillet, cook at 350°; slowly brown the chops on both sides. Remove chops. Cook onion in drippings until tender, but not brown. Add rice, broth and water. Return chops to skillet. Season with salt and pepper; cover; reduce heat to simmer, 225°. Cook until chops are tender, 50 to 60 minutes. Place tomato slices on chops; heat thoroughly. Serves 4.

Peggy Kessinger

SALT PORK AND GRAVY

1 lb. salt pork
2 c. milk
½ c. corn meal

3 Tbsp. bacon drippings
2 Tbsp. flour
2 Tbsp. pan drippings

Slice salt pork very thin. Soak in ½ cup milk a few minutes, then dip in corn meal. Heat bacon drippings; fry pork on each side until brown. Drain on paper toweling. Blend flour with 2 tablespoons of the pan drippings. Add 1½ cups milk and cook over low heat until thickened. Stir constantly; add salt and pepper to taste. Serves 6.

Angela Roth

SPANISH PORK CHOPS

Pork chops
Onions
Green peppers

Canned or fresh tomatoes
Uncooked rice

Take any number of pork chops that you may need and brown them in a small amount of fat. On top of each pork chop, place 1 slice of onion, 1 slice of tomato, 1 slice of green pepper and 1 heaping table-spoon of uncooked rice. Add salt and cover with hot water. Place in oven until rice is done and mixture has thickened.

Sherry Lynch

SPICY PORK CASSEROLE

6 pork chops
1 clove garlic
2 tsp. butter
2 cooking apples, peeled,
    cored and cut into ½ inch
    slices
2 onions, sliced

2 Tbsp. flour
1 Tbsp. lemon juice
2 c. applesauce
¼ tsp. ground cinnamon
¼ tsp. ground nutmeg
⅛ tsp. ground cloves

Preheat oven to 350°. Trim chops; rub both sides with a cut clove of garlic and sprinkle with salt and pepper. Put into a lightly buttered skillet and brown on both sides. Put a layer of apples and onions into a buttered casserole dish; arrange chops on top and cover with remaining apple and onion slices. Stir flour into the sediment in the skillet; add 2 cups boiling water and stir until thickened. Add lemon juice, applesauce and spices. Mix well and pour into the casserole. Cover and cook for 1½ hours; remove the lid for the last 20 minutes.

Melanie Davis

POZOLE

2 large fresh pork hocks
2 qt. water
1 (1 lb.) can tomatoes

2 (1 lb.) cans hominy, drained
2 medium onions, chopped
4 tsp. salt

Put pork, water, tomatoes, hominy, onions and salt in large kettle. Simmer 2 to 3 hours. Remove pork; cool both meat and soup. Remove meat from bones, discarding fat and bones. Before serving, return meat to soup and heat. Serve with assortment of chopped fresh vegetables (lettuce, green onions, radishes and lime wedge). Hot sauce may be added also. Serves 8 to 10.

Pablo Briseno

GREEK RICE AND PORK PILAF

¼ lb. pork, diced
3 slices bacon, diced
1 onion, chopped
1 c. uncooked rice
Salt and pepper to taste

2 c. hot water
2 small sweet red peppers,
    cut into 1 inch pieces
½ c. green peas, cooked

In a skillet, cook first 3 ingredients until pork is browned. Add rice, salt and pepper; cook for a few minutes. Pour off excess fat. Add hot water and peppers. Bring to a boil, then simmer, covered, for about 25 minutes or until rice is done. Add peas. Makes 4 servings.

Paula White

GREEK SAUSAGE

1½ lb. ground pork	1 Tbsp. garlic powder
½ lb. ground beef	3 Tbsp. beef bouillon
½ c. dry red wine	¾ tsp. cumin
1 egg	¼ tsp. cinnamon
¼ c. bread crumbs	2 Tbsp. margarine
½ tsp. marjoram	2 c. tomato sauce
3 Tbsp. parsley	1 c. dry red wine
Salt to taste	

Combine all ingredients, except last 3; blend thoroughly. Roll into small sausages. Melt butter in large skillet; add sausages and cook over low heat about 10 minutes. Brown on all sides. Add tomato sauce and 1 cup wine; cover and simmer 20 minutes.

Dee Dee Millen

HUNGARIAN PORK SAUSAGE LOAF

1 c. diced mushrooms	1 lb. fresh bulk pork sausage
1 Tbsp. butter	1 c. dry bread crumbs
1 egg, beaten	1 tsp. paprika

Melt butter in a skillet and add mushrooms. Saute. Combine sausage, mushrooms, egg and crumbs; shape into a loaf. Sprinkle with paprika. Place in a small roaster. Cover. Bake at 350° for ½ hour. Uncover; return to oven and bake 30 more minutes. Serves 4.

Teresa Stroup

INDIAN DAY PORK ROAST

4 lb. pork roast	1 clove garlic, mashed
2 c. tomato puree	1 tsp. dried sage
½ c. raisins	1 tsp. oregano
1 tsp. chili powder	2 tsp. salt
½ c. chopped sweet peppers	⅓ c. flour
1 Tbsp. onion, chopped	

Combine all the seasonings, except the chili powder. Rub into roast. Place roast fat side up in a baking pan and roast in a preheated 350° oven for 2½ to 3 hours. Reduce oven to 250°. Pour off drippings into a skillet and add onions and green pepper; saute until slightly wilted. Combine flour and chili powder. Add to skillet along with tomato puree and raisins and simmer 10 minutes; stir constantly, until sauce thickens. If sauce is too thin, add a little water gradually until sauce thickens. Return roast to pan; baste with sauce and roast 30 minutes more; baste 2 or 3 times. Yield: 6 to 8 servings.

Gwen Mills

ORIENTAL RIBS

3 lb. lean pork ribs
Salt and pepper
1 (7½ oz.) jar junior baby food
   strained peaches
⅓ c. catsup
⅓ c. vinegar

2 Tbsp. soy sauce
½ c. brown sugar
2 tsp. ground ginger
1 tsp. salt
Pepper

Rub ribs on both sides with salt and pepper. Place meaty side up in foil lined shallow pan. Bake at 400° for 45 minutes. Combine other ingredients to make sauce. At end of 45 minutes baking period, spoon off excess fat and cover ribs with sauce. Lower oven temperature to 325° and bake 1¾ hours, basting occasionally.

Terri Ramage

PAPRIKA PORK WITH SAUERKRAUT

2½ lb. pork shoulder meat
3 Tbsp. flour
3 tsp. salt
¼ tsp. pepper
3 Tbsp. oil
3 - 4 onions, sliced

2 Tbsp. paprika
2 (about 15 oz. each) cans
   sauerkraut
1 green pepper, chopped
1 c. sour cream

Preheat oven to 350°. Trim meat and cut into 1½ inch cubes. Mix flour with 1 teaspoon salt and half the pepper; dredge the meat thoroughly. Heat oil and saute meat until brown. Remove to a casserole. Brown onion in remaining oil; add paprika, 1½ cups water and the rest of the pepper. Simmer until all the brown pieces in the skillet are loosened. Add sauerkraut, green pepper and remaining 2 teaspoons salt. Mix well and pour over the meat in the casserole. Cover and cook for 1½ hours. Just before serving, adjust the seasoning and stir in sour cream. Serves 6.

Good served with rice, noodles or mashed potatoes.

Denise Figg

PORK BAR-B-Q

5 or 6 lb. pork loin end roast
1 bottle Kraft hickory smoke
  bar-b-q sauce
1 tsp. Colgen liquid smoke
2 Tbsp. Worcestershire sauce

Cook roast 12 hours on LOW in crock pot. When done, shred with a fork. Add Kraft hickory smoke bar-b-q sauce, liquid smoke and Worcestershire sauce. Return to cleaned crock pot and cook on LOW 3 to 4 hours. Reheat as needed. Freezes well.

I use pork loin end (Pinley Pig) Winn Dixie brand.

Brownie - Lois Bruner

PORK CHOPS IN SOUR CREAM

4 thick pork chops
Flour
½ c. sour cream
1 Tbsp. lemon juice
½ tsp. lemon rind, grated
1 tsp. sugar
½ tsp. powdered thyme
Orange or grapefruit sections
Honey
Salt and pepper

Preheat oven to 350°. Trim excess fat from chops and dredge lightly in flour. Put the fat trimmings into a saute pan and fry to render the fat. Remove the pieces of skin which remain; put the chops in the pan and brown lightly on both sides. Remove to a casserole. Mix cream, lemon juice, lemon rind, sugar, salt, pepper and thyme. Add ½ cup water and pour over the chops. Cover and cook for 45 to 50 minutes. Brush some sections of orange or grapefruit (or both) with a little honey and broil a few minutes. Garnish with the fruit. Serves 4.

Serve with green beans, spinach or sweet potatoes.

Paula White

PORK CUTLET CASSEROLE

1½ oz. drippings
4 pork cutlets
½ lb. mushrooms, sliced
1 onion, sliced
Black pepper
4 tomatoes
1 can condensed vegetable
  soup

Heat drippings and seal cutlets on both sides; put in an ovenproof dish. Turn the mushrooms and onions in the remaining fat and add to casserole. Season with salt and pepper, skin and slice tomatoes; add to casserole and pour in soup. Bake at 375° for about 45 minutes or until meat is tender.

Teresa Stroup

BARBECUE SPARERIBS

4 lb. country style ribs
1 c. sliced onions
1 c. catsup
½ c. chili sauce
2 tsp. salt
1 c. water

3 Tbsp. Worcestershire sauce
¼ c. vinegar
½ c. brown sugar
2 tsp. dry mustard
1 tsp. paprika
Juice of ½ lemon

Cut spareribs into serving pieces. Brown them in baking pan over surface heat. Combine the remaining ingredients and pour over ribs. Cover. Bake at 350° for 1 ¾ hours. Spoon the sauce over the ribs 2 or 3 times during the baking. Bake, uncovered, 20 minutes or until juice gets syrupy.

Nancy A. Thiry

PORK STEAKS WITH MUSHROOM GRAVY

6 lean pork steaks
½ tsp. salt
¼ tsp. pepper
2 Tbsp. cooking oil
1 c. onion, chopped
1 (8 oz.) can mushrooms

1 (10½ oz.) can condensed
    beef broth
2 tsp. Worcestershire sauce
1 c. evaporated milk
2 Tbsp. flour

Season pork steaks with salt and pepper. Brown well in hot oil. Remove steaks. Add onion and saute. Drain mushrooms; reserve liquid. Add reserved mushroom liquid, beef broth, Worcestershire sauce and meat to skillet. Cover and simmer for about an hour or until meat is tender. Remove meat and keep warm. Add mushrooms to pan juices in skillet. Bring mixture to a boil. Combine evaporated milk and flour. Stir slowly into hot liquid. Cook over medium heat; stir constantly until thickened. Serves 6.

Pam Thompson

RICE AND SAUSAGE

3 c. cooked rice
1 lb. sausage, chopped
1 small onion, chopped
1 small green pepper,
    chopped

2 tomatoes, coarsely
    chopped
Grated Cheddar cheese
Salt and pepper

Keep rice warm in colander over boiling water. Saute sausage until light brown; remove and drain; keep warm. Pour off all but about 1 tablespoon sausage fat from the skillet; add onion and green pepper; saute until soft, but not brown. Add tomatoes and saute 2 minutes. Combine rice, sausage and vegetables in a buttered casserole. Sprinkle with cheese and heat in a 350° oven until cheese is melted, 10 to 15 minutes. Season with salt and pepper to taste. Serves 6 to 8.

Melanie Davis

SAUSAGE-BEAN BAKE

1 lb. sweet Italian sausages,
    cut in 1 inch chunks
1 large onion, sliced
1 (16 oz.) jar meatless
    spaghetti sauce
3 medium potatoes
    (unpeeled), cut in ¾ inch
    cubes

1 (20 oz.) can white kidney
    beans, rinsed and
    drained
1 tsp. oregano
½ tsp. salt

In ovenproof skillet or casserole, cook sausages and onions over medium heat until sausages are browned and onion is tender. Stir in spaghetti sauce and potatoes, scraping up browned bits from bottom of skillet. Stir in beans, oregano and salt; cover. Bake in preheated 350° oven 30 minutes or until potatoes are tender. Serve immediately. Serves 4.

Charles T. Thompson

SAUSAGE CASSEROLE

4 slices bread, torn up
Sausage
1 c. grated cheese
6 eggs

2 c. milk
1 tsp. dry mustard
Salt and pepper

Put bread pieces in baking dish. Spoon sausage over bread and sprinkle with grated cheese. Beat eggs and milk; add dry mustard, salt and pepper. Pour over bread mixture. Bake in 350° oven for 35 minutes.

Barbara Montgomery

SAUSAGE EGGPLANT CASSEROLE

1 lb. sausage
1 large eggplant, peeled and
  cubed
1 large onion, sliced
1 large green pepper,
  chopped

1 (28 oz.) can tomatoes,
  chopped
½ c. tomato paste
Salt and pepper to taste
1 c. Romano cheese, grated

Cook sausage, onion and green pepper until sausage is browned; drain. Add remaining ingredients, except cheese. Simmer about 20 to 30 minutes or until eggplant is tender. Pour into a baking dish; sprinkle cheese on top. Put under broiler and let brown a little.

Cristy Lewis

SAUSAGE-NOODLE BAKE

1 lb. bulk pork sausage
4 oz. (2 c.) uncooked fine
  noodles
2 Tbsp. chopped pimento
2 Tbsp. chopped green
  pepper
¼ c. milk

1 can condensed cream of
  chicken soup
1 c. shredded sharp Cheddar
  cheese
1½ c. bread crumbs
1 Tbsp. butter or margarine,
  melted

Form sausage into balls the size of marbles; flatten into patties. Arrange on cooky sheet and bake in 350° oven until browned (or brown in a skillet). Drain. Cook noodles in boiling unsalted water until tender; drain. Combine patties, noodles, pimento, green pepper, milk, soup and cheese. Turn into greased 1½ quart casserole. Mix crumbs and butter; sprinkle over top. Bake in 350° oven about 1 hour. Makes 6 servings.

Mary Quandt

SAUSAGE PIE

Pastry for an 8 or 9 inch (1
  crust) pie
¾ c. margarine
1 small onion, chopped
4 Tbsp. cooked ham,
  chopped
1 c. mushrooms, sliced

1 Tbsp. flour
1 c. milk
⅛ tsp. grated nutmeg
1 egg yolk
2 Tbsp. heavy cream
8 small sausage links
2 - 3 Tbsp. grated cheese

Preheat oven to 450°. Line an 8 to 9 inch pie plate with pastry; prick the bottom and bake for 10 to 15 minutes. Remove from oven. Heat ¼ cup butter and saute onion, ham and mushrooms until onion is transparent, then set aside. Make a sauce with another ¼ cup butter, flour and milk. When smooth and thickened, add salt, pepper and nutmeg. Remove from heat; stir in egg yolk and cream. Saute sausages in remaining butter until light brown. Put onion and ham mixture into pie shell. Arrange sausages in casserole; pour sauce over; sprinkle with cheese and bake about 20 minutes. Serves 4 to 5.

Melissa Jackson

SAUSAGE PIE

Pastry for an 8 or 9 inch (1
  crust) pie
¾ c. margarine
1 small onion, chopped
4 Tbsp. chopped cooked ham
1 c. sliced mushrooms
1 Tbsp. flour

1 c. milk
⅛ tsp. nutmeg
1 egg yolk
2 Tbsp. heavy cream
8 small link sausages
2 to 3 Tbsp. grated cheese

Preheat oven to 450°. Line an 8 or 9 inch pie plate with the pastry; prick bottom and bake for 10 to 15 minutes. Remove from oven. Heat ¼ cup of the butter; saute onion, ham and mushrooms until onion is transparent, then set aside. Make a sauce with ¼ cup of the butter, flour and milk. When smooth and thickened, add salt, pepper and nutmeg. Remove from heat; stir in egg yolk and cream. Saute sausages in remaining butter until lightly browned. Put onion and ham mixture into pie shell. Arrange sausages in spoke fashion on top. Pour sauce over; sprinkle with cheese and bake about 20 minutes.

Heidi Thompson

212

SAUSAGE STUFFED PEPPERS

4 green peppers
1 lb. sausage
1 apple, peeled and diced
1 Tbsp. parsley, chopped

¼ c. dry bread crumbs
1 egg, beaten
1 (8 oz.) can tomato sauce
1 (4 oz.) can mushrooms

Cut tops off peppers and discard seeds and membranes. Fry sausage partially done; drain. Stir in apple, egg and bread crumbs. Fill peppers with mixture. Combine tomato sauce and mushrooms and pour over peppers. Bake in oven at 350° for 30 minutes or until done.

Note: Mushrooms can also be mixed into sausage mixture.

Bill Farris

SAUSAGE AND POTATO CASSEROLE

4 - 6 medium potatoes
1 - 2 onions
1 can creamed corn
1 lb. pkg. sausage

3 - 4 tsp. butter or margarine
Salt and pepper to taste
Ketchup
1 greased casserole dish

Slice potatoes and onions. Arrange in layers. (Potatoes, onions, creamed corn, etc., with pats of butter here and there.) Make sausage patties and place on top. Bake at 350° until sausage and potatoes are done. Dab sausage with ketchup and bake 5 minutes longer. Serve with tossed salad and rolls.

Wynola Sharon Davis

SCALLOPED POTATOES AND SAUSAGE

1 lb. smoked sausage
1 medium onion, sliced
Flour
6 medium potatoes

Salt
Pepper
Milk
Margarine

Wash, peel and slice the potatoes very thin. Place in baking dish. Fill dish ⅔ full with layers of potato and onion slices. Sprinkle each layer with salt, pepper, flour and dots of butter. Add milk until almost covered. Cover dish and place in 350° oven for 45 minutes. Remove and place sausages on top and return to oven for about 20 minutes or until sausage is done and browned.

Heidi Thompson

SAUSAGE QUICHE

1 lb. hot sausage
1 lb. mild sausage
1 small can mushrooms
1 medium onion, chopped
1 can mushroom soup

2 eggs
1 small (8 oz.) jar Cheez Whiz
1 (8 oz.) pkg. Velveeta cheese
2 deep dish frozen pie shells

Brown sausage; drain. Add onion. Saute until transparent. Add drained mushrooms. Divide between pie shells. Mix soup, eggs and half of the Velveeta in a blender. Pour over sausage, dividing between the 2 pies. Drizzle with Cheez Whiz. Slice remaining Velveeta and place on top. Bake 30 to 35 minutes at 350°. Watch edges of pie shell. Don't let them get too brown.

Rose Briseno

SMOKED SAUSAGE AND SAUERKRAUT

1 lb. smoked sausage
1 can sauerkraut
1 tsp. cooking oil
½ pt. water

1 large potato, grated
Salt to taste
½ tsp. sugar
2 onions, chopped

Heat oil in skillet and fry chopped onion; add sauerkraut and simmer a few minutes. Add the water and sausage; cook until done. Add the grated potato, salt and sugar. Cook 45 minutes longer.

Heidi Thompson

STUFFED BAKED SPARERIBS

4 lb. spareribs (2 equal
    pieces)
1 c. apples, chopped
1 c. bread cubes
¼ c. onion, chopped

3 Tbsp. margarine
1 Tbsp. sugar
2 Tbsp. flour
1 tsp. salt
1 tsp. paprika

Brown onion in margarine; add bread cubes and toss gently until lightly browned. Add apples, salt, sugar and paprika; mix well. Spread this mixture on 1 sparerib and cover with the other piece of meat. Tie the 2 pieces together with string to hold stuffing in place. Rub outside of spareribs with salt and flour. Place on rack in roasting pan and bake in 425° oven for 20 minutes. Reduce heat to 325° and bake for 1 hour. Baste every 10 minutes or so with drippings.

Peggy Kessinger

STUFFED PORK CHOPS

4 thick pork chops
⅓ c. bread crumbs
1 tsp. dried sage
1 small onion, chopped fine
¼ c. golden raisins

½ lemon rind, grated fine
1 egg, beaten
Salt
Pepper
1¼ c. cider

Cut a slit in each chop to make a pocket for stuffing. Brown chops on each side quickly. Mix bread crumbs, sage, onion, raisins and lemon rind with the egg, seasoned well. Stuff into the pockets; arrange in a casserole and season well. Pour over the cider and cook in the oven.

Teresa Stroup

SWEET AND SOUR PORK

Sweet and Sour Pork:

1½ lb. pork, cubed
2 c. water
¼ c. soy sauce
2 Tbsp. sugar
2 medium tomatoes, cut into
    wedges

1 green pepper, diced
½ c. chopped green onions
⅔ c. pineapple cubes
¼ c. butter

Simmer pork in water, soy sauce and sugar for 45 minutes; drain. Remove seeds and juice from tomatoes; combine vegetables and pineapple. Cook in butter for a few minutes, keeping vegetables crisp. Dip pork in batter and fry in deep hot fat (360°) until golden brown. Arrange pork on platter; mix with vegetables. Pour Sweet and Sour Sauce over all.

Dipping Batter:

1 egg, beaten
⅔ c. milk
1 c. sifted flour

2 tsp. baking powder
½ tsp. salt

Combine egg and milk. Add sifted dry ingredients and beat until smooth.

Sweet and Sour Sauce:

½ c. vinegar
½ c. water
¼ c. brown sugar

¼ c. granulated sugar
¼ c. cornstarch
½ c. pineapple juice

Bring vinegar, water and sugars to a boil. Combine cornstarch and pineapple juice; add to hot mixture and cook until thickened. Pour over pork and vegetables. Serves 8.

Bridget Pumphrey

POULTRY

ALMOND CHICKEN BREASTS

Skin and bone chicken breasts; season to taste with salt and pepper. Dip in flour, then beaten egg, then flat slivered almonds that have been mixed with a little flour and fry in butter Crisco.

Helen Russman

CHICKEN CASSEROLE

½ lb. Velveeta cheese, cubed
1 c. milk
½ c. Miracle Whip salad
   dressing
2 c. chopped cooked chicken
   or turkey

1 (10 oz.) pkg. frozen peas
   and carrots, cooked and
   drained
5 oz. spaghetti, cooked and
   drained
1 Tbsp. chopped chives

Heat chopped cheese, milk and salad dressing over low heat; stir until sauce is smooth. Add remaining ingredients. Mix well. Pour into 2 quart casserole and bake at 350° for 35 to 40 minutes or until hot. Serves 6 to 8.

Bessie Litchford

CHICKEN CASSEROLE

2 chickens, deboned (approx.
   5 c.)
3 cans water chestnuts,
   sliced
1 medium jar pimento
4 stalks celery
1 small to medium onion
Chicken bouillon cubes
3 tsp. lemon juice

Salt to taste
3 c. cooked rice, cooked in
   some broth
1½ c. Hellmann's
   mayonnaise
2 or 3 cans cream of chicken
   soup *(undiluted)*
Parsley flakes
1 bag crushed potato chips

When chicken is boiled, use 3 bouillon cubes. Put some onion and parsley flakes into water. Take 1 cup broth; simmer with onion and celery until tender. Slice water chestnuts. Mix all ingredients well. Pour into buttered 9x13 inch baking dish. Before baking in 325° oven for 20 to 30 minutes, add 1 bag of crushed potato chips on top. *Delicious!*

Wilma Crowdus

CHICKEN BREAST

Cut chicken breasts in halves. For 6 to 12 pieces, use 1 can cream of chicken soup and 1 can cream of mushroom soup. For less pieces, just use 1 can cream of chicken soup. In a little margarine in skillet, saute chicken breasts until coated all over. In bowl, mix soup, 8 ounces sour cream and ¼ to ½ cup of white wine; also, a little Kitchen Bouquet for color. Put sauteed breasts in casserole and pour soup mixture over chicken. Bake at 350° for 45 minutes. Serve with rice.

Flo Gish

BRUNSWICK STEW

2 medium onions, chopped
1½ qt. water
1 (1 lb.) can tomatoes
½ tsp. ground ginger
1 Tbsp. salt (or to suit taste)
2 (10 oz.) pkg. frozen lima
    beans

2 oz. chicken fat
3 lb. chicken breasts
¼ tsp. Tabasco
1 Tbsp. Worcestershire sauce
2 (10 oz.) pkg. frozen corn

In Dutch oven, saute chopped onion in chicken fat until soft. Add water, chicken breasts, tomatoes, Tabasco, ginger, Worcestershire sauce and salt. Bring to a boil; reduce heat to simmer and cook until chicken is almost tender, 35 to 45 minutes. Remove chicken. Discard skin and bones, then shred chicken with fingers and return to pot. Add frozen vegetables; bring to a boil; reduce to simmer and cook until beans are soft, about 20 minutes. Serve hot. Serves 10 to 12.

Unless you plan to freeze part of it or are having guests in, cut this recipe in half.

Ruth Ackerman

CHICKEN WITH BISCUIT TOPPING

Filling:

2 Tbsp. vegetable oil
1 small onion, chopped
½ green pepper, chopped
    fine
⅔ c. sliced mushrooms

2 Tbsp. cornstarch
1½ c. milk
1½ - 2 c. cooked chicken,
    cubed

Heat oil; add onion, green pepper and mushrooms; saute for a few minutes. Add cornstarch and cook for 1 minute; stir constantly. Add milk gradually; stir until boiling. Add chicken and seasoning. Turn into a deep 8 or 9 inch pie plate.

Biscuits:

2 c. flour
1 tsp. salt
2½ tsp. baking powder

⅓ c. shortening
About ⅔ c. milk

To make biscuits, sift flour, salt and baking powder; cut in shortening until mixture looks like coarse bread crumbs. Stir in enough milk to make a soft, but not sticky, dough. Knead lightly on a floured board; roll out about ½ inch thick and cut into 1½ inch rounds with a cookie cutter. Place the rounds on top of the chicken mixture in a circle around the edge; let each biscuit overlap the next one. Brush with milk and bake for 10 to 15 minutes.

Cristy Lewis

BAKED CHICKEN AND BROCCOLI

1 lb. fresh broccoli, cooked
and drained
2 chicken breasts or leftover
chicken, cooked and
deboned

½ c. Cheddar cheese (or
Velveeta)
½ c. bread crumbs

Then mix the following together:

½ tsp. curry powder
1 can cream of chicken soup

½ tsp. lemon juice
½ tsp. mayonnaise

Put cooked broccoli in buttered baking dish. Then spread chicken over broccoli. Then spread cheese over chicken, then soup mixture. Sprinkle crumbs on top. Bake at 350° for 25 minutes.

Flora Montgomery

CHICKEN BERCY

4 boned chicken breasts,
split
Salt and pepper
4 Tbsp. butter
3 Tbsp. shallots (green
onions)

¼ lb. sliced mushrooms
¾ c. sauterne wine
2 tsp. minced parsley

Wash and dry chicken breasts. Sprinkle with salt and pepper. Brown chicken in 2 tablespoons butter. Take up chicken and set aside. Add shallots and mushrooms. Lightly brown. Add wine; simmer for 5 minutes until liquid is reduced to ½ cup. Turn off heat. Stir in 2 tablespoons butter. Spoon sauce over chicken. Sprinkle with parsley.

Rose Briseno

BRANDICOT CHICKEN

2 Tbsp. cornstarch	¼ tsp. ground ginger
¼ c. soy sauce	Dash of pepper
¼ c. apricot preserves	1 Tbsp. orange juice
2 Tbsp. sugar	1 Tbsp. brandy
2 Tbsp. white vinegar	1 broiler-fryer (3½ - 4 lb.), cut
1 medium size clove garlic, minced	into serving pieces

Preheat oven to 375°. Stir together cornstarch and soy sauce in a saucepan. Stir in apricot preserves, sugar, vinegar, garlic, ginger and pepper. Cook over medium high heat until thick and bubbling, about 2 minutes. Remove from heat; stir in orange juice and brandy. Place chicken, skin side down, in a 3 quart baking dish or 9x13 inch baking pan. Pour sauce over top. Bake 30 minutes; turn chicken; baste with sauce. Bake additional 30 minutes or until tender. Serves 6.

Charles T. Thompson

CHICKEN BROCCOLI CASSEROLE

6 chicken breasts (or thighs)	2 Tbsp. lemon juice
2 pkg. frozen broccoli (spears or chopped)	¾ tsp. curry powder
	1 pkg. Pepperidge Farm corn bread stuffing mix
2 cans cream of chicken soup	
1 c. mayonnaise	1 stick melted butter

Simmer chicken until tender and remove from bones. Place in bottom of 9x12 inch baking dish and cover with a layer of cooked and drained broccoli. Combine mayonnaise, soup, lemon juice and curry powder. Pour mixture over broccoli and chicken. Cover top of casserole with the stuffing mix and then pour the melted butter over the stuffing. Bake 30 minutes at 350°. Serves 4 to 6.

Betty Jo Yeary

CHICKEN BREASTS FOR 10

10 chicken breasts
¼ c. warm sherry or brandy
2 Tbsp. butter
1 Tbsp. finely chopped
   shallots or onions
1 c. split blanched almonds
1 tsp. tomato paste

1 tsp. Kitchen Bouquet
3 Tbsp. flour
3 c. chicken stock
½ c. white wine
Salt and pepper to taste
Little tarragon
1 c. shredded almonds

Remove skin and bones from chicken. Brown in butter. Pour sherry or brandy over breasts. Remove the breasts. To the juice in pan, add 2 tablespoons butter and 1 tablespoon finely chopped shallots or onions. Cook for 1 minute; add blanched almonds. Cook until almonds begin to brown. Stir in tomato paste, Kitchen Bouquet and flour; add gradually, stirring constantly, chicken stock and white wine; bring to a boil. Season with salt and pepper; return breasts to sauce. Add tarragon. Cover and simmer for 25 minutes. Before serving, sprinkle with almonds.

Helen Russman

CHICKEN BREAST CASSEROLE

8 chicken breasts
1 stick butter
1 c. celery, chopped
1 c. onion, chopped
1 small pkg. Pepperidge Farm
   seasoned dressing mix

½ lb. mild sausage
2 cans cream of chicken soup
2 cans cream of mushroom
   soup
1 small jar pimentos

Boil chicken breasts until well done; let cool; skin and debone. Use chicken broth and stick of butter and cook celery and onion in it until tender. Add dressing mix and sausage; mix well. Place dressing mixture in bottom of baking dish. Place chicken on top of mixture. Mix cream of chicken and cream of mushroom soups together and pour over top. (Do not dilute soups.) Add pimento as garnish. Bake at 375° for 45 minutes.

Note: If you like, you may boil 1 or 2 fryers until tender; let cool, then debone and add to recipe.

Mary Baxter

CHICKEN AND BROCCOLI CASSEROLE

2 chicken breasts, stewed
 and chopped
1 pkg. Cheddar cheese,
 grated
1 can cream of chicken soup

½ c. Kraft salad dressing
2 pkg. chopped or whole
 broccoli
Rice
Croutons

Mix all but broccoli, rice and croutons. Put layer of broccoli on bottom of pan. Put chicken mixture on top. Cover with croutons. Bake at 350° until brown. Serve over rice.

Bina Cloyd

CHICKEN CHEESE CASSEROLE

1 can cream of mushroom
 soup
1 can cream of chicken soup
1 can water chestnuts, sliced
1 small can evaporated milk

1 small can mushrooms
1 large can chow mein
 noodles
4 or 5 chicken breasts

Season and bake chicken breasts. Cut up and mix all but noodles. Put in buttered dish and bake for 1 hour at 325° to 350°. Take out and top with Cheddar cheese and cook for 15 or 20 minutes. Serve over noodles.

Betty Volz

CALIFORNIA CHICKEN

2 Tbsp. salad oil
1 c. catsup
1 tsp. paprika
1 tsp. mustard
1 Tbsp. brown sugar

1 tsp. Worcestershire sauce
1 c. pineapple juice
1 c. chopped onion
1 spring chicken, cut up

Saute onion in oil until medium brown. Blend the rest of the ingredients, except chicken, well. Add to sauteed onion and simmer for 10 minutes. Lay chicken pieces in casserole dish; sprinkle with salt to taste. Spoon sauce over chicken. Cover and bake at 450° for 15 minutes, then 1 hour at 350°. Serves 6 at 55 cents per serving.

Denise Figg

CHICKEN CASSEROLE

3 c. cooked chopped chicken
(medium size)
1 c. chopped celery
½ c. almonds
½ tsp. salt
2 tsp. grated onion
½ c. chopped green peppers

½ c. mayonnaise
2 tsp. lemon juice
½ c. cream of chicken soup
½ c. sharp Cheddar cheese,
chopped
2 c. crushed potato chips

Mix all but the cheese and potato chips. Put in baking dish, then sprinkle with crushed chips and cheese. Bake at 325° for 25 minutes.

Jean Lyle

CHICKEN CASSEROLE

1 small pkg. Pepperidge Farm
dressing (corn bread)
1 stick melted oleo
1 whole chicken or 4 breasts

1 can cream of chicken soup
1 can cream of celery soup
2 c. chicken broth

Boil chicken. Remove bones and cut in bite-size pieces. Mix dressing with oleo. Spread half of dressing in a 9x13 inch baking dish. Spread layer of chicken. Mix both cans of soup with chicken broth. Pour over chicken. Spread remainder of dressing over top. Bake at 400° for 30 minutes or until brown.

Barbara Swank

CHINESE CHICKEN

4 large chicken breasts,
boned
2 green peppers, cut in large
pieces
4 large carrots, cut in large
pieces

1 green onion, chopped
About ½ c. cashews
1 Tbsp. soy sauce
1 Tbsp. cornstarch
1 tsp. salt
2 tsp. wine (if desired)

Cut chicken into bite-size pieces. Add salt, soy sauce and the wine. Add cornstarch; let set for 10 minutes. Then pour 2 tablespoons oil over chicken and mix well. Pour a little oil in skillet. Let it get hot. Cook onion for a few seconds. Add chicken and cook about 2 minutes on high, stirring constantly. Remove chicken from the skillet and put the vegetables in the oil; add ¼ cup water. Cook vegetables about 2 minutes on high, stirring constantly. Pour off water. Add cashews and chicken. Serve over rice immediately.

Laverne Hollingsworth

CHICKEN CORDON BLEU

2 lb. boned chicken breasts (4
   oz. each, about 5x4
   inches)
¼ lb. Swiss cheese
¼ lb. Prosciutto ham

Flour
Beaten egg
½ c. bread crumbs
Oil

Lay each chicken breast out flat and put equal amounts of cheese and ham in center. Roll and insert toothpick to hold. Lay on a sheet pan and partially freeze until firm enough to handle. Then roll in flour; dip in beaten egg and roll in bread crumbs. Deep-fry in a pan which has enough oil to cover. Brown and finish baking in a 350° oven for 10 minutes. Serve with mushroom gravy on top. Serves 2.

Paula White

BAKED CRUNCHY CHICKEN

Chicken, cut in serving size
   pieces
2 c. Pepperidge Farm Herb
   seasoned stuffing mix

2 c. Parmesan cheese
Melted butter

Mix together herb seasoned stuffing mix and Parmesan cheese. Dip raw chicken in melted butter and roll in mixture. Place chicken on cookie sheet. Bake at 375° for 1 hour.

Debbie Rigdon

CHICKEN CURRY

6 c. coconut milk or milk
½ c. curry powder
½ c. chutney
1 tsp. paprika

2 chickens, cut in pieces
6 tsp. soy sauce
2 tsp. flour

Cook coconut milk at boiling point for a few minutes; put in curry powder, chutney and paprika; cook down. Saute pieces of chicken in it; cook down. Season with soy sauce and thicken with flour. Serve with rice. Serves 4.

Denise Figg

224

ONE DISH CHICKEN DINNER

4 chicken breasts, lightly
    salted
1 can tiny peas, drained
1 Tbsp. instant onion (if
    desired)

3 potatoes, sliced
1 can cream of mushroom
    soup

Put chicken in a large casserole. Cover with peas; add sliced potatoes. Pour mushroom soup over all. Cover and bake at 375° for 1 hour or until tender.

Clara Nance

CHICKEN DIVAN

1½ c. cooked cut up chicken
2 tsp. oil
1 c. water
1 Tbsp. dry sherry wine
1 (10 oz.) pkg. broccoli
    flowerets

1 (10¾ oz.) can condensed
    cream of chicken soup
1½ c. Minute rice
1 Tbsp. grated Parmesan
    cheese

Brown chicken lightly in oil. Add water, wine, broccoli and soup. Bring to a full boil, separating broccoli pieces. Stir in rice. Cover; remove from heat and let stand 5 minutes. Sprinkle with cheese. Makes 4 servings.

Mary Quandt

MY FAVORITE GRILLED CHICKEN

1 chicken, cut up (or
    whatever chicken parts
    you like)

1 large bottle Kraft Zesty
    Italian dressing

Marinate chicken in dressing for at least 2 hours. I usually put my chicken in a bowl in the morning when I leave for work and let it marinate in dressing until I come home. Grill on gas or charcoal grill, brushing with dressing as you turn the pieces. It usually takes 35 to 45 minutes. Test for doneness with fork. Serve.

Wilma Lutts

CHICKEN AND DUMPLINGS

1 (5 lb.) stewing hen
1 stalk celery
Salt to taste

1 pod red pepper (optional)
2 onions

Cut hen in serving pieces; place in roaster. Cover with water; add celery, red pepper (if used), salt and onions. Cook on top of stove until chicken is tender. Always keep it covered with water.

Dumplings:

2 c. flour
1 Tbsp. salt

½ tsp. soda
¾ c. buttermilk

Knead well. Roll very thin and cut in strips. Remove chicken from broth and place dumplings in broth. Cover and cook 20 minutes. Remove dumplings and thicken broth for gravy. Combine flour and cold water in a cup; stir into broth until as thick as you like. Season to taste. Put gravy in dish with dumplings; spoon some over chicken if desired.

Ruthie Marty

POTATO DUMPLINGS

2 eggs
1½ tsp. salt
2 Tbsp. grated onion
⅓ c. potato flour

3 Tbsp. matzo meal
4 c. grated raw potatoes,
   drained

Beat eggs, salt and onion together. Stir in potato flour, matzo meal and potatoes. Shape into 1 inch balls. Drop dumplings into hot broth and cook until they rise to the top. Makes 20 dumplings.

Cristy Lewis

KELLEY'S HILLBILLY DRESSING

5 or 6 c. cold corn bread,
   crumbled
5 or 6 c. soft bread, crumbled
1 c. diced celery
½ c. or more chopped onion
2 tsp. salt
½ tsp. pepper
No eggs (eggs are in the corn
   bread)

1 (1 lb.) can peas with liquid
1 (1 lb.) can carrots with
   liquid, sliced
Rubbed sage (to your taste,
   careful)
Cooled giblet broth

Crumble both breads in large container. Add onion, celery, 1 (1 pound) can peas with liquid and 1 (1 pound) can sliced carrots with liquid. Mix well. Add salt and pepper and your rubbed sage. Mix well. Add giblet broth. Mix well again. Stuff lightly into breast region and body cavity of around 12 pound bird. May also be baked in separate pan.

Mary Beeler

CORN BREAD DRESSING

2 cake pans corn bread (use
    buttermilk in the mix)
10 canned buttermilk
    biscuits, baked as usual
1 heart of celery with leaves
6 eggs, beaten
3 or more c. turkey broth
1 big onion, chopped fine

2 pieces wheat toast,
    crumbled
½ tsp. poultry seasoning or
    to taste
½ tsp. salt
½ tsp. pepper
½ tsp. sage or to taste

Mix all ingredients together; add about 3 cups turkey broth or more if needed to make dressing thin and moist. Put in ungreased 13x9 inch pan and bake at 325° for approximately 30 minutes or until lightly browned.

Deborah Rigdon

cook cornbread like you always do —

MOTHER'S CORN BREAD DRESSING

3 c. corn bread
2 slices loaf bread
1 egg
3 sticks celery, chopped

2 Tbsp. sage
½ small onion
¼ tsp. pepper
Beef or chicken broth

Mix all ingredients together; add broth until mixture is slightly thinned. Put in a buttered baking dish and bake until golden brown, about 350°.

Gwen Bond

CHICKEN ENCHILADA

1 pkg. flour tortillas
1 (4 oz.) can green diced
    chiles
1 pt. sour cream
2 (10½ oz.) cans cream of
    chicken soup
1 (1 lb.) pkg. Monterey Jack
    cheese, shredded (or you
    can use Cheddar)

1 (3 lb.) chicken, boiled,
    boned and cut in pieces
1 (4 oz.) can sliced black
    olives

Mix chiles, sour cream, soup and half of cheese together. Divide mixture in half. To one half of mixture, add chicken. Roll into 12 tortillas and place in 13x9 inch (greased) baking pan. Cover tortillas with remaining half of mixture and top with remaining cheese and olives. Bake at 350° for 15 minutes or until well heated through. Serve with a green salad.

Judy Ebelhar

CHICKEN FIDEO

1 large onion, chopped (1 c.)
2 large cloves garlic, crushed
3 Tbsp. oil
8 oz. fideo or vermicelli
    clusters

1 (8 oz.) can tomato sauce
3 c. water
2 c. strips cooked chicken
½ tsp. salt
Pepper to taste

In large deep skillet over medium heat, saute onion and garlic in oil until onion is tender. Add fideo; cook, stirring to break up clusters, until lightly browned. Stir in tomato sauce and water; simmer, uncovered, 10 minutes. Stir in chicken, salt and pepper; heat through. Cooking time: 15 minutes. Serves 4.

Charles T. Thompson

CHICKEN FLAVORED RICE

1 c. rice
4 c. water
2 chicken bouillon cubes
4 Tbsp. margarine

¼ tsp. parsley or ¼ tsp.
    celery
Salt to taste

Dissolve bouillon cubes in water. Add rice and cook until tender. Add seasonings.

Deborah E. Robertson

FRIED CHICKEN

Skin chicken. Dip in beaten egg and water mixture. Roll in flour mixture and fry. Very good.

Flour Mixture: Flour, oatmeal, salt, pepper, garlic powder, poultry seasoning and parsley flakes.

Mary Beeler

CHICKEN FRIED RICE

2 c. chopped onion	3 Tbsp. salad oil
4 eggs, slightly beaten	2 c. chicken, diced fine
6 Tbsp. soy sauce	2 Tbsp. chopped chives
4 c. cold cooked rice	Salt and pepper to taste

Brown onion in 1 tablespoon oil. Add eggs. Stir until slightly set. Set this combination aside. Saute chicken in 2 tablespoons oil; add soy sauce and rice. Mix with egg mixture. Serve with tiny green onions on top and add soy sauce to suit taste.

Vicki Bennett

JAPANESE FRIED RICE

½ c. chopped mushrooms	½ c. chicken broth
6 green onions, chopped	2 tsp. Japanese soy sauce
4 c. cooked rice	Salt (optional)
1 c. cooked diced chicken	

Saute mushrooms and onions in a small amount of salad oil for a few minutes. Add rice and chicken; cook over medium heat; stir constantly for 3 to 4 minutes. Add broth, soy sauce and salt. Cover until liquid is absorbed and rice is hot.

Melissa Jackson

GRILLED CHICKEN

1 (2½ - 3 lb.) broiler-fryer, cut up	Smoky Barbeque Sauce

Place chicken on greased grill, skin side up, 5 to 7 inches from coals. Grill over low coals (coals should be ash gray) 30 minutes; turn and grill 10 minutes. Turn; continue grilling 30 minutes longer, turning and brushing with sauce every 10 minutes. Serves 3 to 4.

Smoky Barbeque Sauce:

½ c. chopped onion
2 Tbsp. butter or margarine
1 (14 oz.) bottle catsup
¼ c. vinegar
¼ c. brown sugar

1 Tbsp. Worcestershire sauce
1 Tbsp. liquid smoke
½ tsp. salt
¼ tsp. pepper

In small saucepan, saute onion in butter until crisp tender. Add remaining ingredients, mixing until blended. Cover; simmer 20 minutes. Yield: 1⅓ cups.

Mary V. Stanley

HERBED CHICKEN CASSEROLE

4 chicken breast halves
1 can cream of chicken soup
1 c. chicken broth

½ stick butter, melted
½ pkg. Pepperidge Farm
   stuffing mix

Boil chicken; bone, skin and cube. Place in casserole. Combine soup and ½ cup chicken broth; pour over chicken and mix slightly. Combine melted butter, ½ cup chicken broth and ½ bag stuffing. Mix and place on top of chicken. Bake at 400° for about 25 minutes.

Wilma Crowdus

HOT CHICKEN SALAD

2 c. chopped chicken, packed
1 c. chopped celery
2 eggs
1 small can water chestnuts,
   sliced

1 tsp. chopped onion
½ c. slivered almonds
1 c. mushroom soup
1 c. mayonnaise
Salt and pepper to taste

Mix ingredients together. Place in 9x12 inch baking dish. Bake at 350° for 15 minutes. Mix 1 cup buttered bread crumbs and 1 cup Cheddar cheese. Place on top of chicken mixture and bake an additional 15 minutes or until brown.

Shirley Cates

HOT CHICKEN SALAD SOUFFLE

2 c. cooked, cubed chicken
8 slices bread, cubed
1 medium onion, chopped
   and sauteed
1 c. celery, chopped and
   sauteed

4 eggs
1 c. milk (all or part
   evaporated best)
½ c. mayonnaise
1 can chicken soup
Grated cheese

Cut bread into cubes; spread half on bottom of greased casserole. Mix chicken, celery, onion and mayonnaise; spread over bread cubes and cover with remaining bread. Beat eggs; add to milk and pour over chicken in casserole. *Important:* Cover with waxed paper and refrigerate overnight, next day spread chicken soup over all and sprinkle with grated cheese. Bake 1 hour at 300°. Serves 8 to 10.

Jean Lyle

HUNTER'S CHICKEN

1 chicken (about 3 lb.)
2 Tbsp. olive oil
½ c. mushrooms, sliced

2 large onions, chopped
Mixed dried herbs
1 Tbsp. tomato paste

Cut chicken in serving pieces. Saute in oil until well browned and tender, about 25 minutes. Remove from pan and keep warm. In the same pan, saute mushrooms and onions. Add tomato paste and herbs. Cook about 4 minutes, then pour over the chicken.

Note: Serve with boiled noodles with poppy seed and a green salad.

Pam Thompson

IMPOSSIBLE CHICKEN AND BROCCOLI PIE

1 (10 oz.) pkg. frozen
   chopped broccoli
3 c. (12 oz.) shredded
   Cheddar cheese
1½ c. cut up cooked chicken
⅔ c. chopped onion

1⅓ c. milk
3 eggs
¾ c. Bisquick baking mix
¾ tsp. salt (if desired)
¼ tsp. pepper

Heat oven to 400°. Grease pie plate, 10 x 1½ inches. Rinse broccoli under running cold water to thaw; drain thoroughly. Mix broccoli, 2 cups of the cheese, the chicken and onion in plate. Beat milk, eggs, baking mix, salt and pepper until smooth, 15 seconds in blender on high or 1 minute with hand beater. Pour into plate. Bake until knife inserted in center comes out clean, 25 to 35 minutes. Top with remaining cheese. Bake just until cheese is melted, 1 to 2 minutes longer. Cool 5 minutes. Serves 6 to 8.

Mary V. Stanley

CHICKEN JAMBALAYA

¼ c. oil
2 medium chopped onions
1 bunch chopped green
   onions
2 green peppers
2 lb. chicken (meat only)
½ lb. chopped ham
½ lb. sliced smoked sausage
1 (6 oz.) can tomato paste
1 (16 oz.) can tomatoes, cut
   up

1 tsp. salt
2 bay leaves
½ tsp. thyme
2 sprigs parsley
1¾ c. uncooked rice, cooked
   according to package
   directions
½ c. water

Heat oil in large kettle. Add onions, green onions, and peppers. Simmer about 10 minutes until transparent. Add chicken and brown on all sides. Add ham and sausage; cook 10 minutes. Add tomatoes, tomato paste and seasonings. Cover and simmer 10 minutes. Stir in cooked rice by the spoonfuls. Add water. Cover and cook on low for 1 hour, stirring frequently. You may have to add additional water. Before serving, you may add ¾ teaspoon of Tabasco sauce. Serves 6.

Note: You may substitute shrimp, crab or other seafoods if you wish.

Peggy Graviss

CHICKEN LITTLE FINGERS

6 whole chicken breasts,
   boned
1½ c. buttermilk
2 Tbsp. lemon juice
2 tsp. Worcestershire sauce
1 tsp. soy sauce
1 tsp. paprika
1 Tbsp. Greek seasoning

1 tsp. salt
1 tsp. pepper
2 cloves garlic, minced
4 c. soft bread crumbs (I use
   homemade biscuits)
½ c. sesame seed
¼ c. margarine, melted
¼ c. shortening, melted

Cut chicken into ½ inch strips. Combine next 9 ingredients; add chicken, mixing well. Cover and refrigerate overnight. Drain chicken. Combine bread crumbs and sesame seed, mixing well. Add chicken and toss to coat. Place chicken in 2 greased 13x9x2 inch baking dishes. Combine margarine and shortening; brush on chicken. Bake at 350° for 35 to 40 minutes. Serve with Plum Sauce. (Recipe follows.)

Plum Sauce:

1½ c. red plum jam   1½ tsp. lemon juice
1½ Tbsp. prepared mustard
1½ Tbsp. prepared
    horseradish

Combine all ingredients in a small saucepan, mixing well. Place over low heat just until warm, stirring constantly. Dip chicken fingers into sauce.

Brownie - Lois Bruner

CHICKEN LIVERS WITH APPLES AND ONION

¾ lb. chicken livers   3 medium apples
3 Tbsp. flour   ¼ c. vegetable oil
½ tsp. salt   ¼ c. sugar
¼ tsp. pepper   1 large onion, sliced thin
⅛ tsp. cayenne pepper

Rinse chicken livers and drain on paper towels. Coat livers with a mixture of flour, salt, pepper and cayenne pepper. Set aside. Wash and core apples; cut apples into ½ inch circles. Heat 2 tablespoons vegetable oil in pan over medium heat. Add apple rings and cook until lightly browned. Turn slices carefully and sprinkle with sugar. Cook, uncovered, over low heat until tender. Remove from pan. Heat remaining 2 tablespoons vegetable oil over low heat. Add chicken livers and onion rings. Cook over medium heat, turning mixture often to brown all sides. Transfer to a warm serving platter. Serve with apple rings. Makes 4 servings.

Denise Figg

MEXICAN CHICKEN

1 boiled chicken
1 pkg. tortillas
1 can cream of chicken soup
1 can cream of mushroom
    soup
1 can Ro-Tel (tomatoes and
    chillies)

1 bell pepper, chopped fine
1 onion, chopped fine
½ lb. Velveeta cheese, grated
    or sliced thin

Remove bones from chicken and set aside. Mix soups, Ro-Tel, pepper and onion. Break tortillas in bite-size pieces. In the bottom of an oblong, greased pan, put a layer of tortillas, then a layer of chicken, then a layer of mixture. Continue the layers until all are used. Cover with cheese and bake 45 minutes at 350°.

Laverne Hollingsworth

ORIENTAL CHICKEN

1 c. mushrooms, sliced
1 c. onions, chopped

1 c. celery, diced
2 Tbsp. butter

Saute the preceding for 3 to 5 minutes. Then turn into a 2 quart casserole.

Add the following:

1 (6 oz.) can mixed Chinese
    vegetables
2 c. chicken, cooked and
    chopped
1 can cream of mushroom
    soup

2 Tbsp. soy sauce
3 c. rice, cooked
½ tsp. pepper
½ tsp. garlic salt

Bake at 350° for 25 minutes in a 2 quart covered casserole. Remove cover and top with 1 cup Chinese noodles. Bake 5 more minutes uncovered. Serves 6.

Louise Ball

PENNSYLVANIA HONEY BAKED CHICKEN

1½ c. melted oleo or butter
Garlic powder to taste
1 Tbsp. Accent
¼ c. parsley
1 c. Parmesan cheese

3 c. crushed corn flakes
1 Tbsp. honey
1 Tbsp. lemon juice
12 chicken breasts, deboned
    and skin removed

234

Wash and pat dry chicken; dip in oleo/butter; roll in dry mix and roll up and place in pan lined with foil. Combine leftover butter/oleo, honey, and lemon juice and pour over chicken in baking pan. Bake at 350° for 45 to 50 minutes, covered with foil. Uncover for 15 minutes to brown.

Dolores Phillips

CHICKEN POT PIE

3 Tbsp. butter or margarine	3 or 4 cooked potatoes,
¼ c. flour	cubed
1¼ c. chicken broth	1½ tsp. salt
1 c. milk	¼ tsp. poultry seasoning
2 c. cubed chicken	⅛ tsp. pepper
1⅔ c. cooked peas and	1 boiled egg, chopped
carrots	Flaky Pastry

Melt butter in large skillet. Blend in flour. Cook over low heat until bubbly, stirring constantly. Gradually add broth and milk; cook until thick, stirring constantly. Stir in vegetables and seasonings and egg. Heat. Spoon chicken mixture into 1½ quart dish and top with pastry. Cut slits in pastry to let steam escape. Bake at 400° for 30 minutes or until pastry is golden brown.

Flaky Pastry:

1 c. flour	⅓ c. shortening
¾ tsp. baking powder	3 Tbsp. ice water
½ tsp. salt	

Combine dry ingredients. Cut in shortening until mixture resembles coarse corn meal. Add ice water and stir lightly. (Dough will be just moist enough to shape in a ball.) Flop dough onto a floured surface. Roll out and lay over your mixture in casserole dish. Tuck the ends under and press firmly to sides of dish.

Lisa Pitts

CHICKEN-RICE CASSEROLE

4 chicken breasts	1 box Stove Top stuffing
2 cans cream of mushroom	Cooked rice
soup (undiluted)	

Simmer chicken breasts until done. In bottom of 10x10 inch casserole, spread about ½ inch of cooked rice. Spread 1 can of soup over rice. Break chicken breasts and spread over soup. Spread 1 can soup over chicken. Top with Stove Top stuffing prepared by instructions on box. Cover and bake 1 hour at 350°.

Newland Stanfill

CHICKEN AND RICE

1 (10½ oz.) can cream of
    mushroom soup
1 soup can milk
¾ c. uncooked regular rice

1 (4 oz.) can mushrooms
1 env. onion soup mix
2 chicken breasts

Heat oven to 350°. Mix mushrooms, soup and milk; reserve ½ cup of the mixture. Mix remaining soup mixture, the rice, mushrooms (with liquid) and half the onion soup. Pour into ungreased baking dish. Place chicken breasts on top. Pour reserved soup over chicken breasts; sprinkle with remaining onion soup mix. Cover with aluminum foil; bake 1 hour. Uncover; bake 15 minutes longer.

Kathy Ryan

CHICKEN SUPREME CASSEROLE

1 c. uncooked instant rice
1 carrot, scraped and
    shredded
1 stalk celery, finely chopped
1 Tbsp. minced fresh parsley
1 (15 oz.) can cut asparagus
    (undrained)
6 chicken breasts, halved,
    skinned and boned

1 Tbsp. soy sauce
⅛ tsp. salt
⅛ tsp. pepper
1 (10¾ oz.) can cream of
    celery soup (undiluted)
1 c. water
1 c. herb seasoned stuffing
    mix

Layer first 5 ingredients in lightly greased 9x13 inch baking dish. Arrange chicken on top. Sprinkle with soy sauce, salt and pepper. Cover and bake at 350° for 45 minutes. Combine soup and water, mixing well. Uncover chicken and pour soup mixture on top. Sprinkle with stuffing mix. Bake, uncovered, 15 minutes more or until lightly browned. Yield: 6 servings.

Dot Berry

SOUFFLE PIE

3 Tbsp. butter
1 c. sliced mushrooms
2 Tbsp. cornstarch
1 chicken bouillon cube
1 c. milk
1 egg

1 c. cooked chicken, chopped
   fine
4 slices cooked bacon,
   chopped
1 (8 inch) baked pastry shell

Preheat oven to 400°. Heat the butter in a pan; saute mushrooms. Add cornstarch and crumble bouillon cube; cook for 1 minute. Gradually add milk and stir until boiling. Remove from heat; add egg yolk, chicken and bacon. Beat egg white stiffly and fold into the mixture. Turn into the baked pastry shell and cook for 25 to 30 minutes. Serves 4.

Denise Figg

CHICKEN SUPREME

4 chicken breasts, skinned,
   boned, split (8 pieces)
1 c. sour cream
1 can cream of mushroom
   soup

½ - ¾ can evaporated milk
8 strips bacon (uncooked)
2 (2.5 oz.) pkg. chipped beef

Line bottom of casserole dish with chipped beef. Wrap 1 bacon strip around each piece of chicken and place on top of beef. Mix other ingredients and pour over chicken. Bake at 300° to 325° for 1½ hours. Serves 8.

Bunny Williamson

QUICK AND EASY CHICKEN STUFFING CASSEROLE

2 c. herb seasoned stuffing
   mix, prepared as directed
2 (7 oz.) cans boned chicken
   (or 1½ to 2 c. leftover
   chicken)

1 (10½ oz.) can cream of
   chicken soup
Small can of mushrooms
¼ tsp. poultry seasoning

Place half of prepared stuffing in 1½ to 2 quart ovenproof serving dish. Combine chicken, soup, mushrooms and seasoning; pour over stuffing. Top with remaining stuffing and bake, uncovered, 20 to 30 minutes at 350°. Serves 3.

Jimmie Dillman

CHICKEN RICE CASSEROLE

2 green peppers, chopped
4 c. chicken, boiled and
    cubed
2 c. brown and white rice,
    cooked
2 c. finely chopped celery
1 lb. chopped mushrooms
½ c. slivered almonds

2 onions, chopped fine
1 green onion
Pimentos
¼ lb. butter
1½ c. white wine
2 cans cream of mushroom
    soup

Saute onions, green peppers, mushrooms and celery in butter until transparent. Put in casserole. Saute almonds until lightly browned; add almonds, chicken, pimentos, celery and cooked rice to casserole. Mix wine and soup; pour over all. Mix well. Sprinkle with paprika and bake at 350° for 1 hour and 45 minutes.

Helen Russman

CHICKEN AND RICE

Chicken
1 can mushroom soup or 4
    oz. can mushrooms and
    ½ can cream of
    mushroom soup
1 can cream of chicken soup

1 c. chopped celery
¼ c. margarine
1½ c. Minute rice (uncooked)
½ c. water
Paprika

Mix and add cut up chicken to the top layer, buttered and sprinkled with paprika. Cover with Reynold's Wrap. Bake in a 200° oven for 2 hours or at 300° for 1½ hours.

Mary Jane Molter

CHICKEN STROGANOFF

2 chicken breasts, cooked
    and cubed
1 c. sour cream
1 can mushroom soup
¼ c. milk
4 oz. extra wide noodles,
    cooked 9 to 10 minutes

¾ pkg. slightly thawed peas
⅓ c. grated onion
½ tsp. salt
Few shakes of pepper
½ c. chopped celery

Combine sour cream, soup and milk until smooth. Add salt and pepper. Add peas and chicken, grated onion and chopped celery. If any chicken stock, add a little. Mix well and put into a long casserole.

238

Topping:

½ c. bread crumbs
¼ c. butter

Parmesan cheese

Bake at 325° for 40 or 50 minutes.

Nellie Ross

CHICKEN WRAP-UPS

1 (8 oz.) pkg. cream cheese,
   softened
4 green onions, minced
Garlic powder or curry
   powder to taste

6 boneless, skinless chicken
   breasts
12 bacon strips (uncooked)

Mix cream cheese, green onions and garlic or curry powder thoroughly. Roll mixture into 6 balls. Place balls in center of flattened chicken breasts. Fold chicken around ball. Wrap 2 bacon strips around each chicken breast, securing with toothpicks. Place in baking dish. Bake at 350° for about 1 hour. Serves 6.

Sandy Lee

CHICKEN SAUSAGE PATTIES

2 c. cooked rice
1 tsp. grated peel of lemon
¾ tsp. fresh ground black
   pepper
½ tsp. fennel seeds, crushed
Dash of ground red pepper
2 Tbsp. plus 2 tsp.
   unsaturated calorie
   margarine, melted

1¼ lb. skinned and boned
   chicken breast, coarsely
   ground
Salt to taste

Put rice in crockery bowl; add lemon peel, salt, seasonings, and melted butter; toss lightly. Add chicken; mix lightly, but thoroughly. Divide into 2 portions and shape into 2 rolls. Wrap tightly in foil; refrigerate at least 24 hours before using. To cook, cut each roll into 8 patties. Preheat heavy skillet; raise heat and brown 4 minutes on each side. Serves 4.

Terry White

DUMPLINGS

2 c. flour
1 tsp. salt
4 tsp. baking powder

3 Tbsp. shortening
¾ c. milk

Mix together flour, salt and baking powder. Cut in shortening. Add ¾ cup milk and drop by teaspoonful into boiling chicken broth. Cover and do not peek for 20 minutes.

Donna Browning

KENTUCKY HOT BROWNS

Arrange thinly sliced turkey and ham slices on trimmed toast. Cover with hot Cheese Sauce (recipe follows). Top with tomato slices and partially cooked bacon strips. Sprinkle with Parmesan cheese.

Cheese Sauce: Melt 2 tablespoons oleo. Add ¼ cup flour. Stir well. Slowly add 2 cups milk, ½ cup grated cheese (I like sharp Cheddar), ¼ cup Parmesan, ¼ teaspoon salt and ½ teaspoon Worcestershire sauce. Cook, stirring constantly, until thick.

Anita Picklesimer

TURKEY OR CHICKEN CASSEROLE

1 (8 oz.) jar Cheez Whiz
    process cheese spread
½ c. milk
7 oz. spaghetti, broken into
    thirds, cooked, drained
2 Tbsp. margarine
1 (10 oz.) pkg. frozen
    chopped broccoli,
    cooked, drained

1 c. chopped cooked turkey
    or chicken
1 (4 oz.) can mushrooms,
    drained
2 Tbsp. chopped pimiento
¼ tsp. poultry seasoning
¼ tsp. onion salt

Combine process cheese spread and milk; mix well. Toss spaghetti with margarine. Combine all ingredients; mix well. Spoon into 2 quart casserole. Cover; bake at 350° for 30 to 35 minutes or until hot. Stir before serving. Makes 6 servings.

Martha Harper

HOT BROWN

Toast bread. Add sliced breast of turkey. Cover with Cheese Sauce. Add slices of tomato and 2 slices of crisp bacon per serving. Place on cookie sheet and heat thoroughly under broiler just before serving.

Cheese Sauce:

6 tsp. melted butter	½ tsp. pepper
2 c. milk	2 heaping tsp. flour
¼ lb. boxed process American cheese	½ tsp. salt

Cook in double boiler or heavy skillet.

Phyllis L. Davis

HOT BROWN

Bacon	2 Tbsp. sharp Cheddar cheese
Slices turkey breast	
Bread, buttered	Dash of pepper
Mushroom caps	Dash of paprika
2 Tbsp. butter	½ c. milk
2 Tbsp. flour	½ c. chicken broth
½ tsp. salt	Tomato slices (optional)
Dash of Tabasco	

Cook bacon crisp. Saute mushrooms; arrange buttered bread slices on baking sheet. Toast bread on bottom. Place turkey slices and bacon on bread. Top with sauce (recipe follows). Place in oven until brown on top. Garnish with mushrooms and tomato slices if desired.

Sauce: Melt 2 tablespoons butter over low heat; stir in 2 tablespoons flour, ½ teaspoon salt, dash of pepper, dash of paprika and dash of Tabasco until smooth. Gradually stir in milk and broth; cook, stirring constantly, until smooth and thickened. Add Cheddar cheese. (I use more than 2 tablespoons cheese.) This is great!

Wilma Crowdus

TURKEY-CHEDDAR CASSEROLE

4 oz. broad noodles, cooked
2½ c. diced cooked turkey
4½ oz. jar mushrooms,
   drained
1 Tbsp. instant minced onion
   (or 1 medium onion,
   chopped)

1 c. milk
11 oz. can condensed
   Cheddar cheese soup
1 c. finely crushed cheese
   crackers
3 Tbsp. butter, melted

Butter a 2 quart casserole and put cooked noodles in bottom. Combine mushrooms and turkey; arrange on top of noodles. Blend together onion (lightly sauteed if fresh onion is used), milk and soup. Pour over the turkey. Combine cracker crumbs and butter; sprinkle over casserole. Bake in a 350° oven for 35 minutes. Makes about 6 servings.

Ruth Ackerman

MOM'S TURKEY DRESSING

1 pkg. corn bread dressing
   crumbs
1 pkg. bread crumbs dressing
1 stick butter
1 drumstick
1 bunch celery
2 onions
1 can cream of mushroom
   soup

1 can onion soup
Sage
Poultry seasoning
Salt
Pepper
2 eggs

Boil drumstick in 4 quarts water; add 1 stick butter to water. When done, remove drumstick from liquid and let cool (keep broth). Cut up onions and celery; add to dressing crumbs. Add onions, eggs, onion soup, cream of mushroom soup and liquid from turkey. Mix well. Add in meat from drumstick and season to taste. Bake at 325° for 1 hour. Enjoy!

Carol Wilson

CHICKEN OR TURKEY TETRAZZINI

4 oz. thin spaghetti, broken, cooked and drained
1 can cream of mushroom soup
½ c. milk
1½ - 2 c. chopped chicken or turkey
¼ c. chopped pimentos
¼ c. minced green pepper
1 Tbsp. minced onion
Pepper to taste
1 c. shredded process sharp Cheddar cheese

Mix all together and bake at 400° for 30 to 40 minutes.

Martha Harper

SHANGHAI DUCK

1 (4 - 5 lb.) duckling
8 black mushrooms (optional)
1 bunch green onions
3 slices ginger root or 1 tsp. powdered dry ginger
5 cloves star anise
2 Tbsp. brown sugar
1 Tbsp. wine (your favorite)
¾ c. soy sauce
2½ tsp. salt
½ c. water

Wash black mushrooms and soak in warm water until soft. Cut off the stems. Cut the top into 4 parts. Remove and discard any large pieces of fat from cavity; soak duckling and giblets in boiling water for several minutes. Then rinse. Put green onions, ginger root, star anise, and giblets in bottom of Dutch oven. Put duckling in with breast side down. Add brown sugar, salt, wine, soy sauce, black mushrooms, and ½ cup water. Cover tightly; bring to a boil and simmer 1 ½ hours or until tender (turn duckling breast side up halfway through cooking). Take cover off and skim excess fat from liquid. Turn heat to medium and baste duckling frequently for 10 minutes until the skin is dark brown with ½ cup of the liquid remaining. Cut into pieces and top with black mushrooms and remaining liquid.

Delicious and sure to be a favorite.

Sarah A. Drewes

ROASTED QUAIL OR CORNISH HEN

6 quail or Cornish hens
1 c. onions, chopped
1 c. bell peppers, chopped
4 cloves garlic
1 c. lemon juice
1 lb. mushrooms, cleaned and sliced
1 c. water
1 c. sauterne wine
5 tsp. Worcestershire sauce

The quail or Cornish hens should be cooked in an oven cooking bag (self-basting). The cooking bag should be put in a deep dish. The quail should be put in first. The other ingredients, such as the onions and bell peppers, should be sliced. The garlic should be crushed and mushrooms should be sliced. Preheat oven to 350° and cook for 1 hour. Eat it with rice and red wine. (Favorite.)

Erich W. Drewes

PHEASANT

1 pheasant, cut into pieces　　**Onions, sliced thin**
Flour　　　　　　　　　　　　**Salt to taste**
1 stick butter　　　　　　　　**Pepper to taste**

Flour pheasant lightly; add salt and pepper. Slice ½ stick butter into bottom of casserole. Cover with layer of onions. Arrange pheasant over onions. Cover with layer of onions; dot with remaining butter. Add ½ cup water. Bake, covered, from 250° to 275° for 4 to 5 hours. Yield: 6 to 8 servings.

Mary Baxter

GROUND BEEF

BEST BARBECUE

3 - 4 lb. ground beef
1 large onion
½ c. chopped celery
1 large bottle Brooks tangy
    catsup

Salt to taste
Chile powder to taste

Brown ground beef in skillet. Add rest of ingredients. Cook in slow cooker or simmer on stove for 2 hours.

Dianne Rice

BAR-B-CUE MEATLOAF

1½ lb. ground chuck
1 medium onion, chopped
¾ c. seasoned bread crumbs
1 egg
Salt and pepper

1 c. ketchup
2 Tbsp. brown sugar
2 Tbsp. mustard
2 Tbsp. cider vinegar

Mix meat, onion, bread crumbs, egg, salt, pepper and ½ cup ketchup in bowl. Form into 9x5 inch loaf and place in shallow baking dish. Mix ½ cup ketchup, brown sugar, mustard and vinegar together; pour over meatloaf. Bake at 350° for 1 hour. Let stand a few minutes before slicing.

Pat Sherrard

BARBECUE MEAT LOAVES

1½ lb. ground beef
1 egg, beaten
½ c. skim milk
1 c. soft bread crumbs
¼ c. onion, chopped
1 tsp. salt

½ tsp. oregano (dried)
⅔ c. catsup
1 Tbsp. brown sugar
1 Tbsp. prepared mustard
1 Tbsp. lemon juice
1 Tbsp. Worcestershire sauce

Mix together ground beef, egg, milk, bread crumbs, onion, salt and oregano. Divide mixture into 6 portions and shape into small loaves. Cook in 350° oven until partially done. Mix catsup, brown sugar, mustard, lemon juice and Worcestershire sauce; pour over meat and continue cooking until done.

Peggy Kessinger

PIZZABURGER MEATLOAF

½ c. chopped onion
1 (6 oz.) can tomato paste
1 c. water
1½ lb. ground beef
1 egg
1 c. bread crumbs

1 tsp. salt
1 tsp. oregano
¼ tsp. basil
Mozzarella cheese (or mix
    Cheddar and Mozzarella)

    Combine onion, tomato paste and water in saucepan. Simmer 20 minutes. Mix together beef, egg, bread crumbs, salt, oregano and basil. Add ½ cup prepared sauce; blend well. Form into loaf. Place in 10x6x2 inch baking dish. Bake at 375° for 50 minutes. Pour remaining sauce and arrange cheese on top. Bake 15 minutes longer.

Ruby Junker

GRANDMA'S MEAT LOAF

8 oz. skinned and boned
    chicken breast
8 oz. boneless beef chuck
8 oz. boneless pork loin
3 oz. white bread, soaked in 6
    Tbsp. water
2 oz. bacon, chopped
2 oz. sausage
1 medium onion, chopped
1 large garlic clove
2 oz. fresh bread crumbs

2 eggs, beaten to blend
1 Tbsp. minced fresh parsley
2 tsp. salt
¼ tsp. freshly ground pepper
¼ tsp. dried marjoram,
    crumbled
All-purpose flour
1 egg, beaten to blend (for
    glaze)
1½ c. (or more) water

    Preheat oven to 350°. Grease roasting pan. Grind chicken, beef, pork, bread, bacon, sausage, onion and garlic through fine plate of meat grinder into large bowl. Mix in bread crumbs, 2 eggs, parsley, salt, pepper, and marjoram. Shape into 9x5 inch loaf. Roll in flour, shaking off excess. Transfer to prepared pan. Brush with beaten egg. Pour in 1½ cups water. Bake (at 350° approximately 1½ hours) until juices run clear when meat loaf is pierced with skewer, basting occasionally and adding water if necessary. Let stand at room temperature 10 minutes before serving. Makes 6 servings.

Charles T. Thompson

MEATLOAF

1½ lb. hamburger	1 egg
1½ tsp. salt	½ c. bread crumbs
½ tsp. black pepper	½ (8 oz. size) can tomato
1 onion	sauce

Mix together and form into a loaf.

Sauce:

½ (8 oz. size) can tomato	2 Tbsp. vinegar
sauce	2 Tbsp. mustard
½ c. water	3 Tbsp. brown sugar

Mix all of preceding ingredients well. Pour over meatloaf. Bake 1½ hours at 350°.

Hazel V. Elrod

MEAT LOAF

1½ lb. ground beef	½ c. green pepper, chopped
1 (8 oz.) can tomato sauce	1 tsp. marjoram leaves
2 eggs, lightly beaten	3 Tbsp. parsley
½ c. carrot, chopped	1 c. cracker crumbs
½ c. celery, chopped	1 tsp. salt
½ c. onion, chopped	⅛ tsp. black pepper

Mix all ingredients together well. Press into a baking pan. Bake in a preheated 400° oven for about 1 hour and 15 minutes or until done.

Peggy Kessinger

MEAT LOAF

2½ lb. meat loaf mix (equal	1 egg, beaten
parts of ground beef,	1 medium can tomato sauce
pork and veal)	½ c. water
½ green pepper, chopped	Cracker crumbs
Small onion, chopped	

Mix all ingredients together. Put in baking dish; put cracker crumbs over top and sides. Mix ½ can of tomato sauce and ½ cup water together; pour over meat loaf. Bake 1 hour at 350°. Then add rest of the tomato sauce and bake another hour.

Debbie Rigdon

MEATLOAF

1½ lb. hamburger
¾ c. uncooked oats
1 pkg. Lipton's onion soup
    mix
1 c. tomato juice (or ½ c.
    catsup, mixed with ½ c.
    water)

½ tsp. black pepper
2 eggs

(Do not use any salt in this recipe. The soup mix makes it salty enough.) Combine all ingredients and mix thoroughly. Pack firmly into a loaf pan. Bake at 350° for 1 hour.

Ruth Ackerman

MEAT LOAF

1 lb. fresh pork, ground
2 lb. beef, ground
1 c. milk
⅛ tsp. pepper
1 onion, chopped fine
Dash of celery salt or sage (if
    desired)

1 lb. veal, ground (may be
    omitted)
1 c. bread crumbs
4 tsp. salt
3 eggs, slightly beaten
4 slices fat salt pork or bacon

Mix the ingredients thoroughly. Shape in loaf; put in pan and lay slices of salt pork or bacon across it. Brown the loaf in the uncovered pan at 400°, then cover and cook for 1¾ hours at 350°. Irish potatoes may be added around the loaf when put in to bake. Remove to platter; pour tomato sauce or brown sauce around the meat and garnish with parsley.

Mary T. Thompson

MEXACALI MEATLOAF

1 can Tostitos brand picante
    sauce
2 eggs
1 c. bread or cracker crumbs
2 lb. ground beef
½ lb. Monterey Jack cheese,
    sliced

1 (4 oz.) can whole green
    chilies (remove seeds),
    cut into strips (use mild
    chilies)
Salt and pepper to taste

Mix ground beef with picante sauce, salt, pepper, bread crumbs and eggs. Spread half of meat mixture into loaf pan. Spread cheese and chilies over meat and top with remaining meat mixture. Bake at 350° for 1½ to 2 hours.

Wanda Harris

MEATBALLS IN TOMATO SAUCE

2 lb. minced beef
1 small can tomato puree
1 tsp. sugar
1 onion, sliced
3 cloves garlic
2 eggs

Parsley
1 oz. flour
Salt
Pepper
Oil for frying

Saute onion and garlic. Mince together with parsley. Place ground meat and eggs in a bowl; add onion and garlic; mix well. Form meatballs of about 1 ounce each (1 inch diameter). Put 2 cups water in a saucepan; bring to a boil; add tomato puree, salt, pepper and sugar. Dilute flour in water; add to sauce while boiling; stir and add meatballs. Cook over medium heat for 15 minutes. Serve as a main course with mashed potatoes and cooked vegetables. Preparing time: 15 minutes. Cooking time: 30 minutes. Serves 6.

Denise Figg

MACARONI AND HAMBURGER

1 medium onion, chopped
½ lb. hamburger
2 c. macaroni

1 c. celery, chopped fine
3 - 4 Tbsp. butter
1 can tomato soup

Cook macaroni; place butter in frying pan; add onion and fry slightly. Add hamburger in bits and fry until nearly done. Add tomato soup or puree and celery. Season. Cover frying pan and let simmer while macaroni is boiling. When tender, drain (don't chill) and pour the hot sauce over immediately. This is quick and very easy to fix.

Denise Figg

FRITO PIE

1 can chili (no beans)
½ bag Fritos (dip size)

4 oz. Cheddar cheese

Heat chili in saucepan. Put Fritos in casserole dish; pour chili over Fritos. Slice cheese and lay on top of chili. Place in oven until cheese is melted. Serve immediately.

Alma Gentry

MEXICAN BEEF PIE

Pastry for 9 inch (2 crust) pie
2 Tbsp. vegetable oil
½ c. chopped onion
½ c. chopped green onion
1 lb. ground beef
1 tsp. salt
¼ tsp. black pepper
1 tsp. chili powder
1 (8 oz.) can Spanish style
  tomato sauce
½ c. sliced stuffed olives

Preheat oven to 400°. Line a 9 inch pie plate with half the pastry. Heat the oil; saute onion and green pepper for 5 minutes. Add beef and cook until brown; stir frequently. Add seasoning and tomato sauce; cook over low heat for 15 minutes. Let cool. Add olives, then turn the mixture into the pastry shell. Roll out remaining pastry and cut into thin strips. Arrange over the meat in a lattice pattern. Bake 35 to 40 minutes or until pastry is well browned.

Heidi Thompson

GROUND BEEF AND MUSHROOMS

1 lb. ground beef
2 Tbsp. shortening
⅔ c. onion, chopped
3 oz. can mushrooms
1 tsp. salt
⅛ tsp. pepper
2 tsp. catsup
½ tsp. oregano
½ c. water or milk
2 Tbsp. chopped parsley
4 slices toast

Melt shortening; add ground beef and onion. Cook until meat is browned. Add rest of the ingredients. Simmer for 10 minutes. Serve on toast.

Peggy Kessinger

GROUND BEEF STEW

2½ lb. ground beef
1 c. chopped onions
1½ qt. sliced carrots
3 qt. cubed potatoes (small)
3 c. canned tomatoes
1 Tbsp. salt

Saute ground beef and onions over low heat in a dry skillet or oven pan. Add carrots, potatoes, tomatoes and salt. Cover and cook in a preheated 350°F. oven for 45 minutes or until vegetables are tender.

Brenda Chitty

HAMBURGER CASSEROLE

1 onion, chopped
1 lb. ground beef
1 can mixed vegetables
¼ tsp. pepper
Corn bread batter

2 Tbsp. shortening
1 c. tomato sauce
1 tsp. salt
Dash of chili powder

Simmer onion in shortening until tender. Stir in ground beef. Add tomato sauce, vegetables, salt, pepper and chili powder. Bring to boil. Pour into a casserole dish. Spread corn bread batter over top. Bake at 375° for about 25 minutes or until brown.

Sue Tipton

HAMBURGER CRUNCH

1 lb. ground beef
½ c. onion, chopped
1 c. parboiled rice
1 can mushroom soup
1 c. evaporated milk

1 c. water
¼ c. soy sauce
Pepper to taste
1 (3 oz.) can chow mein
   noodles

Brown beef and onion in a skillet. Drain. Add rice, mushroom soup, evaporated milk, water, soy sauce and pepper. Simmer, stir occasionally, about 30 minutes, or until rice is done. Sprinkle chow mein noodles on top. Serves 4.

Heidi Thompson

HAMBURGER NOODLE BAKE

2 lb. ground beef
1½ c. onions, chopped
8 oz. medium noodles,
  cooked and drained
8 oz. sharp process American
  cheese, shredded (2 c.)
2 (4 oz.) cans condensed
  tomato soup
⅓ c. chopped green pepper
¼ c. chili sauce

2 Tbsp. chopped canned
  pimento
¾ tsp. salt
1½ c. soft bread crumbs
3 Tbsp. butter or margarine,
  melted
1 c. water
Dash of pepper
Green pepper rings (optional)

In skillet, cook beef and onions until meat is lightly browned and onion is tender. Drain off fat. Combine meat and onions with noodles, cheese and soup. Add water, green pepper, chili sauce, pimento, salt and pepper. Mix well. Turn into a 13x9x2 inch baking dish. Combine crumbs and butter; sprinkle on top. Bake in 350° oven for 40 to 45 minutes. Trim with green pepper rings if desired. Serves 12.

Thelma Barnett

HOBO CASSEROLE

1½ lb. ground beef
¼ c. canned milk
Salt and pepper
6 large potatoes

2 large onions
¼ lb. American cheese
1 can cream of mushroom
  soup

Press the ground beef into the bottom of a 2½ quart casserole. Sprinkle with canned milk, salt and pepper to taste. Slice potatoes on meat; slice onions onto potatoes. Cube the cheese onto onions and cover with mushroom soup. Bake in a covered dish 1 hour at 350°. Makes 6 servings.

Lil Pasinski

POLENTA

3 lb. ground beef
2 onions, chopped
1 large can tomatoes
1 (6 oz.) can tomato paste
4 tsp. chili powder

2 tsp. salt
½ tsp. hot sauce
1 (12 oz.) pkg. corn muffin
  mix
¼ c. grated Parmesan cheese

Saute beef and onions in skillet, stir occasionally, until beef is browned, about 10 minutes; drain. Pour into 3 quart casserole; add tomatoes, tomato paste, chili powder, salt and hot sauce. Prepare corn muffin mix according to package directions; spread over top of casserole. Sprinkle with cheese. Bake at 400° for 35 to 40 minutes or until crust is brown. Yield: 12 servings.

Beth Howard

ITALIAN MEAT BALLS AND SAUCE

1½ lb. ground hamburger
½ lb. ground pork
Dash of garlic
Parsley to taste

1 egg
Salt and pepper to taste
2½ Tbsp. Romano cheese

Mix and let stand ½ hour in refrigerator. Make meat balls and brown.

2 or 3 balls garlic, fried until
    brown
2 cans tomato sauce

½ can water (or 1 can if you
    like it thinner)

Simmer 1 hour.

3 cans tomato paste

2 cans water

Leave uncovered. Add meat balls. Simmer 1½ hours. Makes 28 meat balls.

Kathy Hummel

INDIAN MEAT ROLL WITH MUSHROOMS

1 lb. ground chuck or bottom
    round
½ lb. sausage
1 tsp. salt
⅛ tsp. pepper
¼ tsp. celery salt
1 egg, beaten
2 Tbsp. chopped onion

¼ lb. sliced mushrooms
2 Tbsp. margarine
1 c. bread crumbs
1 Tbsp. chopped parsley
½ tsp. salt
¼ tsp. marjoram
Hot water
3 slices bacon

Combine meats, seasonings, ¼ cup water and egg. Spread on a piece of waxed paper and pat into a rectangle ½ inch thick. Saute onion and mushrooms in margarine; add bread crumbs, parsley, ½ teaspoon salt, marjoram and hot water to moisten. Spread stuffing on meat and roll like a jelly roll; fasten with string. Place on a greased baking pan. Cover top with bacon strips, cut in halves, and bake in 350° oven for 1 hour.

Heidi Thompson

MEAT BALLS

1½ lb. ground chuck	3 Tbsp. chopped onions
¾ c. oats	1½ tsp. salt
1 c. evaporated milk	¼ tsp. pepper

Form meat balls and cook until done, about 45 minutes, at 350°. Makes 12 to 14.

Sauce:

2 Tbsp. Worcestershire sauce	1 c. catsup
3 Tbsp. vinegar	½ c. water
2 Tbsp. sugar	

Combine sauce ingredients and pour over cooked meat balls. Cook over low heat at least ½ hour longer. Turn meat balls frequently so sauce covers them.

Terri Ramage

QUICK HAMBURGER CASSEROLE ✓

1 lb. hamburger meat	1 can chili-beef soup
1 small onion	1½ c. canned tomatoes
1 c. cooked macaroni	4 slices American cheese

Fry hamburger meat and onion until brown. Add cooked macaroni, tomatoes, and chili-beef soup to meat. Let come to boil. Lay cheese on top of casserole. Let melt. Serve.

Sharon McGeorge

SPAGHETTI AND MEAT BALLS
(Easy)

When leaves begin turning shades of red and gold and the air turns cool, hearty appetites often crave that all time favorite - spaghetti. This version of meat balls and spaghetti has all the flavorsome goodness of its Italian counterpart, but the streamlined cookery method is definitely American. Meat balls, sauce and spaghetti are all cooked in 1 skillet.

Meat Balls and Spaghetti:

1 recipe Meat Balls	**1 tsp. chili powder**
¼ c. chopped green pepper	**1 (7 oz.) pkg. spaghetti,**
½ c. chopped onion	**broken into small pieces**
4½ c. tomato juice	**(2½ c. uncooked)**
1 tsp. salt	**Parmesan cheese, grated**

After Meat Balls are browned, push to sides of skillet. Place green pepper and onion in center of pan and cook over low heat until tender. Pour tomato juice over Meat Balls. Sprinkle with salt and chili powder. Bring to a boil over high heat. Add spaghetti and stir to moisten. Cover skillet tightly; turn heat as low as possible and cook until spaghetti is tender, about 40 minutes. When ready to serve, sprinkle with Parmesan cheese. Makes 6 servings.

Meat Balls (basic recipe):

1 lb. ground beef	**Dash of pepper**
¼ c. fine dry bread crumbs	**⅔ c. evaporated milk**
½ c. finely chopped onion	**2 Tbsp. butter**
1 tsp. salt	

In a medium size mixing bowl, add crumbs, onion, salt and pepper to ground beef. Add evaporated milk and mix ingredients lightly, but thoroughly. Divide and shape meat mixture into 12 balls (a scant ¼ cup meat mixture for each ball). Melt butter in a large skillet over medium heat. Add Meat Balls, turning occasionally to brown on all sides.

Ouida Brown

HAMBURGER AND RAGU CASSEROLE

2 lb. ground beef	**1 small onion**
1½ Tbsp. oregano	**1 (15 oz.) jar Ragu sauce**
¾ c. grated Cheddar cheese	**Parmesan cheese**
2½ c. noodles	

Cook beef, chopped onion and oregano until done. Drain grease. Mix Ragu and Parmesan into meat mixture. Simmer 10 minutes. Cook noodles and drain. Pour meat into dish; layer with noodles, then cheese, then more meat, noodles and cheese. Cook at 350° for 30 minutes. Serves 8.

Patricia Jewell

HAMBURGER OPEN FACE SANDWICH

4 slices bread
4 hamburgers (size of bread)

1 can mushroom soup

Make hamburger patties with salt and pepper to your taste. Broil them (do not fry, they will be too hard). Place on slice of bread. Add a very small amount of liquid to soup. Warm and pour over your sandwich. Add salad and you have a quick lunch.

Jamie Beeler

YUMMY CHILI BAKE

Chili (medium to thick
    consistency; no beans)
2 c. sharp Cheddar cheese,
    grated

1 medium onion, diced
Fritos (large dip chips, $1.39
    bag)

Grease bottom of casserole dish. Line with Fritos. Layer with chili, then onions, then cheese. Repeat and be sure to top with extra cheese.

This is a good recipe for leftover chili.

Lou Ann Crouch

HAMBURGER PIE

1 lb. ground beef
1 large onion, chopped
½ green pepper, chopped
1 can cream of mushroom
    soup
1 egg
Grated cheese

Mashed potatoes
Several crackers, crushed
Pinch of marjoram
Pinch of oregano
Salt as you desire
Pepper as you desire
Garlic as you desire

Mix the preceding ingredients, using half of the cream of mushroom soup. Press into a 9 inch pie plate. Bake at 350° until ground beef is done. Remove from oven and spread mashed potatoes over mixture. Spread the remaining half can of mushroom soup over the potatoes. Sprinkle grated cheese over the potatoes. Return to oven and bake until cheese is bubbly.

Linda Y. Borden

EASY MEXICAN DISH

1 can Ro-Tel tomatoes with
   chilies
1 can mushroom soup
1 can tomato soup
1 can Cheddar cheese soup
1 lb. lean ground beef
1 large pkg. corn chips
1 onion, diced
½ green bell pepper, diced
8 oz. shredded Cheddar
   cheese

Brown ground beef, onion and pepper. Mix in tomatoes and soups (do not add water to soup). In a large dish, layer alternating chips and meat and soup mixture. Top with shredded cheese. Cover for 5 to 10 minutes until cheese melts. Serve immediately.

Shirley Cates

ENCHILADAS CASSEROLE

1½ lb. ground beef
1 medium onion, chopped
½ lb. Cheddar cheese, grated
1 tsp. chili powder
1 tsp. salt
½ tsp. pepper
1 medium size can enchilada
   sauce
1 (6¼ oz.) bag tortilla chips
½ c. chopped black olives
   (optional)

Brown ground beef and drain. Add onions and seasonings to skillet and saute until onions are almost transparent. Reserve 2 tablespoons of cheese for topping. Add olives to cheese. Put a layer of tortilla chips in a greased 9x12 inch baking dish. Pour in half the ground beef mixture, half the cheese mixture and half the enchilada sauce. Repeat layers and top with reserved cheese. Bake at 350° for 20 to 25 minutes. Makes 6 servings.

Good served with Mexican rice and tossed salad.

Sharon Elmore

CROCK POT ITALIAN MEAT SAUCE

1½ lb. ground beef, browned
1½ c. onion, chopped
2 garlic cloves
1 (14½ oz.) can tomatoes
2 (6 oz.) cans tomato paste
2 ribs celery (with tops),
    chopped

1½ tsp. salt
2 tsp. dried oregano
¼ tsp. dried thyme
1 bay leaf

Put all ingredients in crock pot. Stir thoroughly. Cover and cook on LOW 10 to 12 hours (HIGH 4 to 5 hours).

Judy Smith

CHILI

2 lb. hamburger
1 small onion, diced
¼ c. chili powder
1 small can tomato sauce

1 can tomato soup
2 cans Brooks chili beans
7 oz. spaghetti

Brown 2 pounds hamburger with 1 onion. Add tomato sauce, tomato soup, and Brooks chili beans in a large kettle. Simmer about 10 minutes while you cook spaghetti according to package directions; drain. Add to chili and add 1 cup water only.

Mary Lauder

CHILI

2 lb. ground beef
1 large can tomatoes,
    chopped
3 Tbsp. margarine
Salt and pepper to taste
2 large cans red kidney
    beans, rinsed and
    drained

2 large onions, chopped
1 (8 oz.) can tomato sauce
Chili powder to suit taste
Enough water for desired
    consistency

Brown onions and beef in heavy skillet or Dutch oven. Drain off any grease and put onions and beef in a large pot. Add remaining ingredients. If you are in a hurry, cook over medium-high heat for 30 minutes, stirring often. If not in a hurry, cook over low heat for 1 hour or longer.

Ruth Ackerman

BEST-EVER CHILI

2 lb. ground beef
1 c. chopped onion
1 c. chopped green pepper
1 c. sliced celery
2 (15 oz.) cans (about 4 c.)
  kidney beans

2 (6 oz.) cans (4 c.) tomatoes,
  cut up
1 (6 oz.) can tomato paste
2 cloves garlic, minced
1 - 1½ Tbsp. chili powder
2 tsp. salt

In Dutch oven, cook beef, onion, green pepper and celery until meat is brown and vegetables are tender. Drain kidney beans, reserving liquid. Add beans and remaining ingredients. Cover; simmer 1 to 1½ hours. If desired, stir in some reserved bean liquid.

Jerry Evans

BAKED CHILI

2 Tbsp. shortening
⅓ c. diced onion
1 lb. ground beef
1 (No. 2½) can tomatoes
½ c. uncooked rice

1 (No. 2) can kidney beans
1 tsp. salt
½ tsp. pepper
2 tsp. chili powder

Heat shortening; add onion and cook slowly until golden brown. Add meat; stir until well done. Add tomatoes, beans and seasonings. Pour into casserole; add uncooked rice. Bake for 1 hour and 30 minutes in a 325° oven. Makes 6 servings.

Martha Harper

CHEESEBURGER PIE

1 lb. ground beef
1½ c. onions, chopped
1½ c. milk
¾ c. Bisquick baking mix
3 eggs

1 tsp. salt
¼ tsp. pepper
2 tomatoes, sliced
1 c. shredded Cheddar
  cheese

Cook beef and onions over medium heat until beef is brown; drain. Spread on greased pie plate. Beat together until smooth milk, baking mix, eggs, salt and pepper. Pour into plate. Bake 25 minutes. Top with tomato slices; sprinkle with cheese. Bake about 8 minutes longer or until knife inserted in center comes out clean. Serves 6.

Helen Sykes

CASSEROLE MEXICANA

1 Tbsp. salad oil
½ lb. ground chuck
1 env. taco, chili or sloppy joe
  seasoning mix
1 (1 lb. 4 oz. size) can kidney
  beans (undrained)
1 (8 oz. size) can tomato
  sauce
1 (3½ oz. size) can pitted
  black olives
1 (6½ oz. size) pkg. tortilla
  chips
¼ c. grated Cheddar cheese

Preheat oven to 350°F. Heat salad oil in large skillet. Add ground chuck and saute until browned. Stir in the seasoning mix, then the kidney beans and the tomato sauce. Bring to boil; stir often. Pour into 2 quart casserole. Drain olives and sprinkle over top of meat mixture. Arrange about half of the tortilla chips around edge, then sprinkle cheese on chips. Bake casserole 10 minutes or until the cheese is melted. Makes 6 servings.

Denise Figg

CORN BREAD PIE

1 lb. ground beef
1 large onion, chopped
1 can tomato soup
1 tsp. salt
2 c. water
¼ tsp. pepper
1 c. drained kernel corn
1 tsp. chili powder
½ c. chopped green pepper
¾ c. corn meal
1 Tbsp. flour
1 Tbsp. sugar
1½ tsp. baking powder
½ tsp. salt
1 Tbsp. melted shortening
1 egg
½ c. milk

Saute beef and onion until brown. Add soup, 1 teaspoon salt, water, pepper, corn, chili powder and green pepper. Simmer 15 minutes. Place in lightly greased 1½ quart casserole. Set aside. Combine corn meal, flour, sugar, ½ teaspoon salt and baking powder. Add remaining ingredients. Mix well and spoon corn bread mixture over meat. Bake at 400° about 25 minutes. Serves 6 to 8.

Donna Browning

260

CABBAGE PATCH STEW

1 lb. ground beef
2 c. chopped cabbage
1 c. water
1 can pinto beans
1 medium onion, chopped

1 can tomatoes
Chili powder to taste
Salt and pepper to taste
1 tsp. sugar
Corn bread

Brown beef with chopped onion. Add cabbage and water. Cook for 15 minutes, slowly and covered. Add pinto beans, tomatoes and remaining ingredients. Cook for about 20 minutes. Serve with hot corn bread. Serves 4 to 6.

Mary Harrod

BEEF CASSEROLE

2½ lb. ground beef
3 c. cooked rice
1 tsp. salt
¼ tsp. pepper
1 onion, minced
3 Tbsp. butter
2 tsp. vinegar

2 garlic cloves, crushed
¼ lb. fresh mushrooms, sliced
1 (10½ oz.) can mushroom soup
2 c. canned tomatoes

Put the cooked rice in a casserole. Saute beef with 2 tablespoons vinegar for a couple of minutes; drain and set aside. Saute onions and mushrooms in butter. Combine with beef; add salt and garlic; mix well and pour over rice. Mix mushroom soup and tomatoes and pour on top. Bake at 350° for about 30 minutes. Serves 6.

Michelle Lewis

BEEF BARBECUPS

1 lb. ground beef
1 Tbsp. brown sugar
1 (8 oz.) can baking powder biscuits

1 c. shredded Cheddar cheese
½ c. barbecue sauce with onion bits

Brown meat lightly and thoroughly. Press biscuits into 12 greased muffin cups, pressing dough up and around the edges of the cups. Add barbecue sauce and sugar to the meat. Mix well. Spoon into biscuit lined cups. Sprinkle cheese on top. Bake at 400° for 10 minutes. Remove from pan at once with a spatula or knife. They stay very hot.

Ruth Ackerman

BEEF-FILLED CORN BREAD SQUARES

1 lb. ground beef
⅓ c. chopped onion
1 clove garlic, minced
¼ c. catsup
1 (10 oz.) pkg. corn bread mix
½ c. shredded American
   cheese
2 tsp. cornstarch

1 (7½ oz.) can tomatoes, cut
   up
2 Tbsp. chopped canned
   green chili peppers
2 Tbsp. chopped green
   pepper
1 tsp. Worcestershire sauce

In skillet, cook ground beef, onion and garlic until meat is browned; drain off fat. Stir in catsup and ¾ teaspoon salt. In bowl, prepare corn bread mix according to package directions. Spread half of the batter in a greased 8x8x2 inch baking pan. Spoon meat mixture over batter in pan; sprinkle with cheese. Spread remaining batter over cheese. Bake, uncovered, in 350° oven for 30 to 35 minutes. Let stand 5 minutes before cutting.

Meanwhile, in small saucepan, combine cornstarch and 2 tablespoons cold water. Stir in undrained tomatoes, chili peppers, green pepper, and Worcestershire. Cook and stir until thickened and bubbly. Cut corn bread into squares; serve tomato mixture atop. Makes 6 servings.

Debbie Wilhelmus

GROUND BEEF STEW

Heat in skillet 1 tablespoon salad oil.

Add:

1 lb. ground beef
1 Tbsp. minced onion

1 tsp. minced green pepper

Mix well. Cook over medium heat until lightly browned.

Add:

1 (1 lb. 12 oz.) can tomatoes
1 (1 lb.) can mixed vegetables

1 c. cooked medium noodles
½ tsp. salt

Mix well. Cook over medium heat 20 minutes or until thoroughly heated.

Wanda Frankenberger

SEVEN LAYER CASSEROLE

4 carrots, sliced
⅔ c. rice, boiled in water 10
   minutes
2 large potatoes, sliced

1 onion, sliced
1 lb. ground beef
1 can tomato soup
½ can water or a little more

Preheat oven to 350°. Boil rice. In large, greased casserole, place sliced carrots, rice, potatoes, then ½ onion, ground beef, and rest of onion. Top with tomato soup which has been mixed with water. Cover with lid or foil and bake 1½ or 2 hours. Serve with tossed salad and rolls.

Mary K. Amyx

POOR MAN'S CHOP SUEY

1 lb. hamburger
2 c. chopped onions
1½ Tbsp. cornstarch
1½ c. water
1 bunch celery

¼ c. sugar
3 Tbsp. soy sauce
1 can bean sprouts, drained
1 can chow mein noodles
Salt to taste

Brown hamburger and onions. Add celery, water, salt and sugar. Let simmer until celery is tender. Add bean sprouts and heat thoroughly. Add cornstarch until thickened. Serve over chow mein noodles.

Stella Moore

PECAN-CHEESE BURGERS

1½ lb. ground beef
2 Tbsp. Worcestershire sauce
2 tsp. salt
1 tsp. black pepper

Dash of cayenne pepper
2 Tbsp. ice water
1 c. Cheddar cheese, grated
1 c. pecans, chopped

Combine beef with Worcestershire sauce, salt, pepper and ice water. Mix lightly and add grated cheese and pecans. Shape into 6 patties, but don't pack down. Grill to desired cooking time.

Pam Thompson

SLOPPY JOES

1 lb. ground beef
½ c. onion, chopped
½ c. celery, chopped
½ c. green pepper, chopped
½ c. catsup
½ c. water

1½ Tbsp. Worcestershire
  sauce
3 Tbsp. brown sugar
⅛ tsp. red pepper sauce
1 tsp. salt

Cook the ground beef and onion until beef is brown and onion is tender. Drain. Stir in the remaining ingredients. Cook until vegetables are tender, about 15 minutes.

Opal Willis

NACHOS

1 lb. ground beef
1 pkg. Old El Paso taco
  seasoning mix
1 can Old El Paso refried
  beans
1 jar Old El Paso green chiles
  and peppers
1 lb. Nacho chips
Salt to taste

Pepper to taste
1 small onion, diced
¼ c. green pepper, diced
1 small can mushrooms
½ lb. sharp Cheddar and
  Monterey Jack cheeses
½ head lettuce, shredded
Paprika
Extra taco sauce

Brown ground beef; add salt and pepper; drain. Add to the beef and let simmer 1 package Old El Paso taco seasoning mix, 1 can Old El Paso refried beans, 1 jar Old El Paso green chilies, onion, green pepper and can of mushrooms. Spread Nacho chips on a large tray; pour meat sauce over them. Top with shredded lettuce, shredded cheese and paprika sprinkled on top. Have extra taco sauce.

Debbie Rigdon

SALISBURY STEAK

1 can condensed golden
  mushroom or cream of
  chicken soup
1½ lb. ground beef
½ c. fine bread crumbs

1 egg, slightly beaten
¼ c. finely chopped onion
½ c. water
Dash of pepper

Combine ¼ cup of soup with rest of ingredients, except water. Mix thoroughly. Shape into patties. Place in shallow baking dish and bake at 350° for 30 minutes. Spoon off fat. Combine remaining soup and water; pour over meat. Bake 10 minutes more. *Very good.*

Mary Harrod

SALISBURY STEAK

For each pound of ground beef:

1 egg
¼ c. cream
1 tsp. salt
1 tsp. pepper
2 Tbsp. cornstarch
1 tsp. parsley
1 slice bread in fine crumbs
    (¼ c.)

½ tsp. Worcestershire sauce
½ tsp. prepared mustard
4 oz. can mushrooms
1 bouillon cube, dissolved in
    1 c. water

Mix egg, meat, cream, crumbs and seasoning. Form into patties and brown slowly in heavy skillet sprinkled with salt. Remove to warm plate. Mix cornstarch with a little mushroom liquid. Pour off accumulated fat from skillet and put in the mushroom liquid, cornstarch mixture and bouillon. Stir and cook until transparent and slightly reduced in volume. Pour over steaks. Sprinkle with parsley. Cook about 30 minutes.

Flo Gish

SMOTHERED HAMBURGER STEAKS

1 lb. ground beef
1 pkg. brown gravy mix

1 large Bermuda onion, sliced
Salt and pepper to taste

Season hamburger with salt and pepper. Shape into 4 large patties and brown in large skillet. (I use a large iron skillet.) Mix brown gravy mix with water it calls for, plus half cup extra and bring to boil according to directions. Drain off grease from hamburgers. Pour gravy over hamburgers. Slice onion; place over burgers. Bring to a boil. Cover pan and simmer for 15 minutes. Makes 4 servings.

Allouise Davidson

SLUMGULLION

1 lb. ground beef
½ lb. bacon
1 large onion
2 cans (1 qt.) tomatoes

¼ lb. American cheese
Salt
Pepper

Dice the bacon; fry until crisp and put into kettle. (I use old fashioned black Dutch oven.) Brown the ground beef in skillet; when done, add to kettle. Pour in tomatoes and cook 15 minutes. Cut the cheese into fine cubes and stir in until cheese is soft. Eat immediately.

Note: This is good for cold winter days and easy to fix.

Allouise Davidson

SWEDISH MEAT BALLS

1 env. Lipton onion soup mix
1 lb. hamburger

1 (12 oz.) jar chili sauce
1 jar red currant jelly

Mix together onion soup mix and hamburger; shape in small balls and brown. Mix together chili sauce and red currant jelly. Pour in casserole dish and add meat balls. Bake at 350° for 30 minutes.

Sue Skelton

STUFFED GREEN PEPPERS

8 large green peppers
1 Tbsp. butter
1 onion, chopped
1 lb. ground beef

1 c. canned tomatoes
2 c. cooked rice
Salt and pepper to taste
⅓ c. dry bread crumbs

Cut green peppers in halves; remove seeds and white membrane. Saute chopped onion and ground beef in butter. Add canned tomatoes and rice. Season with salt and pepper. Fill peppers with mixture. Top with bread crumbs. Bake in a moderate oven (350°) for 15 minutes; increase temperature to 400° and continue baking until tops are brown, about 10 minutes.

Zora Lawson

266

TACO PIE

1 lb. ground beef
1 pkg. taco seasoning mix
1 (4 oz.) can chopped green
  chilies, drained
½ c. onion, chopped
1¼ c. milk
¼ c. Bisquick baking mix

3 eggs
2 tomatoes, sliced and 2,
  chopped
1 c. shredded Cheddar
  cheese
Sour cream
Shredded lettuce

Cook beef and onion until beef is browned; drain. Stir in seasoning mix. Spread on greased pie plate; sprinkle with chilies. Beat milk, baking mix and eggs until smooth. Pour on plate. Bake 25 minutes in a 400° oven. Top with tomato slices, sprinkled with cheese. Bake about 10 minutes longer or until knife inserted comes out clean. Cool about 5 minutes. Serve topped with sour cream, chopped tomatoes and shredded lettuce. Serves 6.

Helen Sykes

SPANISH DELIGHT CASSEROLE

½ c. Wesson oil
2 chopped onions
2 chopped green peppers
2 Tbsp. chili sauce
1 medium pkg. small noodles,
  cooked
1½ lb. ground beef

1 can tomato paste
2 small cans sliced
  mushrooms
1 can creamed corn
½ lb. grated cheese
1 medium bottle olives

Brown ground beef, onions and peppers. Add all other ingredients, including cooked noodles. Simmer 10 minutes in skillet. Pour into baking dish; sprinkle cheese and sliced olives over top. Bake about 30 minutes at 350°.

For smaller amount, use ½ of all ingredients.

Mark A. Cowan

SPAGHETTI

1 lb. hamburger, drained
1 onion, finely chopped
4 Tbsp. bouillon powder
½ tsp. salt
Pepper to taste
1 can tomato sauce

1 can tomato paste
2 c. hot water
2 tsp. sugar
½ tsp. basil
½ tsp. oregano
Dash of garlic

Simmer for 1 hour and serve over 1 pound cooked spaghetti.

Donna Browning

SPAGHETTI PIE

6 oz. spaghetti
2 Tbsp. butter
⅓ c. grated Parmesan cheese
2 eggs, well beaten
1 c. cottage cheese
1 lb. ground beef or pork
  sausage
½ c. onions, chopped

¼ c. green pepper
1 (8 oz.) can tomatoes, cut up
1 (6 oz.) can tomato paste
1 tsp. sugar
1 tsp. dried oregano
½ tsp. garlic salt
½ c. shredded Mozzarella
  cheese

Cook spaghetti according to package directions; drain. Stir butter into hot spaghetti. Stir in Parmesan cheese and eggs. Form spaghetti mixture into a crust in buttered 10 inch pie plate. Spread cottage cheese over bottom of spaghetti crust. In skillet, cook ground beef or sausage, onion and green pepper until vegetables are tender and meat is brown. Drain off excess fat. Stir in undrained tomatoes, paste, sugar, oregano and garlic salt; heat through. Turn mixture in spaghetti crust. Bake in 350° oven for 20 minutes. Sprinkle Mozzarella cheese on top. Bake 5 minutes until cheese melts.

Wanda Harris

BAKED LASAGNA

Meatballs:

1 lb. hamburger
2 Tbsp. chopped onion
2 cloves garlic, crushed
2 Tbsp. chopped parsley
1 tsp. oregano

¾ tsp. salt
Dash of pepper
2 Tbsp. grated Parmesan
  cheese
1 egg

1. Mix ingredients together; shape into balls ¾ inch in diameter.

Tomato Sauce:

¼ c. olive oil
¼ c. chopped onion
1 clove garlic, crushed
1 (12 oz.) can whole tomatoes
2 (6 oz. size) cans tomato
    paste

2 tsp. oregano
1 tsp. basil
1 Tbsp. sugar
2 tsp. salt
1 tsp. garlic powder
¼ tsp. pepper

2. In hot oil, in large heavy skillet, brown meatballs; remove. Add onion and garlic; saute 5 minutes.

3. Add rest of sauce ingredients with ½ cup water and meatballs; stir. Bring to boil; reduce heat and simmer, uncovered, 1½ hours, stirring occasionally.

½ pkg. lasagna
1 lb. Mozzarella cheese,
    diced

1 lb. cottage cheese
1 c. grated Parmesan cheese

4. Heat oven to 350°F. Grease baking dish. Cook lasagna as label directs. Drain; rinse in water.

5. In baking dish, layer all ingredients (lasagna, Mozzarella, cottage cheese, tomato sauce) with meatballs and Parmesan cheese. Repeat. Bake 30 to 35 minutes.

Alice Ritchey

EASY LASAGNE

1 lb. ground beef
⅛ tsp. garlic powder
1 Tbsp. parsley flakes
½ tsp. oregano
4 c. hot water

1 pkg. Betty Crocker Lasagne
    Hamburger Helper
½ c. cottage cheese
¼ c. grated Parmesan cheese
2 c. (8 oz.) Mozzarella cheese

Brown and drain 1 pound ground beef. Add ⅛ teaspoon garlic powder, 1 tablespoon parsley flakes, ½ teaspoon oregano, 4 cups hot water and package of Betty Crocker Hamburger Helper. Heat to boiling, stir constantly; reduce heat; cover and simmer 20 to 25 minutes. Stir occasionally. Stir in ½ cup cottage cheese. Sprinkle ¼ cup grated Parmesan cheese over top and 2 cups Mozzarella cheese. Slide under broiler until cheese is lightly browned and bubbly.

Mary Baxter

IMPOSSIBLE LASAGNE PIE

½ c. creamed cottage cheese
¼ c. grated Parmesan cheese
1 lb. ground beef, cooked and
    drained
1 tsp. oregano leaves
½ tsp. basil leaves
1 (6 oz.) can tomato paste

1 c. shredded Mozzarella
    cheese
1 c. milk
⅔ c. Bisquick baking mix
2 eggs
1 tsp. salt
¼ tsp. pepper

Heat oven to 400°. Grease pie plate, 10 x 1½ inches. Layer cottage and Parmesan cheeses in plate. Mix cooked beef, herbs, paste and ½ cup Mozzarella cheese; spoon over top. Beat remaining ingredients until smooth, 15 seconds in blender on high or 1 minute with hand beater. Pour into plate. Bake until knife inserted in center comes out clean, 30 to 35 minutes. Sprinkle remaining cheese on top. Cool 5 minutes. Serves 6 to 8.

Mary V. Stanley

LASAGNE PIE

1 lb. ground beef
1 tsp. basil
1 (6 oz.) can tomato sauce
1 c. Mozzarella cheese,
    shredded
½ c. cottage cheese
⅓ c. Parmesan cheese,
    grated

1 c. milk
⅔ c. Bisquick baking mix
2 eggs
1 tsp. salt
¼ tsp. pepper
1 tsp. oregano

Cook beef until browned; drain. Stir in oregano, basil, tomato paste and ½ cup Mozzarella cheese. Layer cottage cheese and Parmesan cheese in greased pie plate. Spoon beef mixture over top. Beat together milk, baking mix, eggs, salt and pepper until smooth. Pour on top. Bake about 35 minutes in a preheated 400° oven. Pie is done when knife inserted comes out clean. Serves 6.

Sharon Duke

LASAGNA

2 lb. ground chuck
½ lb. ground pork
1 clove garlic, minced
1 Tbsp. basil
2 Tbsp. chopped parsley
1½ tsp. salt
1 large can tomatoes
2 (6 oz.) cans tomato paste
2 c. Ricotta cheese or cream
   style cottage cheese

⅓ c. Parmesan cheese
2 eggs, beaten
1 tsp. salt
½ tsp. pepper
1 lb. Mozzarella cheese
10 strips lasagna, cooked,
   drained and rinsed in
   cold water

Cook meat until brown; drain off excess fat. Add garlic, parsley, basil, salt, tomatoes and tomato paste. Simmer for ½ hour, stirring occasionally. Combine Ricotta and Parmesan cheese; add eggs, salt and pepper. To assemble lasagna, pour a thin layer of tomato sauce in bottom of 13x9x2 inch baking dish. Cover with a layer of lasagna. Spread half the cheese mixture over lasagna; lay half the Mozzarella over the cheese. Spread a layer of tomato sauce over all. Repeat layers, ending with the tomato sauce. Cover with foil and bake in a 350° oven for 20 minutes. Uncover and bake 20 minutes longer. Let set 15 minutes before serving.

Ladonna Darnell

LASAGNA

Brown 1½ pounds ground beef, onion and garlic powder to taste. Add 2 bay leaves, 1 can tomatoes, 1½ small cans Hunt's tomato sauce and mushrooms, and 1 small can tomato paste. Add oregano. Bring to a boil; turn down heat and let simmer 1½ to 2 hours. Boil lasagna noodles and let stand in cold water. Place in baking dish; layer sauce, lasagna noodles, small curd cottage cheese, Mozzarella cheese, grated Parmesan cheese and repeat layers. Bake at 350° for 20 minutes.

Kathy Ryan

LASAGNA

1 box lasagna noodles (¾)
1 lb. can tomatoes
1 (6 oz.) can tomato paste
1 Tbsp. sugar
2 (1½ oz.) env. French's
   spaghetti sauce mix
1 c. cottage cheese (cream
   style)

2 lb. ground beef
1 (8 oz.) can tomato sauce
1 (6 oz.) can water
2 tsp. minced garlic
1 (8 oz.) pkg. Mozzarella
   cheese
½ c. Parmesan cheese

Mix; mash can of tomatoes with potato masher. Mix tomato sauce, tomato paste with cup water, sauce mix, and garlic. Let simmer 30 minutes. While this is simmering, brown meat in little olive oil slowly. Pour in sauce; add little water if necessary and a little salt. Stir occasionally and cook for 15 minutes. Cook noodles. Cook a little longer than it is on package. Rinse after cooked. Use pan 7 x 11 x ½ inch deep. In bottom of pan, place half of noodles (lay flat), half of sauce, half of Mozzarella cheese (cut in strips), and half of cottage cheese. Repeat first layer for second layer. Sprinkle with Parmesan cheese when ready to bake. Bake at 350° for 25 to 30 minutes or until cheese starts to brown. Let cool a few seconds, then cut.

Oleta Bryan

LASAGNE MEAT SAUCE

2 slices bacon
4 Tbsp. butter
1 clove garlic (if desired)
½ onion
2 Tbsp. finely chopped carrot
1 Tbsp. finely chopped celery
1 tsp. chopped parsley
1 lb. lean ground beef
¼ tsp. marjoram
½ lb. sliced Mozzarella
   cheese

2 c. fresh or canned peeled
   Italian egg tomatoes
½ c. tomato paste, diluted in
   1⅓ c. water
½ c. dry white wine
½ lb. cottage cheese
¼ tsp. salt
1 egg, beaten
½ c. Parmesan cheese
Salt and pepper to taste

Place bacon, butter, garlic, onion, carrot and celery in saucepan and saute gently for 4 to 5 minutes. Discard garlic and add beef, marjoram and parsley; simmer, stirring occasionally, until meat is browned. Add wine and cook until wine has evaporated. Be patient here. Add tomatoes and tomato paste mixture. Simmer, uncovered, for 30 minutes. Season to taste and cook 15 minutes more or until sauce is thick. Mix cottage cheese, egg, Parmesan cheese, pepper and salt into smooth paste. Prepare lasagne noodles as directed on package. In a large rectangular baking dish, put a layer of meat sauce, a layer of cooked noodles, a layer of cottage cheese paste, and a layer of Mozzarella cheese. Repeat, ending with topping of meat sauce. Bake in 350° oven for 30 minutes. Let stand 10 minutes before serving.

This is also good prepared ahead and frozen until ready to serve.

Shirley Cates

SAUSAGE LASAGNA WRAPS

Cook and drain 6 lasagna noodles. Divide 1 pound Hillshire Farm smoked sausage into 6 pieces. Split lengthwise and stuff with ½ slice of Mozzarella cheese. Wrap each piece in a lasagna noodle. Place in baking dish and cover with 1 (16 ounce) jar of Italian cooking sauce. Bake at 350° for 30 minutes. Serve with grated Parmesan cheese.

Marsha Ratliff

LASAGNE AND CHEESE CASSEROLE

1 (½ lb.) pkg. lasagne
½ c. seedless raisins
1 - 2 Tbsp. rum
1 c. sour cream

1 c. cottage cheese
2 - 3 Tbsp. blanched, slivered almonds

Preheat oven to 350°. Soak raisins in rum. Cook noodles in boiling salted water until just tender. Drain; rinse with cold water; drain again and put in a deep buttered casserole. Sprinkle with a little salt and pepper. Mix sour cream, cottage cheese and raisins; pour over the noodles and toss together lightly. Sprinkle with the almonds and cook for 20 minutes.

Paula White

BEEF

BEEF STROGANOFF

1½ lb. sirloin steak
Flour
1½ tsp. salt
½ tsp. pepper
2 onions, finely chopped
½ lb. mushrooms, chopped

1 Tbsp. Worcestershire
1 clove garlic, crushed
6 Tbsp. butter
1 (10 oz.) can consomme
1 pt. sour cream
1 tsp. paprika

Cut steak into strips and dredge with flour. Season with 1 teaspoon salt and ¼ teaspoon pepper. Saute onions, mushrooms and garlic in butter in skillet for 5 minutes. Add steak and cook over high heat 3 minutes, stirring constantly. Then remove steak and vegetables from skillet. Blend 2 tablespoons flour into 2 tablespoons drippings in the skillet; add consomme and cook, stirring, until smooth and thickened. Stir in the sour cream and remaining salt and pepper; place over low heat. Add the paprika, Worcestershire sauce, beef and vegetables; heat thoroughly. Serve over noodles or rice. Serves 4.

Sandi Freeman

TZIMMES

3 lb. lean beef short ribs
2 medium onions, cut in
    chunks
1 c. water
¼ c. packed brown sugar
1 tsp. salt

½ tsp. cinnamon
3 medium size sweet
    potatoes (2 lb.), peeled
    and cut in chunks
1 c. medium size prunes

In Dutch oven, brown ribs well on all sides; drain off fat. Push ribs to side; add onion; saute until tender. Add water, sugar, salt and cinnamon. Cover and bake in preheated 350° oven 1½ hours or until beef is almost tender. Add potatoes and prunes. Cover and bake 45 minutes longer or until meat and vegetables are tender. Serve immediately or let stand covered in turned off oven up to 1 hour. Makes 4 servings.

Charles T. Thompson

STUFFED FLANK STEAK

1½ - 2 lb. flank steak
1½ c. soft bread cubes
1½ c. mashed potatoes
4 Tbsp. instant minced onion
3 Tbsp. parsley flakes
¾ tsp. salt

1 tsp. poultry seasoning
¼ tsp. pepper
3 slices crisp cooked bacon,
    crumbled
¼ c. hot water
¾ c. water

Combine bacon drippings, bread cubes, potatoes, instant minced onion, parsley, salt, poultry seasoning, pepper and bacon; mix well. Gradually add ¼ cup hot water. Score steak lightly on both sides in 1½ inch squares. Beat on both sides with a meat mallet. Spread with stuffing to within ½ inch of edge. Roll up jelly roll fashion. Tie roll in 3 or 4 places with string and place, seam side down, in pan. Add ¾ cup water. Cover and bake slowly 1 hour and 15 minutes or until meat is tender. To serve, cut in crosswise slices. Serves 6.

Cristy Lewis

STUFFED BEEF ROLL

1 - 1½ or 2 lb. flank steak or 2
    lb. round steak
    (boneless), cut ½ inch
    thick
3 medium size onions,
    chopped (1½ c.)
4 Tbsp. (½ stick) butter
2 c. (4 oz.) ready-mix bread
    stuffing
¼ c. chopped parsley
2 Tbsp. grated Parmesan
    cheese

½ tsp. garlic salt
½ c. water
¼ c. flour
¼ c. salad oil
2 env. spaghetti sauce mix
4 c. tomato juice
1 (2 lb.) can Italian tomatoes
2 (4 oz.) cans mushroom
    stems and pieces

Ask meatman to split flank steak, butterfly fashion. Or you can do it yourself with a sharp long bladed knife. Work slowly, cutting with a sawing motion, as evenly as possible. (If using round steak, pound very thin with a mallet or rolling pin.) Saute ¼ cup onion in butter, just until soft, in medium size saucepan. (Save remaining onions for sauce.) Stir in bread stuffing, parsley, Parmesan cheese, garlic salt, and water; toss with fork until moist and well mixed. Lay steak flat on counter top; spread stuffing over steak to within 1 inch of edges. Starting at one end, roll up, jelly roll style; fasten with 2 or 3 picks. Fold up ends of roll to hold in stuffing; fasten with more wooden picks. (Can be tied with string.) Rub roll well with flour; brown in salad oil in heavy kettle or Dutch oven. Stir in saved 1¼ cups onions; saute just until soft. Stir in spaghetti sauce mix, tomato juice, tomatoes and mushrooms with liquid; cover. Simmer 1½ hours or until meat is tender. Remove roll to carving board; take out picks (or remove string). Carve meat in ½ inch thick slices. Measure out and chill 6 cups of sauce; serve remaining with meat.

I like spaghetti served with this, use the extra sauce. Or reserve extra sauce to use another time.

Ruthie Marty

TOURNEDOS CORDON ROUGE

8 (3 inch) patty shells
1 c. Bearnaise sauce
1 c. sauteed mushrooms
½ c. ham in julienne strips

8 tournedos (¾ oz. each from
   tenderloin of beef)
8 mushroom caps
1 c. Madeira sauce

Mix Bearnaise sauce with mushrooms and ham julienne and fill patty shells with the mixture. Bake in 400° oven until puffed up and souffle like. Season and saute pieces of tenderloin to desired point. Saute mushroom caps. Top filled patty shells and tournedos and pin mushroom caps on. Pour Madeira sauce over all. Serves 4.

D. L. Bond

TOURNEDOS CREOLE STYLE

1 (9 oz.) fillet of beef, cut in
   half horizontally
1 Tbsp. butter
2 green onions, chopped fine
1 fresh tomato, skinned,
   seeds removed and
   chopped

1 tsp. green pepper, chopped
   fine
¼ inch piece bay leaf
1 Tbsp. sliced mushrooms
2 oz. dry red wine
Salt to taste
Pepper to taste

Saute fillet in butter on both sides for 2 minutes; remove from pan. Add green onions and saute lightly. Add tomato, green pepper, bay leaf, mushrooms and red wine. Simmer over low flame for 15 minutes or until sauce is reduced one half. Return fillets to skillet and saute a few minutes longer. Serve with rice or pasta. Serves 2.

Paula White

STEAK AND RICE

1½ lb. tenderized boneless
    steak
1½ Tbsp. vegetable oil
2 large onions, cut in ½ inch
    slices, separated into
    rings
1 (4 oz.) can sliced
    mushrooms, drained
    (reserve liquid)

1 (10¾ oz.) can condensed
    cream of mushroom soup
½ c. dry sherry
1½ tsp. garlic salt
3 c. cooked rice

Cut steak into thin strips. In a large skillet, brown meat in oil, using high heat. Add onions. Saute until tender crisp. Blend soup, sherry, liquid from mushrooms, and garlic salt. Pour over steak. Add mushrooms. Reduce heat. Cover and simmer for 1 hour or until steak is tender. Serve over beds of fluffy rice. Makes 6 servings.

Betty King

STEAK AND KIDNEY STEW

2 lb. chuck or sirloin beef,
    cubed
2 pork or lamb kidneys, sliced
2 medium size onions, sliced
2 Tbsp. flour

1 sprig thyme or ½ tsp. dried
1 Tbsp. chopped parsley
Salt and pepper to taste
1 c. water
½ lb. sliced mushrooms

Toss beef cubes and kidney slices in flour seasoned with salt and pepper. Place in casserole. Add onions, thyme, and parsley. Pour water over this. Cover with foil. Cook at 300° for 1½ hours. Add mushrooms and stir stew. Recover with foil and cook for another 30 minutes. Dust stew with chopped parsley. Serve with boiled potatoes, baby carrots, and peas. Serves 6.

Alice Alessio

PIZZA SWISS STEAK

2 lb. round steak (1 inch
    thick)
1 (8 oz.) can tomato sauce
1 (5 oz.) can pizza sauce
1 can mushrooms

1 fried pepper
Oregano
Flour
Salt
Black pepper

Mix flour, salt and pepper in a bowl. Sprinkle over steak and pound both sides. Brown in hot fat. Remove from fry pan and place in baking pan. Mix the sauces; add mushrooms, fried pepper and oregano. Pour this over meat in oven. Bake for 45 minutes to 1 hour in 325° oven.

Sarah A. Drewes

PIZZA STEAK

2 lb. round steak
1 (8 oz.) can tomato sauce
1 (5½ oz.) can pizza sauce
½ c. water
½ tsp. crushed oregano
1 onion, sliced
1 green pepper, sliced

½ c. sliced mushrooms
¼ c. all-purpose flour
2 tsp. salt
¼ tsp. pepper
3 Tbsp. fat
8 oz. Mozzarella cheese

Combine ¼ cup all-purpose flour, 2 teaspoons salt and ¼ teaspoon pepper. Pound into steak. Cut steak into serving pieces. Brown slowly on both sides in 3 tablespoons fat. Combine tomato sauce, pizza sauce, water and spices. Put steak in baking dish. Place slices of onion, pepper and mushrooms on top of steak. Pour on tomato sauce mixture. Cover. Bake about 1 hour until tender. Add cheese last 10 minutes.

Patti Roby

PINWHEEL STEAKS FOR GRILL

1 round or flank steak
About 10 mushrooms

1 env. favorite marinade

Marinate steak about 4 hours. Cut steak into 10 strips. Wrap each strip around a mushroom and secure with toothpicks. Place on grill about 4 inches from heat. Cook 3 to 5 minutes on each side, brushing with marinade several times.

Patti Roby

STEAK MARINADE

1 c. soy sauce
2 large onions, coarsely
    chopped (about 1 c.)
2 cloves garlic, halved

¼ c. Kitchen Bouquet
2 tsp. Beau Monde
    seasoning*

Combine soy sauce, onion and garlic in blender. Process at high speed 1 minute or until smooth. Stir in Kitchen Bouquet and Beau Monde. Makes 2½ cups.

* Can substitute 1 teaspoon monosodium glutamate (Accent) and 1 teaspoon seasoning salt.

SueAnn Maynard

STEAK WITH GRAVY

3 lb. beef (1 inch thick round
   or sirloin steak)
⅓ c. flour
3 Tbsp. oil

1 env. dry onion soup mix
½ c. water
1 can cream of mushroom
   soup

Sprinkle meat with half the flour. Pound in. Cut meat into 6 or 8 serving pieces. Melt oil in skillet; brown meat about 15 minutes. Sprinkle onion soup over meat; mix water and mushroom soup; pour over meat and cover tightly. Simmer for 1½ hours or until tender.

Dollie D. Billiter

SPICED BEEF

4 or 5 lb. chuck roast
Cider vinegar
2 onions, sliced
½ bay leaf
1 tsp. cinnamon
1 tsp. allspice
1 tsp. cloves

1½ tsp. salt
1 tsp. pepper
2 onions
4 large carrots
1 medium turnip
1 rib of celery

Cover beef roast with cider vinegar, 2 onions, ½ bay leaf, cinnamon, allspice and cloves. Let the roast marinate for 12 hours or more. Drain. Reserve liquor. Place the meat in a roasting pan. Heat to a boiling point half of the vinegar marinade and 2 cups of water; pour over roast. Bake in slow oven at 275° for 3 hours. Take 2 onions, 4 carrots, 1 turnip and 1 rib of celery; put through a grinder, then saute in butter until golden brown. Add to the roast for the last half hour of cooking. Add salt if needed. The stock may be thickened with flour.

Peggy Kessinger

SNOW PEAS WITH BEEF

1½ lb. beef tenderloin, sliced
    thin
Peanut oil or salad oil
Salt to taste
4 Tbsp. cornstarch

4 c. chicken bouillon
1 tsp. sorghum molasses
½ lb. snow peas
1 c. sliced water chestnuts

Saute beef in peanut oil. Season with salt. Blend cornstarch with chicken bouillon. Add to meat; add remaining ingredients. Cook until sauce thickens. Adjust seasoning to taste. Serves 6.

Lynnette Bonn

SAUCY STEAK

1 lb. round steak, cut in
    serving pieces
¼ c. all-purpose flour
1 Tbsp. cooking oil
1 c. onion, chopped
1 (16 oz.) can whole potatoes,
    drained (reserve liquid)
⅓ c. catsup
2 Tbsp. Worcestershire sauce
¼ c. green pepper, chopped

1 or 2 tsp. instant beef
    bouillon
1 tsp. salt
1 tsp. dried marjoram leaves
¼ tsp. black pepper
1 (10 oz.) pkg. frozen Italian
    green beans
1 (2 oz.) jar pimento, sliced
    and drained

Coat beef steaks with flour; pound into beef. Brown beef in cooking oil; push beef to side. Cook and stir onion in oil until tender; drain. Add enough water to reserved potato liquid to measure 1 cup. Mix potato liquid, catsup, Worcestershire sauce, green pepper, instant bouillon, salt, marjoram and pepper; pour on beef and onion. Heat to boiling and reduce heat. Cover and simmer until beef is tender, about 1½ hours. Rinse frozen beans under cold water to separate. Add potatoes, beans and pimento to the steak. Heat to boiling; reduce heat. Cover and simmer until beans are tender, about 15 minutes.

Peggy Kessinger

YOCIANNE'S BANGKOK DINNER

1 lb. beef, cubed
¼ small head cabbage, cut in
    1 inch pieces
2 - 3 stalks broccoli, cut in 1
    inch pieces

1 large onion, diced
2 tsp. Ajinomoto
    (monosodium glutamate)
Thai rice noodles

Cook noodles in boiling salt water; drain and set aside. (Noodles are irregular shaped, but roll up when cooked.) These cook very quickly, about 5 or 6 minutes. Sprinkle beef with 1 teaspoon Ajinamoto and brown very fast; set aside. Sprinkle vegetables with 1 teaspoon Ajinamoto. Cook broccoli in hot cooking oil about 1 minute, before adding cabbage and onion. Cook vegetables fast; do not overcook. Cook about 4 or 5 minutes. Combine noodles, beef and vegetables. Serve immediately, plain or with soy sauce.

Note: Use no salt. Ajinamoto takes care of this.

Pam Thompson

MEAT CHUNKS - SNIAH

1 lb. beef, cubed
4 ripe tomatoes, sliced
2 summer squash, cubed
1 small eggplant, cubed
3 potatoes, peeled and cubed

1 small onion, chopped
Salt
Pepper
3 Tbsp. oil

Grease a baking dish and place in all onion. Top with a layer of vegetables (but not tomatoes); add layer of meat; repeat layers in this order until used up. Top with tomato slices; pour over oil and sprinkle with salt and pepper. Bake in a moderate oven for an hour, until meat is tender. Serve hot as a main course. Use moderate oven about 350°. Preparing time: 15 minutes. Cooking time: 60 minutes. Serves 5 or 6.

Paula White

MINUTE STEAK SCRAMBLE

4 cube steaks, cut in strips
¼ tsp. garlic salt
¼ tsp. ginger
¼ c. salad oil
2 green peppers, cut into
   strips
1 c. bias cut celery slices

3 Tbsp. cornstarch
1 c. cold water
6 Tbsp. soy sauce
3 tomatoes, peeled and cut
   into eighths
Rice

Season meat with garlic salt and ginger. Heat half of the oil in skillet; add meat and brown quickly on all sides. Remove the meat. Add remaining oil; heat. Add the peppers and celery; cook just until slightly tender (about 3 minutes). Mix cornstarch, water and soy sauce. Add to skillet; cook and stir until mixture thickens. Add meat and tomatoes; heat. Serve with hot rice.

Maxine Welch

MINUTE STEAK MEXICANA

2 eggs
¼ c. milk
1 tsp. cooking oil
¾ c. all-purpose flour
4 beef cube steaks
3 Tbsp. cooking oil

½ c. chopped onions
½ c. chopped green pepper
1 Tbsp. butter or margarine
1 c. American cheese
Sliced green onion (optional)

Combine eggs, milk and the 1 teaspoon oil. Stir together flour, ¼ teaspoon salt and ¼ teaspoon of pepper. Dip meat in flour-egg mixture, then flour again. Heat the 3 tablespoons cooking oil in large skillet. Add meat; cook over medium heat 8 to 10 minutes on each side. Remove to platter and keep warm. Cook onions, green pepper and ¼ teaspoon pepper in 1 tablespoon butter until tender. Add undrained tomatoes; heat. Stir in cheese until melted. Pour over steaks. Garnish with green onions.

Jean Lyle

ROUND STEAK WITH GRAVY

Place a round steak in an oblong pan; salt and pepper it. Slice an onion (thin) and place over steak. Pour a small can Franco-American beef gravy or mushroom gravy over steak. Cover with Reynold's Wrap and bake at 350° for 2 hours. Serve with mashed potatoes. *Very good.*

Frances Crum

ROUND STEAK WITH MUSHROOM GRAVY

2 lb. round steak
2 tsp. salt
Pepper to taste
Flour

1 medium onion, chopped
2 Tbsp. water
1 can mushroom soup

Cut steak into individual serving pieces. Sprinkle salt and pepper on each piece. Dip in flour. Brown steak on both sides. Mix water with soup. Alternate layers of steak, onion and soup. Cover and cook at 350° for 2 hours or until tender. Yield: 6 servings.

Madeline Ogden

ROUND STEAK BAKE

2 lb. round steak
½ env. dried onion soup

1 can condensed cream of
mushroom soup

Place steak in heavy frying pan. Sprinkle with onion soup. Spread with mushroom soup. Remember, the onion soup is salty, so salt sparingly. Cover pan. Bake in 325° oven about 2 hours or until tender.

Allouise Davidson

RICHARD'S TENDERLOIN FOR TWO

2 Tbsp. butter
1 clove garlic, minced
¾ - 1 tsp. dried basil, crushed
Salt and pepper
2 (4 oz.) slices beef tenderloin

2 large fresh mushrooms,
fluted
2 slices French bread,
buttered and toasted

Melt butter in a heavy skillet. Stir in garlic and basil. Sprinkle meat with salt and freshly ground pepper. Add to skillet along with mushrooms. Pan broil over medium high heat (4 minutes on each side for rare, 6 minutes on each side for medium). Serve on toasted bread. Pour pan drippings over toast and top with mushrooms.

Richard Nannie

GLAZED CORNED BEEF

8 lb. corned beef brisket
2 medium onions, peeled and
quartered
2 bay leaves

1 tsp. salt
10 whole black peppers
1 clove garlic
4 whole cloves

Glaze:

½ c. dark corn syrup

1 Tbsp. prepared mustard

1. Day before serving: Put brisket in large kettle; cover with cold water.

2. Add onions, bay leaves, salt, black peppers, garlic and cloves. Bring to boiling.

3. Reduce heat and simmer, covered, about 4 hours, or just until corned beef is fork tender.

4. Remove corned beef from cooking liquid. Cool completely. Refrigerate, covered, overnight.

5. Next day, make glaze. In small saucepan, combine corn syrup and mustard.

6. Bring to boiling over medium heat, stirring constantly. Reduce heat and simmer, uncovered, 10 minutes, stirring occasionally. Remove from heat and let cool.

7. Trim any excess fat from corned beef. Place meat on rack in broiler pan. Brush top and sides with some of the glaze.

8. Run under broiler, 5 or 6 inches from heat, 10 minutes. Brush several times with remaining glaze.

9. Let corned beef cool. Refrigerate until ready to serve. Makes 12 servings.

Sarah A. Drewes

REBEL STEAK

Use any thick cut steak desired. Marinate at room temperature for 3 hours before grilling. Marinate steak in genuine Chinese soy sauce. (This can be purchased in any Chinese grocery store.) After marinating, drain steak; sprinkle with garlic salt and cover with fine ground black pepper. Grill-sear 3 minutes close to coals on each side with lid on. Raise grill. Cook 5 to 8 minutes on each side, depending on desired doneness.

It won't be salty from soy sauce. It won't be hot from the pepper. Just good and tender.

Pablo and Rose Briseno

KENTUCKY BURGOO

2 lb. lean beef
1 medium size stewing
    chicken
1 lb. veal
4 qt. water
2 c. chopped okra
2 green peppers, chopped
1 small red pepper
1 qt. tomatoes
6 ears corn, cut off cobs

2 c. diced raw potatoes
2 c. onions, diced
3 large carrots, diced
1 garlic clove, mashed
1 c. minced fresh parsley
1 bunch celery, chopped
    (with leaves)
Salt and pepper to taste
3 c. dry sherry

Boil beef, chicken and veal in water until tender. Remove meat from bones and replace meat in pot. Add other ingredients, except sherry, and cook over slow heat for 2 hours. The mixture should be very thick. Stir it up from the bottom occasionally. Before serving, add sherry and stir well. Serves 12.

Paula White

KOREAN STEAK

1½ lb. round steak
¼ c. soy sauce
3 Tbsp. cooking oil
½ c. onion, chopped fine
2 Tbsp. toasted sesame
   seeds

1 or 2 garlic cloves, minced
2 tsp. sugar
½ tsp. ground ginger
¼ tsp. pepper

Beat meat with meat mallet. Score meat on both sides by criss-crossing shallow diamond shaped cuts. Cut into 3x4 inch pieces. Combine other ingredients and mix well. Pour over meat and marinate at room temperature for 1 hour. Arrange meat on broiler rack 3 inches from flame. Broil for 6 minutes; turn once; baste with marinade as necessary. Serves 6.

Pam Thompson

PEPPY CURRY BEEF

6 Tbsp. vegetable oil
1½ c. sliced green peppers
1½ c. sliced Spanish onions
1 c. celery
1 lb. beef sirloin, cut in thin
   strips
¼ c. beef broth

1 medium garlic clove
½ tsp. cinnamon
2 tsp. cornstarch
3 tsp. water
4 tsp. soy sauce
4 Tbsp. madras or hot
   Jamaican curry powder

Heat oil in large fry pan. Add green peppers, celery and onions. Cook 8 minutes, stirring occasionally. Remove vegetables with a slotted spoon. Place in a saucepan or bowl. Cover to keep warm. Add beef strips to same fry pan. Saute until brown. Remove with slotted spoon. Add to cooked vegetables. Keep warm. Combine cornstarch and water in small bowl. Stir until smooth. Add remaining ingredients to bowl and stir. Pour sauce mixture into the fry pan and cook, stirring constantly, until mixture thickens. Return beef and vegetables to fry pan; heat thoroughly. Serve over rice.

Pat Vinscom

HUNGARIAN GOULASH - TAIVSHIL GOULASCH HUNGARI

2 lb. lean steak, cubed
3 carrots, diced
1 onion, diced
½ c. celery, diced
½ c. ketchup
2 Tbsp. brown sugar
3 Tbsp. Worcestershire sauce
1 tsp. paprika

2 Tbsp. vinegar
½ tsp. powdered mustard
1 tsp. salt
2 Tbsp. flour
1 clove garlic, grated
2 Tbsp. fat
3 c. hot water
Parsley

Brown meat, onion and garlic in fat. Set aside. Put ketchup and next 6 ingredients (preceding) in a mixing bowl. Place pan with meat and onion on low heat. Add celery and carrots. Pour the hot water over the meat; add the rest of the ingredients from the mixing bowl and mix well. Cover and simmer for 2 hours. Mix the flour with cold water and thicken gravy in pot. Garnish with parsley. Serve as a main dish, all you need is salad, bread and dessert for a complete meal. Preparing time: 25 minutes. Cooking time: 2 hours. Serves 6.

Denise Figg

GARLIC FRIED STEAK

6 sandwich steaks
Garlic powder
Salt

Pepper
1 can mushroom soup
1 can water

Sprinkle garlic powder, salt and pepper on steak; beat into the steaks. Mix mushroom soup and water; pour over steaks and cook in 325° oven for about 1½ hours or until done.

Denise Figg

RUMP ROAST

Using approximately 3 to 5 pound roast, insert meat thermometer in middle from end to end. (Tenderize meat by poking all over with fork; sprinkle with Adolph's tenderizer.) Start to wrap with foil. Sprinkle all over with Lipton's Cup-a-Soup onion mix (1 large or 2 small packages). Lay celery around and on top of meat, preferably the green leafy tops, finish wrapping foil, enclosing all but end of meat thermometer. Cook until indicator on thermometer reaches the temperature where you like doneness of meat.

Rump Roast Gravy: Save juices to make gravy. Use all liquids in gravy, such as, water left over from cooking potatoes, green beans, peas, etc. Thicken gravy with flour-water mixture and add "Kitchen Bouquet" to brown.

Doris Beeler

LEFTOVER ROAST CASSEROLE

Slice fresh carrots enough to cover bottom of casserole. Then slice potatoes enough to cover carrots, then slice a large onion over that. Slice leftover roast over that. Then pour 1 can of mushroom soup (rinse can with some milk) over it. Bake until potatoes and carrots are done.

Kitty Wright

BARBECUED BEEF

Cook roast beef until tender. Tear into pieces after cooking. In skillet, add chopped onion and 2 tablespoons Crisco and fry.

In large pan, add:

2 Tbsp. vinegar	1 tsp. mustard
2 Tbsp. brown sugar	1 medium size bottle ketchup
2 Tbsp. ReaLemon juice	Salt and pepper to taste
2 tsp. Worcestershire sauce	

Add water from time to time and cook on low heat approximately 1½ hours.

Debbie Hunter

CROCK POT BARBECUE

2 lb. beef stew meat	Heinz barbecue sauce
Chopped onion (to taste)	Water

Put meat into pot. Pour in just enough water to cover meat. Chop onion and put in. Let set for 8 hours on HIGH. Drain water and pull meat apart. Mix barbecue sauce in with meat and let set ½ hour on HIGH.

Patricia Jewell

BETSY'S BEEF STEW

Beef cubes	Onions
Potatoes	Small can of peas, drained
Carrots	

Mix ingredients, all but peas. Put peas on top, then cover with 1 can (undiluted) tomato soup. Cover with Reynold's Wrap and bake 4½ hours at 250°.

Betsy Wells

BAKED STEW

1 lb. stew meat
2 small carrots
3 small potatoes
1 onion
1 pkg. frozen green peas

Brown stew meat in 1 teaspoon margarine; season with salt, season salt, and pepper as you brown meat. Remove meat and place in a baking dish with potatoes, carrots, green peas, and onion which are cut up. Use drippings from browned meat and make gravy. Put 1 teaspoon flour in a cup of cold water and pour into drippings (bouillon cubes may be added for additional flavor). Simmer until thick. Pour over ingredients in baking dish until completely covered. Bake for 1 hour at 350°.

Marsha Vaughn

CROCK POT STEW

1½ lb. beef stew meat, cut in 1 inch cubes
1 tspb. salt
Dash of pepper
½ tsp. paprika
4 medium zucchini, cut in 1 inch slices
2 c. hot water
2 Tbsp. bottled steak sauce
2 c. canned whole kernel corn, drained
3 Tbsp. cornstarch
3 Tbsp. cold water

Sprinkle beef with salt, pepper and paprika. Place in crock pot, along with zucchini. Pour hot water and steak sauce over. Cover and cook on LOW 7 to 9 hours or until tender. Turn control to HIGH. Stir in corn. Dissolve cornstarch in cold water. Add to meat mixture. Cook on HIGH 15 to 20 minutes.

Denise Figg

CROCK POT BEEF CASSEROLE

2 lb. stew beef, cut into 1 inch pieces
1 (1⅜ oz.) env. dry onion soup mix
½ c. red wine
1 (10¾ oz.) can cream of mushroom soup
1 (4 oz.) can whole mushrooms, drained
¼ c. quick cooking tapioca

Combine all ingredients in crock pot. Stir together well. Cover and cook on LOW 8 to 12 hours. Serve over noodles or rice. (HIGH 4 to 6 hours.)

Judy Smith

CHIPPED BEEF CREOLE

5 oz. chipped beef, shredded
⅓ c. minced onion
¼ c. minced celery
¼ c. minced green pepper

2 Tbsp. minced parsley
3 Tbsp. margarine
1 (16 oz.) can tomatoes
Salt and pepper to taste

Saute onion, celery, and green pepper in margarine. Mash up tomatoes and add to vegetables; add parsley and shredded beef. Let it reach a boil and then simmer for a few minutes. Add salt and pepper to taste. If beef is salty, you may not need to add salt. Serve over rice or noodles.

Helen Sykes

CHIPPED BEEF IN CREAM

½ lb. chipped beef
4 Tbsp. green onions, minced
2 Tbsp. green pepper, minced
3 Tbsp. margarine
3 Tbsp. flour

2 c. milk
3 Tbsp. parsley, minced
½ tsp. paprika
Pepper to taste
Toast

Saute onions and green pepper until golden. Add flour and mix; add milk and stir constantly. Add beef which has been shredded. Simmer until thickens. Add parsley, paprika, and pepper. Serve on toast.

Note: Don't add salt since beef is salty.

Angela Roth

CHUCK ROAST AU GRATIN

3½ lb. chuck roast (2 inches thick)
6 medium potatoes, peeled, cut in halves
3 or 4 small onions

2 cans cream of mushroom soup
½ c. grated Cheddar cheese
Paprika

1546-85

289

Trim fat from meat; place in large baking pan. Roast at 350° for 1 hour; spoon off fat. Arrange potatoes around roast. Pour soup over meat, potatoes, and onions. Cover; bake 2 hours more or until meat and potatoes are tender. Sprinkle with cheese and paprika; bake until cheese melts. Makes 6 servings.

Jerry Evans

BURGOO

2 lb. beef
1 lb. salt pork, diced
2 lb. veal
2 lb. lamb
4 lb. chicken
2 c. onion, chopped
4 c. potatoes, diced
3 c. tomato puree
2 c. lima beans

2 c. celery, diced
2 c. okra, sliced
3 c. whole grain corn
2 c. green pepper, diced
5 bay leaves
Tabasco to taste
1 c. parsley
Salt and pepper to taste

Put all meat in a large kettle with 1 gallon water and simmer until meat falls off the bones. Remove; cool and debone. Return meat to broth. Add all vegetables and simmer until thick. Season only when soup is nearly done. Add parsley shortly before serving.

Lila White

BEEF TENDERLOIN
(Old French Market style)

⅓ medium onion, chopped
   fine
½ tsp. shallot, chopped fine
⅓ tsp. garlic, chopped fine
⅛ lb. mushrooms, sliced
2¾ oz. butter

⅛ c. flour
1⅓ c. beef broth
½ c. stewed tomatoes
Salt and pepper
1¼ lb. beef tenderloin, sliced
½ c. burgundy wine

Saute onion, shallots, garlic and mushrooms in half of the butter. When light brown in color, sprinkle flour in gradually and stir. Add beef stock, tomatoes, salt and pepper to taste. Saute beef in remaining butter in another pan; brown both sides. Add wine and simmer a couple of minutes. Add the preceding sauce and bring to a boiling point. Serves 2.

Cristy Lewis

BEEF STROGANOFF

2 lb. sirloin, cut into ½ inch
   strips
½ tsp. salt
¼ c. flour
¼ c. margarine
1 lb. mushrooms, sliced

¾ c. onion, minced
1 garlic clove, crushed
2 Tbsp. tomato paste
1 c. consomme
2 c. sour cream
¼ c. sherry

Mix salt with 1 tablespoon flour and roll the beef in the mixture. Brown beef quickly in 2 tablespoons real hot margarine. Add mushrooms, onion and garlic. Cook 4 or 5 minutes. Heat the remaining margarine in a separate pan. Blend in the remaining flour. When smooth, add the tomato paste and consomme. Cook and stir until smooth. Pour over the beef. Stir in sour cream and sherry; heat without boiling.

Sharon Duke

BEEF STROGANOFF WITH RICE

2 lb. beef tenderloin
½ lb. mushrooms
2 garlic cloves, chopped
3 c. White Sauce

2 c. sour cream
4 tsp. red wine
Salt and pepper to taste

White Sauce:

2 Tbsp. margarine
1 qt. milk

2 Tbsp. flour

Cut tenderloin into 1 inch long strips ½ inch wide. Brown both sides. Add garlic and mushrooms. When mushrooms are done, add White Sauce, red wine and sour cream. To make White Sauce, melt margarine; add flour and stir well. Add milk slowly; stir constantly, until thickens to right consistency. After all ingredients are mixed, simmer 5 minutes and serve with rice. Serves 4.

Paula White

BEEF AND SHELL CASSEROLE

½ box shell macaroni
1½ lb. chopped chuck
1 finely chopped onion
1 tsp. salt
1 c. cubed American or
   Cheddar cheese

1 can Campbell's vegetable
   soup
1 large can whole tomatoes
Crumbled corn flakes

Cook ½ box of macaroni; drain. Brown chopped chuck in small amount of fat with chopped onion and salt. Combine macaroni and beef mixture in casserole with vegetable soup, tomatoes and cheese cubes. Toss. Top with corn flakes. Bake at 350° for 30 minutes.

Heidi Thompson

BEEF STEW SUPREME

2½ lb. beef cubes	1 Tbsp. sugar
1 c. onion, chopped	1½ tsp. salt
2 c. mushrooms, sliced	1 tsp. Worcestershire sauce
1 can tomatoes	½ tsp. pepper
1 (6 oz.) can tomato paste	2 c. sour cream
½ c. water	⅓ c. margarine, melted
2 Tbsp. cooking oil	2 c. plus 2 Tbsp. Bisquick

Cook beef and onion in cooking oil in Dutch oven or heavy kettle until brown. Stir in mushrooms, tomatoes, tomato paste, water, sugar, salt, Worcestershire sauce and pepper. Heat to boiling; reduce heat; cover and simmer. Stir occasionally until beef is tender, about 1½ hours. Mix 1 cup sour cream and 2 tablespoons baking mix; stir into the stew. Heat to boiling. Mix remaining ingredients, 1 cup sour cream, 1 cup Bisquick and melted margarine; beat about 1 minute. Drop by spoonfuls on top of stew. Bake at 450° until brown, about 10 minutes. Yield: 6 servings.

Peggy Kessinger

BEEF ROAST

1 beef roast	1 can mushroom soup
1 pkg. onion soup mix	Salt

Salt roast lightly; put it in a baking pan and sprinkle onion soup mix on it and then pour mushroom soup over all. Cover and turn oven on 425°. When it starts to cooking, turn down to 300°. Cook 2 hours or until tender. (Don't add any water.)

Peggy Kessinger

BEEF AND ONIONS WITH RICE

1 lb. steak
2 tsp. fresh ginger, chopped
 fine
2 Tbsp. dry sherry
2 Tbsp. sugar
1 Tbsp. cornstarch

2 Tbsp. soy sauce
Salt
¾ c. rice
Vegetable oil
2 large onions, sliced

Cut meat lengthwise into pieces about ¼ inch thick. Make a marinade of all the other ingredients, except the onion, oil and rice; soak the beef in the marinade for an hour. During that time, boil the rice; drain and keep warm. Heat a couple spoons of oil in a pan and fry the onions until tender, but not browned. Remove onions and keep warm, then add a little more oil; drain the beef and fry it in the oil for about 1½ minutes. Then add onion; mix it well with the beef and cook for 1 minute more. Serve with a bed of rice. Serves 4.

Gwen Mills

BEEF BURGUNDY

2 lb. beef chuck or round
2 Tbsp. flour
2 Tbsp. oil
1 c. chopped lean bacon
15 - 18 small white onions
5 - 6 small carrots

1 clove garlic, crushed
1 Tbsp. tomato paste
¼ c. red wine
1 c. beef broth or bouillon
1 c. sliced mushrooms

Preheat oven to 250°. Cut meat in 2 inch cubes and dredge in flour mixed with some salt and pepper. Heat oil; saute meat until well browned and remove to casserole. Saute bacon; add onions, carrots and garlic. Cook until onions begin to brown. Put bacon and vegetables into the casserole with the meat. Stir remaining flour into fat left in skillet and cook until it begins to brown. Add tomato paste, wine and broth; stir until boiling. Taste for seasoning, then pour over meat and vegetables. Cover and cook about 3 hours. Add mushrooms and cook 15 to 20 minutes more. Serves 5 to 6.

Melissa Jackson

BEEF CURRY

½ c. onion, chopped
1 Tbsp. curry powder
1 Tbsp. butter
1½ c. cooked roast beef,
    cubed

1 green pepper, cut in strips
1 can beef gravy
½ tsp. salt
Pepper to taste

Saute onion and pepper in butter. Stir in curry powder, gravy, salt and roast beef. Cover and simmer 10 to 15 minutes; stir occasionally. Serve over rice or noodles.

Trudy Frazier

BEEF CASSEROLE

3 c. cooked beef, chopped
4 potatoes, peeled and sliced
    thin
2 onions, sliced thin
2 apples, peeled and sliced
    thin

3 Tbsp. margarine
1 tsp. salt
¼ tsp. pepper
1½ c. beef broth
¼ c. bread crumbs

Butter a baking dish. Make layers of potatoes, meat, onions and apples, with potatoes on top. Sprinkle potatoes with salt and pepper; pour the broth over. Sprinkle with bread crumbs and dot with 3 table-spoons margarine. Bake in 350° oven for about 1 hour. Serves 4.

Helen Sykes

BEEF BOURGUIGNON

½ lb. mushrooms
¼ c. butter
3 slices bacon, fried crisp
2 lb. boneless beef (2 inch
    cubes)
¾ c. beef stock or broth
2 Tbsp. flour
1 Tbsp. sugar
¼ tsp. salt

¼ tsp. thyme
1 bay leaf
1 peppercorn
1½ c. Holland House red
    cooking wine
Cherry tomatoes (optional)
½ lb. whole small white
    onions

Add 1 bay leaf, 1 peppercorn, ¾ cup beef stock or broth and 1½ cups Holland House red cooking wine. Cover and simmer 1 hour, stirring occasionally. Add ½ pound whole small white onions, mushrooms and bacon. Simmer 1 hour longer; add more cooking wine if liquid has evaporated. Garnish with cherry tomatoes and serve over rice. Serves 4 to 5.

Jean Lyle

BERGHOFF RAGOUT

¾ c. butter
3½ lb. round steak, cut in thin
   strips
1 c. chopped onion
1½ c. chopped green pepper
1 lb. mushrooms, sliced

½ c. flour
2 c. beef broth
1 c. white wine
1 tsp. salt
1 tsp. Worcestershire sauce
Tabasco sauce to taste

Melt ½ cup butter. Brown meat over medium high heat; remove browned meat. Saute onion for 2 minutes in remaining butter. Add green pepper and mushrooms. Cook 3 more minutes. Melt ¼ cup butter and add flour. Slowly add beef broth; cook until thickened. Stir in wine and seasonings. Add meat and mushroom mixture. Cover and simmer about 1 hour or until meat is tender. Serve with noodles or dumplings. Serves 8.

Denise Figg

BEEF CASSEROLE

2 Tbsp. drippings
1½ - 2 lb. beef chuck
12 small white onions, peeled
1 Tbsp. flour
¼ c. red wine
Bouquet garni
1 clove garlic

1½ - 2 c. beef bouillon
1 small bunch celery
1 Tbsp. butter
¼ c. walnut meats
Rind of ½ orange, shredded
   and blanched

Preheat oven to 325°. Heat drippings in a pan and brown the meat. Remove to casserole. Saute onions in remaining fat until they just begin to color, then add to meat. Pour off excess fat; leave about 1 tablespoon. Stir in flour; add wine, bouquet garni, garlic (crushed with a little salt) and 1½ cups bouillon. Stir until boiling and pour over contents of casserole. Add the extra bouillon if necessary, just to cover meat. Add a little seasoning. Cover tightly and cook about 2 hours. Trim celery and cut in strips crosswise. Heat butter; add celery, walnuts and a pinch of salt. Toss over heat for a few minutes. When ready to serve, scatter celery, walnuts and orange rind over the meat. Serves 4.

Denise Figg

BEEF BRISKET

2½ - 3 lb. beef brisket
1½ tsp. celery, onion and
   garlic seasoning (or
   amount to taste)

1 (18 oz.) barbecue sauce

Sprinkle meat with celery, onion and garlic seasoning. Marinate overnight with a bottle of liquid smoke poured over brisket; cover tightly with foil. Next morning, turn over and place in a 275° oven for 4 hours. Remove foil and cover meat with an 18 ounce bottle of barbecue sauce and bake for 1 more hour. Remove to platter and slice across the grain in very thin slices. Serve with more sauce if desired.

Patricia Jewell

DAUBE OF BEEF

3 lb. top round beef
¼ lb. carrots, peeled and
   sliced lengthwise
1 Tbsp. chopped fresh or 1
   tsp. dried oregano

1 Tbsp. chopped fresh or 1
   tsp. dried basil
Few slices of bacon
3 tomatoes, peeled and
   chopped

Marinade:

1 c. salad oil
1 onion, chopped
4 shallots, chopped
1 stalk celery, cut in pieces
1 carrot, chopped
½ c. dry red wine
6 white peppercorns

2 garlic cloves, crushed
1 bay leaf
1 Tbsp. fresh or 1 tsp. dried
   thyme
1 Tbsp. fresh or 1 tsp. dried
   marjoram
2 sprigs parsley

Preheat oven to 275°. Put all marinade ingredients into a skillet and simmer gently for 15 to 20 minutes. Cool, then pour over meat in a large bowl. Leave for 12 to 24 hours; pierce meat and turn it over occasionally. Transfer meat to a casserole; add 1 cup of the liquid from the marinade. Arrange carrots and herbs around the meat and cover with bacon slices. Cover casserole tight with foil, then put on lid and cook about 2½ hours. Add tomatoes and cook another ½ hour. Adjust seasoning and serve with buttered noodles and a green vegetable. Serves 6 to 8.

Dee Dee Millen

DEVILED SWISS STEAK

1½ lb. round steak
1 Tbsp. dry mustard
½ c. flour
1 tsp. salt
½ tsp. pepper
½ c. shortening

1 Tbsp. Worcestershire sauce
1 c. onion, chopped
2 c. canned tomatoes,
   mashed
2 Tbsp. brown sugar

Mix dry mustard, salt and pepper with flour and pound into steak. Melt shortening on medium heat and brown meat on both sides. Place in a baking dish. Combine onions, tomatoes, Worcestershire sauce and brown sugar. Pour over steak and bake in 325° oven for 1½ hours or until tender. Serves 6 to 8.

Judy Smith

ECUADORIAN BAKED BEEF

2½ lb. round steak, cut 1 to
   1½ inches thick
2 tsp. salt
2 large onions, chopped
1 green pepper, chopped
2 Tbsp. butter
2 tomatoes, peeled and
   chopped or 1 c. canned

1 Tbsp. paprika
¼ tsp. pepper
¼ c. peanut butter
3 c. milk
6 potatoes, peeled and cut
   into ½ inch cubes

Put the meat in a roasting pan with 1 cup water and 1 teaspoon salt; bake, covered, about 2 hours or until tender. Saute onions and green pepper in butter. Add tomatoes, paprika, remaining salt, pepper and peanut butter. Add the milk slowly. Simmer slowly for 10 minutes. Boil potatoes in salted water. Place meat on a platter; surround with potatoes and pour sauce. Serves 6.

Opal Willis

FRUITED SWISS STEAK

2 lb. round steak
3 Tbsp. flour
1 tsp. salt
⅛ tsp. pepper
2 Tbsp. cooking oil
¼ c. lemon juice
1 or 2 tsp. Worcestershire
   sauce

½ c. water
1 (16 oz.) can whole
   cranberry sauce
½ c. chopped celery
2 garlic cloves, minced
1 Tbsp. sugar
1 tsp. grated lemon rind

Dredge meat with combined flour, salt and pepper. Brown in hot oil. Combine lemon juice, Worcestershire sauce and water; mix well. Pour over steak. Bring to a boil; reduce heat; cover and simmer about 45 minutes. Mix together cranberry sauce, celery, garlic, sugar and lemon rind. Pour over meat; cover and simmer for 1 hour or until meat is tender. Serves 6.

Dee Dee Millen

VEAL CUTLET "CORDON BLEU"

2 (6 oz.) veal cutlets
4 slices imported Swiss
   cheese
2 slices ham

2 c. bread crumbs
2 raw eggs
Cooking oil for frying

Pound veal cutlets as flat as possible. On ½ of meat, place 1 slice of cheese, 1 slice of ham and second slice of cheese. Fold second half of meat over the first and bread the cutlet on both sides. Dip into beaten eggs and brown in hot skillet. When meat is brown, place in baking pan and bake in 400° oven for about 15 minutes. Serve with fresh parsley and lemon slices. Serves 2.

Paula White

VEAL CUTLETS WITH CHERRY SAUCE

4 veal cutlets
1 Tbsp. vegetable oil
½ tsp. salt
⅛ tsp. white pepper

¼ c. red wine
2 Tbsp. condensed milk
1 (16 oz.) can tart cherries,
   drained

Heat vegetable oil and brown cutlets on each side, about 3 minutes. Season with salt and pepper; remove cutlets from pan and keep warm. Blend wine and milk in pan and simmer for 3 minutes. Add cherries; heat through and adjust seasonings. Return cutlets to sauce and heat, but don't boil. Arrange cutlets on a preheated platter and pour cherry sauce around them. Serves 4.

Denise Figg

VEAL STEAK WITH MUSHROOMS AND CHICKEN LIVERS

1½ lb. (750 grams) mushrooms
1½ lb. (750 grams) chicken livers
2 Tbsp. butter
½ c. chopped onions
Pinch of garlic powder
1 bay leaf
Pepper
Pinch of paprika

Pinch of thyme
2 Tbsp. brandy
2 Tbsp. dry white wine
¼ c. flour
1 c. veal stock
¼ c. heavy cream
4 (¼ lb.; 120 grams) veal steaks
¼ c. grated Gruyere cheese

Chop fine mushrooms and chicken livers; mix. Saute in butter with chopped onions, garlic powder, bay leaf, pepper, paprika and thyme. Flame with brandy. Add white wine. Add flour and veal stock. Finish with cream. Set aside to cool. Grill veal steaks lightly. Then place duxellos on top and add grated cheese. Place in a warm (200°) oven for 5 minutes or until cheese is bubbly. Serves 4.

Heidi Thompson

LIVER AND ONIONS

1½ lb. beef or calves liver, sliced ¼ inch thick
4 Tbsp. oleo
3 medium size onions, sliced

2 - 4 Tbsp. olive oil
2 Tbsp. cider or wine vinegar
1½ tsp. salt
¼ tsp. ground pepper

Trim membrane from liver (if chilled it is easier to slice); rinse in cold water and dry on paper toweling. Cut into 1x2 inch strips. Heat butter in a large skillet. Add onions; saute over medium heat until soft and light brown. Remove with slotted spoon to a plate; keep warm. Add 2 tablespoons oil to skillet; turn heat to high. Add liver; cook, stirring constantly, until liver loses its red color and starts to brown, about 3 to 4 minutes. Return onions to skillet; stir in vinegar, salt and pepper; toss with fork to blend. Cook 1 to 2 minutes.

This recipe is best if cooked quickly.

Mrs. Reg Lowery

LIVER AND ONIONS WITH GRAVY

Pork liver, sliced
Flour
Water
Onion, sliced

Salt to taste
Pepper to taste
Sage to taste
Cooking oil

Sprinkle liver with salt, pepper and sage; roll in flour. Heat oil in skillet and fry liver and onions slowly until done on both sides. Remove liver and pour enough water for the amount of gravy desired. Mix a little flour, about 2 tablespoons, in a little water and add to liquid. Stir until gravy thickens; remove from heat and pour over liver and serve.

Denise Figg

VENETIAN LIVER

1 lb. liver
1 onion, chopped
2 oz. drippings
1 tsp. mixed herbs

1 tsp. chopped parsley
4 oz. mushrooms, sliced
Lemon juice
¼ pt. stock

Cut liver in strips. Heat drippings and fry onion lightly. Add liver and turn in hot fat for 1 minute. Put half the liver and half the onion in an ovenproof dish. Sprinkle with mixed herbs, parsley and lemon juice. Cover with half the mushrooms. Add rest of liver and onions; top with remaining mushrooms. Pour in stock and cover dish. Bake at 375° for 45 minutes.

Jeffrey Cox

BAKED LIVER IN SOUR CREAM

1½ lb. liver
½ c. flour
1 tsp. salt

¼ tsp. pepper
2 Tbsp. margarine
1½ c. sour cream

Soak liver in boiling water for 5 minutes. Mix flour, salt and pepper together. Roll liver in flour. Melt butter in skillet; brown liver on both sides. Put in greased baking dish. Blend 2 tablespoons flour with sour cream. Pour over liver and cover. Bake in 350° oven for 15 minutes. Uncover and bake 25 minutes longer. Serves 4.

Rosemary Ramirez

FISH - SEAFOOD

TUNA CASSEROLE

1 can cream of chicken soup
1 can cream of mushroom
  soup

1 small can evaporated milk
1½ c. shell macaroni
1 large can tuna

Mix mushroom soup, chicken soup, tuna and evaporated milk together. Cook macaroni on top of stove for 20 minutes. Pour into tuna mixture (with water) and bake in oven 1 hour at 350°.

Ruth Noe

TUNA CASSEROLE

½ (8 oz.) pkg. noodles,
  cooked
1 c. fancy white tuna (packed
  in spring water)
2 chopped hard-boiled eggs

1 (8 oz.) pkg. sour cream
Salt and pepper to taste
Paprika
Chopped onion or onion
  powder (if desired)

Combine all ingredients and put into greased casserole dish. Bake at 300° for 30 minutes.

Ruth Ackerman

BROCCOLI TUNA ROLL-UPS

1 (10¾ oz.) can condensed
  cream of mushroom soup
1 c. milk
1 (10 oz.) can tuna fish,
  drained and flaked
1 (10 oz.) pkg. frozen broccoli
  spears, thawed, drained,
  cut in 1 inch pieces*

1 (4 oz.) c. shredded Cheddar
  cheese
1 (2.8 oz.) can Durkee's
  French fried onions
1 tomato, chopped (optional)
6 small (7 inch) flour tortillas

Combine soup and milk; set aside. Combine tuna fish, broccoli, ½ cup cheese and ½ can French fried onions. Stir in ¾ cup soup mixture. Divide tuna mixture evenly between the tortillas and roll up; place, seam side down, in a lightly greased 9x13 inch baking dish. Stir tomato into remaining soup and pour over top of tortillas. Bake, covered, at

350° for 35 minutes. Top center of tortillas with remaining cheese and onions; bake, uncovered, 5 minutes longer. Makes 6 servings.

* Two and one half cups cut up broccoli, cooked, may be substituted. (Ham or chicken could also be substituted for the tuna.)

Debbie Wilhelmus

TUNA CROQUETTES

3 c. drained canned
  chickpeas
½ c. water
2 (6½ oz.) cans tuna
½ c. whole wheat cracker
  crumbs

3 Tbsp. parsley, chopped
1 egg, slightly beaten
¼ tsp. pepper
Cooking oil
1 tsp. crushed garlic

Put chickpeas with water in a blender. Pour into a bowl; add tuna, cracker crumbs, parsley, egg, garlic and pepper. Mix well. Shape into 16 balls and flatten slightly. Chill 2 hours or overnight. Heat oil to 375°. Fry a few balls at a time until golden brown, about 5 minutes. Drain well.

Note: Serve as appetizers with cocktail picks or make sandwiches by placing in pita bread with shredded lettuce and a little lemon juice.

Peggy Kessinger

CURRIED TUNA

2 (10½ oz.) cans cream of
  chicken soup
¼ c. green pepper
2 tsp. curry powder
1 (8¾ oz.) can crushed
  pineapple

2 Tbsp. chives, snipped
2 (6½ oz.) cans tuna, drained
Hot cooked rice

Heat first 5 ingredients to boiling. Add tuna and heat thoroughly. Serve over rice.

Denise Figg

CHOPSTICK TUNA

1 can condensed cream of
    mushroom soup
¼ c. water
1 (3 oz.) can chow mein
    noodles

1 (6½ or 9¼ oz.) can tuna
1 c. celery, sliced
½ c. salted cashews
¼ c. chopped onion
Dash of pepper

Combine 1 can condensed cream of mushroom soup and ¼ cup water. Add 1 cup chow mein noodles, 1 can tuna, 1 cup sliced celery, ½ cup salted cashews, ¼ cup chopped onion and dash of pepper. Toss lightly. Place in baking dish. Sprinkle 1 cup chow mein noodles over top. Bake at 375° for 15 minutes.

Marilyn Williams

CHOPSTICK TUNA

1 can cream of mushroom
    soup
¼ c. water
2 c. chow mein noodles
1 (6½ oz.) can tuna, drained
    and flaked

1 c. celery, sliced
¼ c. chopped onion
Dash of pepper

Combine soup and water in mixing bowl. Add 1 cup of chow mein noodles, tuna, celery, onion and pepper. Toss lightly. Pour into a greased baking dish. Sprinkle remaining noodles on top. Bake in 375° oven for 30 minutes or until casserole is heated through. Serves 4.

Mary Lauder

TUNA DELIGHT

2 (6½ oz.) cans tuna, drained
1 (10 oz.) pkg. frozen peas,
    cooked and chilled
1 c. diced celery
1 small onion, chopped
¾ c. mayonnaise

1 Tbsp. lemon juice
1 tsp. soy sauce
⅛ tsp. garlic salt
⅛ tsp. curry powder
1 c. chow mein noodles

Mix together all of the ingredients, except noodles. Chill for at least 1 hour. Just before serving, combine with noodles. Serves 6.

Perfect for a luncheon.

Brownie - Lois Bruner

DEVILED TUNA CASSEROLE

2 (6½ oz.) cans tuna
1 onion, chopped
1 medium size green pepper,
  chopped
3 - 4 Tbsp. butter
1 c. milk
3 Tbsp. flour

1 tsp. or more Beau Monde
1 tsp. or more Worcestershire
  sauce
1 tsp. hot sauce
1 egg, beaten slightly
2 Tbsp. parsley
Ritz cracker crumbs (topping)

Heat oven to 400°. Lightly grease baking dish. Saute onion and green pepper in butter. Blend in flour; gradually stir in milk until mixture thickens. Add remaining ingredients; mix. Pour into casserole. Cook about 20 minutes until casserole is bubbly hot and cracker crumbs are browned. Serve immediately.

Gwen Mills

TUNA LOAF

8 oz. canned tuna
2 sweet pickles, minced
¾ c. bread crumbs
¾ c. water
¼ c. chopped parsley

1 onion, chopped
1 egg, beaten
1 Tbsp. Worcestershire sauce
1 tsp. salt

Preheat oven to 350°. Flake tuna with a fork. Add remaining ingredients. Mix well. Place in a greased 3½ x 7½ inch loaf pan and shape into a loaf. Bake 30 minutes. Serve with tomato sauce. Serves 4.

Pam Thompson

TUNA NOODLE CRISP

4 oz. uncooked noodles
¼ c. Crisco
⅓ c. onions, chopped
2 Tbsp. green pepper,
  chopped
1 (10½ oz.) can cheese soup

½ c. milk
1 Tbsp. pimiento, chopped
⅛ tsp. pepper
1 (6½ oz.) can tuna
½ c. bread crumbs

Preheat oven to 350°. Cook noodles in boiling salted water according to package directions. Drain. Melt Crisco in large skillet; add onion and green pepper; cook until tender. Stir in soup, milk, pimento, salt and pepper. Bring to a boil. Add uncooked noodles and tuna. Place mixture in a 1½ or 2 quart casserole. Sprinkle bread crumbs on top. Bake at 350° for 25 to 30 minutes.

Peggy Kessinger

ORIENTAL TUNA

2 onion bouillon cubes
¾ c. boiling water
1 (10½ oz.) can condensed
   cream of mushroom soup
1 c. chow mein noodles

1 (6½ or 7 oz.) can tuna
1½ c. diagonally sliced celery
⅛ tsp. pepper
2 Tbsp. diced pimento
Hot cooked rice

Dissolve onion bouillon cubes in water in skillet. Add mushroom soup, ½ cup of the chow mein noodles, tuna, celery and peppers. Mix well. Bring to a boil. Cover; reduce heat and simmer 20 minutes. Add pimiento. Serve over rice, topped with remaining ½ cup chow mein noodles. Serves 3.

Terry White

PITA POCKET TUNA

1 (6½ oz.) can tuna (in spring
   water)
½ carrot, shredded
½ zucchini, shredded
1 small apple, chopped fine
3 Tbsp. chopped green onion
4 Tbsp. reduced calorie
   mayonnaise

1 tsp. Dijon mustard
1 tsp. poppy seed
2 whole wheat pitas
Garnish with relish and
   parsley

Combine all ingredients. Cut pita bread in half and fill with mixture. Garnish with relish and parsley.

Terry White

SUNSHINE CHEDDAR TUNA CASSEROLE

2 c. grated carrots
1½ c. cooked rice (not instant)
2 regular size cans chunk tuna
1½ c. shredded Cheddar
1 Tbsp. minced onion (or more)

1 tsp. parsley
3 eggs, beaten
1½ c. milk, scalded
1 tsp. salt
⅛ tsp. pepper
6 slices Cheddar cheese

Preheat oven to 350°. Toss together carrots, rice, tuna, onion and grated cheese. Turn into greased 2 quart casserole. Blend eggs, milk, salt and pepper; pour over mixture in casserole. Bake 50 to 60 minutes or until knife inserted in center comes out clean. Add cheese slices and bake 5 minutes. Remove from oven and sprinkle with parsley. Serves 6 to 8.

Ruthie Marty

SEAFOOD GUMBO

5 Tbsp. bacon drippings
2 onions, chopped fine
1 garlic pod
1 can tomato sauce
3 tsp. salt
2 lb. shrimp (fresh or frozen)
1 pkg. cut okra (frozen)
6 Tbsp. flour

1½ c. finely chopped celery
1 large can tomatoes
5 - 6 c. water
1 tsp. pepper
2 lb. crabmeat (fresh or frozen)
1 pt. oysters (optional)
3 Tbsp. Worcestershire sauce

Brown flour in bacon drippings to make roux. Add onions, celery and garlic and brown for 5 minutes. Add tomatoes, tomato sauce, water, salt and pepper; boil for 1 hour over medium fire. Add shrimp, crabmeat and okra; cook 20 minutes longer. Add Worcestershire sauce. Stir well and serve over steamed rice.

FISH PATTIES

1 can tuna
1 egg
2 - 3 Tbsp. flour
1 - 2 Tbsp. meal

1 small onion, chopped
¼ c. milk (use only as
    needed)

Mix tuna, egg, flour, meal and onion. Add only enough milk to mix together. Roll in bread crumbs or meal and fry.

Wynola Sharon Davis

CODFISH CAKES

½ lb. codfish, shredded
2½ c. potatoes, sliced thin
¼ c. onion, chopped
1 - 2 Tbsp. milk
⅓ c. cooking oil

Salt to taste
Pepper to taste
Dash of cayenne pepper
1 egg, beaten

Combine fish, potatoes and onion in saucepan; cover with water. Cover and cook on medium heat until potatoes are tender. Drain. Put in bowl and mash. Combine milk, salt, pepper and egg. Stir into potato mixture and blend well. Shape into 6 cakes and saute in skillet with heated oil until golden brown on each side. Serve hot.

Peggy Kessinger

ESCABECHE DE PESCADO - MARINATED FISH

2 lb. whitefish, sole or
    flounder, filleted
1 c. lime or lemon juice

6 Tbsp. butter
2 Tbsp. cooking oil
1 c. flour

Dip the whitefish in the lime or lemon juice; save the juice. Melt butter in skillet and add the oil. Dip the fillets in flour and saute until golden brown. Arrange in a serving dish and pour over the fish the following sauce.

Sauce:

½ c. olive oil
3 Tbsp. reserved lime juice
⅓ c. orange juice
6 green onions, chopped fine
1 bunch fresh coriander,
    chopped or 1 Tbsp. dried
    ground coriander

Cayenne pepper to taste
Lemon or lime, quartered
Parsley, chopped

Combine the olive oil, reserved lime juice, orange juice, green onions, coriander and a few grains of cayenne to taste. Mix well. Pour over the fish and refrigerate for 24 hours before serving. Use as a first course with lemon or lime quarters and chopped parsley.

Peggy Kessinger

MARINATED SHRIMP

4 lb. peeled, cooked shrimp	2 medium onions
1 c. Wesson oil	Salt
1 c. tarragon vinegar	Black pepper
2 cloves garlic	Red pepper

Mix shrimp, Wesson oil and vinegar to which garlic has been crushed with salt, black pepper and red pepper. Slice onions thin; place over shrimp in bowl. Marinate in refrigerator overnight. Drain most of juice off; place in bowl; serve with toothpicks and crackers as an hors d'oeuvres.

Peggy Larrison

POOR BOY SHRIMP COCKTAIL
(If you like shrimp, you'll love this dish)

Slice most any good fish filet (cod, perch, etc.) into large shrimp sized pieces. Put these in boiling water (approximately 1 pound of fish to 1 quart of water) and wait exactly 3 minutes. Remove and chill or let cool. Serve with your favorite shrimp sauce. Don't put this off - this is delicious!

This dish can aptly be named Kentucky Lake Shrimp, Nolin River Shrimp, etc., depending entirely on where your "shrimp" came from.

Andy Herdt

SOUTHERN FRIED FISH

Fish	Red hot sauce
Salt and pepper	Corn meal
3 - 4 Tbsp. mustard or more	

Salt and pepper fish. Mix hot sauce and mustard; spread all over fish. Let set 30 minutes or longer. Roll in corn meal and fry in deep, hot fat.

Denise Figg

CREAMED HADDOCK

1 lb. haddock fillets
2 tomatoes, sliced
4 oz. sliced mushrooms

2 Tbsp. grated cheese
¾ pt. white sauce
1 oz. butter

Lay the fish in ovenproof dish. Cover with sliced mushrooms and pour over the white sauce. Arrange sliced tomatoes over the top and sprinkle evenly with cheese. Dot with butter. Bake at 375° in oven for 20 minutes.

Terry White

OYSTERS BIENVILLE PORT ST. LOUIS

Ice cream salt
1 doz. oysters on the half
    shell
4 green onion tops, chopped
    fine
2 Tbsp. butter

3 Tbsp. flour
⅓ c. dry white wine
⅔ c. milk
½ c. chopped shrimp
½ c. mushrooms, chopped
Parmesan cheese

Place ice cream salt in a pie plate; arrange oysters in shells atop the salt. Fry onions in butter until lightly browned; add flour slowly; stir well and place over low heat; add milk and wine; stir constantly. Add shrimp and mushrooms; cook about 10 minutes over low heat; stir constantly as mixture thickens. Season to taste. Spoon a little sauce over each oyster. Sprinkle bread crumbs and grated cheese (Parmesan) thick on top of each oyster. Place under broiler until just lightly browned. Serves 2.

Paula White

OYSTERS BIENVILLE A LA PITTORI

Ice cream salt (coarse salt)
1 doz. oysters on half shell
1 bunch shallots, chopped
1 Tbsp. butter
1 Tbsp. flour
½ c. chicken broth
½ c. shrimp, chopped

⅓ c. mushrooms, chopped
1 egg yolk
⅓ glass white wine
Bread crumbs
Paprika
Grated cheese

Place ice cream salt in pie plate and place oysters on half shell on salt. Bake oysters in 350° oven until partially done, about 6 to 8 minutes. For the sauce, fry shallots in butter until brown. Add flour and heat until brown. Add chicken broth, shrimp and mushrooms. Beat egg yolk with wine and slowly add to sauce; beat rapidly. Season to taste. Simmer 10 to 15 minutes; stir constantly. Pour sauce over each oyster; cover with bread crumbs, paprika and grated cheese mixed. Place in oven to brown, about 12 minutes. Serves 2.

Cristy Lewis

SALMON CROQUETTES

2 c. canned salmon
3 Tbsp. chopped parsley
1 Tbsp. lemon juice
1 tsp. Worcestershire sauce
¼ tsp. salt

Few grains of pepper
1 c. thick white sauce (No. 2004)
1 c. bread crumbs
1 egg

Drain salmon. Remove skin and bones. Flake. Add parsley, lemon juice, Worcestershire sauce, salt, pepper and white sauce. Blend well. Chill. Shape into croquettes; roll in bread crumbs; dip in slightly beaten egg to which a little water has been added and roll again in crumbs. Fry in deep, hot fat (390°) 3 to 5 minutes. Drain on absorbent paper. Serves 4.

Mary Stanley

BAKED SALMON

1 whole salmon or piece of salmon
8 oz. cream
4 oz. sherry wine

Melted butter
Salt and pepper
Chopped parsley

Preheat oven to 350°. Wash salmon and pat dry. Brush with melted butter. Place in baking dish. Pour cream and sherry over salmon. Season with salt and pepper. Cover and bake at 350°. Allow 12 to 15 minutes per pound. Baste occasionally during cooking. Allow 2 servings per pound of salmon. Spoon cream over salmon and then sprinkle with chopped parsley.

Alice Alessio

MACARONI AND SALMON LOAF

2 eggs, beaten
¼ c. sliced olives
1 Tbsp. grated onion
1 c. drained salmon

½ c. bread crumbs
2 c. cooked macaroni
½ c. melted margarine
1 can Cheddar cheese soup

Preheat oven to 350°. Combine eggs, olives, onion, salmon and bread crumbs. Mix in macaroni, soup and margarine. Pour into a well greased baking dish and bake for 1 hour. Very good one dish meal.

Stella Moore

SHRIMP ORLEANS

2 chopped onions
2 Tbsp. butter
1 c. boiled shrimp
2 Tbsp. flour
1 c. sour cream

¼ c. liquid from shrimp
Salt and pepper to taste
Buttered toast
Pan liquor for sauce

Saute onions in butter to a light brown. Drain fish, reserving ¼ cup liquid. Dredge shrimp with flour and add to onions. Cook slowly 5 minutes without browning. Add sour cream and simmer slowly 20 minutes. Add shrimp liquid and season to taste with salt and pepper. Heat thoroughly. Serve on buttered toast with pan liquor for sauce. Serves 6.

Mary Stanley

SHRIMP SCAMPI WITH WINE

1 lb. jumbo shrimp
¼ c. minced onion
1 clove garlic, minced
1 tsp. salt

1 Tbsp. chopped parsley
¼ tsp. pepper
¼ c. dry white wine
¼ c. butter

Remove shells of shrimp if desired. Split shrimp down back with sharp knife almost all the way through. Place shrimp in 1 layer in shallow pan. Sprinkle with onion, garlic, salt and pepper. Drizzle with wine. Dot with butter; sprinkle with parsley. Broil, turning once, until done (takes 10 minutes for shrimp measuring 15 to a pound, or 15 minutes for shrimp measuring 10 to a pound). Remove to a platter and garnish with parsley.

Alice Walsh Alessio

SPANISH RICE WITH SHRIMP

1 (6 oz.) pkg. Spanish rice mix
3 c. canned tomatoes
3 Tbsp. butter
3 (4½ oz.) cans shrimp, drained

2 (3 oz.) cans sliced mushrooms, drained
5 oz. Cheddar cheese, grated
Salt to taste

Cook Spanish rice mix with the canned tomatoes and butter according to package directions. When rice is almost tender, add shrimp, mushrooms and grated cheese. Stir constantly over low heat until shrimp and mushrooms are hot and cheese melts; salt to taste.

Pam Thompson

TRUIT VAL DU CHOUES

4 Tbsp. butter
4 trout
2 c. cream
Salt
Pepper

2 tsp. fresh chopped dill
2 tsp. chives, chopped
2 tsp. parsley
Pinch of tarragon
3 egg yolks, beaten

Butter pan well; place trout on it and add 2 cups of cream, salt and pepper. Cover and let cook slowly for 10 minutes, turning once. Remove from pan; skin trout and place on serving dish. Add herbs to the cream and cook gently to reduce. Add egg yolks to cream mixture to thicken and pour sauce over trout before serving. Serves 4.

Paula White

VIEUX CARRE SCAMPI

1½ lb. extra large raw
   deveined shrimp
2 Tbsp. lemon juice
½ tsp. lemon pepper
   marinade
½ tsp. salt
1 green onion, chopped fine

4 sprigs parsley, chopped
¼ tsp. mace
⅛ tsp. garlic powder
3 Tbsp. butter
2 oz. Longhorn cheese,
   sliced thin

Place shrimp in a buttered baking dish. Pour lemon juice over shrimp. Sprinkle with the lemon pepper marinade and salt. Combine the green onion, parsley, mace, and garlic powder. Sprinkle over shrimp. Top with butter and cheese. Bake at 350° for 15 to 20 minutes. Serve immediately.

Denise Figg

FROG LEGS IN MUSHROOM SAUCE

6 large frog legs
2 thin slices lemon
½ tsp. salt
⅛ tsp. pepper
2 Tbsp. onion, diced
2 Tbsp. parsley, chopped
2 Tbsp. celery, diced
3 Tbsp. butter
1 c. sliced mushrooms

1½ Tbsp. flour
1½ c. chicken stock or stock
    substitute
Salt
Paprika
3 egg yolks, beaten
3 Tbsp. rich cream
1½ tsp. lemon juice

Clean and skin frog legs and cut each leg into 3 or 4 pieces. Put them in a saucepan and cover with boiling water and add 2 thin slices of lemon, ½ teaspoon salt, ⅛ teaspoon pepper, onion, parsley and celery. Simmer until frog legs are tender; drain them well. Melt butter; add 1 cup sliced mushrooms and saute until light brown. Stir in 1½ tablespoons flour; stir in slowly chicken stock. Season with salt and paprika. When the sauce reaches the boiling point, add the frog legs and reduce heat to simmer for a few minutes. Mix beaten egg yolks and rich cream and slowly pour into mixture, stirring constantly. Add 1½ teaspoons lemon juice slowly and stir. Serve immediately.

Peggy Kessinger

MISCELLANEOUS MEATS AND MAIN DISHES

LAMB STEW

2 or 3 c. lamb, cut in cubes
½ large green pepper,
  chopped
3 large onions, chopped
1 c. celery, chopped
Cooking oil

1 can tomato soup
1 tomato can water
1 or 2 tsp. Kitchen Bouquet
Salt and pepper to taste
1 or 2 Tbsp. flour
Soy sauce

Saute in cooking oil the green pepper, onion, and celery; add cubed lamb and cook until browned. Add 1 can tomato soup, 1 can of water, 1 or 2 teaspoons of Kitchen Bouquet, and salt and pepper to taste. Simmer about 30 minutes or until lamb is tender. Thicken gravy with 1 or 2 tablespoons flour; add a little boiling water if necessary. Serve over boiled rice. Add soy sauce to individual taste.

Note: Two cups of boiled rice serves six.

Paula White

HUNGARIAN LAMB CASSEROLE

2 lb. stewing lamb
3 Tbsp. oil
1 large onion, sliced
1 sweet red pepper, sliced
3 Tbsp. flour
1 Tbsp. paprika

3 chicken bouillon cubes
⅓ c. lima or navy beans,
  soaked overnight
5 potatoes, peeled and cut
  into slices

Preheat oven to 350°. Trim meat and cut into small pieces. Heat oil; add meat, onion, red pepper and saute a few minutes. Then remove to casserole. Add flour, paprika, crumbled bouillon cube and a little salt to the pan drippings; mix well. Add 2 cups water and stir until boiling. Add drained beans and simmer for 5 minutes. Pour all over the casserole. Cover and cook for 2 hours. Arrange potatoes in overlapping slices on top of the casserole and cook for another 25 to 30 minutes or until potatoes are tender. Serves 4 to 5.

Paula White

PARMESAN LAMB CUTLETS

8 lamb cutlets
1½ oz. butter
½ lb. mushrooms

1½ oz. Parmesan cheese,
  grated
1 Tbsp. minced onion

Fry cutlets in hot butter on both sides, don't cook completely. Mince mushrooms and mix with cheese and onion. Cover one side of cutlet with mixture; press down firm. Bake at 400° for 20 to 25 minutes. Serves 4 to 8.

Jeffrey Cox

BARBECUE FRANKS

10 frankfurters
1 Tbsp. butter
1 small onion, cut in thin
    strips
1 small green pepper,
    seeded, cut in thin strips

½ c. ketchup
½ c. water
2 Tbsp. cider vinegar
1 Tbsp. Worcestershire sauce
1 tsp. paprika

Slash each frank diagonally in several places, but not all the way through. In a large skillet, in the hot butter, gently cook the onion and green pepper until wilted. Stir in the ketchup, water, vinegar, Worcestershire and paprika. Add the franks and spoon the sauce over them. Simmer, covered, until the franks are hot through, about 10 minutes.

Dollie D. Billiter

BARBECUED FRANKFURTERS

1 lb. pkg. frankfurters
½ c. onions, chopped
2 Tbsp. cooking oil
2 Tbsp. brown sugar
1 tsp. dry mustard
8 Tbsp. chili sauce
2 Tbsp. Worcestershire sauce

1 Tbsp. paprika
6 Tbsp. water
4 Tbsp. vinegar
1 tsp. salt
½ tsp. black pepper
Dash of Tabasco

Saute onions in cooking oil. Add all the rest of the ingredients and simmer 15 minutes. Score the frankfurters and marinate them in the sauce for a couple hours.

Pam Thompson

BAR-B-Q WIENERS

¾ c. tomato ketchup
½ c. vinegar (white or apple
   cider)
½ c. water

½ c. light brown sugar
Pepper to taste
1 lb. beef wieners, cut in 1
   inch lengths

Combine ingredients; simmer on low heat for 30 minutes or longer.

Shirley Cates

BOURBON WIENERS

1 pkg. wieners, cut up
½ bottle Kraft barbeque
   sauce (plain)

½ c. bourbon

Mix together in saucepan and let it reach a boil, then let it simmer for a few minutes.

Annell Maze

CORN DOGS

1 c. flour
2 tsp. baking powder
1 tsp. salt
1 c. milk
1 lb. wieners

1 c. corn meal
2 Tbsp. sugar
1 egg
2 Tbsp. shortening, melted

Sift together flour and corn meal, baking powder, sugar and salt. Beat egg slightly and add milk. Stir into dry ingredients. Add shortening. Dip wieners into batter, holding with a fork or skewer. Drain excess batter back into bowl. Fry in a wire basket in oil heated to 375° until golden brown. Drain on absorbent paper. Serve hot.

Helen Sykes

SWEET AND SOUR HOT DOGS

1 lb. (8 to 10) frankfurters or
   cocktail wieners

1 c. currant jelly
⅓ to ½ c. prepared mustard

Cut frankfurters into 1 inch pieces. Melt jelly and mustard over medium heat. Stir in frankfurters until well glazed. Keep hot in chafing dish. Serves 8.

Daisy Mace

CORN DOGS

1 pkg. wieners
1 c. flour
2 Tbsp. sugar
1½ tsp. baking powder
1 tsp. salt

⅔ c. corn meal
1 egg
2 Tbsp. oil
¾ c. milk

Dry wieners between paper towels. Combine flour, sugar, baking powder, salt and corn meal. Add oil, egg and milk. Stir until mixed. Dip wieners into mixture to coat and deep-fry until golden brown. Drain on paper towels. Serves 8.

Kathy Chesser

CHILI SAUCE FOR HOT DOGS

3 - 3½ lb. ground beef
2 pkg. French's Chili-O-Mix
1 (15 oz.) can tomato sauce

2 cans Mexican style
   Manwich

Mix all ingredients together and simmer 1 hour on low, stirring occasionally.

Note: This is a very good and easy sauce to make. Everyone will like it.

Ann Crum

PRONTO PUPS

1 egg
½ c. milk
1 c. Bisquick
2 Tbsp. yellow corn meal

¼ tsp. paprika
½ tsp. dry mustard
⅛ tsp. cayenne pepper
1 lb. frankfurters

Heat deep fat to 375°. Blend eggs and milk; mix well. Stir in dry ingredients. Dip frankfurters in batter. Fry until brown, 2 to 3 minutes on each side.

Elaine Cady

BRATWURST

¾ lb. fresh veal
1½ lb. pork loin
2 tsp. pepper
¾ tsp. grated nutmeg

½ tsp. mace
Pork casings
Milk

1546-85

Combine all ingredients, except casings and milk, put through grinder 3 times. Mix with about ½ cup water; fill pork casings. Cover bratwurst with hot water. Bring to a boil and remove from heat immediately. Let stand in hot water for a few minutes until firm. Drain. Dip Bratwurst in milk. Place in broiler and cook until golden brown under low to medium heat.

Brenda Chitty

BRATWURST

½ lb. ground veal
½ lb. ground pork
½ lb. ground beef
2 Tbsp. beef bouillon
1½ tsp. dry mustard

½ tsp. mace
¼ tsp. nutmeg
Dash of ginger
Salt and black pepper to taste
1 egg, lightly beaten

Combine all ingredients, except egg. Mix in blender, a little at a time. Add egg and blend thoroughly. Form into patties; fry until browned on both sides.

Dee Dee Millen

BRATWURST IN PASTRY - BRATWURST IN TEIG

1 recipe Salty Tart Pastry or
  Puff Pastry

12 Bratwursts
2 egg yolks, well beaten

Parboil Bratwurst 5 minutes, then brown slowly and evenly in a skillet, about 8 minutes. Let cool completely. Roll out dough and cut into 12 rectangular strips to fit around Bratwurst. Place 1 Bratwurst on each strip of dough and roll securely. Brush dough with egg yolks. Bake at 375° for 15 to 20 minutes or until dough is flaky and golden brown.

Paula White

GERMAN BURGERS

Mash out 2 hamburger patties. On one patty, put chili pepper and sliced onions. (Cheese may be added if desired.) Lay second patty over the first patty. Crimp together both patties to hold ingredients inside while cooking. Fry in skillet until thoroughly cooked. Serve on buns.

Wanda Frankenberger

WELSH RAREBIT

1½ Tbsp. margarine
1½ c. milk
1 c. grated cheese
¼ tsp. paprika

1½ tsp. salt
1½ Tbsp. all-purpose flour
½ tsp. dry mustard
Toast or crackers

Make a white sauce of the margarine, flour, salt and milk. Add the cheese and stir over low heat until cheese is melted. Add seasoning and serve over toast or crackers.

Stella Moore

WELSH RAREBIT WITH MUSHROOMS

2 oz. butter
½ tsp. mustard
Dash of cayenne pepper

4 oz. cheese, grated
2 slices toast
4 oz. mushrooms

Melt 1 ounce butter, then remove from heat. Stir in mustard, cayenne and salt to taste. Add cheese and stir thoroughly to make a spreading consistency. Spread mixture on one side of toast. Heat remaining butter and grill the mushrooms. Put the Welsh Rarebit under the hot grill until golden. Top with mushrooms and serve at once.

Lynnette Bonn

RAREBIT

1 can Cheddar cheese soup
¼ tsp. prepared mustard
¼ c. milk

4 slices tomato
4 slices toast

Mix soup and mustard in saucepan until smooth. Stir in milk gradually. Place over low heat; stir often until heated through. Arrange tomato slices on toast on serving plates and pour cheese sauce over top. Yield: 4 servings.

Paula Childress

A MAN'S CASSEROLE

1 (12 oz.) pkg. thin egg
   noodles
2 onions, chopped
2 Tbsp. melted margarine
2 lb. ground chuck
1 Tbsp. salad oil
2 tsp. salt

1 tsp. pepper
1 tsp. thyme
1 (10¾ oz.) can tomato or
   celery soup
½ c. evaporated milk
1½ c. (6 oz.) shredded
   Cheddar cheese

Cook noodles according to package directions; drain, and rinse in cold water. In large skillet, saute onion in margarine over medium flame; set aside. Brown meat in same skillet in oil over medium high flame; drain. Add salt, pepper, thyme and sauteed onions to meat. Combine soup and milk. Arrange ⅓ of noodles, ½ of meat-onion mixture, and ½ of soup mixture in layers in a greased 4 quart casserole. Repeat layers. Arrange remaining noodles on top; sprinkle with cheese. Bake in 350° oven for 1 hour or until lightly browned. Yield: 8 large servings.

Sue Sympson

CHEESY HOT QUICHE

8 eggs
½ c. flour
1 tsp. baking powder
¾ tsp. salt
4 c. (1 lb.) shredded Monterey
   Jack pepper cheese

1½ c. cottage cheese
¼ c. chopped jalapeno
   peppers or 1 small can
   green chilies

Beat eggs 3 minutes. Combine flour, baking powder and salt. Add to eggs and mix well. Stir in cheese and chilies. Pour into greased 13x9x2 inch baking pan. Bake at 350° for 30 minutes. Let cool 10 minutes; cut into squares.

Mrs. Ron Martin

EGGS A LA CARDINAL HILL

1 c. onions, sliced
1 c. mushrooms, sliced
2 green peppers, sliced
5 Tbsp. butter
1 pimiento, sliced
12 hard-boiled eggs, sliced

1 c. condensed celery soup
   (undiluted)
¼ tsp. marjoram
¼ tsp. ground sage
Salt and pepper

Saute onions, mushrooms and green peppers in butter until onions are soft, but not brown. Add pimiento and cook 5 minutes longer. Take from heat and mix with eggs, celery soup and seasonings. Mix well and add salt and pepper to taste. To serve, reheat in oven for about 20 minutes and keep hot on buffet table in a chafing dish over hot water. Serves 6.

Paula White

EGGS AU GRATIN

4 Tbsp. butter
1 Tbsp. grated onion
3 Tbsp. green pepper, minced
4 Tbsp. flour
3 c. scalded light cream
3 Tbsp. mushrooms,
    chopped fine
1 tsp. salt
½ tsp. coarse ground black
    pepper

¼ tsp. nutmeg
6 hard-boiled eggs, sliced
2 Tbsp. canned pimiento,
    chopped
3 Tbsp. dry sherry
Dry bread crumbs
Grated cheese

Melt butter; add onion and green pepper; saute. Stir in flour. When well blended, stir in cream. Add mushrooms and seasonings. When sauce has thickened, cook gently 5 minutes longer; stir frequently. Add eggs, pimiento and sherry. Cook gently until mixture is heated thoroughly. Pour into a buttered casserole and sprinkle with bread crumbs and grated cheese. Brown quickly under broiler. Serves 6.

Paula White

YOCIANNE'S BANGKOK EGGS

2 eggs, beaten
1 small onion, diced
1 tsp. Ajinomoto
    (monosodium glutamate)

1 tsp. fish sauce (Nam Pla)

Blend all ingredients together; pour into hot, well greased skillet. Brown lightly. When mixture sets, turn and brown lightly on other side. Serve immediately.

Note: Use no salt. Ajinomoto and fish sauce take care of this.

Pam Thompson

EGGS BENEDICT

6 thin slices Old Kentucky
   ham or baked ham
2 Tbsp. butter
6 split toasted English muffin
   halves
6 poached eggs

Famous Old House
   Hollandaise sauce
Cracked black pepper
Chopped fresh or dried
   tarragon

Saute ham in butter for 5 minutes until lightly browned. Place a slice of ham on each muffin half. Top with poached egg and liberally spoon Hollandaise sauce over it. Place on serving dish under broiler 1 minute. Remove from broiler and sprinkle, just before serving, with cracked black pepper and tarragon to taste. Excellent for lunch or late supper. Serves 6.

Paula White

CURRIED EGGS

4 Tbsp. margarine
4 Tbsp. onion, minced
¼ c. flour
1 Tbsp. curry powder
1¼ c. chicken broth
1 c. milk

¼ tsp. ground ginger
½ tsp. garlic powder
8 hard-boiled eggs
3 c. cooked rice
2 Tbsp. fresh parsley, minced

Melt margarine; saute onion in it for 3 or 4 minutes. Blend in flour; cook 2 minutes longer. Stir in curry powder, chicken broth, milk, ginger and garlic powder. Cook, stir constantly, until mixture thickens. Cut eggs lengthwise into halves. Add to sauce just to heat. Serve over hot rice. Garnish with parsley. Serves 8.

Cristy Lewis

EGGS WITH DRIED BEEF

2½ oz. pkg. dried beef
2 Tbsp. butter
1 onion, chopped fine

4 eggs
4 Tbsp. heavy cream

Pour boiling water over beef; drain and tear into pieces. Saute onion in butter. Add beef and cook slowly for 2 or 3 minutes. Beat eggs with the cream and scramble into beef mixture. Cook over low heat; stir constantly until eggs are set, about 3 or 4 minutes. Serves 2.

Note: Beef is salty so you probably won't need any salt added to the eggs; taste before you do.

Helen Sykes

EGGS-SAUSAGE SOUFFLE

6 - 8 eggs, slightly beaten
6 slices cubed bread
1 c. sharp Cheddar cheese
1 lb. cooked sausage

2 c. milk
1 tsp. salt
1 tsp. dry mustard

Beat eggs; add other ingredients. Put in a 9x13 inch baking dish. Refrigerate at least 12 hours. Bake at 350° for 35 minutes or until done.

Norma Combs

FETTUCCINE ALFREDO

1 (12 oz.) pkg. fettuccine,
   cooked according to pkg.
4 Tbsp. butter
¾ c. grated Parmesan cheese
½ c. heavy cream, slightly
   whipped

Additional Parmesan cheese,
   grated
Freshly ground pepper

Cook fettuccine until almost tender. In small saucepan, melt butter; add cheese and cream. Beat together with wire whisk. Drain fettuccine. Place ¼ of cheese mixture in deep, heated platter. Top with fettuccine, then rest of cheese mixture. Toss quickly with fork and spoon, adding Parmesan cheese and dash of pepper as you toss. Serve on warm plates. Makes 4 servings.

Alice Walsh Alessio

FRITTATA

2 Tbsp. butter
6 eggs
½ tsp. salt
¾ c. Swiss cheese, grated
3 Tbsp. parsley, chopped
½ c. diced ham

1 c. mushrooms, sliced
3 Tbsp. green onions,
   chopped
2 Tbsp. chopped green
   pepper
Dash of pepper

Beat eggs, salt and pepper. Stir in grated cheese; add rest of the ingredients. Melt butter in a 10 inch skillet. Add egg mixture and lower heat. Cook undisturbed until bottom is golden brown when edges are lifted. Put the skillet in the broiler for about 30 seconds or until the top is golden brown. Serves 4.

Mildred Zack

SOUFFLE DE FROMAGE PRINCESSE BIRGITTA - SWISS CHEESE SOUFFLE

¾ c. heavy cream
2 eggs, separated
6 Tbsp. grated Parmesan
    cheese
3 Tbsp. grated Swiss cheese

2 Tbsp. brandy
Salt
Pinch of cayenne
Grated Parmesan cheese

Whip cream not too stiff. Mix in egg yolks, cheese, brandy, salt and cayenne. Beat egg whites and add. Butter and sprinkle with additional grated Parmesan in four individual souffle pots and fill almost to brim with cheese mixture. Put more grated cheese on top and bake in moderately hot oven (375°) for 8 to 10 minutes. Serve immediately. Serves 4.

As there is no flour in mixture, the souffle will not stay puffed many minutes after it has left the oven.

Teresa Stroup

QUICHE

12 slices bacon, fried and
    crumbled
1 c. Swiss cheese, shredded
½ c. onion, chopped
2 c. milk

1 c. Bisquick baking mix
4 eggs
½ tsp. salt
¼ tsp. pepper

Grease pie plate; sprinkle bacon, cheese and onion in plate. Beat remaining ingredients together until smooth. Pour into plate. Bake in preheated 400° oven for about 40 minutes or until a knife inserted comes out clean. Serves 6.

Sharon Duke

WARM CHEESE AND BREAD DISH
(Dutch)

10 slices whole wheat bread   1 c. milk
6 slices cheese   2 Tbsp. butter
2 eggs   ¼ tsp. salt

Place 5 slices of bread in a buttered ovenproof dish. Cover with cheese and top with rest of bread. Beat eggs with milk and salt; pour over bread. Let soak for 30 minutes. Dot with butter and bake in 350° oven for 30 minutes. Serve warm or cold.

Note: Diced up boiled ham can be layered on top of the cheese.

Gwen Mills

BARBECUED GROUND HOG

1 ground hog, dressed and   2 Tbsp. lard (approx.)
  cut into bite-size chunks   Barbecue sauce

Brown meat in lard in heavy skillet. Drain off excess lard and drippings. Pour barbecue sauce over meat until each piece is covered. Simmer on stove until meat is tender. Serve with vegetables and bread.

Linda Cloyd

Notes

Breads,
Rolls,
Pastries

BREAD BAKING GUIDE

The pleasure of baking homemade bread is matched only by eating it, except when something goes wrong. Most problems can be determined and easily avoided the next time.

Problem...	Cause...
Bread or biscuits are dry	Too much flour; too slow baking; over-handling
Bread has too open texture or uneven texture	Too much liquid; over-handling in kneading
Strong yeast smell from baked bread	Too much yeast; over-rising
Tiny white spots on crust	Too rapid rising; dough not covered properly while rising
Crust has bad color	Too much flour used in shaping
Small flat loaves	Old yeast; not enough rising or rising much too long; oven temperature too hot
Heavy compact texture	Too much flour worked into bread when kneading; insufficient rising time; oven temperature too hot
Coarse texture	Too little kneading
Crumbly texture	Too much flour; undermixing; oven temperature too cool
Yeasty sour flavor	Too little yeast; rising time too long
Fallen center	Rising time too long
Irregular shape	Poor technique in shaping
Surface browns too quickly	Oven temperature too hot
Bread rises too long during baking and is porous in center and upper portion of loaf	Oven temperature too cool

BREADS, ROLLS, PASTRIES
PANCAKES, FRITTERS, ETC.

ELEPHANT EARS

1½ c. milk
2 Tbsp. sugar
1 tsp. salt
6 Tbsp. shortening
2 pkg. dry yeast
4 c. flour

Oil for frying
Sugar mixture (½ c.
    granulated sugar mixed
    with 1 tsp. ground
    cinnamon)

Heat, but do not boil, milk, sugar, salt and shortening until shortening is melted. Cool to lukewarm. Add yeast to milk mixture and stir until dissolved. Stir in flour, 2 cups at a time, beating until smooth after each addition. Put in greased bowl; cover with a damp cloth and let rise until doubled (about 30 minutes). Dust hands with flour and pinch off pieces of dough about the size of golf balls. Stretch each ball into a thin 6 to 8 inch circle. Fry, 1 at a time, in 350° oil until it rises to the surface; turn and fry other side until light brown. Drain on absorbent paper and sprinkle generously with sugar mixture.

Erdean Lee

ELEPHANT EARS

Dissolve 1 package dry yeast in 2 cups warm milk.

Add:

1 Tbsp. shortening
1 egg

2 Tbsp. sugar
1½ tsp. salt

Mix in 6 cups flour (plain). Mix well to form dough. Let rise until doubled. Pinch off dough the size of an egg. Roll very thin. Fry in hot oil until brown on both sides. Dough will form bubbles on top. Drain. Sprinkle with sugar and cinnamon.

QUICK DOUGHNUTS

Oil or shortening for frying
Can of biscuits

Powdered sugar

Heat oil or shortening for frying. Make doughnuts with holes out of biscuits. Cook until golden, then turn and finish cooking. Dip in powdered sugar while still warm. Place on plate to cool a little.

You may sprinkle with other spices also. Nice snack.

Jamie Beeler

BACON BITS

1 pkg. unbaked crescent rolls
½ tsp. onion salt
½ c. sour cream

½ lb. bacon, fried crisp and
   crumbled

Open rolls into rectangles (2 rolls together). Spread with sour cream; sprinkle with onion salt and bacon crumbles. Roll into jelly roll style and cut into 6 sections. Bake 12 to 15 minutes in 375° oven. Serve hot.

Ruth Ackerman

NEW ORLEANS CALAS

3 c. cooked rice
3 beaten eggs
¼ tsp. vanilla
¼ tsp. nutmeg
¼ tsp. cinnamon

¼ tsp. grated lemon rind
½ c. sifted flour
½ c. sugar
3½ tsp. baking powder
½ tsp. salt

Mix rice, eggs, vanilla, spices and lemon rind. Sift flour with sugar, baking powder and salt. Stir into the rice mixture; blend well. Drop from tablespoon into hot shortening; fry until brown on both sides. Drain on paper; sprinkle with confectioners sugar and serve hot. Makes about 2 dozen calas.

Hot rice Calas were sold on the streets in the Vieux Carre section by Negro vendors.

Dee Dee Millen

TEA SCONES

2 Tbsp. butter
1 tsp. baking powder
2 Tbsp. sugar
½ c. milk (approx.)

2 c. flour
½ tsp. salt
1 egg

Place flour in bowl; add baking powder and salt. Mix together. Rub butter into flour mixture. Add sugar and mix together. Beat egg and add to milk. Mix liquid into dry ingredients. Dough should not be too moist. Place on floured board. Roll to 1 inch thick. Cut into rounds with pastry cutter. Arrange on lightly floured baking sheet. Bake at 400° until golden brown, approximately 15 to 20 minutes.

If you desire, ½ cup golden raisins may be added to mix.

YORKSHIRE SCONES

8 oz. flour	3 oz. butter or lard
¼ tsp. soda	2 oz. sultanas
½ tsp. cream of tartar	½ oz. chopped candied peel
¼ tsp. salt	1 egg
3 oz. sugar	Little milk

Sift all dry ingredients together; rub in the fat. Add sultanas and peel; stir in beaten egg and mix to stiff dough with milk. Divide in 2; roll into rounds on floured board. Place on baking sheet and mark each round into triangles. Bake in moderately hot oven (375°) for 15 or 20 minutes.

Melissa Jackson

STREUDEL

2 c. flour	1 Tbsp. vinegar
2 sticks (½ lb.) oleo	¼ c. water
3 egg yolks	

Mix oleo and flour as for pie crust. Mix egg yolks, water and vinegar together, then add to flour mixture. Mix. Separate in 2 pieces (balls). Roll out 1 real thin and cover with filling (½ can Solo). Roll up and put on ungreased cookie sheet; paint with egg whites. Do the same with the other piece. Bake at 325° to 350° for 25 to 30 minutes. While baking, mix together ⅓ cup XXX sugar, 1 teaspoon oleo, couple drops of vanilla and milk enough to mix it up. When streudel is done, slip onto platter and while real hot put sugar mixture over. Makes 2 streudel.

Vinnette Grennan

LAYERED STRAWBERRY STRUDEL

1 qt. fresh strawberries,
   hulled
1 c. granulated sugar
2 c. water
⅛ tsp. salt
8 oz. heavy whipping cream,
   chilled

1 tsp. vanilla extract
16 (9 inch) rounds strudel
   (phyllo) dough
3 c. cooking oil
Confectioners sugar to
   sprinkle

Slice strawberries lengthwise. Bring sugar, water and salt to a boil in a large saucepan. Stir over low heat until sugar completely dissolves. Increase heat and boil 5 minutes without stirring. Remove from heat and add berries. Set aside.

The cream should be very cold for whipping. In hot weather, chill the bowl and beaters in addition to the cream. Whip cream to soft peaks, adding vanilla, and refrigerate until you are ready to use it.

Frozen, store bought strudel dough should be thoroughly thawed before it is unwrapped. You'll need 16 rounds of dough to assemble the strudel; you may want to prepare extra sheets in case you lose a few during frying. Carefully rewrap the remainder and refreeze.

Using a 9 inch circle pattern, a plate or pan lid, carefully cut rounds of dough with a pastry cutter or sharp knife. Heat the vegetable oil to 375°. Lift a round of dough from the work table with both hands and drop it horizontally onto the surface of the oil. Don't attempt to slip the dough edgewise into the fat or it will buckle. If there is a wrinkle or fold, immediately try to straighten the round. It will become brittle after 5 seconds of cooking. The round should firm and turn tan within 20 seconds. Do not allow it to turn dark brown, which means it is close to scorching. Using tongs or wooden spoons, lift the dough from the fat and hold it over the kettle momentarily to let it drain. Stack on absorbent paper. Repeat with remaining rounds.

Assemble the strudel on a serving plate in this order: 3 rounds fried phyllo, whipped cream, 2 rounds, strawberries, 3 rounds, whipped cream, 2 rounds, strawberries, 3 rounds, whipped cream, 3 rounds and a dust of confectioners sugar. If some rounds crack during assembly, it won't matter because they won't be seen. Spread the whipped cream with a spatula; there are 3 layers, so don't spread each too thickly. Place the strawberries by hand evenly over the surface. If some fruit remains, spread the balance on the last layer of whipped cream.

Refrigerate the strudel until ready to serve. It will be beautiful, so present it to guests for a visual feast before cutting it into pie shaped pieces. The delicate rounds will crack and break when the knife is pressed through the strudel, but this will not affect the taste - or the delight.

HOMEMADE CRACKERS

1 pt. flour	½ tsp. salt
1 tsp. baking powder	1 egg white, beaten
4 Tbsp. melted butter	1 c. milk

Sift baking powder into flour. Add melted butter, salt, egg white, and milk. Mix in more flour if needed to make a stiff dough. Knead for 25 minutes. Roll thin and cut round or square. Bake quickly to a light brown in a hot oven (400°).

Teresa Stroup

CRACKERS

3 c. rolled oats	¾ c. salad oil
2 c. unsifted flour	1 c. water
1 c. raw wheat germ	1 egg white, slightly beaten
3 Tbsp. sugar	Sesame seed
1 tsp. salt	Garlic salt

Combine oats, flour, wheat germ, sugar and salt. Add oil and water; stir until mixture leaves sides of bowl. Divide dough into quarters. Roll out each quarter onto a lightly floured board to make a rectangle of 12x10 inches. Roll dough loosely around a rolling pin and place on lightly greased baking sheet. Cut into desired shapes, squares, triangles or rectangles. Brush with egg white; sprinkle with sesame seed and garlic salt. Bake in 350° oven for about 15 minutes or until golden brown. Makes about 8 dozen.

Lora Martin

FRENCH TOAST

6 eggs	½ c. pecan pieces
1 c. half & half	1 tsp. vanilla
2 tsp. cinnamon	1 loaf French bread
1 (4 oz.) pkg. cream cheese, softened	

Mix first 3 ingredients well and set aside. Cream the cheese with mixer and fold in nuts and vanilla. To prepare, cut bread into inch wide pieces. Slit top of pieces and put approximately a tablespoon of cheese mixture in each piece. Dip bread in egg mixture and cook on hot griddle until lightly browned. Sprinkle with powdered sugar (optional) and serve with warm Apricot Syrup.

Apricot Syrup: Heat 12 ounce jar apricot or peach preserves and 1 cup orange juice just until warm.

Galena Gronefeld

CHEESE TOAST

1 egg yolk
1 tsp. butter
Pumpernickel, rye or whole
   wheat bread

1 Tbsp. grated Parmesan
   cheese

Mix egg yolk and butter to a paste. Trim crusts from 2 or 3 slices of bread. Spread with paste; sprinkle with Parmesan. Cut slices into triangles and toast under broiler until golden.

Pam Thompson

FRENCH TOAST

Day old bread (preferably
   French)
Milk
Sugar
Vanilla

Grand Marnier (optional)
Beaten eggs
Flour
Butter

Soak slices of day old bread in a little lukewarm milk, sweetened with a few tablespoons of sugar and flavored with a few drops of vanilla, and, if you like, Grand Marnier. Beat eggs in a soup plate. Dip soaked bread into beaten eggs, then in flour. Shake off excess flour. Fry in butter on both sides. Sprinkle with sugar and top with a lump of butter.

Jeffrey Cox

FRIAR TUCK'S TOAST

12 slices white bread
¾ c. Cheddar cheese, grated
¼ c. butter

1 tsp. dry mustard
2 tsp. Worcestershire sauce
8 slices bacon

Trim crusts off. Combine cheese, butter, dry mustard, and Worcestershire sauce. Cook bacon until crisp; drain and crumble; add to the cheese mixture; mix well. Spread mixture on the bread and roll each slice into a jelly roll. Secure the rolls with toothpicks. Place under broiler and brown on both sides.

Pam Thompson

PANCAKES STUFFED WITH COCONUTS AND RAISINS - CHAVITAT EGOZEI KOKAS

3 c. flour
1½ c. sugar
1½ c. milk
3 oz. raisins

½ lb. shredded coconut
3 eggs
1 oz. vanilla sugar
Oil

In a bowl, combine flour, sugar, vanilla sugar and milk. Mix well. Beat eggs and add to mixture. Grease a frying pan lightly, place on low heat, and, when hot, pour in 1 tablespoon of batter. Tilt pan to allow batter to cover pan entirely. Remove and repeat until all batter is used. Place some coconut mixed with raisins on the fried side of pancake. Roll around raisins and return to pan to brown lightly. Serve hot as a dessert or for late meals. Preparing time: 10 minutes. Cooking time: 15 minutes. Serves 6.

Cristy Lewis

APPLE YOGURT PANCAKES

1¼ c. sifted all-purpose flour
½ tsp. salt
1 tsp. baking soda
Pinch of baking powder
8 oz. plain yogurt

¼ c. milk
1 egg yolk, slightly beaten
2 egg whites
½ c. thin sliced apples

Sift flour, salt, baking soda and baking powder together. Combine yogurt, milk and egg yolk. Stir in flour mixture only until ingredients are moistened; batter will be lumpy. Beat egg whites until stiff, but not dry; fold into batter. Gently fold in apple slices. Heat a non-stick skillet that has been sprayed with cooking spray. Drop by tablespoons to make 3 inch pancakes. Cook over low heat until bubbles appear on the surface, then flip and brown other side. Serve immediately. Makes 25 pancakes.

Rosetta Humphries

BANANA PANCAKES

1 c. flour
1½ tsp. baking powder
½ tsp. salt
1 egg, beaten
2 Tbsp. melted butter
3 Tbsp. sugar

¼ tsp. nutmeg
4 or 5 over-ripe bananas (fruit very soft, skins dark brown)
Butter or vegetable oil for frying

Sift together flour, baking powder, and salt. Add egg, butter, sugar, and nutmeg. Mix well. Mash bananas; add to batter. Heat pan over moderate heat; grease lightly with butter. Drop batter by table-spoonful into pan. Brown lightly on both sides. Serve hot with butter, confectioners sugar, honey or syrup. Serves 4 to 6.

Paula White

LUMBERJACK PANCAKE

1 c. pancake mix
1 c. regular beer (any brand)

1 egg
1 Tbsp. cooking oil

Mix all ingredients in large bowl until all lumps disappear. Pour on hot, lightly greased griddle. Turn over when bubbles begin to break on surface and the edges look cooked.

John H. Drewes

SOURDOUGH PANCAKES

2 pkg. dry granular yeast
1 qt. lukewarm water
6 c. sifted flour
2 tsp. salt

1 tsp. baking soda
3 Tbsp. molasses
½ c. hot water
5 eggs, beaten

Dissolve yeast in 1 quart warm water. Stir in flour; let stand 24 hours at room temperature. Add salt, soda, molasses, and the hot water. Add eggs. Do not beat, but mix well. Let stand ½ hour and the batter is ready to serve. Cook on dry griddle or in iron skillet. Test your griddle or skillet with a drop or 2 of water. When the water drops jump around in your cookware, it is hot enough.

Great for camping!

Mary Beeler

PANCAKES

1 c. milk
2 Tbsp. melted butter
1 egg, beaten
1 c. flour

2 tsp. baking powder
1½ Tbsp. sugar
½ tsp. salt

Mix milk, butter and egg. Sift together dry ingredients. Add to milk mixture. Stir enough to dampen flour. Heat frying pan or griddle over moderate heat. If needed, grease very lightly with butter. Drop batter by tablespoonful. Cook until top side is full of bubbles and underside is nicely browned. Brown other side. Yield: 4 cakes.

Dee Dee Bond

ZUCCHINI PANCAKES

3 medium zucchini
2 eggs
3 Tbsp. flour
2 Tbsp. Parmesan cheese

1 Tbsp. chopped chives
¼ tsp. chopped parsley
1 pinch of garlic powder
Salt and pepper to taste

Grate zucchini and drain thoroughly. Add rest of ingredients. If mixture looks too liquid, add 1 tablespoon flour. Drop batter on oiled grill or skillet for small pancakes. Cook until browned on one side. Turn and brown on other side. Makes 8 to 9 pancakes.

Dorothy O'Neal

BLACKBERRY FRITTERS

2 c. flour
1 Tbsp. baking powder
1 tsp. salt
¼ c. sugar
2 eggs, beaten lightly

1 c. milk
2 c. fresh blackberries
Cooking oil for deep-frying
Powdered sugar

Fill deep fryer with oil to at least 6 inches. Heat oil to 375°. Combine flour, baking powder, salt and sugar. Stir in eggs and milk; blend and fold in berries. Drop by spoonful into hot oil and cook, turning once, 2 or 3 minutes or until golden. Drain on paper towel and keep warm if not served at once. Sprinkle powdered sugar over.

Pam Thompson

CORN FRITTERS

2 c. boiled corn, cut from cob
    (2 cans)
2 cans whole kernel corn
2 c. flour
½ c. milk

1⅛ tsp. salt
3 tsp. baking powder
1 Tbsp. melted butter
2 eggs

Add milk to corn. Sift flour with baking powder; add to corn mixture. Add well beaten eggs and melted butter. Mix well. Heat fat to 375° and drop by spoonfuls into fat. Cook until browned. Drain on paper towel.

Wanda Harris

SQUASH FLOWER FRITTERS

16 - 20 summer squash
    flowers or enough to
    make 2 c. when coarsely
    chopped
2 c. all-purpose flour
3 Tbsp. baking powder

1 tsp. granulated sugar
1 egg
½ c. water
¼ c. milk
Vegetable oil
Salt

Sift together flour, baking powder and sugar. Beat together egg, water and milk. Stir the liquid ingredients into the dry ingredients, then beat until the batter is smooth and stiff. Stir in the chopped flowers and drop the batter by tablespoon into ¼ inch deep hot oil. Fry 2 or 3 minutes on each side. When golden brown, remove from oil; drain on paper towels; sprinkle with salt and serve immediately.

Paula Childress

CORN PUFFS

1 c. corn meal
½ tsp. salt
1½ c. boiling water

4 egg whites, beaten
1 tsp. baking powder

Mix together corn meal, salt and boiling water. Blend well and let cool. Beat egg whites until stiff and blend in baking powder. Fold egg white mixture into cooled corn meal. Drop by teaspoonful on a greased baking dish. Bake at 350° for 20 to 30 minutes or until light brown. Serve hot with butter.

Helen Sykes

SPICY SUGAR PUFFS

4 Tbsp. margarine	4 tsp. baking powder
½ c. sugar	½ tsp. salt
1 egg	¼ tsp. nutmeg
1 tsp. lemon peel	1 c. milk
2 c. flour	½ c. melted butter

Set dial on mixer at 1. Cream margarine and sugar. Beat in egg and lemon peel. Sift together flour, baking powder, salt and nutmeg. Add dry ingredients alternately with milk. Beat briefly after each addition. Pour batter into muffin tins. Bake at 375°F. for 15 minutes. While muffins are hot, dip each in melted butter, then in sugar-ginger mixture (2 teaspoons ginger and ¾ cup sugar).

Martha Hooper

HUSHPUPPIES

1 c. corn meal	1 c. Bisquick
1 tsp. salt	1 tsp. sugar
1 tsp. baking soda	1 egg
1 chopped onion	1 small can cream corn

Make into balls and deep-fry until golden brown.

Peggy Graviss

HUSH PUPPIES

1 c. flour	1 egg
⅔ c. corn meal	2 Tbsp. oil
2 Tbsp. sugar	¾ c. milk
1 tsp. baking powder	1 large onion, minced
1 tsp. salt	

Combine all ingredients with spoon or whisk. Drop by teaspoon into hot oil until browned. Drain on paper towels.

Kathy Chesser

HUSH PUPPIES

1 c. water	1 Tbsp. lard, melted
½ tsp. salt	½ onion, minced
1 c. white corn meal	Bacon fat or vegetable oil for
1 tsp. baking powder	frying

Boil water; add salt. In a bowl, mix water, meal, baking powder, lard, and onion. Shape into flat cakes about the size of a silver dollar. In a pan, heat enough oil for deep fat frying. Oil should be very hot. Fry cakes until golden. Serve hot. Serves 4.

Helen Sykes

SQUASH HUSH PUPPIES

2¼ c. self-rising corn meal mix
3 Tbsp. self-rising flour
1 Tbsp. finely chopped onion (more if desired)*

½ c. buttermilk
1 egg
Fresh cooked, cooled and drained squash or canned drained squash

Combine corn meal, flour and onion; add egg. Gradually beat in buttermilk. Drain squash and stir into the regular hushpuppies mix. Mixture should be rather medium batter. To be dropped from spoon in hot fat. Puppies should float and fry to golden brown. Should be cooked in hot fish fat. Serve with fish and cole slaw.

* One half package of dried onion soup mix can be used instead of fresh onion if you wish.

Mary Beeler

BREADS

APPLE PECAN BREAD

2 c. sugar
2½ c. flour
1½ tsp. soda
¾ tsp. salt
½ tsp. cinnamon

3 eggs
1½ c. salad oil
2 tsp. vanilla
3 c. sliced apples
½ c. pecans

Mix dry ingredients; add eggs, salad oil, vanilla, and apples. Bake 40 minutes at 350°.

Patricia Embry

APPLESAUCE NUT BREAD

2 c. flour, sifted
¾ c. sugar
1 tsp. baking powder
1 tsp. salt
½ tsp. soda

½ tsp. nutmeg
1 c. nuts
1 egg, beaten
1 c. applesauce

Add all ingredients and stir just enough to moisten. Bake 1 hour in slow oven, about 350°.

Peggy Larrison

AYRSHIRE SHORTBREAD

1 c. rice flour
⅔ c. sugar
2 Tbsp. thin cream
1 c. flour

½ beaten egg (I use whole
egg)
4 oz. butter

Sieve the flours into mixing bowl and rub in butter with the fingers. Mix in the sugar and bind to a stiff consistency with egg and cream. Roll out thin; prick with fork and place on greased paper on a greased baking sheet and bake in steady oven for 15 minutes until pale golden color. Cool on a wire tray; dust with sugar.

Teresa Stroup

PULL APART BACON BREAD

3 cans (10 per can) buttermilk
    biscuits
1 c. each chopped green
    pepper, onions and
    chives

½ lb. bacon
½ c. Parmesan cheese
½ c. margarine, melted

Fry and crumble bacon. Saute chopped vegetables in bacon drippings. Drain on paper towels, absorbing as much of the grease as possible. Cut biscuits into fourths with scissors. Mix all ingredients in a bowl. Pour into lightly greased Bundt pan or a 12 cup angel food cake pan and bake for 30 minutes at 350°.

The bread can be made ahead and reheated.

Paula White

BANANA NUT BREAD

½ c. shortening
3 well ripened bananas
2 c. all-purpose flour
2 eggs
Dash of salt

1 c. sugar
1 Tbsp. vanilla
1 tsp. soda
½ c. chopped pecans or
    walnuts

Cream shortening and sugar; add mashed bananas and beaten eggs, 1 at a time, then add vanilla, dry ingredients and nuts. Line a loaf pan with waxed paper; bake at 350° for 45 to 50 minutes. Let cool 10 minutes before removing from pan.

Lillian White

BANANA NUT BREAD

⅓ c. margarine
2 eggs
1 c. mashed bananas

½ c. sugar
1¾ c. self-rising flour
½ c. chopped pecans

Mix together all ingredients; put in ungreased loaf pan. Bake at 325° approximately 45 minutes or until done. When you stick a toothpick in center and it comes out clean, it is done.

Troy Rigdon

BANANA NUT BREAD

2 sticks oleo
2 c. sugar
4 c. flour
4 egg yolks
4 egg whites

2 Tbsp. water with 2 tsp. soda
    dissolved in it
6 large bananas
1½ c. nuts

Mix oleo, sugar, egg yolks, soda with water, and bananas; beat well. Add flour to mixture; mix well. Beat egg whites and fold in. Bake at 350° for 1¼ hours. Makes 2 small pans or 1 large pan.

Can be baked in a Bundt or tube pan. Recipe can be halved for smaller amount.

Zama Picklesimer

BEER BREAD

3 c. self-rising flour
3 Tbsp. sugar
1 (12 oz.) can beer

1 egg
Baker's Joy

Spray Baker's Joy on a 9x5 inch loaf pan. In a large bowl, combine flour, sugar, beer and egg. Mix well. Pour into pan and bake for 45 to 50 minutes at 350°. Bread will turn golden brown and pull away from sides of pan when done.

Peggy Kessinger

BOSTON BROWN BREAD

2 c. buttermilk
¾ c. dark molasses
¾ c. seedless raisins
1 c. rye flour
1 c. whole wheat or graham
    flour

1 c. yellow corn meal
¾ tsp. baking soda
1 tsp. salt
1 Tbsp. butter, softened

In a deep bowl, beat the buttermilk and molasses together vigorously with a spoon. Stir in the raisins. Combine the rye flour, whole wheat or graham flour, corn meal, soda and salt; sift them into the buttermilk mixture, 1 cup at a time, stirring well after each addition.

Thoroughly wash and dry 2 empty 2½ cup (Number 2) tin cans. Then, with a pastry brush, spread the softened butter over the bottom and sides of the cans. Pour the batter into the cans, dividing it evenly between them. The batter should fill each can to within about 1 inch of the top. Cover each can loosely with a circle of buttered wax paper and then with a larger circle of heavy duty aluminum foil. The foil should be puffed like the top of a French chef's hat, allowing an inch of space above the top edge of the can so the batter can rise as it is steamed. Tie the wax paper and foil in place with kitchen string. Stand the cans on a rack set in a large pot and pour in enough boiling water to come about ¾ of the way up the sides of the cans. Return the water to a boil over high heat; cover the pot lightly, and reduce the heat to low. Steam the bread for 2 hours and 15 minutes. Remove the foil and paper from the cans at once, and turn the bread out on a heated platter if you plan to serve it immediately or leave the bread in the cans with the foil and paper in place, and steam it for 10 to 15 minutes to reheat the loaves before you serve them. Steamed loaves, with covers in place, can be kept in the refrigerator for a week to 10 days. Makes 2 (5½ x 3 inch) cylindrical loaves.

CARROT BREAD

1 c. sugar
¾ c. oil
2 eggs
2 c. flour
1 tsp. cinnamon

1 tsp. baking powder
1 tsp. soda
1¼ c. carrots, shredded
½ c. nuts or raisins

Cream sugar and oil together. Blend in eggs. Add alternately dry ingredients with shredded carrots. Grease and flour 3 (6x3 inch) pans. Bake 1 hour at 325°.

Mary Lauder

CINNAMON BREAD

2 c. flour
1 c. sugar
4 tsp. baking powder
1½ tsp. cinnamon
1¼ tsp. salt

1 c. buttermilk
⅓ c. oil
2 tsp. vanilla
2 eggs

Grease and flour loaf pans. In large bowl, combine all bread ingredients; beat 3 minutes at medium speed. Pour batter into pans. In small bowl, combine all Streusel ingredients until crumbly; sprinkle over batter and swirl lightly. Bake at 350°F. for 40 to 45 minutes. Remove from pans immediately.

Streusel:

2 Tbsp. sugar	**2 tsp. margarine**
1 tsp. cinnamon	

Martha Hooper

COCONUT PUMPKIN BREAD

2 c. sugar	**2 c. all-purpose flour**
1 tsp. baking soda	**1 tsp. ground nutmeg**
1 tsp. salt	**1½ c. vegetable oil**
1 tsp. ground cinnamon	**⅔ c. flaked coconut**
2 (3½ oz.) pkg. coconut pie	**2 c. (about 1 lb.) cooked**
filling (regular)	**pumpkin**
5 eggs	

Mix together the first 8 ingredients in a large mixing bowl. In another bowl, mix together eggs, vegetable oil, and pumpkin, blending well. Add egg mixture to dry ingredients; mix well. Grease 2 (8½ x 4½ x 2½ inch) loaf pans and cover bottom with greased wax paper. Divide dough evenly between pans and place on middle rack of a preheated 350° oven. Bake for 50 minutes to 1 hour and 10 minutes. Tester should come out clean! Cool in pan for 10 minutes. Carefully turn out onto cake rack and remove wax paper; cool completely. *Freezes well!*

Patricia Jewell

CRACKLING CORN BREAD

1½ c. corn meal	**1 egg, beaten**
½ c. flour	**1½ c. milk**
2 tsp. baking powder	**½ c. cracklings**
½ tsp. salt	

Sift together corn meal, flour, baking powder and salt. In another bowl, combine beaten egg, milk and cracklings. Combine with dry ingredients. Beat well and pour into a hot, greased pan. Bake in moderate oven until done and brown.

Sue Tipton

CORN CAKES

Fried on a griddle (spider), these cakes were served with butter as a bread or with sorghum molasses as pancakes.

1 egg, beaten slightly	**1 c. hot water (or milk)**
1 c. corn meal	**1 Tsp. fat or lard**
½ c. flour	**1 tsp. sugar**
1 tsp. salt	

Mix dry ingredients, then stir in the others. Drop or pour on hot, greased surface. Fry to a golden brown on both sides.

CORN CAKES OR LACE CAKES

1 egg	**1 rounded tsp. salt**
1 level tsp. baking soda	

Beat well and add 1 pint rich buttermilk and 3 heaping tablespoons self-rising flour. Add enough white corn meal to make a thin batter. Grease griddle and, when smoking hot, put batter on by the tablespoon, leaving room to turn. When brown on one side, turn and brown the other.

Never turn but once. The secret is to have the batter thin and the griddle hot.

Mrs. Marion Kiess

CRANBERRY-NUT BREAD

1 c. fresh cranberries, chopped	**½ c. chopped walnuts**
	2 eggs
2 c. sifted flour	**1 c. milk**
¾ c. sugar	**¼ c. melted margarine**
3 tsp. baking powder	**1 tsp. vanilla**
¼ tsp. salt	

Sift flour with sugar, baking powder and salt into large bowl. Stir in cranberries and walnuts. In small bowl, with rotary beater, beat eggs with milk, butter and vanilla. Make well in center of cranberry mixture. Pour in egg mixture; with fork, stir until dry ingredients are moistened. Turn into 2 (7 x 3½ x 2 inch) pans, greased. Bake 40 to 45 minutes or until cake tester inserted in center comes out clean. Cool in pans 10 minutes. Remove from pans and cool on wire rack. Oven temperature: 350°F.

Martha Hooper

DATE-NUT-MARMALADE BREAD

1 c. chopped dates
½ c. nuts
3 c. sifted flour
1 egg
1¼ c. milk

¼ c. oil
⅓ c. sugar
⅔ c. orange marmalade
1 tsp. salt
3 tsp. baking powder

Mix ½ cup flour with dates and nuts; set aside. Blend together the egg, milk, oil, sugar and baking powder into the bowl with liquid mixture and mix quickly, only enough to moisten flour. Add dates and nuts. Put dough into greased loaf pans and bake at 350°F. for 1 hour. Cool for 30 minutes before turning out of pans. Cool thoroughly before wrapping to store.

Martha Hooper

GERMAN CORN BREAD

2 c. self-rising corn meal
1½ c. flour (self-rising)
1 can cream style corn
1 onion
1 sweet pepper (green)
2 red hot peppers (fresh or
    canned)

1 c. grated cheese (American)
1 Tbsp. oil
1 c. buttermilk
1 c. milk

Bake in oblong pan or round skillet (well greased) at 400° to 450° until done.

Frances Crum

GERMAN STOLLEN

¼ oz. (¼ cake) fresh
   compressed yeast
½ c. warm milk
2 c. all-purpose flour
½ tsp. salt
¼ c. butter
¼ c. sugar
1 egg, beaten
½ c. raisins
⅓ c. currants or chopped
   candied cherries

3 Tbsp. mixed candied peel,
   chopped
¼ c. blanched almonds,
   chopped
Grated rind of ½ lemon
1 Tbsp. butter, melted
Icing (confectioners sugar for
   dusting)

Cream the yeast with 2 tablespoons of milk. Sift flour and salt into a warmed bowl. Make a well in the center. Cream the butter with the sugar; add egg and beat well. Add to the flour, with the remaining milk, yeast liquid, fruit, peel, nuts and lemon rind. Mix ingredients together and beat until dough comes cleanly away from the sides of the bowl. Turn onto a lightly floured surface and knead well for 5 minutes. Place in a clean bowl; cover with a damp cloth and leave in a warm place for 1½ hours or until doubled in size. Turn onto a lightly floured surface and knead well for 5 minutes. Roll to an oblong about 10x8 inches. Brush with melted butter. Fold over lengthwise so the top layer is 1 inch from the edge of the bottom, forming a split loaf shape. Place on a greased baking sheet and put inside an oiled plastic bag. Leave in a warm pace fo 30 minutes until doubled in size. Remove from the bag. Bake in a moderate hot oven (375°) for 35 to 45 minutes until golden brown. Turn onto a wire rack to cool. Sprinkle the top generously with icing sugar before serving. Makes 1 (10 inch) stollen.

Gwen Mills

GINGERBREAD

½ c. butter
1 c. sugar
2 eggs
½ c. molasses
3 c. flour

2 tsp. soda
½ tsp. salt
1½ tsp. ginger
½ c. boiling water

Cream ½ cup butter and 1 cup sugar. Beat in 2 eggs. Sift 3 cups flour, 2 teaspoons soda, ½ teaspoon salt and 1½ teaspoons ginger. Add to creamed mixture alternately with ½ cup water and ½ cup molasses. Bake at 350° for 35 to 40 minutes.

Sauce:

1 c. sugar	**1 tsp. vanilla**
3 Tbsp. flour	**2 Tbsp. butter**
1 c. boiling water	**Ginger to taste**

Mix flour and sugar. Add boiling water gradually. Boil for about **7** minutes. Remove from heat and add butter and vanilla. Add ginger to taste. Serve over warm gingerbread.

Sue Tipton

GOURMET CORN BREAD

1 c. self-rising meal	**1 (8 oz.) can cream style corn**
½ c. sour cream	**Salt (optional)***
½ c. salad oil	**Jalapeno peppers (optional)**
2 eggs, well beaten	

Mix all at once. Beat well; pour into a well greased 8 inch square pan. Bake at 425° until brown, about 25 minutes.

* Note: Some self-rising corn meal contains very little salt. Taste batter and add if necessary.

Mary Baxter

HOMINY BREAD

2 c. hominy	**2 eggs, well beaten**
3 c. boiling water	**1 pt. milk**
1 Tbsp. butter	**1 Tbsp. lard**
3 Tbsp. corn meal	

Put 2 cups fine hominy into double boiler with 3 cups boiling water and cook until hominy is tender and water absorbed. Let cool and add 1 tablespoon butter, 3 tablespoons corn meal, 2 eggs (well beaten), and 1 pint milk. Mix thoroughly to a smooth batter. Melt 1 tablespoon lard in a skillet; pour in batter while lard is hot and bake 30 minutes in 350° oven.

Note: Take 2 cups of canned hominy and grate and use.

Helen Sykes

IRISH SODA BREAD

4 c. bread flour
2 c. buttermilk
1½ c. raisins
¼ tsp. salt

2 tsp. baking powder
1 tsp. baking soda
1 Tbsp. caraway seed

In large bowl, mix all ingredients, except buttermilk, together. Make well in center and add buttermilk. Mix well. If too sticky, add a bit more flour. Knead gently and shape into a round loaf. Make cross on top of loaf. Place on a heavy greased flat pan and bake at 375° for about 40 minutes. Cool, but while still warm, place in plastic bag. Let rest overnight. Slice thinly and serve with butter.

Alice Alessio

KUCHEN COFFEE CAKE

2 c. plain flour
1½ c. light brown sugar,
     packed down
½ c. Crisco

1 c. buttermilk with scant 1
     tsp. soda stirred in
1 whole egg

Mix flour, sugar and Crisco with fingers until crumbly and blended well. Add 2 teaspoons cinnamon and 1 teaspoon nutmeg. Save ¾ cup of this mixture to spread evenly on top, before baking. Pour in buttermilk and egg to rest of mix; beat well. Pour in long baking pan. Bake 25 minutes or until done. (Glass dish takes a little longer.)

Doris Beeler

MARMALADE NUT BREAD

2½ c. unsifted flour, stirred
     before measuring
⅓ c. sugar
3½ tsp. baking powder
1 tsp. salt
1 c. coarsely chopped
     walnuts

1 egg
1 c. sweet orange marmalade
1 c. orange juice
3 Tbsp. vegetable oil

Mix together flour, sugar, baking powder and salt. Add nuts and stir to coat evenly. Mix in another bowl marmalade, juice, oil and egg. Add flour to mixture; stir only until dry ingredients are moistened. Divide batter evenly between 2 well greased loaf pans (8½ x 4½ x 2½ inches). Bake in preheated 350° oven for 1 hour or until toothpick inserted in center comes out clean. Cool in pans on rack 10 minutes; remove from pans; cool thoroughly on rack. Wrap tightly in foil. Allow flavors to mellow overnight before serving.

Mary Goff

HOT MEXICAN CORN BREAD

2 eggs
1 c. corn
1 c. soured cream or 1 c.
    buttermilk plus 3 Tbsp.
    sugar

½ c. salad oil
4 large jalapeno peppers
1 c. self-rising corn meal
1 c. grated Cheddar cheese
    (optional)

Mix together first 5 ingredients in blender and then add corn meal without blending. Pour half of the batter into a greased 9 inch square pan. If using cheese, sprinkle grated cheese over batter. Pour remaining batter on top. Bake in a 350° (moderate) oven for approximately 1 hour.

Mrs. Lindey (Abbie) Mercer

MEXICAN CORN BREAD

1½ c. corn meal
3 tsp. baking powder
1 tsp. salt
2 eggs
⅔ c. salad oil

1 c. buttermilk
3 jalapeno peppers, chopped
1 (1 lb.) can cream style corn
1 c. grated Cheddar cheese

Mix all ingredients, except cheese in order listed. Pour half the batter into greased 9 inch square baking dish. Sprinkle with half the cheese. Add remaining batter. Cover with remaining cheese. Bake in preheated 350° oven for 45 minutes or until done.

Note: One can whole green chilies, drained and chopped, may be substituted for jalapeno peppers.

Deborah E. Robertson

MEXICAN CORN BREAD

2 c. corn bread mix
2 eggs
1 Tbsp. sugar
½ c. cooking oil

1 can cream style corn
1 c. chopped onion
1 c. grated Longhorn cheese
1 hot pepper, chopped

Mix together and bake same as corn bread.

Wanda Frankenberger

MEXICAN CORN BREAD

1 c. self-rising corn meal
1 c. cream style corn
1 c. buttermilk
1 Tbsp. green pepper
2 chopped jalapeno peppers
   or small can green chili
   peppers

2 eggs
1½ c. cheese
⅔ c. oil

    Mix well all preceding ingredients, except for cheese. Pour half of batter in a hot greased skillet. Sprinkle half of cheese over batter. Then pour in the rest of the batter and top with cheese. Bake at 400° for 20 to 25 minutes.

Jenny Carp

MONKEY BREAD

1 pkg. dry yeast
½ c. lukewarm water
½ c. shortening
⅜ c. sugar
¾ tsp. salt

½ c. boiling water
1 egg, beaten
3 c. plain flour
1 stick melted butter

    Dissolve yeast in lukewarm water and set aside. Mix shortening, sugar and salt together. Add boiling water and mix well. Add egg to this mixture and stir. Add flour and yeast mixture alternately to shortening mixture until all is well mixed. Let rise until dough doubles in size. Punch down. Roll dough out on floured board until ½ to ¼ inch thick. Cut dough into various shapes and dip each piece in melted butter. Lay pieces in tube pan layer on layer. Let rise about 2 hours. Bake at 350° about 45 minutes, until top is real brown.

    This bread is easier to pull apart than slice.

Hazel Walker

NAVAJO FRY BREAD

4 c. all-purpose flour
3 tsp. baking powder
1 tsp. salt

1⅓ c. warm water (approx.)
Vegetable oil for deep-frying
Corn meal or flour

    Combine flour, baking powder and salt. Add warm water in small amounts until mixture reaches the consistency of bread dough. Knead thoroughly until smooth and elastic; cover the bowl, and let the dough rest for 10 minutes. Heat 2 or 3 inches of vegetable oil in a deep fryer to 400°. Pull off 2 inch round pieces of dough and roll out ¼ inch thick and about 8 to 10 inches round on a board lightly dusted with flour or corn meal. Punch a hole in the center of each piece. Fry bread, 1 at a time, on each side until golden. Serve hot.

Will freeze up to 3 months.

Gwen Mills

NEW MEXICAN CORN BREAD

2 Tbsp. oil
2 c. corn kernels, briefly
  chopped in food
  processor
3 eggs
1 c. sour cream

1 c. yellow corn meal
1 c. green chilies, chopped
1 tsp. baking soda
1 tsp. salt
2 c. Monterey Jack cheese,
  grated

Preheat oven to 400°. Put 2 tablespoons oil in 10 inch cast iron frying pan. Set in oven to heat while you mix bread. Combine all ingredients; mix thoroughly. Pour into well heated frying pan. Bake 45 minutes or until firm.

New Mexican corn bread is good with winter soups and stews. With its extra corn, green chilies, and cheese, the bread is almost a main dish. Cut in small squares, it is a tasty party hors d'oeuvres.

Wilma Crowdus

NO FAT BREAD

2½ c. water
2 pkg. dry yeast

6½ - 7 c. plain flour
1 Tbsp. salt

Use 1 cup of the 2½ cups of water. Warm the water and dissolve the yeast. Mix all the ingredients and allow to stand until it has doubled in bulk. Beat down and let rise again. Beat down a second time, then roll out on a floured board to about ½ inch thick. Then roll up the dough like a jelly roll. Place on a cookie sheet and let rise again until big and fat. Mix 1 egg white with 1 tablespoon of water. Beat until foamy. Brush the mixture on top of the dough. Place in a 350° to 375° oven for about 40 minutes or until golden brown.

J. W. Borden, Jr.

ONION CORN BREAD CASSEROLE

4 c. onions, chopped
¼ c. butter, melted
1 c. sour cream
1 c. shredded Cheddar
   cheese in 2 parts
1½ c. self-rising corn meal
2 Tbsp. sugar
¼ tsp. dill weed
2 eggs, beaten
1 c. cream style corn
¼ c. milk
¼ c. oil
Dash of hot pepper sauce

Brown onions in butter until tender; remove from heat and set aside. Stir together corn meal, sugar, and dill weed. Combine eggs, corn, milk, oil, and hot pepper sauce. Add all at once to corn meal mixture, stirring until blended. Pour batter into greased iron skillet or 9 inch square pan. Spoon onion mixture on top. Sprinkle remaining cheese on top. Bake at 400° for 25 to 30 minutes.

Shirley Cates

ORANGE CANDY BREAD

2 c. flour
1 c. sugar
4 tsp. baking powder
1 tsp. salt
1 c. buttermilk
⅓ c. oil
2 tsp. vanilla
2 eggs
1 c. candy orange slices, cut
   up

Grease and flour loaf pans. Toss candy in ½ cup of the flour. Combine rest of ingredients; beat 3 minutes at medium speed. Fold in orange candy. Pour batter into prepared pans. Bake at 350°F. for 45 to 50 minutes. Remove from pans immediately.

Martha Hooper

PEANUT BUTTER BANANA BREAD

1¾ c. flour
2 tsp. baking powder
½ tsp. soda
½ tsp. salt
⅓ c. margarine
¾ c. peanut butter (crunchy)
⅔ c. sugar
2 eggs
1 c. mashed bananas
¼ c. buttermilk

Preheat the oven to 350°F. Combine flour, baking powder, soda and salt; sift together. Cream together the peanut butter and shortening in large mixing bowl. Add eggs and beat well, then add dry ingredients alternately with banana pulp and buttermilk. Mix thoroughly, but do not beat. Pour batter into a well greased loaf pan and bake 1 hour or until done. Cool before slicing.

Martha Hooper

PINEAPPLE ZUCCHINI BREAD

3 eggs
1 c. salad oil
2 c. sugar
2 tsp. vanilla
2 c. zucchini, coarsely
    shredded
1 (8¼ oz.) can pineapple,
    drained

3 c. unsifted flour
2 tsp. soda
1 tsp. salt
½ tsp. baking powder
2 tsp. cinnamon
1 c. chopped nuts
1 c. raisins

Beat eggs; add oil, sugar and vanilla; beat mixture until light and foamy. Stir in zucchini and pineapple. Combine flour, soda, salt, baking powder, cinnamon, nuts, and raisins. Stir gently into zucchini mixture. Pour batter into a greased and floured 9x5 inch loaf pan. Bake at 350° for 1 hour. Cool in pans.

Cristy Lewis

PITA BREAD

2 pkg. active dry yeast
2 tsp. sugar
1½ c. warm water

4 c. flour
1 tsp. salt

Put yeast and sugar in the warm water and stir until dissolved. Add flour and salt. Mix well. Knead the dough generously for 5 minutes. Then divide into equal parts to make 12 balls. Roll out each ball on a floured board until about 7 inches in diameter and about ⅓ inch thick. Let the pitas rise in a warm place for ½ hour or until puffy. Bake a few at a time in a 500° oven for no more than 5 minutes.

Any leftovers can be put in a plastic bag and frozen for later use. Good served with Moussaka.

Mary Goff

PUMPKIN CORN BREAD

1¼ c. all-purpose flour
1 Tbsp. baking powder
1 c. corn meal
½ tsp. salt
1 tsp. ginger
¾ c. brown sugar, packed

¼ c. margarine, melted
2 eggs, beaten lightly
1 c. cooked, mashed
   pumpkin
⅔ c. buttermilk

Preheat oven to 350°. Grease 8x8 inch baking pan or muffin pan. Stir together all ingredients; mix well, but don't overmix batter. Bake about 45 minutes.

Annette Anderson

PUMPKIN BREAD

1 c. oil
2 c. sugar
2 tsp. cinnamon
2 c. cooked pumpkin

2 c. self-rising flour
4 eggs, beaten lightly
1 c. raisins

Mix all ingredients together. Bake at 325° about 60 minutes or until done.

PUMPKIN BREAD

3½ c. flour
2 tsp. soda
1½ tsp. cinnamon
1½ tsp. nutmeg
¾ tsp. cloves
1½ tsp. salt

3 c. white sugar
1 c. Crisco oil
4 eggs
⅔ c. water
2 c. pumpkin
1 c. nuts, chopped (optional)

Sift dry ingredients into a large bowl. Add remaining ingredients. Mix well and pour into well oiled pans. Bake 1 hour at 350°.

Zella Mae Cox

PUMPKIN BREAD

1 (16 oz.) can pumpkin
4 eggs
1 c. vegetable oil
⅓ c. water
3½ c. flour
1 tsp. pumpkin pie spice

3 c. sugar
2 tsp. baking soda
1½ tsp. salt
Sugar glaze (optional)
Cherries (optional)
Nuts (optional)

Combine pumpkin, eggs, oil and water. Mix well. Add combined dry ingredients to pumpkin mixture; mix well. Pour into 2 greased and floured 9x5 inch loaf pans. Bake at 350° for 1 hour and 10 minutes. Cool 10 minutes and remove from pan. Top with sugar glaze, cherries and nuts if desired.

Wanda Harris

PUMPKIN BREAD

3½ c. flour (plain)
3 c. sugar
4 eggs, well beaten
2 tsp. soda
1 tsp. baking powder
2 tsp. salt
2 tsp. cinnamon

1 tsp. nutmeg
1 tsp. allspice
½ tsp. cloves
½ tsp. ginger
1 (16 oz.) can pumpkin
1 c. oil
⅔ c. water

Mix dry ingredients; add rest and mix well. Bake in loaf pan at 350° for about 1 hour. (Can also use Bundt pan or muffin tins, adjust time accordingly.)

Cream Cheese Frosting:

1 (8 oz.) pkg. cream cheese,
   softened
1 stick butter, softened
1½ tsp. vanilla

1 tsp. lemon juice
2 - 3 c. powdered sugar (to
   taste)

Cream first 4 ingredients. Add sugar a little at a time until smooth and spreading consistency. Add nuts if desired.

Galena Gronefeld

RICE CORN BREAD

4 Tbsp. (½ stick) butter, melted
1 c. corn meal
2½ tsp. baking powder
1 tsp. salt
1 c. cooked rice
1 egg, well beaten
1 c. cold milk

Preheat oven to 400°. Pour half the melted butter in a 9 x 9 x 2½ inch baking pan. Set aside. Combine the corn meal, baking powder and salt in a sifter. Sift over the cooked rice. Mix well with a fork, separating the rice kernels. Combine the beaten egg and milk. Stir well into the rice mixture alternately with the remaining butter. Pour into the baking pan and again mix well. Bake for 30 to 40 minutes or until nicely browned. Serve, cut into wedges, with lots of butter. Serves 6.

Kim Clinton

RHUBARB BREAD

1½ c. brown sugar
⅔ c. Wesson oil
1 egg
1 c. sour milk
1 tsp. salt
1 tsp. soda
1 tsp. vanilla
2½ c. flour
1½ c. finely diced rhubarb
½ c. chopped nuts

Combine brown sugar and oil; stir in sour milk and vanilla; add sifted dry ingredients. Stir in rhubarb and nuts. Pour into well greased pans. Combine topping ingredients and sprinkle on top. Bake at 325° for 40 minutes. Cool in pan. Bake in 2 (9x5x3 inch) pans.

Topping:

½ c. brown sugar
½ tsp. cinnamon
1 Tbsp. butter

Dollie D. Billiter

SOUR CREAM CORN BREAD

2 c. self-rising corn meal
2 eggs, slightly beaten
½ c. oil
½ c. cream style corn
1 c. sour cream
¼ tsp. salt

Mix first 4 ingredients, then fold in sour cream. Bake in iron skillet at 450° for 25 minutes.

Annette Anderson

356

SOURDOUGH STARTER

2 c. flour   **6 tsp. dry yeast**
1¾ c. warm water   **2 Tbsp. honey**

Combine flour and dry yeast in a bowl. Mix honey in warm water and gradually add to dry ingredients. Store in earthenware pot at room temperature for 2 days to 1 week.

SOURDOUGH BREAD

The night before baking, combine 1 cup of starter (preceding recipe) with 2 cups warm water. Sift in 2½ cups flour and beat well. Cover and leave 12 hours in warm place. (Then, before adding any other ingredients, return 1 cup of batter to the storage pot for future use.) Add enough flour to make stiff dough. Turn out onto lightly floured board; knead vigorously until smooth and elastic, about 10 minutes. Place in greased bowl, turning to grease top. Cover. Place in warm place. Let it rest 20 minutes. Form into loaves. Let rise until doubled. Bake at 400° about 25 minutes.

SOUTHERN SPOON BREAD

3 c. milk   **3 level tsp. baking powder**
3 eggs, well beaten   **1 tsp. salt**
1 c. water ground corn meal   **Butter (size of a walnut)**

Stir meal into 2 cups milk. Let come to a boil, making a mush. Add remainder of milk, well beaten eggs, salt, baking powder and melted butter. Bake in moderate oven for 30 minutes or until brown. Serve in dish in which it has been baked.

Barbara Haddix

SOUTHERN SPOON BREAD

Stir together:

1 c. yellow corn meal   **½ tsp. salt**
1½ tsp. baking powder

In greased (1 quart size) casserole, pour:

2 eggs, beaten   **2 Tbsp. butter, melted**

In medium size pan, heat 2¼ cups milk (stir to avoid scorching). As it starts boiling, sprinkle in the dry ingredients, stirring vigorously with wooden spoon. Cook and stir for 2 or 3 minutes, as it thickens. Mix with eggs in casserole. Bake at 425° for 45 minutes. Serve from casserole with spoon. Add butter. Eat with fork.

SOUTHERN STYLE CORN BREAD

2 Tbsp. bacon drippings
1¼ c. corn meal
1 (7½ oz.) pkg. corn muffin
   mix
2 tsp. baking powder
1 tsp. salt
1½ c. buttermilk
2 eggs, beaten

Pour bacon drippings into 8 inch square baking pan; place in 400° oven. Combine dry ingredients; add remaining ingredients, mixing until moistened. Pour into hot pan. Bake at 400° for 25 to 30 minutes or until golden brown.

To double recipe: Substitute 13x9 inch baking pan for 8 inch square baking pan.

Mary V. Stanley

SPICY PEACH NUT BREAD

2 c. flour
⅔ c. sugar
2 tsp. baking powder
½ tsp. salt
½ tsp. soda
½ tsp. ground cloves
2 Tbsp. melted margarine
2 eggs
2 c. (16 oz. can) chopped
   peaches
1 c. chopped nuts
1 c. raisins (optional)
½ c. peach syrup

Grease and flour bottom of loaf pan. In large bowl, combine flour, sugar, baking powder, salt, soda, ground cloves, margarine, eggs, peaches, and syrup. Beat 2 minutes at medium speed. Stir in nuts and raisins. Pour into prepared pans. Bake at 350°F. for 60 minutes. Remove from pans. Cool completely.

Martha Hooper

SPOON BREAD

2 c. evaporated milk, mixed
    with water (equal
    amounts of both) or 2 c.
    whole milk
½ c. white corn meal

1 tsp. salt
2 Tbsp. butter
½ tsp. baking powder
2 eggs, separated

Preheat oven to 375°. Boil milk. Gradually stir in corn meal. Add salt and butter. Turn off heat. Add baking powder. Add egg yolks. Beat egg whites until stiff. Fold in batter. Pour batter into a hot greased 2 quart casserole. Bake 35 to 40 minutes. Serve hot with butter. Serves 4 to 6.

Cristy Lewis

STRAWBERRY NUT BREAD

2 c. all-purpose flour
1 tsp. baking soda
1 tsp. salt
1 Tbsp. ground cinnamon
2 c. sugar

4 eggs, beaten
1¼ c. vegetable oil
2 c. thawed, sliced frozen
    strawberries
1½ c. chopped pecans

Combine dry ingredients. Add eggs, oil, strawberries and pecans. Stir until all ingredients are just moistened. Spoon batter into 2 well greased 9x5x3 inch loaf pans. Bake at 350° for 60 to 70 minutes or until bread tests done. Cool in pans for 5 minutes; remove to wire rack to cool. Yield: 2 loaves.

Melanie Davis

STRAWBERRY BREAD

2 (10 oz.) pkg. frozen
    strawberries
4 eggs
1¼ c. oil
3 c. flour

1 tsp. baking soda
1 tsp. salt
3 tsp. ground cinnamon
2 c. sugar
1¼ c. chopped nuts

Thaw berries. Mix undrained berries, eggs, and oil. Sift dry ingredients into strawberry mixture, reserving about ½ cup flour to sprinkle over nuts. Blend thoroughly. Add flour to nuts, coating well. Add to batter. Pour into well greased and floured 9x5 inch loaf pans. Bake at 350° for 1 hour. If top browns too quickly, cover with tent shaped aluminum foil. Yield: 2 loaves.

Pam Thompson

STRAWBERRY BREAD

1 (10 oz.) pkg. sweetened
   frozen strawberries,
   thawed
2 eggs, beaten
½ c. plus 2 Tbsp. oil
1½ c. all-purpose flour

½ tsp. baking soda
½ tsp. baking powder
½ tsp. salt
1½ tsp. ground cinnamon
1 c. sugar (optional)
½ c. chopped pecans

   Mix together undrained strawberries, eggs and oil. Combine dry ingredients. Reserve about ½ cup dry ingredients and add remaining to strawberry mixture. Stir to blend well. Stir nuts into reserved dry ingredients and add to batter; stir well. Pour into a well greased and lightly floured 9x5 inch loaf pan and bake in a preheated oven at 350° for 1 hour or until done. If top starts to overbrown before bread is done, make a tent of foil and cover pan loosely.

Sharon Elmore

SWEET POTATO BREAD

3 c. sugar
1 c. oil
4 eggs
3 c. flour
1 tsp. soda
½ tsp. salt

½ tsp. cinnamon
½ tsp. nutmeg
2 c. mashed sweet potatoes
¾ c. water
1 c. chopped nuts (optional)

   Cream together sugar and oil. Add eggs, 1 at a time. Cream after each addition. Add other ingredients. Pour into greased and floured loaf pans. Bake at 350°F. for about 45 minutes.

Martha Hooper

WHOLE WHEAT BREAD

2 c. scalded milk
⅓ c. molasses
2 tsp. salt

1 Tbsp. yeast
¼ c. warm water
4⅔ c. whole wheat flour

   Add molasses to milk. Let cool to lukewarm. Dissolve yeast in the lukewarm water. Put liquids together. Add them, as you stir, to the flour into which the salt has already been mixed. Beat well and cover. Let rise to double in bulk. Again beat and turn into greased bread pans so that pans are half full. Allow to rise in warm place until almost doubled. Bake at 400° about 50 minutes until it shrinks from sides of pans. Butter the top a few minutes before removing from oven.

HOMEMADE YEAST BREAD

1 tsp. yeast
¼ c. warm water
¾ c. cold water

1 egg
1 c. self-rising flour

Mix all ingredients together. Let stand 30 minutes. Bake at 350° until done.

Rose Liplitte

ZUCCHINI BREAD

3 eggs
2 c. sugar
1 Tbsp. cinnamon
½ tsp. baking powder
3 c. flour
½ c. chopped nuts

1 c. oil
1 tsp. salt
1 tsp. soda
1 tsp. vanilla
2 c. peeled, grated zucchini

Mix together thoroughly. Bake 40 to 45 minutes at 375°. Mix glaze together and pour over the top.

Glaze:

1 c. powdered sugar   ½ c. orange juice

Prick loaves with fork. Pour glaze over hot loaves. Makes 2 loaves.

Barbara Sumner

NUTTY ZUCCHINI BREAD

3 eggs
1 c. salad oil
1 c. packed brown sugar
1 c. granulated sugar
1 tsp. vanilla
2 c. coarsely shredded,
    peeled zucchini

3 c. all-purpose flour
1½ tsp. baking soda
1 tsp. salt
1 tsp. baking powder
1 c. chopped walnuts

Beat together the first 5 ingredients until foamy. Stir in remaining ingredients. Pour into 2 greased and floured 9x5 inch loaf pans. Bake at 350° for 1 hour. Cool in pans for 10 minutes, then remove. Freezes well. Excellent with cream cheese.

ZUCCHINI BREAD

3 eggs, beaten
2½ c. sugar
1 c. oil
3 c. flour
½ Tbsp. cinnamon
1 tsp. soda

1 tsp. salt
1 tsp. baking powder
1 Tbsp. vanilla
2 c. grated zucchini
1 c. chopped nuts

Mix eggs, sugar and oil. Add all at one time the flour, cinnamon, soda, salt and baking powder. Next, add vanilla, zucchini and nuts. Bake for 1 hour at 350° in 2 greased loaf pans.

Mary Francess Stayton

ZUCCHINI BREAD

3 eggs
1 c. oil
2 c. sugar
1 Tbsp. sugar
2 c. zucchini, grated
3 c. flour

1 tsp. baking powder
1 tsp. soda
2 tsp. salt
1 tsp. cinnamon
¾ c. walnuts, chopped

Beat first eggs, oil, sugar and zucchini. Add the rest of ingredients. Bake at 325° for 1 hour. Makes 2 (9x5x3 inch) pans.

Dollie D. Billiter

ZUCCHINI BREAD

3 eggs
1 tsp. vanilla

1 c. oil

Beat and set aside.

Mix:

3 c. flour	2 c. sugar
1½ tsp. baking powder	½ c. raisins (white)
1 tsp. salt	½ c. chopped nuts
1 tsp. soda	2 c. grated zucchini
1 tsp. cinnamon	(including skin)

Mix *dry* ingredients and add to egg mixture. Add zucchini. Pour into 3 small loaf pans. Bake at 350° for 1 hour.

J. W. Borden, Jr.

ZUCCHINI BREAD

3 eggs	2½ c. self-rising flour
2 c. sugar	2 c. raw, unpeeled zucchini
1 c. oil	3½ tsp. cinnamon
1 Tbsp. vanilla	

Beat eggs until fluffy. Add other ingredients in order and beat well. Bake at 350° for 1 hour. Makes 2 loaves or I have used a Bundt cake pan and it makes a pretty design when sliced and placed on a doily covered plate and served with whipped cream cheese.

Marion Goodmann

ROLLS, BISCUITS, MUFFINS

BEER ROLLS

2 c. plus 2½ Tbsp. Bisquick   **1 Tbsp. sugar**
1 c. beer

Mix all ingredients well. Bake at 375° in a greased muffin pan for 15 to 18 minutes.

Paula White

BEER ROLLS

Dissolve completely one cake of dry yeast in one cup of warm water. Place in large pan.

Add:

2 Tbsp. sugar   **1 tsp. salt**
1 slightly beaten egg   **2 Tbsp. melted shortening**
⅔ c. milk

Gradually add small amount of flour to this mixture until you have used about 4 ½ cups. While adding the small amounts of flour, add also 2 tablespoons of beer at a time until you have used 6 tablespoons of beer. Mix thoroughly after each addition. Do not use too much flour. When dough is just dry enough to knead, and it should be slightly moist, knead until bubbles appear in the dough. Then dip entire batch of dough in melted butter; cover and let rise for 1½ hours in a warm place. Roll out dough and make rolls of your choice, Parker House or cloverleaf. Let them rise in a warm place for about 1½ hours. Bake in 475° oven until they are brown. This makes about 30 Parker House rolls or 18 cloverleaf rolls.

You had better keep a sharp eye on them because they bake quickly (the quicker, the better).

BISQUICK ROLLS

2 c. Bisquick   **¾ c. beer**
2 Tbsp. sugar

Mix all ingredients together. Pour into greased muffin pan and bake in hot oven (350°) for about 10 minutes or until done. Makes 12 rolls.

Mary Baxter

BRAN ROLLS

1 c. All-Bran cereal or Bran Buds	1 c. lukewarm water
	2 eggs
1 c. melted fat (Crisco)	¾ c. sugar
6 c. flour (plain)	2 cakes yeast
1 c. boiling water	1½ tsp. salt

Pour boiling water over bran; let soak 30 minutes. Put yeast in lukewarm water. Combine eggs, sugar, salt and fat; add to bran mixture. Add yeast and 3 cups flour; beat until smooth. Add rest of flour; let rise 2 hours. Punch down. Then you can make rolls or put in refrigerator (covered) to make out later. Stays good for several days. Let rolls rise 1 hour. Cook at about 350° until brown.

Patsy S. Brown

HOT ROLLS

1 cake yeast, dissolved in ¼ c. cold water	1 heaping tsp. salt
	¼ c. sugar
2 c. hot water	4½ c. plain flour
½ c. lard	

Mix together the hot water, lard, salt and sugar. Add dissolved yeast when preceding mixture is cooled. Sift in flour, stirring all the time. Let set until rises to top of bowl. Stir down and let set in refrigerator all night. Make into rolls and let rise. Bake at 450° until done.

Erdean Lee

ICEBOX ROLLS

2 cakes compressed yeast	1 c. boiling water
1 c. cold water	2 eggs
½ c. lard	6 c. all-purpose flour
½ c. butter or margarine	(self-rising can be used)
¾ c. sugar	2 tsp. salt

Dissolve yeast in cold water. Cream lard and margarine or butter, slowly add sugar and boiling water. When cool, add yeast, well beaten eggs. Add flour, sifted with salt. Beat mixture thoroughly. Place in greased mixing bowl; set in refrigerator overnight. Let rise 2 hours. Bake in hot oven.

These rolls are the best.

Bessie Litchford

MAYONNAISE ROLLS

1 c. self-rising flour
2 Tbsp. mayonnaise

½ c. milk

Mix well. Spoon into greased muffin pan. Bake at 400° for 20 minutes. Yields 6 rolls.

Peggy Graviss

REFRIGERATOR ROLLS

1½ c. lukewarm water
⅔ c. sugar
1½ tsp. salt
2 cakes compressed yeast (or dry)

2 eggs, slightly beaten
⅔ c. soft shortening
1 c. lukewarm mashed potatoes
7 - 7½ c. flour

Mix together lukewarm water, sugar and salt. Crumble 2 cakes compressed or dry yeast into mixture. Stir until dissolved and add 2 slightly beaten eggs and ⅔ cup soft shortening. First mix with spoon and then by hand 1 cup lukewarm mashed potatoes and 7 or 7½ cups flour. After mixing thoroughly, place in refrigerator. About 2 hours before baking, shape dough into desired shape. Cover and let rise until light and doubled in size. Bake at 400° until brown, about 12 or 15 minutes. Makes 4 dozen rolls.

Can be used in smaller quantities and will store in refrigerator for about 4 days.

Erdean Lee

REFRIGERATOR ROLLS

2 eggs, beaten
¾ c. sugar
1 c. cold water
2 tsp. salt
¾ c. shortening

1 c. boiling water
2 pkg. yeast
½ c. lukewarm water
7½ c. plain flour

Beat eggs, sugar, salt and cold water in large bowl. Melt shortening in hot water. Dissolve yeast in lukewarm water. Make sure water is *only lukewarm* not too hot. Add shortening mixture to bowl with eggs; stir, then add yeast mixture to bowl. Sift 7½ cups plain flour into mixture. Stir. Cover with cloth and let rise to doubled in size (approximately 1½ hours). Push dough down. Put on floured area and knead well. Roll dough out ¼ inch thick. I cut dough with glass and pull into oblong form. Brush soft margarine on one end and fold over for Parker House rolls. Refrigerate until ready to use. Let rise in warm area for about an hour or two before baking. Bake at 350°.

Judy Damron

REFRIGERATOR ROLLS

1 pkg. dry or cake yeast	1 tsp. salt
¼ c. lukewarm water	1 c. scalded milk
½ c. sugar	1 egg, beaten
¼ c. margarine	About 4 c. flour

Soften yeast in water. Add ½ teaspoon sugar. Add margarine, rest of sugar and salt to hot milk. Stir until sugar is dissolved. Cool, then add egg. Stir in softened yeast. Stir flour into liquid ingredients until well mixed. Turn dough out onto lightly floured board. Knead quickly until smooth and elastic. Place in greased bowl and let rise 1 hour and knead again. Refrigerate until used.

Sharon McGeorge

SPOON ROLLS

1 pkg. dry yeast	1 stick margarine
2 c. warm water (105° to 115°)	1 egg
¼ c. sugar	4 c. self-rising flour

Dissolve yeast in water in medium size mixing bowl; add remaining ingredients. Mix well and store in refrigerator until ready to bake. Spoon into greased muffin tins. Bake at 425° for 20 minutes. Yields 1½ to 2 dozen.

Daisy Mace

ANGEL BISCUITS

5 c. plain flour*
3 tsp. baking powder
1 tsp. baking soda
1 tsp. salt
3 Tbsp. sugar

¾ c. margarine
2 c. buttermilk
1 pkg. yeast, dissolved in ½
   c. warm water

Sift dry ingredients together. Cut in margarine until well mixed. Add buttermilk and dissolved yeast, all at once. Stir until all flour is moistened. Store in Tupperware container in refrigerator at least 2 hours before using. On floured board, roll desired amount to ½ inch thick and cut with 2 inch biscuit cutter. Bake at 400° on a cookie sheet for 12 minutes or until golden brown.

Note: Batter will keep 2 to 3 weeks in refrigerator.

* Self-rising flour may be used. Omit salt, baking powder and baking soda.

Kathy Chesser

ANGEL BISCUITS

5 c. all-purpose flour
¾ c. shortening
1 tsp. baking soda
1 tsp. salt
3 tsp. baking powder

3 Tbsp. sugar
1 cake yeast, dissolved in ½
   c. lukewarm water
2 c. buttermilk

Sift dry ingredients together. Cut in shortening until mixed thoroughly. Add buttermilk and dissolved yeast. Mix all ingredients thoroughly. Cover bowl and put in refrigerator until ready to use as needed. Roll out on floured board to ½ inch thickness and cut. Bake at 400° in a shallow pan until brown or about 12 minutes.

Dough will keep in refrigerator for about 2 weeks.

Bessie Litchford

APRICOT BISCUITS

2 Tbsp. margarine
½ c. brown sugar
¼ c. chopped nuts
2 Tbsp. orange rind

1 (16 oz.) can drained apricot
   halves
1 pkg. refrigerator biscuits

Combine margarine, brown sugar, nuts and orange rind. Put 1 drained apricot half in each muffin cup. Divide brown sugar mixture among 10 muffin cups. Place a biscuit on each apricot. Bake at 425° for 8 to 12 minutes. To remove, let stand for about 1 minute, then invert pan on waxed paper and allow to cool slightly before lifting pan. Makes 10.

Heidi Thompson

CHEESE BISCUITS

Pecan halves
1 lb. sharp Cheddar cheese,
   grated
1 lb. butter

5½ c. plain sifted flour
½ tsp. salt
½ tsp. cayenne pepper

Blend mixture *very* well with hands. Chill. To make biscuits, roll out dough and cut with a small cookie or biscuit cutter. Bake at 300° for 25 to 30 minutes. Remove from oven and place a pecan half on top.

Ladonna Darnell

CHEESE BISCUITS

2 c. flour
3 tsp. baking powder
1 tsp. salt

¼ c. shortening
½ c. grated cheese
¾ c. milk

Mix flour, baking powder and salt in mixing bowl. Cut in shortening with 2 knives until mixture looks like coarse corn meal. Stir in grated cheese. Add milk and mix enough to hold dough together. Knead dough on lightly floured surface; roll out to about ½ inch thickness; cut and bake on ungreased cookie sheet in hot oven (425°) for 15 minutes or until brown.

Wanda Harris

KEEPSAKE BISCUIT

1 qt. milk or cream
1½ c. butter or lard
2 Tbsp. white sugar
1 good tsp. salt

1 tsp. cream of tartar
Enough flour to make stiff
   dough

Knead well and mold into neat, small biscuits with your hands. Bake well and you have a good, sweet biscuit that will keep for weeks in a dry place. They are fine for a traveling lunch.

PINEAPPLE TURNOVER BISCUITS

½ c. crushed pineapple,
   drained
¼ c. brown sugar

2 Tbsp. butter, melted
½ tsp. cinnamon
1 pkg. refrigerator biscuits

Combine pineapple, sugar, butter and cinnamon; divide into 10 muffin cups. Center each with either a pecan or walnut half. Add 1 teaspoon pineapple juice to each cup; top with refrigerated biscuit. Bake at 425° for 12 to 15 minutes. Invert pan immediately on serving plate. Cool 1 minute before removing from pan. The goodies are on the bottom.

Jeffrey Cox

POTATO BISCUITS

1 c. mashed potatoes
2 Tbsp. butter
½ tsp. soda
1 c. buttermilk

1 Tbsp. honey
2 c. flour
2 tsp. baking powder
1 Tbsp. brown sugar

Stir butter into potatoes. Dissolve soda in buttermilk; add honey. Mix baking powder, sugar and flour, adding in milk as you go. Press into ¾ inch pad; cut biscuits. Bake at 400°.

YEAST BISCUITS

4 - 5 c. flour
2 c. buttermilk
Scant ⅔ c. shortening
2 tsp. baking powder

3 Tbsp. sugar
½ tsp. salt
½ tsp. soda

Sift dry ingredients together. Cut in shortening. Add buttermilk. After this is well mixed, add 1 package dry yeast that has been dissolved in ¼ cup warm water. Mix well. Cover and store in refrigerator. Keep at least overnight before using. Use as needed. Makes enough for 4 or 5 makings.

J. W. Borden, Jr.

DERBY BREAKFAST YEAST BISCUITS

1 c. warm buttermilk (I use
   powdered buttermilk
   mix)
1 pkg. yeast (or cake)
½ tsp. soda

1 tsp. salt
2 Tbsp. sugar
2½ c. flour (self-rising)
½ c. shortening

Dissolve yeast in warm buttermilk; set aside. Sift soda, salt, sugar and flour in a bowl; cut in shortening. Add yeast mixture. Stir until blended. Knead and roll ½ inch thick. Cut biscuits and dip in melted butter. Place on greased pan. Let rise 1 hour. Bake at 400° for 12 minutes.

Patsy S. Brown

BEER MUFFINS

4 c. biscuit mix
3 Tbsp. sugar

1 egg
1 (12 oz.) can beer

Mix all ingredients and drop in greased loaf pan or 12 count muffin pan. Bake in a preheated 400° oven 18 minutes for muffins, 30 minutes for loaf.

Patricia Jewell

CORN MUFFINS

1½ c. biscuit mix
½ c. corn meal
2 Tbsp. sugar

2 beaten eggs
⅔ c. milk

Mix first 3 ingredients thoroughly; add eggs and milk. Mix until moistened. Pour in greased muffin tin. Bake 15 to 20 minutes in 400° oven. Yield: 1 dozen.

Jackie Webb

EASY CORN BREAD MUFFINS

⅓ c. shortening
1 Tbsp. sugar
1 well beaten egg
1¼ c. milk

1 c. flour
½ tsp. salt
4 tsp. baking powder
1 c. corn meal

Cream shortening and sugar; add egg and milk. Add flour sifted with salt and baking powder. Add corn meal, stirring only enough to mix. Fill greased hot muffin pan two thirds full; bake in hot oven (425°) for 25 minutes. Makes 1 dozen muffins.

Ruth Ackerman

CRANBERRY MUFFINS

Preheat oven to 400°.

Bowl 1:

1 c. raw chopped fresh cranberries	**½ c. sugar**

Mix together and set aside.

Bowl 2:

2 c. sifted flour	**¾ c. milk**
¾ tsp. soda	**¼ c. shortening, melted, or**
¼ tsp. salt	**oil**
¼ c. sugar	**1 egg, beaten**

Sift dry ingredients together. Add milk, shortening and egg. Mix until blended. (Do not overmix.) Add bowl 1 to bowl 2. Stir until blended. Fill greased muffin pan ⅔ full. Sprinkle cinnamon-sugar mixture over top of batter. Bake at 400° for approximately 20 minutes. Makes 12.

Sherry Greer

FRENCH BREAKFAST MUFFINS

Mix thoroughly:

⅓ c. margarine	**1 egg**
½ c. sugar	

Sift together:

1½ c. flour	**½ tsp. salt**
1½ tsp. baking powder	**¼ tsp. nutmeg**

Stir in alternately with ½ cup milk. Pour into muffin tins. Bake at 375°F. for 15 minutes. Immediately after baking, roll in ½ cup melted butter, then cinnamon sugar (½ cup sugar and 1 teaspoon cinnamon).

Martha Hooper

MAYONNAISE MUFFINS

2 c. self-rising flour	1 c. milk
¼ c. real mayonnaise	1 Tbsp. sugar

Combine ingredients and spoon into a greased muffin pan. Bake in preheated oven (400°) for 15 to 20 minutes. Should be golden brown in color.

Donna Browning

MOLASSES MUFFINS

2 c. Bisquick	1 egg
¼ c. brown sugar, packed	½ c. pecans, chopped
½ c. milk	½ c. raisins
¼ c. molasses	

Heat oven to 400°. Line muffin cups with paper baking cups. Mix all ingredients and beat fast for 30 seconds. Fill muffin cups about ⅔ full and bake about 15 minutes or until a toothpick inserted in center comes out clean. Yield: 12 muffins.

Peggy Kessinger

PECAN MUFFINS

1 egg	½ c. milk
¼ c. oleo or butter	1½ c. flour (self-rising)
⅔ c. sugar	½ c. chopped pecans

Cream sugar and oleo. Add egg and milk. Add dry ingredients. Dredge nuts in flour and add to mixture. Fill muffin tins half full. Bake 20 minutes at 400°. Yields 12.

Ruby Junker

PINEAPPLE MUFFINS

Add to 1 small box plain muffin mix an 8 ounce can of crushed pineapple in juice (juice and all), as the amount of juice it is packed in substitutes perfectly for the ⅓ cup of water the box calls for, and ¼ cup of dark brown sugar and 1 egg. Bake as directed.

Recipe can be doubled easily!

Patricia Jewell

PINEAPPLE CHEESE MUFFINS

1 (8¼ oz.) can crushed
   pineapple
2 c. Bisquick baking mix
1 Tbsp. sugar

½ c. milk
1 egg
½ c. shredded Cheddar
   cheese

Heat oven to 400°. Line 12 medium size muffin cups with paper baking cups. Mix pineapple (with syrup) and the remaining ingredients; beat fast for 30 seconds. Fill muffin cups about ⅔ full. Bake until golden brown and toothpick inserted in center comes out clean, about 15 minutes. Yield: 12 muffins.

Peggy Kessinger

SALLY LUNN MUFFINS

¼ c. soft shortening
4 tsp. baking powder
2 eggs, separated
2 c. flour

⅓ c. sugar
1 tsp. salt
¾ c. milk

Cream shortening and sugar. Add unbeaten egg yolks into mixture and heat until light, thick, and lemon colored. Add dry ingredients to mixture with milk. Fold in stiffly beaten egg whites. Fill greased muffin tins ¾ full and bake in hot (400°) oven for 25 minutes.

May also be baked in loaf or tube pan.

Daisy Mace

WHOLE WHEAT MUFFINS

Terrific for breakfast or break time. Add some raisins or chopped nuts to the dough if desired.

2 eggs, beaten
½ c. yogurt
⅔ c. warm milk
⅓ c. honey

⅓ c. oil
2 c. whole wheat flour
1 tsp. baking soda

In a mixing bowl, combine eggs, yogurt and milk. Beat thoroughly with a wooden spoon, then add the honey and oil. Add the dry ingredients and blend thoroughly. Pour into greased muffin tins. Bake at 425°F. for 15 minutes. Yield: 12 large muffins.

Sue Parker

YELLOW SQUASH MUFFINS

2 lb. (2 c.) yellow squash,
   cooked and mashed
2 eggs
1 c. butter or margarine,
   melted

1 c. sugar
3 c. plain flour
1 Tbsp. plus 2 tsp. baking
   powder
1 tsp. salt

Combine squash, eggs and butter. Stir well; set aside. Combine remaining ingredients in large bowl. Make well in center of mixture. Add squash mixture to dry ingredients, stirring just enough until moistened. Spoon into greased muffin tins, filling ¾ full. Bake at 375° for 20 minutes or until wooden pick inserted comes out clean. Makes 2 dozen regular muffins.

Barbara C. Hendrick

Notes

Cakes,
Cookies,
Desserts

CAKE BAKING GUIDE

Problem...	Cause...	
	Butter-Type Cakes	**Sponge-Type Cakes**
Cake falls	Too much sugar, liquid, leavening or shortening; too little flour; temperature too low; insufficient baking	Too much sugar; over-beaten egg whites; egg yolks underbeaten; use of greased pans; insufficient baking
Cake cracks or humps	Too much flour or too little liquid; overmixing; batter not spread evenly in pan; temperature of oven too high	Too much flour or sugar; temperature too high
Cake has one side higher	Batter spread unevenly; uneven pan; pan too close to side of oven; oven rack or range not even; uneven oven heat	Uneven pan; oven rack or range not level
Cake has hard top crust	Temperature too high; overbaking	Temperature too high; overbaking
Cake has sticky top crust	Too much sugar or shortening; insufficient baking	Too much sugar; insufficient baking
Cake has soggy layer at bottom	Too much liquid; eggs underbeaten; undermixing; insufficient baking	Too many eggs or egg yolks; underbeaten egg yolks; undermixing
Cake crumbles or falls apart	Too much sugar, leavening or shortening; batter undermixed; improper pan treatment; improper cooling	
Cake has heavy, compact quality	Too much liquid or shortening; too many eggs; too little leavening or flour; overmixing; oven temperature too high	Overbeaten egg whites; underbeaten egg yolks; overmixing
Cake falls out of pan before completely cooled		Too much sugar; use of greased pans; insufficient baking

CAKES, COOKIES, DESSERTS
CAKES AND FROSTINGS

$100.00 CAKE

½ c. butter or margarine
2 c. sugar
4 sq. bitter chocolate
2 eggs
2 c. cake flour

1 tsp. salt
2 tsp. baking powder
2 tsp. vanilla
1½ c. milk
1 c. pecans

Cream butter and sugar until soft and fluffy. Add chocolate which has been melted over hot water. Add eggs which have been thoroughly beaten. Add flour, salt, baking powder, vanilla, nuts and milk. Pour into 2 (9 inch) pans and bake at 375° about 35 minutes.

Cake Icing:

1 box confectioners sugar
½ c. butter or margarine
2 sq. bitter chocolate
2 tsp. lemon juice

¼ tsp. salt
1 egg
1 tsp. vanilla
½ c. nuts

Mix sugar and butter, then add chocolate which has been melted over hot water. Add lemon juice and thoroughly beaten egg. Add vanilla, salt and nuts. Beat until smooth, then spread.

Mrs. Ken Ford

CAKE

Bake 1 box yellow butter cake mix in 2 round pans. Let cool completely and cut in 4 layers.

Topping:

1 small bag coconut
1 large Cool Whip

1 c. sour cream
1 c. sugar

Mix together and put between layers.

Dollie D. Billiter

ANGEL FOOD CAKE WITH STRAWBERRY FILLING

1 large angel food cake
2 (10 oz. each) pkg. frozen
    strawberries

½ pt. whipping cream
2 pkg. strawberry Jello
2 c. boiling water

Cut cake into 3 layers. In a large bowl, pour 2 cups boiling water over Jello; stir until blended. Add frozen strawberries, stirring until strawberries are separated. Whip cream until it stands in peaks. Fold into Jello mixture. Refrigerate until firm. Put top layer of cake in tube pan. Add half of filling. Put on second layer of cake; add remaining filling. Put on last layer of cake and refrigerate several hours or overnight. Run knife around edge of cake and lift out cake and tube.

Kathy Chesser

BEST ANGEL FOOD CAKE

1 c. sifted cake flour	¾ tsp. salt
¾ c. sugar	¾ c. sugar
1¾ c. (about 12) egg whites	1 tsp. vanilla
1½ tsp. cream of tartar	¼ tsp. almond extract

Sift together flour and ¾ cup sugar. Beat egg whites, cream of tartar and salt until foamy. Add ¾ cup sugar, 1 tablespoon at a time, beating at high speed until stiff glossy peaks form. Blend in vanilla and almond extract. Add your mixture in 4 parts, folding about 15 strokes after each addition. Spoon batter into ungreased 10 inch tube pan. Pull metal spatula through batter once to break large air bubbles. Bake in 375° oven for 35 minutes or until cake tests done. Invert tube pan on funnel or bottle to cool. When completely cooled, remove from pan.

Bessie Litchford

APPLE CAKE

3 c. flour	1 tsp. vanilla
1 c. sugar	3 c. chopped apples
1 c. brown sugar	1 c. oil
2 tsp. cinnamon	2 eggs
1 tsp. soda	1 c. nuts
¼ tsp. salt	

Combine all ingredients in a large bowl. Mix by hand. Put in a 9x13 inch pan or a loaf pan. Bake at 350° for 45 minutes for 9x13 inch pan and 1 hour for loaf pan.

Rosetta Humphries

378

APPLE CAKE

¼ lb. (1 stick) margarine
1 c. sugar
1 tsp. vanilla
2 eggs
2 c. flour, sifted
1 tsp. baking powder

1 tsp. baking soda
1 c. sour cream
2 apples, chopped fine
1 pear, chopped fine
½ tsp. salt

Cream sugar and margarine. Add vanilla and eggs; beat well. Sift flour, salt, baking powder and baking soda together. Add to egg mixture and alternate when adding sour cream. Fold in pear and apples. Grease a pan, 13x9x2 inches, and pour in the mixture, spreading out evenly.

Topping:

1 tsp. cinnamon
1 c. brown sugar

2 Tbsp. margarine
½ c. nuts, chopped

Combine mixture and spread on top of batter. Bake at 350° for ¾ of an hour.

David Terry

CHOPPED APPLE CAKE

1½ c. salad oil
2 c. sugar
2 eggs
3 c. flour
1 tsp. salt
1½ tsp. soda

1 tsp. cinnamon
3 c. chopped fresh apples,
    chopped fine
1 c. chopped nuts
2 tsp. vanilla

Mix oil, sugar and eggs. Sift flour with salt, soda and cinnamon. Gradually add to oil mixture. Stir in apples, nuts and flavoring. Bake at 350° for approximately 1 hour.

Icing:

½ c. butter
1 (8 oz.) pkg. Philadelphia
    cream cheese
1 (1 lb.) box sifted powdered
    sugar

1 tsp. vanilla
1 c. chopped nuts

Beat butter and cream cheese until light. Blend in remaining ingredients. Frost cake.

Barbara Haddix

COUNTRY APPLE COFFEE CAKE

This was the $40,000.00 winner in a Pillsbury Bake-Off. The recipe appeared in the food section of a national newspaper several years ago. This is also good as a dessert served with cream or ice cream.

2 Tbsp. oleo, softened
1½ c. chopped, peeled
　　apples
10 oz. can biscuits
⅓ c. firmly packed brown
　　sugar

½ c. pecan pieces
¼ tsp. cinnamon
⅓ c. light corn syrup
1½ tsp. whiskey
1 egg

Glaze:

⅓ c. powdered sugar
¼ tsp. vanilla

1 - 2 tsp. milk

Preheat oven to 350°. Using 1 tablespoon of the oleo, grease bottom and sides of 9 inch round cake pan. Spread 1 cup of the apples in pan. Separate the biscuits. Cut each one into 4 pieces. Arrange *point* side up over apples. Top with remaining apples. In small bowl, combine remaining 1 tablespoon oleo, brown sugar, cinnamon, corn syrup, whiskey and egg. Beat well. Stir in pecans. Spoon over biscuit pieces. Bake 35 to 45 minutes or until brown. Drizzle glaze over coffee cake.

Anita Picklesimer

DRIED APPLE CAKE

2 c. dried apples
2 c. molasses
1 c. raisins
1 c. butter
1 c. sour milk
1 c. brown sugar

2 eggs, well beaten
1½ tsp. soda
2 tsp. cinnamon
½ tsp. cloves
½ tsp. grated nutmeg
3 c. self-rising flour

Soak dried apples overnight in cold water; drain them in the morning. Chop fine and cook slowly with molasses 1 hour. Then add raisins; stir well and let cool. Cream butter; add sugar gradually, beaten eggs, cooled mixture, sour milk and flour mixed and sifted with soda and spices. Turn into a well buttered loaf pan and bake in a 350° oven.

Lena March

DRIED APPLE STACK CAKE

Cake:

1 c. sugar	2 tsp. soda in 1 Tbsp. vinegar
1 c. shortening	½ tsp. salt
1 c. sorghum molasses	1 tsp. cinnamon
¼ c. buttermilk	½ tsp. ginger
Flour (about 5 c.)	1 egg

Cream sugar, shortening and molasses. Add egg and buttermilk; mix well. Stir in dry ingredients together with vinegar-soda mixture. Divide dough into 6 balls; press each ball of dough into a well greased 8 inch cake pan. Bake at 350° for about 15 minutes or until brown. Remove from pans while warm and set aside to cool.

Filling:

1 qt. dried apples, cooked	Sugar to taste
4 Tbsp. cream	

Cook and drain dried apples. Sweeten to taste. Mash apples and add cream to make a thin paste. Spread apple mixture between cake layers, leaving top plain. Let stand at least 12 hours before serving.

Sue Tipton

FRESH APPLE CAKE

1½ c. salad oil	1 tsp. soda
2 c. granulated sugar	½ tsp. salt
2 eggs	2 tsp. cinnamon
3 c. apples, chopped	2 tsp. vanilla
(Winesap preferred)	2½ to 3 c. all-purpose flour
1 c. nuts (optional)	

Combine oil, sugar and eggs. Add apples and nuts. Stir thoroughly; add salt, soda, cinnamon and vanilla. Stir in flour until batter is very stiff. Bake in tube pan at 350° for 1 hour (35 to 40 minutes in oblong pan may be okay).

Glaze:

½ stick margarine	½ c. light brown sugar
½ tsp. vanilla	2 Tbsp. milk

Combine ingredients; boil for 1 minute. Spread on hot cake.

Betty Castle

FRESH APPLE CAKE

1 c. Crisco oil
2 c. sugar
3 eggs
2 c. self-rising flour
1 tsp. vanilla

1 c. pecans or black walnuts
1 tsp. cinnamon
1 tsp. nutmeg
3 c. chopped apples

Combine oil, sugar and eggs. Add vanilla. Add flour; beat thoroughly. Add remaining ingredients and stir to blend well. Turn into a greased and floured 9x13 inch pan. Bake in preheated 350° oven for 40 to 45 minutes.

Ann Duke

HONEY APPLE CAKE

3 eggs
2 c. sugar
1 c. oil
¼ c. honey
3 c. flour
1 tsp. soda

1 tsp. salt
1 tsp. cinnamon
¼ tsp. nutmeg
1 tsp. vanilla
1 c. chopped nuts
3 c. chopped apples

Beat together eggs, sugar, oil and honey. Sift together dry ingredients and add to honey mixture. Mix thoroughly. Add vanilla, nuts and apples. Mix gently and pour into a large cake pan (13x9x2 inches) which has been lightly greased and floured, or a tube pan, or 3 layers. Bake for 45 minutes at 350°.

Topping:

1 stick margarine
1 c. light brown sugar

¼ c. milk
¼ c. honey

Boil ingredients together 2½ minutes and pour over cake while it is still hot. It is extra moist with the honey and apples. It will keep moist for days.

Here's another good icing recipe:

½ c. margarine
1 c. brown sugar

¼ c. milk
2 c. powdered sugar

Melt margarine; add brown sugar and bring to boil. Boil 2 minutes; add milk and bring to boil. Set off heat and let cool. Add powdered sugar and beat.

Bessie Litchford

APPLESAUCE CAKE

½ c. melted butter
1⅓ c. sugar
2 eggs
1 c. applesauce
2 c. flour
1 tsp. baking soda

1 tsp. baking powder
1 tsp. cinnamon
½ tsp. nutmeg
¼ tsp. cloves
1 c. raisins

Mix all ingredients well. Bake in 350° oven for 35 to 40 minutes.

Peggy Hunter

APPLESAUCE CAKE

4 c. flour
1 tsp. allspice
2 c. brown sugar
1 Tbsp. cocoa
½ lb. dates
2 tsp. cinnamon
1 tsp. nutmeg
2 c. unsweetened applesauce

1 c. raisins
½ lb. figs
¼ tsp. soda
Few grains of salt
1 c. Crisco
1 bottle maraschino cherries
1 c. nuts

Cream Crisco and sugar; stir in applesauce. Mix dry ingredients; sift into the creamed Crisco and sugar mixture. Flour the fruits and nuts; stir into batter. Pour into a well greased paper lined and floured pan. Bake in a moderate oven (350°). Bake 2½ hours.

Mattie Hammack

APPLESAUCE PRUNE CAKE

3 c. flour
1½ tsp. soda
1⅛ tsp. salt
¾ c. shortening
1½ tsp. cinnamon
¾ tsp. cloves
1½ c. sugar

2 eggs, beaten
1½ c. applesauce
1½ c. cooked, pitted prunes
¾ c. chopped nuts (optional)
Cream Cheese Frosting (if
    desired)

Sift flour, soda, salt and spices. Cream shortening and sugar; add eggs and applesauce; blend well. Add flour mixture to creamed mixture a little at a time; blend well. Add prunes and nuts, if used, by hand. Pour into well greased 9x13 inch pan and bake at 350° for 50 to 55 minutes at 350°. Makes 20 servings.

Frost if desired or sprinkle with powdered sugar. Keeps well.

Ruthie Marty

APPLESAUCE FRUIT CAKE

1 c. butter
1½ c. sugar
2 tsp. cinnamon
1 tsp. cloves
1 tsp. allspice
3 c. flour
½ tsp. salt
1½ tsp. soda

1 c. chopped raisins
½ c. chopped dates
½ c. chopped figs
½ c. mixed candied fruit,
  chopped
½ c. chopped nuts
2 eggs
2 c. applesauce

Cream butter; add sugar gradually with spices. Cream until light. Sift flour, salt and soda together. Dredge nuts and fruit with ½ cup of the flour. Beat eggs until light and add alternately with remaining flour. Blend well. Add fruit, nuts and applesauce. Bake in greased pan for 1½ hours at 325°.

For a holiday look, put only ½ cup chopped dates and figs and use 1 cup candied fruit.

Mrs. Morris (Laura) Futrell

OLD FASHIONED STACK-UP APPLESAUCE CAKE

3 eggs
¾ c. shortening
½ c. molasses

1 c. brown sugar
1 Tbsp. mixed spices
½ c. buttermilk

Combine ingredients and add flour to make a stiff enough dough to roll. Roll as thin as possible and cut into large circles with a fluted pie pan. Bake on large cookie sheet until golden brown at 375°. Spread each layer with seasoned applesauce or cooked apples and stack. Put in covered container and store at least 12 hours before cutting.

Martha Hooper

APRICOT NECTAR CAKE

1 box Duncan Hines Lemon
  Supreme cake
½ c. sugar

1 c. apricot nectar juice
⅔ c. Crisco oil
4 eggs

Stir together; beat for 2 minutes. Preheat oven to 325°; bake 45 minutes. Cool 25 minutes. Use Bundt pan or tube pan. Mix ½ pound powdered sugar and juice of 3 lemons or nectar juice. Pour over cake.

Martha Harper

APRICOT NECTAR CAKE

1 box Duncan Hines Lemon
   Supreme cake mix
1 c. apricot nectar juice

4 eggs
½ c. sugar
¾ c. Wesson oil

Mix cake mix, apricot juice and oil. Add eggs and sugar. Mix well. Bake in tube pan at 325° for 1 hour.

Topping:

1 c. confectioners sugar   Juice of 2 lemons

Mix well and pour over hot cake. Let cool and remove from pan.

Virginia Moran

BANANA CAKE

½ c. shortening
1½ c. sugar
2 large eggs
1¾ c. flour
1 tsp. soda in warm water
   (about ¼ c.)

¼ tsp. salt
5 Tbsp. buttermilk
1 c. mashed bananas
1 tsp. vanilla

Bake at 350° for 30 to 35 minutes.

Frosting:

2 Tbsp. shortening
1 Tbsp. butter
¼ tsp. salt
½ tsp. grated lemon rind
3 c. sifted confectioners
   sugar

1 large banana, mashed
3 Tbsp. scalded cream
   (about)

Combine shortening, butter, salt and grated lemon rind; blend. Add ½ cup sugar gradually, creaming well. Add mashed banana and blend. Add remaining sugar alternately with cream, beating until smooth and creamy and stiff enough to spread.

Mattie Hammack

BANANA CAKE

2½ c. flour
1⅔ c. sugar
1¼ tsp. soda
1¼ tsp. baking powder
1 tsp. salt

⅔ c. buttermilk
⅔ c. oil
2 eggs, beaten
1½ c. mashed bananas

Stir first 5 ingredients together. Beat buttermilk, oil and eggs, then add to dry ingredients and beat 2 minutes. Add bananas and beat 1 minute. Pour into 2 cake pans. Bake at 350° for 45 to 50 minutes.

Banana Icing:

1 stick margarine
1 lb. box powdered sugar
½ banana, mashed with 1
　Tbsp. lemon juice

½ c. chopped nuts

Melt margarine; beat in sugar and mix in banana well. Add milk if necessary for desired spreading consistency.

Donna Browning

BANANA BUTTER PECAN CAKE

1 box Duncan Hines yellow
　cake mix
1 box Jell-O butter pecan
　instant pie mix
4 eggs

1 c. water
¼ c. oil
1 c. chopped pecans
½ c. bananas, mashed fine

Bake at 350° for 50 minutes.

Frosting:

1 stick butter

1 lb. brown sugar

Melt slow in warm pan. Let cook for 3 minutes. Add ¾ cup Pet milk. Cook a few minutes longer. Do not overcook.

Mary H. Tuttle

BANANA LAYER CAKE

2½ c. cake flour, sifted before
    measuring
1 tsp. baking powder
1 tsp. soda
½ c. shortening
1½ c. sugar

2 eggs
½ c. buttermilk
1 tsp. vanilla
1 c. ripe bananas, mashed
    (then measured)

Sift flour with soda and baking powder. Cream shortening; add sugar and cream together until light and fluffy. Add eggs, beating well after the addition of each. Add buttermilk and vanilla to bananas. Add the flour and banana mixture alternately to creamed shortening and sugar mixture, beginning and ending with the dry ingredients. Beat until smooth and well blended. Do not overmix. Pour into greased and floured cake pans (2 (9 inch) round cake pans). Bake in preheated oven (375°) for 25 to 30 minutes. Remove from pans immediately after baking. Cool on racks.

Delores Darnell

BANANA PECAN CAKE

Cream 1 stick butter or margarine with 1 cup sugar. Beat in 2 eggs, 1 at a time. Add 2 cups flour, sifted with 1 teaspoon each of baking powder, baking soda and cinnamon, and ½ teaspoon each of ground cloves and salt. Mash 1 cup banana in 1 cup buttermilk, and add to bowl. Stir in 1½ teaspoons vanilla, 1 teaspoon orange peel and ½ - ⅔ cup coarsely chopped pecans. Pour all into greased and floured Bundt pan, and bake in 350° oven for about 45 minutes or until toothpick tests "clean." In shallower, or layer pans, test about 10 minutes earlier.

This cake will be better the second day and even better the third day.

Patricia Jewell

BANANA SPLIT CAKE

1 stick oleo
2 c. graham cracker crumbs
1 pkg. instant vanilla pudding
    (large pkg.)
3 - 4 bananas, sliced
1 large can crushed
    pineapple, drained

1 large ctn. Cool Whip
1 c. chopped pecans
½ c. chopped maraschino
    cherries

Melt oleo and mix with graham crumbs to make crust. Press into 13x9x2 inch pan. Make vanilla pudding according to directions on package. Pour over crust. Arrange sliced bananas on top of pudding; top with pineapple. Cover with Cool Whip; sprinkle with nuts and cherries. Cover and chill overnight.

Dianne Rice

BANANA SPLIT CAKE

1½ pkg. graham crackers (about 15), crushed
1 stick margarine, melted
4 or 5 bananas
1 can Eagle Brand milk
Juice of 2 lemons or ReaLemon

1 can crushed pineapple, drained
Cool Whip
Cherries
Peanuts

Mix together the graham crackers and melted margarine. Press into a greased 9x13 inch pan. For first layer of cake, slice 4 or 5 bananas and put on top of graham cracker crust. For second layer, mix Eagle Brand milk with lemon juice. Beat this for 2 minutes. Spread on bananas. For third layer, put crushed pineapple on top of Eagle Brand milk mixture. Top with Cool Whip and cherries. Sprinkle on crushed nuts. Chill and cover with *foil*. (Must be covered with *foil* or it won't set properly.)

Bernadette Mills

FLUFFY BANANA CAKE

2 large bananas, mashed
2 c. flour
½ tsp. baking powder
¾ tsp. soda
½ tsp. salt

½ c. shortening
1½ c. sugar
2 eggs (unbeaten)
1 tsp. vanilla
¼ c. buttermilk

Cream shortening and sugar; add eggs and vanilla; beat until fluffy. Add sifted flour mixture, buttermilk and bananas. Bake at 350° for 30 to 35 minutes in either 2 (9 inch) pans or 13x9x2 inch rectangular pan.

Penuche Icing:

1 stick butter	¼ c. milk
2 c. brown sugar	

Mix and bring to a boil; let boil for 2 or 3 minutes. Add enough powdered sugar to make of spreading consistency.

Willie Summers

BACARDI RUM PINA COLADA CAKE

1 pkg. white cake mix	½ c. water
1 (4 serving size) pkg. Jello	⅓ c. rum
coconut cream pudding	¼ c. Wesson oil
4 eggs	

Blend all ingredients in large mixing bowl. Beat 4 minutes at medium speed. Pour into 2 greased and floured 9 inch layer pans. Bake at 350° for 25 to 30 minutes. Do not underbake. Cool in pan 15 minutes. Remove cake and cool on rack. Fill and frost. May sprinkle coconut. Chill. Refrigerate leftover cake.

Frosting:

1 (8 oz.) can crushed	⅓ c. rum
pineapple (in juice)	1 large container Cool Whip,
1 (4 serving size) pkg. Jello	thawed, or 2 pkg. Dream
coconut cream pudding	Whip

Combine all ingredients, except Cool Whip in a bowl. Beat until well blended. Fold into thawed topping.

Hint: Instead of ½ cup water in cake, you may add some pineapple from frosting and ⅓ cup water.

Peggy Graviss

BETTER THAN SEX CAKE

1 box yellow cake mix	6 oz. pkg. chocolate chips
1 box instant vanilla pudding	1 German's chocolate bar,
mix	grated
½ c. oil	8 oz. sour cream
½ c. water	4 eggs

Mix cake mix, pudding mix, oil, water, sour cream and eggs together. Grate chocolate bar and add along with chocolate chips to mixture. Mix by hand. Bake in a tube pan in a 350° oven for 55 minutes. Frost.

Frosting:

1 stick butter
1 (8 oz.) pkg. cream cheese
1 box powdered sugar

1 tsp. vanilla
½ c. pecans

Cream butter and sugar together and add powdered sugar, vanilla and pecans. Frost cake and then sprinkle grated German's chocolate on top of cake.

Bill Dean

BETTER THAN SEX CAKE

Crust:

2 c. flour
2 sticks margarine

1 c. chopped pecans

With a fork, cream margarine, flour, and nuts together until it is crumbly. Spread mixture evenly in greased 9x13 inch baking pan. Bake crust at 350° for about 20 minutes or until golden brown. Let crust cool completely before filling.

Second Layer:

1 (8 oz.) container frozen
   non-dairy whipped
   topping

1 (8 oz.) pkg. cream cheese
½ c. peanut butter
2 c. powdered sugar

Cream peanut butter, sugar, and cream cheese. Add whipped topping and mix with electric mixer until smooth and creamy. Place in cooled crust.

Third Layer:

3 small boxes instant
   chocolate pudding

4½ c. milk

Mix pudding and milk with mixer at high speed until thick. Spread pudding over Second Layer.

Topping:

1 large container frozen non-dairy whipped topping

½ c. chopped pecans

Spread whipped topping over Third Layer and sprinkle pecans on top of this.

Marsha Ratliff

BLACKBERRY JAM CAKE

2 c. jam
1 c. brown sugar
1 c. sorghum
1 c. butter or shortening
1 lb. raisins
1 lb. nuts, chopped
6 whole eggs

8 Tbsp. buttermilk
1 tsp. soda
½ tsp. cinnamon
1½ tsp. cloves
1½ tsp. allspice
3 c. flour

Anna L. Smyth

BLACK FOREST CAKE

1 box Duncan Hines chocolate cake mix

1 can cherry pie filling
1 large container Cool Whip

Prepare a Duncan Hines chocolate cake mix according to package directions. Bake in 3 (9 inch) layer pans. Cool and remove. Spread cherry pie filling between layers. Layer plentifully on top layer. Ice sides with Cool Whip and refrigerate. Use 1 can cherry pie filling and 1 large container Cool Whip.

Melissa Jackson

BLACK WALNUT CAKE

½ c. butter or margarine, softened
½ c. Wesson oil
2 c. sugar
5 eggs, separated
1 c. buttermilk

1 tsp. soda
2 c. all-purpose flour
1 tsp. vanilla
1½ c. chopped black walnuts
1 (3 oz.) can flaked coconut
½ tsp. cream of tartar

Cream butter and oil; add sugar and beat until light and fluffy. Add egg yolks and beat well. Combine buttermilk and soda; stir until soda dissolves. Add flour to mixture alternately with buttermilk. Stir in vanilla.

Add walnuts and coconut, stirring well. Beat egg whites with cream of tartar until stiff peaks form. Fold egg whites into batter. Pour batter into 3 greased and floured 9 inch round pans. Bake at 350° for 30 minutes or until done. Cool in pans 10 minutes; remove and cool completely. Frost with Cream Cheese Frosting.

Brownie - Lois Bruner

BROILER CAKE

2 eggs	1 tsp. baking powder
1 c. sugar	1 Tbsp. butter
½ c. milk	Few grains of salt
1 c. flour	

Beat eggs; add sugar to eggs and beat 10 minutes. Heat milk; stir in butter; add flour. Mix well and pour into well greased pan. Bake 30 minutes in 350° oven. Remove from pans and let cake cool. Spread over top 4 tablespoons melted butter, 3 tablespoons cream and 6 tablespoons brown sugar; cover with nuts. Coconut may be added. Brown under the flame.

Mattie Hammack

BROWNIE CAKE

2 c. sugar	½ c. buttermilk
2 c. flour	6 Tbsp. cocoa
1 tsp. salt	4 Tbsp. milk
3 sticks margarine	1 box confectioners sugar
2 eggs, beaten	1 c. water
1 tsp. vanilla	Nuts
1 tsp. soda	

Mix 2 cups sugar, 2 cups flour and 1 teaspoon salt. Set aside. In a saucepan, put 2 sticks of margarine, 3 tablespoons cocoa and 1 cup water; bring to a boil. Add to dry ingredients. Then add 2 beaten eggs, 1 teaspoon vanilla, 1 teaspoon soda and ½ cup buttermilk; mix well. Pour in a greased pan and bake at 350° for 20 to 30 minutes or until done. Frost while still warm.

For frosting, mix: 1 stick margarine, 3 tablespoons cocoa and 4 tablespoons milk; bring to a slow boil. Add 1 box confectioners sugar while still boiling. Take off stove; beat and add nuts.

Mary Baxter

CARROT CAKE

Wet Ingredients:

2 junior size Beechnut carrots
2 c. sugar

1½ c. Wesson oil
4 eggs, beaten in 1 at a time

In a separate bowl, sift dry ingredients:

2 c. flour (self-rising still add
   extras)
1 tsp. cinnamon

1 tsp. soda
½ tsp. salt

Sift dry ingredients and add to wet ingredients. Add 1 cup pecan pieces. Bake at 350° for 30 to 35 minutes.

Cream Cheese Frosting:

8 oz. cream cheese, softened
   real well
2 tsp. vanilla

1 stick margarine
1 box confectioners sugar

Blend well.

Patricia Jewell

CARROT CAKE

2½ c. sifted flour
2 tsp. soda
2 tsp. cinnamon
1 tsp. salt
2 c. sugar

1½ c. Wesson oil
3 c. grated raw carrots
   (loosely)
4 eggs
1 c. nuts

Sift dry ingredients. Beat oil and sugar well. Add carrots and blend. Add eggs, 1 at a time; beat well. Add dry ingredients and mix well. Add nuts. Makes 3 layers. Bake at 350° for 30 minutes.

Icing:

1 lb. powdered sugar
½ stick butter or margarine,
   melted
1 (8 oz.) pkg. cream cheese
   (room temperature)

Pinch of salt
2 tsp. vanilla

Mix all together and ice cake.

Bessie Litchford

OLD FASHIONED CARROT CAKE

1 pkg. Pillsbury Plus Carrot
   'N Spice cake mix
1¼ c. water
⅓ c. oil
3 eggs
1 c. finely chopped nuts
½ c. raisins

8¼ oz. can crushed
   pineapple, well drained
1 can Pillsbury
   ready-to-spread cream
   cheese vanilla frosting
   supreme

Heat oven to 350°F. Grease and flour 13x9 inch pan. In large bowl, blend cake mix, water, oil and eggs until moistened. Beat 2 minutes at highest speed. By hand, stir in nuts, raisins and drained pineapple. Pour into prepared pan. Bake at 350°F. for 35 to 45 minutes or until toothpick inserted in center comes out clean. Frost completely cooled cake with Cream Cheese Frosting. Store loosely covered. Makes 12 servings.

Tip: For Old Fashioned Applesauce Carrot Cake, substitute 1 (15 ounce) jar (1 ⅔ cups) applesauce for water and oil. Omit pineapple. Bake as directed.

Phyllis L. Davis

AMARETTO CHEESECAKE

1½ c. graham cracker
   crumbs
2 Tbsp. sugar
1 tsp. ground cinnamon
¼ c. plus 2 Tbsp. butter or
   margarine, melted
3 (8 oz.) pkg. cream cheese,
   softened
1 c. sugar

4 eggs
⅓ c. Amaretto
1 (8 oz.) ctn. commercial sour
   cream
1 Tbsp. plus 1 tsp. sugar
1 Tbsp. Amaretto
¼ c. toasted sliced almonds
1 (1.2 oz.) chocolate candy
   bar, grated

Combine graham cracker crumbs, 2 tablespoons sugar, cinnamon, and butter; mix well. Firmly press mixture into bottom and ½ inch up the sides of a 9 inch springform pan.

Beat cream cheese with electric mixer until light and fluffy. Gradually add 1 cup sugar, mixing well. Add eggs, 1 at a time, beating well after each addition. Stir in ⅓ cup Amaretto; pour into prepared pan. Bake at 375° for 45 to 50 minutes or until set.

Combine sour cream, 1 tablespoon plus 1 teaspoon sugar, and 1 tablespoon Amaretto; stir well, and spoon over the cheesecake. Bake at 500° for 5 minutes. Let cool to room temperature, then refrigerate 24 to 48 hours. (Cheesecake is best when thoroughly chilled and flavors have time to ripen.) Garnish with almonds and the grated chocolate. Yield: About 12 servings.

Crust:

1 c. all-purpose flour	**4 Tbsp. sugar**
1 beaten egg	**¼ c. melted butter**
1 Tbsp. baking powder	

Mix together and pat bottom of pan (lemon peel).

Crust:

2 c. vanilla wafer crumbs	**2 Tbsp. sugar**
¼ c. butter	**½ tsp. cinnamon**

Mix and press in bottom of pan.

Note: Either crust is very good.

Clarine Ballard

CHEESECAKE

¼ c. sugar plus 2 Tbsp.	**1 tsp. grated lemon peel**
½ c. Bisquick baking mix	**1 c. sour cream**
2 eggs	
4 tsp. vanilla	
2 (8 oz.) each pkg. cream cheese, cut into 1 inch cubes and softened	

Blend together ¼ cup sugar, ½ cup Bisquick, 2 eggs, 2 teaspoons vanilla, 2 packages cream cheese, and 1 teaspoon grated lemon peel, until smooth, 2 or 3 minutes. Pour into a greased pie plate and bake in 350° oven for about 30 minutes or until puffed and center is dry. (Don't overbake.) To make cheesecake topping, mix 1 cup sour cream, 2 tablespoons sugar and 2 teaspoons vanilla. Spread topping over top and refrigerate at least 3 hours.

Sharon Duke

CHEESE CAKE

4 (8 oz.) pkg. cream cheese
1½ c. sugar
½ c. cornstarch

2 sticks butter, softened
6 eggs
1 pt. heavy whipping cream

Cream butter and cheese together. Add rest of ingredients, 1 at a time, mix until smooth. Pour into a 10 inch spring form pan. Place pan in 1 inch of water; bake 1 hour until brown on top (wiggles). Cool in spring form pan for 3 hours. Remove and chill.

Debbie Rigdon

CHEESE CAKE

Layer dish with graham cracker crust (graham cracker crumbs, sugar and melted margarine to taste).

1 large pkg. Philadelphia
**   cream cheese, softened**
¾ c. sugar
1 small pkg. lemon Jello
¾ c. boiling water

1 large can Carnation milk
**   (cold)**
1 small can crushed
**   pineapple, drained**

Cream together cream cheese and sugar. Dissolve Jello in boiling water. Mix with cream mixture. Beat cold milk until stiff; add pineapple; fold in cheese and Jello mixture. Top with graham cracker crumb mixture. Best chilled overnight before serving.

Barb Haddix

DELUXE CHEESECAKE

Use 1 graham cracker crust in 10 inch tube pan or springform.

Mix together:

3 (8 oz.) pkg. cream cheese
1 c. sugar

5 eggs (1 at a time)
1½ tsp. vanilla

Pour in crust. Bake for 1 hour at 300°.

Topping - Mix together:

1½ pt. sour cream
½ c. sugar

1½ tsp. vanilla

Pour on top and return to oven and bake 10 minutes more. Refrigerate 24 hours. Serve with fresh strawberries. Makes a large cheesecake.

Sarah A. Drewes

HAWAIIAN CHEESE CAKE

1 box yellow cake mix
1 (8 oz.) ctn. Cool Whip
1 (8 oz.) pkg. cream cheese
1 (16 oz.) can crushed
    pineapple

½ c. chopped nuts
1 (4 oz.) pkg. instant vanilla
    pudding
1¼ c. milk

Make cake in 13x9 inch pan as directed on cake box. Combine in bowl the pudding mix, milk and softened cream cheese; spread on cake. Drain pineapple. (I use this juice as a substitute for water that is called for in cake mix.) Spread only crushed pineapple over pudding mixture; sprinkle nuts and top with Cool Whip. Refrigerate overnight.

Bonnie Ryan

HEAVENLY KAHLUA CHEESECAKE

1¼ c. graham cracker
    crumbs
¼ c. sugar
¼ c. cocoa
⅓ c. butter or margarine,
    melted
2 (8 oz.) pkg. cream cheese,
    softened
¾ c. sugar
½ c. cocoa

2 eggs
¼ c. strong coffee
¼ c. Kahlua or other coffee
    flavored liqueur
1 tsp. vanilla extract
1 c. commercial sour cream
2 Tbsp. sugar
1 tsp. vanilla extract
6 - 8 chocolate curls
    (optional)

Combine first 4 ingredients; mix well. Firmly press mixture into bottom of a 9 inch springform pan. Bake at 325° for 5 minutes; cool. Beat cream cheese with electric mixer until light and fluffy; gradually add ¾ cup sugar, mixing well. Beat in ½ cup cocoa. Add eggs, 1 at a time, beating well after each addition. Stir in next 3 ingredients. Pour into prepared pan. Bake at 375° for 25 minutes. (Filling will be soft, but will firm up as cake stands.)

Combine sour cream, 2 tablespoons sugar, and 1 teaspoon vanilla; spread over hot cheesecake. Bake at 425° for 5 to 7 minutes. Let cool to room temperature on a wire rack; chill 8 hours or overnight. Remove sides of springform pan. To garnish, place 3 chocolate curls in center of cheesecake; gently break remaining chocolate curls, and sprinkle over cheesecake, if desired. Yield: 10 to 12 servings.

RENA'S CHEESE CAKE

1 (8 oz.) pkg. cream cheese
½ c. sugar
3 eggs, separated
1 tsp. vanilla
1 (8 oz.) pkg. sour cream

1 tsp. vanilla
¼ c. sugar
1 graham cracker crumb
    crust

Mix together cream cheese, ½ cup sugar, eggs and 1 teaspoon vanilla. Pour into graham cracker crumb crust and bake at 300° until filling has lost its shine. Next, mix sour cream, 1 teaspoon vanilla and ¼ cup sugar together; pour over cheese cake and bake until slightly set.

Lil Pasinski

CHERRY DELIGHT

2 cans pie cherries
1 box white cake mix

1 stick margarine
Crushed pecans (own choice)

Take a long cake pan about 9½ x 13 inches long and grease with butter, then pour cherries into cake pan. Take 1 box cake mix and spread it evenly over cherries. Cut 1 stick margarine into thin slices; scatter over cake mix, then place crushed or whole pecans over buttered cake mix. Bake at 325° about 45 minutes.

Betty Robinson

QUICK CHERRY CRISP

1 can cherry pie filling
1 c. yellow or white cake mix

½ stick melted butter
½ c. chopped nuts (optional)

Oven ready in only 2½ minutes. Just pour cherry pie filling into an 8 inch pie pan. Sprinkle with 1 cup yellow or white cake mix. Pour melted butter over all. Bake at 400° for 30 minutes. For extra flavor, add ½ cup chopped nuts over top after butter.

Terri Ramage

CHESS CAKE

1 box yellow cake mix
3 eggs
1 stick margarine, melted

1 (8 oz.) pkg. cream cheese
1 box powdered sugar
1 tsp. vanilla

Combine cake mix, 1 egg and 1 stick melted margarine. Press into a 9x13 inch pan, forming slight ridges at sides. Mix together cream cheese, 2 eggs, 1 box powdered sugar and 1 teaspoon vanilla; pour on top of cake base and bake in preheated 350° oven for 30 or 35 minutes or until slightly browned.

Erdean Lee

CHESS CAKE

1 box yellow cake mix
1 egg
1 stick butter (room
    temperature)

1 box powdered sugar
1 (8 oz.) pkg. cream cheese
2 eggs

Mix together cake mix, 1 egg and butter to crumbly stage. Put in a 9x13 inch pan. Next, mix together the powdered sugar, cream cheese and 2 eggs; pour over top of cake. Bake in 325° oven for 45 to 50 minutes.

Bev Sowders

CHESS CAKE

1 box butter cake mix
1 egg
1 stick melted butter
1 box powdered sugar

3 eggs
1 (8 oz.) pkg. cream cheese,
    softened

Mix and press in 9x13 inch pan the first 3 ingredients. Mix and pour over top the next 3 ingredients. Bake 50 minutes in 350° oven. If using glass baking dish, oven should be 325°.

Terri Ramage

CHESS CAKE

1 box yellow cake mix
1 stick margarine, melted

1 egg
¼ c. water

Mix and spread evenly in 9x13 inch pan.

1 (8 oz.) pkg. cream cheese   2 eggs
1 box powdered sugar   1 tsp. vanilla

Mix and spread over cake mix mixture. Bake for 25 to 30 minutes at 325° to 350°.

Donna Browning

COCA-COLA CAKE

2 c. flour   ½ c. buttermilk
2 c. sugar   2 eggs
2 sticks margarine or butter   1 tsp. soda
2 Tbsp. cocoa   1½ c. miniature
1 tsp. vanilla   marshmallows
1 c. cola drink

Combine the sugar and flour. Heat the butter with the cocoa and cola to boiling point. Pour this over the flour and sugar mixture and mix thoroughly. In another bowl, add buttermilk, eggs, soda, vanilla and marshmallows. Combine the 2 mixtures. Bake in a greased and floured tube pan at 350° for 50 to 60 minutes.

Cocoa-Cola Icing: Boil 6 tablespoons Coke, 3 tablespoons cocoa and 1 stick margarine. Remove from heat and add 1 box confectioners sugar, 1 cup nuts and 1 teaspoon vanilla. Wait until cake is cooled before icing.

Donna Browning

COCONUT CAKE

1 pkg. yellow cake mix with   2 c. coconut
   pudding   3½ c. or 8 oz. Cool Whip,
1½ c. milk   thawed
½ c. sugar

Prepare cake mix as directed on package, baking in 13x9 inch pan. Cool 15 minutes, then punch holes down through the cake with a utility fork. Meanwhile, combine milk, sugar and ½ cup of the coconut in saucepan. Bring to a boil; reduce heat and simmer 1 minute. Carefully spoon over warm cake, allowing liquid to soak down through holes. Cool completely. Fold ½ cup of the coconut into whipped topping and spread over cake. Sprinkle with remaining coconut. Chill overnight. Store leftover cake in refrigerator.

Clara Nance

MOIST 'N CREAMY COCONUT CAKE

1 (2 layer size) pkg. yellow
    cake mix or pudding
    included cake mix
1½ c. milk
½ c. sugar

2 c. Baker's Angel Flake
    coconut
3½ c. or 1 (8 oz.) container
    Cool Whip

Prepare cake mix as directed on package, baking in 13x9 inch pan. Cool 15 minutes, then poke holes down through cake with utility fork. Meanwhile, combine milk, sugar and ½ cup of the coconut in saucepan. Bring to a boil; reduce heat and simmer 1 minute. Spoon over warm cake, allowing liquid to soak into the holes. Cool completely. Fold ½ cup coconut into Cool Whip and spread on cake. Sprinkle with remaining coconut. Chill overnight. Store leftover cake in refrigerator.

Patricia Jewell

COCONUT SOUR CREAM DREAM CAKE

1 (8½ oz.) pkg. butter
    flavored cake mix
2 c. sugar
1 (8 oz.) ctn. commercial sour
    cream

1 (12 oz.) pkg. frozen
    coconut, thawed
1½ c. whipped cream or
    frozen whipped topping,
    thawed

Prepare the cake according to directions, making 2 (8 inch) layers. Split both layers horizontally after they have cooled. Blend together the sugar, sour cream and coconut. Chill. Spread all but 1 cup of the sour cream mixture between the 4 layers. Blend the remaining cup of the mixture with the whipped cream and spread on top and sides of cake. Seal in airtight container and refrigerate for 3 days before serving. Keep refrigerated after cutting.

Nora Stith

COCONUT-PINEAPPLE CAKE

Sift 1 box yellow butter cake mix with ½ cup brown sugar. Make well and beat 2 eggs; pour into well. Add 16 ounce can crushed pineapple (juice and all). Add 1 cup Angel Flake coconut. Mix well. Bake 45 minutes in 325° oven.

Frosting: Make while cake is baking. Melt 1 stick of butter in pan. Add ½ cup white sugar and ½ cup milk. Bring to boil and boil 2 minutes. Pour over cake as soon as removed from oven. Sprinkle with 1 to 1½ cups coconut. Allow to stand overnight for more moist cake.

Katherine Ray

RAVE REVIEWS COCONUT CAKE

1 (2 layer size) pkg. yellow
    cake mix
1 small pkg. vanilla instant
    pudding
1⅓ c. water

4 eggs
¼ c. oil
2 c. coconut
1 c. chopped walnuts or
    pecans

Blend cake mix, pudding mix, water, eggs and oil in large mixer bowl. Beat at medium speed 4 minutes. Stir in coconut and walnuts. Pour into 3 greased and thawed 9 inch layer pans. Bake at 350° for 35 minutes. Cool in pans 15 minutes; remove and cool on racks.

Coconut-Cream Cheese Frosting:

4 Tbsp. margarine
2 c. coconut
1 (8 oz.) pkg. cream cheese

2 tsp. milk
3½ c. confectioners sugar
½ tsp. vanilla

Melt 2 tablespoons margarine in skillet. Add coconut; stir constantly over low heat until golden brown. Spread coconut in paper towel to cool. Cream 2 tablespoons margarine with cream cheese. Add milk; beat in sugar gradually. Blend in vanilla; stir in 1¾ cups of the coconut. Spread on tops of cake layers. Stack and sprinkle with remaining coconut.

Donna Browning

WHITE COCONUT CAKE

Bake 1 box white deluxe cake mix (Duncan Hines) as directed. While still hot, prick all over with a fork.

Mix together:

**1 (8 oz.) can cream of
coconut**

1 can Eagle Brand milk

Pour over cake while hot and cover with 1 large carton Cool Whip. Sprinkle with coconut. Refrigerate overnight.

Dollie D. Billiter

CHOCAROON CAKE
(Tastes like a coconut chocolate candy bar)

2 egg whites
⅓ c. sugar
2 Tbsp. flour
**1¾ c. Baker's Angel Flake
coconut**
**1 (2 layer size) pkg. chocolate
cake mix**

⅓ c. oil
**1 (4 serving size) pkg. Jell-O
chocolate instant
pudding and pie filling**
2 eggs
2 egg yolks

Beat egg whites until foamy. Gradually add sugar and beat until mixture forms stiff shiny peaks. Blend in flour and coconut; set aside. Combine remaining ingredients in large mixer bowl. Blend, then beat at medium speed of electric mixer for 2 minutes. Pour ⅓ of the batter into a greased and floured 10 inch Bundt pan. Spoon in coconut mixture and top with remaining batter. Bake at 350° for 50 to 55 minutes or until cake tester inserted in center comes out clean. Cool in pan about 15 minutes. Remove from pan and finish cooling on rack. Top with glaze.

Confectioners Sugar Glaze: Gradually add 1 tablespoon milk to 1 cup sifted confectioners sugar in a bowl. Makes ⅓ cup.

Patricia Jewell

CHOCOLATE CAKE

2 c. flour
2 c. sugar
2 sticks margarine, melted
1 c. water
½ c. cocoa

½ c. buttermilk
2 eggs
½ tsp. soda
1 tsp. vanilla

Mix together and bake at 350° for 40 minutes or until done.

Ruth Noe

CHOCOLATE CHIP CAKE

¼ lb. butter
1 c. granulated sugar
2 eggs
1 c. sour cream

1 tsp. vanilla
2 c. flour
1½ tsp. baking powder
1 tsp. baking soda

Preheat oven to 350°. Cream butter, sugar, and eggs. Add sour cream and vanilla. Sift flour, baking powder and baking soda. Add dry ingredients to butter mixture and beat. Pour half of batter into a greased oblong pan.

In separate bowl, mix:

½ c. granulated sugar
1 c. chocolate chips

1 tsp. cinnamon

Spoon half of mixture over top of cake batter already in pan. Pour in remaining cake batter and then rest of chocolate chip mixture. Bake approximately 25 minutes.

Nancy A. Thiry

BACARDI RUM CHOCOLATE CAKE

1 (18½ oz.) pkg. chocolate
   cake mix
1 pkg. Jello chocolate instant
   pudding
4 eggs

½ c. dark rum
½ c. Wesson oil
¼ c. slivered almonds
   (optional)
½ c. water

Mix and bake at 350° for 30 minutes or until done.

Frosting for Bacardi Rum Chocolate Cake:

1½ c. cold milk
½ c. dark rum

1 pkg. chocolate pudding
1 env. Dream Whip

Put ingredients in mixing bowl and whip. Frost rum cake.

Ruby Junker

GERMAN SWEET CHOCOLATE CAKE

1 (4 oz.) bar Baker's sweet chocolate
½ c. boiling water
1 c. butter or margarine
2 c. sugar
4 egg yolks (unbeaten)
1 tsp. vanilla
2½ c. sifted Swans Down cake flour
½ tsp. salt
1 tsp. baking soda
1 c. buttermilk
4 egg whites, stiffly beaten

Melt chocolate in boiling water. Cool. Cream butter and sugar until fluffy. Add egg yolks, 1 at a time, and beat well after each. Add melted chocolate and vanilla. Mix well. Sift together flour, salt and soda. Add alternately with buttermilk to chocolate mixture. Beat well. Beat until smooth. Fold in egg whites. Pour into 3 (8 or 9 inch) layer pans. Bake 30 to 40 minutes at 350°. Cool. Frost tops only.

Coconut-Pecan Frosting:

1 c. evaporated milk
1 c. sugar
3 egg yolks
1 tsp. vanilla
1½ c. Baker's Angel Flake coconut
1 c. chopped pecans
½ c. butter or margarine

Combine evaporated milk, sugar, egg yolks, butter and vanilla. Cook and stir over medium heat until thickened, about 12 minutes. Add coconut and pecans. Beat until thick enough to spread.

Bessie Litchford

CHOCOLATE CHEESECAKE

1 c. flour
½ c. ground walnuts or pecans
½ c. melted butter
1 (8 oz.) pkg. cream cheese
1 c. powdered sugar
1 large container Cool Whip
2 pkg. chocolate or butterscotch pudding
Nuts for top

Mix together 1 cup flour, ½ cup ground walnuts or pecans and ½ cup melted butter. Press into bottom and sides of a 9 inch pie pan. Bake at 350° for 20 to 25 minutes. Mix 1 (8 ounce) package cream cheese and 1 cup powdered sugar; beat until creamy; fold in a large container of Cool Whip. Pour over cooled, baked crust. Cook 2 packages of chocolate or butterscotch pudding, less ½ cup milk. Cool before pouring on top of cheese layer. Pour Cool Whip on top of cooled pudding and sprinkle with nuts.

Mary Baxter

CHOCOLATE ZUCCHINI CAKE

2½ c. sifted flour
½ c. cocoa
1 tsp. cinnamon
2½ tsp. baking powder
1½ tsp. baking soda
¾ c. butter

2 c. sugar
3 eggs
2 tsp. vanilla
2 c. shredded zucchini
¼ c. milk
1 c. chopped pecans

Sift together the sifted flour, cocoa, cinnamon, baking powder and soda. Set aside. In mixing bowl, cream butter, and sugar until light and fluffy. Add eggs and beat well. Add vanilla and zucchini; blend thoroughly. Blend in flour mixture alternately with milk. Fold in the pecans. Bake in a well greased and floured Bundt pan for 1 hour in a preheated 350° oven. Remove from pan and cool. Drizzle with a glaze made from 1 cup confectioners sugar mixed with 1 tablespoon orange juice.

Jayne Haws

CREAM CHEESE FUDGE CAKE

1 c. flour
½ tsp. salt
1 c. sugar
¾ c. milk
1 (3 oz.) pkg. cream cheese
2 tsp. baking powder

2 Tbsp. butter
2 eggs
1 tsp. vanilla
2 sq. melted unsweetened
   chocolate

Heat oven to 350°. Generously grease and flour a 9x5x3 inch loaf pan. Sift together flour, baking powder and salt. Cream butter until light and blend in cheese. Gradually beat in sugar. Beat in eggs, 1 at a time. Stir in dry ingredients alternately with milk and vanilla. Blend in chocolate. Bake 1 hour. Cool and frost if desired.

Frosting:

1 (3 oz.) pkg. cream cheese
2 c. powdered sugar
Dash of salt

1 sq. unsweetened
   chocolate, melted

Soften cream cheese. Gradually beat in powdered sugar and salt. Stir in melted unsweetened chocolate. Spread on cake.

Ruth Ackerman

DATE CAKE

1 pkg. dates (small pieces)
1 c. cold water
1 c. sugar
½ stick butter
1 egg

1½ c. flour
1 c. nuts
1 tsp. vanilla
1 tsp. soda

Mix water with baking soda. Add dates. Let stand for 1 hour. Then add the rest of the ingredients; place in a baking dish and bake in a 225° oven for 2 hours.

Barbara Montgomery

DATE CAKE

4 eggs
1 c. sugar
½ lb. candied pineapple,
    chopped
½ lb. candied cherries,
    chopped

1 lb. dates, chopped
1 c. flour
1 tsp. vanilla
1½ c. pecans

Cut fruit together with flour and sugar in bowl. Mix well, using hands. Separate eggs. Beat yolks and vanilla until light. Beat whites until stiff. Add yolks to fruit and mix well. Fold whites into fruit mixture. Turn into a greased and floured tube pan. Bake 2 hours at 250°.

Rose Briseno

DOODLE CAKE

Combine in mixing bowl:

2 c. self-rising flour
2 c. sugar
2 eggs

1 (No. 2) can crushed
    pineapple (do not drain)

Bake in 350° oven for 30 to 35 minutes. *(Do not preheat oven.)*

Icing:

1½ c. sugar
1 stick margarine

1 small can evaporated milk

Boil 3 minutes.

Add:

1 c. pecans
1 c. cocoanut

½ tsp. vanilla

Pour over warm cake. Cool and serve. Very moist and good.

Judy Seeders

DUMP CAKE

**1 (8 oz.) can crushed
pineapple**
1 stick margarine

**1 (14 oz.) box butter pecan
cake mix**
9 inch pie pan

Dump pineapple into bottom of pie pan (9 inches). Spread over bottom. Next, spread cake mix over first layer. Pour melted margarine on top of dry mix. Bake at 350°F. for 45 minutes.

Mary T. Thompson

DUMP CAKE

Dump all ingredients in a bowl and mix:

1 can apple pie filling
2 c. sugar
2 c. all-purpose flour
2 tsp. cinnamon
2 tsp. baking soda

1 c. oil
½ tsp. salt
1 c. chopped pecans
2 beaten eggs

Bake at 350° for 60 minutes.

Peggy Graviss

DUMP CAKE

**1 (20 oz.) can crushed
pineapple**
1 can flaked coconut

1 box yellow cake mix
1½ sticks margarine
1 c. broken nuts

Put in 9x13 inch baking dish in order given. Bake at 350° for 35 to 45 minutes until top is golden brown.

Donna Browning

EASY REFRIGERATOR CAKE

½ to 1 c. chopped nuts
1 c. flour
1 stick melted butter
1 c. powdered sugar
1 (8 oz.) pkg. cream cheese,
    softened

1 large container Cool Whip
3 small pkg. instant pudding
    (chocolate is best)
3 c. cold milk

Bottom layer: Melt butter; mix with flour and nuts. Press into a 9x12 inch pan. Bake at 350° for 20 to 25 minutes; cool.

Second layer: Beat powdered sugar, cream cheese and half of the Cool Whip. Spread on bottom layer.

Third layer: Beat pudding and milk until stiff and cover second layer.

Fourth layer: Frost with remaining Cool Whip. Sprinkle with chopped nuts. Refrigerate. Serves 8 to 12.

Wilma Crowdus

FIVE FLAVOR CAKE

2 sticks butter
½ c. Crisco
3 c. sugar
5 eggs, well beaten
3 c. plain flour
½ tsp. baking powder

1 c. sweet milk
1 tsp. coconut extract
1 tsp. butter
1 tsp. rum
1 tsp. vanilla
1 tsp. lemon

Cream butter, Crisco and sugar together; add eggs. Combine flour and baking powder; add to creamed mixture alternately with milk. Stir in flour; add remaining ingredients and mix well. Bake in tube pan 1½ hours at 325°.

Glaze:

1 c. sugar
1 tsp. lemon extract
1 tsp. butter extract
1 tsp. vanilla extract

1 tsp. rum extract
1 tsp. coconut extract
½ c. water

Combine all of the preceding. Bring to a boil. Stir until sugar is dissolved. Pour over *hot* cake and let cool, then remove it from pan.

Lil Pasinski

FRIENDSHIP CAKE

1 can peaches with juice   **1½ c. starter**
2½ c. sugar

Place in a gallon container, loosely covered. Leave at room temperature. Stir each day for 10 days.

On tenth day, add:

1 large can chunk or grated   **2½ c. sugar**
   pineapple

Stir each day for 10 days. On twentieth day, add: 2 (8 ounce) jars maraschino cherries, *drained.* Add *no* sugar. Stir each day for 10 days. On thirtieth day, drain mixture well. Divide juice into 1½ cups to give to friends. Should be 4 starters.

Cake Recipe:

1 box yellow cake mix   **4 eggs**
1 box vanilla instant pudding   **1 c. raisins (that have been**
1 c. chopped nuts   **"plumped" in boiling**
⅓ c. cocoanut   **water for 15 minutes and**
1½ c. drained fruit   **drained)**
⅔ c. cooking oil

Mix cake according to package directions. Stir in fruit and nuts. Bake in well greased and floured Bundt pan at 350° for 40 to 60 minutes.

You should have approximately 3 cups fruit remaining. This cake freezes well; should you want to use your fruit in cake. The brandied fruit is good as an ice cream topping or the following dessert.

Mix 1½ sticks melted margarine, 4 tablespoons sugar, 1½ cups flour and 1 cup chopped pecans. Spray 9x13 inch baking dish with Pam. Mixture is pressed firmly into dish and baked for 20 to 25 minutes or until golden brown, at 350°.

Filling:

1 large pkg. cream cheese   **1 lb. powdered sugar**
2 large pkg. Cool Whip

Spread over cooled crust. Top with fruit. Dob with more Cool Whip and sprinkle with toasted pecans.

Margarete Miller

THIRTY DAY FRIENDSHIP CAKE

A friend gives you a cup and a half of fermented juice starter or you can try using a cup and a half of rum or some other alcohol that you would use in making a fruit cake.

Mix in a gallon jar with a lid:

1½ c. starter
2½ c. sugar

1 large can sliced peaches
with the juice.

Stir once a day for 10 days. On the tenth day, add a large can of pineapple chunks with the juice and 2½ cups of sugar. Stir once a day for 10 days. On the twentieth day, add 2 large jars of maraschino cherries, drained. Stir once a day for 10 days. Bake cakes on the thirtieth day. *Drain fruit.* (Save drained fruit juice, you have enough to start another cake and give starters (1 ½ cups each) to 3 friends.) There is enough fruit to bake 3 cakes, 1½ cups each to make *1* cake.

Mix:

1 pkg. yellow or white cake
mix (with pudding in the
mix)
4 eggs

⅔ c. oil
1½ c. drained fruit
1 c. chopped pecans

Fold fruit and nuts in last by hand. Bake at 350° for 45 to 50 minutes (test with toothpick). You can use a Bundt pan or oblong cake pan, greased.

Anna Mae Rutledge

FRUIT CAKE

1 box butter brickle cake mix
½ c. cherries
2 c. candied fruit

1 c. raisins
1 c. nuts

Combine cake mix according to package directions. Add remaining ingredients. Bake for 1 hour at 325°.

Sheila Duke

FRUIT CAKE

2 c. brown sugar
⅔ c. shortening
2 c. water
2 c. raisins
2 c. currants

2 tsp. cinnamon
1 tsp. cloves
1 tsp. nutmeg
½ tsp. allspice
1 tsp. salt

Stir together and boil 3 minutes. Cool. Add 4 cups flour, 2 cups nutmeats, 2 teaspoons baking powder and 2 teaspoons soda. Bake at 350° for 45 minutes in 2 well greased tins. Cool and frost with a butter cream frosting.

Pat Whisman

FRUIT COCKTAIL CAKE

2 c. all-purpose flour
½ tsp. salt
½ c. coconut
1½ c. sugar

2 tsp. soda
2 eggs
2 c. fruit cocktail

Mix all ingredients. Sprinkle ½ cup light brown sugar on top of batter. Bake in a 9x13 inch pan for 40 minutes at 325°.

Topping:

1 stick butter
¾ c. sugar

¾ c. condensed milk
1 tsp. vanilla

Over medium heat, bring to a boil. Boil 5 minutes, stirring constantly. Pour over cake. Sprinkle with coconut and pecans.

Ina Gray (submitted by Robert Gray)

FRUIT COCKTAIL CAKE

1 c. flour
1 c. sugar
1 tsp. soda
1 egg

1 can fruit cocktail
¼ stick butter
½ c. milk
1 c. sugar

Mix flour, sugar, soda, egg and fruit cocktail together. Bake at 350° until done. Then mix butter, sugar and milk; bring to a boil, then pour over cake while hot.

Lil Pasinski

412

FRUIT COCKTAIL CAKE

2 c. flour	Pinch of salt
1½ c. sugar	2 eggs
2 level tsp. soda	1 (No. 303) can fruit cocktail

Stir all ingredients together with a spoon; do not use electric mixer. Place ingredients in a 13x9x3 inch pan. Bake at 325° until done, when toothpick comes out clean.

Icing:

1 stick margarine	1 c. white sugar
½ or 1 c. Pet milk	½ c. brown sugar
1 tsp. vanilla	½ c. nuts
1 can Angel Flake coconut	

Make icing and pour over cake while still hot. Holes may be made in cake to allow icing to run into cake.

Mark A. Cowan

FRUIT COCKTAIL CAKE

1 (No. 2) can fruit cocktail	2 tsp. soda
2 c. plain flour	¼ tsp. salt
1½ c. sugar	2 eggs

Mix together by hand. Pour into greased 9x13 inch pan. Sprinkle ½ cup brown sugar over cake. Bake 40 minutes at 350°, after 10 minutes, turn to 325°.

Sauce:

1 c. sugar	1 small can Pet milk
1 stick margarine	

Cook until thick and starts to stick. Take off and set in cold water and stir until thick. Then pour over cake in pan. Sprinkle with pecans if desired.

Jenny Carp

FRUIT CRUMB COFFEE CAKE

1 (18.25 oz.) pkg. deluxe
  white cake mix
1 c. flour
1 pkg. active dry yeast
⅔ c. warm water
2 eggs
1 (18 oz.) jar red raspberry
  preserves or apricot

preserves (any favorite
  flavor of preserves)
¼ c. sugar
1 tsp. cinnamon
6 Tbsp. butter or margarine
1 c. sifted powdered sugar
1 Tbsp. corn syrup
1 Tbsp. milk

Preheat oven to 375°. Reserve 2½ cups dry cake mix. In a large bowl, combine remaining cake mix, flour, yeast, water and eggs. Mix by hand 100 strokes. Spread batter evenly in a greased 13x9x2 inch pan. Spoon red raspberry preserves or other flavor evenly over dough in pan.

In medium bowl, combine reserved cake mix, sugar, cinnamon and butter with fork until fine. Sprinkle over preserves. Bake 30 to 35 minutes or until golden brown. In small mixing bowl, blend powdered sugar, corn syrup and milk. Drizzle over warm or cool cake. Makes 12 to 16 servings.

Mary Quandt

FUDGE-PUDDING CAKE

1 c. flour
¾ c. sugar
2 tsp. baking powder
½ tsp. salt
2 tsp. cocoa
½ c. milk
1 tsp. vanilla

2 tsp. melted margarine
½ c. chopped nuts
½ c. sugar (granulated)
½ c. brown sugar
2 tsp. cocoa
1 c. boiling water

Heat oven to 350°. Butter a 9 inch square cake pan. Sift flour, ¾ cup granulated sugar, baking powder, salt and 2 teaspoons cocoa together. Add milk, vanilla, and margarine; beat until smooth. Stir in the nuts. Spread in pan. Mix ½ cup granulated sugar, brown sugar, and 2 teaspoons cocoa; sprinkle on top of cake batter, then pour the boiling water on this. Bake 50 to 60 minutes. Serves 6 to 8.

J. Faye Blevins

HOT FUDGE CAKE

2 c. flour
2 c. sugar
1 stick oleo
4 Tbsp. cocoa
½ c. Crisco oil

1 c. water
2 eggs
1 tsp. soda
1 tsp. cinnamon
½ c. buttermilk

Mix flour and sugar. Take oleo, cocoa, Crisco oil and water; bring to a boil. Pour over sugar and flour mixture. Mix well, then add 2 eggs, soda, cinnamon and buttermilk. Pour in oblong pan, well greased. Bake at 400° for 25 minutes. Five minutes before cake is finished, make icing.

Hot Fudge Cake Icing - Put in pan:

1 stick butter
6 Tbsp. milk

4 Tbsp. cocoa

Bring to a boil. Remove from heat.

Add:

1 pkg. powdered sugar
1 tsp. vanilla

1 c. pecans

Put on cake while hot.

J. Faye Blevins

FUNNEL CAKE

1⅓ c. flour
1¼ tsp. salt
½ tsp. soda

2 Tbsp. sugar
¾ Tbsp. baking powder

Sift together in bowl.

1 egg, beaten

⅔ c. milk (or more if too thick)

Mix egg and milk together and add to dry ingredients. Beat until smooth. Hold finger over bottom of funnel; pour in some batter; remove finger, letting batter drop in spiral motion into pan with 1 to 2 inches of hot oil. Fry until golden. Turn once. Drain on paper towel. Sprinkle with cinnamon sugar or powdered sugar. Serve hot.

Rose Briseno

GERMAN CHOCOLATE CAKE

1 pkg. German's chocolate
½ c. boiling water
2½ sticks butter (no
   substitute)
2 c. granulated sugar
5 eggs, separated

½ tsp. vanilla
½ tsp. salt
1 tsp. baking soda
2½ c. sifted cake flour
1 c. sour cream

Shave chocolate and melt in boiling water. Cool. Cream butter and sugar until fluffy. Add egg yolks, 1 at a time, and beat well after each addition. Add chocolate and vanilla. Mix well. Sift together sifted flour, salt and baking soda. Add alternately with sour cream to chocolate mixture. Beat well until smooth. Beat egg whites until stiff and fold into batter with a wire whisk. Pour into 3 (9 inch) cake pans that have been buttered and lined with generously buttered waxed paper. Bake in a preheated 350° oven for 30 to 35 minutes or until cake tests done.

Filling:

½ pt. coffee cream
1 c. granulated sugar
3 egg yolks, lightly beaten
1 stick butter (no substitute)
1 tsp. vanilla

1⅓ c. freshly grated coconut
1 c. finely chopped black
   walnuts
1 lb. confectioners sugar

Combine coffee cream, granulated sugar, beaten egg yolks, butter and vanilla. Cook and stir over medium heat until thickened. Remove from heat and add fresh coconut and black walnuts. Add confectioners sugar, a little at a time, beating until it's of spreading consistency. Spread filling between layers and on top of cake.

Frosting:

½ stick butter (no substitute)
1 pkg. German's chocolate
3 c. confectioners sugar
¼ tsp. salt

½ c. coffee cream
1¼ tsp. vanilla
½ c. finely chopped black
   walnuts

Melt ½ stick butter and chocolate over medium heat. Stir in all other ingredients. Beat until it's of spreading consistency. Frost sides of cake and edge around top layer.

Wilma Crowdus

GERMAN SWEET CHOCOLATE CAKE

1 (4 oz.) pkg. Baker's German's brand sweet chocolate
½ c. boiling water
1 c. butter or margarine
2 c. sugar
4 egg yolks
1 tsp. vanilla

2¼ c. sifted all-purpose flour (or use 2½ c. sifted Swans Down cake flour)
1 tsp. baking soda
½ tsp. salt
1 c. buttermilk
4 egg whites, stiffly beaten

Melt chocolate in boiling water. Cool. Cream butter and sugar until fluffy. Add yolks, 1 at a time, beating well after each. Blend in vanilla and chocolate. Sift flour with soda and salt; add alternately with buttermilk to chocolate mixture, beating after each addition until smooth. Fold in beaten whites. Pour into 3 (9 inch) layer pans, lined on bottoms with paper. Bake at 350° for 30 to 35 minutes. Cool. Frost tops only.

Coconut-Pecan Frosting:

1 c. evaporated milk
1 c. sugar
3 slightly beaten egg yolks
½ c. butter or margarine

1 tsp. vanilla
1⅓ c. Baker's Angel Flake coconut
1 c. chopped pecans

Combine evaporated milk, sugar, egg yolks, butter or margarine and vanilla. Cook and stir over medium heat until thickened, about 12 minutes. Add Baker's Angel Flake coconut and chopped pecans. Cool until thick enough to spread, beating occasionally. Makes 2½ cups.

Vickie McDaniel

GOOEY BUTTER CAKE

1 pkg. butter recipe cake mix
1 stick butter
4 eggs

1 (8 oz.) pkg. sour cream
1 box confectioners sugar

Mix the cake mix, butter and 2 of the eggs together by hand and pour in an ungreased 13x9 inch pan. Then mix the sour cream, confectioners sugar and the other 2 eggs also by hand and pour the second mixture over the first. Bake for 45 minutes at 350° in a preheated oven.

Sue Johnson

GRANNY'S BAKING POWDER SPONGE CAKE

3 egg yolks
¼ c. cold water
1½ c. sugar
½ tsp. lemon extract
1 c. cake flour

¼ c. cold water
1 c. cake flour
2 tsp. baking powder
½ tsp. salt
3 egg whites

Beat the egg yolks, then add each ingredient in order given, adding baking powder and salt with the last cup of flour. Then fold in very thoroughly the egg whites beaten light. Bake in a tube sponge cake pan for 45 minutes or a biscuit pan or larger pan for 15 minutes.

Can be used for shortcake or jelly roll also.

Jewell Hundley

GRANNY CAKE

1½ c. white sugar
2 c. flour (plain)
2 eggs
1 tsp. soda

1 tsp. salt
1 c. crushed pineapple
    (undrained)

Pour preceding mixture into 9x13 inch pan. On top sprinkle ½ cup brown sugar and ½ cup nuts. Bake 45 minutes at 350°.

Meanwhile, prepare sauce:

1 can Milnot
1 stick butter

½ c. sugar
1 tsp. vanilla

When cake is done, prick with fork. Pour warm sauce over warm cake. Make tonight, serve next day.

Dianne Rice

GRANNY GOO BUTTER CAKE

1 box Duncan Hines yellow
    butter cake mix
1 stick butter

3 eggs
8 oz. pkg. cream cheese
1 box confectioners sugar

Mix by hand cake mix, butter and 1 egg; press in baking dish. Beat in mixer until creamy the cream cheese, 2 eggs and ¾ box confectioners sugar. Pour over the first mixture in baking dish. Bake in 350°

oven 30 to 35 minutes. Sprinkle rest of confectioners sugar over hot cake when baked. Cool. Refrigerate; better if left overnight. Cut in bars or squares.

Deborah E. Robertson

GOLD MINES

1 box brownie mix
1 egg
½ c. brown sugar
1 c. pecans, chopped

1 c. coconut
½ c. sweetened condensed
  milk

Preheat oven to 350°. Prepare brownie mix according to package directions for cake like brownies. Set aside. In a separate bowl, mix together remaining ingredients. Paper line a 2 dozen cupcake tin. Divide the brownie mixture equally among the cups. Place a heaping teaspoon of the coconut mixture in the center of each cup and press lightly into brownie mixture. Bake for 25 to 30 minutes, being careful not to overbake.

Mrs. Dennis G. Ebelhar

GRAHAM STREUSEL CAKE

2 c. graham cracker crumbs
¾ c. chopped nuts
¾ c. brown sugar, packed
1¼ tsp. cinnamon
¾ c. margarine, melted

1 pkg. white cake mix
1 c. water
¼ c. vegetable oil
3 eggs
Vanilla Glaze

Grease 13x9 inch pan. Mix crumbs, nuts, brown sugar, cinnamon and butter. Blend cake mix, water, oil and eggs on low speed until moistened. Beat on medium speed, stirring occasionally 3 minutes. Pour half of batter into pan; sprinkle with half of reserved crumb mixture. Spread remaining batter evenly over crumb mixture; sprinkle with remaining crumb mixture. Bake at 350° for 45 to 50 minutes; cool. Drizzle cake with Vanilla Glaze.

Vanilla Glaze:

1 c. powdered sugar

1 - 2 Tbsp. water

Mix powdered sugar and water until desired consistency.

Phyllis L. Davis

GRAHAM STREUSEL CAKE

2 c. (approx. 26) graham
    cracker crumbs
¾ c. chopped nuts
¾ c. packed brown sugar
1¼ tsp. cinnamon
¾ c. melted margarine

1 pkg. Duncan Hines cake
    mix (any flavor you like, I
    use yellow)
1 c. water
⅓ c. vegetable oil
3 eggs

Heat oven to 350°. Grease and flour 9x13 inch pan. Mix cracker crumbs, nuts, brown sugar, cinnamon and margarine; reserve. Beat cake mix, water, oil and eggs in large mixer bowl on low speed, scraping bowl until moistened. Beat 2 minutes on medium, scraping bowl frequently. Pour half of batter into prepared pan; sprinkle with half of cracker mix. Spoon remaining cake batter over crumb mix; top with remaining crumb mixture. Bake until cake springs back when touched in center or until tests done. Drizzle with Powdered Sugar Glaze. Cool completely. Cover until serving time.

Powdered Sugar Glaze: Mix 1 cup powdered sugar and 1 tablespoon milk or water. Stir in additional liquid and 1 tablespoon soft margarine until smooth and of desired consistency.

Ruthie Marty

GRAND MARNIER CAKE

1 box Duncan Hines white
    cake mix
½ c. Crisco oil
1 (3½ oz.) pkg. Royal instant
    vanilla pudding

4 eggs
¾ c. orange juice
¾ c. Grand Marnier

Mix to blend, then heat 1 minute at maximum speed. Pour into greased and floured tube pan (10 inch). Bake at 350° for 45 to 50 minutes. Cool slightly.

Topping - Mix:

½ c. sifted powdered sugar
1 Tbsp. orange juice

2 Tbsp. Grand Marnier

Punch holes in cake to the bottom. Pour mixture over the cake.

Helen Russman

HARVEY WALLBANGER CAKE

Orange cake mix (2 layers)
3¾ oz. size vanilla pudding
4 eggs
½ c. orange juice

½ c. Liquore Galliano
2 Tbsp. vodka
½ c. cooking oil

In a large bowl, combine cake mix and pudding. Add eggs, oil, orange juice, Liquore Galliano and vodka. Beat on low speed of electric mixer for ½ minute; beat on medium speed for 5 minutes, scraping bowl frequently. Pour into greased and floured 10 inch Bundt pan. Bake at 350° for 45 minutes. Cool in pan for 10 minutes. Remove and pour on icing while cake is still warm.

Icing:

1 c. sifted confectioners
   sugar
1 Tbsp. orange juice

1 Tbsp. Liquore Galliano
1 tsp. vodka

Mix all of the preceding well.

Peggy Hunter

HAWAIIAN CAKE

1 box white or yellow cake
   mix
1 small can mandarin oranges
   and juice

3 eggs
½ c. oil

Mix and bake at 350°.

Topping:

1 pkg. vanilla instant pudding
1 c. (16 oz.) crushed
   pineapple

1 ctn. Cool Whip

Irene Bennett

HERSHEY'S DISAPPEARING CAKE

¼ c. butter
¼ c. shortening
2 c. sugar
1 tsp. vanilla
2 eggs
¾ c. Hershey's cocoa

1¾ c. unsifted all-purpose
   flour
¾ tsp. baking powder
¾ tsp. baking soda
⅛ tsp. salt
1¾ c. milk

Generously grease and flour 2 (9 inch) round cake pans. Cream butter, shortening, sugar and vanilla until fluffy; blend in eggs. Combine cocoa, flour, baking powder, baking soda and salt in bowl; add alternately with milk to batter. Blend well. Pour into pans; bake at 350° for 30 to 35 minutes or until cake tester inserted in center comes out clean. Cool 10 minutes; remove from pans.

Sue Sympson

HUNTING CAKES FROM BOONE TAVERN

1 c. sugar
½ c. butter
1 c. sour cream
2 eggs
½ tsp. cloves
1 tsp. soda

1 tsp. cinnamon
1 c. raisins, cut with scissors
½ c. walnuts
2 c. flour, sifted before
   measuring

Cream butter and sugar. Add eggs; beat well. Sift flour and spices; mix in raisins and nuts. This will separate the particles. Mix soda with sour cream and add alternately with flour mixture. Mix well. Bake in cupcakes for 20 to 30 minutes in 350° oven. Frost each cake with boiled icing and place a half date on top of each cake. These keep well.

Barbara Terranova

FREDIA CONLEY'S IGLOO CAKE

¼ c. cold water
⅓ c. sugar
1¾ c. milk
1 Tbsp. vanilla
⅓ c. sugar
1 Tbsp. plain gelatin
¼ tsp. salt
3 egg *yolks*

3 egg *whites*
1 pkg. German's sweet
   chocolate
Chocolate cake mix (any
   kind)
Dream Whip
Hershey's candy bar

Mix ¼ cup water and gelatin. Let set. Mix ⅓ cup sugar, salt, milk, chocolate and egg yolks. Cook over low heat until slightly thickened. Add gelatin mix and chill. Beat egg whites, ⅓ cup sugar and vanilla until stiff. Fold in chocolate mixture and chill 2½ hours or overnight, in mixing bowl. Fix layer cake (any chocolate cake mix). Dip bowl with chocolate mixture in hot water to loosen. Unmold on top of chocolate cake layer. Frost with Dream Whip and top with chocolate curls. (Use Hershey's candy bar for making curls.)

Ruth Ackerman

ITALIAN CREAM CAKE

1 stick margarine
½ c. shortening
2 c. sugar
5 egg yolks
2 c. sifted flour
1 tsp. soda

½ tsp. salt
1 c. butterm
1 c. cocon
1 c. chopp
5 egg whi'

Beat cr
well. Add va
and sides

Blend margarine, shortening and sugar, 1 at a time. ⌐
Sift together flour, soda and salt. Add the flour mixture and buttermilk ⌐
the blended ingredients. Mix well. Stir in coconut and nuts. Beat the egg
whites until stiff and fold in mixture. Pour batter into 3 (9 inch) cake pans
greased and floured. Bake at 350° for 35 minutes.

Frosting:

½ stick margarine
1 tsp. vanilla

1 lb. powdered sugar
8 oz. pkg. cream cheese

Cream margarine and cream cheese; beat in sugar and vanilla. If
mixture is too thick, add a few drops of cream.

Dianne Rice

ITALIAN CREAM CAKE

1 stick butter
½ c. vegetable shortening
   (Crisco)
2 c. sugar
5 egg yolks
2 c. cake flour
1 tsp. soda

1 c. buttermilk
1 tsp. vanilla
1 small can Angel Flake
   coconut
1 c. chopped pecans
5 egg whites, stiffly beaten

Cream butter and shortening. Add sugar and beat until smooth.
Add egg yolks. Beat well. Combine flour and soda. Add to cream mixture
alternately with buttermilk. Stir in vanilla. Add coconut and nuts. Fold in
egg whites. Pour into 3 greased and floured 8 inch pie plates. Bake at
350° (preheated) for 25 minutes or until tests done. Thoroughly cool and
frost.

Cream Cheese Frosting:

1 (8 oz.) pkg. cream cheese,
   softened at room
   temperature
½ stick butter, softened

1 box powdered sugar
1 tsp. vanilla
Chopped pecans (optional)

am cheese and butter until smooth. Add sugar and mix
illa and beat until smooth. Spread between layers on top
of cake. Sprinkle nuts on top if desired.

Ann Duke

ITALIAN CREAM CAKE

1 c. buttermilk	½ c. shortening
1 tsp. soda	2 c. flour
5 eggs, separated	1 tsp. vanilla
2 c. sugar	1 c. pecans
1 stick butter	1 small can coconut

Combine buttermilk and soda. Let stand. Cream sugar, butter
and shortening. Add egg yolks, 1 at a time, beating after each addition.
Add buttermilk and soda with flour. Add vanilla. Fold in beaten egg
whites. Gently fold in pecans and coconut. Bake 25 to 30 minutes at
325° in 3 (9 inch) pans.

Frosting:

1 stick butter	1 box confectioners sugar
1 (8 oz.) pkg. cream cheese	1 tsp. vanilla

Soften cheese and butter. Cream this and gradually add sifted
sugar. When smooth, add vanilla. Sprinkle pecans and coconut between layers and on top.

Sue Casey

MRS. CREASON'S JAM CAKE

5 eggs, beaten	½ c. cinnamon
2 c. sugar	1½ c. cloves
3 c. flour	1½ c. allspice
1 c. butter or shortening	1 c. raisins or chopped dates
1 c. buttermilk	1 c. chopped nuts
1 tsp. soda	1 c. jam
¼ tsp. salt	

Cream butter and gradually add sugar; cream together until light
and fluffy. Add well beaten eggs. Sift flour before measuring and add to it
the salt and spices. Dissolve the soda in buttermilk and add it and the
flour alternately to the egg, sugar, butter mixture and beat after each addition. Lightly dredge the fruit and nuts with extra flour and add. Next,

add the jam. Stir to get good distribution. Grease and paper line 2 (9 inch) cake pans. Bake at 325° for 40 to 50 minutes. Ice with Caramel Icing.

Helen Russman

JAM CAKE

4 c. flour (plain)	1 tsp. cloves
2 c. sugar	6 eggs
1 c. shortening (½ butter and	1 c. buttermilk
½ Crisco or lard)	1 tsp. soda
½ tsp. salt	1 pt. jam
2 tsp. nutmeg	1 c. nuts, crushed
2 tsp. cinnamon	1 c. raisins

Cream shortening and sugar. Add salt and spices. Beat eggs into mixture, 1 egg at a time. In another container, mix soda and buttermilk. Add to shortening mixture alternately with flour. Beat jam into mixture. Coat nuts and raisins with 2 tablespoons flour (I shake them in a bag) and add to mixture. Pour into 3 (10 inch) cake pans or tube pan. Bake at 350° for 1 hour to 90 minutes or until toothpick is clean when inserted. Top with Caramel Icing.

Marianne E. Albright

JAM CAKE

6 egg whites	2 c. or more pecans
2 c. sugar	2 c. seedless blackberry or
1½ c. (3 sticks) butter or	strawberry jam
margarine	2 tsp. soda
1 c. buttermilk	2 tsp. cinnamon
4 c. plain flour	2 tsp. allspice
½ c. raisins	2 tsp. nutmeg

Cream sugar and butter together. Flour raisins lightly. Mix all dried ingredients together. Combine creamed sugar and butter, raisins, pecans, jam, and buttermilk; mix well. Fold in egg whites that have been beaten lightly together. Bake at 325° for about 2 hours.

Debbie Rigdon

JAM CAKE

1 Duncan Hines Deluxe II
   spice cake mix
5 eggs
1 can blackberry pie filling or
   blackberries in heavy
   syrup*

1 - 1½ c. nuts

Bake in tube (greased) pan at 350° for 50 to 60 minutes.

* Can substitute strawberry pie filling.

Wynola Sharon Davis

MOM'S OLD FASHIONED JAM CAKE

1 c. butter, melted
2 c. sugar
1 tsp. allspice
1 tsp. cinnamon
1 c. nuts
1 c. raisins
1 c. jam

1 c. pear preserves
1 c. peach preserves
4 eggs, separated
1 c. buttermilk
2 tsp. soda, added to
   buttermilk
4 c. flour

Cream butter and sugar. Add spices, nuts, raisins, jam and beaten egg yolks; mix well. Combine milk and soda until dissolved. Add to mixture with flour. Fold in well beaten egg whites. Mix well and bake at 300° for 1 hour and 15 minutes.

Peggy Larrison

MR. BORDEN'S JAM CAKE

2 c. sugar
1 c. butter
6 eggs, separated
1 c. buttermilk
1 tsp. baking powder
2 tsp. soda
4 c. flour

1 tsp. cinnamon
1 tsp. cocoa
1 tsp. allspice
1 tsp. vanilla
2 c. blackberry jam
1 c. raisins
2 c. black walnut kernels

426

Combine butter and sugar. Add egg yolks; beat until light and fluffy. Add sifted dry ingredients alternately with milk. Mix until smooth; add jam, raisins and walnuts. Mix thoroughly. Bake 3 hours in 275° oven.

Note: Fold beaten egg whites into cake last (just before baking).

J. W. Borden, Jr.

JAM CAKE

2 c. white sugar
1 c. shortening (use solid
    Crisco)
3½ c. flour
2 c. buttermilk
2 tsp. soda, stirred into
    buttermilk
3 Tbsp. cocoa

3 eggs
1 pt. jam
1 Tbsp. cinnamon
1 Tbsp. cloves
1 Tbsp. nutmeg
1 c. nuts
Raisins (optional)

Mix all ingredients and bake at 375° for 1 hour or until cake springs back when touched.

Caramel Icing:

1 stick butter
1 c. brown sugar (use light
    brown)

¼ c. milk

Cook butter and sugar together for 2 minutes. Add milk; let cool and mix about 1 box confectioners sugar. If too thick, add a little hot water.

B. Plunkett

JAMAICAN CAKE AND ICING

2 c. sugar
3 c. all-purpose flour
1½ c. vegetable oil
1 (8 oz.) can crushed
    pineapple (including
    juice)

2 c. mashed bananas
3 beaten eggs
1 tsp. salt
1 tsp. soda
1 tsp. cinnamon
1 c. pecans

Mix all ingredients in a large bowl. Bake in a greased tube pan for 1 hour and 15 minutes at 350°. Let cool 3 to 4 hours.

Icing:

1 box powdered sugar   ¼ lb. margarine
½ c. pecans   2 tsp. vanilla
6 oz. cream cheese

    Cream margarine with cheese; add remaining ingredients.

Elizabeth Hensley

LEMON COCONUT CAKE

1 pkg. yellow cake mix   1 Tbsp. flour
2 c. heavy cream, whipped   ½ c. sugar
    stiff   ⅔ c. water
1 c. flaked coconut   1 egg yolk, slightly beaten
Citron slices   3 Tbsp. lemon juice
Candied red cherries, halved   1 tsp. grated lemon peel
2 Tbsp. cornstarch   1 Tbsp. margarine

    Preheat oven to 350°. Grease and flour 2 (8 x 1½ inch) round layer cake pans. Make and bake cake according to package directions. Remove from oven and let cool 10 minutes before removing from pans. To make filling, in a small saucepan, combine cornstarch, flour and sugar; mix well. Gradually add water; stir until smooth. Bring to a boil over medium heat; stir occasionally; boil 1 minute. Remove from heat. Stir some of the hot mixture fast into the beaten egg yolk. Return it to the hot mixture and blend together. Return to heat; cook over low heat about 5 minutes until stiff; stir occasionally. Remove from heat. Stir in lemon juice, lemon peel and margarine. Pour into a small bowl; place bowl in a bowl of ice water; stir occasionally until chilled and stiff, about 30 minutes. Makes about 1¾ cups. Take out ¾ cups filling for the top.

    Combine rest of the filling with 1 cup of whipped cream and mix with a wire whisk until smooth. Slice layers in halves horizontally to make 4 layers. Place a layer, cut side up, on cake plate. Spread with ⅓ of filling. Repeat with remaining layers; end with top layer with cut side down. Spread top with the reserved lemon filling. Sprinkle with coconut. Decorate top with citron and cherries. Refrigerate until ready to serve. Serves 12.

Wanda Alton

LEMON LAYER CAKE

3 c. sifted cake flour
3 tsp. baking powder
¾ c. (1½ sticks) butter
1½ c. granulated sugar

1 tsp. vanilla
3 large eggs
1¼ c. milk

Sift together the flour and baking powder. Cream the butter, granulated sugar and vanilla. Thoroughly beat in the eggs, 1 at a time. Stir in the flour mixture in 4 additions, alternately with the milk, just until smooth each time. Turn into 3 greased and floured round (9 inch) layer cake pans. Bake in a preheated 350° oven until a cake tester inserted in the center comes out clean, 20 to 25 minutes. Cool cakes in pans on wire racks for 5 minutes. Loosen edges and turn out on racks. Cool completely. Spread 1 layer with ½ cup of the Lemon Fill and Frost; add another cake layer and spread with another ½ cup of the Lemon Fill and Frost. Add the last cake layer. Whip the cream with the confectioners sugar until stiff; fold in the remaining Lemon Fill and Frost and use generously to cover top and sides of cake. Store in refrigerator.

Lemon Fill and Frost:

1½ c. heavy cream   ⅓ c. confectioners sugar

In a 1 quart saucepan, over low heat, stir together about 1 tablespoon grated lemon rind, ¼ cup lemon juice, 1⅓ cup granulated sugar and ½ cup (1 stick) butter until sugar is dissolved and butter melted. Off heat, gradually whisk in until blended, 3 slightly beaten large eggs. Over medium heat, stirring constantly, cook until slightly thickened; do not boil. Cover and chill. Use as directed in Lemon Layer Cake recipe.

Mrs. Clarence Ebelhar

LEMON VELVET CAKE

1 box Betty Crocker lemon
    velvet cake mix
1 pkg. lemon instant pudding
¾ c. cooking oil
4 eggs

¾ c. water
½ c. orange juice
2 Tbsp. melted butter
2 c. powdered sugar

Mix together 1 box Betty Crocker lemon velvet cake mix and lemon instant pudding, ¾ cup cooking oil, 4 eggs and ¾ cup water; beat 4 minutes. Bake in greased pan in 300° or 325° oven for 50 minutes. Mix orange juice, melted butter and powdered sugar; pour over cake while hot. Leave cake in pan until cool.

Peggy Kessinger

MEXICAN PECAN CAKE

1¼ c. sugar
⅔ c. ground pecans
¼ tsp. salt
1 c. butter

1 Tbsp. lemon juice
5 eggs
1¾ c. sifted flour

Place sugar, pecans, salt, butter and lemon juice in a mixing bowl. With an electric mixer, cream mixture well, until fluffy. Add eggs and beat thoroughly until mixture is light and airy. Add flour and beat well again. Spoon batter into a greased and floured 10 inch spring form pan and bake in a preheated 325° oven for about 1 hour or until cake tests done. Cool and serve with warm Butter Lemon Glaze drizzled over or Mexican Fudge Sauce.

Lemon Butter Glaze:

¼ c. butter
1 c. honey or sugar
5 tsp. lemon juice

¼ c. coarsely chopped
   pecans

Combine butter, honey and lemon juice in a small pan. Boil gently for 2 minutes; remove from heat; cool for 10 minutes; stir in the pecans; drizzle over cooled cake.

Mexican Fudge Sauce:

1 (14½ oz.) can evaporated
   milk
1¾ c. sugar
4 oz. (4 sq.) unsweetened
   chocolate
¼ c. butter

1 tsp. vanilla
½ tsp. salt
1 tsp. cinnamon
¼ tsp. cloves
⅛ tsp. nutmeg

Heat milk and sugar; stir constantly, until mixture simmers. Add the chocolate and stir until melted. Beat until smooth (if sauce has slightly curdled appearance, beat vigorously, it will become creamy smooth). Remove from heat and stir in the butter, vanilla, salt, cinnamon, cloves and nutmeg. Serve warm.

Gwen Mills

MILKY WAY CAKE

8 Milky Way bars
2 sticks oleo
2 c. sugar
4 eggs

2½ c. flour
½ tsp. soda
1¼ c. buttermilk
1 c. chopped pecans

Melt Milky Way bars and 1 stick oleo, then set aside. Cream sugar and 1 stick oleo. Add eggs. Add alternately flour and soda with buttermilk. Add melted candy and oleo mixture. Add pecans. Bake in tube pan at 325° for 1 hour and 10 minutes or until done.

Icing:

2 (6 oz.) pkg. cream cheese
3 c. confectioners sugar
1 egg yolk

1 tsp. vanilla
⅛ tsp. salt

Combine cream cheese, egg yolk, salt and 1 cup of the sugar; add vanilla. Stir in remaining sugar, 1 cup at a time.

Mrs. Ben Allen (Mary Ella) Burns

MILKY WAY CAKE

8 Milky Way bars
2½ sticks butter
2 c. sugar
4 eggs, well beaten
½ tsp. baking soda

1½ c. buttermilk
2½ c. cake flour, sifted
½ tsp. salt
2 tsp. vanilla
1 c. chopped nuts

Melt bars over very low heat with 1 stick butter. Cool. Cream sugar and remaining butter thoroughly. Add eggs. Dissolve soda in buttermilk. Add sifted flour and salt; mix into batter; stir thoroughly. Add vanilla, nuts and bars. Beat together well. Bake in a greased and floured 9 inch tube pan at 325° for an hour or until done. Frost with Cream Cheese Frosting.

Cream Cheese Frosting:

1 (8 oz.) pkg. cream cheese
1 box 4X sugar
1 tsp. vanilla

½ stick oleo
1 c. pecans (small pieces)

Cream together cream cheese and oleo; add sugar, nuts and vanilla. Spread between layers and on top.

JoAnn Thompson

MOLASSES CAKE

1½ c. molasses
1 c. brown sugar
4 eggs
1 tsp. ginger
1 tsp. allspice

Cooked apples, mashed fine
1 c. oil
1 tsp. salt
1 tsp. soda
½ c. buttermilk

Mix together molasses, brown sugar and eggs. Mix together ginger, allspice and cinnamon; add to the molasses mixture. Dissolve soda in buttermilk; add salt and oil; combine mixtures. Pour mixture into greased and floured skillet and bake at 350° until done. Make either 2 or 3 layers. When done, let cool. Take cooked, mashed apples and spread between the layers and on top.

Opal Thompson

MOLASSES CAKE

1 c. butter
¾ c. sugar
3 eggs, beaten slightly
1 c. molasses
3 c. all-purpose flour
1 tsp. baking soda

1 tsp. cinnamon
¾ tsp. nutmeg
¾ tsp. allspice
¾ tsp. ground cloves
1 c. milk
1 c. raisins

Preheat oven to 350°. Cream butter with sugar. Beat in eggs and molasses. Sift all dry ingredients together. Alternately beat dry ingredients and milk, a little at a time, into the batter. Mix well. Add raisins. Pour batter into a greased 9 inch square baking pan. Bake for 50 to 60 minutes. Serves 6 to 8.

Beth Howard

MONKEY COFFEE CAKE

1 can biscuits
½ c. brown sugar

2 or 3 Tbsp. cinnamon
3 Tbsp. butter, melted

Take canned biscuits and cut each biscuit into several pieces. Grease baking pan lightly and put cut up pieces in it. Mix sugar and cinnamon together; sprinkle over biscuits and between them. Melt butter and pour over top and let it run down in the sugar mixture. Bake in about 350° oven for about 20 minutes or until done.

Mrs. Conder

MOUNTAIN DEW CAKE

1 box orange layer cake mix
1 box instant coconut cream
    pie filling
1 c. pure vegetable
    shortening

4 eggs
1 can Mountain Dew

Mix ingredients. Pour batter into 3 greased and floured layer cake pans. Bake at 350° for 30 minutes.

Filling:

1 (8 oz.) can crushed pineapple 1½ c. sugar	1 stick butter 1 (3½ oz.) can coconut 3 Tbsp. flour

Bring to a boil about 5 minutes and stir. Let cool and ice cake.

Phyllis L. Davis

NANNY'S CHOCOLATE CAKE

½ c. shortening 1¼ c. sugar 2 eggs 2 sq. chocolate, melted	1¾ c. flour ½ tsp. salt 1 tsp. baking soda ¾ c. milk

Cream shortening and sugar. Add eggs, 1 at a time, and beat well. Add dry ingredients and milk alternating. Stir in melted chocolate. Bake in tube pan or square pan for 45 to 50 minutes at 350°.

Wilma Crowdus

NUTTY ORANGE-GLAZED DELIGHT

2 c. *sifted* self-rising cake
   flour*
1 c. coarsely chopped pecans
1 tsp. ground cinnamon
⅛ tsp. ground allspice
1 c. vegetable oil
	4 eggs
	2 (4½ oz. each) jars baby
	   food plums with tapioca
	1½ c. sugar
	Orange Glaze (recipe follows)

1. Preheat oven to slow (325°). Grease and flour a 12 cup (10 inch) kugelhopf or Bundt pan.

2. Combine ½ cup of the flour and pecans in a bowl; stir well to coat pecans; reserve.

3. Sift remaining 1½ cups flour, cinnamon and allspice onto wax paper; reserve.

4. Beat oil, eggs, plums and sugar in large bowl until light and fluffy. Mix in flour-spice mixture, ⅓ at a time, until blended. Stir in pecan mixture. Turn into prepared pan.

5. Bake in preheated slow oven (325°) for 1½ to 1¾ hours or until top springs back when lightly touched with fingertip, and cake tester inserted in cake comes out clean. Let cool in pan on wire rack 10 minutes.

Loosen around edges with thin spatula; invert onto rack. Cool to room temperature. Drizzle Orange Glaze over top. Garnish with orange slices, pecans and grated orange rind, if you wish.

Orange Glaze: Combine 1 cup 10X (confectioners) sugar and ¼ teaspoon finely grated orange rind in small bowl. Gradually stir in about 2 tablespoons orange juice until smooth and pouring consistency.

Note: This cake has been popular in Alabama for many years. The original recipe called for prunes instead of plums, but the cake can be made with prunes and apricots too.

* For the self-rising cake flour, you can substitute the following: Sift together 2 cups *sifted* cake flour, 1 teaspoon baking powder, 1 teaspoon baking soda and ½ teaspoon salt.

Rowena Pipes

OATMEAL CAKE

Pour 1¼ cups hot water over 1 cup regular oats; let stand until cool.

Cream together:

1 stick butter
1 c. brown sugar

1 c. white sugar

Mix with oats and add:

2 eggs
1 tsp. vanilla
1⅓ c. flour

1 tsp. cinnamon
½ tsp. salt

Beat and bake in greased or floured pan 30 minutes at 350°. Spread top of cake when done and brown in oven.

Topping:

1 c. brown sugar
1 c. coconut
½ c. nuts

4 Tbsp. butter
½ c. cream

Jan Campbell

OATMEAL CAKE

1 c. oats
1¼ c. boiling water
½ c. margarine
1 c. brown sugar
1 c. white sugar
2 eggs

1½ c. flour
1 tsp. cinnamon
½ tsp. salt
1 tsp. soda
1 c. chopped nuts

Pour oats in bowl; add boiling water and let stand for 20 minutes. Combine margarine, eggs, sugar and oats. Mix flour, cinnamon, salt, and soda. Add to oat mixture. Stir in nuts. Pour in greased 13x9 inch pan and bake at 350° for 35 minutes or until done.

Icing - Mix together:

½ c. margarine
1 c. packed brown sugar
½ c. milk

1 tsp. vanilla
½ c. chopped nuts

Spread on cake. Cook under broiler about 3 minutes or until golden brown.

Madeline Ogden

OATMEAL CAKE

1⅓ c. boiling water
1 c. quick cooking oats
½ c. margarine, softened
1 c. granulated sugar
1 c. light brown sugar
2 eggs

1⅓ c. all-purpose flour
1 tsp. soda
1 tsp. salt
½ tsp. cinnamon
1 tsp. vanilla

Pour boiling water over oats and let stand 15 minutes. Cream margarine with sugar; add eggs, flour, spices, oatmeal and vanilla. Mix well. Grease and flour a 9x12x2 inch baking pan. Bake at 325° for 35 minutes or until toothpick inserted comes out clean.

Topping:

1½ c. light brown sugar
6 Tbsp. margarine, melted
¼ c. evaporated cream (Pet, etc.)

½ c. chopped pecans
½ c. coconut
1 tsp. vanilla

Mix together and spread on cake while warm. Put under broiler for 5 minutes.

Brownie - Lois Bruner

OATMEAL CAKE

1¼ c. boiling water
1 c. quick oats
1 stick margarine
1 c. brown sugar
1 c. granulated sugar
2 eggs, beaten

1½ c. plain flour
1 tsp. soda
¼ tsp. salt
1 tsp. cinnamon
½ tsp. nutmeg
1 tsp. vanilla

Pour boiling water over oats. Then add margarine. Stir until melted. Add the rest of the ingredients and pour into a greased and floured 9x13 inch pan. Bake at 350° for 30 to 40 minutes.

Topping:

1 (4 oz.) pkg. or can coconut
1½ c. brown sugar
1 small pkg. chopped pecans

1 small can Pet milk
5 Tbsp. margarine

Bring to boil and boil 8 to 10 minutes; add nuts and coconut. Spread on cake while still hot. Put back into oven for just a short time. Remove when topping starts a bubbly stage.

Donna Browning

DUTCH OATMEAL CAKE

1½ c. boiling water
1 c. quick rolled oats
½ c. shortening
1 c. packed brown sugar
1 c. sugar

1⅓ c. sifted flour
1 tsp. soda
½ tsp. salt
1 tsp. cinnamon
2 eggs, well beaten

Pour boiling water over dates; allow to cool. Cream shortening; add sugar; beat until fluffy. Sift flour, soda, salt and cinnamon together and add eggs to cream mixture. Mix well; add oats and flour; mix well. Pour into greased and floured 9x11 inch pan. Bake at 350°.

Frosting:

6 Tbsp. melted butter	1 tsp. vanilla
¼ c. canned cream	1 c. flaked coconut
½ c. packed brown sugar	½ c. chopped nuts

Combine all ingredients; spread on cooled cake and place in oven (on broil) until frosting bubbles.

Dollie D. Billiter

OLD FASHION CAKE

2 c. plain flour	1 c. sugar
1 Tbsp. baking powder	2 eggs
½ tsp. salt	1 tsp. vanilla
½ c. margarine	¾ c. milk

Sift flour, baking powder and salt together. Cream together margarine and sugar until light and fluffy. Beat in eggs, 1 at a time. Add vanilla to milk and alternate with flour, mixing enough to blend. Pour into 2 greased 8 inch pans. Bake in preheated 350° oven for 25 to 30 minutes. Cool and frost.

Caramel Icing:

3½ c. brown sugar	½ c. margarine
½ pt. cream	1 Tbsp. vanilla

Mix all ingredients together; cook icing mixture to soft boil stage. Pour in platter; let stand about 5 minutes. Beat until spreading consistency.

Travis Robertson

OLD FASHION STACK CAKE

½ c. shortening	2 tsp. baking powder
½ c. sugar	½ tsp. soda
½ c. molasses	½ tsp. salt
1 egg, well beaten	1 tsp. ginger
½ c. buttermilk	1 tsp. nutmeg
3½ c. flour	Dried apples

Cream sugar and shortening together. Add eggs, molasses and buttermilk; mix well. Sift flour, baking powder, salt, soda, ginger and nutmeg together. Add to the other mixture. Mix well. This makes a stiff dough. Roll out and cut to fit a 9 inch pan. Bake at 350° for 10 to 12 minutes. When cool, stack the layers with old fashion dried apples that have been cooked, mashed, sweetened and spiced to taste.

Note: Highly spiced and sweetened applesauce can be used instead of the old fashion dried apples.

Louisa Rosser

ORANGE CAKE

1 orange	1½ c. flour
1 c. sugar	¾ c. milk
1 egg	1 tsp. vanilla
1½ tsp. baking powder	½ c. walnuts
½ tsp. salt	½ c. white raisins
½ c. shortening	

Heat oven to 350°. Grease and flour 2 (8 inch) cake pans. Remove thin outer layer of peel from orange. Set orange aside for juice in frosting. Place peel in blender and chop at low speed. Remove and set aside. Place remaining ingredients plus 1 tablespoon of the chopped peel into blender container. Set speed on high and blend for 30 seconds. Pour into prepared pans and bake for 25 minutes or until cake is done. Cool 10 minutes before removing cakes from pans. When completely cooled, frost with Creamy Orange Frosting.

Creamy Orange Frosting:

½ c. (1 stick) butter, softened	3 Tbsp. orange juice
1 tsp. reserved orange peels	3 c. powdered sugar
2 tsp. vanilla	

In large bowl, mix all ingredients until smooth. If using an electric mixer, blend 30 seconds on low speed. Beat 3 minutes on high speed, scraping bowl occasionally. Spread between layers and over top and sides of completely cooled cake.

Norma T. Hibbs

ORANGE CHIFFON CAKE DESSERT

1 orange chiffon cake	1 pt. whipped cream,
1 small can frozen orange	whipped stiff
juice	1 pkg. frozen coconut
1 small bottle 7-Up	
1 (15 oz.) bag miniature	
marshmallows	

Melt orange juice in 7-Up over low heat. Add marshmallows and stir until almost melted. Cool. Whip cream and fold in preceding. Put ½ cake, broken in pieces, in large pan. Then layer cream mixture, then rest of cake, then rest of cream mixture on top. Cover with coconut. Put in icebox for several hours or overnight. Serves 15 to 20.

This freezes well.

Betsy Wells

MANDARIN ORANGE CAKE

1 box Duncan Hines yellow
    cake mix
1 stick butter
4 eggs

Juice of 2 small cans
    mandarin oranges
Mandarin oranges

Mix together at medium speed, use 3 (8 inch) cake pans. Place oranges in batter. Put cake mix over oranges to keep from burning. Bake 20 to 25 minutes at 375°. Do not overcook.

Icing:

1 large can crushed
    pineapple (including
    juice)
2 small boxes instant vanilla
    pudding

¾ ctn. large Cool Whip
    (frozen kind)

Mix all of preceding together. Make sure cake has cooled before icing. Keep cake in refrigerator.

Bev Sowders

ORANGE PINEAPPLE CAKE

1 box Duncan Hines yellow
    butter cake mix
4 eggs
¾ c. cooking oil
1 can mandarin oranges and
    juice

1 box instant vanilla pudding
1 can crushed pineapple,
    drained
1 small ctn. Cool Whip

Combine cake mix, eggs, cooking oil and mandarin oranges. Mix well. Mix about 5 minutes. Grease and flour 3 (8 inch) cake pans and bake in 350° oven for 30 to 35 minutes. Cool and ice. Mix pudding and pineapple well and add Cool Whip, then ice layers. Refrigerate cake.

Mary Baxter

ORANGE SLICE CAKE

1 c. butter or margarine
2 c. sugar
4 eggs
1 tsp. soda
½ c. buttermilk
3½ c. all-purpose flour
1 lb. dates, chopped

1 lb. candy orange slices,
  chopped
2 c. chopped nuts
1 can flaked coconut
1 c. fresh orange juice
2 c. powdered sugar

Cream butter and 2 cups sugar until smooth. Add eggs, 1 at a time, beating well after each addition. Dissolve soda in buttermilk and add to creamed mixture. Place flour in large bowl and add dates, orange slices and nuts; stir to coat each piece. Add flour mixture and coconut to creamed mixture. This makes a very stiff dough that should be mixed with the hands. Put in a greased and floured 13x9x3 inch pan. Bake at 250° for 2½ to 3 hours. Combine orange juice and powdered sugar; pour over hot cake. Let stand in pan overnight.

Mark A. Cowan

OUT OF THIS WORLD CAKE

4 c. graham cracker crumbs
2 c. sugar
4 beaten eggs
2 sticks melted margarine
1 tsp. baking powder

1 c. milk
1 c. coconut
1 c. chopped pecans
1 tsp. vanilla

Combine graham cracker crumbs and sugar. Add melted margarine, then beaten eggs. Add rest of ingredients in order given. Pour into greased and floured 9x13 inch pan. Bake at 350° for 35 to 40 minutes.

Icing:

1 (No. 2) can crushed
  pineapple (undrained)

1 c. sugar
4 Tbsp. flour

Cook over medium heat until thick and pour over warm cake. Cake best when set a couple of days.

Donna Browning

PEA PICKING CAKE

1 box Duncan Hines yellow
   cake mix
1 can (regular) mandarin
   oranges and juice

1½ c. oil
4 eggs

Mix all this and pour into 3 cake pans. Bake in 350° oven.

Icing:

1 large can crushed
   pineapple, drained

1 box instant vanilla pudding
1 large ctn. Cool Whip

Mix all this together and put on cake.

Clara Nance

PEANUT BUTTER BROWNIE CAKE

½ c. butter, softened
1 c. sugar
1 tsp. vanilla
2 eggs

1¼ c. unsifted flour
⅛ tsp. baking soda
¾ c. chocolate syrup
2 c. peanut butter chips

Cream butter, sugar and vanilla. Add eggs. Beat well. Combine flour and soda. Add alternately with chocolate syrup to creamed mixture. Stir in 1 cup of chips. (Save the other cup for frosting.) Pour batter into greased 13x9 inch pan. Bake at 350° for 30 to 35 minutes.

Frosting:

⅓ c. sugar
¼ c. evaporated milk
2 Tbsp. butter

1 c. peanut butter chips
1 Tbsp. vanilla

Combine sugar, evaporated milk and butter in a small saucepan. Stir over medium heat until it comes to a full boil. Remove from heat and quickly add peanut butter chips and vanilla. Beat and spread while cake is still warm.

Donna Barrett

PICNIC DELIGHT CAKE

2 c. sifted flour
2½ tsp. baking powder
½ tsp. salt
½ c. butter
1 egg
1 c. sugar
¾ c. buttermilk

1 tsp. vanilla
12 marshmallows, cut up
½ c. semi-sweet chocolate
  bits
½ c. brown sugar
2 Tbsp. butter
1 c. chopped nuts

Sift together flour, baking powder and salt. Cream butter and 1 cup sugar until well blended. Add egg and beat 1 minute. Combine buttermilk and vanilla; add alternately with dry ingredients to creamed mixture, beginning and ending with dry ingredients. Blend thoroughly after each addition. Add marshmallows and chocolate bits, blending into batter evenly. Spread in a well greased, floured 12x8x2 inch pan. Combine brown sugar, butter, and nuts. Sprinkle over batter in pan. Bake in moderate oven, 350°F., 45 to 50 minutes. Cut in squares for serving.

Martha Hooper

PINEAPPLE CAKE

In a large mixing bowl, beat 2 eggs until light and fluffy. Add contents of 20 ounce can of crushed pineapple (undrained), 2 cups of all-purpose flour, 1 cup of granulated sugar, 1 cup of brown sugar, and 2 teaspoons of baking soda. Mix well by hand. Then stir in 1 cup of chopped nuts and spread evenly in an ungreased 13x9x2 inch baking pan. Bake in 350° oven for 45 or 50 minutes, or until toothpick inserted in middle comes out clean. After cake cools, cover with frosting.

Cream Cheese Ginger Frosting: In small mixer bowl, beat together 3 ounce package of cream cheese (softened), ¼ cup of butter or margarine, and 1 teaspoon of vanilla. Mix with electric mixer, if desired, add 2 cups of powdered sugar and ½ teaspoon of ground ginger. Spread on cooled cake and sprinkle few nuts on top.

Mattie Hammack

442

PINEAPPLE COCONUT CAKE

1½ c. sugar
2 c. flour
2½ tsp. cinnamon
1 tsp. baking soda
1½ c. oil
1 (4 oz.) can shredded
    coconut
1 (8 oz.) can crushed
    pineapple
½ tsp. salt
4 eggs

Combine all ingredients in a large bowl. Blend with electric mixer at low speed until all ingredients are combined. Turn mixer to medium and continue until smooth, scraping the side of the bowl. Pour into 3 greased and floured 9 inch round pans. Bake about 30 minutes in pre-heated oven (350°).

Cream Cheese Icing:

⅔ stick margarine
1 (8 oz.) pkg. cream cheese
1 lb. powdered sugar
2 tsp. vanilla
1 c. chopped pecans

Whip margarine and cream cheese together. Add remaining ingredients and beat well.

Bridget Pumphrey

PINEAPPLE UPSIDE DOWN CAKE

¼ lb. butter
1 c. brown sugar
1 can sliced pineapple
3 eggs
1 c. sugar
5 Tbsp. pineapple juice
1 c. cake flour
1 tsp. baking powder

Melt butter in 9 inch cake pan. Spread brown sugar evenly over butter, then place sliced pineapple over brown sugar. Beat egg yolks, and add sugar, pineapple juice and flour sifted with baking powder, then fold in stiffly beaten egg whites. Pour over pineapple and brown sugar; bake in moderate oven (375°) for 20 minutes.

Wanda Harris

PINEAPPLE UPSIDE DOWN CAKE

1 stick margarine
1 c. brown sugar
Pineapple slices
3 eggs, separated
5 Tbsp. pineapple juice

1 c. sugar
1 c. flour
1 tsp. baking powder
¼ tsp. salt

Melt margarine in heavy skillet. Add brown sugar and arrange pineapple slices and maraschino cherries to cover bottom of skillet. Blend together egg yolks, pineapple juice and sugar. Add flour, baking powder and salt. Fold in 3 stiffly beaten egg whites. Pour batter over pineapple slices. Bake 30 to 35 minutes at 350°.

Donna Browning

PINEAPPLE WHIPPED CREAM CAKE

1 (8 inch) angel food cake
8¼ oz. can crushed
    pineapple
1 c. milk

½ pt. whipping cream,
    whipped
3¾ oz. pkg. vanilla pudding

Whip cream and fold in pineapple. Prepare instant pudding, using cup of milk instead of amount called for on package. Fold into cream-pineapple mixture. Slice cake crosswise twice, making 3 layers. Spread pineapple filling between layers; cover top and sides of cake. Refrigerate for several hours. Then serve.

Oleta Bryan

EFFIE'S PINEAPPLE CAKE

2 c. flour
2 c. sugar
2 eggs
2 tsp. baking soda

1 (1 lb. 4 oz.) can crushed
    pineapple in heavy syrup
    (*do not* drain)

Mix preceding ingredients and bake in a greased oblong pan 25 to 30 minutes at 350°.

Icing:

8 oz. cream cheese
½ stick butter or oleo
1 tsp. vanilla

1½ c. confectioners sugar (or
    more until reaches
    spreading consistency)

Nancy A. Thiry

444

PINEAPPLE UPSIDE-DOWN CAKE

⅓ c. butter
¾ c. brown sugar
Pineapple slices (and juice)
Maraschino cherries
2 eggs

1 c. sugar
1½ c. flour
¼ tsp. salt
2 tsp. baking powder
¼ c. melted butter

Cook ⅓ cup butter and ¾ cup brown sugar a short time. Spread evenly over bottom of cake pan. Place drained pineapple slices over sugar and butter mixture. Place a maraschino cherry in each hole of pineapple slice. Beat 2 egg yolks and add 1 cup sugar and ½ cup juice. Sift 1½ cups flour with ¼ teaspoon salt and 2 teaspoons baking powder. Add flour mixture to eggs and sugar. Add ¼ cup melted butter. Fold in 2 stiffly beaten egg whites. Bake for 30 to 35 minutes at 375°.

Mrs. Morris (Laura) Futrell

PISTACHIO CAKE

1 box white cake mix
1 c. vegetable oil
3 eggs
1 (8 oz.) bottle club soda or
    Coke

2 boxes instant pistachio
    pudding

Mix well. Bake at 350° in preheated oven until cake tests done.

Icing:

1 pkg. dry Dream Whip
1 pkg. pistachio instant
    pudding

1 c. milk

Mix all of preceding. Beat until spreading consistency.

Sharon Shepherd

PLUM CAKE

3 c. sifted flour
2 c. sugar
1 c. buttermilk
1 c. plum juice
1 c. black walnuts
2 eggs

1 tsp. salt
2 tsp. soda
1 tsp. nutmeg
1 tsp. cinnamon
½ c. Wesson oil

Put all ingredients into a bowl. Mix well. Bake in a 350° oven in a 13½ x 9 ½ inch pan, loaf pan or large tube pan.

Opal Willis

LITTLE PLUM CAKES

4 c. flour, sifted
1 lb. powdered sugar
1 lb. butter
1 lb. currants
1 lb. raisins

1 tsp. nutmeg
Rind of 1 lemon, grated
12 eggs (unbeaten)
3 Tbsp. milk

Mix 1 cup flour with the fruit. Cream the butter until soft. Add lemon rind and nutmeg. Add flour, sugar, and eggs alternately. Mix in fruit. Drop into small cookies. Bake at 450° until brown, then reduce heat to 350° and finish baking.

Cristy Lewis

PURPLE PLUM CAKE

2 c. self-rising flour
2 c. sugar
1 c. oil
1 large can purple plums,
    drained and seeds
    removed

1 tsp. cinnamon
1 tsp. cloves
3 eggs
1 c. chopped pecans
1½ c. powdered sugar
Lemon or orange juice

Combine flour, sugar, oil, plums, cinnamon, cloves, eggs, and pecans. Bake in Bundt pan in 350° oven for 1 hour. Glaze with powdered sugar mixed with lemon or orange juice.

Hazel Walker

446

SOUTHERN PLUM CAKE

2 c. sugar
2 c. self-rising flour
1 c. Crisco oil
1 c. chopped pecans
3 eggs

1 c. raisins
1 tsp. cinnamon
½ tsp. cloves
2 small jars plum baby food
  (Heinz)

Mix all together; bake in Bundt or tube pan at 350° for 1 hour.

Glaze:

1 c. confectioners sugar

2 Tbsp. milk

Mix and pour over cake.

Mary T. Thompson

POUND CAKE

3 sticks margarine
3 c. sugar
6 eggs
3 c. self-rising flour

1 c. evaporated milk
  (undiluted)
2 Tbsp. lemon juice
1 tsp. vanilla

Cream margarine and sugar until light and fluffy. Add eggs; beat after adding each one. Add flour alternately with milk. Add juice and vanilla; mix well. Pour into a 10 inch tube pan and bake at 350° for 1 to 1½ hours or until done, when a toothpick comes out clean.

Daisy Mace

BROWN SUGAR POUND CAKE

3 sticks butter
1 lb. light brown sugar
½ c. white sugar
5 eggs

2 tsp. vanilla
3 c. flour
½ tsp. baking powder
1 c. milk

Cream butter and sugar thoroughly. Add eggs, 1 at a time, beating at medium speed. Add flavoring. Sift dry ingredients together; add to creamed mixture alternately with milk. Mix well. Place in a large tube pan. Bake at 325° for 1 ½ hours.

Mary Lauder

BUTTERNUT POUND CAKE

6 eggs, separated
3 sticks butter
3 c. cake flour
3 c. sugar

1 (8 oz.) pkg. cream cheese
2 tsp. vanilla butternut
 flavoring

Beat egg whites until stiff. Cream butter, cream cheese and sugar. Beat until light and fluffy. Add egg yolks and flavoring, then flour. Beat well. Fold in egg whites. Pour into lightly greased tube pan or loaf pans.

Anita Picklesimer

CHERRY CHIP POUND CAKE

2½ c. Bisquick
3 eggs, beaten
2 c. sugar
2¼ c. shortening

1¼ c. milk
1 tsp. salt
1 Tbsp. vanilla
1½ jars maraschino cherries

Blend sugar and shortening together; add flour, vanilla and salt. Add beaten eggs. Chop cherries and add cherries and juice to batter; gradually blend milk in. Preheat oven to 350° and bake 25 to 30 minutes.

Ann Brawand

CREAM CHEESE POUND CAKE

3 sticks butter
1 (8 oz.) pkg. cream cheese
3 c. sugar
6 eggs

1 tsp. vanilla
1 tsp. almond flavoring
3 c. flour

Cream butter, cream cheese and sugar. Add eggs, 1 at a time, and blend. Add flavorings and flour and blend until smooth. Do not overbeat. Pour into a greased and floured tube pan. Bake at 325° for 1¼ hours or until tests done.

Francele Black

FOOLPROOF POUND CAKE

3 sticks butter
1 lb. pkg. 4X sugar
7 eggs

1 lb. flour
¼ tsp. salt
2 tsp. vanilla

Cream butter; add sugar all at once; cream well. Add eggs, 1 at a time; beat well after each. Fill sugar box with flour not sifted. Add gradually, mixing well. Add vanilla and salt; beat 1 minute. Bake at 325° for 1½ or 1¾ hours. Ice if preferred.

Cristy Lewis

IRISH POUND CAKE

Mix together:

½ lb. creamed butter	**½ tsp. mace**
1⅔ c. sugar	**1 tsp. vanilla**

By hand, beat in 5 eggs (room temperature), 1 at a time. Add 2 cups sifted flour. Grease shallow baking dish. Bake at 350° for 25 to 30 minutes. Sprinkle lightly with powdered sugar.

Patricia Ryan

LEMON POUND CAKE

4 eggs	**¾ c. water**
1 (2 layer size) pkg. yellow cake mix	**⅓ c. salad oil**
1 (3¾ or 3⅝ oz.) pkg. *instant* lemon pudding mix (dry)	**Lemon Glaze**

Beat eggs until thick and lemon colored. Add cake mix, pudding mix, water, and oil; beat 10 minutes at medium speed on electric mixer. Pour into ungreased 10 inch tube pan with removable bottom. Bake at 350° about 50 minutes. *Leaving cake on pan bottom,* remove sides of pan from hot cake. Using 2 tined fork, prick holes in top of cake. Drizzle Lemon Glaze over top and spread on sides of cake. Cool completely; remove pan bottom. Garnish with *thin* slices of lemon.

Lemon Glaze: Heat 2 cups sifted confectioners sugar and ⅓ cup lemon juice to boiling.

Velma Pace

SEVEN-UP POUND CAKE

3 c. sugar	**1 tsp. coconut flavoring**
3 sticks margarine	**1 tsp. vanilla extract**
5 eggs	**½ tsp. salt**
1 tsp. lemon extract	**3 c. self-rising flour**
1 tsp. butter flavoring	**7 oz. 7-Up**

Mix all ingredients together well. Bake at 300° in well greased and floured tube or Bundt pan 1½ hours or until done, starting in a *cold* oven. Cool on wire rack before removing from pan.

Mary Lauder

PRALINE CHEESECAKE WITH PRALINE CREAM TOPPING

½ c. ground pecans
1 pkg. (10) graham crackers,
   finely crushed
¼ c. brown sugar
½ stick butter, melted
2 (8 oz.) blocks cream cheese
   (room temperature)
½ lb. (½ box) brown sugar,
   sieved

4 eggs
½ c. heavy cream
1 tsp. vanilla
1 tsp. praline liqueur
   (optional)
¼ c. sifted flour
1 c. heavy cream
½ c. sieved brown sugar

Heat oven to 350°. In the bottom of an 8 or 9 inch spring form pan, stir together the pecans, cracker crumbs and ¼ cup brown sugar. Pour melted butter over mixture. Use fingers to fuse butter and crumbs into a somewhat dry mixture. Use knuckles to press crumbs on bottom of pan and partially up sides. Bake 10 minutes. Remove and cool. Reduce oven temperature to 300°.

Meanwhile, beat cream cheese and ½ pound brown sugar until smooth. Beat in eggs, 1 at a time, then beat in cream. Fold in remaining ingredients; pour over baked crust and bake between 1 hour and 75 minutes. Remove from oven; cool and chill.

For topping, whip cream to soft peaks. While beating, gradually add brown sugar until cream forms medium stiff peaks and is smooth. Spread over cheesecake. Chill well, at least 2 hours. Remove springform band and slice in wedges.

Shirley Harrison

PRUNE CAKE

2½ c. flour
2 c. sugar
1 c. buttermilk
1 c. Wesson oil
3 whole eggs
1 tsp. soda, mixed in
   buttermilk

1 tsp. cinnamon
1 tsp. allspice
1 tsp. nutmeg
½ tsp. salt
1 c. pecans, chopped
1 c. cooked chopped prunes

Mix all ingredients together well. Pour into a buttered cake pan and bake in slow oven (350°), for about 30 minutes or until done.

Icing:

½ c. buttermilk
½ tsp. soda, mixed in
   buttermilk

1 c. sugar
1 Tbsp. white Karo syrup
1 stick butter

Mix all ingredients and cook until it reaches a boil. Boil until it forms soft ball in cold water. Pour over cake while hot. (Do not beat.)

Peggy Kessinger

PRUNE CAKE

2 c. sugar
2 c. flour (all-purpose)
1 tsp. salt
1 tsp. vanilla
1 tsp. soda
1 tsp. cinnamon
1 tsp. allspice

1 tsp. nutmeg
3 well beaten eggs
1 c. Mazola oil
1 c. buttermilk
1 c. prunes, cooked, cut in
   pieces

Stir all ingredients together with a spoon; do not use electric mixer. Place ingredients in a 13x9x3 inch pan. Bake in 350° oven for 1 hour (when toothpick comes out clean). Then make icing and pour over cake while still hot. Holes may be made in cake to allow icing to run into cake.

Icing:

½ c. buttermilk
1 c. sugar
1 stick margarine

½ tsp. soda
1 tsp. vanilla

Cook 10 minutes.

Mark A. Cowan

PRUNE CAKE

1 c. Wesson oil
1½ c. sugar
3 eggs
1 c. buttermilk
2 c. sifted cake flour
1 c. cooked prunes
1 c. chopped nuts

1 tsp. soda
1 tsp. salt
1 tsp. cinnamon
1 tsp. nutmeg
1 tsp. allspice or cloves
1 tsp. vanilla

Mix Wesson oil, sugar, and eggs; blend well. Sift dry ingredients. Add to Wesson oil mixture, alternating with buttermilk. Add vanilla; blend. Fold in prunes and nuts. Bake in 9x13 inch ungreased pan or 2 (9x7 inch) ungreased pans. Bake 1 hour at 300°. Serve from pan.

Topping:

1 c. sugar	1 tsp. white corn syrup
1 stick oleo	½ tsp. soda
½ c. buttermilk	1 tsp. vanilla

Combine ingredients in saucepan. Cook over medium heat; stir while cooking. Cook to a soft ball stage. Do not beat. Pour over cake. Be careful not to overcook.

Zama Picklesimer

PRUNE CAKE

1½ c. white sugar	1½ tsp. nutmeg
1 c. salad oil (Wesson oil)	1½ tsp. cinnamon
3 eggs	1½ tsp. vanilla
1 c. buttermilk	2 c. flour
2 small jars baby food prunes	1 c. nuts
1½ tsp. soda	

Mix each ingredient as added; bake for 20 minutes at 350°.

Icing:

1 c. white sugar	1 stick butter
½ c. buttermilk	5 Tbsp. Karo syrup (white)

Cook all together and boil hard for 2 minutes. Pour over cake while both are hot. Pour icing slowly over cake and lift up corners of cake with tablespoon to allow icing to soak into cake; also may punch holes to allow icing to soak into cakes. This makes cake more moist.

Patsy Akers

PUDDING CAKE

1 box yellow cake mix	1 c. water
1 box lemon instant pudding mix	4 eggs
¾ c. Wesson oil	½ c. orange juice
	1 c. sugar

Mix all ingredients well. Add 4 eggs (beaten). Pour into Bundt pan. Bake at 350° for about 30 minutes or until done. Let cake cool. Leave in pan and punch holes in top with sharp object. Dissolve ½ cup orange juice and 1 cup sugar in saucepan. Leave cake in pan and pour glaze over cake.

Tina Slone

PUMPKIN CAKE

4 eggs
1 c. oil
2 tsp. baking soda
½ tsp. salt

2 c. sugar
2 c. flour
2 tsp. cinnamon
2 c. pumpkin

Beat eggs together with sugar until blended. Add oil. Continue to beat. Sift dry ingredients together and thoroughly mix with egg mixture. Add pumpkin. Blend well and pour into greased and floured pan. Bake at 350° for 55 minutes. Let stand to cool.

Cream Cheese Icing:

1 (8 oz.) pkg. cream cheese
1 stick margarine, softened
1 lb. powdered sugar

1 tsp. vanilla
1 c. pecans, broken

Combine all ingredients.

Lila Mae White

PUMPKIN CAKE

4 eggs
1 c. oil
2 tsp. soda
½ tsp. salt
2 c. sugar

2 c. flour (all-purpose)
2 tsp. cinnamon
2 c. pumpkin
½ c. chopped nuts

Beat eggs and sugar together; add oil and mix well. Add dry ingredients and beat well. Add pumpkin and nuts. Mix well. Pour into greased Bundt pan. Bake at 350° for 55 minutes. Cool 10 minutes, then turn out on rack.

Icing:

1 (8 oz.) pkg. cream cheese
1 stick butter

1 lb. box confectioners sugar
1 tsp. vanilla

Mix all ingredients well.

Gwen Levell

PUMPKIN CAKE

4 eggs
2 c. sugar
1 tsp. soda
2 tsp. cinnamon
2 c. flour

1 c. cooking oil
½ tsp. salt
2 c. pumpkin or 1 can
  pumpkin

Beat eggs with sugar. Add all rest of the ingredients, pumpkin last. Bake in Bundt cake pan 50 to 55 minutes at 350°.

Cream Cheese Frosting:

¾ box powdered sugar
1 stick margarine (room
  temperature)
1 tsp. vanilla

3 oz. pkg. cream cheese
1 c. chopped pecans or
  walnuts

Combine margarine and powdered sugar. Add vanilla and cream cheese. Mix well. Add nuts last. Frost cooled cake.

Donna Browning

PUNCH BOWL CAKE

1 small jar maraschino
  cherries
1 small pkg. nuts (pecans,
  walnuts or whatever you
  desire)
1 box pineapple cake mix
2 large boxes instant vanilla
  pudding, mixed

according to pkg.
  directions
2 cans cherry pie filling
1 large can crushed
  pineapple, drained
1 large ctn. Cool Whip

Bake cake in 9x13 inch pan. Cool; cut in half. Crumble half of cake in bottom of punch bowl. Top with half (1 box) of pudding. Then add 1 can pie filling on top of cake. Next, add ½ can crushed pineapple.

Then layer cake, pudding, pie filling, and crushed pineapple again. Top and spread with Cool Whip. Garnish with cherries with stems up and chopped nuts. Refrigerate.

Norma T. Hibbs

RED DEVILS FOOD CAKE

1 c. sugar	2 tsp. soda
2 c. cake flour	Pinch of salt
4 Tbsp. cocoa	1 c. Miracle Whip dressing
1 tsp. vanilla	1 c. hot water

Add dry ingredients, then dressing and water. Add vanilla and stir well. Bake in oven (350° or 400°) until done or about 30 minutes.

Spice Cake - Use recipe for Red Devils Food, but leave out cocoa and add:

1 tsp. cinnamon	1 c. raisins, soaked
1 tsp. allspice	1 c. jam
½ tsp. nutmeg	1 c. nuts
½ tsp. cloves	

Mattie Hammack

SAUSAGE CAKE

3 c. brown sugar	1 c. fresh coconut
1 c. jam	¼ c. cocoa
1 c. pork sausage	2 tsp. soda
1 c. raisins	1 tsp. nutmeg
3½ c. flour	1 tsp. cinnamon
1 c. coffee	½ tsp. cloves

Bake from 1½ to 3 hours. This cake is better if kept 3 or 4 weeks before cutting. Bake in a slow oven.

Elizabeth Shellman, Paula White

SEVEN-UP CAKE

1 box yellow cake mix	1 box vanilla instant pudding
4 eggs	1 (10 oz.) bottle 7-Up

Mix together cake mix, 4 eggs, vanilla pudding and 7-Up. Grease and flour 2 cake pans and pour batter into pans. Bake in a preheated 350° oven until done. Let cool a few minutes, then put on a cake plate.

Frosting:

2 eggs
1½ c. sugar
1 Tbsp. flour
1 stick butter or margarine,
    melted

1 small can crushed
    pineapple

Mix together.

Linda Thompson

SEVEN-UP CAKE

1 box Duncan Hines lemon
    supreme cake mix
1 box instant pineapple
    pudding

¾ c. Wesson oil
4 eggs
1 (10 oz.) 7-Up

Mix well. Bake at 300° for 35 to 40 minutes. Makes 3 layers.

Icing:

1 stick butter
1 c. crushed pineapple (do
    not drain)
1½ c. sugar

1 Tbsp. flour
1½ c. coconut
1 c. pecans

Bring sugar, flour, butter and crushed pineapple to a boil and cook until thick. Boil no more than 5 minutes. Add coconut and pecans and ice cake.

Ollie Childress

SNOWBALL CAKE

2 env. Knox unflavored
    gelatine
4 Tbsp. cold water
1 c. boiling water
1 large can crushed
    pineapple (with juice)

1 c. sugar
3 tsp. lemon juice
Pinch of salt
4 pkg. Dream Whip
1 angel food cake

Mix together unflavored gelatine, 4 tablespoons cold water and 1 cup boiling water; set aside to cool. Tear the angel food cake into pieces and place in bottom of 13x9 inch pan. Make Dream Whip according to instructions on package. Fold the Dream Whip into other ingredients and pour over cake and chill in refrigerator overnight.

Pam Duer

456

SNOWBALL CAKE

2 env. Knox unflavored
   gelatine
4 Tbsp. cold water
1 c. boiling water
1 large can crushed
   pineapple (with juice)

1 c. sugar
3 tsp. lemon juice
Pinch of salt
4 env. Dream Whip
1 angel food cake

Add the Knox gelatine, cold water and boiling water together and set aside to cool. Break up the angel food cake into pieces and place in bottom of 13x9 inch pan. Make Dream Whip according to instructions on package. Fold together Dream Whip with all other ingredients and pour over cake. Chill in refrigerator overnight.

Bessie Litchford

SOUR CREAM CAKE

3 c. flour
3 c. sugar
1 c. butter

½ pt. sour cream
¼ tsp. soda
6 eggs, separated

Cream butter, sugar and egg yolks. Beat well. Add soda and flour alternately with sour cream. Beat egg whites and fold in. Bake at 300° for 1½ hours in greased and floured tube pan.

Filling and Topping:

⅓ c. brown sugar
¼ c. granulated sugar

1 tsp. cinnamon
1 c. nuts

If desired, pour half of batter into tube pan, then sprinkle with half of sugar mixture. Pour in remaining batter and top with remaining sugar mixture.

Donna Browning

SOUR CREAM CAKE

3 c. sifted flour
1 c. (8 oz. pkg.) sour cream
¼ tsp. soda
½ tsp. vanilla

3 c. sugar
1 c. butter
6 eggs, separated
½ tsp. mace (if desired)

Cream butter and sugar. Add egg *yolks,* 1 at a time, beating well after each addition. Sift flour. Add soda to sour cream and mix well. Add cream alternately with flour to sugar mixture. Beat egg *whites* until stiff, but not dry. Gently fold into cake batter. Add vanilla and mace. Put in a greased tube pan or 2 greased loaf pans. Bake in a 300° oven about 1 hour and 15 minutes or until cake tester comes out clean.

Ruth Ackerman

SOUR CREAM COFFEE CAKE

Cake:

½ c. butter or margarine, softened	1 tsp. baking soda
1 c. sugar	1 tsp. baking powder
2 eggs	½ tsp. salt
2 c. plain flour	1 c. sour cream
	1½ tsp. vanilla

Topping:

⅔ c. brown sugar	2 tsp. cinnamon
½ c. granulated sugar	2 c. chopped nuts (optional)

Cream butter and sugar; add eggs. Sift flour, soda, baking powder and salt together. Add to butter mixture alternately with sour cream. Add vanilla. Put half of batter into a buttered pan (11¾ x 7½ x ¾ inches). Sprinkle half of topping over batter. Add remaining batter and top with remaining topping. Bake in 325° oven for 40 minutes or until done.

Judy Damron

OLD FASHION STACK CAKE

¾ c. shortening	½ tsp. soda
1 c. sugar	2 tsp. baking powder
1 c. sorghum molasses	1 tsp. salt
3 eggs	3 c. applesauce, seasoned
1 c. milk	with spices
4 c. flour	

Mix flour, salt, soda and baking powder. Cream shortening; add sugar slowly; blend well. Add sorghum; mix well. Add eggs, 1 at a time; beat well. Add flour and milk alternately and beat until smooth. Pour mixture about ⅜ inch deep in a 9 inch greased and floured pan. Bake at 375° for 18 minutes. Makes 6 layers. When cool, spread applesauce generously between each layer and stack.

Gwen Mills

STRAWBERRY CAKE

1 box white cake mix
1 small box strawberry Jello
¾ c. Wesson oil
¾ c. milk

4 eggs, separated
1 c. shredded coconut
1 c. pecans, chopped
2 c. strawberries, halved

Combine cake mix and Jello. Mix together by hand. Add oil, milk and egg yolks; beat just enough to mix. In a separate bowl, mix coconut, nuts and strawberries. Put half of this mixture in batter; reserve the remaining half for frosting. Beat egg whites until stiff, but not dry. Fold into batter. Pour into 3 (8 or 9 inch) greased and floured cake pans. Bake 20 to 25 minutes at 350°.

Frosting:

½ stick margarine, softened
1 box powdered sugar

½ strawberry mixture

Cream margarine. Stir in powdered sugar. Add remaining half of strawberry mixture and beat well. Ice cooled cake.

Melanie Davis

STRAWBERRY CAKE

1 box white or yellow cake
    mix, sifted
4 eggs

1 c. Wesson oil
1 c. (10 oz. pkg.) strawberries
1 pkg. strawberry Jello

Mix all ingredients and pour in cake pans. Bake at 325° approximately 30 to 35 minutes.

Frosting:

1 box powdered sugar
1 stick margarine

½ c. frozen strawberries

Paula White

STRAWBERRY CAKE
(Three layer)

1 box white cake mix
4 Tbsp. self-rising flour
½ tsp. salt
1 c. Wesson oil
½ c. water

4 eggs
1 small box or 1 c.
    strawberries
1 (3 oz.) box strawberry Jello

Mix dry ingredients; add strawberries. Bake at 350° for 30 to 35 minutes.

Frosting:

1 small can Carnation milk
2 c. sugar
1 stick butter

1 large Tbsp. marshmallow
    cream

Cook milk, sugar and butter slowly for 15 minutes. Put in cold water and let stand for awhile, then beat rapidly until thickens. Beat in marshmallow cream and beat until thick enough to spread.

Mattie Hammack

STRAWBERRY CAKE

1 pkg. white cake mix
½ c. water
½ (10 oz.) pkg. frozen
    strawberries

¾ c. Wesson oil
1 pkg. strawberry Jello
4 eggs

Mix cake mix, water, Wesson oil, Jello and strawberries. Add whole eggs; beat well. Bake at 350° for 30 to 40 minutes.

Icing:

1 box confectioners sugar
½ pkg. strawberries

1 stick butter

J. W. Borden, Jr.

STRAWBERRY COOL WHIP CAKE

1 box white cake mix
1 small ctn. Cool Whip

1 box strawberry Jello
Fresh strawberries

Mix cake according to package directions. Bake in 9x13 inch pan. When cool, punch holes in cake. Mix Jello according to package directions and pour over cake. Cover with Cool Whip and top with fresh strawberries. Refrigerate.

Elaine Cady

STRAWBERRY FLAN CAKE

1 box yellow cake mix
  (pudding in the mix)
1 small box vanilla instant
  pudding

2 c. whipping cream
Fresh strawberries
1 can whipped cream
  (optional)

Bake yellow cake according to directions on box in 9x13 inch pan.

Topping: Mix vanilla instant pudding and whipping cream (instead of milk) according to directions on box. Spread on cooled cake. Cover topping with slices of fresh strawberries. Refrigerate for 2 hours.

Note: Add whipped cream as you serve if you wish. Keep leftover cake in refrigerator.

J. Faye Blevins

STRAWBERRY ICEBOX CAKE

Prepare yellow cake mix according to directions and bake in 13x9 inch pan. Prepare Jello (strawberry) using 1 cup boiling water, then 1 cup tap water. While cake is still warm, poke holes in it with fork. Pour Jello through holes. Use chilled glass bowl. Put 1 package French vanilla pudding (instant) and 1 package Dream Whip in bowl with 1 cup cold milk. Beat until stiff. Spread this mixture on cake. Use 1 package (or more if wanted) of fresh strawberries. Cut in halves and place on top of pudding mixture. Refrigerate and eat!

Peggy Van Meter

STRAWBERRY JAM CAKE

½ c. shortening
1 c. sugar
2 eggs
⅔ c. strawberry jam
⅔ c. chopped nuts
⅔ c. seedless raisins
2⅔ c. sifted flour
1 tsp. salt

4 tsp. baking powder
1½ tsp. cinnamon
½ tsp. cloves
1 tsp. nutmeg
½ tsp. allspice
⅔ c. milk
1 tsp. vanilla

Cream shortening and sugar. Add eggs; beat well. Add jam, nuts, and raisins. Beat well. Add dry ingredients with milk and vanilla. Bake about 40 minutes in a 375° oven.

When cool, cover with this frosting:

1½ c. brown sugar   3 Tbsp. butter
½ c. milk   ½ tsp. vanilla

Boil sugar, milk and butter together until syrup forms soft ball in water. Remove from fire; add vanilla and beat.

Lil Aarvig

TEXAS SHEET CAKE

Step 1:

2 c. sugar   ½ tsp. salt
2 c. plain flour

Mix.

Step 2:

2 eggs, beaten   1 tsp. baking soda
½ c. sour cream

Step 3 - Bring to boil 2 sticks butter and add:

4 Tbsp. cocoa   1 c. water

Pour Step 3 into Step 1. Then add Step 2. Stir well. Bake at 375° about 20 minutes in large cookie sheet.

Icing - Boil:

1 stick margarine   1 box powdered sugar
4 Tbsp. cocoa   1 tsp. vanilla
5 Tbsp. milk   ½ c. chopped nuts

Frost cake.

Mrs. Ron Martin

TEXAS SHEET CAKE

1 c. margarine   2 c. sugar
1 c. water   2 c. flour
4 Tbsp. cocoa   1½ tsp. salt
1 tsp. soda   1 tsp. vanilla
2 eggs   ½ c. buttermilk

Melt margarine. Add cocoa and water; bring to boil. Remove from heat and add rest of ingredients. Bake in sheet pan 20 to 25 minutes at 400°.

Frosting:

1 stick margarine	1 lb. box confectioners sugar
4 Tbsp. cocoa	1 tsp. vanilla
6 Tbsp. milk	1 c. nuts

Bring to boil. Add box of confectioners sugar, 1 teaspoon vanilla and nuts last. Pour over cake while hot.

Donna Browning

THE CAKE

1 pkg. lemon or yellow cake mix	4 eggs
	1 c. chopped nuts
1 c. oil	1 c. chocolate chips
1 c. sour cream	1 c. miniature marshmallows
1 pkg. vanilla instant pudding mix	Bread crumbs

Mix the cake mix, oil, sour cream, vanilla instant pudding and eggs for 3 minutes on low speed. Grease a 10 inch tube pan with oil and dust lightly with fine bread crumbs. Next, mix nuts and chocolate chips together. Pour half of batter in pan. Over this, pour half of the nuts and chocolate chips and 1 cup miniature marshmallows. Pour in rest of the batter and top with the rest of the nuts and chocolate chips. Bake for 1 hour at 350° or until toothpick comes out clean.

Ruth Ackerman

THREE DAY COCONUT CAKE

1 (2 layer) yellow butter cake mix	1 pt. sour cream
	2 c. sugar
6 or 7 oz. can coconut	1 large ctn. Cool Whip

Bake cake according to package instructions. Mix coconut mixture (coconut, sour cream, sugar and Cool Whip) and set aside. Split layers of cake when cool. (Makes 4 layers.) Spread mixture between layers. Then sprinkle extra on outside too if you like. Place in refrigerator in an airtight container for 3 days.

Maxine Welch

TIAMARIA CAKE

1 box Duncan Hines fudge
   cake mix
½ c. Crisco oil
1 (3 oz.) pkg. instant
   chocolate pudding mix
   (dry)
4 eggs
¾ c. strong coffee
¾ c. Tiamaria and creme de
   cacao (mixed equal
   parts)

½ c. powdered sugar
1 Tbsp. strong coffee
2 Tbsp. Tiamaria
⅓ c. butter or margarine
⅛ tsp. salt
3 c. powdered sugar
3 unsweetened chocolate
   squares (Hershey's)
¼ c. half & half
1 tsp. vanilla
1½ Tbsp. Tiamaria

To the cake mix, add the Crisco, instant chocolate pudding, 4 eggs, ¾ cup strong coffee and ¾ cup Tiamaria and creme de cacao, mixed equal parts. Mix, then beat 4 minutes at medium speed on mixer. Pour into greased and floured tube pan. Bake at 350° for 45 to 50 minutes. When removed from oven, this cake will fall. Cool. Punch holes all over top to bottom of the cake and drizzle the following mixture over the cake: Mix ½ cup sifted powdered sugar, 1 tablespoon strong coffee and 2 tablespoons Tiamaria.

Icing: Melt chocolate squares with butter; add salt and sugar; mix well. Then add ¼ cup half & half, 1 teaspoon vanilla and 1½ tablespoons Tiamaria. Mix well and put on cake.

Ann LaDuke (submitted by Brownie - Lois Bruner)

TURTLE CAKE

1 German chocolate cake mix
⅔ c. evaporated milk
¼ c. margarine

1 (14 oz.) pkg. caramels
6 oz. chocolate chips
1 c. nuts

Mix cake according to directions, but add ⅓ cup evaporated milk and ¼ cup margarine in addition to the oil and water the mix calls for. Put half of batter in a 9x13 inch pan and bake 15 minutes at 350°. Melt caramels and ⅓ cup evaporated milk. Pour over warm cake. Sprinkle chocolate chips and nuts over this. Pour remainder of batter over this and bake 15 to 20 minutes or until done.

Louise Atherton

VANILLA WAFER CAKE

1 c. coconut
1 c. sugar
3 c. vanilla wafer crumbs
1 tsp. baking powder
½ c. shortening or 1 stick
    butter, melted

3 eggs
¾ c. milk
1 c. chopped pecans
1 tsp. vanilla

Combine all ingredients. Cook in 13x9 inch pan, greased. Cook at 350° for 35 to 40 minutes.

Frosting:

1 stick oleo
¼ c. half & half

1 c. brown sugar

Cook 5 minutes after coming to a boil. Add 2 cups powdered sugar and 1 teaspoon vanilla.

Ruby Junker

WELFARE CAKE

2 c. plain flour
½ tsp. soda
1 Tbsp. cocoa
2 c. brown sugar

1 stick margarine
1 c. buttermilk
2 well beaten eggs

Sift flour and soda 3 times; add cocoa and brown sugar and sift again. Melt 1 stick margarine in 1 cup buttermilk to boiling point. Add dry ingredients to milk mixture and 2 well beaten eggs. Mix well and add 1 teaspoon vanilla. Bake in square 8x13 inch pan at 300° for 30 minutes.

Topping:

1 stick margarine
1 c. brown sugar
½ c. Pet milk

1 c. coconut
1 c. nuts
1 tsp. vanilla

Melt 1 stick margarine; add 1 cup brown sugar, ½ cup Pet milk, 1 cup coconut, 1 cup nuts, and 1 teaspoon vanilla. Mix well; pour over hot cake. Turn oven to broil. Cook until brown.

Phyllis L. Davis

YUMMY CAKE

1 c. oatmeal
1¼ c. boiling water
1¾ sticks butter
1½ c. brown sugar
1½ c. white sugar
1⅓ c. sifted flour
1 tsp. soda

1 tsp. cinnamon
½ tsp. salt
½ tsp. nutmeg
¼ c. canned milk
1 tsp. vanilla
1 c. shredded coconut and
    chopped pecans, mixed

Pour 1¼ cups boiling water over 1 cup oatmeal and 1 stick of butter. Let stand 10 to 20 minutes. Add 1 cup brown sugar, 1 cup white sugar, 1⅓ cups sifted flour, 1 teaspoon soda, 1 teaspoon cinnamon, ½ teaspoon salt, and ½ teaspoon nutmeg. Stir gently, *do not* use mixer. Pour in buttered pan and bake 35 minutes at 350°.

Mix together for the icing ¾ stick butter, ½ cup brown sugar, ½ cup white sugar, ¼ cup canned milk, 1 teaspoon vanilla, and 1 cup coconut and pecans mixed. Pour icing on cake after it is baked, brown under the broiler about 10 minutes. Leave in pan and serve. Cut in squares.

Mary Lauder

ZUCCHINI CAKE

2 c. flour
2 tsp. baking soda
1 tsp. salt
¼ tsp. baking powder
3 tsp. ground cinnamon
3 eggs
1 c. vegetable oil

1½ c. sugar
2 medium size zucchini,
    grated (2 c.)
2 tsp. vanilla
1 c. raisins or currants
1 c. chopped walnuts

Sift flour, baking soda, salt, baking powder and cinnamon onto wax paper. Combine eggs, oil, sugar, zucchini and vanilla in a large mixing bowl; beat until well mixed. Stir in the flour mixture until smooth. Stir in raisins and nuts. Pour into a well greased 9x13 inch pan; bake at 350° for 40 to 45 minutes or until center springs back when lightly pressed with fingertips. Cool. Makes 20 servings.

Can be frosted if desired or serve plain. Freezes well.

Ruthie Marty

ZUCCHINI CHOCOLATE CAKE

1 c. brown sugar	4 Tbsp. cocoa
1½ c. sugar	½ tsp. allspice
1 stick butter	½ tsp. salt
½ c. oil	2½ c. plain flour
3 eggs	½ tsp. cinnamon
1 tsp. vanilla	3 c. zucchini, grated
½ c. buttermilk	1 c. nuts
2 tsp. soda	Chocolate icing (any kind)

Mix together 1 cup brown sugar, 1½ cups sugar, 1 stick butter, ½ cup oil, 3 eggs and 1 teaspoon vanilla. Mix in another bowl ½ cup buttermilk and 2 teaspoons soda; mix and set aside. Mix 4 tablespoons cocoa, ½ teaspoon allspice, ½ teaspoon salt, 2½ cups plain flour and ½ teaspoon cinnamon. Grate 3 cups zucchini and add 1 cup nuts. Combine all ingredients. Bake at 350° for 45 to 50 minutes in greased cake pan. Ice with chocolate icing.

Mary Baxter

CUSTARD FILLING FOR CAKES

⅓ c. cornstarch	⅓ c. honey
⅔ c. skim milk powder	2 egg yolks, lightly beaten
¼ tsp. salt	1 tsp. vanilla extract
1¾ c. water	

Combine cornstarch, skim milk powder and salt in a medium size saucepan. Add ¼ cup water; stir with wooden spoon until mixture is smooth. Add remaining 1 ½ cups of water; mix well. Add honey and place over medium heat; stir constantly until it thickens, about 10 to 12 minutes. Remove from heat. Add 3 tablespoons of hot mixture to beaten egg yolks; mix well. Gradually pour yolk mixture into custard; blend well. Return to medium heat and cook 3 minutes; stir constantly. Remove from heat; add vanilla and cool custard completely before using to fill cake. Yield: 2 cups.

Crystal Duke

PINEAPPLE FILLING

½ c. water	1 c. crushed pineapple
¼ c. cornstarch	1 tsp. vanilla
½ c. sugar	

Bring water to a boil. Add cornstarch and sugar. When they are dissolved, add pineapple and vanilla. Mix well. Cool. Spread between layers of an 8 or 9 inch layer cake.

Denise Figg

CHOCOLATE FUDGE FROSTING

1 Tbsp. butter
2 sq. (2 oz.) unsweetened
   chocolate, cut up
1½ c. sugar

½ c. water
1 Tbsp. light corn syrup
1 tsp. vanilla

Mix in a saucepan butter, chocolate, sugar, water and corn syrup. Cover pan and cook slowly until mixture boils; remove cover and cook, without stirring, until a little dropped into cold water forms a soft ball. Remove from heat; let stand until cold. Add 1 teaspoon vanilla. Beat until thick enough to spread.

Debbie Rigdon

AUNT LILLIE'S BOILED ICING

4 egg yolks, beaten
¼ c. white syrup

2 c. sugar
¾ c. water

In double boiler, cook sugar, syrup, and water until it spins a thread. Cool. Pour the cooled syrup mixture over egg yolks and beat. Add 1 teaspoon lemon (or orange) flavoring. Serve on cake of your choice.

Shirley Cates

BROWN SUGAR FROSTING

2 leftover egg whites
1½ c. dark brown sugar,
   packed firm

⅓ c. water
1 tsp. vanilla

Mix all ingredients, except vanilla, in the top of double boiler until smooth. Place over brisk boiling water and beat vigorously for 7 minutes with a rotary beater or 4 minutes with an electric one. Frosting at this point looks fluffy and holds a soft shape. Take it off the heat and stir in the vanilla. Continue beating until mixture holds a precise point when you lift up the beater. Spread frosting between layers, around sides and over top of cake. Makes enough to frost 2 (9 inch) cake layers.

Seafoam Frosting: To make this frosting, use only 1 cup dark brown sugar and ½ cup granulated sugar.

Paula White

BUTTER FROSTING

¼ c. butter or margarine (at
   room temperature)
1 egg yolk
4 - 5 Tbsp. milk, scalded

1 tsp. vanilla, lemon or
   almond extract
3 c. confectioners sugar

Cream butter and egg yolk. Stir in milk and extract. Add sugar in small amounts and beat until creamy. Frosts a 2 layer (9 inch) cake.

Denise Figg

CHOCOLATE ICING

½ c. butter
½ c. cocoa
2 c. sugar

½ c. milk
⅓ c. light corn syrup
1 tsp. vanilla

Melt the butter in a saucepan. Add remaining ingredients. Bring to a boil and cook 1 minute. Cool to lukewarm. Beat to desired consistency. Frosts a 2 layer (9 inch) cake.

Denise Figg

COCONUT ICING

½ c. butter
Rind of 1 lemon, grated
1 Tbsp. lemon juice

3 Tbsp. milk
2 lb. confectioners sugar
2 c. grated coconut

Melt butter in a saucepan. Gradually stir in the rind, juice, milk, sugar and coconut. Cool. Makes enough icing for a 2 layer (9 inch) cake.

Denise Figg

CREAM CHEESE ICING

1 stick butter, melted
1 (8 oz.) pkg. cream cheese,
   softened

1 box powdered sugar
1 tsp. vanilla
1 c. pecans, chopped

1546-85

Melt butter. Mash up cream cheese and add melted butter and mix. Add powdered sugar and vanilla; mix well. Add pecans and mix again.

Lila Mae White

DECORATOR ICING

1 c. Crisco
2 boxes powdered sugar
2 egg whites

1 tsp. vanilla
¼ tsp. salt
⅓ c. water

Mix Crisco, egg whites, vanilla, salt and water. Add powdered sugar gradually until well blended.

Thelma Barnett

EASY CARAMEL ICING

½ c. margarine
1 c. firm packed light brown
  sugar

½ c. evaporated milk
2 - 2½ c. powdered sugar
1 tsp. vanilla or ½ tsp. maple

Melt margarine over low heat. Remove and add brown sugar. Stir until smooth; boil; stir 1 minute. Remove from heat; add cream over low heat and return to boil. Remove from heat and let cool to room temperature. Beat in confectioners sugar and vanilla.

Donna Browning

WHITE ICING

2 c. sugar
1 c. water
1 tsp. vanilla

4 egg whites
¼ tsp. cream of tartar

Boil 1½ cups sugar and the water to a syrup. Beat in vanilla. Beat egg whites until foamy. Add cream of tartar. Continue beating until stiff. Gradually beat in the remaining ½ cup sugar. Gradually beat in the sugar syrup. Makes enough icing for a 2 layer (9 inch) cake.

Kim Clinton

COOKIES

ALMOND COOKIES

2 c. flour
1 c. lard or butter
⅔ c. sugar
1 Tbsp. almond extract
⅓ c. fine crushed and
    blanched almond nuts
    (food processor works
    best)

1 egg
½ tsp. baking soda
1 tsp. baking powder
⅓ c. almonds for cookie
    centers
¼ tsp. salt

Cream lard and sugar together. Add almond extract, egg, flour, crushed almonds, baking soda, baking powder, and salt. Knead dough until very smooth. Form into small balls. Press. Lay on ungreased cookie sheet 1 inch apart. Press on almond half gently, but firmly, in the center of each. Bake 15 to 20 minutes in 350° oven or until golden brown. Makes 4 dozen. Serve with hot Jasmin Tea.

Sarah A. Drewes

BROWNIES

2 sticks margarine
10 Tbsp. cocoa
2 c. sugar
4 eggs, beaten

1½ c. flour
Dash of salt
½ c. nuts

Melt margarine and add cocoa, then sugar and beat well. Add eggs, flour and salt. Mix well and stir in nuts. Spread in 9x12 inch greased pan. Bake at 350° for 25 to 30 minutes.

Donna Browning

BUTTERSCOTCH BROWNIES

1 c. butter
2 c. flour

2 c. brown sugar

Mix well.

Add:

2 tsp. baking soda
2 tsp. vanilla

2 eggs

Mix well.

Add:

12 oz. chocolate chips   **1 c. pecans**

Bake at 350° for 25 to 30 minutes in 9x13 inch pan. Cool and cut in squares.

Ladonna Darnell

CARAMEL SQUARES

Use chocolate cake mix with pudding. Mix and bake ½ according to directions.

Melt:

1 stick butter   **1 (14 oz.) pkg. caramels**
1 can Eagle Brand milk

Pour over baked cake. Add remaining cake mix and bake again according to package directions. Let cool completely.

Myrna Blackman

CHERRY CRUNCH COOKIES

2¼ c. sifted flour   **2 eggs**
1 tsp. baking powder   **1 c. chopped nuts**
½ tsp. baking soda   **1 c. chopped pitted dates**
½ tsp. salt   **½ c. chopped cherries**
¾ c. soft margarine   **2½ c. frosted flakes**
1 c. sugar   **12 - 15 cherries, quartered**
3 Tbsp. maraschino cherry   **(red and green cherries**
** syrup**   ** make prettier cookies)**

Sift together flour, baking powder, soda and salt. Blend butter and sugar. Add eggs, 1 at a time, beating well after each one. Stir in cherry syrup. Add dry ingredients, nuts, dates and chopped cherries. Crush frosted flakes slightly with rolling pin. Roll teaspoon of dough in crumbs. Place on cookie sheet and press fourth of cherry lightly into top of each cookie. Bake at 375° for 15 minutes.

Grace Murphy

CHESS SQUARES

1 box yellow cake mix   **1 stick oleo, softened**
1 egg

Mix together and pat in greased pan (9x13x2 inches).

3 eggs
8 oz. cream cheese, softened

1 lb. powdered sugar
1 tsp. vanilla

Mix and pour over cake mix; bake at 325° for 45 minutes. Makes 48 squares.

Vinetta Wills

GRAHAM CRACKER CHOCOLATE CHIP COOKIES

2 cans Eagle Brand milk
2 c. graham cracker crumbs

2 tsp. vanilla
Chocolate chips (to taste)

Mix thoroughly and pour into a 13x9x2 inch baking pan and bake at 350° for 25 to 30 minutes. Cut into squares and serve.

Mrs. Bill (Jo) Barron

CHOCOLATE CHIP COOKIES

⅔ c. shortening
3 c. flour (if using self-rising
    flour omit soda and salt)
⅔ c. softened butter or
    margarine
1 c. granulated sugar
1 tsp. soda
1 tsp. salt

1 c. brown sugar, packed
1 c. chopped nuts
2 eggs
2 tsp. vanilla
2 (6 oz. each) pkg.
    semi-sweet chocolate
    pieces

Heat oven to 375°. Mix thoroughly shortening, butter, sugars, eggs and vanilla. Blend in remaining ingredients. (For a softer, rounder cookie, add ½ cup flour.) Drop dough by rounded teaspoonfuls 2 inches apart onto ungreased cookie sheet. Bake 8 to 10 minutes or until light brown. Cool slightly before removing from cookie sheet. Yield: About 7 dozen cookies.

Patricia Jewell

CHOCOLATE HALFWAY COOKIES

½ c. shortening
½ c. granulated sugar
½ c. brown sugar
2 egg yolks, slightly beaten
  with 1 Tbsp. water
1 tsp. vanilla
2 c. all-purpose flour, sifted
  before measuring

¼ tsp. salt
1 tsp. baking powder
¼ tsp. baking soda
1 (6 oz.) pkg. semi-sweet
  chocolate

Cream shortening and sugars. Add egg yolk, to which water has been added, and vanilla. Blend well. Sift flour with salt, baking powder and baking soda. Thoroughly blend dry ingredients with creamed shortening mixture. Put in greased 2 (8 inch) square pans; sprinkle the chocolate morsels on top, and press down slightly into the dough. Next, spread topping over the dough. Bake in preheated oven (350°F.) for 30 minutes. Cool before cutting. Yields about 3 dozen cookies.

Topping:

2 egg whites

1½ c. brown sugar

Beat egg whites until stiff. Blend in the brown sugar and fold ingredients together until well blended.

Delores Darnell

CHOCOLATE-FILLED BONBONS

¾ c. Crisco
½ c. granulated sugar
¼ c. packed brown sugar
1 egg
2 tsp. vanilla extract
½ tsp. almond extract
1¾ c. unsifted all-purpose
  flour

½ tsp. baking powder
½ tsp. salt
½ c. finely chopped pecans
  or blanched almonds
3½ to 4 doz. milk chocolate
  kisses

Preheat oven to 350°. Using electric mixer, cream Crisco and both sugars until fluffy. Add egg and extracts; beat well. Add flour, baking powder, salt and nuts; mix until blended. Form dough into 1 inch balls. Press each ball around a Hershey's kiss so that kiss is completely enclosed by dough. Bake 12 minutes on ungreased cookie sheet. (Do *not* overbake!) Cool on wire racks. Frost or decorate as desired or leave them plain. Makes 3½ to 4 dozen cookies.

Patricia Jewell

COCONUT CONES

¼ c. butter or margarine
2¼ c. sifted confectioners
   sugar
¼ c. evaporated milk

3 c. flaked coconut
1 (6 oz.) pkg. (1 c.) chocolate
   morsels

Melt butter over low heat until lightly browned. Stir in confectioners sugar, evaporated milk and coconut. Drop from teaspoon onto a waxed paper lined cookie sheet. When cool, shape into cones. Melt chocolate morsels over hot, not boiling, water. Dip the bottoms of each cone into the melted chocolate. Return to waxed paper until chocolate hardens. Yield: 3 dozen cookies.

Patricia Jewell

COCONUT WREATHS

⅔ c. unsalted butter or
   margarine, softened
½ c. granulated sugar
1 tsp. vanilla
1 egg

1¾ c. all-purpose flour
1 c. flaked coconut
Silver dragees and red icing
   (for decoration)

With electric mixer, beat butter and sugar in medium size bowl until pale and fluffy. Beat in vanilla and egg. Stir in flour and coconut until well blended. Chill 20 minutes. Put dough into cookie press fitted with large star tip. Press out 3 inch wreath shapes, 1 inch apart, onto ungreased cookie sheet. Bake in preheated 350° oven for 10 to 12 minutes until lightly browned. Cool on rack. Makes 24.

Patricia Jewell

CHRISTMAS COOKIES

2½ c. flour
½ tsp. baking powder
½ tsp. salt
½ tsp. cinnamon
¾ c. shortening

3 eggs
¾ c. sugar
1½ c. raisins
1½ c. nuts

Cream shortening and sugar. Add eggs, then flour with dry ingredients sifted in. Last, add raisins and nuts. Just barely cook until brown edges in 350° oven. Store in tight container.

Izetta Stephens

CHRISTMAS ROCKS

1 c. butter
1½ c. sugar
1 tsp. cinnamon
1 tsp. cloves
3 eggs
1 tsp. soda, dissolved in 2
    Tbsp. hot water

1 lb. nuts (pecans)
1 lb. raisins
1 lb. dates
½ c. cherries (maraschino)
3 c. flour

Mix all together and drop teaspoon size onto a greased pan. Bake at 350° (10 to 12 minutes for crisp and 7 to 10 minutes for chewy rocks).

Patsy Akers

CONGO BARS

1 lb. box light brown sugar
1½ sticks butter
3 eggs

2⅔ c. self-rising flour
1 c. pecans
1 large bag chocolate chips

Blend sugar, butter, flour and eggs; beat. Fold in nuts and chips. Bake in 9 inch square pan for 25 to 30 minutes at 350°.

Peggy Graviss

CONGO SQUARES

2¾ c. sifted flour
2½ tsp. baking powder
½ tsp. salt
⅔ c. shortening
1 (6 oz.) pkg. semi-sweet
    chocolate chips

2¼ c. (1 lb. box) light brown
    sugar
3 eggs
1 c. chopped pecans

Mix and sift flour, baking powder and salt. Melt shortening and add brown sugar. Stir until well mixed. Allow to cool slightly (so as not to cook eggs). Add eggs, 1 at a time, beating well after each addition. Add dry ingredients, then pecans and chocolate chips. Pour into a greased pan about 10½ x 15½ x ¾ inches (or larger pan if you have it). Bake at 350° for about 25 to 30 minutes.

Note: Batter will be extremely thick. Place a sheet of wax paper over batter in pan and press it into corners and edges with your hands. Remove wax paper before putting in oven.

Ruth Ackerman

DATE-NUT ROLL COOKIES

Filling:

2½ c. chopped pitted dates   **1 c. water**
1 c. granulated sugar

Combine and cook over low heat about 10 minutes or until thick. Add 1 cup chopped nuts and cool while you mix dough.

Dough Mixture:

1 c. Crisco   **4 c. flour**
2 c. brown sugar   **½ tsp. salt**
3 eggs, well beaten   **½ tsp. soda**

Cream shortening and sugar, then add eggs. Add all dry ingredients. Chill thoroughly. Divide into 2 equal parts; roll like for biscuits, only thinner (about ¼ inch thick). Spread date mixture (filling) on rolled out dough mixture and roll like a jelly roll. Put in wax paper or aluminum foil and set in refrigerator overnight. Cut into thin slices. Bake at 400° on cookie sheet (greased) for 8 to 10 minutes.

Zama Picklesimer

DELICIOUS BARS

2 sticks butter   **1 tsp. vanilla**
1 c. brown sugar   **¼ tsp. salt**
1 egg yolk   **15½ oz. Hershey's bar**
2 c. plain flour

Cream butter and sugar; add egg yolk, flour, vanilla and salt. Put in greased 9x13 inch pan. Bake at 350° for 20 minutes. Remove from oven and top immediately with chocolate bars. Smooth with knife when melted. Cool. Cut in bars. Makes 3 dozen.

Dot Berry

DOUBLE CHOCOLATE CHIP OATMEAL COOKIES

3 eggs   **2 c. cocoa**
1½ c. self-rising flour   **Pkg. Nestle's chocolate chips**
2 c. sugar   **½ c. water**
2½ c. oatmeal   **1 Tbsp. vanilla**
1 c. cooking oil

Beat eggs and sugar together. Mix flour, oatmeal and cocoa together, then add to egg and sugar mixture. Add vanilla and cooking oil; mix well. Mix in chocolate chips. Gradually add water to the batter. Drop by spoonful on a greased baking sheet and bake in a preheated 350° oven about 8 to 10 minutes.

Ann Brawand

CHOCOLATE COOKIES

1 box confectioners sugar
1 c. coconut
1 tsp. vanilla
1 c. graham cracker crumbs
½ c. crunchy peanut butter

2 sticks butter
½ block paraffin
1 (6 oz.) pkg. semi-sweet
   chocolate chips
1 c. nuts (optional)

Mix first 6 ingredients together and form cookies. Melt chocolate chips and paraffin in double boiler. Dip cookies in chocolate and lay on wax paper to cool.

Debbie Rigdon

CHOCOLATE-COVERED CHERRY COOKIES

1½ c. all-purpose flour
½ c. cocoa
¼ tsp. salt
¼ tsp. baking powder
¼ tsp. soda
½ c. butter or margarine,
   softened
1 c. sugar

1 egg
1½ tsp. vanilla
1 (10 oz.) jar (about 48)
   maraschino cherries
1 (6 oz.) pkg. chocolate chips
½ c. Eagle Brand sweetened
   condensed milk

In large bowl, stir together flour, cocoa, salt, baking powder and soda. In mixer bowl, beat together butter and sugar on low speed of mixer until fluffy. Add egg and vanilla; beat well. Gradually add dry ingredients to creamed mixture; beat until well blended. Shape dough into 1 inch balls; place on greased cookie sheet. Press down center of dough with thumb. Drain maraschino cherries, reserving juice. Place a cherry in the center of each cookie. In small saucepan, combine chocolate chips and sweetened condensed milk; heat until chocolate is melted. Stir in 4 teaspoons of the cherry juice. Spoon about 1 teaspoon frosting over each cherry, spreading to cover the cherry. (Frosting may be

thinned with additional cherry juice, if necessary.) Bake in a 350° oven about 10 minutes or until done. Remove to wire rack to cool. Makes about 48 cookies.

Maxine Welch

COCONUT COOKIES

1 stick margarine or butter
1 c. sugar
3 tsp. coconut flavoring

1 small pkg. Bix-Mix
1 small pkg. Spudflakes

Cream together butter, sugar and flavoring. Add egg and beat. Stir in Bix-Mix and Spudflakes. Cover bowl and chill about an hour. Heat oven to 375°. Shape dough into marble size balls and place about 2 inches apart on a greased cookie sheet. Bake 12 to 14 minutes. Makes about 4 dozen cookies.

Maxine Welch

FILLED CUPCAKES

3 c. flour
2 c. sugar
1 tsp. salt
⅔ c. vegetable oil

½ c. cocoa
2 c. water
2 Tbsp. vinegar
2 tsp. vanilla

Fill cups ½ way with mixture and add heaping teaspoons of filling in the middle. Bake at 350° about 15 minutes. Makes approximately 3 dozen.

Filling:

1 (8 oz.) pkg. Philadelphia
   cream cheese
⅓ c. sugar

1 egg
⅛ tsp. salt

Mix together and add 6 ounces of chocolate chips.

Sue Sympson

FILLED PASTRIES
(Cookies)

⅓ c. jam or jelly (any flavor)
1 c. margarine
3 Tbsp. cream
3 Tbsp. water
¼ tsp. vinegar

2 c. sifted flour
2 egg whites
¼ c. almonds, chopped
¼ c. sugar

Cream margarine; add cream, water and vinegar. Blend in flour; mix well. Roll dough out ¼ inch thick; cut half of dough into rings with doughnut cutter. Cut other half into circles. Brush rounds with slightly beaten egg whites; place a ring on each circle. Brush top of circles with beaten egg white and sprinkle with chopped almonds and sugar. Put jam in centers. Bake in hot oven (400°) for 15 minutes. Cool.

Pretty addition to a cookie tray.

Ruthie Marty

FORGOTTEN COOKIES

Preheat oven to 375°. Put mixer beaters in freezer a *couple of hours before* making dough.

2 egg whites	**Pinch of salt**
1 tsp. vanilla	**1 c. chocolate chips**
¾ c. pecans	**¾ c. sugar**

1. Oven must be turned on *before* gathering ingredients.
2. Beat egg whites until stiff.
3. Add sugar and beat again until stiff peaks form.
4. Add salt and vanilla; beat until peaks again.
5. Fold in chips and nuts, preferably with a wooden spoon.
6. Turn oven *off.*
7. Drop by heaping teaspoon onto greased cookie sheet.
8. Oven door must not be opened for 7 hours. Make at bedtime and forget until morning.

Patricia Jewell

FRUIT CAKE COOKIES

1 c. brown sugar	**¾ lb. white raisins**
3 eggs, well beaten	**2 c. cherries, chopped**
3 c. flour	**7 c. chopped pecans**
1 tsp. cinnamon	**1 tsp. soda**
½ c. milk	**2 c. dates**
1 c. butter	**6 slices candied pineapple**

Dredge fruit in flour after cutting. Cream butter and sugar; sift flour and spices. Add eggs and flour alternately with milk. Stir in fruit and nuts. Drop from teaspoon onto greased cookie sheet. Space so cookies will not run together. Bake at 300° for 20 to 30 minutes. Cool and store in closed container.

Wilma Crowdus

GINGER COOKIES

1 c. sugar	1 tsp. ginger
¾ c. margarine or Crisco	2 tsp. soda
2 c. flour	1 egg
¼ c. molasses	¼ tsp. salt
1 tsp. cinnamon	

Cream margarine and sugar. Add molasses and beaten egg. Add sifted dry ingredients. Mix well. Drop by teaspoon on greased cookie sheet. Bake at 350° about 8 minutes. Watch carefully and do not over-bake.

Maxine Welch

GINGERSNAPS

2 eggs	1 tsp. soda
1 c. molasses	1 Tbsp. ginger
⅔ c. soft margarine	1 tsp. each cloves, cinnamon
1 c. sugar	4 c. sifted flour

Beat eggs; add molasses, margarine and sugar; beat thoroughly. Add sifted dry ingredients. Blend well. Make balls the size of walnuts and roll in granulated sugar. Place on greased cookie sheet 2 inches apart. Bake about 11 to 13 minutes at 350°.

Brenda Chitty

GOBS

Cream:

2 c. sugar	2 eggs
½ c. Crisco	

Sift and add:

2 tsp. soda	4 c. flour
¼ tsp. salt	½ c. cocoa
½ tsp. baking powder	

Then add:

1 c. buttermilk	1 c. boiling water
1 tsp. vanilla	

Drop this mixture by teaspoon on baking sheet and bake at 350° to 375° for 10 minutes.

Filling - Cook until thick, then cool:

1 c. sweet milk   **5 Tbsp. flour**

Cream and add to cooled mixture:

1 c. powdered sugar   **1 tsp. vanilla**
½ c. Crisco   **¼ tsp. salt**
½ c. plus 1 tsp. margarine

Spread filling between 2 Gobs.

Regina Reck

GOOEYS

1 (14 oz.) pkg. caramels   **¾ c. margarine**
⅔ c. evaporated milk, divided   **1 c. chopped nuts**
18 oz. pkg. German chocolate   **6 oz. semi-sweet chocolate**
     cake mix   **chips**

Combine caramels and ⅓ cup milk in double boiler, stir constantly, until melted; remove from heat. (This can also be melted in the microwave.) Combine cake mix and ⅓ cup milk and margarine. Mix with mixer until dough holds together. Stir in nuts. Press half of the mixture into a greased 9x13 inch pan. Bake at 350° for 6 minutes. Remove from oven and sprinkle chocolate chips over the top. Pour the caramel mixture over this and drop the rest of the cake mixture by tablespoons on top. Cook in oven 15 to 18 minutes.

Sue Sympson

GOOEY COOKIES

1 box yellow cake mix   **1 lb. powdered sugar**
1 stick butter   **2 eggs**
1 (8 oz.) pkg. cream cheese

Mix together cake mix and butter thoroughly. Press into 13x9 inch pan. Beat other ingredients together and pour on top. Bake at 350° for 40 minutes.

Tina Surgenor

EASY GRAHAM COOKIES

24 graham crackers   **1 c. light brown sugar, packed**
½ lb. butter or margarine   **1 c. finely chopped pecans**

Preheat oven to 350°. Place graham crackers on baking sheet, side by side (15 ½ x 10½ x 1 inch). Melt butter or margarine (can use 1 stick of each). Add brown sugar and cook mixture 3 minutes or until butter and sugar are well blended. Remove from heat and add nuts. Spread immediately on crackers. Bake 10 minutes. Cool thoroughly (in pan), then cut into small bars using cracker indentations as a guide.

Comment: Very good for something so easy!

Nellie Ross

ICEBOX COOKIES

Whole graham crackers
2 sticks butter
1 c. sugar
1 beaten egg
½ c. undiluted evaporated
    milk

1 c. pecans
1 c. coconut
1 c. graham cracker crumbs

Line a large, shallow pan with whole graham crackers. Melt in a saucepan 2 sticks butter, then add 1 cup sugar, 1 beaten egg and ½ cup undiluted evaporated milk. Bring to boil and cook 1 minute. Then add 1 cup pecans, 1 cup coconut and 1 cup graham cracker crumbs. Pour over crackers in bottom of pan. Top with whole graham crackers and refrigerate until set. Frost with Buttercream Frosting. Cut into squares to serve.

Ruth Ackerman

LEMON SOURS

½ c. butter
½ c. brown sugar, sifted
1 c. self-rising flour plus 2
    Tbsp.
2 eggs
1 c. chopped pecans

1 c. shredded coconut
1 tsp. vanilla
⅛ tsp. salt
1½ tsp. lemon rind, grated
3 Tbsp. lemon juice
1 c. confectioners sugar

Preheat oven to 350°. Cream butter and sugar; add flour and mix well. Press in a greased pan; bake 10 minutes. While baking, beat eggs until frothy. Add sugar and beat until thick. Add pecans and coconut which has been tossed with 2 tablespoons flour. Flavor with vanilla and salt; spread over first mixture. Bake 20 minutes at 350°. While cookies are baking, mix rind, juice and sugar. After cookies have baked 20 minutes, spread icing over hot cookies. Cool and cut into 24 squares.

Note: Be sure to use self-rising flour and sift sugar, this is part of the secret of making these cookies.

Lila White

LEMON SQUARES

Crust:

2 c. flour
½ c. powdered sugar

1 c. butter or margarine
Pinch of salt

Sift flour with powdered sugar and salt. Cut in margarine until consistency of coarse corn meal. Pat into 13x9 inch pan with a slight ridge of crust up the sides. Bake at 350° for 25 minutes.

Note: Keep eye on crust, I usually leave mine in for only 25 minutes.

Filling:

4 eggs
1¾ c. granulated sugar
6 Tbsp. lemon juice

4 Tbsp. flour
½ tsp. baking powder

Beat eggs slightly, adding sugar gradually. Stir in lemon juice, then sift flour mixed with baking powder; stir until smooth. Pour over baked crust and bake 25 minutes at 350°. Cool and sprinkle powdered sugar on top.

Jeanine Sharp

M & M HOLIDAY PARTY COOKIES

1 c. shortening
2 eggs
2 tsp. vanilla
1 tsp. salt
1 c. brown sugar, firmly
   packed

½ c. granulated sugar
2¼ c. sifted all-purpose flour
1 tsp. baking soda
1½ c. M & M's plain chocolate
   candies

Blend shortening and sugars in large bowl. Beat in vanilla and eggs. Sift dry ingredients together; add to mixture, blending well. Stir in ½ cup of candies. Drop by teaspoon on ungreased baking sheet; decorate with remaining candy. Bake at 375° for 10 minutes or until golden brown. Makes about 72 (2½ inch) cookies.

Patricia Jewell

M & M COOKIES

1 c. shortening
1 c. brown sugar, firmly
    packed
½ c. granulated sugar
2 eggs

2 tsp. vanilla
2¼ c. all-purpose flour
1 tsp. baking soda
1 tsp. salt
1½ c. (¾ lb. pkg.) M & M's

Cream shortening, sugar, eggs, and vanilla thoroughly. Sift together flour, soda and salt. Add dry ingredients gradually to creamed mixture; mix well. Stir in ½ cup M & M's. Reserve remaining candy for decorating. Drop by teaspoon on ungreased baking sheet. Decorate tops of cookies with remaining candy after baking. Bake at 375° for 10 to 12 minutes. Makes about 6 dozen.

Sharon Dukes

MACAROONS

2 egg whites
½ c. sugar
¼ tsp. salt
1 tsp. almond extract

1 tsp. aniseed or sesame
    seed
2 c. oven toasted rice cereal

Beat egg whites until stiff. Beat in sugar and salt. Fold in almond extract, aniseed and cereal. Drop by teaspoonful 2 inches apart onto greased baking sheet. Bake in very slow oven, 250°, for 25 minutes for crisp cookies or 15 minutes for soft ones. Remove from baking sheet and cool on racks. Makes 2 dozen.

Cristy Lewis

MOLASSES COOKIES

½ c. shortening
½ c. sugar
1 tsp. grated lemon rind
1 tsp. lemon extract
1 egg, beaten

⅔ c. dark molasses
2 c. all-purpose flour, sifted
½ tsp. ginger
½ tsp. salt
½ tsp. baking soda

Preheat oven to 350°. Cream shortening and sugar until fluffy. Add lemon rind and extract. Mix in egg and molasses. Sift together the remaining ingredients. Mix into batter. Drop by teaspoonfuls onto a lightly greased cookie sheet. Yield: Approximately 3 dozen.

Denise Figg

MOLASSES SPICE CRISPS

2½ c. sifted flour	¾ c. shortening
2 tsp. soda	1 c. sugar
2 tsp. cloves	1 egg (unbeaten)
2 tsp. ginger	4 Tbsp. molasses
2 tsp. cinnamon	

1. Sift flour once. Measure; add soda and spices. Sift together 3 times.
2. Cream shortening; add sugar gradually and cream until light.
3. Add egg; beat thoroughly; add molasses.
4. Add flour gradually. Mix well after each addition. Chill dough.
5. Roll into balls the size of walnuts; dip in sugar. Place sugar side up on greased cookie sheet. Bake at 350° for 10 to 15 minutes.

Mary Beeler

RYAN'S NO BAKE COOKIES

½ c. milk	½ c. butter
2 c. sugar	3 c. oats (add more to thicken
3 Tbsp. cocoa	if needed)
3 Tbsp. chunky style peanut butter	1 tsp. vanilla

Wipe inside of saucepan with butter just below rim. Combine milk, sugar, cocoa, peanut butter and butter in pan. Stir and bring to a boil over medium heat. Boil for 1½ minutes without stirring. Remove from heat. Stir in oats and vanilla. Stir until well blended. Drop by teaspoon onto buttered baking sheets or waxed paper. Cool before serving. Makes 4 to 5 dozen small cookies.

Ryan Sowders

FAMOUS OATMEAL COOKIES

Mix with beater:

¾ c. shortening	1 egg
½ c. sugar (granulated)	¼ c. water
1 c. brown sugar	1 tsp. vanilla

Add - stir in:

3 c. oats (uncooked)	½ tsp. soda
1 c. all-purpose flour	Chocolate chips
1 tsp. salt	

Dip by teaspoonfuls (rounded) onto cookie sheet (375°). Bake approximately 12 minutes or until light brown.

Doris Beeler

OATMEAL COOKIES

1 c. raisins	½ tsp. soda
1 c. shortening	1 Tbsp. cocoa
1 c. sugar	3 eggs
1 c. nuts	6 Tbsp. raisin juice
2 c. oatmeal	1 tsp. cinnamon
½ tsp. salt	1 tsp. allspice
½ tsp. cloves	2 c. flour

Cover raisins with boiling water. Cook 5 minutes. Cream shortening and sugar. Add eggs. Add all dry ingredients and raisin liquid. Last, stir in oats, raisins and nuts. Drop on baking sheet by teaspoonfuls. Bake 8 to 10 minutes in 350° to 375° oven. Makes 5 dozen.

Donna Browning

OATMEAL CRUNCHIES

¾ c. shortening	1 tsp. salt
1 c. flour	½ c. sugar
1 c. packed brown sugar	1 egg
1 tsp. vanilla	1 tsp. cinnamon
¼ c. water	½ tsp. soda
1 c. chocolate chips	3 c. oatmeal

Heat oven to 350°. Mix thoroughly sugars, egg, shortening, water and vanilla. Stir in remaining ingredients. Drop dough by rounded teaspoonful 1 inch apart onto greased baking sheet. Bake 12 to 15 minutes; remove immediately from sheet. Yield: 5 dozen.

Patricia Jewell

PEANUT BLOSSOMS

1¾ c. flour
1 tsp. soda
½ tsp. salt
½ c. Crisco
½ c. peanut butter

½ c. brown sugar
1 egg
2 Tbsp. milk
1 tsp. vanilla
36 Hershey's kisses

Cream together Crisco, peanut butter, sugar and brown sugar. Add egg, milk and vanilla; beat well. Blend in dry ingredients gradually and mix thoroughly. Shape by teaspoonfuls into balls. Roll in sugar and place on ungreased cookie sheet. Bake at 375° for 8 minutes. Remove from oven and place candy kiss on top of each cookie, pressing down so that the cookie cracks around the edge. Return to oven 2 to 5 minutes longer. Makes 3 dozen.

Grace Murphy

PEANUT BUTTER CHIP COOKIES

⅔ c. soft margarine
½ c. sugar
½ c. brown sugar
1 egg, beaten
1 tsp. vanilla

1¾ c. flour
½ tsp. salt
¾ tsp. baking soda
1 c. peanut butter chips

Preheat oven to 375°. Cream margarine and sugars. Add egg and vanilla. Mix well. Add dry ingredients. Mix until blended thoroughly. Drop by teaspoonfuls onto ungreased baking sheet. Bake 8 to 10 minutes at 375°.

Sherry Greer

PEANUT BUTTER COOKIES

Ritz crackers
Peanut butter

Chocolate almond bark

Spread Ritz crackers with peanut butter. Put another cracker on top to make a sandwich. Melt chocolate almond bark in top of double boiler. Dip cracker sandwiches in melted chocolate. Cool.

Barbara Swank

PEANUT BUTTER COOKIES

1 c. shortening	1 c. peanut butter
1 c. sugar	2 eggs
1 c. brown sugar	2½ c. flour
1 tsp. soda	½ tsp. salt
1 tsp. vanilla	

Mix together all ingredients. Roll dough to size of a walnut. Press with a fork on cookie sheet. Bake in 350° oven for 10 minutes.

Chasteen Thompson

PEANUT BUTTER CRISSCROSSES

1 c. shortening	1 c. peanut butter
1 c. granulated sugar	3 c. sifted all-purpose flour*
1 c. brown sugar	2 tsp. soda
2 eggs	½ tsp. salt
1 tsp. vanilla	

Thoroughly cream shortening, sugar, eggs and vanilla. Stir in peanut butter. Sift dry ingredients. Stir into creamed mixture. Drop by rounded teaspoons on ungreased cookie sheet; press with back of floured fork to form crisscrosses. Bake in moderate oven (350°) for about 10 minutes. Makes about 5 dozen cookies.

   * For richer cookies, use 2 cups flour.

Erdean Lee

PEANUT BUTTER KISSES

1 c. peanut butter	2 eggs
1 c. Crisco shortening	1 c. light brown sugar
3½ c. all-purpose flour	2 tsp. baking soda
1 c. granulated sugar	1 tsp. salt
¼ c. milk	⅓ c. granulated sugar (for
2 tsp. vanilla	rolling cookies)
11 oz. pkg. Hershey's kisses	

Preheat oven to 375°. Combine peanut butter, Crisco, and sugars. Stir in milk, vanilla, and eggs. Add combined flour, soda, and salt. Mix thoroughly using your hands if necessary. Shape dough into 1 inch balls; roll in ⅓ cup of granulated sugar. Place on ungreased baking sheet. Bake at 375° for 8 minutes. Remove from oven and press a milk chocolate kiss (unwrapped) on the center of each cookie. Return to oven and bake another 3 minutes. Remove to racks to cool. Makes 7 to 8 dozen cookies.

Patricia Jewell

PECAN TASSIES

1 stick margarine (less 1 inch)   **1 c. flour**
1 (3 oz.) pkg. cream cheese

Mix well and roll into small balls (about ¾ inch). Press into tassie pans.

Filling:

1 egg, beaten   **1 inch margarine (left from**
¾ c. sugar   **stick)**
¾ c. nuts   **Pinch of salt**
1 tsp. vanilla

Mix filling ingredients well and put 1 teaspoon in each cup. Makes 24. Bake 25 to 30 minutes at 350°.

Laverne Hollingsworth

PERSIMMON COOKIES

1 c. persimmon pulp   **2¼ c. flour**
1 c. nuts   **½ tsp. cinnamon**
1 c. raisins   **½ tsp. cloves**
1 c. sugar   **½ tsp. nutmeg**
½ c. shortening   **1 egg**
1 tsp. soda, dissolved in pulp

Cream shortening and sugar. Add egg, soda and persimmon pulp. Add dry ingredients, nuts and raisins. Drop with teaspoon on greased cookie sheet. Bake for 10 minutes in 350° to 375° oven. Makes approximately 90 cookies.

Dee Dee Millen

PINWHEEL COOKIES

½ c. sugar
¼ c. butter
½ egg (2 Tbsp.)

½ tsp. vanilla
⅔ c. flour
1 tsp. baking powder

Cream butter and sugar. Add beaten egg. Mix baking powder and flour; stir into creamed butter and sugar. Divide dough into 2 equal parts; melt and cool ½ square Baker's chocolate. Add to half of dough, if dough is soft, chill so it may be rolled between sheets of waxed paper. Roll white dough and chocolate separate into oblong shapes to thickness of ⅛ inch. Place dark on light and roll like a jelly roll. Slice and bake on greased tin in moderate oven.

Mattie Hammack

POLKA DOT MERINGUE

¼ tsp. salt
2 egg whites
1 c. sugar
¼ tsp. vanilla

½ c. chopped nuts
2 c. corn flakes
1 pkg. semi-sweet chocolate

Add salt to egg whites and beat until frothy. Add sugar (about 2 tablespoons at a time) and continue to beat until very thick. Beat in vanilla and fold in nuts, corn flakes, and ⅔ package of semi-sweet chocolate. Drop by teaspoonfuls on a greased cookie sheet. Top each with 3 or 4 chocolate pieces. Bake in very slow oven (300°) for 20 minutes. Makes 3 dozen cookies.

Betty Volz

POLYNESIAN COOKIES

1 c. shortening
1½ c. sugar
1 egg
1 (8½ oz.) can crushed
   pineapple
3½ c. Gold Medal flour*

1 tsp. soda
½ tsp. salt
¼ tsp. nutmeg
½ c. chopped macadamia
   nuts

Heat oven to 400°. Mix shortening, sugar and egg. Stir in pineapple (with syrup) and remaining ingredients. Drop dough by teaspoonfuls about 2 inches apart onto ungreased baking sheet. Bake 8 to 10 minutes or until golden brown and no imprint remains when touched lightly with finger. Makes about 5 dozen cookies.

* If using self-rising flour, omit soda and salt.

Substitution: For macadamia nuts: ½ cup chopped walnuts or pecans.

Variations - Pineapple Coconut Cookies: Omit nutmeg and stir in 1 cup flaked coconut. Pineapple Raisin Cookies: Stir in 1 cup raisins.

Barbara C. Hendrick

POTATO CHIP COOKIES

1 c. sugar
1 c. brown sugar
1 c. shortening
2 eggs

2 - 2½ c. flour
2 tsp. soda
1 tsp. vanilla
2 c. crushed potato chips

Cream sugar and shortening; add eggs; beat well. Add flour, soda and vanilla. Stir in potato chips. (Add variations now.) Drop by teaspoon onto greased cookie sheet. Bake at 350° until lightly browned. Sprinkle with powdered sugar. Yield: 5 dozen.

Variations: Nuts, coconut or chocolate chips.

Lilly Brown

BRANDIED PRUNE TARTS

1 c. pitted prunes
⅓ c. brandy
⅓ c. water
2 Tbsp. granulated sugar
½ tsp. cornstarch

1 tsp. grated orange peel
2 - 3 oz. pkg. cream cheese, softened
3 Tbsp. orange juice
8 baked (3 inch) tart shells

Cut prunes into quarters in saucepan. Combine prunes with brandy and water. Heat to boiling; cover and simmer 5 minutes. Combine sugar and cornstarch; stir into prunes and cook over moderate heat until slightly thickened. Add ½ teaspoon of the orange peel; cool. Mix cream cheese with orange juice and remaining peel. Spoon evenly into tart shells. Top with prune mixture. Yield: 8 tarts.

Peggy Kessinger

QUICK "COOKIES"

24 graham crackers
1 stick butter
1 stick margarine

½ c. granulated sugar
½ c. chopped nuts

Melt until it clarifies. Spread mixture over crackers that are placed on a cookie sheet. Sprinkle nuts over mixture. Bake for 10 minutes at 350°.

Linda Y. Borden

ROCKY ROAD FUDGE BARS

Step 1:

½ c. butter
1 oz. sq. chocolate
1 c. sugar
1 c. flour

¾ c. nuts
1 tsp. baking powder
1 tsp. vanilla
2 eggs

Melt over low heat. Mix well. Spread in greased and floured pan.

Step 2:

1 (8 oz.) pkg. cream cheese
  (reserve 2 oz. for
  frosting)
½ c. sugar
2 Tbsp. flour
¼ c. butter

1 egg
½ tsp. vanilla
¼ c. nuts
6 oz. chocolate chips
2 c. miniature marshmallows

Combine cream cheese, flour, sugar, butter, eggs, and vanilla. Stir in nuts and spread over Step 1. Sprinkle chocolate chips over. Bake at 350° for 25 to 30 minutes. Remove. Sprinkle marshmallows and bake for 2 minutes.

Step 3 - Frosting for Rocky Road Fudge Bars:

¼ c. butter
1 oz. sq. chocolate
2 oz. cream cheese

¼ c. milk
3 c. confectioners sugar
1 tsp. vanilla

Over low heat, melt butter, chocolate, cream cheese and milk. Remove from heat. Stir in sugar and vanilla. Spread over fudge bars.

Deloris White

SAND TARTS

1 c. butter
2 c. plain flour
1½ c. crushed nuts

1 tsp. vanilla
6 Tbsp. powdered sugar

Cream butter and sugar; add flour and vanilla. Mix well. Roll into balls or fingers. Bake 15 minutes at 350°. Roll in powdered sugar. Grease pan. Makes about 30; roll small.

Patsy Akers

SANDIES

¾ c. butter
5 Tbsp. confectioners sugar
2 c. sifted cake flour

1 Tbsp. ice water
1 tsp. vanilla
1 c. chopped pecans

Cream butter; add sugar; cream together. Add flour, water, vanilla and pecans. Mix well. Chill. Shape into rolls about 1 inch long and ½ inch thick. Bake in slow oven until very light brown. Roll in confectioners sugar while hot. Makes about 2 dozen.

Heidi Thompson

SEVEN LAYER COOKIES

Layer in 13x9x2 inch pan:

1 stick margarine, melted
1 c. graham crackers
1 c. cocoanut
1 c. chocolate chips

1 c. butterscotch chips
1 c. pecan chips
1 can Eagle Brand condensed
  milk

Bake 30 minutes at 350°. Cool and slice.

Judy Seeders

SEVEN LAYER BARS

1 stick butter

Graham cracker crumbs

Mix together and make crust.

1 (6 oz.) pkg. chocolate chips
1 (6 oz.) pkg. butterscotch
  chips

1 can Eagle Brand milk
1 c. nuts
1 c. coconut

Bake at 350° for 30 to 35 minutes.

Wynola Sharon Davis

SUGAR COOKIES

1 c. butter or oleo
1½ c. sifted confectioners
  sugar
1 egg
1 tsp. vanilla

2½ c. sifted flour (plain)
1 tsp. soda
1 tsp. cream of tartar
Dash of salt

Cream butter and sugar. Add eggs and vanilla; continue to beat. Sift dry ingredients and blend into sugar mixture. Chill dough and slice. Sprinkle with sugar. Preheat oven to 400°. Bake 10 to 12 minutes at 375°.

Katherine Ray

SUGAR COOKIES

3 c. all-purpose flour
½ tsp. baking soda
½ tsp. baking powder
1 c. butter

2 eggs
1 c. sugar
1 tsp. lemon extract

In a mixing bowl, sift together flour, soda and baking powder on low speed of mixture. Cut in butter until mixture resembles corn meal. In small mixing bowl, beat eggs. Add sugar and lemon extract; beat thoroughly. Blend egg mixture into flour and butter. Chill dough. On a lightly floured surface, roll dough 1 inch thick. Cut with floured cookie cutters. With wide spatula, transfer to baking sheet. Sprinkle with sugar if desired. Bake in 375° oven for 6 to 8 minutes or until lightly browned. Yield: 6 dozen.

Peggy Kessinger

AMY'S SUGAR COOKIES

1 egg
⅓ c. vegetable oil
1 tsp. vanilla
1 tsp. baking powder

6 Tbsp. sugar
1 c. flour, sifted
¼ tsp. salt
¼ tsp. soda

Beat egg; stir in vanilla and oil. Blend in sugar. Mix flour, baking powder, soda and salt into mixture. Drop by teaspoonful 2 inches apart on ungreased baking sheet. Gently press each cookie flat with the bottom of a glass moistened with vegetable oil and dipped in sugar. Bake at 400° for 8 to 10 minutes or until brown. Remove immediately from baking sheet and place on a cooling rack.

Virginia Moran

DROP SUGAR COOKIES

1 c. margarine or butter
1 c. granulated sugar
1 c. confectioners sugar
1 c. oil
2 eggs

4 c. plus 4 Tbsp. flour
1 tsp. cream of tartar
1 tsp. soda
1 tsp. pure almond extract
½ tsp. salt

Cream margarine; add sugar and mix well. Add eggs, oil and almond extract; mix well. Add dry ingredients that have been sifted together and mixed well. Chill for several hours or overnight. Roll into walnut size pieces; put on ungreased cookie sheet; flatten with a small juice glass that has been dipped in granulated sugar and bake at 350° for 8 to 10 minutes. Yield: 6 dozen.

Betty Coogle

GRANNY'S SUGAR COOKIES

½ c. butter
1 c. sugar
1 large egg
2 - 2¼ c. all-purpose flour

2 tsp. baking powder
½ tsp. salt
½ tsp. vanilla

Cream together ½ cup butter and 1 cup sugar. Blend in 1 large egg. Sift together and add to mixture 2 to 2¼ cups all-purpose flour, 2 teaspoons baking powder, ½ teaspoon salt and ½ teaspoon vanilla. Divide dough in 2 parts. Chill 1 to 2 hours so it will be easy to handle. Roll dough, 1 part at a time, to ⅛ inch thick and cut cookies out with cookie cutters. Transfer to cookie sheet and bake in preheated 375° oven 8 to 10 minutes. Frost with Confectioners Sugar-Water Glaze. Makes approximately 2 dozen cookies. (Keep other part of dough chilled until ready to roll out.)

Confectioners Sugar-Water Glaze:

1 c. sifted confectioners
  sugar

Food coloring (optional)
5 - 6 tsp. water

Blend together 1 cup sifted confectioners sugar and 5 to 6 teaspoons water. Add food coloring if desired. Brush glaze over cookies while still warm.

Peggy Kessinger

ROCKIE ROAD COOKIES

1 (6 oz.) pkg. chocolate bits
½ c. margarine
2 eggs
1 c. sugar
1½ c. flour

½ tsp. baking powder
½ tsp. salt
½ tsp. vanilla
¾ c. chopped nuts

Melt half the chocolate bits and margarine over low heat. Cool. Sift together flour, baking powder and salt. Add remaining chocolate bits and nuts to flour mix. Coat with flour mix; set aside. Beat eggs; add sugar and vanilla and mix. Add chocolate mixture and blend well. Add flour, chocolate bits and nut mixture. Mix until well blended. Drop by teaspoon 2 inches apart on greased baking sheet. Bake for 8 minutes at 400°. Yield: 2 dozen.

Sharon Dukes

SPICE COOKIES

1½ c. sugar
1 c. shortening
½ c. black coffee
½ c. dark corn syrup or
    molasses
5 c. sifted flour
2 tsp. baking soda

1 tsp. baking powder
1 tsp. allspice
1 tsp. cloves
1 tsp. cinnamon
1 tsp. vanilla
Jelly (flavor to suit you)

Cream sugar and shortening. Combine coffee and syrup. Sift together dry ingredients. Add flour mixture to creamed mixture alternately with coffee mixture. Add vanilla and other spices and additional flour mixture to make a stiff dough. Chill. Roll out on floured board about ¼ inch thick. Cut with round cookie cutter, about 2½ inches in size. Place on cookie sheet. Dent center of each cookie with thumb and dot with jelly. Bake 10 to 12 minutes at 350°. Cool on racks.

Kathy Chesser

TEXAS RANGERS COOKIES

1 c. shortening
1 c. white sugar
1 c. brown sugar
2 eggs
2 c. corn flakes
2 c. oats

2 c. flour
2 tsp. soda
1 tsp. baking powder
½ tsp. salt
1 c. shredded coconut
1 tsp. vanilla

Mix ingredients in order given. Drop by teaspoon on lightly greased cookie sheet. Bake 8 to 10 minutes in 375° oven. Yield: 6 dozen cookies.

Denise Figg

SNAPPY TURTLE COOKIES

1½ c. flour (all-purpose)
½ c. firmly packed brown
    sugar
¼ tsp. salt
¼ tsp. soda

½ c. butter or margarine,
    softened
¼ tsp. vanilla
1 egg

Frosting:

1 (1 oz.) sq. unsweetened
    chocolate
1 Tbsp. butter or margarine

3 Tbsp. milk
1½ c. powdered sugar
2 c. pecan halves

Combine first 7 ingredients; blend well. Chill dough. Heat oven to 350°. On greased cookie sheets, arrange pecan halves in groups of 3 or 5 to resemble head and legs of a turtle. Shape dough into 1 inch balls; press lightly onto nuts (tips of pecans must show when cookie is baked). Bake 10 to 15 minutes until bottom is lightly browned. Cool, in small saucepan; heat first 3 frosting ingredients, stirring constantly, until chocolate melts. Remove from heat. Add powdered sugar; blend until smooth. Frost tops of cookies generously.

Wilma Crowdus

UGLIES

Melt 1 stick of butter in baking dish.

Layer:

Graham cracker crumbs
12 oz. chocolate chips
12 oz. Reese's peanut butter
    chips (or butterscotch
    chips)

1 small can coconut
1 c. cut up pecans

Pour 1 can of Eagle Brand milk over all. Bake in preheated oven at 350° for *only* 30 minutes. If you cook any longer, they get too hard.

Doris McCord

DESSERTS

APPLE CRISP

2 sticks margarine, melted
1½ c. brown sugar

1½ c. flour
1 c. oatmeal

Stir mixture in large mixing bowl. Use 9x13 inch pan. Use approximately 4 to 5 apples, sliced. Spread mixture over apples. Bake 40 minutes at 350°.

Donna Barrett

APPLE CRISP

2 cans fried apples (or 4 c.
　sliced, pared tart apples,
　cooked)
½ c. flour
¾ tsp. cinnamon
⅓ c. softened margarine

½ c. raisins
⅔ - ¾ c. brown sugar
½ c. uncooked oats
¾ tsp. nutmeg
½ c. chopped pecans

Place apples in a baking dish. Combine all other ingredients and mix well. Sprinkle mixture over the top of the layer of apples. Bake in a 375° oven for 10 minutes. Can be served warm or cold.

Ruth Ackerman

APPLE DUMPLINGS

Use 6 apples, peeled and cut in halves.

Dough:

2 c. flour
2½ tsp. baking powder
½ tsp. salt

⅔ c. shortening
½ c. milk

Sauce:

2 c. brown sugar
2 c. water

¼ c. butter
½ tsp. cinnamon

Roll out dough. Cut in squares. Place apple half on each square. Wet edges of dough and press into a ball around the apple. Set dumplings in pan. Pour sauce over and bake at 350° to 375° for 20 to 25 minutes.

Donna Browning

APPLES OF EDEN

6 large apples
¾ c. raisins
½ c. white wine

Rind of 1 orange
¼ c. butter
½ c. granulated sugar

Wash apples and remove cores. Grease a baking dish with butter and arrange apples in it. Rinse raisins well; boil for a few seconds in ¼ cup wine. Stuff apples with raisins; top with dried peel or few chips of butter, and a sprinkling of sugar. Pour wine over each apple and bake in a moderate oven about 350° for ½ hour. Serve hot. Preparing time 20 minutes. Cooking time 30 minutes. Serves 6.

Denise Figg

DELUXE APPLE TART

Crust:

1½ c. all-purpose flour
½ tsp. baking powder
½ tsp. salt

¼ c. each butter and
   shortening
3 - 4 Tbsp. milk

Combine flour, baking powder and salt. Cut in butter and shortening; sprinkle milk over mixture and stir with fork until moist. Form into a ball and chill at least 1 hour. Roll out and fit in 11 x 7½ x 1 inch pan.

Fillings:

½ c. plus 2 Tbsp. blanched,
   slivered almonds
½ c. sugar

1 egg, beaten
1 Tbsp. melted butter

Process almonds in food processor until fine; add other ingredients; pour into prepared shell.

5 - 7 cooking apples
2 c. water
2 Tbsp. lemon juice

¼ c. sugar
¼ c. butter
½ tsp. cinnamon

Peel and slice apples into water with lemon juice. When all sliced, drain and arrange in rows in crust. Combine sugar and cinnamon; sprinkle over apples; dot with butter. Bake at 400° for 1 hour.

Glaze:

½ c. apricot or peach
   preserves

2 Tbsp. water (add more if not
   spreadable)

Combine preserves with water; cook, stirring constantly, until melted. Press through sieve. Reserve syrup. Discard solids. Carefully brush syrup over tart. Makes 16 servings.

Ruthie Marty

APRICOT BARS

1 lb. dried apricots
1 unpeeled seeded orange
1 c. sugar

1 c. pecans, chopped
Sifted powdered sugar

Put apricots and orange through food chopper twice. Combine with sugar in top of double boiler and cook, covered, over hot water for 30 minutes or longer, until quite stiff. Cool and stir in nuts. Shape into rolls ½ inch wide and 1 ½ inches long; roll in powdered sugar.

Note: Don't store in covered container as they will become sticky. Put them on a cookie sheet or wax paper in refrigerator until they become firm.

Helen Russman

APRICOT BARS

1 c. dried apricots
1 c. flour, sifted
¼ c. sugar
½ c. margarine
⅓ c. flour, sifted
½ tsp. baking powder

¼ tsp. salt
2 eggs
1 c. brown sugar, packed
⅔ c. pecans, chopped
½ tsp. vanilla
Confectioners sugar

Cook apricots in boiling water for 10 minutes; drain. Cool and cut up; set aside. Combine 1 cup flour, sugar and butter; mix until crumbly. Press into greased 9 inch square pan. Bake in 350° oven for about 18 minutes. Sift together ⅓ cup flour, baking powder and salt. Beat eggs well. Slowly beat in brown sugar and blend well. Add flour mixture; stir well. Add apricots, nuts and vanilla. Spread over baked layer. Bake at 350° for 25 minutes or until golden brown. Cool in pan on rack. Cut into bars with a buttered knife. Roll in confectioners sugar.

Lora Martin

BAKED ALASKA

1 (8 inch) layer pound cake
3 egg whites
¼ tsp. salt

¾ c. sugar
1 qt. pistachio ice cream

Ice cream should be firmly frozen. Cover thick wooden board with heavy brown paper. Place cake on center of board. Beat egg whites and salt until foamy. Beat in sugar a tablespoon at a time, beating until satiny. Take firmly frozen ice cream and place on cake. Cover ice cream and cake with thick coating of meringue. Bake at 500° for 3 to 5 minutes, until delicately browned. Slip onto cold platter. Serve in wedges immediately. Makes 6 to 8 servings.

Alice Walsh Alessio

BANANA PUDDING

1 small *instant* vanilla
  pudding
1 can Eagle Brand milk

1 (8 oz.) ctn. Cool Whip
6 bananas
Box of vanilla wafers

Mix instant pudding with 2 cups cold milk; add Eagle Brand milk, then add Cool Whip (room temperature). Whip lightly with wire beater until creamy. Place layer of wafers, layer of bananas and layer of mixture. Repeat until mixture is used. May crumble wafers on top. Makes 10 to 12 servings.

Can make 2 puddings if desired.

Mindy Crook

BANANA SPLIT DESSERT

2 c. graham cracker crumbs
3 sticks butter or margarine
2 eggs
1 lb. confectioners sugar
1 tsp. vanilla

Sliced bananas
1 can crushed pineapple
1 (9 oz.) bowl Cool Whip
Nuts

Melt 1 stick of butter and mix with graham cracker crumbs and press in a 9x13 inch dish. Next, mix eggs, 2 sticks butter or margarine, confectioners sugar and vanilla. Beat 15 minutes. Spread over crumb mixture. Put sliced bananas over creamed mixture. Drain can of crushed pineapple and spread over bananas. Spread Cool Whip over pineapple and sprinkle with nuts.

Best to make the night before.

Mary Frances Stayton

BANANA WALNUT LOAF

¾ c. granulated sugar
¼ c. shortening
2 eggs
1 c. mashed bananas
2 c. sifted all-purpose flour

2 tsp. baking powder
½ tsp. salt
1 c. chopped walnuts
¼ tsp. baking soda

Beat sugar, shortening and eggs together until light and fluffy. Add mashed bananas. Resift flour with baking powder, salt and soda. Add to banana mixture. Beat until smooth. Add walnuts. Turn into greased 9x5x3 inch loaf pan. Bake at 350° for 55 to 65 minutes. Cool on rack. Makes 1 loaf.

Bessie Litchford

BLUEBERRY JELLO DESSERT

2 small pkg. raspberry or
   grape Jello
2 c. hot water

1 can blueberry pie filling
1 (20 oz.) can crushed
   pineapple

Combine and chill.

Topping:

1 (8 oz.) pkg. cream cheese
1 c. sour cream
½ tsp. vanilla

½ c. sugar
½ c. chopped nuts

Spread topping on Jello. Can be topped with Cool Whip.

Donna Barrett

HODGENVILLE BOURBON BALLS

1 c. chopped pecans
¾ c. bourbon
1 stick butter

2 lb. powdered sugar, sifted
1 box semi-sweet chocolate
½ cake paraffin

Soak pecans in bourbon overnight. Cream butter with ½ box powdered sugar. Add remaining sugar and nut mixture. Place mixture in refrigerator to chill slightly. Form into small balls and refrigerate 1 hour until firm. In top of double boiler, melt chocolate and paraffin. Dip balls into chocolate and place on wax paper until firm. Store in refrigerator. Makes 6 to 8 dozen.

Helen Russman

BOURBON BROWNIES

1 (15½ oz.) box brownie mix
2 eggs, beaten
3 Tbsp. water

⅓ c. bourbon
½ c. soft butter

Follow recipe on cake box for brownies, using 2 eggs and 3 tablespoons water. Spread mixture in the bottom of a 9x13 inch pan, greased and floured. Bake according to directions and transfer to a rack to cool. Brush with ⅓ cup bourbon.

Icing:

3 Tbsp. bourbon
3 c. confectioners sugar
1 (16 oz.) pkg. semi-sweet
   chocolate chips

⅓ c. butter plus 2 Tbsp.

Mix the ⅓ cup butter with 3 tablespoons bourbon and the confectioners sugar. Spread on top of bourbon brushed brownies. Melt chocolate chips with 2 tablespoons butter. Cool a little and spread on top. Slice into finger size bars while topping is still creamy. Place in refrigerator or freezer.

Helen Russman

BREAD PUDDING

2 c. dry bread cubes
1 Tbsp. butter
¾ c. sugar
1 tsp. vanilla extract

4 c. milk, scalded
¼ tsp. salt
4 slightly beaten eggs

Soak bread in milk 5 minutes. Add butter, salt and sugar. Pour slowly over eggs; add vanilla and mix well. Pour into greased baking dish. Bake in pan of hot water in moderate oven (350°) until firm, about 50 minutes. Serve warm with Lemon Sauce. Add ½ cup seeded raisins if desired.

Lemon Sauce:

½ c. sugar
⅛ tsp. salt
1 c. boiling water
1½ Tbsp. lemon juice

1 Tbsp. cornstarch
⅛ tsp. nutmeg
2 Tbsp. butter

Mix sugar, cornstarch, salt and nutmeg; gradually add water and cook over low heat until thick and clear. Add butter and lemon juice; blend thoroughly.

Oleta Bryan

BREAD PUDDING

10 oz. French bread	2 c. milk
6 eggs	½ c. cream (half & half)
½ tsp. cinnamon	2 tsp. vanilla extract
1 Tbsp. nutmeg	1½ c. seedless raisins
¼ c. sugar	2 sticks butter

In bowl, combine eggs, cinnamon and nutmeg. Mix well. Add to this mixture sugar, milk, cream and vanilla extract. Mix well. Cut up bread in bite-size pieces in baking dish (about 1½ quarts). Add raisins and melted butter to bread. Pour mixture over bread. Bake about 30 minutes or until it is golden brown. Serves about 12.

Rum Sauce:

2½ c. milk, scalded	Dash of cinnamon
¾ c. sugar	Dash of nutmeg
6 Tbsp. flour	1 tsp. vanilla flavor
4 eggs, beaten well	1 tsp. rum flavor
1 stick butter	1 oz. rum

In saucepan, melt butter; add flour. Mix well. Add scalded milk and sugar. Cook over low heat until thick. Beat in eggs and remove from heat. Add nutmeg, cinnamon, vanilla and rum. Serve over pudding.

BROWNIES

1 stick (½ c.) butter	1 c. plain flour
1 c. sugar	4 eggs
16 oz. can Hershey's chocolate syrup	2 tsp. vanilla
	½ c. nuts

Cream butter and sugar together; add rest of ingredients. Bake at 325° for 30 minutes.

Icing:

6 Tbsp. butter
6 Tbsp. milk

1⅓ c. sugar
½ c. chocolate chips

Bring butter, milk and sugar to boil; cook for 1 minute. Add chocolate chips and stir until it melts. Pour over brownies.

Peggy McKeehan

NESTLE'S QUIK BROWNIES

4 c. Nestle's Quik chocolate
** mix**
6 eggs
½ c. sugar
2½ c. self-rising flour

1 Tbsp. vanilla or 2½ tsp.
** peppermint flavoring**
½ tsp. salt
1 c. cooking oil
½ c. milk

Beat eggs and sugar together; add flour, salt and vanilla. Stir in Nestle's Quik chocolate, then blend cooking oil and milk into the batter. Beat the batter about 10 minutes; pour into greased pan and bake in a preheated oven of 350° about 25 to 30 minutes.

Ann Brawand

CARAMEL CRISPY TREATS

¼ c. Parkay margarine
4 c. Kraft miniature
** marshmallows**

5 c. Rice Krispies
2 wrapped caramel sheets

Melt margarine in saucepan over low heat. Add marshmallows; stir until melted and well blended. Remove from heat. Add cereal; stir until well coated. Press half of cereal mixture into a 9 inch square pan. Cover with caramel sheets, stretching slightly to cover top. Top with remaining cereal mixture. Press lightly. Cool and cut into squares.

Bev Sowders

FROSTED CARROT BARS

2 c. flour
2 c. sugar
2 tsp. baking soda
1½ tsp. cinnamon
1¼ c. oil

½ tsp. salt
2 jars junior baby carrots
4 eggs
1½ c. nuts (optional)
1½ c. raisins (optional)

Mix flour, sugar, cinnamon, salt, oil, eggs and carrots. Bake on greased cookie sheet at 350° for 20 to 25 minutes. Ice when cool.

Icing:

8 oz. cream cheese
1 box powdered sugar

1 stick margarine
1 tsp. vanilla

Mix and spread on cookie bars. Cut in squares.

CHARLOTTE RUSSE

4 eggs, separated
1 c. sugar
½ c. cold water
1 env. plain gelatin plus 1 tsp.
3 (½ pt.) ctn. whipping cream

1 pkg. Dream Whip, fixed
according to instructions
on pkg.
1 tsp. vanilla
2 pkg. ladyfingers

Put whipping cream (in boxes), milk for Dream Whip (in separate bowl), bowl for whipping cream, and beaters in freezer until *cold.* Cream whips better and so does Dream Whip. Put gelatin in ½ cup cold water for 5 minutes in small Pyrex custard cup. Set in boiling water until gelatin dissolves, stirring occasionally. Beat egg yolks and sugar in large mixer bowl until creamy and sugar is not grainy. Beat egg whites until stiff; add to egg mixture with wooden spoon and fold in gently until well distributed. Beat whipping cream until stiff; add vanilla and fold into egg white mixture; fold in Dream Whip. Line large bowl (tall salad size) with ladyfingers (pull ladyfingers apart). Makes 2 quarts.

Mrs. Doris Buckner

CHARLOTTE RUSSE

1½ c. milk
1 c. sugar
4 egg yolks
3 Tbsp. flour
1½ env. clear gelatin, soaked
in ½ c. cold water

3 tsp. vanilla
4 egg whites, whipped
1 qt. cream (half & half)
Ladyfingers

Heat milk in double boiler; add sugar, egg yolks and flour. Cook until thickens. Add the gelatin; stir in vanilla; whip egg whites and add to mixture. Fold in cream and let stand in refrigerator for 6 hours. Serve over ladyfingers.

Peggy Hunter

CHERRY CRUNCH

1 pkg. Duncan Hines white
    deluxe cake mix
1 can cherry pie filling
1 tsp. lemon juice

½ c. chopped nuts
1 stick melted butter
Whipped cream or ice cream
    or coffee cream

Spread pie filling in a 9 inch square pan. Sprinkle with lemon juice. Combine cake mix, nuts and melted butter; sprinkle over pie filling. Bake at 350° for 40 to 50 minutes or until golden brown. Serve with whipped cream, ice cream or coffee cream.

Peggy Kessinger

CHERRY DELIGHT

3 c. graham cracker crumbs
1½ sticks margarine, melted
¾ c. sugar
1 large pkg. cream cheese
2 pkg. Dream Whip, mixed
    according to pkg.
    directions

1 c. cold milk
2 cans cherry pie filling

Mix graham crackers, margarine and sugar. Press in bottom of a 9x13 inch pan. Mix Dream Whip with cream cheese and cold milk. Spread this on top of graham cracker crust. Then spread cherry pie filling on top of cream cheese-Dream Whip mixture. Refrigerate until chilled.

Bernadette Mills

CHERRY DELIGHT

1 (8 oz.) pkg. cream cheese
1 small ctn. sour cream
1 can cherry pie filling

1 can pineapple chunks
2 small boxes cherry Jello

Mix pie filling and pineapple together and let set. Mix Jello according to directions. When partially set, pour pie filling mixture on top and let set until jelled. Mix softened cream cheese and sour cream together until well blended, then spread on top of Jello. Chill.

Carol Mills

508

CHERRY DESSERT

1 c. flour	1¼ c. sugar
1 can cherries	1 tsp. soda
½ c. nuts	1 tsp. cinnamon
1 Tbsp. melted butter	1 egg, beaten

Cream sugar, butter and egg. Add dry ingredients. Drain cherries (save juice) and add to mixture. Add nuts now too. Mix well. Bake at 350° for 45 minutes.

Cherry Sauce:

Cherry juice plus water to equal 1 c.	¼ tsp. salt
½ c. sugar	1 Tbsp. melted butter
	1 Tbsp. cornstarch

Mix sugar with cherry juice. Add this to rest of ingredients in a saucepan. Cook over medium heat until it starts to thicken (very little).

Barbara Montgomery

CHERRIES IN THE SNOW

2 c. all-purpose flour	1 (8 oz.) pkg. cream cheese
2 sticks margarine (do not use whipped)	½ c. powdered sugar
½ c. light brown sugar	Cherry pie filling
1½ c. chopped pecans	
2 pkg. Dream Whip, prepared according to pkg. directions	

Crust is very important for perfection. Blend butter and flour real well. Add brown sugar and nuts; press into 13x9x2 inch ungreased pan. Bake at 400° for 15 minutes. Remove from oven; cool, then chip up. Next, blend cream cheese and powdered sugar; fold in Dream Whip. Spread crust evenly in an 11x8x2 inch Pyrex baking dish. Spread topping (cream cheese mixture) over crust, then top with any brand of prepared cherry pie filling.

Ann LaDuke (submitted by Brownie - Lois Bruner

CHOCOLATE DESSERT

1 stick margarine
1 c. flour
1 c. nuts, chopped
1 (8 oz.) pkg. cream cheese
1 c. confectioners sugar
1 ctn. Cool Whip
1 pkg. instant vanilla pudding
    mix

1 pkg. chocolate instant
    pudding mix
2 c. milk
1 tsp. vanilla
Chocolate syrup
Slivered almonds

First layer: Mix together 1 stick margarine, 1 cup flour and 1 cup chopped nuts. Pack into 9x9 inch pan. Bake at 325° for 25 minutes. Cool.

Second layer: Mix together 8 ounce package cream cheese and 1 cup confectioners sugar. Add Cool Whip; pour this over first layer. (Leave enough Cool Whip for fourth layer.)

Third layer: Beat together until thick 1 package instant vanilla pudding mix, 1 package instant chocolate pudding mix, 2 cups milk and 1 teaspoon vanilla; pour over second layer.

Fourth layer: Cover third layer with remaining Cool Whip. Dribble chocolate syrup over top, then sprinkle slivered almonds over this. Refrigerate 12 hours; cut in squares. It's super!

Mary Harrod

DOUBLE CHOCOLATE CRUMBLE BARS

½ c. butter or margarine
¾ c. sugar
2 eggs
1 tsp. vanilla
¾ c. all-purpose flour
½ c. chopped pecans
2 Tbsp. cocoa

¼ tsp. baking powder
2 c. tiny marshmallows
1 (6 oz.) pkg. chocolate chips
1 c. peanut butter
1½ c. Rice Krispies
¼ tsp. salt

Cream butter and sugar. Beat in eggs and vanilla. Stir together flour, chopped nuts, cocoa, baking powder and ¼ teaspoon salt; stir into egg mixture. Spread on bottom of greased 13x9 inch pan. Bake in 350° oven for 15 to 20 minutes or until bars test done. Sprinkle marshmallows evenly on top of bars; bake 3 minutes longer. Cool. In a small saucepan, combine chocolate chips and peanut butter. Cook and stir over low heat until chocolate is melted. Stir in the cereal. Spread mixture over the top of cooled bars. Chill; cut into bars. Makes 3 to 4 dozen.

Maxine Welch

CHOCOLATE RUM BALLS

1 c. vanilla wafer crumbs
1 c. pecans, ground
2 Tbsp. cocoa
2 Tbsp. white corn syrup
¼ c. Jamaica rum
Powdered mixture composed
    of 1 tsp. cocoa and ½

tsp. cinnamon to every
rounded Tbsp. sifted
powdered sugar
Powdered sugar

Mix cookie crumbs with ground nuts; add cocoa, corn syrup and rum. Mix well. Mold into balls, 1 teaspoonful at a time. Roll in cocoa-cinnamon-sugar mixture. Place balls on baking sheet for 3 hours to dry. Roll in plain powdered sugar. Makes 20 balls.

Denise Figg

CINNAMON COFFEE CAKE

1 c. butter
2 eggs
2 c. sugar
1 c. sour cream
4 tsp. sugar
¾ c. pecans

2 c. flour
1 tsp. baking powder
Pinch of salt
½ tsp. vanilla
1 Tbsp. cinnamon

Cream butter and sugar; add eggs and sour cream. Sift together flour and baking powder; add salt and vanilla. In another bowl, stir together 4 teaspoons sugar and 1 tablespoon cinnamon and ¾ cup pecans. Pour half of batter in tube pan and half of cinnamon mixture on top, then add the rest of batter and top with remaining cinnamon mixture. Bake at 350° for 50 to 55 minutes. When finished, sprinkle powdered sugar on top.

Martha Harper

COCOA DROPS

2 c. sugar
½ c. milk
1 stick margarine
4 Tbsp. cocoa

2 tsp. vanilla
½ c. peanut butter
2½ c. Quaker Quick oats

Bring sugar, cocoa, margarine and milk to a boil in a 1½ quart saucepan. Boil 1½ minutes, no more. Remove from heat. Add vanilla, peanut butter and oats. Beat with a spoon until well blended. Drop by teaspoon on wax paper and cool.

Note: May be spread into an oiled 9x13 inch shallow pan. Cut into desired sizes when cool.

Kathy Chesser

COCONUT DESSERT

½ c. margarine
1 c. flour

2 Tbsp. sugar
½ c. chopped nuts

Mix all ingredients together and put in 9x13 inch pan. Bake at 350° for 10 to 15 minutes. Let cool.

1 (8 oz.) pkg. cream cheese
1 c. powdered sugar

1 c. Cool Whip

Mix well and put on cooled baked layer.

2 small pkg. instant coconut
   pudding

3 c. cold milk

Mix and pour over last layer. Sprinkle with coconut.

Dianne Rice

CREAM CHEESE CUPCAKES

2 (8 oz.) pkg. cream cheese,
   softened
¾ c. sugar
2 eggs
1 Tbsp. lemon juice

1 Tbsp. vanilla
1 pkg. Nabisco vanilla wafers
Pie filling (strawberry,
   blueberry, etc.)

Beat together first 5 ingredients until light and fluffy. Line muffin tins with cupcake liners (tea size). Place vanilla wafers in bottom of each cup. Fill ⅔ cup with cream cheese mixture. Bake at 375° for 15 to 20 minutes or until set. When ready to serve, fill with pie filling of your choice. Makes 25 to 30 cupcakes.

Crystal Duke

CUPCAKES

1¾ c. sifted flour*	½ c. sugar
3 tsp. baking powder	1 tsp. vanilla
½ tsp. salt	3 eggs
⅔ c. milk	½ c. shortening

Sift dry ingredients into mixing bowl. Add shortening and milk. Beat for 2 minutes. Add eggs and vanilla. Beat for 2 minutes. Pour batter into well greased muffin pans. Bake at 375° for 20 to 25 minutes. Frost as desired. Makes 18 medium cupcakes.

* If using self-rising flour, omit baking powder and salt.

Sue Tipton

ANGEL CUSTARD

3 egg yolks, beaten	3 egg whites, beaten stiff
1 c. sugar	¾ large angel food cake,
¼ tsp. salt	broken up
1 c. milk	Chopped nuts
1 env. gelatin	Coconut
¼ c. cold water	Cherries
1 c. heavy cream, whipped	

Combine egg yolks, sugar, salt and milk. Cook 6 to 8 minutes in double boiler until mixture coats spoon. Remove from heat. Dissolve gelatin in ¼ cup cold water. Stir into hot custard mixture. Cool. Reserve enough whipped cream to use for topping. Sweeten this portion only. Fold remaining whipped cream into custard mixture. Add beaten egg whites. Grease a 12x8x2 inch dish with butter. Alternate layers of broken cake with custard, beginning with cake and ending with custard. Top with reserved whipped cream. Garnish with chopped nuts, coconut and cherries. Chill in refrigerator for at least 12 hours. This keeps well and improves in flavor for 3 or 4 days.

Sue Tipton

513

OLD FASHION BOILED CUSTARD

1 qt. milk
¾ c. sugar
4 egg yolks

4 Tbsp. flour, sifted before
    measuring

Mix sugar, flour and egg yolks until smooth. Heat milk to luke-warm and add to preceding. Then cook in double boiler until correct thickness. Add vanilla.

Heidi Thompson

DATE BALLS

To 3 sticks melted butter, add 1 cup sugar. Cook until sugar is dis-solved. Add 2 pound dates, cut up, and cook until dates are like thick mashed potatoes. Stir constantly or it will stick. Remove from fire and add 1 teaspoon salt and 1 teaspoon vanilla. Add 2 cups pecans, cut up. Add 4 or 5 cups Rice Krispies. Make into balls or little larger than mar-bles.

Clara Nance

DATE BONBONS

1 lb. pitted dates
½ c. pecan halves
1 (10 oz.) can flaked coconut,
    toasted

1 c. white corn syrup

Boil syrup 2 or 3 minutes. Cool. To toast coconut, place on flat pan and bake at 350° for 7 to 10 minutes, stirring frequently, until lightly toasted. Cool. Insert nut into each date, dip in syrup, roll in coconut, and place on waxed paper to dry.

Jean Lyle

DATE NUT ROLL
(Can be used as either a dessert or candy)

2 c. (½ lb.) vanilla wafer
    crumbs
1 c. chopped dates
½ c. chopped nutmeats

½ c. sweetened condensed
    milk
2 tsp. lemon juice

Combine wafer crumbs, dates and nutmeats. Blend milk and lemon juice. Add to crumb mixture and knead well. Form into roll 3 inches in diameter and cover with waxed paper. Chill in refrigerator for 12 hours or longer. Cut in slices. Garnish with whipped cream or hard sauce if using as a dessert.

Martha Hooper

FRUIT BAKE

1 (No. 303) can peach halves	⅓ c. butter
1 (No. 303) can pear halves	¾ c. brown sugar
1 (No. 2) can pineapple slices	1 tsp. curry powder

Drain fruit well. Place fruit in casserole dish. Melt ⅓ cup butter; add ¾ cup brown sugar and 1 teaspoon curry powder. Pour mixture over fruit. Bake 1 hour at 325°.

Mary Baxter

FRUIT PIZZA

1 pkg. yellow cake mix	¼ c. butter
¼ c. water	¼ c. brown sugar
2 eggs	½ c. chopped nuts

Should be stiff. Put wax paper on 2 pizza pans, greased and floured. Spread mixture. Bake at 350° for 15 to 20 minutes. Spread Cool Whip over cooled cake. Cover with fruit (grapes, bananas, fresh strawberries, pineapple chunks, etc.) Pour glaze over and refrigerate.

Glaze:

½ c. apricot preserves	2 Tbsp. water

Heat, then strain.

Peggy Graviss

FRUIT PIZZA
(This is a cool, refreshing summertime dessert; it is also pretty)

1 box Duncan Hines golden sugar cookie mix	1 c. powdered sugar
	1 banana
1 egg	1 peach
1 (8 oz.) pkg. Philadelphia cream cheese	A few strawberries
	Watermelon
½ stick margarine or butter	Seedless grapes

Mix cookie mix according to package directions, *without* water. Pat out on a pizza pan and bake about 4 to 5 minutes at temperature on package, until lightly browned at edges. Cool. Whip cream cheese together with butter and powdered sugar. Spread on cooled cookie. Cut up fruit onto pizza. Chill and serve.

I use the preceding combination, but feel free to use the fruits of your choice. I always toss my bananas in lemon juice to keep them from turning brown or put them on at serving time.

Wilma Lutts

GERMAN KUCHEN

Mix:

2 c. flour	**1 tsp. vanilla**
1½ c. sugar	**½ tsp. salt**
1 c. margarine or 2 sticks	**2 eggs**

Spread half of mixture in greased and floured 9x12 inch pan. Spread 1 can instant pie filling (apricot or pineapple or peach). Then spread rest of the batter on top. Bake at 350° about 45 minutes. Let cool a little and dust with powdered sugar. Good served warm.

Clara Nance

GLORIFIED RICE

1 c. cold, cooked rice	**1 c. whipping cream,**
½ c. sugar	**whipped**
1½ c. crushed pineapple,	**1 c. small marshmallows**
drained	**1 small jar maraschino**
½ tsp. vanilla	**cherries**

Mix all ingredients. Chill overnight. Serve.

Sherry Lynch

GRAHAM CRACKER DELIGHT

Graham crackers	**1 stick margarine**
1 c. sugar	**¾ c. pecans, chopped**
1 stick butter	

516

Break graham crackers apart and lay on cookie sheet. Melt butter and margarine; pour in sugar; stir to dissolve. Stir in pecans and mix. Spoon mixture on graham crackers. Bake 10 minutes at 375°.

Note: It is necessary to use both 1 stick of butter and 1 stick of margarine to get the right effect.

Betty Coogle

ELOQUENT HARLEQUIN

1 (3 oz.) pkg. orange, lime and strawberry flavor gelatin
1 (6 oz.) pkg. lemon flavor gelatin
1½ c. boiling water

½ c. lemon juice
1 c. cold water
2 (9 or 10 oz.) pkg. frozen whipped topping
8 ladyfingers, split

Early in day or day before, prepare orange, lime and strawberry gelatins separately, as directed on the package. Pour into 3 (8 inch) square pans; chill until firm. In a large bowl, dissolve lemon gelatin in the 1½ cups boiling water, cold lemon juice and cold water. Chill until mixture begins to mound from spoon. Fold in the whipped topping. To assemble dessert, cut orange, lime and strawberry gelatins into ½ inch cubes; fold in the lemon gelatin mixture. Line the sides of a 9 inch spring pan with waxed paper, then ladyfingers, rounded sides out. Spoon mixture into pan; chill until firm. To serve, remove pan and waxed paper. Serves 10.

Beth Howard

HIMMEL FUTTER - HEAVENLY FOOD

1 c. nuts
½ c. flour
1 tsp. baking powder
2 eggs, beaten lightly

1 c. chopped dates
½ c. sugar
⅛ tsp. salt

Mix together; bake in a pan. When done, it is turned out and sprinkled with pulverized sugar. Homemade citron made from watermelon rinds can be added if desired; this makes it more moist.

Note: This recipe came from Miss Mary E. Johnson of Sylva, home demonstration agent of Jackson County.

Beth Howard

HUNGARIAN NUT TORTE

12 egg yolks	6 Tbsp. graham cracker
12 egg whites	crumbs
12 Tbsp. sugar	12 Tbsp. walnuts, ground
6 Tbsp. flour	1 tsp. vanilla

Beat yolks and sugar until thick and lemon colored. Fold in flour, crumbs, nuts and vanilla. Beat egg whites until stiff; fold in batter. Bake in 3 (9 inch) pans (floured and greased) at 350° until cake springs back when touched, about 35 minutes. Cool, frost and fill. Split layers if desired.

Frosting:

1 can Eagle Brand milk	½ c. oleo*
½ c. Spry*	1 tsp. vanilla

Dump in bowl and mix 10 minutes.

* Must be cold.

Katherine Ray

DURGIN-PARK'S INDIAN PUDDING

1 tsp. butter, softened, plus 4	½ c. dark molasses
Tbsp. butter, cut into ½	¼ c. sugar
inch bits	¼ tsp. baking soda
2 eggs	¼ tsp. salt
6 c. milk	1 c. yellow corn meal

Preheat oven to 350°. With a pastry brush, spread the teaspoon of softened butter over the bottom and sides of a 2 quart souffle or baking dish. Set aside. In a heavy 4 to 5 quart saucepan, beat the eggs with a wire whisk until they are well mixed. Stirring constantly with the whisk, add 4 cups of the milk, the molasses, sugar, baking soda and salt. Then bring to a simmer over moderate heat, stirring until the molasses and sugar dissolve. Pour in the corn meal very slowly, making sure the simmering continues, and stirring constantly to keep the mixture smooth. Cook, uncovered, stirring from time to time, until the pudding is thick enough to hold its shape solidly in a spoon. Beat in the 4 tablespoons of butter bits and remove the pan from the heat. Then pour in the remaining 2 cups of milk in a thin stream, beating constantly. Pour the pudding into the buttered dish and bake in the middle of the oven for 1 hour. Reduce oven temperature to 300° and continue baking for 4 hours longer or until the pudding is very firm when prodded gently with a finger. Serve the pudding at once, directly from the baking dish; or let it cool and serve at room temperature. It may be topped with unsweetened whipped cream or vanilla ice cream if you like. Serves 6.

IRISH MISTY

1 container heavy whipping
    cream
½ tsp. vanilla extract
2 Tbsp. Irish Mist liqueur
1 (3 oz.) pkg. Jello, made with
    1 c. water

1 Tbsp. sugar
2 oz. slivered almonds
1 can mandarin orange
    sections, drained

Cut Jello into 1 inch cubes when completely firm. Whip cream until stiff. Stir in sugar, vanilla and Irish Mist liqueur. Fold in almonds, orange sections and Jello cubes. Serve with cookies (almond or butter cookies) if desired.

Alice Alessio

LEMON HEAVEN SALAD

Bottom Layer:

1 (6 oz.) pkg. lemon Jello   1 c. boiling water

Stir to dissolve well. Add 2 cups cold water. Add 4 diced bananas and 1 cup crushed pineapple (drain juice and reserve). Jell.

Middle Layer - Cook until thick and let cool:

1 c. sugar, mixed with 2
    tablespoons cornstarch
2 c. pineapple juice (use
    reserve juice and add
    water to make 2 c.)

4 eggs, well beaten
2 Tbsp. butter

Pour over first layer.

Top Layer: Top with 2 cups Cool Whip or Dream Whip. Top with nuts and cherries.

Kathy Ryan

LEMON SQUARES

1 c. flour
⅓ c. confectioners sugar

½ c. butter (room
    temperature)

Cream butter and sugar. Gradually add flour and mix well. Spread into lightly greased 9x9 inch pan. Level with spatula. Bake at 350° for 20 minutes. Remove and set on rack.

Topping:

2 eggs (room temperature)
1 c. milk
1 Tbsp. sugar
4 Tbsp. lemon juice
1 tsp. grated lemon rind

2 Tbsp. flour
½ tsp. salt
Confectioners sugar to
    sprinkle on top

Helen Russman

MARSHMALLOW DELIGHT

36 large marshmallows
15 graham crackers
¾ c. milk

1 pt. cream, whipped
9 oz. can crushed pineapple

Heat milk and dissolve marshmallows. Add pineapple and let cool. Fold in whipped cream. Line pan or dish with graham cracker halves; pour in filling and top with graham cracker crumbs. Refrigerate.

Jewell Hundley

MERINGUE SHELLS

3 egg whites
Dash of salt
½ tsp. vinegar

¼ tsp. vanilla
1 c. sugar

Add salt, vinegar and vanilla to egg whites; beat until mixture forms peaks. Add sugar gradually. Continue beating until very stiff. Spoon into 6 large mounds or cookie sheet covered with plain ungreased paper. (I use brown paper bag.) Shape cups with spoon. Bake in slow oven (300°) for 45 minutes. Remove from paper immediately. Cool. Serve with ice cream and any fruit.

Clara Nance

520

ORANGE STICKS

2 Tbsp. butter
1 c. brown sugar, packed firm
2 eggs
2 Tbsp. grated orange rind
2 Tbsp. orange juice
⅓ c. chopped nuts
1¼ c. sifted flour

½ tsp. baking powder
½ lb. orange candy (the kind that looks like orange sections)
Juice of 1 large orange
4 Tbsp. granulated sugar

Cream butter and sugar; add eggs and mix well. Add orange rind and mix well. Sift flour and baking powder together. Mix with orange candy which has been cut into small pieces and nuts. Add to cream mixture with orange juice. Pour into 8 ½ x 11 inch pan which has been greased with wax paper. Bake at 350° about 30 minutes or until done. Turn out. Mix juice of 1 large orange with granulated sugar and pour over hot cake. Cool and cut into finger like pieces. Roll in additional granulated sugar.

Note: This is a specialty of Mrs. Hoyle Ripple of Winston Salem.

Helen Sykes

OREO COOKIE DESSERT

24 Oreo cookies
½ stick butter
½ gal. vanilla ice cream
1 can Hershey's syrup

1 can Eagle Brand milk
1 stick butter
Cool Whip
Pecans

Press crushed cookies and melted butter in 9x13 inch pan. Add softened ice cream and refreeze. Combine syrup, milk and butter; cook 1 minute. Cool. Add to crust and freeze. Add Cool Whip and nuts; refreeze.

Dot Berry

OVERNIGHT BAKES

2 egg whites with pinch of cream of tartar or baking powder
⅔ c. sugar

1 tsp. flavoring (vanilla or almond)
⅔ c. course chopped nuts
1 c. chocolate chips

Beat egg whites until stiff, slowly blend in sugar until mixed. Stop mixer, clean beaters and scrape down bowl. Fold in nuts and chips. Drop by spoonfuls onto prepared oven racks.* Slip into preheated 300° oven and immediately turn off the oven. Leave cookies in oven for 12 hours. Do not peek!

    * When you start to turn on oven, remove the racks. Wrap them in foil, front to back (so will slide back into oven easily). Punch holes with pronged fork evenly, so heat will penetrate over the area. This is a much better way than using cookie sheets.

Rosetta Humphries

PEANUT BUTTER PILE UPS

1 c. peanut butter	**1 egg**
½ c. sugar	**Chocolate chips**

    Blend together peanut butter, sugar and egg. Press into ungreased 10x7 inch pan. Bake at 325° for 20 minutes. Remove from oven. Cover with chocolate chips and cover pan with aluminum foil. Let stand 3 minutes; remove foil and spread chocolate.

Francele Black

PEANUT BUTTER LOGS

Cake:

1 c. sugar	**1 tsp. vanilla**
2 eggs	**1½ tsp. baking powder**
½ c. cold water	**Scant c. flour**

    Separate eggs; beat yolks. Add sugar, a little at a time. Add water, a little at a time. Add vanilla, baking powder, and flour. Beat cake mixture with mixer on high speed for 3 minutes. Beat egg whites and fold in cake mixture last. Bake at 325° to 350° about 20 minutes in an 11 x 7½ x 1¾ inch deep pan. Grease edge of pan; line with wax paper, then grease and flour wax paper. Cut cake *cold* in 3 inch long and 6 inch wide squares.

Topping:

1 lb. salted peanuts, ground	**1 lb. powdered sugar**
using small holes on	**½ stick butter**
grinder or use can of mix	**½ - 1 tsp. vanilla**
of nut topping mix	**Milk to spread well**

    Mix sugar, butter, vanilla and milk; spread icing on cakes, then roll them in the ground peanuts.

Brenda Bishop

QUICK CRESCENT PECAN PIE BARS

8 oz. Pillsbury refrigerator
   quick crescent dinner
   rolls
1 egg, beaten
½ c. chopped pecans

½ c. sugar
½ c. corn syrup
1 Tbsp. margarine, melted
½ tsp. vanilla

Heat oven to 375°. Lightly grease, not oil, a 13x9 inch pan. Separate crescent dough into 2 large rectangles. Press rectangles over bottom of pan and ½ inch up sides of greased pan to form a crust. Seal perforations. Bake crust at 375° for 5 minutes. In medium bowl, combine remaining ingredients. Pour over partially baked crust. Bake at 375° for 18 to 22 minutes or until brown. Cool and cut into bars.

J. Sanders

PEPPERMINT WHIP

14 chocolate wafers, crushed
   fine
1¼ c. miniature
   marshmallows

½ c. crushed peppermint
   candy
½ pt. heavy cream, whipped

Cover bottom of 9x9 inch dish with half the chocolate crumbs. Fold marshmallows and candy into whipped cream and spoon onto crumbs. Sprinkle remaining crumbs on top and refrigerate for at least 12 hours. Serves 6.

Paula White

PERSIMMON WHIP

½ c. persimmon pulp
2 env. unflavored gelatin
1½ Tbsp. honey
2 tsp. lemon juice

1½ c. persimmon pulp
⅛ tsp. salt
2 egg whites, beaten stiff

Put ½ cup persimmon pulp into the top of a double boiler. Sprinkle gelatin over it and let it soak for 5 minutes. Heat over boiling water; stir until gelatin is dissolved. Remove from heat. Add honey, lemon juice, remaining persimmon pulp and salt. Pour into a bowl and cool. Refrigerate until almost set. Fold in stiffly beaten egg whites. Pour into serving dish and refrigerate several hours until it is set. Yield: 6 servings.

Opal Willis

PORCUPINES

2 c. pecans
1 c. dates
2 c. shredded coconut

1 c. brown sugar
2 eggs (unbeaten)

Grind pecans and dates in food chopper. Mix in 1½ cups coconut and remaining ingredients. Shape into roll ½ inch thick and 4 inches long. Roll each porcupine in remaining coconut. Place on greased baking sheet and bake 10 minutes at 350°. Makes 40 porcupines.

Denise Figg

PINEAPPLE AU GRATIN

1 c. shredded Cheddar
  cheese
¾ c. sugar
1 (20 oz.) can pineapple
  chunks in juice

3 Tbsp. flour
1 pack or ⅓ small box Ritz
  crackers
Butter

Drain pineapple chunks, reserving ½ cup juice. Combine cheese, sugar and flour. Mix well. Add pineapple juice, then pineapple. Crumble Ritz crackers over top. Melt ½ stick butter and spoon over cracker crumbs. Bake in moderate oven (350°) until bubbly. Serves 4. Side dish.

Norma Combs

SCALLOPED PINEAPPLE

1 (No. 2) can diced pineapple
2 eggs
2 c. sugar

½ c. melted margarine
2 c. bread crumbs

Combine ingredients (except pineapple juice) in a greased casserole. Pour pineapple juice over top. Bake 1 hour at 350°. Serves 6.

Dorothy O'Neal

PINEAPPLE TAPIOCA

2½ c. crushed pineapple
¼ c. Minute tapioca
⅓ c. sugar

⅛ tsp. salt
Whipped cream

Mix all ingredients and cook in a double boiler until tapioca is clear, about 20 minutes. Chill. Serve with whipped cream.

Annette Anderson

PLUM BAVARIAN CREAM

2½ c. canned red plums
1 pkg. pineapple gelatin
½ c. heavy cream

2 Tbsp. sherry
2 egg whites

Drain syrup from plums and add enough water to make 2 cups of liquid. Heat to boiling point. Remove from heat and add gelatin; stir until dissolved. Chill until mixture starts to congeal. Whip cream and fold into gelatin mixture. Add sherry and then fold in the stiffly beaten egg whites. Remove seeds from plums and cut them in halves and add to mixture. Chill until firm.

Wanda Alton

PUMPKIN ROLL

3 eggs
1 c. sugar
⅔ c. cooked mashed
   pumpkin
1 tsp. lemon juice
¾ c. all-purpose flour
2 tsp. ground cinnamon
1 tsp. baking powder
½ tsp. salt

1 tsp. ground ginger
1 tsp. ground nutmeg
1¼ c. powdered sugar,
   divided
1 (8 oz.) pkg. cream cheese,
   softened
¼ c. butter or margarine,
   softened
1 tsp. vanilla

Beat eggs 5 minutes at high speed with electric mixer. Gradually add sugar, beating well. Stir in pumpkin and lemon juice. Combine flour, cinnamon, baking powder, salt, ginger and nutmeg. Add to pumpkin mixture and blend well. Spoon batter into greased and floured pan; spread evenly to corners. Bake at 350° for 10 minutes. Turn cake onto a towel sprinkled with ¼ cup powdered sugar. Roll up and cool. Combine 1 cup powdered sugar, cream cheese, butter and vanilla. Beat until smooth and creamy. Unroll cake and spread filling. Roll up again and put in Reynold's Wrap.

Betty Franklin

SHORT'NIN' BREAD

2 c. all-purpose flour, sifted
½ c. light brown sugar

1 c. butter (at room
   temperature)

Preheat oven to 350°. Mix the ingredients. Place the dough on wax paper and pat to ½ inch thickness. Cut into desired shapes. Bake on lightly greased cookie sheet for 25 to 30 minutes. Yield: Approximately 2 dozen.

Teresa Stroup

SPICY PEACH DUMPLINGS

3½ c. sliced peaches
¼ c. granulated sugar
2 Tbsp. butter
1 Tbsp. lemon juice
1⅓ c. biscuit mix

⅓ c. brown sugar
½ tsp. nutmeg
¼ tsp. ginger
⅓ c. milk
2 Tbsp. cooking oil

In a large saucepan, combine peaches, granulated sugar, butter and lemon juice. Heat to boiling. Meanwhile, stir together the biscuit mix, brown sugar, nutmeg and ginger. Combine milk and oil; add to dry ingredients. Mix well. Drop by tablespoonfuls into the simmering peaches. Cover and cook over low heat for 15 minutes. Serve immediately.

Sharon Elmore

STRAWBERRY CHIFFON SQUARES

⅓ c. butter or margarine
1½ c. (about 45) finely
    crushed vanilla wafers
1 (3 oz.) pkg. strawberry
    flavored gelatin
¾ c. boiling water
1 (14 oz.) can Eagle Brand
    sweetened condensed
    milk (not evaporated)

1 (10 oz.) pkg. frozen sliced
    strawberries in syrup,
    thawed
4 c. miniature marshmallows
1 c. (½ pt.) whipping cream,
    whipped

In small saucepan, melt butter; stir in crumbs. Pat firmly on bottom of 11x7 inch baking dish. Chill. In large bowl, dissolve gelatin in boiling water. Stir in sweetened condensed milk and undrained strawberries. Fold in marshmallows and whipped cream. Pour into prepared pan. Chill 2 hours or until set. If desired, garnish with whipped topping and strawberries. Delicious. Serves 12.

Whipped topping or cream and fresh strawberries are optional.

Bessie Litchford

STRAWBERRY LOAF

2 c. flour	½ c. honey
1 Tbsp. baking powder	½ c. oil
1 tsp. salt	1½ c. strawberries (fresh or
2 tsp. lemon juice	frozen)
½ tsp. cinnamon	½ c. English walnuts
2 eggs, beaten	

Stir together dry ingredients. Combine eggs, honey and oil. Stir in strawberries and nuts. Add liquid all at once to flour mixture, stirring only until flour is moistened. Pour into loaf pan. Bake at 350° in preheated oven for 55 minutes. Let cool and slice.

Martha Tipton

STRAWBERRY MOUSSE

4 egg yolks	1 c. fresh or frozen
1 c. sugar	strawberries, mashed
1 c. milk	1 Tbsp. lemon juice
2 env. unflavored gelatin	2 c. heavy cream, whipped
¼ c. water	1 pt. whole strawberries

In top of double boiler, beat the yolks and sugar until well blended. Stir in milk. Cook until thickened, stirring constantly. Remove from heat. Add gelatin to water to soften. Stir softened gelatin into cooked mixture until dissolved. Pour into a bowl and cool. Blend in mashed strawberries and lemon juice. Fold in whipped cream. Pour into mold (2 quart) and freeze until firm. Serve in wedges with whole strawberries for garnish. Serves 6 to 8.

Alice Walsh Alessio

STRAWBERRY SWIRL

1 c. chocolate cookie crumbs	1 c. boiling water
4 Tbsp. butter	½ lb. marshmallows
1 Tbsp. sugar	½ c. milk
2 c. fresh strawberries, sliced	1 c. whipping cream
3 oz. pkg. strawberry gelatin	9 inch pie shell

Combine crumbs and butter; press into pie shell. Sprinkle sugar over berries; let stand 30 minutes. Dissolve gelatin in boiling water. Drain berries and reserve juice. Add water to juice to make 1 cup and add to gelatin. Chill until partially set. Heat marshmallows and milk; stir until marshmallows melt. Cool thoroughly; whip cream and fold in. Add berries to gelatin, then swirl in marshmallow mixture. Pour into pie shell. Chill until set.

Paula White

SUMMER DELIGHT

1 angel food cake
1 pkg. frozen strawberries

1 small pkg. cherry Jello
1 pkg. Dream Whip

Add 1 cup boiling water to Jello. Let it set until it becomes a soft jell. Mix Dream Whip and strawberries to Jello. Slice cake. Cover on all sides with your Jello mixture.

Mary Beeler

SWEDISH NUTS

2 egg whites
1 c. sugar

1 lb. pecans or mixed nuts
1 stick butter

Beat 2 egg whites stiff. Add 1 cup sugar. Beat again. Mix in 1 pound pecans. Melt 1 stick butter; mix with nuts. Put in 325° oven and stir every 15 minutes. Remove from oven in 1 hour or when nuts are slightly browned.

Beth Howard

TAFFY APPLES

1 c. granulated sugar
½ c. boiling water
1 c. brown sugar
½ c. cream

2 Tbsp. butter
6 apples
6 wooden skewers

Melt ½ cup of granulated sugar over a direct flame. Add the boiling water and cook to a smooth syrup. In a separate pan, cook the cream with the remaining sugar and butter to the soft ball stage or to 236°. Combine the 2 syrups and cook until drops of syrup will form a hard ball when dropped into cold water or to a temperature of 250°. Cool the syrup to lukewarm. Place apples on skewers and twirl them in the syrup. Dip them immediately in ice water to harden the syrup.

Gary Lee Figg

TWENTY-FOUR HOUR DESSERT

1 c. sugar
½ c. powdered sugar
2 egg yolks
1 can crushed pineapple,
    drained

1 c. chopped nuts
About 32 vanilla wafers
Whipped topping or whipped
    cream

Cream sugar and butter. Add egg yolks, 1 at a time, until light and fluffy. Add pineapple and nuts. Line 8 inch square pan with half of vanilla wafers. Spread half of fruit mixture over wafers. Add the rest of wafers and the rest of fruit mixture. Chill 24 hours or overnight. Top with a layer of whipped topping or whipped cream. Serves 9.

Daisy Mace

VANILLA BAVARIAN CREAM

2 pkg. unflavored gelatin
½ c. cold water
9 Tbsp. sugar
1 Tbsp. cornstarch
2 eggs, beaten

1½ c. milk, scalded
1 c. vanilla ice cream
1 tsp. vanilla
1 c. heavy cream, whipped

Sprinkle gelatin over cold water to soften. Heat to dissolve completely. Mix sugar and cornstarch together. Add eggs; beat for 2 minutes. Slowly add warm milk; beat constantly. Pour into 1 quart saucepan. Cook over medium heat until custard coats a spoon. Add gelatin and ice cream while custard is hot. Cool until slightly thickened. Add vanilla. Fold in whipped cream. Pour into 1 quart mold; chill until set. Unmold carefully and serve garnished with fresh fruit. Serves 6 to 8.

Michelle Lewis

YUMMIE DESSERT

3 egg whites
1 c. sugar
¾ c. chopped nuts
1 tsp. vanilla

¾ c. soda crackers, crumbled
½ pt. whipped cream
Powdered sugar

Beat egg whites until stiff. Add vanilla and sugar. Mix gradually at low speed. Fold in soda cracker crumbs. Add nuts. Pour into a 9 inch pan and bake 20 minutes at 350°. Cool completely, then top with whipped cream, sweetened with powdered sugar. Cover with plastic wrap and let set overnight in refrigerator. Cut and serve.

Double for family.

Sue Tipton

PIES

ANGEL PIE

1 c. chocolate cookie crumbs
3 Tbsp. melted margarine
1 env. unflavored gelatin
¼ c. cold water
¼ c. boiling water

1 tsp. vanilla
¼ tsp. aniseed
3 egg whites
½ c. sugar
1 c. heavy cream, whipped

Combine cookie crumbs and melted butter. Set aside 1 table-spoon crumb mixture for garnish. Press remaining crumbs into a 9 inch pie pan; chill. Soften gelatin in cold water; add boiling water, vanilla and aniseed; stir to dissolve gelatin. Beat egg whites until soft peaks form; add sugar, 1 tablespoon at a time; beat well after each addition. Beat until stiff peaks form. Fold in gelatin, then fold in whipped cream. Refrigerate until mixture starts to set, then spoon into crumb crust. Sprinkle top with reserved crumbs; chill until set. Serves 6.

Cristy Lewis

APPLE PIE

2 c. flour
4 egg yolks, lightly beaten
4 Tbsp. shortening
5 Tbsp. white sugar
Pinch of salt
1 egg, beaten

7 apples
2 tsp. lemon juice
Grated rind of 1 lemon
4 Tbsp. peach jam
3 Tbsp. brown sugar
2 tsp. cinnamon

Mix flour with lightly beaten egg yolks, shortening, white sugar, and a pinch of salt. Stir and knead until smooth, blended dough. Roll out ⅛ inch thick on a floured board and cut in half. Line a greased pie plate with half the pastry and brush the edges with the beaten egg. Peel and slice apples; combine with lemon juice, lemon rind, peach jam and brown sugar. Stir and pour into lined pie plate. Sprinkle with cinnamon. Cover pie with top crust; prick several places with a fork and brush with the remainder of the beaten egg. Bake about 45 minutes or until golden brown.

Denise Figg

APPLE PIE IN CHEDDAR CRUST

Cheddar Cheese Pastry:

2 c. sifted flour
1 c. shredded Cheddar
  cheese
½ tsp. salt

⅔ c. shortening
6 Tbsp. cold water
1 egg yolk, beaten
1 Tbsp. water

Combine flour, Cheddar cheese and salt in a large bowl. Cut in shortening until mixture resembles coarse crumbs. Add cold water, 1 tablespoon at a time, mixing until dry ingredients are moistened and dough can be gathered in a ball. Reserve egg yolk and water. Divide dough in half. Roll out ½ to a 13 inch circle on a lightly floured surface. Line a 9 inch pie plate with pastry. Trim edges to ½ inch beyond rim of plate.

Apple Filling:

9 c. sliced, pared cooking
  apples
⅓ c. packed light brown
  sugar
⅓ c. granulated sugar

2 Tbsp. all-purpose flour
1 tsp. ground cinnamon
¼ tsp. ground nutmeg
¼ tsp. salt
2 Tbsp. margarine

Combine apples, sugars, flour, cinnamon, nutmeg and salt in a large bowl. Mix well. Arrange in the unbaked pie shell. Dot with butter. Preheat oven to 400°. Roll out remaining pastry to an 11 inch circle. Place the top crust over apples and trim edge to 1 inch beyond rim of pie plate. Fold top crust under lower crust and form a ridge. Flute edge. Cut slits for steam to escape. Combine egg yolk and water. Brush over crust. Bake at 400° for 40 minutes or until apples are tender and crust is golden brown. Cool on a rack. Serve warm or cold with ice cream or Cheddar cheese.

Peggy Kessinger

AUSTRALIAN PIE

Pastry for an 8 or 9 inch (1
  crust) pie
2 Tbsp. butter
2 Tbsp. flour
1 c. milk
¼ c. heavy cream

1 c. grated cheese
1 egg
1½ c. chopped cooked
  chicken
⅔ c. raisins
Egg or milk to glaze

Preheat oven to 400°. Line a deep 8 or 9 inch pie plate with half the pastry. Make a sauce with the butter, flour, and milk; add cream, cheese and seasoning. Remove from heat; stir in beaten egg. Put alternate layers of chicken and raisins into the pastry shell and pour the sauce over. Cover the pie with remaining pastry, pressing the edges together. Make 2 or 3 cuts in the top and bake for about 30 minutes.

Dee Dee Millen

BLACKBERRY JAM PIE

2 c. white sugar
3 Tbsp. flour
6 egg yellows

1 c. blackberry jam
1 c. sweet milk
⅔ c. butter

Mix the first 5 ingredients. Drop butter into mixture and heat filling just enough to melt butter. Then pour into unbaked crust. Bake about 1 hour at 325° or until the filling is almost firm. Use your egg whites for meringue; put meringue on pie when you take pie out of oven.

Ann Williams

BROWNIE PIE

4 eggs
4 oz. chocolate, melted and
    cooled
½ c. Bisquick baking mix

½ c. granulated sugar
½ c. brown sugar, packed
¼ c. margarine, softened
1 c. pecans, chopped

Beat all ingredients together, except pecans, until smooth, about 2 minutes in the blender. Pour into a greased pie plate; sprinkle nuts on top. Bake in a preheated 350° oven for about 30 to 35 minutes or until a knife inserted in center comes out smooth.

Cristy Lewis

BROWN SUGAR PIE

3 c. brown sugar
3 Tbsp. flour
¼ tsp. salt
4 egg yolks, beaten
3 c. milk

1 tsp. vanilla
½ stick butter, melted or
    softened
1 baked pie shell

Beat eggs, sugar and flour until light and fluffy. Add milk, vanilla and butter. Mix at highest speed on blender or electric mixer until well blended. Cook until done. Pour into baked pie shell. Bake at 350°.

Topping:

4 egg whites
4 tsp. sugar

1 tsp. vanilla

Beat egg whites until thick. Add sugar and vanilla. Bake until brown.

Lil Pasinski

BROWN SUGAR CUSTARD PIE

2 c. brown sugar, packed
¼ c. margarine
3 Tbsp. flour
1 tsp. ground cinnamon
¼ tsp. cream of tartar

¹/₁₆ tsp. salt
3 eggs
3 c. milk
1 tsp. vanilla
2 unbaked (8 inch) pie shells

Cream brown sugar and margarine until light and fluffy. Mix flour, cinnamon, cream of tartar and salt. Add eggs and beat well; add to brown sugar and butter mixture. Slowly beat in milk and vanilla. Pour into pie shells. Bake in 375° oven for about 40 minutes or until a knife inserted in the center comes out clean. Cool.

Lora Martin

BUTTERMILK PIE

1 stick (¼ lb.) butter
2 c. sugar

2 Tbsp. flour

Cream together.

Add:

4 eggs
1 tsp. vanilla

⅔ c. buttermilk

Pour in 2 unbaked pie crusts. Bake for 45 minutes at 350°.

Peggy Graviss

BUTTERMILK PIE

½ c. margarine
1½ c. sugar
3 eggs, separated
4 Tbsp. flour

1 pt. buttermilk
1 tsp. vanilla
2 (9 inch) unbaked pie shells

534

Cream butter, sugar, and egg yolks well. Add flour; beat. Add buttermilk and vanilla; stir well. Add well beaten egg whites and mix gently. Pour into pie shells and bake in a preheated 450° oven for 10 minutes, then lower heat to 350° and bake 30 minutes or until an inserted knife comes out clean.

Rosetta Humphries

BUTTERMILK PIE

1½ c. sugar
1 c. buttermilk
½ c. Bisquick baking mix

⅓ c. margarine, melted
1 tsp. vanilla
3 eggs

Heat oven to 350°. Beat all ingredients until smooth, about 30 seconds in a blender. Pour into a greased pie plate. Bake about 30 minutes or until a knife inserted in center comes out clean.

Sharon Duke

BUTTERMILK PIE

1½ c. sugar
1 c. buttermilk
½ c. Bisquick baking mix

⅓ c. margarine, melted
1 tsp. vanilla
3 eggs

Heat oven to 350°. Grease pie plate, 9 x 1¼ inches. Beat all ingredients until smooth, 30 seconds in blender on high. Pour into plate. Bake until knife inserted in center comes out clean, about 30 minutes. Cool 5 minutes. Serve with mixed fresh fruit.

Mary Baxter

CHART HOUSE MUD PIE

½ pkg. Nabisco chocolate
    wafers
½ cube butter, melted
1 gal. coffee ice cream

1½ c. fudge sauce
Whipped cream
Slivered almonds

Crush wafers and add butter. Mix well. Press into a 9 inch pie plate. Cover with soft coffee ice cream. Put into freezer until ice cream is firm. Top with cold fudge sauce (it helps to place in freezer for a time to make spreading easier). Store in freezer approximately 10 hours. To serve, slice mud pie into 8 portions and serve on a chilled dessert plate with a chilled fork. Top with whipped cream and slivered almonds.

Wilma Crowdus

CHESS PIE

1 stick butter, melted over
   low heat
1½ c. sugar
1 Tbsp. corn meal

1 Tbsp. vinegar
1 tsp. vanilla
3 eggs, slightly beaten
1 uncooked pie shell

Melt 1 stick butter over low heat. Add 1½ cups sugar. Mix all other ingredients with butter/sugar mixture. Bake at 325° in uncooked pie shell for 45 minutes.

Betty Carrier

CHESS PIE

1 (9 inch) unbaked pie crust
3 eggs
1 stick butter, melted
1 tsp. vanilla

1½ Tbsp. corn meal
2 Tbsp. vinegar
1½ c. sugar

Beat eggs; add sugar, corn meal, vanilla, butter and vinegar. Mix well. Let stand 10 minutes, then stir gently and bake for 35 minutes in a 350° oven.

Allouise Davidson

CHESS PIE

2 c. sugar
2 Tbsp. corn meal
2 Tbsp. flour
5 egg yolks

1 can Carnation milk
1 tsp. vanilla
1 stick butter

Mix all of the preceding. Bake in 425° oven for 15 minutes, then bake for 45 minutes at 350°.

Barbara Montgomery

CHESS PIE

6 eggs, beaten
3 c. sugar
1 large can Carnation milk
⅔ c. butter, melted

3 Tbsp. corn meal
1 tsp. vanilla
2 pie crusts

Combine eggs, sugar, corn meal, milk and vanilla. Add melted butter. Mix well. Bake in a 350° oven for 50 to 60 minutes or until browned and set. Makes 2 pies.

Mrs. Sam (Linda) Martin

CARAMEL PIE

1 c. sugar
4 Tbsp. flour
1 pt. milk
4 egg yolks

1 c. sugar, caramelized
2 Tbsp. butter
2 tsp. vanilla

Combine sugar and flour. Add milk and egg yolks; cook until thick. Remove from heat and add caramelized sugar. Beat as you add the hot sugar. When mixture is smooth, add butter and vanilla. Pour in a partially baked pie shell. Bake enough for shell to be done and pie to thicken, approximately 15 to 20 minutes at 350°. Beat egg whites. Add ½ cup sugar. Pour over pie and brown lightly.

Dorothy Mullins

CHOCOLATE PIE

3 Tbsp. cocoa
6 c. sugar
1 c. flour

1 tsp. vanilla
4 egg yolks
1 Tbsp. butter

Mix with small amount of cold water. Then add 2 cans cream and 1 can water.

Coconut Pie: Delete 3 tablespoons cocoa and substitute a package of coconut.

Meringue:

4 egg whites
¾ c. sugar

1 tsp. vanilla

Beat egg whites until stiff. Add sugar and vanilla.

Cat Moore

CHOCOLATE PIE

2 c. sugar
2 heaping Tbsp. flour
3 eggs
1 tsp. vanilla

½ c. cocoa
Dash of salt
2 c. milk

Make pie crust and bake. Mix sugar, flour, salt and cocoa. Add 3 beaten *egg yolks* and 2 cups milk. Microwave or stir on top of stove until thick. Pour in pie shell. Make meringue and bake until brown.

Alice Ritchey

CHOCOLATE CREAM PIE

3 eggs, separated
¾ c. sugar
3 heaping Tbsp. Hershey's
chocolate

2 c. milk
¼ or ½ stick margarine
3 Tbsp. cornstarch
1 tsp. vanilla

Heat milk in double boiler until hot (reserve some milk, about ⅛ cup). Cream together egg yolks and sugar. Add other ingredients and mix together until smooth and no lumps. Pour into hot milk slowly, stirring all the time. Add margarine and cook until thickened; add vanilla. If lumpy, beat until smooth.

Meringue:

3 egg whites
¼ c. sugar

¼ tsp. cream of tartar
¼ tsp. vanilla

Beat egg whites until stand in peaks. Add sugar, vanilla and cream of tartar; mix together well. Spread over pie and bake at 325° for 15 minutes.

Martha Denning

CHOCOLATE MOUSSE PIE

2 Tbsp. chocolate
3 Tbsp. cornstarch
1 c. sugar
3 eggs

½ stick margarine
½ tsp. vanilla
Baked pie shell

Mix dry ingredients together. Melt butter. Pour butter over ingredients. Add just enough milk to make moist. Add 3 beaten egg yolks. Add 2 cups of milk. Cook until very hot. Add all ingredients to hot milk. Stir until it becomes thick. Remove from heat. Add ½ teaspoon vanilla.

Meringue:

3 egg whites
1 tsp. sugar

¼ tsp. cream of tartar
¼ tsp. vanilla

Beat egg whites until stiff. Gradually add 1 teaspoon of sugar while beating egg whites. Add ¼ teaspoon cream of tartar and ¼ teaspoon vanilla. Pile lightly on filling in baked pie shell. Bake at 350° until delicately browned.

Randy Riggs

DELICIOUS CHOCOLATE MERINGUE PIE

3 c. sifted all-purpose flour
1 c. shortening
6 Tbsp. ice water
1 egg, well beaten
2 c. milk
1 c. sugar
¼ c. plus 2 Tbsp. all-purpose
    flour
¼ c. plus 2 Tbsp. cocoa
¼ tsp. salt
3 egg yolks, slightly beaten
1 Tbsp. butter or margarine
1 tsp. vanilla flavoring
3 egg whites
¼ tsp. cream of tartar
¼ c. plus 2 Tbsp. sugar

Crust: Place 3 cups flour in mixing bowl; cut in 1 cup shortening until mixture resembles coarse meal. Add 6 tablespoons ice water and 1 egg. Stir with a fork until all dry ingredients are moistened. Shape dough into a ball; roll out to fit a 9 inch pie pan. Bake at 450° for 10 to 12 minutes or until golden brown. Shape leftover dough into a ball; wrap and store in refrigerator. (I usually make 2 pies and use it up.)

Pie Filling: Place 2 cups milk in double boiler. Combine sugar (1 cup), ¼ cup plus 2 tablespoons all-purpose flour, ¼ cup plus 2 tablespoons cocoa and ¼ teaspoon salt; add to milk. Cook until thickened, stirring constantly. Stir a small amount of hot milk mixture into egg yolks until well combined. Add egg mixture to hot mixture and cook 2 or 3 minutes, stirring constantly. Remove from heat; add 1 tablespoon butter and 1 teaspoon vanilla. Cool. Pour into cooled 9 inch baked pastry shell. Top with meringue. Brown meringue. (I don't beat with mixer after it is cooked.)

Meringue: Combine 3 egg whites and ¼ teaspoon cream of tartar; beat until foamy. Gradually add sugar, beating until stiff (¼ cup plus 2 tablespoons sugar).

This recipe sounds like a lot of work, but it's worth it.

Bessie Litchford

MOTHER'S CHOCOLATE PIE

4 egg yolks
2 c. sweet milk
4 Tbsp. flour
2 c. sugar
4 Tbsp. grated chocolate
    (less 1 tsp.)

Mix sugar, flour and chocolate; pour into milk and eggs. Cook in double boiler until thick and pour into baked crust. Makes 2 pies.

Pie Crust:

1 c. flour
⅓ c. water

⅓ c. shortening
⅓ tsp. salt

Mix well by cutting shortening and water with flour, rather than using your hands. This is a pastry that never fails if mixed and rolled properly. Makes enough for a 2 crust pie.

Mary T. Thompson

MOTHER'S CHOCOLATE PIE FILLING

2 c. milk (evaporated milk and
**   water)**
1½ c. sugar
4 egg yolks

3 Tbsp. cocoa
1 tsp. vanilla
3 Tbsp. cornstarch
1½ Tbsp. butter

Cook in double boiler until thick. Pour in 9 inch baked shell. The preceding ingredients can be used for lemon or coconut pie. Just eliminate the cocoa and add 1 tablespoon of lemon juice or 1 cup of coconut.

Meringue:

4 Tbsp. sugar
4 egg whites

Pinch of cream of tartar
1 tsp. vanilla

Beat egg whites and cream of tartar until stiff; add sugar and vanilla; spread over pie filling. Bake at 350° until brown.

Shirley Cates

COCONUT PIE

3 eggs
1½ c. sugar
½ c. butter, melted
1 tsp. vinegar

1½ tsp. vanilla
Dash of salt
1 c. flaked coconut
1 (9 inch) unbaked pie shell

Beat eggs slightly and add sugar, butter, vinegar, vanilla, salt and coconut; mix well. Pour into pie shell and bake in preheated 350° oven for about 45 minutes.

Rosetta Humphries

COCONUT SUPREME CREAM PIE

¼ c. cornstarch
⅔ c. sugar
3 eggs, separated
¾ c. flaked coconut
6 Tbsp. sugar

½ tsp. salt
3 c. milk
1 tsp. vanilla
1 baked (9 inch) pie shell
¼ c. flaked coconut

Combine cornstarch, ⅔ cup sugar, and salt in top of double boiler. Gradually add milk, stirring until smooth. Cook over boiling water, stirring constantly, until thickened. Cover; cook 10 minutes longer, stirring occasionally. Beat egg yolks. Blend a small amount of hot mixture into egg yolks, mixing well; stir egg yolks into remaining hot mixture. Cook over boiling water 2 minutes, stirring constantly. Remove from water; stir in vanilla and coconut. Cool; pour into pie shell.

Patricia Jewell

FRENCH COCONUT PIE

1 stick melted butter
1½ c. sugar
3 whole eggs, well beaten
1 can flaked coconut

1 Tbsp. vinegar
1 tsp. vanilla (I use coconut
  extract)

Mix all ingredients; pour into *unbaked* 9 inch pie shell. Bake for 1 hour at 325°.

Patricia Jewell

FRESH COCONUT CREAM PIE

1 c. sugar
½ c. cornstarch
¼ tsp. salt
3 c. hot milk
2 egg yolks, beaten

1 tsp. vanilla extract
½ tsp. almond extract
2 c. coconut
1 (9 inch) baked pie shell

Combine sugar, cornstarch and salt; gradually add to hot milk in medium saucepan, stirring until smooth. Cook until it thickens. Pour some of thick mixture over egg yolks. Pour back into pan and cook until mounds from spoon. Remove from heat and add vanilla, almond and a little yellow food coloring; stir; add coconut. Turn into bowl; cover with waxed paper directly on filling; refrigerate. Turn into baked pie shell and top with meringue when set and cooled. Sprinkle coconut on top and lightly brown under broiler.

Dora C. Thompson

COCONUT PIE

3 eggs
1 stick butter
½ c. milk
1 c. brown sugar, packed

1 c. coconut
1 Tbsp. corn meal
1 unbaked pie shell

Mix all ingredients well. Pour into unbaked pie shell and bake about 1 hour in a very slow oven.

This is *not* a cream pie. Tastes similar to pecan pie.

Ruth Ackerman

COOL WHIP PIE

1 large can crushed
   pineapple
1 can sliced peaches, diced
1 can mandarin oranges

1 large box Cool Whip
1 can Eagle Brand milk
¼ c. lemon juice
Graham cracker crust

Combine Eagle Brand milk and lemon juice. Add Cool Whip. Add drained fruit. Pour in graham cracker crust. Makes 2 pies.

Mark A. Cowan

BASIC CREAM PIE AND VARIATIONS

⅔ c. sugar
3 Tbsp. cornstarch
2 c. milk
3 beaten egg yolks
1 tsp. vanilla

1 Tbsp. butter
Dash of salt
9 inch baked pie shell
3 stiffly beaten egg whites
6 Tbsp. sugar

Combine ⅔ cup sugar and cornstarch. Add milk gradually. Stir until smooth. Cook, stirring, until thickened. Add small amount of hot mixture to egg yolks; blend well. Return to hot mixture. Cook until thickened, stirring, over medium heat. Remove from heat. Blend in vanilla, butter, and salt. Cool 15 to 20 minutes. Pour into baked pie shell. Top with meringue made by beating egg whites with 6 tablespoons sugar. Brown meringue at 375° (moderate) for 10 to 15 minutes; cool.

Pineapple Cream Pie: Fold 9 ounce can drained, crushed pineapple into filling just before pouring into pie shell.

Cocoa Cream Pie: Mix 3 tablespoons cocoa with dry ingredients in basic recipe. Proceed as basic recipe indicates.

542

Banana Cream Pie: Follow basic recipe. Slice 2 large bananas into baked pie shell. Add filling. Proceed as indicated in basic recipe.

Butterscotch Pie: Follow basic recipe, except substitute 1 cup brown sugar for granulated sugar. Increase butter to ¼ cup. Proceed as indicated in basic recipe.

Coconut Pie: Follow basic recipe. Add ½ cup cut, shredded coconut just before adding filling to pie shell. Proceed as indicated in basic recipe.

Phyllis L. Davis

CREAM PIE

1 c. sugar	2 egg yolks, beaten
1 heaping Tbsp. flour	1 Tbsp. butter
1 c. milk	½ tsp. vanilla

Mix in order and cook over medium heat, stirring *constantly,* or in double boiler until thick. Pour into baked pie shell. Top with meringue and brown. *Delicious!*

Izetta Stephens

CRUMB PIE

¾ c. sugar	½ c. molasses
1¾ c. flour	¼ c. boiling water
½ c. butter	½ tsp. soda
1 egg	

Mix the sugar, flour and butter together. Save out ½ cup of this mixture for the crumbs to be used on the top of the pies. Beat the egg and add the molasses and boiling water in which the soda has been dissolved. Add to the sugar mixture. Pour into 2 unbaked pastry shells. Sprinkle the crumbs over the top and bake at 375° for 40 minutes. Yield: 2 (9 inch) pies.

Cristy Lewis

CRUNCH TOP APPLE PIE

1¼ c. sugar
1 Tbsp. flour
3½ c. cooking apples, peeled
   and chopped
2 Tbsp. butter
½ tsp. cinnamon

Dash of salt
1 (16 oz.) can applesauce
1 Tbsp. lemon juice
Pastry for double crust (9
   inch) pie

Roll half of pastry ⅛ inch thick; fit into 9 inch pie pan; trim. Combine sugar, flour, cinnamon and salt. Stir in apples, applesauce and lemon juice. Spoon into pie pan and dot with butter. Roll out remaining pastry to ⅛ inch thickness and cut into strips. Arrange in lattice design over apples. Sprinkle Crunch Topping over top crust. Bake at 425° for 10 minutes; reduce heat to 350° and bake about 45 minutes or until crust is golden brown.

Crunch Topping:

3 Tbsp. all-purpose flour
Dash of salt

1 Tbsp. sugar
1 Tbsp. butter

Combine flour, sugar and salt. Cut in butter until mixture resembles crumbs.

Mary Francess Stayton

DIXIE PIE

3 eggs
1 c. Karo syrup
1 c. nuts (walnuts)
6 oz. chocolate chips

½ c. sugar
2 Tbsp. butter
1 tsp. vanilla
1 unbaked pie shell

Heat oven to 350°. In large bowl, beat eggs until well combined. Add syrup, walnuts, chocolate chips, sugar, butter and vanilla; mix until well blended. Pour evenly into pie shell. Bake at 350° until slightly more set around the edges than in the center, 50 to 60 minutes. Cool completely.

Lil Pasinski

FIRST SATURDAY OF MAY PIE

1 c. sugar
2 eggs
½ c. flour
1 stick margarine, melted and
  cooled
1 c. pecans or English
  walnuts

1 unbaked pie shell
1 tsp. vanilla
1 c. miniature chocolate
  chips

Combine sugar and eggs. Beat until well blended. Add flour. Add margarine slowly. Add vanilla. Stir in chocolate chips and nuts. Pour into unbaked pie shell and bake 30 minutes at 350°.

Kathy Chesser

FRUIT COBBLER

1 c. flour
½ c. sugar
1 tsp. baking powder
½ c. milk
1 qt. fruit (should be 2 c. fruit
  and 2 c. juice, boiling
  hot)

2 Tbsp. margarine (or more)
Pinch of salt

Melt margarine in baking dish. Mix flour, sugar, baking powder, milk and salt. Pour batter in butter. Pour fruit over batter. Bake in preheated oven at 450° until done.

Sheila Duke

FRUIT COBBLER

1 stick butter or margarine
1 c. flour
1 c. sugar

2 tsp. baking powder
1 c. milk
1 qt. sweetened fruit, heated

Melt butter in a 9 inch square pan and set aside. Mix flour, sugar, baking powder and milk. Beat well. Pour over top of melted butter or margarine. Do not stir. Pour heated fruit over flour mixture. Bake at 375° until pastry rises to top and is brown, about 30 minutes.

This cobbler is delicious.

Bessie Litchford

FRUIT WHIP PIE

½ c. lemon juice
1 large ctn. Cool Whip
1 c. crushed pineapple

1 can Eagle Brand milk
1 c. sliced peaches
1 c. mandarin oranges

Put lemon juice in bowl and add milk. Mix well. Add Cool Whip and stir well. Drain fruit and cut in small pieces. Add fruit to mixture and pour into graham cracker pie shell. Makes 2 pies.

Sue Sympson

FUDGY CHOCOLATE PIE

To ½ cup melted margarine, add:

¾ c. sugar
⅓ c. cocoa

¼ c. flour

Stir well; beat in 2 eggs, 1 at a time. Add 1 teaspoon vanilla. Pour into greased 8 or 9 inch pie pan. Bake 15 minutes at 350°, center will become firm upon standing, cool 10 minutes. Serve with ice cream if desired. Serves 6 to 8.

Do *not* bake ahead; should be served when baked.

Ruthie Marty

GRAHAM CRACKER PIE

Crust:

20 graham crackers
½ c. brown sugar

½ c. butter

Roll graham crackers and stir in sugar and melted butter. Mix well and pat into pie tin forming crust.

Filling:

2 c. milk
2 Tbsp. cornstarch or 4 Tbsp.
    flour
½ c. sugar

3 egg yolks
1 tsp. vanilla
Few grains of salt
1 c. coconut

Mix sugar and dry ingredients. Beat egg yolks and stir into milk. Stir in dry materials and cook over hot water until thick. Remove from heat and add vanilla and coconut. Pour into crust and cover with meringue. Sprinkle over the meringue some of the buttered crumbs.

Meringue: Beat egg white until stiff. Beat 3 tablespoons sugar into them. Brown pie in oven. Remove from oven and set in cool place overnight.

Mattie Hammack

HARVEST PIE

1 lb. potatoes, peeled and
   sliced
1 lb. cooking apples, peeled
   and sliced
2 - 3 onions, sliced

¾ lb. bacon or ham, diced
1 c. broth or consomme
   (approx.)
Pastry for 8 - 9 inch (1 crust)
   pie

Preheat oven to 425°. Arrange potatoes, apples, onions, and bacon in layers in a deep baking dish. Sprinkle each layer with pepper and a little salt. Add broth, then cover with pastry. Make a slit in the top; decorate as desired. Bake for ½ hour, then reduce heat to 375° and bake for 1 hour. Serves 4 or 5.

This recipe comes from a very old English recipe. The pie was served in the farmhouses as a supper dish for the harvesters. In those days, home cured ham was used.

Heidi Thompson

HAWAIIAN PIE

1 c. sugar
½ c. sifted flour
¼ tsp. salt
2 - 3 tsp. lemon rind
1¼ c. water
¼ - ⅓ c. lemon juice

1 c. crushed pineapple
3 eggs, separated
1 Tbsp. butter
1 baked pie shell
½ tsp. cream of tartar
6 Tbsp. sugar

Combine first 4 ingredients in a saucepan. Add the next 3 liquid ingredients. Bring to a boil over medium heat and cook until thick, stirring constantly. Blend in the 3 slightly beaten egg yolks and add the butter. Pour into pie shell. Top with meringue. Bake at 350° for 12 to 15 minutes.

Mary Baxter

HERSHEY BAR PIE

6 Hershey bars with almonds   **16 regular size marshmallows**
½ c. milk

Melt and blend together in top of double boiler. Cool. Add ½ pint cream, whipped. Put into baked pie shell and chill.

Patricia Jewell

HEAVENLY PIE

1 c. flour   **1 tsp. vanilla**
1 c. sugar   **1 c. chocolate chips**
2 eggs   **1 c. walnuts**
1 stick soft butter or
  margarine

Mix all together; pour into unbaked pie shell. Bake for 30 minutes at 350°. Makes 2 pies.

Patti Roby

INNKEEPER'S PIE

1½ oz. unsweetened   **1 tsp. baking powder**
  chocolate   **½ tsp. salt**
½ c. water   **½ c. milk**
⅔ c. sugar   **1 egg**
1 stick butter (room   **1 unbaked (9 inch) pie shell**
  temperature)   **½ c. chopped walnuts**
2 tsp. vanilla   **1 c. whipping cream,**
1 c. all-purpose flour   **whipped**
¾ c. sugar

Preheat oven. Melt chocolate with water in small saucepan over hot water, stirring frequently. Add ⅔ cup sugar. Remove from over water; increase heat to medium and bring to boil, stirring constantly. Remove from heat. Add 4 tablespoons butter and stir until melted. Add 1½ teaspoons vanilla. Set aside. Combine flour, ¾ cup sugar, baking powder and salt in medium bowl of electric mixer. Add milk and remaining butter and vanilla; beat 2 minutes. Add egg and beat 2 more minutes. Pour batter into pie shell. Stir chocolate sauce and carefully pour over batter. Sprinkle with nuts. Bake approximately 55 minutes at 350°, until tester inserted in center comes out clean. Serve warm or at room temperature with whipped cream. Makes 8 to 10 servings.

Charles T. Thompston

LAZY DAY COBBLER

1 stick butter
1 c. sugar
1 c. self-rising flour*

¾ c. milk
Any kind of fruit

Melt butter in a 9 inch deep pan. Mix other ingredients to smooth batter; pour over melted butter, but do not stir. Empty fruit over batter. Sprinkle with ½ cup sugar. Bake at 350° for 30 to 45 minutes.

* Note: If using plain flour, add 1½ teaspoons baking powder and ¼ teaspoon salt.

Mark A. Cowan

LEMON PIE

3 eggs, well beaten
½ c. butter, melted
3 Tbsp. lemon juice

1 Tbsp. grated lemon rind
1 c. sugar
9 inch unbaked pie shell

Preheat oven to 325°. Blend all of filling ingredients. Pour into the pie shell. Bake 25 minutes or until crust is light brown. Remove from oven. Let cool. The filling will congeal as it cools. Serves 4 to 6.

Denise Figg

LEMON CHESS PIE

2 c. sugar
¼ c. milk
1 Tbsp. all-purpose flour
1 Tbsp. white corn meal
1 scant Tbsp. grated lemon
    peel

4 eggs
¼ c. butter, melted
¼ c. lemon juice
9 or 10 inch unbaked pie shell

Put sugar, flour and corn meal in a large bowl and toss lightly with a fork. Add eggs, melted butter, milk, lemon juice and peel. Beat until smooth and thoroughly blended. Pour into unbaked pie shell. Bake at 350° for 35 to 40 minutes until top is golden brown.

Brownie - Lois Bruner

EASY LEMON MERINGUE PIE

1 graham cracker crust
3 eggs, separated
1 (14 oz.) can Eagle Brand
   sweetened condensed
   milk

½ c. lemon juice
1 tsp. grated lemon rind
¼ tsp. cream of tartar
¼ c. sugar

Preheat oven to 350°. In medium bowl, beat egg yolks; stir in sweetened condensed milk, lemon juice and rind. Turn into shell. In small bowl, beat egg whites with cream of tartar until foamy; gradually add sugar, beating until stiff, but not dry. Spread meringue on top of pie, sealing carefully to edge of shell. Bake 15 minutes or until meringue is golden brown. Cool and chill before serving.

Bev Sowders

SELF-FROSTING LEMON PIE

1 lemon (juice and grated
   rind)
1 c. sugar
2 egg yolks, well beaten

2 egg whites, stiffly beaten
3 Tbsp. flour
¾ c. milk
Small piece butter, melted

Stir together lemon, pulp, juice, and rind with sugar, egg yolks, flour, and milk. Add butter; fold in beaten egg whites. Pour into an unbaked pie shell and bake at 350° for 40 minutes.

Lila White

LEMONADE PIE

1 (12 oz.) can frozen
   lemonade
1 large container Cool Whip

1 can Eagle Brand milk
2 graham cracker pie crust
   shells

Mix the thawed lemonade and milk. Add Cool Whip. After mixing all ingredients, pour into pie shell and refrigerate. Makes enough for 2 pies.

Lynnette Bonn

LIME PIE

1 small can frozen limeade
1 can Eagle Brand milk
1 (8 or 9 inch) pkg. Cool Whip

Baked 9 inch pie shell
Grated chocolate

Put limeade in milk. Stir to combine. Fold in all but ½ cup of Cool Whip. Pour into baked 9 inch pie shell. Spread reserved Cool Whip (½ cup) over top. Sprinkle with grated chocolate.

Green coloring may be added if desired.

Dorothy O'Neal

MILLIONAIRE PIE

2 graham cracker crusts
1 (9 oz.) container whipped
    cream
1 can Eagle Brand condensed
    milk

1 small can crushed
    pineapple, drained
3 Tbsp. lemon juice (real or
    bottled)
1 c. pecans

Mix (don't beat) all ingredients and spoon into crusts. Let set in refrigerator and chill for at least 2 hours before serving.

Jerry Evans

MOONSHINE PIE

1¼ c. sugar
4 Tbsp. flour
1 c. sweet milk
½ stick margarine

Vanilla
3 eggs
Coconut
2 baked pie crusts

Mix flour and sugar together. Add milk, butter and vanilla. Cook until thick. Then beat the whites of 3 eggs stiff and mix through filling before putting into baked pie crust. Sprinkle with coconut and set in the oven to brown. This will make 2 pies. (Filling is a bit thin.)

Wynola Sharon Davis

MUD PIE

25 Oreo chocolate cookies   ⅓ c. melted butter

Crush cookies. Mix crumbs with butter and press into a 9 or 10 inch pie pan. Freeze 15 minutes.

Filling: Soften 1½ quarts of coffee ice cream and spoon into frozen crust. Freeze until very firm.

Topping:

2 sq. unsweetened chocolate
½ c. sugar

2 Tbsp. butter
1 small can evaporated milk

Put all preceding ingredients into a double boiler and cook and stir until thickened. When thoroughly cooled, spread over frozen pie. Freeze until ready to serve. Let stand at room temperature 15 minutes before serving.

Mattie Hammack

NESTLE'S CRUNCH PIE

1 lb. Nestle's crunch bar
1 lb. bowl Cool Whip

1 Johnston's Ready pie crust
(graham cracker)

Melt Nestle's crunch bar over medium heat. Add Cool Whip to chocolate, mixing well. Spoon into pie crust. Place in refrigerator until firm.

Teresa Redmon

NEXT BEST THING TO ROBERT REDFORD
(Make day before)

1 c. flour
1 stick (½ c.) butter or
    margarine, softened
1 c. chopped nuts (optional)
1 (8 oz.) pkg. cream cheese
1 c. confectioners sugar
1 (12 oz.) ctn. Cool Whip,
    thawed and divided in
    half

1 large pkg. *instant* vanilla
    pudding
1 large pkg. *instant* chocolate
    pudding
3 c. milk

Combine flour, butter and nuts; press into bottom of ungreased 9x13x2 inch pan. Bake at 350° for 15 to 20 minutes. Let cool. Combine cream cheese, sugar and half Cool Whip. Blend until smooth and spread over cooked crust. Beat together the 2 puddings and milk.* Whip until well blended. Pour into crust. Spread remainder of whipped topping on top. Keep refrigerated.

* Puddings can be prepared separately and layered. If this is done, you will need an additional 3 cups of milk for pudding as each flavor will require 3 cups.

Fred Eaton

552

OATMEAL PIE

8 inch unbaked pie shell
2 eggs, beaten
½ c. butter or margarine
⅔ c. light brown sugar, packed

⅔ c. light corn syrup
⅔ c. uncooked oatmeal
¼ tsp. salt
1 tsp. vanilla

Mix ingredients and pour into unbaked pie shell. Bake in pre-heated 350° oven for 50 to 60 minutes, until set. Cook, eat and be fat.

Linda Cloyd

OATMEAL PIE

2 whole eggs
⅔ c. white sugar
⅔ c. white Karo syrup

⅔ c. melted butter
⅔ c. quick oats
2 tsp. vanilla

Combine all ingredients and place in unbaked pie shell. Cook about 45 minutes at 300°.

Brenda Bishop

OATMEAL PIE

2 eggs, beaten
⅔ c. melted butter
⅔ c. sugar
⅔ c. white syrup

⅔ c. oats
1 tsp. vanilla
¼ tsp. salt
1 unbaked pie shell

Mix and pour into pie shell and bake at 350° for 1 hour.

Sue Parker

OATMEAL PIE

2 eggs, beaten
¾ c. maple syrup
¾ c. sugar
¾ c. quick oats

1 stick margarine, softened
1 tsp. vanilla
Coconut
Nuts (optional)

Stir ingredients together, except coconut and nuts. Pour into un-baked pie crust. Sprinkle with coconut and nuts if preferred. Bake 40 minutes at 350°.

Opal Willis

OATMEAL PIE

3 egg whites
½ tsp. cream of tartar
1 c. sugar
6 crackers, crushed
½ c. quick cooking oatmeal

½ c. pecans, chopped
1 tsp. vanilla
Whipped cream
Fresh strawberries

Beat egg whites and cream of tartar until foamy. Add sugar gradually; beat constantly until stiff. Fold in crackers, then oatmeal, then pecans. Gently stir in vanilla. Pour into greased 9 inch pie pan. Bake in preheated 375° oven for 25 minutes. Top with whipped cream and fresh strawberries.

This pie makes its own crust.

Rosetta Humphries

OZARK PIE

2 beaten egg whites
1½ c. sugar
¼ tsp. salt
3 tsp. baking powder
½ c. all-purpose flour

1 c. chopped walnuts
1 c. chopped apples
2 large Heath bars
1 qt. vanilla ice cream

Combine first 5 ingredients; beat well. Stir in nuts and apples. Grease pie pan. Bake at 350° for 25 minutes, then cool completely. Fill with ice cream. Top with crushed Heath bars and store in freezer.

Linda Y. Borden

PEACH PIE

Cream:

1 c. sugar
⅓ c. butter
⅓ c. flour

1 egg
½ tsp. vanilla

Slice peaches in unbaked pie shell. Pour creamed mixture over peaches. Bake at 400° until golden brown.

Ruby Junker

PEACH PIE

6 - 8 large peaches, peeled
   and sliced
⅔ c. white sugar
⅓ c. brown sugar
1 egg yolk, beaten

3 Tbsp. evaporated milk
   (undiluted)
½ tsp. cinnamon
2 unbaked (9 inch) pie crusts

Preheat oven to 450°. Combine pie filling ingredients. Mix well. Pour into pie shell. Top with other crust. Flute the edges. Brush top with milk. Prick crust with fork. Bake 10 minutes in 450° oven. Reduce heat to 400° and bake 35 minutes or until crust is delicately browned. Serves 4 to 6.

Denise Figg

OLD FASHION DRIED PEACH PIE

2 c. cooked, dried peaches,
   sweetened to taste
4 eggs, separated
9 Tbsp. sugar

2 c. milk
2 tsp. vanilla
Pinch of baking powder

Line pie pan with pastry. Pour in cooked peaches. Beat together the egg yolks, 4 tablespoons sugar, milk and vanilla; pour over peaches. Bake at 450° until crust browns, then turn heat down until done. Beat egg whites with 5 tablespoons of sugar and a pinch of baking powder until it holds a peak. Pour over baked custard and return to slow oven (300°) to brown.

Cristy Lewis

FRESH PEACH PIE

⅓ c. flour
½ c. sugar

1 stick butter

Mix and put in uncooked pie shell. Add fresh peach halves (turn upside down) and bake at 350° for approximately 45 minutes, or additional 15 minutes if peaches are extra firm.

Mattie Hammack

FRESH PEACH PIE

1 c. sugar
1 c. water
3 c. fresh peaches
2½ Tbsp. cornstarch
Pinch of salt

½ tsp. almond flavoring
2½ Tbsp. peach gelatin
1 Tbsp. lemon juice
Yellow food coloring

Mix sugar, salt and cornstarch. Add water and cook together until thickened. Add peach gelatin and stir until dissolved. Add a few drops of yellow coloring and almond flavoring. Cool; fold in peaches and pour into 9 inch baked pie shell. Chill.

Mattie Hammack

PEACH COBBLER

2 c. sifted flour
½ tsp. salt
½ c. shortening
¼ c. cold water

1 (No. 2½) can peaches
½ c. sugar
4 or 5 pats butter

Mix 2 cups sifted flour, ½ teaspoon salt, ½ cup shortening and ¼ cup cold water. Roll out on floured board, about ¼ inch thick. Put a layer in a buttered baking dish. Mix peaches with ½ cup sugar and pour on the crust. Fold another layer of crust on top of peaches. Cut 4 or 5 pats of butter up on top of crust. Sprinkle lightly with sugar. Bake in 400° oven for about 20 minutes or until golden brown.

Peggy Kessinger

DEEP DISH PEACH COBBLER

2 c. flour
½ tsp. salt
Margarine
4 - 6 Tbsp. water
2 (29 oz.) cans peach slices
½ c. packed brown sugar

2 Tbsp. flour
½ tsp. cinnamon
¼ tsp. nutmeg
⅛ tsp. allspice
Dash of salt
1 Tbsp. lemon juice

Combine flour and salt; cut in ⅔ cup margarine until mixture resembles coarse crumbs. Sprinkle with water while mixing lightly with a fork; form into a ball. On lightly floured surface, roll out ⅔ of dough to 13 inch square. Place in 8 inch square baking dish. Drain peaches, reserving ½ cup syrup. Combine sugar, flour and spices. Add peaches, reserved syrup and lemon juice; mix lightly. Place in pastry shell; dot with 2 tablespoons margarine. Roll out remaining dough to 9 inch square; cut into 8 strips. Place strips across fruit to form lattice; press edges to seal. Flute edges. Bake at 400° for 40 minutes or until golden brown.

Mary V. Stanley

PEANUT BUTTER PIE

1 c. peanut butter (add more
   if you like)
1 c. cream cheese
1 can "Eagle Brand"
   sweetened condensed
   milk

1 pt. Cool Whip

Whip with a mixer; place in a graham cracker crust. Chill and serve.

Sue Parker

PEANUT BUTTER PIE

1 c. chunky peanut butter
2 (3 oz.) pkg. cream cheese
1 c. sifted powdered sugar
1 tsp. vanilla

3 Tbsp. milk
1 (9 oz.) container Cool Whip
1 baked pie shell

Mix all ingredients, except Cool Whip. Blend thoroughly. Add Cool Whip and blend. Pour into a baked pie shell. Refrigerate at least 2 hours before serving.

Lynnette Bonn

JANET'S PECAN PIE

¼ c. margarine (room
   temperature)
½ c. granulated sugar
¾ c. Karo syrup (white)

¼ tsp. salt
¾ c. chopped pecans
3 eggs

Cream margarine and sugar until fluffy. Add syrup and salt. Mix well. Add eggs, 1 at a time. Beat well. Add pecans. Pour in unbaked 9 inch pie shell. Bake for 50 minutes at 350°. May bake longer for a chewier pie.

Melissa Ratliff

PECAN PIE

1 c. white corn syrup
1 c. dark brown sugar
⅓ c. melted butter
1 c. shelled pecans

3 whole eggs
A dash of vanilla
A pinch of salt

Mix preceding ingredients well; pour into an unbaked 9 inch pastry pie shell and bake in 350° oven for 45 to 50 minutes. Cool and top with whipped cream or ice cream.

Dollie D. Billiter

PECAN PIE

1 c. dark syrup
1 c. sugar
3 eggs, beaten

1 c. pecans
1 lump butter (size of walnut)
1 tsp. vanilla

Mix sugar and syrup and bring to boil. Add slightly beaten eggs, butter, and vanilla to sugar and syrup mixture; beat while adding. Cool and pour into unbaked pie shell. Bake at 450° for 10 minutes; reduce heat to 350° and bake until filling thickens.

Pie Crust:

1 c. all-purpose flour, sifted
½ tsp. salt

⅓ c. Crisco
3 or 4 Tbsp. ice water

Blend flour, salt and Crisco until the consistency of meal; add water and mix.

Teresa Denning

PECAN PIE

¼ c. margarine, melted
3 eggs, well beaten
1 c. dark corn syrup
½ c. sugar
½ tsp. cinnamon
1 tsp. vanilla

1 Tbsp. flour
½ tsp. salt
1 c. chopped pecans
1 unbaked (8 inch) pastry
    shell

To the well beaten eggs, add margarine, syrup, sugar, cinnamon, vanilla, flour, salt, and pecans. Pour into unbaked pie shell. Bake in moderate oven (350°) until filling is set, about 45 minutes.

Mattie Hammack

PECAN PIE

½ c. sugar
¼ c. butter or margarine
1 c. light corn syrup
¼ tsp. salt

3 eggs
1 c. pecans
1 recipe Plain Pastry

Cream sugar and butter; add syrup and salt; beat well. Beat in eggs, 1 at a time; add pecans. Pour into 9 inch pastry lined pie pan. Bake in a moderate oven (350°) for 1 hour and 10 minutes or until knife comes out clean.

I've tried this and it is very good.

Wilma Crowdus

PECAN PIE

3 eggs
⅔ c. sugar
½ tsp. salt

⅓ c. butter, melted
1 c. light or dark corn syrup
1 c. pecan halves

Beat eggs, sugar, salt, butter and syrup with rotary beater. Pour into pie shell and bake about 350° until done.

Myrtle Logsdon

SOUTHERN PECAN PIE

1 c. sugar
¾ c. dark corn syrup
½ tsp. vanilla
1 stick margarine, melted

3 eggs, slightly beaten
1½ c. chopped pecans
1 (9 inch) unbaked pie shell

Mix all together and bake at 350° for 45 or 50 minutes.

Sue Johnson

PERSIMMON PUDDING

3 eggs
1¼ c. light brown sugar
1½ c. all-purpose flour
1 tsp. baking powder
1 tsp. baking soda
½ tsp. salt

½ c. melted butter
2½ c. half & half
2 tsp. cinnamon
1 tsp. ginger
½ tsp. ground nutmeg
1 c. chopped nuts

Bake at 325° about 1 hour or until firm in a 9x9 inch baking dish. Serve with whipped cream.

J. W. Borden, Jr.

PUMPKIN PIE

Pastry shell
1½ c. canned pumpkin
¾ c. sugar
½ tsp. salt
1¼ tsp. cinnamon
1 tsp. ginger

½ tsp. nutmeg
½ tsp. ground cloves
3 eggs, slightly beaten
1¼ c. milk
1 (6 oz.) can evaporated milk

Combine pumpkin, sugar, salt, cinnamon, ginger, nutmeg and cloves. Blend in eggs, milk and evaporated milk. Pour into pastry shell and bake in hot oven of 400° for 50 minutes or until knife inserted comes out clean. Cool.

Peggy Kessinger

PUMPKIN PIE

1 (9 inch) unbaked pie shell
¾ c. brown sugar
½ tsp. salt
1 tsp. cinnamon
½ tsp. ginger

½ tsp. cloves
½ tsp. nutmeg
1½ c. pumpkin
2 eggs, beaten
1 Tbsp. molasses

Combine brown sugar, salt and spices. Add remaining ingredients and mix until smooth. Pour in shell and bake at 425° for 30 to 40 minutes or until done.

Allouise Davidson

560

PUMPKIN PIE

¾ c. brown sugar
¾ c. white sugar
1 can pumpkin
1 tsp. pumpkin pie spices
1 tsp. cinnamon
5 eggs
1½ cans Milnot cream
3 pie shells

Mix; beat with mixer until smooth. Pour mixture into pie shells. Bake at 350° until done. Makes 3 pies.

Lil Pasinski

PUMPKIN PIE

1 c. sugar
1½ tsp. cinnamon
½ tsp. cloves
½ tsp. allspice
½ tsp. nutmeg
½ tsp. ginger
½ tsp. salt
2 eggs
1½ c. cooked pumpkin
1⅔ c. (1 tall can) undiluted Carnation evaporated milk
9 inch unbaked pie shell

Blend sugar, spices and salt together. Beat eggs with milk and combine with sugar, spice mixture and pumpkin. Pour into unbaked pie shell. Bake in hot oven (425°F.) 15 minutes; reduce to moderate heat (350°) and continue baking about 40 minutes or until knife inserted in pie mixture comes out clean. Cool.

Mattie Hammack

PINEAPPLE PIE

2 eggs
½ c. melted butter
2 heaping Tbsp. flour
2 c. sugar
1 small can pineapple
Unbaked pie shell

Cream butter and sugar with flour. Cream eggs in mixture, 1 at a time. Add pineapple. Pour into unbaked pie shell. Bake at 400° for 10 minutes, then at 350° for 50 minutes.

Lillian White

PINEAPPLE PARFAIT PIE

1 pkg. lime gelatin
1¼ c. hot liquid (juice or water)
1 pt. vanilla ice cream
1 c. drained crushed pineapple
1 baked pie shell

Dissolve gelatin in hot liquid. Add ice cream, a spoon at a time. Stir until melted; chill until thickened, 25 to 30 minutes. Fold in pineapple. Turn into a baked pie shell. Chill 20 minutes. Top pie with whipped cream if desired.

Variations: Recipe may be varied such as strawberries with strawberry gelatin; also, orange gelatin and coconut are a good combination.

Kim Clinton

QUICK AND EASY COBBLER

1 stick butter
1 c. flour
1 c. sugar

1 c. water or milk
1 large can fruit

Put fruit on to boil. Melt butter in oven in large baking dish. Make batter with flour, sugar and water or milk. Pour batter into melted butter. Pour boiling fruit into dish. Ingredients will mix as you pour them in. Bake in 350° oven until brown on top.

Claudia G. Myles

RAISIN PIE

2 eggs
1 c. sugar
2 Tbsp. butter, softened
½ c. milk

1½ c. raisins
½ c. chopped nuts
Unbaked (9 inch) pie shell

Beat eggs until fluffy. Gradually add sugar and beat well. Beat in softened butter. Add milk, raisins and nuts. Pour into unbaked pie shell and bake at 350° for 30 to 35 minutes.

Wanda Harris

SOUR CREAM RAISIN PIE

1 baked (9 inch) pastry shell
1 c. raisins
2 Tbsp. water
1 c. granulated sugar

3 egg yolks
2 tsp. flour
½ tsp. ground cinnamon
1 c. sour cream

Prepare pastry shell and set aside. Boil raisins and water; allow water to boil away completely. Remove from heat and stir in sugar, yolks, flour, cinnamon and sour cream. Blend well and stir constantly; bring to a gentle boil. Cook and stir until thickened to consistency of soft whipped cream. Don't overcook; mixture will thicken as it cools. Remove from heat and stir occasionally; let cool slightly. Mound into prepared pastry shell. Serve at room temperature.

Gwen Mills

ROBBIE'S FRUIT PIZZA

1 pkg. sugar cookie dough
12 oz. cream cheese
2 Tbsp. sugar
1 small can crushed
    pineapple, drained

Pineapple juice
1 can cherry pie filling
3 large bananas
¼ c. chopped pecans

Before you start, have the cookie dough and the cream cheese at room temperature. Spread cookie dough over a large pizza pan and bake at 375° for about 8 minutes or until golden brown. Let cookie dough completely cool. Blend cream cheese, sugar, and enough pineapple juice to make a spreading consistency; spread over cooked dough completely covering it. Place cherries on outer ring of dough about 2 inches. Layer 2 rings of bananas sliced, then fill remaining center circle with crushed pineapple. Sprinkle chopped nuts over the pineapple; ready to eat or can be refrigerated.

Robbie Castleman

RUM ICEBOX PIE

15 chocolate cream filled
    cookies, crushed
⅓ c. melted butter
5 egg yolks
1 c. sugar

1 env. unflavored gelatin
1 pt. whipping cream
Dark rum
Chopped pecans

Mix cookie crumbs with melted butter and pat into a 9x9 inch pie pan; chill in refrigerator. Beat egg yolks and add sugar. Soak gelatin and water over low heat and bring to a boil. Pour over eggs and sugar, stirring. Whip cream until stiff and fold into egg mixture. Add ½ cup dark rum and mix well. Cool filling until it begins to set, then pour into a pie shell. Chill until firm. Sprinkle top with chopped pecans that have been soaked for 24 hours in enough dark rum to cover them.

Paula White

SKILLET PIE

1½ c. granulated sugar
1½ c. milk
3 Tbsp. flour
3 egg yolks

1 tsp. vanilla
2 heaping Tbsp. cocoa
1 Tbsp. butter

Mix sugar, flour and cocoa together. Add egg yolks and mix slightly. Add milk, vanilla and butter. Cook over medium heat in iron skillet for about 5 minutes or until thick. Pour into baked pie shell. Top with meringue.

Variation: Butterscotch Pie - Omit granulated sugar and cocoa. Add 1½ cups packed brown sugar.

Variation: Coconut Cream Pie - Omit cocoa and add 1 package flaked coconut. Save small amount to sprinkle on meringue.

Janis Anderson

STRAWBERRY PIE

1 c. sugar
1 c. self-rising flour
2 Tbsp. butter, melted
1 tsp. vanilla

1 egg, beaten slightly
1 box frozen strawberries,
    partially defrosted

Mix sugar and flour. Melt butter; beat egg and combine; add vanilla. Gradually add flour to mixture. Pour batter into pan; pour strawberries on top. Cook at 300° about 1 hour or until brown.

Mary Lou Fentress

AUNT FRANCES' STRAWBERRY PIE

1¼ c. water
¾ c. sugar

3 Tbsp. cornstarch

Cook until thick and add 1 box strawberry Jello and 1 quart strawberries. Cool. Pour in 9 inch baked pie shell.

Mary Beeler

STRAWBERRY PIE

1 c. sugar
4 Tbsp. cornstarch
4 Tbsp. (small pkg.)
    strawberry Jello

1 c. water

Cook until thick and cool. Spoon over strawberries. Drain water from berries real well. Lay berries on cooled baked pie shell and spread cooled filling over berries.

Clara Nance

STRAWBERRY ICEBOX PIE

1 (17 oz.) pkg. marshmallows
1 box strawberries or 2 c.
   fresh, sweetened to taste
1 c. whipping cream or Cool
   Whip
1 cooled pastry shell

Put marshmallows in double boiler; add 2 tablespoons of strawberry juice. Cook until marshmallows are dissolved. Mix strawberries and marshmallows thoroughly. Chill about 2 hours. Fold in whipped cream to marshmallow mixture and pour into pastry shell. Chill until firm.

Mrs. Wendell (Jean) Ford

STRAWBERRY ICEBOX PIE

1 (10 oz.) box frozen
   strawberries, thawed
1 can condensed milk
⅓ c. lemon juice
1 large ctn. Cool Whip
1 c. chopped pecans
2 graham cracker crusts

Combine milk, lemon juice, and Cool Whip; mix thoroughly. Fold in strawberries and pecans. Pour into crusts. Chill until ready to serve.

Denise Figg

BUTTERNUT SQUASH PIE

1 c. squash
2 c. brown sugar
½ c. sugar
½ c. flour
½ tsp. vanilla
3 eggs
2 c. milk
1 stick butter
Pie shell, baked
1 tsp. allspice

Mix sugar, flour, and allspice. Gradually add milk to dry ingredients. Add melted butter, then squash, beaten eggs and vanilla. Cook until thick. Pour into pie shell, baked. Bake at 350° until knife comes out clean when inserted in the center.

Chasteen Thompson

SWEET POTATO PIE

8 or 9 medium sweet potatoes
3 Tbsp. light cream
¼ tsp. ground cinnamon
¾ tsp. salt

¾ c. chopped dates or
  pineapple
Marshmallows

Cook potatoes in hot boiling water until tender. Peel and mash while hot. Add cream, cinnamon, salt and dates or pineapple. Mix well. Put in casserole. Top with marshmallows. Bake in 350° oven about 15 or 20 minutes or until just brown.

Patti Roby

FRESH SWEET POTATO PIE

2 c. (4 medium) mashed,
  cooked sweet potatoes
3 eggs
1 c. packed brown sugar
1 tsp. salt
1 c. evaporated milk or light
  cream

1 unbaked (9 inch) pastry
  shell
Pecans for garnish
½ tsp. ground cinnamon
½ tsp. ground nutmeg
¼ tsp. ground ginger
⅛ tsp. ground cloves

Cook sweet potatoes. Bake in preheated 350°F. oven 40 minutes or boil in water to cover for 20 minutes, until soft. Cool, peel and mash until smooth. In large bowl, beat eggs with sugar, salt and spices. Add mashed sweet potatoes and evaporated milk; mix well. Turn into unbaked pastry shell. Bake in preheated 350°F. oven 1 hour and 15 minutes or until the tip of a silver knife inserted in center comes out clean. Garnish with pecans. Serve with whipped cream or ice cream if desired.

Mattie Hammack

TRANSPARENT PIE

3 c. brown sugar
3 eggs
½ c. butter

½ c. cream
1 tsp. vanilla
1 pinch of salt

Cream butter, eggs and sugar together and then add cream, vanilla and salt. Pour into 9 inch pastry lined pie plate and bake at 450° for 10 minutes and then about 25 minutes at 350°.

Kim Clinton

VINEGAR PIE

1 c. sugar
2 eggs
2 Tbsp. vinegar
2 Tbsp. flour or cornstarch
1 c. water
Small lump butter or margarine
½ tsp. lemon extract
Baked pie shell
Whipped cream (optional)

Combine sugar, eggs, vinegar, flour and water in double boiler and cook until thick and smooth, stirring occasionally. Just before removing from heat, stir in butter and lemon extract. Pour into baked pie shell. Top with whipped cream if desired.

Sue Tipton

GREEK YOGURT PIE

1 graham cracker crust (I buy mine)
12 oz. Ricotta or Farmers cheese
1½ c. plain yogurt
3 Tbsp. honey
1 tsp. vanilla
Fresh strawberries or blueberries

Let Ricotta or Farmers cheese set out until room temperature. Put into medium size mixing bowl and beat well, then add yogurt, a little at a time, mixing well. Stir in honey and vanilla. Pour into graham cracker crust and refrigerate for 24 hours before serving. Serve with fresh strawberries or blueberries. Serves 8.

Mary Goff

ZUCCHINI PIE

First Set of Ingredients:

5 c. sliced raw zucchini
½ c. water
¾ c. sugar
¼ c. lemon juice
2 tsp. cinnamon

Second Set of Ingredients:

6 Tbsp. margarine
1 c. flour
½ c. brown sugar, packed
1 tsp. baking powder
1½ tsp. salt

Cook first set of ingredients in saucepan for 10 minutes. Pour into greased 9 inch square pan. Combine next set of ingredients until crumbly and sprinkle on top. Bake 45 minutes at 350° or until brown and bubbly.

This tastes like apple.

Kathy Chesser

GRAHAM CRACKER CRUST

1½ c. graham cracker crumbs

⅓ c. butter, melted

Mix; press into pie pan. Bake 10 minutes in 350° oven. Cool before using for chiffon type pies.

Peggy Kessinger

PIE CRUST

5½ c. flour
2 c. shortening
1 tsp. salt

1 Tbsp. sugar
1 egg
Water

Beat 1 egg in measuring cup; fill with water to make 1 cup. Mix flour and shortening. Add the egg and water. Beat well. Add enough flour to roll out. Place in pans and freeze. Makes 6 crusts.

Erdean Lee

PIE CRUST

1⅓ c. flour
1 tsp. salt
⅓ c. lard

⅓ c. butter
⅓ c. ice water

Sift dry ingredients together. Cut lard and butter into flour mixture. They should be cut in pieces about the size of small peas. Stir in ice water. Handle dough as little as possible. Roll dough into balls; wrap in foil and refrigerate ½ hour or more. Divide ball in half. Roll thin. Yields 2 pie crusts.

Denise Figg

LEMON PIE CRUST

1½ c. flour
1 tsp. baking powder
1 tsp. salt

⅓ c. lard
¼ c. lemon juice, chilled

Sift dry ingredients together. Cut lard into dry mixture about the size of small peas. Stir in lemon juice. Handle dough as little as possible. If desired, roll dough into a ball; wrap in foil; refrigerate dough for ½ hour. Divide dough in half. Roll thin. Yields 2 pie crusts.

Denise Figg

NEVER FAIL PIE CRUST

4 c. flour
1½ tsp. salt
1 egg, beaten
½ c. water

1 Tbsp. sugar
1½ c. Crisco
1 Tbsp. vinegar

Blend flour, sugar and salt; cut in Crisco. Mix eggs, vinegar and water. Add to flour mixture. Chill before you roll out (best overnight). Keeps for several days. Makes enough for 2 (9 inch) pies.

Donna Browning

PERFECT MERINGUE

1 Tbsp. cornstarch
1 Tbsp. cold water
½ c. water

3 egg whites
6 Tbsp. sugar

Dissolve cornstarch in 1 tablespoon cold water. Add ½ cup water and cook until thick and clear. Cool thoroughly. Beat 3 eggs until foamy; add 6 tablespoons sugar and beat until stiff. Add cooled mixture to beaten egg whites and spread on pie. Bake at 350° until brown, 12 to 15 minutes.

Donna Browning

ICE CREAM, SHERBETS AND PUDDINGS

HOMEMADE ICE CREAM

2¼ c. sugar
3 Tbsp. flour
¾ tsp. salt
6 c. milk

6 eggs
6 tsp. vanilla
6 c. cream

Mix flour, sugar and salt. Stir into milk. Cook over boiling water until slightly thickened. Cover and cook 10 minutes more. Stir a little hot milk into eggs and then add to milk. Cook 5 minutes more or until mixture coats spoon. Chill. Add vanilla and cream. Freeze in ice cream freezer (gallon freezer).

Lenora Crafton

HOMEMADE ICE CREAM

6 eggs
2 c. sugar
2 cans Carnation milk

1 Tbsp. vanilla
6 - 8 peaches, bananas

Blend in blender. Pour in bucket and finish filling to fill line in container with milk. Freeze.

Phyllis L. Davis

LEMON VELVET ICE CREAM

2 c. sugar
3 Tbsp. flour
6 egg yolks, slightly beaten
⅔ c. lemon juice

¼ tsp. salt
3½ c. milk
2 Tbsp. grated lemon rind
3 c. heavy cream

Combine sugar, salt and flour in a large saucepan. Add milk gradually. Cook over medium heat, stirring constantly, until mixture thickens and bubbles. Remove from heat. Stir half of the mixture slowly into beaten egg yolks. Stir back into remaining mixture in saucepan. Cook, stirring constantly, for 1 minute. Remove from heat; pour into a large bowl and cool. Add lemon rind and lemon juice. Stir in cream and chill. Pour in a 4 to 6 inch quart freezer can.

FRESH PEACH ICE CREAM

2 eggs
1¼ c. sugar
1 c. milk
1 tsp. vanilla extract

⅛ tsp. almond extract
6 large ripe peaches, peeled
  and chopped
1 c. whipping cream

Beat eggs until thick and lemon colored, about 5 minutes. Beat in sugar. Stir in milk, vanilla and almond extract; set aside. Puree peaches in a blender. Stir into egg mixture. Stir in whipping cream. Pour into freezer trays. When frozen to mushy stage, take out and beat. Put back into trays and freeze.

OLD FASHION VANILLA ICE CREAM

3 c. sugar
4 eggs
1 Tbsp. vanilla

Milk (add enough to fill your
  freezer container ¾ full)

Stir and put in electric or hand crank ice cream freezer until it hardens.

Mrs. Max (Gloria) Rhoads

VANILLA ICE CREAM

4 eggs
2½ c. sugar
6 or 7 c. milk

¾ c. light cream
1½ or 2 Tbsp. vanilla
½ tsp. salt

Beat eggs until light. Add sugar. Beat until thickens. Add other ingredients. Freeze. Yield: 1 gallon.

J. W. Borden, Jr.

VANILLA ICE CREAM
(Uncooked)

4 eggs
2¼ c. sugar
5 c. milk
4 c. cream (half pint of half &
   half and half pint of
   whipping cream)

4½ tsp. vanilla
½ tsp. salt

Beat eggs. Gradually add sugar and beat stiff. Add cream and beat. Add milk and vanilla. Put in ice cream freezer and freeze.

Lenora Crafton

BUTTERMILK SHERBET

2 c. buttermilk
1 c. crushed pineapple
⅔ c. sugar

1 tsp. vanilla
¹/₁₆ tsp. salt
1 egg white

Mix buttermilk, all but 2 tablespoons sugar, salt, pineapple and vanilla. Freeze to a mush. Beat egg white until stiff and add the 2 tablespoons sugar. Transfer mixture to a cold mixing bowl; beat until fluffy. Add egg white and return to freezing tray. Freeze quickly without further stirring.

Lila White

CIDER SHERBET

Peelings from 4 or 5 apples,
   chopped coarse
2 c. cider

1 c. applesauce
Juice of 2 lemons, strained
2 c. syrup*

Puree the apple peel with a cup or so of the cider in an electric blender. Combine with the applesauce, remaining cider, lemon juice and syrup. Taste to see if enough sugar. Pour into 2 ice cube trays and place in freezer. When ice has frozen around the edges, pour into a large bowl. Beat with an electric or rotary beater. Return to the trays and continue to freeze until hard. Serves 6 to 8 people.

* To make the syrup: Combine 2 cups sugar with 1 cup of water in a saucepan. Bring to a boil; reduce heat somewhat, then boil until the syrup reaches 220° on a candy thermometer. Makes about 2 cups.

Paula White

LIME SHERBET

1 Tbsp. gelatin
2 Tbsp. cold water
1 c. sugar
4 c. lime carbonated
    beverage

½ c. boiling water
3 egg whites, whipped stiff
½ c. pistachio nuts

Soak gelatin in 2 tablespoons cold water for 5 minutes. Add ½ cup boiling water and stir until dissolved. Cool. Add sugar and lime beverage. When partially frozen, a thick mush stage, add egg whites and nuts. Freeze. Serves 8.

Gwen Mills

PLUM SHERBET

2 lb. ripe plums, pitted
½ c. sugar (or more)
1 tsp. unflavored gelatin

1 c. water
½ tsp. almond extract

Cook plums in heavy saucepan over medium heat until soft, about 10 minutes; stir occasionally and add 1 tablespoon water if needed to prevent burning. Cool plums; puree in a blender. You should have about 2 cups. Mix sugar and gelatin in a saucepan. Add water; stir over low heat until sugar and gelatin are dissolved completely. Remove from heat; stir in extract. Mix plum puree and sugar mixture. Pour into freezer container. When almost frozen, take out and beat; put back in freezer and finish freezing.

Gwen Mills

PINEAPPLE SHERBET

2 c. unsweetened pineapple
    juice
⅓ c. honey
2 Tbsp. lemon juice
1 Tbsp. unflavored gelatin

1 c. unsweetened crushed
    pineapple, drained
2 egg whites
⅛ tsp. salt

Combine pineapple juice, honey, and lemon juice in a saucepan. Sprinkle gelatin over juice and blend together. Place over medium heat and stir until gelatin dissolves. Remove from heat and cool mixture. Stir in drained, crushed pineapple. Pour mixture into freezer tray and freeze until almost firm, but still mushy. Remove from freezer and dump into large mixing bowl; add unbeaten egg whites and salt; beat until fluffy, but still thick. Return mixture to freezer for several hours or until firm. To

1546-85

573

retain a light and fluffy consistency, spoon sherbet into a cold mixing bowl, about 1 hour before serving, and beat until smooth. Return to freezer. Yield: 6 servings.

Crystal Duke

PINEAPPLE SHERBET

8 oz. pineapple juice
2 beaten egg whites

24 oz. water
6 Tbsp. sugar (or to taste)

Mix all ingredients together, except egg white. Freeze to semi-hard stage in ice tray or other container. Add egg white. Place back in freezer until hard.

Paula White

ALABAMA ICEBOX PUDDING

1 c. pineapple juice
½ c. orange juice
25 marshmallows
1 env. unflavored gelatin
Chopped pecans

1 lb. vanilla wafers
1 c. heavy whipped cream
Pinch of salt
Whipped cream

Heat 1 cup pineapple juice and ½ cup orange juice; add pinch of salt. Add marshmallows and dissolve partially; remove from heat. Soften 1 envelope unflavored gelatin in 2 tablespoons cold water, then add to hot mixture until well dissolved. Cool thoroughly, then fold in 1 cup heavy whipped cream. Place layer of vanilla wafer crumbs on bottom of 8x12 inch casserole dish and spread with half of mixture. Sprinkle nuts, another layer of crumbs, rest of the mixture, nuts and crumbs on top. Chill in refrigerator overnight and serve cut in squares topped with whipped cream.

Gwen Bond

BANANA PUDDING

¾ c. sugar
3 Tbsp. all-purpose flour
Dash of salt
2 c. milk
½ tsp. vanilla extract
Vanilla wafers

5 - 6 medium size bananas, sliced
1 egg
3 egg yolks
3 egg whites

574

Combine ½ cup sugar, flour and salt in top of double boiler or a Club aluminum stewer. Mix in 1 whole egg and 3 egg yolks. Stir in milk; cook uncovered over boiling water, stirring constantly, until thickened. Remove from heat; add vanilla. Spread small amount on bottom of 2 quart casserole. Cover with layer of vanilla wafers. Top with bananas. Continue to layer wafers, bananas and custard to make 3 layers of each, ending with custard. Beat remaining 3 egg whites stiff, but not dry; gradually add remaining ¼ cup sugar and beat until mixture forms stiff peaks. Pile on top of pudding, covering entire surface. Bake in preheated oven at 425° until delicately browned. Makes 8 servings.

Bessie Litchford

MOTHER'S BANANA PUDDING FILLING

1½ c. sugar	3 Tbsp. cornstarch
3 egg yolks	1 Tbsp. butter
2 c. milk	3 bananas
1 tsp. vanilla	

Cook in double boiler until thick. Layer graham crackers or vanilla wafers, layer bananas, then filling. Repeat until all filling is used. Cover with meringue and place in oven at 350° until brown.

Meringue: Beat 3 egg whites until stiff; add 3 tablespoons sugar; cover to edge of dish; place in 350° oven until brown.

Shirley Cates

BLACKBERRY PUDDING

¼ c. shortening	¼ c. milk
¾ c. sugar	1 tsp. vanilla
1 c. sifted flour	2 egg whites, beaten
¼ tsp. salt	3 c. blackberries
1 tsp. baking powder	

Cream the shortening and stir in ½ cup sugar gradually. Sift dry ingredients together and add alternately with the milk to the first mixture. Fold in stiffly beaten egg whites. Add vanilla. Mix blackberries with the remaining ¼ cup sugar. Place in a greased baking dish. Pour batter over them and cover. Bake at 350° for 1¼ hours. Serves 4 to 6.

Lynnette Bonn

BREAD PUDDING

2 c. (8 or 9 slices) dry bread
   crumbs, toasted
1 pt. milk
½ box raisins

1 c. sugar
2 eggs
1 tsp. vanilla extract
2 tsp. banana extract

Scald milk in saucepan. Add bread crumbs. Beat eggs with sugar and add to mixture. Cook short time over low heat. Add flavorings just before pouring into a greased baking dish. Bake in a 350° oven for 45 minutes.

Peggy Kessinger

DIRT PUDDING

Crunch up 1 small package Oreos (scrape off icing). Place in bottom of 9x13 inch pan (save handful of cookies for top of dessert).

In small bowl, mix:

1 (8 oz.) pkg. Philadelphia
   cream cheese

½ stick butter
1 c. powdered sugar

Mix really well!

In *big* bowl, mix:

1 (8 oz.) ctn. Cool Whip
2 boxes instant French vanilla
   pudding

3 c. milk

Combine small and big bowls. Pour over crumbs. Top with extra crumbs. Chill.

Patricia Jewell

FRENCH PUDDING

1½ c. powdered sugar
2 eggs
½ lb. vanilla wafer crumbs
½ c. oleo
½ pt. whipping cream

1 c. chopped pecans
2 c. fruit (peach or cherry pie
   filling, or crushed
   pineapple)

Thoroughly cream oleo and powdered sugar. Then add eggs and beat. Put layer of ½ vanilla wafer crumbs in bottom of greased pan, layer of mixture, layer of whipped cream, layer of fruit, then a layer of other ½ vanilla wafer crumbs. Sprinkle nuts on top. Chill. Serves 10 to 12.

Barbara Swank

JAM PUDDING

½ c. margarine
3 beaten eggs
1 c. jam
1½ c. flour

1 c. sugar
1 tsp. soda
1 c. buttermilk
½ tsp. cinnamon

Cream butter with eggs and jam. Add flour slowly, beating to blend. Add sugar and beat light. Dissolve soda in buttermilk and add to batter. Add cinnamon and beat light. Pour into greased baking pan. Bake at 350° for about 20 minutes. Serve hot with Cream Sauce.

Cream Sauce:

1 c. sugar
1 egg white
3 egg yolks

1 c. cream
1 tsp. vanilla

Combine ingredients and beat until very light. Heat over hot water; beat until foamy. Remove from heat; add vanilla; stir well.

Lynnette Bonn

NUT PUDDING

1 c. raisins
1 c. bread crumbs
1 c. milk
1 c. nuts (black walnuts)

1 Tbsp. shortening
1 egg
1 c. sugar

Bake until brown, about 30 minutes at 350°. Top with white sauce.

Margaret Hunter

PRUNE PUDDING

4 egg whites, beaten stiffly
4 tsp. sugar
⅛ tsp. salt

15 stewed prunes
¼ tsp. cream of tartar
Whipped cream

Beat sugar and salt into egg whites. Mash prunes, adding cream of tartar; beat into first mixture. Pour into buttered baking dish. Bake at 350° for 20 minutes. Serve hot or cold with whipped cream.

Rosemary Ramirez

TWINKIES PUDDING

1 box (12) vanilla Twinkies
2 large pkg. instant vanilla
   pudding
1 large can crushed
   pineapple, drained

2 - 3 sliced bananas
1 large Cool Whip
6 maraschino cherries
Nuts (if you like)

1. Line 9x12 inch glass Pyrex with the Twinkies.
2. Mix 4 cups of cold milk and vanilla pudding, then spread on Twinkies.
3. Then layer the drained pineapple.
4. Add sliced bananas.
5. Add Cool Whip on top of that.
6. Put cherries and nuts on top. Make the day ahead.

Flo Gish

QUICK PUDDING

1 c. flour
1 c. sugar
2 tsp. baking powder

Pinch of salt
1 c. raisins
½ c. milk

Mix preceding ingredients and place in greased baking dish.

Mix together:

1 c. brown sugar
2 c. boiling water

1 Tbsp. butter

Pour over batter. Bake 30 to 40 minutes at 350° to 375°.

Jewell Hundley

Candy,
Jelly,
Preserves

QUANTITIES TO SERVE 100

Baked beans . . . . .5 gallons
Beef . . . . 40 pounds
Beets . . . . 30 pounds
Bread . . . . 10 loaves
Butter . . . . .3 pounds
Cabbage for slaw . . . . 20 pounds
Cakes . . . . 8 cakes
Carrots . . . . 33 pounds
Cauliflower . . . . 18 pounds
Cheese . . . . 18 pounds
Chicken for chicken pie . . . . 40 pounds
Coffee . . . . .3 pounds
Cream . . . . 3 quarts
Fruit cocktail . . . . 1 gallon
Fruit juice . . . . 4 (No. 10) cans
Fruit salad . . . . 20 quarts
Ground beef . . . . .30 to 36 pounds
Ham . . . . 40 pounds
Ice cream . . . . .4 gallons
Lettuce . . . . .20 heads
Meat loaf . . . . 24 pounds
Milk . . . . .6 gallons
Nuts . . . . .3 pounds
Olives . . . . 1¾ pounds
Oysters . . . . 18 quarts
Pickles . . . . 2 quarts
Pies . . . . .18 pies
Potatoes . . . . 35 pounds
Roast pork . . . . 40 pounds
Rolls . . . . 200 rolls
Salad dressing . . . . 3 quarts
Scalloped potatoes . . . . .5 gallons
Soup . . . . .5 gallons
Sugar cubes . . . . .3 pounds
Tomato juice . . . . 4 (No. 10) cans
Vegetables . . . . 4 (No. 20) cans
Vegetable salad . . . . 20 quarts
Whipping cream . . . . 4 pints
Wieners . . . . .25 pounds

CANDY, JELLY, PRESERVES

CANDY

BOSTON CREAM CANDY

3 c. white sugar	1 tsp. vanilla
1½ c. heavy cream	Chopped nuts, raisins or
1 c. white corn syrup	coconut to taste

Combine first 3 ingredients; cook, stirring constantly, to soft ball stage, 235°. Remove from heat; add vanilla. Beat; add nuts. Pour into pan; cut into squares.

Ruth Ackerman

KENTUCKY COLONEL BOURBON BONBONS

This is an old and famous recipe from the Blue Grass Country. For many years these were hand dipped, but with the introduction of the new plastic candy molds in the bonbon shape, this old favorite is now easy and exciting to make.

7 Tbsp. butter	1 c. pecans, soaked in 7
1 lb. powdered sugar	Tbsp. bourbon

Soak broken pecans in bourbon for 3 days if possible. If nuts are not soaked, use 5 tablespoons of bourbon rather than 7. Combine butter and sugar until consistency of coarse meal. Add pecans and bourbon and blend. Refrigerate 1 hour before forming balls for filling. Use this filling in the bonbon mold; first making a shell of semi-sweet chocolate molding candy. Add bourbon filling and cover with melted chocolate and place in freezer to harden.

Lena March

BROWN SUGAR PRALINES

2 c. packed brown sugar	2 Tbsp. margarine
1 c. light cream	2 c. pecan halves

In a large saucepan, combine sugar and cream; bring to a boil; stir constantly. Cook to 238°, soft ball stage; stir when necessary to prevent sticking. Remove from heat; add margarine. Stir in pecans. Beat for about 2 minutes or until candy begins to lose its gloss. Drop by tablespoon onto waxed paper; shape into patties with spoon. If candy becomes too stiff to drop, add a few drops of hot water. Makes 24.

Rosalie Smith

OVEN-MADE CARAMEL CORN

5 qt. popped corn
1 c. (2 sticks) margarine
2 c. brown sugar, firmly
    packed

½ c. light corn syrup
1 tsp. salt
½ tsp. baking soda

Spread freshly popped corn in a large, shallow sheet pan. Put it in a very slow oven (250°) to keep warm and crisp. Combine butter, brown sugar, corn syrup and salt in 2 quart heavy saucepan. Place on medium heat, stirring until sugar dissolves. Continue to boil to the firm ball stage (248°), about 5 minutes. Remove from heat and stir in baking soda. Syrup will foam. Take popped corn from oven and pour hot caramel mixture over it in a fine stream. Stir to mix well. Return to oven for 45 to 50 minutes, stirring every 15 minutes. Cool and serve or store.

To store, pour into airtight container and set in a cold place. Makes about 5 quarts or almost 2 pounds.

Martha Hooper

CHOCOLATE COVERED PRETZELS

1 medium size bag pretzels
White chocolate

Paraffin

Melt chocolate in double boiler with ½ cake paraffin. Dip pretzels; shake off and place on waxed paper to chill.

Helen Russman

CHRISTMAS JEWELS

3 c. sugar
1½ c. non-dairy liquid coffee
    creamer
1 c. light corn syrup
1 tsp. salt

2 tsp. vanilla
2 c. candied fruit
1 c. sliced almonds
1½ c. broken pecan pieces

Combine sugar, creamer, syrup and salt in a heavy saucepan. Stir to dissolve sugar; cook to 236° without stirring. Remove from heat; add vanilla and beat with electric mixer until mixture is creamy and begins to hold its shape. Stir in candied fruit, almonds and pecans by hand. Press into 2 buttered (8 inch) square pans and chill until firm enough to cut. Let stand in refrigerator 24 hours before serving. Makes about 80 pieces.

Annetta Crossfield

COCONUT BONBONS

¾ c. light corn syrup
2½ c. dry macaroon coconut

Colored chocolate

Heat corn syrup just to boiling. Pour over coconut and mix. Set mixture aside for an hour or so. Roll mixture into balls and let air dry slightly. Dip in colored chocolate.

Sue Tipton

QUICK FONDANT 1

½ c. softened butter or
   margarine
1 tsp. vanilla
¼ tsp. salt

⅔ c. sweetened condensed
   milk (not evaporated)
6 c. confectioners sugar
   (about 1½ lb.)

Cream together butter or margarine, vanilla and salt. Gradually add sweetened condensed milk. Add 5 cups of confectioners sugar, 1 cup at a time, blending well after each addition. Turn out on a clean board or marble slab and knead in the remaining 1 cup of sugar. Fondant is ready to use.

Nuts or coconut may be kneaded in for variety.

Renee Wallace

QUICK FONDANT 2
(These make ideal cream centers for molded candies)

⅓ c. softened butter or
   margarine
⅓ c. white corn syrup
¼ tsp. salt

1 tsp. vanilla
4½ c. sifted confectioners
   sugar
Food coloring

In a large mixing bowl, blend softened butter, corn syrup, salt and vanilla. Add sifted confectioners sugar all at once. Mix together first with spoon, then with your hands, kneading until smooth.

By adding food coloring, flavoring, candied or dried fruits, nuts or coconut, many varieties may be made from one batch.

Renee Wallace

CARNATION FIVE MINUTE FUDGE

⅔ c. undiluted Carnation
  evaporated milk
2 Tbsp. butter
1⅔ c. sugar
2 c. miniature marshmallows

½ c. chopped nuts
1½ c. semi-sweet chocolate
  bits
1 tsp. vanilla

Combine ⅔ cup undiluted Carnation evaporated milk, 2 tablespoons butter and 1 ⅔ cups sugar in saucepan; heat to boiling. Cook 5 minutes, stirring constantly. Remove from heat. Add 2 cups miniature marshmallows, ½ cup chopped nuts, 1½ cups semi-sweet chocolate bits and 1 teaspoon vanilla. Stir until marshmallows are melted. Pour into a buttered 8 or 9 inch square pan. Garnish with nuts if desired. Cut in squares.

Bessie Litchford

CHOCOLATE FUDGE

3 blocks unsweetened
  chocolate
1 can Eagle Brand milk
1 box sifted confectioners
  sugar

1½ Tbsp. butter
1 c. chopped pecans (or black
  walnuts)
1 tsp. vanilla

Melt chocolate in a double boiler; put in milk and boil 5 minutes, stirring constantly. Stir in sifted sugar; add butter and vanilla. Stir nuts in and pour into a buttered pan and set in refrigerator.

Ruth Ackerman

MAPLE FUDGE

2 c. maple syrup
¾ c. light cream
1 Tbsp. light corn syrup

1 tsp. vanilla
½ c. nuts, chopped

582

Stir together maple syrup, cream and corn syrup in heavy 2 quart saucepan. Bring mixture to boil over medium heat, stirring constantly. Continue cooking without stirring, until temperature reaches 236° or until small amount of mixture dropped in very cold water forms a small ball that flattens upon removal from water. Remove from heat and cool until lukewarm (110°) without stirring. Beat with electric beater on low speed until candy loses its gloss and thickens. Stir in vanilla and nuts. Turn into lightly buttered 9x5x3 inch loaf pan. When cool, cut into pieces. Makes about 1 pound.

Mary Baxter

PEANUT BUTTER FUDGE

1 c. brown sugar
1 c. sugar
½ c. Carnation evaporated
   milk

2 Tbsp. butter
¾ c. peanut butter
1 c. marshmallow pieces
1 tsp. vanilla

Combine sugars, milk and butter in a heavy saucepan and cook until mixture comes to the soft ball stage. Add peanut butter, marshmallows and vanilla. After marshmallows melt, remove from heat and stir mixture until it begins to thicken, approximately 1 minute. Pour onto buttered dish. Makes 1½ pounds.

Rosetta Humphries

PEANUT BUTTER FUDGE

½ c. butter or margarine
1 lb. Colonial light brown
   sugar
½ c. milk
1 tsp. vanilla extract

¾ c. smooth or crunchy
   peanut butter
1 lb. Colonial confectioners
   sugar

In medium saucepan, melt butter and stir in brown sugar and milk. Bring to a boil; boil and stir 2 minutes. Remove from heat. Stir in peanut butter and vanilla. Mix in confectioners sugar. Beat until smooth. Spread into buttered 9 inch square pan. Chill until firm. Cut into squares.

JoAnn Thompson

PEANUT BUTTER FUDGE

2 c. sugar
1 c. peanut butter

1 c. marshmallow cream
⅔ c. milk

Mix the sugar and milk in a saucepan. Bring to a boil and cook until mixture reaches the soft ball stage, 234° on a candy thermometer. Remove from heat and add peanut butter and marshmallow cream. Beat until well blended, then pour into a buttered shallow pan or dish. When cool, cut into squares.

Patricia Jewell

PEANUT BUTTER FUDGE

Using 1 stick of butter, butter large plate and melt the rest. Add 6 tablespoons Pet milk, dash of salt, 1 tablespoon vanilla, 1 pound box powdered sugar, and 4 heaping teaspoons cocoa. Stir well. Add about ½ cup peanut butter. Stir and pour on buttered plate. Place in refrigerator. Let cool and harden. Cut and enjoy.

PEANUT BUTTER FUDGE

Cook:

2 c. sugar   **⅔ c. milk**
½ c. white corn syrup

Cook until soft ball stage. Add 1 (12 ounce) jar of peanut butter. Stir well. Put in greased 9x9 inch pan. Cool and cut into squares.

Wynola Sharon Davis

PEANUT BUTTER FUDGE

4 c. sugar   **1 mug milk (or large c.)**
1 tsp. vanilla   **3 Tbsp. peanut butter**
2 Tbsp. butter

Cook first 4 ingredients until ball forms in water. Add 3 tablespoons of peanut butter and stir. Pour into buttered pan.

Cat Moore

REMARKABLE FUDGE

4 c. white sugar   **1 jar marshmallow creme**
2 c. butter or margarine   **1 tsp. vanilla**
1 large can condensed milk   **1 c. chopped nuts**
2 (6 oz.) pkg. semi-sweet
**   chocolate chips**

Cook sugar, butter or margarine and milk until soft ball stage. Stir often. Add chocolate pieces until chocolate is mixed well. Add marshmallow creme and vanilla. Beat well. Add nuts. Makes 5 pounds.

Bev Sowders

STOVERS FUDGE

4 c. sugar
1 stick butter

1 large can Pet milk

Let come to boil and cook 6 minutes.

Mix well with:

2 (6 oz.) pkg. chocolate chips
  (semi-sweet)
1 pt. marshmallow cream

1 pkg. nuts
3 large Hershey bars (not
  giant)

Pour on greased sheet and cool.

JoAnn Thompson

VANILLA FUDGE

2 c. sugar
¼ tsp. salt
1⅔ c. half & half

¼ c. light corn syrup
1 tsp. vanilla

Combine dry ingredients, half & half, and corn syrup. Stir constantly until it boils. Then stir occasionally. Cook until it forms a soft ball in cold water or a soft ball on candy thermometer. Then add vanilla and beat.

Ann Williams

MALTED MILK BALLS

1 c. white chocolate
1 c. malted milk powder

1 lb. milk chocolate

In a double boiler, melt white chocolate. Set aside. Measure malted milk powder into a medium size bowl; add 5 or 6 tablespoons of the melted white chocolate to the powder, or enough to form into eggs. Make into balls and chill. Dip into milk chocolate and turn onto waxed paper to air dry.

Peggy Kessinger

MINTS FROM THE BLUEGRASS COUNTRY

4 Tbsp. softened butter
⅓ c. light corn syrup
½ tsp. salt
Food coloring as desired
A few drops to taste oil of
     peppermint (or other oil
     flavoring)

4¾ c. (1 lb. box) sifted
    confectioners sugar

Blend butter, corn syrup, salt and peppermint (use hands to blend). Gradually add 1 box of sifted confectioners sugar. Form into balls; dip in extra fine granulated sugar and press into mold. Fill entire tray, then turn out on waxed paper. (Tap back of tray with spatula handle to release mints.) Dry on cake rack overnight. Store in airtight container.

These can also be frozen. If fine sugar is not available, put granulated sugar in blender for a quick turn on and off only, or you will have powdered sugar.

Crystal Duke

NO COOK MINT PATTIES

⅓ c. light corn syrup
¼ c. margarine, softened
1 tsp. peppermint extract
4 c. sifted powdered sugar

2 drops of red food coloring
2 drops of green food
    coloring

In a small bowl, combine corn syrup, margarine and peppermint; beat until well mixed. Gradually add 2 cups of powdered sugar; beat well. Mix in as much of the remaining powdered sugar as you can mix in with a spoon. Turn out onto a surface coated lightly with a little powdered sugar. Knead in enough of the remaining powdered sugar to make a stiff dough that is smooth. Divide dough into thirds. Take ⅓ of the dough and knead in the red food coloring until evenly distributed. Knead the green food coloring into another third of the dough. Leave the remaining dough white. Shape dough into ¾ inch balls; place 2 inches apart on baking sheet lined with wax paper. Press with tines of a fork. Let dry several hours. Makes about 75 mints.

Lynnette Bonn

SUMMER MINT MELT A WAYS

Instant mix dry candy fondant
Food color

Flavoring
Water or fruit juice

Mix fondant powder with enough water or fruit juice to be able to work with your hands. Add desired flavor and food color; knead. The following are suggestions for flavors and colors that are good combinations for summer mints: White with peppermint, pink with wintergreen, green with spearmint or lime, red with cinnamon or clove, yellow with lemon, orange or pineapple. Sprinkle the mold cavity with granulated sugar before molding. This helps release the mint from the mold. Roll the fondant mix into small uniform size balls. Dip in granulated sugar and press in mold cavity. We suggest using molds with shallow cavities such as the mint leaf, rose mold or small mini mold. Turn out of mold immediately and store in airtight container. These will remain creamy for days.

Crystal Duke

MOLASSES COCONUT CHEWS

½ c. corn syrup
½ c. molasses
1 Tbsp. vinegar

2 Tbsp. butter
2 c. shredded coconut

Combine syrup, molasses, vinegar and butter. Place over low heat and stir until mixture boils. Continue boiling to 240° or until a small amount of syrup becomes brittle in cold water. Remove from heat; add coconut. Drop by teaspoon on greased surface. Chill.

Annette Anderson

NOODLE CLUSTERS

1 lb. chocolate or
   butterscotch candy

1 c. peanuts
2 or 3 c. chow mein noodles

Melt chocolate to almost liquid. Mix all ingredients together. Drop by spoonful onto wax paper.

Debbie Rigdon

PEANUT BUTTER BALLS

2 sticks oleo
8 oz. chunky peanut butter
1 lb. confectioners sugar

3½ c. hand crumbled Rice
   Krispies

Mix into small balls. Refrigerate at least 1 hour. In double boiler, melt ¼ cake paraffin and 1 package semi-sweet chocolate chips. Dip balls and refrigerate on wax paper until firm, then place in airtight container.

Helen Russman

PEANUT BUTTER BONBONS

1 c. crunchy peanut butter
1 c. pecans, crushed
1 box powdered sugar
1 c. graham crackers,
    crushed fine

2 sticks melted butter or
    margarine
1 (6 oz.) pkg. butterscotch
    morsels
½ cake paraffin

Mix graham crackers, powdered sugar, and pecans in bowl and blend well. Pour melted butter over crackers, sugar, and pecans. Add peanut butter. Mix well. You will have a thick batter. Melt paraffin and butterscotch morsels in saucepan over low heat. Dip balls into butterscotch morsels and paraffin mixture with toothpicks or small spoon. Drop on wax paper. Let cool.

Teresa Redmon

PEANUT BUTTER CANDY

3 c. powdered sugar
3 Tbsp. milk or cream

½ tsp. vanilla

Mix and knead into a dough. Spread out with rolling pin like a pie dough. Spread on layer of peanut butter. Roll up like a jelly roll. Slice.

Wanda Frankenberger

A RECIPE FOR A HAPPY FAMILY

1 husband
1 wife
Children
1 Bible
1 home
1 pkg. work
1 pkg. play (together)

1 Tbsp. patience
1 Tbsp. forgiveness
1 Tbsp. understanding
Generous portion of prayer
3 c. love, packed
1 c. kisses

Mix thoroughly and sprinkle with awareness. Bake in moderate oven of everyday life, using as fuel all grudges and past unpleasantness. Cool. Turn out on platter in large helpings. Serve God, country and community.

Wanda Frankenberger

CHOCOLATE PEANUT CLUSTERS

1 pkg. chocolate pudding (not instant)
1 c. chopped nuts

1 c. sugar
½ c. Pet milk
1 Tbsp. butter or margarine

Cook and stir to a full over boil. Lower heat, keep stirring while mixture boils slowly for 3 minutes. Remove from heat. Stir in nuts. Beat until candy starts to thicken. Drop from teaspoon onto wax paper.

If you wish, you can leave the nuts in large chunks. Nuts can be of your choice.

Mary Beeler

PECAN CLUSTERS

12 oz. pkg. chocolate chips

12 oz. pkg. pecans

Line cookie sheets with waxed paper. In a large saucepan, over low heat, melt chips; stir until smooth. Stir in pecans. Drop by teaspoon onto cookie sheets. Chill until set. Store covered in refrigerator.

Beverly Craft

CREOLE PECAN PRALINES

1 lb. (1½ c.) pecan halves
1 Tbsp. melted butter

2 c. brown sugar, packed firm
4 Tbsp. water

Mix pecans with melted butter. Add sugar to water and bring to a boil. Cook until it forms a syrup. Add pecans; stir until mixture bubbles; remove from heat. Butter a sheet of heavy wax paper. Take 1 tablespoon of the mixture at a time and place on buttered sheet, pressing it into a round ¼ inch thick and 4 inches in diameter. Work fast. Leave until it hardens and lift with a knife. Pralines should be light, crisp and flaky. Makes 24.

Cristy Lewis

PECAN ROLL

1 lb. graham crackers,
   crushed
15 oz. raisins
1 lb. pecans

1 jar maraschino cherries
1 lb. marshmallows
¾ c. milk

Mix well ¾ pound graham cracker crumbs, raisins, pecans and maraschino cherries; set aside. Melt marshmallows in ¾ cup milk and pour into dry ingredients and mix well. Shape into rolls, then roll in ¼ pound graham cracker crumbs. Wrap in aluminum foil and refrigerate.

Sue Skelton

TOFFEE

1 c. pecans, chopped
½ c. butter
¾ c. brown sugar, packed
1 (4½ oz.) bar milk chocolate
   candy, broken into pieces

or ½ c. semi-sweet
chocolate pieces

Butter 9x9x2 inch square pan. Spread pecans in pan. Heat sugar and butter to boiling, stirring constantly, for 7 minutes. Immediately spread mixture evenly over nuts in pan. *(Do this quickly, before it hardens!)* Sprinkle chocolate pieces over hot mixture; place baking sheet over pan so contained heat will melt chocolate. Spread melted chocolate evenly over the nuts. While hot, cut into 1½ inch squares. Chill until firm. Makes 3 dozen candies.

Patricia Jewell

JAMS, JELLIES, PRESERVES

APPLE BUTTER

1 bushel apples, peeled,
  cored and quartered
8 lb. sugar
4 Tbsp. cinnamon

¼ tsp. allspice
1 tsp. salt
½ c. red hots

Cook apples in saucepan until tender, then add to roaster. Mix with sauce the sugar, cinnamon, allspice, salt and red hots (will give color and also add to the flavor). Bake at 325° until thick.

Maxine Welch

APRICOT-PINEAPPLE JAM

1 qt. diced canned apricots
4 c. sugar

2 c. drained crushed
  pineapple

Combine apricots and sugar. Stir over low heat until sugar is dissolved; boil 20 minutes. Add drained pineapple; return to a boil. Pour into hot, sterilized jars and seal. Yield: 3 pints.

Gwen Mills

CRANBERRY JELLY

3½ c. cranberry juice cocktail
1 (1¾ oz.) pkg. powdered
  fruit pectin

4 c. sugar
¼ c. lemon juice

In a large kettle, combine cranberry juice and pectin. Bring to a full rolling boil. Stir in sugar. Bring again to a full rolling boil. Boil hard, uncovered, 1 minute; stir constantly. Remove from heat. Stir in lemon juice. Quickly skim off foam with metal spoon. Pour at once into hot, sterilized jars; seal. Makes 6 half pints.

Gwen Mills

CUCUMBER JELLY

4 lb. cucumbers
⅓ c. water
Sugar

Lemons
Ground ginger

Wash cucumbers; cut into pieces. Put into pans with water and simmer until soft. Put cucumbers and juice in a jelly bag and allow to drain overnight. Measure juice and allow 2 cups sugar, juice of 1 lemon and ⅛ teaspoon ginger for each 2 cups juice. Stir over low heat until sugar is dissolved. Then boil rapidly until setting point is reached. Skim any scum from jelly; pour into hot, sterilized jars and seal.

Dee Dee Millen

LEMON AND FIG JAM

2 lb. dried figs
3¼ c. hot water

6¾ c. sugar
Juice of 2 lemons

Wash figs and soak overnight in cold water. Rinse in fresh water and cut into small pieces. Put in a pan of hot water and simmer until tender. Add lemon juice and sugar. Stir over low heat until sugar is dissolved. Boil rapidly until thickened to desired consistency, then pour into hot, sterilized jars and seal immediately.

Dee Dee Millen

ORANGE LEMON JELLY

6 oranges (juice)
6 lemons (juice)

Sugar
1 box pectin

Mix lemon and orange juice; add 3½ times as much water. Add 1¾ cups sugar to each 2 cups of juice. Add pectin. Bring to a boil and boil rapidly to the jelly stage. Pour into hot, sterilized jars and seal.

Gwen Mills

PEACH OR APRICOT BUTTER

5 lb. peaches or apricots
5 c. sugar
Juice and grated rind of 1
  orange

2 tsp. cinnamon
1 tsp. ground cloves
½ tsp. allspice

Wash, peel and pit fruit; crush or cut into small pieces. Add sugar, orange juice and rind of orange. Stir until sugar is dissolved and add spices. Simmer over low heat; stir often, until mixture thickens to spreading consistency. Pour into hot, sterilized jars and seal. Yield: 6 pints.

Gwen Mills

PEACH JAM

6 c. sliced peaches (12
  medium peaches)

3 c. sugar
1 Tbsp. lemon juice

Wash, blanch, peel and slice peaches. Combine all ingredients and let stand, uncovered, 1 hour. Place in kettle and simmer until sugar is dissolved; stir constantly. Bring to a boil and boil rapidly until gel stage is reached. Remove from heat and skim off foam. Pour hot mixture into hot, sterilized jars and seal. Makes 6 or 7 (8 ounce) glasses.

Gwen Mills

PEACH PRESERVES

3½ c. sugar
2 c. water

5 c. (about 5 large) sliced
peaches

Combine sugar and water in a large Dutch oven; cook over medium heat, stirring constantly, until sugar dissolves. Add peaches; bring to a boil and cook for 20 minutes or until peaches are clear. Stir occasionally. Remove from heat; cover and let stand 12 to 18 hours in a cool place. Drain peaches, reserving liquid in pan. Spoon peaches into hot, sterilized jars; set aside. Bring liquid to a boil and cook 2 to 3 minutes, stirring often. Pour over peaches, leaving ¾ inch head space. Cover at once with metal lids, and screw metal bands tight. Process in boiling water bath 15 minutes. Yield: 5 half pints.

Phyllis L. Davis

PEAR HONEY

7 lb. pears, peeled and
ground with course blade
on food chopper
7 lb. sugar

1 (No. 2) can crushed
pineapple
1 can coconut

Mix course ground pears and sugar; cook in a large kettle until thick. Add crushed pineapple; cook until thick. Add 1 can coconut and mix well. Put in jars and seal. Makes 10 pints.

Allouise Davidson

PLUM BUTTER

4 lb. plums
3 c. sugar
1 tsp. ground cloves

1 tsp. cinnamon
½ tsp. allspice

Wash and cook plums in a little water until tender. Press through a strainer. Add sugar and spices to pulp; cook over low heat for about 45 minutes or until mixture thickens; stir often. Pour into hot, sterilized jars and seal. Yield: 4 pints.

Gwen Mills

PLUM JAM

3 lb. plums   6¾ c. sugar
¾ to 2 c. water

Put washed plums into a pan of water. Sweet juicy plums will need only ¾ cup water, but hard cooking varieties will need 2 cups of water. Simmer gently until fruit is soft. Stir in sugar until it dissolves, then boil rapidly. Remove seeds as they rise to the surface. When jam is the right thickness, skim, then pour into hot, sterilized jars and seal.

Gwen Mills

PRUNE MARMALADE

1 lb. dried prunes   Juice and grated rind of 2
2 c. water   small oranges
1½ c. sugar

Pour 2 cups water over prunes and let stand overnight. Drain, but reserve liquid. Remove pits from prunes and chop prunes. Combine prunes, reserved liquid, sugar, orange rind and juice. Bring to a boil; reduce heat and simmer until thick, about 30 minutes. Stir often so mixture won't scorch. Seal in hot, sterilized jars. Yield: 1 pint.

Michelle Lewis

STRAWBERRY JAM

2 qt. crushed strawberries   6 c. sugar

Combine strawberries and sugar; place over low heat until sugar is dissolved. Cook rapidly; stir often. Cook about 45 minutes or until jam is thick. Pour into hot, sterilized jars and seal. Yield: 4 pints.

Paula Childress

FRESH STRAWBERRY PRESERVES
(Microwave)

1 pt. sliced fresh strawberries   ½ medium lemon juice
1 c. sugar
1 Tbsp. powdered pectin or 2
   Tbsp. liquid pectin

Combine the fruit, sugar, pectin and lemon in a 2 quart or 3 quart mixing bowl. Stir to mix. Cook, uncovered, using HIGH power for 7 to 8 minutes, stirring at end of 2 minutes and again at 4. Mixture should come to a rolling boil. Let stand, stirring occasionally for 12 to 24 hours. Put into clean jars and refrigerate for use within 6 weeks or into freezer containers for longer use.

Jean Lyle

STRAWBERRY FREEZER JAM

4 c. berries (whole), capped   1 pkg. Sure-Jell
4 c. sugar   ¾ c. water

Mash berries; pour sugar on top. Let set. Mix Sure-Jell and water; bring to a boil; boil for 2 minutes, stirring constantly. Pour over berries and sugar; mix well. Put in jars or plastic bags. Put in freezer. The night before you plan to use, put in refrigerator to defrost.

Debbie Rigdon

TOMATO GINGER PRESERVES

3 c. peeled, cooked tomatoes   1 box Sure-Jell
¼ c. lemon juice   Candied ginger, chopped
4½ c. sugar

Put 3 cups cooked tomatoes in an 8 quart kettle. Add ginger, lemon juice and Sure-Jell. Measure sugar and set aside. Bring to a full boil over high heat; stir constantly. Bring to a rolling boil that can not be stirred down. Add sugar and bring to a rolling boil again that can't be stirred down. Boil 1 minute; stir constantly. Remove from heat; remove foam. Pour into jars and seal.

Helen Russman

ZUCCHINI JAM

3 c. mashed zucchini
½ c. water
1 large box Jello (any flavor desired)

¼ c. lemon juice
3 c. sugar
1 pkg. Sure-Jell

Peel and chop enough zucchini for 3 cups when mashed. Add ½ cup water to cook. When tender, mash or blend until texture of crushed pineapple. Measure 3 cups and put in large cooking pan. Add box of Jello and ¼ cup of lemon juice. Boil 2 minutes. Add sugar and Sure-Jell; boil 2 minutes. Pour into jelly jars and seal. When cool, set in refrigerator overnight and store.

Strawberry, apricot, peach, wild cherry and cherry Jello are good choices for flavors.

Maxine Welch

Beverages,
Microwave,
Miscellaneous

MICROWAVE TIPS

- Always choose the minimum cooking time. Remember, food continues to cook after it is removed from the microwave.
- Keep your microwave clean. Built-up grease or food spatters can slow cooking times.
- When poaching or frying an egg in a browning dish, always prick the center of the yolk with a fork to keep the egg from exploding.
- Do not try to hard-cook eggs in a shell in a microwave. They will build up pressure and burst.
- Do not use metal dishes or aluminum foil except as specifically recommended by the manufacturer of your microwave.
- Never use a foil tray over ¾ inch deep in your microwave.
- When heating TV-style dinners, remove the foil cover, then place tray back in carton. Food will heat only from the top.
- Be sure to prick potatoes before baking to allow steam to escape.
- Cut a small slit in pouch-packed frozen foods before heating in microwave to allow steam to escape.
- When placing more than one food item in microwave, arrange foods in a circle near edges of oven.
- Cover foods that need to be steamed or tenderized.
- Do not try to pop popcorn without a microwave-approved corn popper.

DID YOU KNOW YOU CAN...?
(Use High setting for the following unless otherwise indicated.)
- Use your microwave oven to melt chocolate, to soften cream cheese and to soften or melt butter.
- Roast shelled nuts for 6 to 10 minutes, stirring frequently.
- Peel fruit or tomatoes by placing in 1 cup hot water. Microwave for 30 to 45 seconds; remove skins easily.
- Plump dried fruit by placing in a dish with 1 to 2 teaspoons water. Cover tightly with plastic wrap. Microwave for ½ to 1½ minutes.
- Precook barbecued ribs or chicken until almost done, then place on the grill to sear and add a charcoal flavor.
- Soften brown sugar by placing in a dish with a slice of bread or apple and microwaving for 30 to 45 seconds, stirring once.
- Dry bread for crumbs or croutons. Place cubed or crumbled bread on paper towels. Microwave for 6 to 7 minutes, stirring occasionally.
- Warm baby food or baby bottles by removing metal lid and microwaving for 10 to 20 seconds. Be sure to test temperature before feeding baby.
- Freshen chips and crackers by microwaving for 15 to 30 seconds. Let stand for 2 to 3 minutes.
- Dry herbs by placing on paper towels and microwaving for 2 to 3 minutes or until herbs are dry.
- Ripen an avocado by microwaving on Low for 2 to 4 minutes.

BEVERAGES, MICROWAVE, MISCELLANEOUS
BEVERAGES

APPLE MINT JULEP

Combine:

2 c. chilled apple juice
1 pt. lime sherbet

A few drops of mint extract

Beat until smooth and pour into tall glasses. Makes 3 to 4 servings. Add a sprig of mint to each glass for a pretty garnish.

Peggy Larrison

BANANA SLUSH

4 c. sugar
6 c. water
5 bananas, mashed
1 (46 oz.) can pineapple juice
1 (12 oz.) can frozen orange
    juice

1 (12 oz.) can frozen
    lemonade
6 qt. ginger ale

Dissolve sugar in water completely. Add juice and bananas. Mix well. Place in 3 (½ gallon) containers and freeze. Place frozen blocks in punch bowl and pour ginger ale over them. Mix to slushy consistency.

Sue Johnson

COCOA MIX

13 c. powdered milk
1 lb. box instant hot
    chocolate powder
    (Nestle's or Hershey's)

11 oz. instant cream powder
    (Cremora or Pream)
4 Tbsp. powdered sugar

Combine all ingredients and store until needed. When serving, put ¼ cup powder into tea cup; fill with hot water and add marshmallows if desired.

Donna Browning

EGGNOG

Separate 12 eggs into 2 bowls. Beat yellows well. Add 1 box confectioners sugar to yellows and stir. In a separate bowl, pour 1 quart of whipping cream and whip until stiff or peaks up. Beat egg whites until real stiff. Pour 1 fifth of bourbon *slowly* into yellows and stir *real well* while pouring. Fold in cream and egg whites. If too thick, add ½ to 1 quart milk or half & half. Add nutmeg if desired or serve to side to be sprinkled on top. Stir before serving (each time). Yields over 1 gallon. *Enjoy!*

Debbie Okiens

FRUIT PUNCH

1½ c. sugar
2 c. boiling water
3 c. cranberry juice
½ c. lemon juice

2 c. orange juice
1 qt. ginger ale
Mint sprigs
Orange and lemon slices

Dissolve sugar in hot water. Add cranberry juice, lemon and orange juice. Chill. Just before serving, pour into a punch bowl; add ginger ale and orange and lemon slices. Decorate with mint sprigs. Serves 10.

Wanda Alton

BLENDED FRUIT PUNCH

27 oz. canned apricot nectar
27 oz. canned pineapple juice
27 oz. canned pear nectar

13½ oz. orange juice
1 c. ginger ale

Mix first 4 ingredients. Chill. Pour over ice cubes. Add ginger ale just before serving. Serves 25.

Wanda Alton

ISLAND FRUIT PUNCH

1 (16 oz.) bottle Hawaiian
    Punch concentrate
2½ qt. (10 c.) cold water
2 (46 oz.) cans pineapple
    juice, chilled

3 qt. (12 c.) orange juice,
    chilled
3 (28 oz.) bottles 7-Up, chilled
Ice or ice ring

In a very large punch bowl, mix Hawaiian Punch concentrate and cold water. Stir in pineapple juice, orange juice and 7-Up. Add ice or ice ring.

Barbara C. Hendrick

FRUIT PUNCH

4 qt. water
2 c. crushed pineapple
2 qt. strong tea or grape juice

2 lb. sugar
3 c. orange juice
1 c. lemon juice

Boil 1 quart water and sugar for 1 minute. Cool. Add all other ingredients. Serve in a punch bowl with ice cubes. Garnish with orange and lemon slices and sprigs of mint. Serves 50.

Note: Freeze punch in ice cube trays and use these cubes in the punch bowl and your punch won't be watered down as the cubes melt.

Lora Martin

FRUIT PUNCH

3 pkg. cherry Kool-Aid
2 c. sugar
2 qt. water

1 large bottle ginger ale
1 large can pineapple juice

Mix together Kool-Aid, sugar and 2 quarts water. Pour into 2 trays and freeze. Refrigerate the rest until ready to use. Also, refrigerate ginger ale and pineapple juice. Mix all ingredients together, including frozen Kool-Aid cubes.

Debbie Rigdon

GOLDEN APRICOT MILKSHAKE

1 c. milk
1 egg
8 oz. canned apricot halves,
    well drained

⅛ tsp. almond extract
Dash of salt

Combine all ingredients in a blender container. Puree until smooth. Makes 1 serving, 395 calories.

Clara Nance

INSTANT GRASSHOPPER

1 pt. vanilla ice cream
½ c. white creme de cacao

½ c. creme de menthe

Blend in blender or electric mixer. Serve at once. Makes 6 after dinner drinks or cocktails.

Daisy Mace

HOT FRUITED TEA

5 c. boiling water
4 tea bags
10 whole cloves
¼ tsp. cinnamon

½ c. sugar
4 Tbsp. lemon juice
⅓ c. orange juice
Orange slices

In a large teapot, pour boiling water over tea, cloves and cinnamon. Cover and let steep 5 minutes. Strain tea; stir in sugar and juices. Heat to simmering. Serve hot with orange slices.

Rosalie Smith

HOT SPICED CIDER

1 gal. apple cider
1 (6 oz.) can frozen lemonade
    concentrate
20 whole cloves
1 tsp. whole allspice
1 (6 oz.) can frozen orange
    juice concentrate

10 cinnamon sticks, broken
    into pieces
¾ c. brown sugar, firmly
    packed

Put all ingredients in a large pot and bring to a boil; reduce heat to simmer and simmer for 20 minutes. Remove spices and serve warm.

Ruth Ackerman

ICED TEA PUNCH

2 c. boiling water
2 tea bags or 2 tsp. loose tea
¼ c. sugar

2 c. cold water
1 c. ginger ale

Pour boiling water over tea bags. Let set 5 minutes or until tea is very strong. Remove tea bags. Stir in sugar while tea is warm. Add cold water; chill. Just before serving, add ginger ale. Serves 4.

Helen Sykes

HOT SPICED TEA

Juice from 3 lemons
1 tsp. whole allspice
2 sticks cinnamon
½ c. tea leaves

Juice from 3 oranges
2½ c. sugar
1 tsp. whole cloves

Pour 1 quart of boiling water over tea leaves and spices. Let stand until nearly cold. Then strain. Strain fruit juice, then add sugar to juice. Add to tea mixture when tea mixture is cold. Lastly, add enough water to make 1 gallon. Store in refrigerator until ready to serve. Then heat and serve "piping hot."

Ruth Ackerman

MEXICAN HOT CHOCOLATE

¼ c. cocoa
¼ c. sugar
½ tsp. cinnamon
Dash of salt
3 c. milk

1 c. half & half
1 tsp. vanilla
Whipped cream
Cinnamon sticks

Combine cocoa, sugar, cinnamon, salt and 1 cup of milk in a saucepan over low heat and mix until smooth. Bring to a simmer and add remaining milk, half & half and vanilla. Heat thoroughly. Remove from heat; beat until frothy. Serve in mugs. Garnish with whipped cream and cinnamon sticks.

Gary Lee Figg

PUNCH

1 large can pineapple juice
1 large can cherry Hawaiian
    Punch
1 large ginger ale

2 small pkg. strawberry
    Kool-Aid (unsweetened)
1 qt. cold water (or ice cubes)
½ gal. vanilla ice cream

Mix together in punch bowl and put ice cream on top.

Ruth Noe

PERCOLATOR PUNCH

1 qt. apple cider
1 pt. cranberry juice
¾ c. lemon juice
1 c. orange juice

1 c. sugar (optional)
1 tsp. whole cloves
1 tsp. whole allspice
3 cinnamon sticks

Combine juices in percolator. Place spices and sugar in percolator basket. Allow to go through perk cycle. Serve hot.

Shirley Harrison

SPICED TEA PUNCH

1 qt. water
2 heaping Tbsp. loose tea or
    7 tea bags
½ tsp. nutmeg
½ tsp. ground cinnamon
½ tsp. allspice

1½ c. sugar
1 c. orange juice
½ c. lemon juice
1 qt. cold cranberry juice
    cocktail
1 qt. chilled club soda

Bring water to a boil; remove from heat. Immediately add tea, nutmeg, cinnamon, and allspice. Cover and steep 10 minutes. Stir and strain into a punch bowl containing sugar and fruit juices. Just before serving, add ice cubes and club soda. Makes 35 punch cups.

Paula White

WASSAIL PUNCH

1 gal. apple cider
1 qt. orange juice
1 c. lemon juice
1 qt. pineapple juice

24 whole cloves
4 sticks cinnamon
1 c. sugar

Mix ingredients and simmer 10 minutes. Yield: 1½ gallons.

Paula White

HOT BUTTERED RUM

1 (16 oz.) box brown sugar
½ c. butter
½ tsp. cinnamon
½ tsp. nutmeg
½ tsp. cloves

Dash of salt
Rum
Lemon slices
Cinnamon sticks

Combine all ingredients, except rum, lemon slices and cinnamon sticks. To make 1 serving, use 1 tablespoon mixture, 1 jigger rum and boiling water. Garnish with lemon slices and a cinnamon stick.

Shirley Harrison

NANCY'S CHRISTMAS LIFT

1 qt. strawberry liqueur
1 liter 7-Up

1 can Hawaiian Punch
Crushed ice

Fill glass with ice. Pour 10 ounce glass ½ full of punch. Add 2 shots of strawberry and finish filling glass with 7-Up. Shake well.

For ½ gallon: Pour all ingredients in container, except ice, and shake well. Pour over ice in 10 ounce glasses.

Nancy Tullis

SMOOTHIE

½ frozen banana
2 large frozen strawberries

1½ c. apple juice
2 ice cubes

Blend in blender until fruits are all liquid and drink is bubbly.

Helpful Hint: Peel bananas and cut in halves; place in Ziploc freezer bags. Clean strawberries and pull off tops. Drain on paper towel. Place berries (whole) in Ziploc freezer bags. Keep these frozen and you'll always be ready for a smoothie.

Doris Beeler

MICROWAVE

MICROWAVE BREAKFAST DISH

This is a recipe I just sort of threw together, but it's good for breakfast.

½ c. milk   6 eggs

Whip in blender. Pour in glass baking dish.

Add:

Lots of Cheddar cheese   Salt
Onion flakes   Dash of pepper
Green pepper   Bacon, sausage or ham
Tomatoes   (already cooked)
Pimentos   Parmesan cheese
Mushrooms

Bake or microwave until set. Serve with homemade tomato juice.

Alice Ritchey

MICROWAVE CARAMEL CORN

4 qt. popped corn   ¼ c. corn syrup
1 c. brown sugar   ½ tsp. salt
1 stick margarine   ½ tsp. soda

Combine brown sugar, margarine, syrup and salt in a 2 quart dish. Place in microwave and bring to a boil, then cook on HIGH for 2 minutes. Remove from microwave and stir in baking soda. Mix well. Put popped corn into heavy brown grocery bag. Pour syrup over corn. Close bag and shake to mix and coat corn. Close bag by turning down top. Cook in bag in microwave on HIGH for 1½ minutes and again shake and cook another 1½ minutes. Place in shallow pan; cool and break apart. Store in closed container.

Mary Baxter

MICROWAVE CHEESE SAUCE

Dump together; do not stir:

2 Tbsp. butter   1 c. milk
2 Tbsp. flour

Cook preceding ingredients at FULL power 2 minutes. Remove and add 1 cup cheese; cook additional 2 minutes. Remove and stir to blend smooth.

Shirley Cates

MICROWAVE FUDGE

3 c. sugar
¾ c. butter
1 (5½ oz.) can evaporated milk (not sweetened condensed milk)
1 pkg. chips (chocolate, peanut butter, butterscotch)

7½ - 8 oz. jar marshmallow cream
1 c. nuts
1 tsp. vanilla

In a big, deep bowl, melt butter; add sugar and milk. Stir thoroughly to dissolve sugar. Cook on HIGH power for 9 to 10½ minutes. During cooking time, stir 3 times. Add other ingredients and stir thoroughly. Pour onto buttered sheet; cool and cut into squares.

Marion Goodmann

TWO MINUTE MICROWAVE CHOCOLATE FUDGE

Dump into bowl:

1 (16 oz.) box confectioners sugar

2 Tbsp. cocoa

Stir to mix cocoa and sugar.

Dump; do not mix or stir:

1 stick butter, cut up

¼ c. milk

Cook 2 minutes in microwave at FULL power. Remove from oven; stir to blend. Add 1 teaspoon vanilla and nuts if desired. Pour into buttered dish; place in refrigerator for 1 hour. Serve.

Shirley Cates

MICROWAVE ORANGE GLAZED CARROTS

6 medium carrots, sliced
¾ c. orange juice, divided
1 Tbsp. sugar

2 tsp. cornstarch
½ tsp. salt

Combine carrots, ¼ cup orange juice and sugar in a 2 quart casserole; cover with Saran Wrap. Microwave at HIGH for 9 to 11 minutes or until carrots are desired degree of doneness. Combine cornstarch and salt; mix well; add remaining orange juice and beat with wire whisk until cornstarch is dissolved. Gradually add orange juice mixture to the carrots, mixing well. Cover and microwave on HIGH for 1½ to 2½ minutes until thick and bubbly, stirring at 1 minute intervals.

Wilma Crowdus

MICROWAVE PEANUT BUTTER HAYSTACKS

6 oz. (1 c.) butterscotch chips
½ c. peanut butter

½ c. salted peanuts
2 c. chow mein noodles

Place chips and peanut butter in 2 quart casserole or bowl. Cover with plastic wrap. Microwave at 50% power (MEDIUM) for 3 to 5 minutes, until most of chips are shiny or soft. Blend well. Stir in peanuts and chow mein noodles with rubber spatula. Drop by forkfuls onto wax paper. Cool until set. Makes 2½ dozen.

Jean Lyle

MICROWAVE VEGETABLES
(Carrots, cauliflower, broccoli)

Add 2½ tablespoons water and season to taste. Place in bowl; lay Saran Wrap across top of bowl. Do not seal down. Cook on FULL power 4½ to 5½ minutes per pint of vegetables. After removing from microwave, leave Saran Wrap on dish until ready to serve. Vegetables will continue to cook. Good with cheese sauce over vegetables.

Shirley Cates

MISCELLANEOUS

HERB BUTTER

1 lb. margarine
4 Tbsp. parsley flakes
1 Tbsp. dried basil leaves

1 Tbsp. dried tarragon leaves
1 Tbsp. chopped fresh or
  frozen chives

Soften margarine to room temperature. Add herbs to margarine and mix thoroughly with electric mixture. Pack into a container with a tight lid. Let stand overnight for flavor to develop. Yield: 1 pound.

Cristy Lewis

HOMEMADE COUNTRY BUTTER

1 lb. margarine, softened
4 oz. Philadelphia cream
  cheese, softened

1 small can condensed cream
½ tsp. salt

Mix in a blender all ingredients together. Continue blending until all of the milk has been worked into the mixture. Store in refrigerator until used.

Gwen Mills

LEMON BUTTER

4 Tbsp. melted butter
1 tsp. lemon juice

⅛ tsp. pepper

Blend all together; serve hot.

Note: Good over baked fish.

Peggy Kessinger

MAPLE BUTTER

½ c. margarine
¼ c. maple syrup

2 Tbsp. powdered sugar

Beat margarine and sugar until light and fluffy. Beat in maple syrup gradually.

Martha Hooper

ORANGE BUTTER

½ c. margarine
2 Tbsp. powdered sugar

¼ c. light corn syrup
2 tsp. grated orange peel

Beat margarine and sugar until light and fluffy. Beat in corn syrup gradually. Stir in orange peel.

Martha Hooper

PEANUT BUTTER VARIATIONS

You might like to try peanut butter with apple butter, jelly, cheese, bacon, bananas, marshmallow fluff. Take your pick!

Mary Beeler

BEER BATTER FOR FRYING FISH

1 c. all-purpose flour
1 tsp. baking powder
1½ tsp. salt
1 Tbsp. peanut or vegetable
   oil

1 c. stale beer
Dash of Tabasco

Sift dry ingredients. Make a well in the center; add the liquids and stir until smooth.

Cristy Lewis

BATTER FOR DEEP-FRYING

1 c. Bisquick

½ c. beer

Mix well. Dredge fish (shrimp, onion rings, vegetables, etc.) in dry Bisquick. Salt to taste. Then dip in batter and deep-fry, a few pieces at a time.

Note: If batter becomes too thick, add a little more beer.

Ruth Ackerman

DUMPLING BATTER

1 c. yellow corn meal
¼ c. all-purpose flour
1 tsp. baking powder
1 tsp. salt

2 eggs, beaten
½ c. milk
1 Tbsp. margarine, melted

Sift dry ingredients together. Add remaining ingredients and mix well.

Greens 'N Dumplings:

½ lb. slab bacon
2 large onions, minced
1 qt. water

3 lb. fresh collard greens, cut
   in small pieces
¼ tsp. black pepper

Simmer the meat and onions in the water for 1 hour. Add remaining ingredients. Cover and cook for 1½ hours. Add teaspoonfuls of dumpling batter on top of greens. Cover and cook 15 minutes. Serves 4.

Brenda Chitty

HERB SALT

¼ c. parsley flakes
1 Tbsp. dried basil leaves
1 Tbsp. oregano

1 Tbsp. paprika
1 tsp. celery flakes
1 c. salt

With blender set at lowest speed, sprinkle parsley, basil, oregano, paprika and celery flakes into blender, a little at a time. Add salt a little at a time and blend mixture until herbs are as fine as salt. Pour into a shaker. Yield: 1 cup.

Cristy Lewis

CONDENSED MILK

Stir until dissolved:

1 c. boiling water
½ c. butter

2 c. sugar
2 c. powdered milk

Beat until smooth. Will be thin, but thickens later on. Can be done in blender. Makes 1 quart.

Donna Browning

HOT CRANBERRY CASSEROLE

Spray a 2 quart casserole with a vegetable spray. Place in it a mixture of 3 cups peeled, cored and chopped apples and 2 cups whole raw cranberries. Sprinkle with 1½ teaspoons lemon juice. Cover with 1½ cups white sugar. In a medium mixing bowl, blend just to moisten 1⅓ cups quick cooking oatmeal, 1 cup chopped walnuts, ⅓ cup packed brown sugar, and 1 stick melted margarine (¼ pound). Pour crumb mixture over fruit. Bake, uncovered, in a 325° oven for 1¼ hours. Serves 8 to 10.

Good with turkey and chicken or serve hot with vanilla ice cream as a dessert.

Debby Trinkle

NEW ZEALAND DEVILED CROISSANTS

6 oz. Puff Pastry
2 oz. ham, chopped fine
1 Tbsp. mustard pickle

1 tsp. mayonnaise
Few drops of Tabasco sauce
1 egg, beaten

Mix ham, pickle and mayonnaise together and season well with Tabasco. Roll out the Puff Pastry into a long narrow strip; trim the edges and cut into 3 inch squares. Cut each square in half diagonally and put ½ teaspoon of filling on each triangle. Roll up and make into a crescent shape. Place on cold, greased tray. Brush with beaten egg and bake at 400° for 8 to 10 minutes or until golden brown and crisp.

Gwen Mills

STUFFED GRAPE LEAVES

8 oz. uncooked rice
4 oz. Romano cheese, grated
1 medium onion, chopped
½ c. chopped fresh parsley
1 tsp. salt
1 tsp. fresh ground black
  pepper

48 grape leaves, rinsed and
  dried
¼ c. olive oil (preferred
  Greek)

In medium bowl, combine first 6 ingredients; set aside. Lay out grape leaves and place equal amounts of stuffing, 1 heaping tablespoon on each. Roll up leaves to enclose filling and wrap the ends under. Place, seam side down, in shallow baking dish in 1 layer. Mix olive oil with enough water to cover the rolled leaves. Bake in preheated 350° oven until rice is tender and liquid is absorbed. Cool in baking pan. Cover and chill. Serves 8.

Terry White

VEGETABLE MARINADE

½ - ¾ c. tomato soup
⅓ c. vinegar
⅓ c. sugar
¼ c. salad oil

1 tsp. dry ground mustard
1 tsp. salt
1 tsp. pepper
1 tsp. Worcestershire sauce

Mix together and let set overnight before using.

Mary Baxter

VEGETABLE SANDWICHES

2 loaves sandwich bread
2 cucumbers, peeled and
    grated
2 carrots, grated

1 large onion, grated
1 c. chopped celery
Juice of ½ lemon
Dash of cayenne pepper

Add 2 cups of mayonnaise. Mix well. Put 1 envelope of clear gelatin in ¼ cup water; mix well. Add ½ cup boiling water and dissolve. Pour into vegetable mixture and chill until well set. Make sandwiches and refrigerate. Will keep 10 days in refrigerator.

Helen Russman

CANNING

APPLE CHUTNEY

2 - 3 lb. apples, peeled and
    cut
2 oz. ginger
3 - 4 hot peppers, chopped
4 tsp. salt

6 - 8 onions, chopped
1 lb. sugar
1 pt. vinegar
½ lb. chopped raisins

Boil vinegar, onions, sugar, salt, ginger and peppers until almost syrup. Add apples. Cook 20 to 30 minutes, stirring constantly, until fairly thick. Add chopped raisins. Put in sterilized jars.

Helen Russman

CANNED BANANA PEPPERS

1 gal. water
2 c. salt

Peppers

Use enough peppers to be covered, weigh down. Next day, drain and pack in jars.

1 gal. water
1 c. vinegar

1 c. salt

Bring all ingredients to boil. Fill packed jars with water/vinegar/salt mixture. Put 1 teaspoon alum in each jar. Process in water bath for 5 minutes.

Mary Raney

CANNED EGGPLANT

Eggplant, peeled and sliced

1 tsp. salt for each jar

Peel and slice eggplant and drop in salted water. Drain. Place eggplant in big mouth quart jars. Add teaspoon salt to each jar; fill with boiling water. Seal. Cook in cold packer for 15 minutes.

Note: If you like fried eggplant, these are very good fried in egg batter.

Rosaleen Robertson

CANNED FRESH PORK

Fresh pork, cut in pieces
    about 2 inches sq.

1 tsp. salt

Brown in 350° oven. Cook about 45 minutes, turning the pork to brown on all sides. Place in quart jars; add 1 teaspoon salt in each jar. Pour all the drippings over the meat. (Never add water to the pork.) Cold pack 2 hours.

Josie Bratcher

CANNED PORK MEAT LOAF

1 qt. canned pork (lean meat), chopped up
½ c. onion, chopped
1 c. chopped potatoes
1 c. bread crumbs
½ c. grated carrots
1 egg, well beaten
½ c. celery
Salt to taste

Mix all ingredients and bake in 350° oven for 30 minutes or until done.

Josie Bratcher

CANNED GREEN TOMATOES

Wash and slice green tomatoes. Pack in sterlized quart jars. Add 1 teaspoon salt to each jar and fill with boiling water. Seal. Process 5 minutes with 5 pounds pressure or cook in cold packer for 8 minutes.

Note: If you like fried green tomatoes, these are better than fresh green tomatoes because the salt has penetrated the tomato.

Gwen Bond

CAULIFLOWER PICKLES

3 heads cauliflower, separated into flowerets
3 pt. white vinegar
3 c. sugar
¾ c. salt
¼ c. mixed pickling spices, tied in cheesecloth bag
5 hot red peppers

Sprinkle salt over the cauliflower and let stand overnight. Place in a colander and rinse thoroughly with cold water. Bring vinegar and sugar to a boil; add spice bag and boil 5 minutes. Add cauliflower and boil 2 or 3 minutes. Remove spice bag. Place in sterile jars; add liquid to within ½ inch of top. Put a pepper in each and seal.

Helen Russman

CRANBERRY CONSERVE

4 c. (1 lb.) fresh cranberries
1 c. water
1 c. raisins, chopped
2½ c. sugar

1 Tbsp. grated orange peel
⅓ c. orange juice
1 c. pecans, chopped

Wash cranberries; put them in a saucepan and add water; bring to a boil and cook about 5 minutes or until all the skins burst. Force cranberries through a sieve. Combine puree in a saucepan with the raisins, sugar, orange peel and orange juice; mix well. Stir over medium heat until sugar is dissolved, then continue cooking about 15 minutes or until thick. Remove from heat; stir in walnuts; pour into hot, sterilized jars; seal. Process by simmering in boiling water bath for 10 minutes.

Melissa Jackson

DILL MIX

3 qt. yellow beans (whole)
3 qt. whole carrots, scraped
3 qt. small pickle onions, peeled

2 qt. water
½ c. salt
½ c. vinegar
Dill

Boil vegetables separately until tender, but not soft. Then combine with water, salt and vinegar and bring to boil. Fill into hot, sterilized jars, put 1 head of dill in top of each and seal.

Gwen Mills

HOME-CANNED POTATOES

If potatoes are about 1 to 1½ inches in diameter, they may be canned whole; dice or slice the larger ones. Wash and scrape freshly dug new potatoes, removing all blemishes (a toothbrush is ideal for cleaning the potatoes). To prevent darkening during preparation, store in salt water (1 teaspoon salt to each quart of water). Fill jars with whole, diced or sliced potatoes, leaving ½ inch headroom; add ½ teaspoon salt to pints, 1 teaspoon salt to quarts. Add boiling water, leaving ½ inch headroom. Adjust lids. Pressure process at 10 pounds (240°F.) whole potatoes in pints or quarts for 40 minutes, diced or sliced potatoes in pints or quarts for 45 minutes. Remove jars; complete seals if necessary. Pour off starch before adding potatoes to other dishes or heating to serve.

Note: Potatoes can also be hot packed.

Phyllis L. Davis

HOMEMADE KRAUT

Cabbage, shredded fine
1 tsp. salt (for each jar)

Boiling water

Shred real fine the amount of cabbage you wish to use and press firmly into quart jars. Put 1 teaspoon salt in each quart jar. Fill with boiling water and seal.

Opal Thompson

MAMMAW'S TOMATO CATSUP

24 large ripe tomatoes
8 large onions, chopped (3 c.)
1 qt. vinegar
8 Tbsp. sugar
4 Tbsp. salt
1 tsp. cloves

1 tsp. cinnamon
1 or 2 Tbsp. black pepper to
taste
2 packs frozen chopped
onion

Peel tomatoes. Grind tomatoes and let stand overnight to drain. Mix all ingredients together and cook on medium heat until thick. Pour into hot, sterilized jars and seal.

Mary Baxter

PEPPER HASH

12 sweet red peppers
12 green peppers
12 small onions

1 qt. cider vinegar
2 Tbsp. canning salt
1 c. light brown sugar

Chop very fine peppers and onions. Add salt and allow mixture to simmer for 10 minutes. Drain well. Add vinegar and brown sugar (more brown sugar if you would like it sweeter). Bring to boiling. Fill clean, hot jars and seal. Great with dried beans.

Brownie - Lois Bruner

PICA LILLI

1 peck green tomatoes
3 small heads cabbage
3 green peppers

4 onions (good sized)
6 large cucumbers
1 c. salt

Grind all ingredients and let stand overnight. Next morning, drain and scald in 1 quart vinegar and 2 quarts water. Drain again. Make a syrup of *1 quart vinegar* and *6 pounds of sugar.* Boil 20 minutes, *add ½ teaspoon cloves* and *2 teaspoons cinnamon.* Can hot.

Sarah A. Drewes

PICKLED CHINESE SNOW PEAS

4 lb. snow peas
2 qt. white vinegar
¼ c. salt

½ c. sugar
2 c. water
3 Tbsp. mixed pickling spice

Wash peas; remove ends and string. Steam 5 minutes over boiling water; immediately rinse under cold water. Combine remaining ingredients in a kettle and bring to a boil. Simmer 10 minutes. Pack pea pods in hot, sterilized jars. Pour strained hot vinegar mixture over them. Seal. Process in hot water bath 5 minutes. Makes 4 quarts.

Gwen Mills

PICKLED EGGS

1 doz. boiled eggs
1½ c. white vinegar
½ c. water
½ c. sugar

6 whole cloves
1 bay leaf
Salt to taste

Heat mixture to boil, then let simmer for 5 minutes. Pour over the eggs. Refrigerate for several days.

Virginia Moran

PICKLED ONIONS

10 lb. small onions
2 qt. plus 1 pt. vinegar
1 c. salt

4 or 5 c. sugar
¼ c. mixed pickle spices

Peel onions. Cover with water. Add the salt and mix well. Let it stand overnight. Place in colander. Pour plenty of cold water over to rinse and let drain. Boil sugar and vinegar and spices; put onions in vinegar mixture; let boil up and fill jars to within an inch of top. Seal hot.

Tip: I put the hot onions in jars, then spoon vinegar and a little spice in each jar. Fill 1 jar at a time and seal. When you start to can the onions, turn your heat down to just enough to keep your onions hot.

J. W. Borden, Jr.

PICKLED STUFFED PEPPERS

24 green bell peppers
2 qt. cabbage, shredded fine
2 cucumbers, chopped
4 red sweet peppers,
  chopped
½ c. horseradish
4 onions, chopped

½ c. carrots, grated
¼ c. salt
¼ c. mustard seed
¼ c. celery seed
¼ c. parsley
24 garlic cloves
Vinegar

Cut the top off of the stem end and set aside. Discard the seed and white membranes from the peppers and pack them firmly with the mixture of cabbage, cucumber, onion, pepper, horseradish, parsley, carrot and spices. Press a garlic clove in the center of each pepper. Replace the tops and fasten them securely with toothpicks. Pack the stuffed peppers into quart or gallon sterilized jars. Fill jars with boiling hot vinegar and seal.

Gwen Mills

PICKLED YELLOW SQUASH

8 c. sliced yellow squash
  (thin)
2 c. chopped onions
1 c. chopped green peppers
1 Tbsp. canning salt

2 c. cider vinegar
1 tsp. celery seed
3½ c. sugar
1 tsp. mustard seed

Combine squash, onions, salt and peppers. Let stand 1 hour, then drain. Combine remaining ingredients; bring to a boil. Put in clean, hot jars and seal.

Brownie - Lois Bruner

SANDWICH SPREAD

4 red peppers, ground
4 green peppers, ground
1 qt. ground green tomatoes
4 - 6 eggs
1½ c. white sugar
1 c. vinegar

4 rounded Tbsp. flour
4 Tbsp. mustard
2 Tbsp. salt
1 c. sour cream
1 doz. medium size sweet
  pickles, ground

Boil in 1 cup water the peppers and ground tomatoes. Drain. Mix sugar, flour and salt. Add vinegar slowly. Beat eggs and add to the mixture; mix and boil for 5 minutes. Mix peppers and tomatoes with all other ingredients, except pickles. Cook for 10 minutes, then add pickles. Simmer until hot again, then pack in hot, sterilized jars and seal.

Louisa Rosser

SANDWICH SPREAD

10 sweet green peppers
10 sweet red peppers
10 onions
10 green tomatoes
2 c. vinegar

2 c. brown sugar
4 Tbsp. prepared mustard
8 Tbsp. flour
1 qt. mayonnaise

Grind vegetables together. Cover with boiling water and let stand for 10 minutes. Drain. Put in large kettle and add vinegar and sugar; cook 8 minutes. Make a batter of mustard and flour and a little water; add to vegetables. Cook 3 minutes; add mayonnaise and cook until desired thickness, about 4 minutes. Seal at once in sterilized jars.

Gwen Bond

SAUCES

BBQ SAUCE

1 qt. vinegar
1 stick butter
1 small bottle Worcestershire
   sauce

1 bottle Tabasco sauce
1 box pickling spice
1 bottle ReaLemon

Mix all the preceding and simmer for 1 hour.

Barbara Montgomery

BARBECUE SAUCE

½ c. light molasses (Karo)
½ c. catsup
½ c. chopped onions, minced
⅓ c. lemon juice or 1 Tbsp.
   vinegar
1 Tbsp. Wesson oil
1 Tbsp. steak sauce

1 Tbsp. butter
½ tsp. mustard
1 Tbsp. Worcestershire sauce
¼ tsp. garlic powder
1 Tbsp. hot sauce
3 whole cloves
Salt and pepper to taste

Mix together. Bring to a boil; reduce heat and simmer 10 minutes. Take cloves out. Salt and pepper to taste. Perfect for outside grilling.

Note: Add Kraft hot barbecue sauce if desired.

Kathy Hummel

BARBEQUE SAUCE

½ c. light molasses (Karo)
½ c. catsup
½ c. chopped onion, minced
⅓ c. lemon juice or 1 Tbsp.
   vinegar
1 Tbsp. Wesson oil
1 Tbsp. steak sauce

1 Tbsp. butter
½ tsp. mustard
1 Tbsp. Worcestershire sauce
¼ tsp. garlic powder
1 Tbsp. hot sauce
3 whole cloves

Mix together; bring to a boil; reduce heat; simmer 10 minutes. Take cloves out; add salt and pepper to taste. Perfect for outside grilling. Add Kraft barbecue sauce as desired.

Kathy Hummel

BARBECUE SAUCE

2 medium onions, chopped
¾ c. melted margarine
1½ c. firmly packed brown
    sugar
1 (24 oz.) jar prepared
    mustard
2 (26 oz.) bottles catsup

2 Tbsp. garlic powder
1 (4 oz.) bottle liquid smoke
1 (7 oz.) bottle
    Worcestershire sauce
¾ c. lemon juice
5 c. water

Saute onion in margarine in a large saucepan. Add brown sugar, mixing well. Add remaining ingredients; bring to a boil and simmer over low heat for 30 minutes. Yield: 4 quarts.

Stores well in refrigerator. Great for chicken, ribs, steaks or hamburgers.

Mrs. Joe (Marie) Hancock

BAR-B-Q SAUCE

1 Tbsp. margarine
½ c. chopped onions
1 tsp. paprika
½ tsp. pepper
4 Tbsp. sugar

1 tsp. prepared mustard
4 tsp. Worcestershire sauce
¼ tsp. Tabasco sauce
¼ c. catsup
3 Tbsp. vinegar

Saute onions; add remaining ingredients and simmer approximately 10 minutes. Good for any kind of meat, pork, hot dogs, hamburgers, etc.

Can double or triple recipe without problems.

Don Borders

BAR-B-QUE FOR 5 CHICKENS

¾ c. shortening
1¼ c. vinegar
1¼ c. Worcestershire
5 lemons (juice; slice rind of 1
    lemon)
3 or 4 Tbsp. black pepper
2 or 3 Tbsp. salt

2 Tbsp. mustard
3 Tbsp. catsup
1 tsp. Frank's red hot sauce
1 bag pickling spice
    (optional)
Dash of chili powder
    (optional)

Clarence "Bunny" Ebelhar

HOT SOUP FOR BEANS

1 large (29 oz.) can tomatoes
1 medium onion, chopped
2 - 3 hot peppers, chopped or
  dried pepper to taste
3 cloves garlic, crushed

2 Tbsp. vegetable oil
1 Tbsp. vinegar
1 tsp. salt
2 tsp. crushed red pepper (or
  more if desired)

Combine all ingredients; bring to a boil; cook about 5 minutes. Serve with pinto or white beans or can be served with chips for hot dip.

Ruthie Marty

CHAMPAGNE MUSTARD

2 eggs
½ c. firmly packed brown
  sugar
½ c. canned consomme

½ c. champagne vinegar
Dash of hot pepper sauce
1½ tsp. flour
¼ c. dry mustard

Beat eggs in medium bowl. Add remaining ingredients and mix well. Pour into saucepan and cook over low heat until thick, stirring often, about 8 to 10 minutes. Pour into a container that has a tight fitting top. Seal and refrigerate. Can be stored in refrigerator for about 2 weeks. Makes 2½ cups.

Ruth Ackerman

BASIC CHEESE SAUCE FOR VEGETABLES

½ stick butter
3 Tbsp. flour
½ tsp. salt

2 c. milk
⅔ c. cheese, diced
Buttered cracker crumbs

Melt butter in a heavy saucepan; stir in flour and salt. Remove from heat; gradually stir in milk. Stir in cheese. Cook over medium heat; stir constantly until thickened. Pour over cooked vegetables.

Good over asparagus, broccoli, Brussels sprouts, cauliflower, peas or potatoes.

Helen Sykes

CHEESE SAUCE

2 Tbsp. butter
2 Tbsp. flour
1 c. milk

Cheese
1 small bay leaf
1 clove garlic

Place butter over low heat in small pan; melt. Add flour and milk. Bring to boil and add cheese, bay leaf, and garlic, stirring constantly, over low heat until desired consistency is obtained.

J. W. Borden

EASY CHEESE SAUCE

⅔ c. evaporated milk   2 c. shredded cheese

Heat evaporated milk in small saucepan over very low heat, just to boiling. Then add the 2 cups of shredded cheese and stir until the cheese is melted and well blended.

This is good with summer vegetables, noodles, rice or potatoes.

Lou Perry

CHILI SAUCE

18 large ripe tomatoes	1 tsp. cinnamon
2 large onions	1 tsp. cloves
4 green peppers	2 c. vinegar
2 Tbsp. plain salt	1 or 2 hot peppers
1 c. sugar	

Peel the tomatoes and onions. Remove seeds from peppers and chop them fine. Stir all ingredients together and add salt, sugar, cinnamon, ground cloves and vinegar. Cook slowly for 45 to 60 minutes or until thick, stirring occasionally. Pour into sterilized jars and seal. Makes 6 pints.

Hazel Stanfield

CHILI SAUCE

18 large ripe tomatoes	1 c. sugar
2 large onions	1 tsp. each cinnamon/cloves
4 green peppers	2 c. vinegar
2 Tbsp. plain salt	1 or 2 hot peppers

Peel the tomatoes and onions. Remove seeds from peppers and chop them fine. Stir all ingredients together and add salt, sugar, cinnamon, ground cloves and vinegar. Cook slowly for 45 to 60 minutes or until thick, stirring occasionally. Pour into sterilized jars and seal. Makes 6 pints.

Hazel Stanfield

COCKTAIL SAUCE

½ c. chili sauce
2 Tbsp. prepared horseradish
2 Tbsp. lemon juice
1 tsp. Worcestershire sauce

½ tsp. minced onion flakes
Tabasco red pepper sauce to
taste

Mix all ingredients together and chill.

Ellen Jones

CRANBERRY SAUCE

2 c. fresh cranberries
½ c. water

¾ c. sugar

Cook cranberries and water until tender, about 2 minutes. Mash with a potato masher. Add the ¾ cup sugar. Cook 1 minute longer. Chill.

FUDGE SAUCE

4 oz. unsweetened chocolate
¼ c. margarine
2 c. sugar

Dash of salt
13 oz. can evaporated milk
1 tsp. vanilla

In medium saucepan, over low heat, melt chocolate and margarine. Stir in sugar and salt. Slowly stir in evaporated milk. Cook; stir constantly until mixture bubbles and is slightly thickened. Remove from heat; stir in vanilla. Cool. Sauce thickens as it cools. Store, covered, in refrigerator. Makes 3 cups.

Rosalie Smith

GINGERBREAD SAUCE

1 Tbsp. flour
¾ c. sugar
Pinch of salt
1 Tbsp. butter

1 c. boiling water
1 egg
1 tsp. vanilla

Combine flour, sugar and salt; mix. Add egg, boiling water and butter; cook until desired thickness. Add vanilla.

Note: Good over apple crisp.

Betty Coogle

THE GLISTEN GLAZE FOR MEATS

½ c. brown or white sugar
¼ c. light corn syrup or
   honey

1½ Tbsp. cornstarch
1 c. water

Mix cornstarch and sugar well together. Add the corn syrup and the water. Mix well and cook, stirring constantly, until the mixture is clear. Use to glaze ham, turkey, Canadian bacon, etc.

Ruth Ackerman

HOLLANDAISE

3 egg yolks
⅓ c. butter

Juice of 1 lemon

Mix the egg yolks, butter and lemon juice together, very lightly. Do not stir vigorously. Let this mixture stand at room temperature for several hours. Then put it into the top of double boiler and add 1 tablespoon boiling water. Bring water in the bottom up to boiling point, but do not boil. (If you do, the sauce is likely to curdle.) Stir sauce constantly and briskly over the hot water until it thickens and becomes of proper consistency. Remove from hot water. The sauce can be reheated later by adding another tablespoon of hot water, or put the jar in a pan of hot water while cooking other vegetables and it will be hot enough for vegetables.

It makes even shoe leather taste good and keeps for days in the refrigerator.

FRESH HORSERADISH SAUCE

½ c. fresh grated horseradish
2 tsp. prepared mustard
2 tsp. vinegar
1 tsp. salt

½ tsp. pepper
1 tsp. sugar
4 Tbsp. cream

Combine and heat fresh grated horseradish, mustard, vinegar, salt, pepper, sugar and cream. Do not boil. Serve with sliced beef or ham.

Eldred Sykes

LEMON SAUCE

¼ c. honey
1 Tbsp. cornstarch
1 c. boiling water

Dash of nutmeg
Dash of salt
2 Tbsp. lemon juice

In small pan, mix honey and cornstarch. Add boiling water and cook 5 minutes; stir constantly. Remove from heat; stir in nutmeg, salt and lemon juice. Yield: 1¼ cups.

Crystal Duke

TRANSPARENT MAPLE SAUCE

½ c. packed brown sugar
2 tsp. flour
½ c. white sugar

1 c. water
¼ c. butter
1 tsp. vanilla

Cook sugar, flour and water until thick and clear. Add butter and vanilla; stir until butter melts. Pour over cake while hot.

Best with yellow, butter or spice cakes.

Wynola Sharon Davis

MUSTARD SAUCE

1 Tbsp. butter
1½ tsp. flour
1 tsp. dry mustard
2 Tbsp. vinegar
1 Tbsp. prepared mustard

1 tsp. sugar
1 c. hot stock
Salt
Pepper

Melt butter; add flour. Cook and stir until smooth. Add dry mustard, vinegar, prepared mustard, sugar and stock. Simmer slowly 10 minutes, stirring occasionally. Season with salt and pepper to taste.

Peggy Kessinger

NUTMEG SAUCE

1 c. sugar
1 Tbsp. flour
Few grains of salt

1 Tbsp. butter
1 tsp. nutmeg
2 c. boiling water

Mix sugar, flour and salt. Add 2 cups boiling water and stir. Add butter. Cook 5 minutes. Add nutmeg.

Peggy Kessinger

RAISIN SAUCE

½ c. brown sugar
1 tsp. dry mustard
1 Tbsp. flour
2 Tbsp. sugar

2 Tbsp. lemon juice
¼ tsp. grated lemon peel
1½ c. water
⅓ - ⅔ c. seedless raisins

Mix first 3 ingredients, slowly add 2 tablespoons sugar. Add rest of ingredients. Cook over low heat until thick; stir constantly.

Note: Good over ham.

Renee Wallace

CELERY ROOT IN REMOULADE SAUCE

1 large celery root, cleaned
 and peeled
Lemon juice
2 egg yolks

1 Tbsp. Dijon mustard
Salt to taste
Pinch of cayenne pepper
2 c. peanut oil

Cut celery root into fine julienne strips, immediately toss with fresh lemon juice to keep it white. Make a mayonnaise: Beat together the egg yolks, mustard, salt and cayenne. Add oil in a slow stream, whisking constantly and rapidly. Toss the mayonnaise and celery root together; taste for seasoning; cover and refrigerate until ready to use. Yield: 6 to 8 servings.

Angela Roth

RHINELAND MARINADE-RHINELAND DRESSING

1 Tbsp. powdered sugar
1 tsp. Worcestershire sauce
1 tsp. tomato ketchup
1½ Tbsp. vinegar
1 Tbsp. olive oil

½ tsp. salt
¼ tsp. prepared mustard
Dash of pepper
¼ tsp. Tabasco sauce
1½ Tbsp. lemon juice

Blend ingredients in the order given and mix well. A perfect all around dressing for vegetables, meat or fish salad.

Gwen Mills

ITALIAN SPAGHETTI SAUCE

4 cans tomato paste
8 cans water (use tomato
    paste can)
1 lb. ground beef
2 carrots, grated fine
2 stalks celery, grated fine

1 onion, grated fine
2 pieces garlic, grated fine
1 small green pepper, grated
    fine
Allspice to taste
Vegetable oil

Fry beef in vegetable oil. Mix all other ingredients in large pot. Add cooked beef. Cook over low heat for 3 hours.

Ann Duke

SWEET SOUR SAUCE

¼ c. brown sugar
¼ c. prepared mustard
¼ c. molasses
¼ c. vinegar

¼ c. Worcestershire sauce
½ c. pineapple juice
½ tsp. lemon juice

Mix together sugar, mustard and molasses. Add vinegar, Worcestershire sauce, pineapple juice and lemon juice. Mix well and heat. Serve hot.

Wanda Alton

SWEET 'N SOUR SAUCE FOR HAM

Combine the following and cook until thick (consistency of sorghum molasses):

2 c. pineapple juice
¾ c. water

¼ c. vinegar
3 Tbsp. cornstarch

Remove from heat and add ½ teaspoon almond extract, ¼ cup soy sauce and 2 to 3 slices ginger root. Blanch 1 chopped green pepper, 1 chopped onion, 1 cup pineapple chunks, and ½ cup sliced carrots for 3 to 4 minutes and add to the preceding sauce. Makes approximately 6 cups.

Barbara C. Hendrick

TARTAR SAUCE

½ c. chopped pickle
¼ c. chopped onion
1 c. mayonnaise
½ c. salad dressing

¼ c. lemon juice
¼ tsp. dry mustard
Pepper to taste

Mix all ingredients together in a covered jar. Store in refrigerator until ready to use.

Bill Farris

TURKISH SAUCE

1 c. fresh bread crumbs
3 egg yolks, lightly beaten
1 small clove garlic, crushed,
   peeled and minced
1½ c. olive oil or vegetable oil
   or half and half

Juice of ½ lemon, strained
   (or to taste)
Salt
Pepper

Mix crumbs, egg yolks and garlic together well. Beat in the oil and lemon juice. Add salt and pepper to taste. Makes about 1⅔ cups.

A fascinating sauce from the other side of the world to serve with hard cooked eggs or cold poached fish.

Bill Farris

HOT WINE SAUCE FOR VEGETABLES

1 Tbsp. minced onion
2 Tbsp. chopped fresh
   parsley

¾ c. mayonnaise
¼ c. dry white wine
1 Tbsp. lemon juice

Combine onion, wine, parsley, lemon juice and mayonnaise in top of double boiler and heat over hot, not boiling, water. Serve over asparagus, broccoli, green beans, and cauliflower that have been cooked crisp.

May be cooked in pan if watched carefully.

Mary Butler Wessel

628

VANILLA SAUCE

1 c. sugar
2 Tbsp. cornstarch
⅛ tsp. salt
2 c. boiling water

4 Tbsp. butter
2 tsp. vanilla
1 tsp. nutmeg

Combine sugar, salt and cornstarch in saucepan. Add boiling water gradually. Simmer until clear and thickened, stirring constantly. Stir in butter, vanilla and nutmeg. Yield: 2½ cups sauce.

This is a fantastic topping for Bread Pudding or Rice Pudding.

Thelma Barnett

Notes

INDEX OF RECIPES

SOUPS, SALADS, VEGETABLES

1546-85

641

642

CANDY, JELLY, PRESERVES

BEVERAGES, MICROWAVE, MISCELLANEOUS

BEVERAGES

MICROWAVE

MISCELLANEOUS

CANNING

SAUCES

Notes

Notes

Notes

You may order as many of our cookbooks as you wish for the price of $10.00 each plus $3.75 postage and handling per book ordered. Mail to:

Kentucky Chapter 32
Telephone Pioneers of America
P.O. Box 32410
534 Armory Place B-9
Louisville, Kentucky 40232

Save postage and handling by picking up your books at the Chapter Pioneer office located in:
Room B-9, 534 Armory Place
Louisville, Kentucky
Tele. No. (502) 582-8319

Number of books ordered _____ Volume I
_____ Volume II
Amount enclosed_____

Please make checks payable to:
Kentucky Chapter 32, TPA

Please Print:

Name _____

Street Address_____

City, State, Zip_____

Your Tele. No. _____
(in case we have questions)